*Delphi Developer's Journal:* Decemb

"...Delphi has gained a solid reputation as a tool for developing sophisticated Windows user interfaces and general Windows applications. *Mastering Delphi* provides the most comprehensive explanations of how Delphi can address these development needs. ...this is a complete (and heavy) reference/tutorial for Delphi and Windows programming.

The runner-up to this book is *Delphi Developer's Guide*. It explains Windows programming topics in simpler terms than most of the other books, but it doesn't quite measure up to *Mastering Delphi*."

## *Delphi Developer's Group Journal—UK:*
## November/December 1995

"Another compendious tome to accompany Delphi, Marco Cantù's *Mastering Delphi* isn't small and isn't lightweight. There is something for every Delphi developer, from the novice to the expert.

In order to achieve this broad appeal, the author has structured the book in a way which gradually introduces those new to Delphi to the capabilities of the language while, at the same time, providing more experienced readers with many useful hints, tips, and code optimizations."

"Throughout the book, Marco Cantù uses sample applications to illustrate the techniques of programming in Delphi, analyses the coding used, suggests improvements and work-arounds, and then asks the reader to build on the program. This approach is ideal for grasping both the fundamentals of Delphi and the more advanced features such as developing custom components. For those with the time, this book would be most beneficial read from cover to cover but, as few of us can afford that luxury, just choose a chapter and start learning.

Overall, this book is to be recommended both as source of advice and as a comprehensive tutor, with the added bonus that the accompanying CD-ROM includes all of the sample programs (more than 200 of them) and some more Delphi components."

## *Sacra Blue*
## *The Magazine of the Sacramento PC Users Group:* December 1995

"This late entry has displaced *Delphi Unleashed* as my favorite. It's a huge tome, but the size enables the author to explore topics in greater depth than any other. Despite its depth, the treatment starts at the beginning, making it suitable for readers of all levels. The examples are well chosen, often illustrating multiple topics, with variations on a single program. Many include multiple ways to treat a given task, with helpful comments on the tradeoffs. If you intend to buy just one book on Delphi, I highly recommend this one."

# Mastering™ Delphi™ 2 for Windows® 95/NT

## Marco Cantù

SYBEX®

San Francisco • Paris • Düsseldorf • Soest

Associate Publisher: Gary Masters
Acquisitions Manager: Kristine Plachy
Developmental Editor: John Read
Editor: Michelle Nance
Project Editor: Shelby Zimmerman
Technical Editors: Alain Tadros, Tim Gooch
Graphic Illustrator: Tony Jonick
Cover Designer: Design Site
Book Designer: Suzanne Albertson
Electronic Publishing Specialist: Dina F Quan
Production Coordinators: Kim Askew-Qasem, Alexa Riggs
Indexer: Nancy Guenther
Cover Photographer: Mark Johann

SYBEX is a registered trademark of SYBEX Inc.

Mastering is a trademark of SYBEX Inc.

Library of Congress Card Number: 95-73074
ISBN: 0-7821-1860-7

Manufactured in the United States of America

10 9 8 7 6 5 4 3 2

*To my wife Lella, with all of my love*

# ACKNOWLEDGMENTS

I spent almost a year working on the previous edition of this book, and another eight months on this new edition. Many things happened during that period, many people got involved with my work and my life, and it is not easy to find the right words to thank all of them.

Probably the first thank you goes to Borland programmers and managers, because they built a great product. The thanks go in particular to Zack Urlocker and David Intersimone (they have helped me in many ways since we met many years ago). I would also like to extend my thanks to all of Borland's Delphi team, including the people I've been in contact with and those I've never met (you can actually see a list of the names of the Borland developers by opening Delphi's About box, holding down Alt, and typing **TEAM** or **DEVELOPERS**).

The book also owes a lot to Nan Borreson at Borland, who first suggested that I have a look at the product and write about it, and who provided me with insightful information. Another person who introduced me to Delphi was Bruce Eckel, a friend and an author of great C++ (and now Java) books. In the last year, Bruce and I spent some time discussing Delphi while wandering in such different places as the small streets of Venice or the woods north of San Francisco.

The next thank you is for Sybex editors. I don't even know everyone who got involved with the book (although I managed to visit Sybex headquarters), but I want to thank them all. Special thanks go to Gary Masters, Barbara Gordon, Kristine Plachy, John Read, and Judy Jigarjian. Thanks also to Jane Reh, Marilyn Smith, Dusty Bernard, and Valerie Potter for the previous edition, and to Shelby Zimmerman and Michelle Nance for this edition.

Next, I want to thank Stefano Maruzzi (who taught me a lot about Windows programming) and his wife Antonella, Andrea Provaglio (another Delphi and C++ guy), Claudio Galletti (also known as Dino), Giovanni Librando (who introduced me to Visual Basic, helping me to understand why Delphi is better), Giorgio Panzeri (editor at PCProfessionale), Marco Miotti (now in the Microsoft camp), Ernesto Franchini, and other Borland people in both Italy and London. Also, a very big thank you to all the attendees of my Delphi programming courses.

Some friends and magazine editors looked at portions of the book, or just examples and ideas for it, discussed Delphi programming with me, and provided some invaluable feedback. They include JD Hildebrand, Jerry Coffrey, Chris Frizelle, Norm McIntosh (my San Francisco host), Bob Arnson, Kevin Weeks (who elected the previous edition as "the current winner of the Manhattan Phone Book Look-Alike Contest"), OLE expert Brian Waters, Steve Tendon (who read the whole manuscript of the previous edition), Bob Swart (better known as Dr. Bob), Johanna and Phil of the UK Delphi Developer's Group, and many others. I also want to thank people *living* on the Delphi CompuServe forum (in particular *TeamB* members) for the support they provide to Delphi programmers.

Danny Thorpe reviewed the previous edition of the book, suggesting improvements, revealing features I was not aware of, and providing many ideas. The second edition was reviewed by Alain Tadros and Tim Gooch. They both contributed many insightful comments, gave me advice, suggested examples and ideas, and helped me find all the new Delphi 2 features. Tim also did most of the Windows NT work. The book owes its quality to my technical reviewers more than any other people, so thank you very much.

Besides those involved with my work and the book, there are many others who helped me. First of all my wife, Lella, who never stopped supporting me in every possible way. Many of her plans, particularly for holidays and weekends, had to change because of the book, and things were really hectic at times. She also improved my self-confidence when things were not working out as planned and forced me to stop working from time to time.

For this same reason, I have to thank many of our friends who sustained my mental health, inviting us to their homes, to eat pizza, or to see a film. The list of the friends is quite long, and includes among others Sandro and Monica, Stefano and Elena, Marco and Laura (and now Matteo), Chiara, Luca and Elena, Chiara and Daniele, and Laura, to name just a few. Our parents, brothers, sisters, and their families were very supportive, too. It was nice to spend some of our limited free time with them and our five nephews, Matteo, Andrea, Giacomo, Stefano, and Andrea; playing with them really helped me to relax.

Finally, I would like to thank all of the people, many unknown, who enjoy life and help to build a better world. If I never stop believing in the future, it is also because of them.

# CONTENTS AT A GLANCE

# TABLE OF CONTENTS

## 6 The Visual Component Library

# INTRODUCTION

It all happened at once. I was a happy C++ programmer and writer when Zack Urlocker showed me a yet-to-be-released product: Delphi. Since the first time I saw it, I liked its fine language, its rich environment, and its ease of use. Pascal was my first serious programming language—the one I used at the University for my first projects—and at that time, Pascal actually meant Turbo Pascal. I have since used other languages, but have come back to Object Pascal and use it frequently in my work. Then, when I was introduced to Delphi (a program written in Object Pascal), I immediately found it to be a very interesting environment. I guess my first impression was accurate.

I used to write, teach, and consult about Windows programming in C and C++; now I still write, consult, and teach courses, but they mostly relate to Delphi. The previous edition of this book was a great success because Delphi was so successful and was rapidly accepted by a diverse group of programmers.

# From Delphi 1 to Delphi 2

This edition is meant for programmers moving to Delphi 2 from Delphi 1, since the book covers the new version of the Borland environment. In the text I'll underline new Delphi features, mentioning the differences between this version and the last. The examples have been rewritten to take advantage of the new Delphi 2 capabilities whenever possible, and many of them won't be compilable with Delphi 1. However, on the companion CD, you'll find (whenever possible) the corresponding examples from the previous edition of the book, which you can use with Delphi 1.

## Delphi? Great!

There are many programming environments you can work with, but Delphi is outstanding for a number of reasons. Here are my top ten reasons to use Delphi (in reverse order):

10. Previous Borland Pascal and C++ compilers

9. Delphi third-party components and tools

8. Delphi programming environment

7. The availability of the VCL source code

6. The form-based and object-oriented approach

5. The super-fast compiler

4. The great database support

3. The close integration with Windows 95 programming

2. Delphi's component technology

1. The Object Pascal language (which actually is the foundation of all the other elements above)

# Delphi 2? Even Better

If you liked Delphi 1, as I did, you'll like Delphi 2 even better. There are many new features, not all relating to Win32 programming. Here is my "best-of" Delphi 2 list:

10. The new 32-bit optimizing compiler and the faster linker

9. Lookup fields, table filtering, and other improved database capabilities and related tools

8. Design-time uses of forms and data modules

7. Multithreading support

6. OLE Controls support

5. The Multi-Record Object and the improved database grid

4. OLE Automation support and the variant data type

3. Full Windows 95 support and integration, including the new Windows 95 controls

2. The new long string data type (which raises the 255-character barrier up into the gigabytes)

1. Visual Form Inheritance—that is, object-oriented programming and visual programming to the max

If you want to know the details about each of these points, and those from the previous list, this book is for you.

# Becoming a Delphi Master (by Reading This Book)

Delphi is a great tool, but it is also a complex programming environment that involves many different elements. This book will help you master Delphi programming, including the Object Pascal language, Delphi components (both using the existing ones and developing new components), database support, and the key elements of Windows programming.

You do not need an in-depth knowledge of any of these topics to read this book. Having some familiarity with Delphi will help you a lot, particularly after the introductory chapters. The book starts going in-depth in Chapter 4, so if you've never used Delphi at all, you'll have to study hard, and if you've used the first version of Delphi, you'll start seeing a lot of new information. Actually, you'll see new Delphi 2 features all the way from Chapter 1 through Chapter 28. There aren't just one or two final chapters or added sections at the ends of the chapters to cover new features: this book has been completely revised from the first to the last page.

What this book does require is a knowledge of the basics of programming, using any language and with any operating system or environment. You should have an idea of what variables and functions are and what the term *"loop"* means. If you've never written a program line in your life, this might not be the book for you right now. First, read a book that provides an introduction to programming using Delphi, and then read this book.

## The Structure of the Book

The book is divided into four parts:

- The first part, "Visual Programming and Language," introduces beginners to Delphi programming and also provides some tips for more experienced users. The focus is on the Delphi development environment, and just a few examples are presented. This part goes on to discuss the Object Pascal language, from a brief overview of Pascal to the object-oriented features of the language. The final chapter in this part examines the key elements of Delphi's Visual Component Library (VCL).

- The second part, "Using Components," explores the use of Delphi components and forms to build Windows applications. It covers standard components, the Windows 95 controls, graphic components, menus, mouse input, graphical output, MDI (Multiple Document Interface), database programming, and many other topics. The chapters include both Delphi-specific topics and related Windows programming ideas.

- The third part, "Advanced Delphi Programming," discusses some advanced Windows programming techniques, such as memory handling, using resources, printing support, file handling, Dynamic Data Exchange (DDE), and OLE. The chapters in this part provide more advanced examples and suggestions for further exploration of Delphi tools, to help you acquire a solid knowledge of the Windows environment.

- The fourth part, "Creating Components and Libraries," covers Delphi components and Dynamic Link Library (DLL) development. Writing components, which is more difficult than using them, constitutes a key element of Delphi programming.

The book has two short appendices, which are both quick introductions to programming concepts. Appendix A deals with OOP (object-oriented programming), and Appendix B covers SQL (Structured Query Language).

## How to Read This Book

This book focuses on examples. After the presentation of each concept and each Delphi component, there is usually an example (sometimes more than one), to let you see how the feature can be used. All told, there are almost 250 examples presented in the book. Most of the examples are quite simple and focus on a single feature. More complex examples are often built step-by-step, with intermediate steps including some solutions that do not work well.

In this book, I've tried to skip reference material almost completely. You'll see just a few tables listing the meanings of different parameters of a procedure. A list of parameters of a function is presented only in a couple of cases where the original Delphi documentation is not correct. Adding a lot of reference material is an easy way to increase the size of the book, but it also makes it obsolete as soon as the software changes slightly.

I suggest that you read this book with the Delphi Help files at hand, to have reference material readily available. Also, if you read it somewhere near a computer, you can test and run the programs immediately, and follow instructions as you come to them. However, I've done my best to allow you to read the book far away from a computer if you prefer (I'll let you choose your favorite place). Screen images and the key portions of the listings should help in this direction. The full listings that were available in the previous edition, however, have been removed. While full listings can be helpful to understand a program, when faced with a choice between listings or new content, I chose new content.

Even if you tend to read books from cover to cover as I do, considering the size of this book and the various topics it covers, you might follow one of these paths for reading it:

- If you are quite new to the whole subject, you might want to read the first three parts, skipping some of the more advanced constructs of the language. Also, read the two appendices, which introduce OOP and SQL. Then re-read the second and third parts, and move along only when you are familiar with the information there.

- If you consider yourself a good programmer, but not a Delphi expert, read the book straight through. You can skip the sections that introduce Windows topics if you are familiar with the API of the system.

- If you are an experienced Delphi programmer and you don't have much time, you can focus on the language chapters, try to locate new Delphi 2 features, and then start from Chapter 9 and read forward from there. You'll probably spend most of your time on the advanced parts of the book, but keep in mind that not all of the examples in the first part of the book are simple (even in the language chapters, I introduce constructs that many Delphi programmers are not aware of).

## Conventions Used in This Book

The book uses a few conventions to make it more readable. Some elements of the language, such as the keywords and the names of constant values, appear in a different font, as in "the `for` keyword." Direct calls of Windows API functions also appear in that font to distinguish them from similarly named Delphi methods. Delphi data types, component names, method names, and property names are in the regular font used for the text (you can easily spot them by their mixed capitalization).

In capitalizing and formatting the source code, I've tried to remain consistent with the most common conventions, but you'll notice that I have my preferences. Code formatting is a topic of much debate, as is any subject that involves personal taste and habits more than fixed rules.

The text generally contains code fragments and partial listings. You'll be able to find all of the source code files on the companion CD. To make it simple to locate the examples on the disk, each chapter has its own directory, and each sample has its own subdirectory. The names of these subdirectories reflect the names of the examples, as indicated in the book.

# The Companion CD

The main reason for the companion CD is to hold the source code of the almost 250 examples discussed in the book. In the text you'll mainly find code excerpts, while on the companion CD you'll be able to see the full code, and also to run the resulting program immediately, since the compiled programs are also on the CD. This way, you can copy only the examples you want to modify onto your hard disk.

Besides the examples for this edition, as I already mentioned, I used some of the empty space on the CD for a copy of all the examples from the previous edition. Since many examples are similar, you'll often find alternative coding solutions compatible with Delphi 1.

On the CD, you'll find a browser application, CDVIEW.EXE (a variation of an example built in Chapter 14), which you can use to look at the source code and run the executable files much more quickly than loading the files in Delphi (although you don't get the syntax highlighting).

Basically, each chapter has its own directory, with subdirectories named after each example. In some cases, the name of an example's project and executable files do not match the name of the directory containing them, particularly for those examples with multiple versions. In these cases, the name of the example mentioned in the text refers to the directory name, not to the project name. Since there is a single Delphi project in each directory (except for a few special cases), it should be quite simple to find a particular example.

## Third-Party Tools

The companion CD holds much more than the source code of the book examples. You'll find many third-party tools, including a number of Delphi components. Some of them are in demo version, others are shareware, and others are public domain versions. Of course, you'll need to register the demo and shareware components (and the other shareware tools) if you use them to build programs. Notice that the third-party components on the CD are the 16-bit versions, so you cannot install them in Delphi 2 (unless they include 32-bit compatible source code). You can try them out in the 16-bit version of Delphi, and if you like them, look for a new edition on CompuServe or the Internet, or directly from the vendor.

The CD contains a variety of Delphi-related tools, ranging from installation programs to resource editors to table viewers. The selection includes only tools that are strictly Delphi-related, and most of them are written in Delphi, too. Again, most of the tools relate to 16-bit Delphi, but some are Windows 95 versions.

The CD also contains some electronic Delphi magazines, provided as Windows Help files or Acrobat files (the Acrobat reader is included, in case you don't have it). I hope you'll enjoy these magazines, subscribe to them, and support the vendors of Delphi-related tools in general.

Some components and tools are ready to use, while others require you to run the proper installation program. You'll need to install them and compile the related examples to see how they work.

Again, you can use the CDVIEW program to browse through the add-on tools. Every directory has a README.TXT file, which is automatically loaded by the CDVIEW program as soon as you reach the directory.

# How to Reach the Author

If you find any problems in the text or examples in this book, or if you have specific questions, I would be happy to hear from you. You can reach me directly via electronic mail (see the address below). You can also find an update on the book, with any necessary changes, and new tips and ideas, on my own World Wide Web home page. This is the address:

`http://ourworld.compuserve.com/homepages/marcocantu`

You might check this page before indicating problems and submitting requests. If you have more general questions and you have a CompuServe account, you can address them to me in the Delphi forum (GO DELPHI), too. I'll reply to them, but others might help you at the same time. You can also check the SYBEX home page at `http://www.sybex.com` and their forum on CIS (GO SYBEX) for more information on this and other books.

I would definitely like to hear from you. Besides reporting errors and problems, give me your unbiased opinion of the book or tell me which example you liked best and which you liked least. Suggestions for future editions are also appreciated. My e-mail address on CompuServe is `100273,2610`. From the Internet, that becomes `100273.2610@compuserve.com`.

I hope you'll enjoy reading this book as much as I've enjoyed writing it.

# PART I

## Visual Programming and Language

# CHAPTER

## ONE

# A Form Is a Window

- Form creation

- Components and properties

- Program compilation

- Events and code

- Delphi as a two-way tool

In this chapter, we will build our first Windows 95 application using Delphi. As the name suggests, Windows applications are usually based on windows. So, how are we going to create our first window? We'll do it by using a form.

A form really is a window in disguise. There is no real difference between the two concepts, at least from a general point of view. If you look closely, though, a form is always a window, but the reverse isn't true.

> **NOTE**  Some Delphi components are windows, too. A push button is a window. A list box is a window. To avoid confusion, I'll use form to indicate the main window of an application or a similar window and window in the broader sense.

## Creating Your First Form

Even though you have probably already created a simple application in Delphi, I'm going to show you the process again, to highlight some interesting points. Creating a form is one of the easiest operations in the system: you only need to open Delphi, and it will automatically create a new, empty form for you, as you can see in Figure 1.1. That's all there is to it.

If you have another project open, you can choose File ➤ New Application to close the old project (you might be asked if you want to save some of the files) and open a new blank project. If you want to start with an existing project template instead,

**FIGURE 1.1:**

The empty form created when you open the Delphi environment.

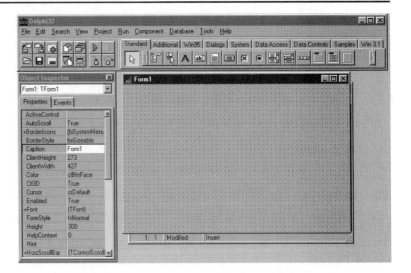

you can select File ➤ New and open the Object Repository (a topic covered in Chapter 3).

Believe it or not, you already have a working application. You can run it, using the Run button on the toolbar or Run ➤ Run menu command, and it will result in a standard Windows program. Delphi creates a stand-alone executable file that you can easily move to another machine. In fact, no run-time libraries are needed. Of course, this application won't be very useful, since it has a single empty window with no capabilities.

## Adding a Title

Before we run the application, let's make a quick change. The title of the form is Form1. For a user, the title of the main window stands for the name of the application. Let's change Form1 to something more meaningful.

When you first open Delphi, the Object Inspector window should appear on the left side of the form (see Figure 1.1, above). If it doesn't, open it by choosing View ➤ Object Inspector. In the Object Inspector window, you can see a list of the properties of the form (the Object Inspector shows the properties of the selected component). At the top of the list, there is a page tab labeled Properties. The other page tab is labeled Events; you can choose this to switch to a list of events that can take place in the form or in the selected component.

We can change the title of the form simply by changing the Caption property, which is selected by default. (The properties are listed in alphabetical order, so it's quite easy to find the ones you want to change.) Type in a new caption for the form. While you type, you can see the title of the form change. If you type Hello, the title of the form changes immediately, as you can see in Figure 1.2.

**FIGURE 1.2:**

The form with a new title.

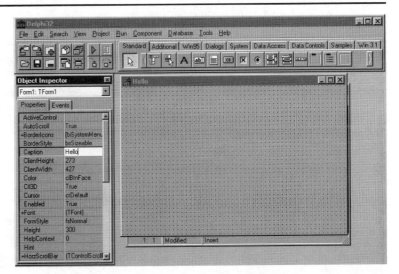

As an alternative, you can modify the internal name of the form by changing its Name property. If you have not entered a new caption, the new value of the Name property will be used for the Caption property, too.

Although we haven't done much work, we have built a full-blown application, with a system menu and the default minimize, maximize, and close buttons. You can resize the form by dragging its borders, move it by dragging its caption, maximize it to full-screen size, or minimize it. It works, but again, it's not very useful.

If you do minimize the window, or simply look at the icon in the TaskBar, you'll see that something isn't right. Instead of showing the caption of the form as the icon caption, it shows the name of the project, something like Project1. We can fix this by giving a name to the project, which we'll do by saving it to disk with a new name.

## Saving the Form

Select the Save Project or Save Project As command from the File menu, and Delphi will ask you to give a name to the source code file associated with the form, and then to give a name to the project file. Since I like the name of the project to match the caption of the form (Hello), I've named the form source file HELLO_F .PAS (see Figure 1.3), which stands for Hello Form. I've given the project file the name HELLO.DPR (see Figure 1.4).

Unfortunately, we cannot use the same name for the project and the form; they must be unique Delphi names. Adding an underscore and the letter f (_f) after the form name is a solution that was common in the 16-bit version of Delphi, because file names could not exceed 8 characters. In Delphi 2, we can use long file names, and we can also name the file HELLO_FORM. You could use a totally different name, or simply call it Mainform. However, I dislike this approach because you will end up with a number of forms (in different projects) that all have the same name, which can become confusing.

**FIGURE 1.3:**

When you save a project, you need to name the Pascal source file first.

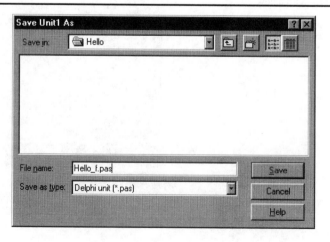

**FIGURE 1.4:**

After you name the source file, name the project file. If the project file name matches the form's caption, the name on the TaskBar will be the same, too.

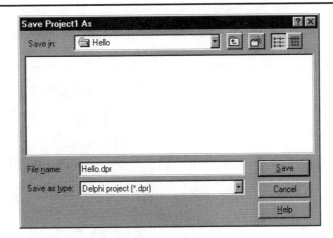

Both files have been placed in a HELLO subdirectory of directory 01 (which stands for Chapter 1). This is the way I'll save source files throughout the book, and you should follow this approach to find the code for the examples on the companion CD.

The name you give to the project file is used by default at run-time as the title of the application, displayed by Windows 95 in the TaskBar while the program is running. For this reason, if the name of the project matches the caption of the main form, it will also correspond to the name on the TaskBar (or application icon in Windows NT). In fact, you can change the title of the application by using the Application page of the Project Options dialog box (choose Project ➤ Options), or by writing a line of code to change the Title property of the Application global object. We will discuss this global object in detail in later chapters (in particular in Chapter 19).

# Using Components

Now it's time to start placing something useful in our Hello form. Forms can be described as component containers. Each form can host a number of components or controls. You can choose a component from the multipage palette above the form, in the Delphi window.

To complete our example, choose the Button component from the Standard page of the Components palette. Click on this component, move the mouse cursor to the form, press the left mouse button to set the upper-left corner of the button, and drag the mouse to set the button's size. You can also simply click on the form to place a button with default height and width—this is actually the more common approach. Now your form should look like Figure 1.5.

**FIGURE 1.5:**

Adding a button to the Hello form.

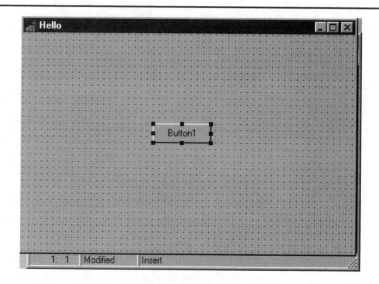

Our form will have only one button, so we'll center it in the form. You can do this by hand, but I'm not that good at it. Fortunately, I have help from Borland. When you choose the View ➤ Alignment Palette, a toolbox with alignment icons appears.

This toolbox makes a number of operations easy. It includes buttons to align controls or to center them in the form. Using the two buttons in the third column, you can place a component in the center of the form.

Keep in mind that although we've placed the button in the center, as soon as you run the program, you can resize the form and the button won't be in the middle anymore. So the button is only in the center of the form at startup. Later on, we'll see how to make the button remain in the middle after the form is resized, by adding some code. For now, our first priority is to change the button's label.

# Changing Properties

Like the form, the button has a Caption property that we can use to change its label (the text displayed inside it). As a better alternative, we can change the name of the button. The name is a kind of internal property, used only in the code of the program. However, as I mentioned earlier, if you change the name of a button before changing its caption, the Caption property will have the same text as the Name property.

Changing the Name property is usually a good choice, and you should generally do this early in the development cycle, before you write much code. However, you often need to change the Caption property, too. There are at least two reasons for this. The first reason to have a caption different from the name is that it's a good habit to have the word Button in the name of the component so that it's easy to identify, but it's not that nice to see the word in the button's text. In the code, it's better to refer to HelloButton than to Hello, since Hello can refer to a form or any other kind of component. At the same time, a caption such as Say hello is certainly better than HelloButton.

The second reason is that captions should be descriptive, and therefore they often use two or more words, as in my Say hello button. If you try to use this text as the Name property, however, Delphi will show an error message, such as the one in Figure 1.6.

**FIGURE 1.6:**

The error message shown when you try to use a space in the Name property of a component.

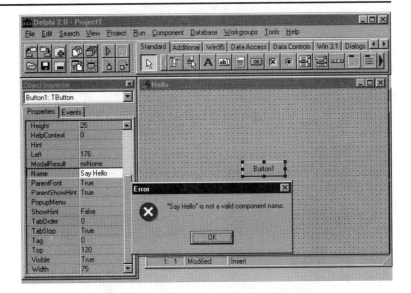

The name is an internal property, and it is used as the name of a variable referring to the component. Therefore, for the Name property, you must follow the rules for naming an identifier in the Pascal language:

- An identifier is a sequence of letters, digits, or underscore characters of any length (although only the first 63 characters are significant).

- The first character of an identifier cannot be a number; it must be a letter or the underscore character.

- No spaces are allowed in an identifier.

- Identifiers are not case-sensitive, but usually each of the words in an identifier begins with a capital letter, as in HelloButton. But hellobutton, HELLOBUTTON, and helloButton refer to this same identifier.

Here is a summary of the changes we have made to the properties of the button and form. At times, I'll show you the structure of the form of the examples as it appears once it has been converted in a readable format (I'll describe how to convert a form into text later in the chapter). I won't show you the entire textual description of a form (which is often quite long), but rather only its key elements. I won't include the lines describing the position of the components, their sizes, or some less important default values. I will also use bold text to highlight the names of the elements (following the object keyword):

```
object Form1: TForm1
  Caption = 'Hello'
  OnClick = FormClick
  object HelloButton: TButton
    Caption = 'Say hello'
    OnClick = HelloButtonClick
  end
end
```

This description shows some attributes of the components and the events they respond to. We will see the code for these events in the following sections.

If you run this program now, you will see that the button works properly. In fact, if you click on it, it will be pushed, and when you release the mouse button, the on-screen button will be released. The only problem is that when you press the button, you might expect something to happen....

# Responding to Events

When you press the mouse button on a form or a component, Windows informs your application of the event by sending it a message. Ignoring Windows behavior, at least for the moment, you should know that Delphi responds by receiving an event notification and calling a proper event-response method or event-handler. As a programmer, you can provide several of these methods, both for the form itself and for the components you have placed in the form (in our case, the button).

Delphi defines a number of different events for each kind of component. The list of the events for a form is different from the list of the events for a button, although some events are common to both components. You can determine the events available for a form or a component by viewing the Events page of the Object Inspector while that element is selected.

Here's how to display a hello message when the button is pressed:

1. Select the button, in the form or in the Object Inspector using the Object Selector (the combo box just below the title of the Object Inspector).

2. Select the Events page.

3. Double-click with the left mouse button in the white area on the right side of the OnClick event. A new method name will appear.

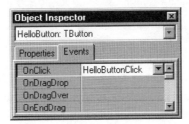

Delphi creates a procedure named HelloButtonClick in the code of the form and opens the source code file in that position, as shown in Figure 1.7. Instead of following the steps above, you can accomplish the same task by just double-clicking on the button in the form.

**FIGURE 1.7:**

The edit window after you have created a procedure to handle the Hello button click.

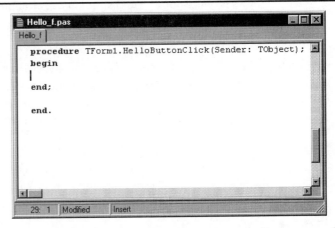

```
procedure TForm1.HelloButtonClick(Sender: TObject);
begin

end;

end.
```

This operation invokes the default action for the component. The default action for a button is to add a procedure to respond to the click event. Even if you are not sure of the effect of the default icon, you can still double-click on the component. If you end up adding a new procedure you don't need, just leave it empty. Empty method bodies generated by Delphi will be removed as soon as you save the project. In other words, if you don't put any code in them, they simply go away.

**TIP**

When you want to remove an event-response method you have written from the source code of a Delphi application, you could delete all of the references to it. However, a better way is to delete all of the code from the corresponding procedure, leaving only the declaration and the begin and end keywords. The text should be the same as what Delphi automatically generated when you first decided to handle the method. When you save or compile a project, Delphi removes any empty methods from the source code and from the form description (including the reference to them in the Events page of the Object Inspector). Conversely, to keep an event-handler that is still empty, consider adding a comment to it, so that it would not be removed.

Now we can start typing some instructions between the begin and the end keywords delimiting the code of the procedure. If you do not know the Object Pascal language, don't worry. We will explore its most important features in Chapters 4 and 5. Writing code is usually so simple that you don't need to be an expert in the language to start to work with Delphi.

For the moment, type the code below. You should type only the line at the middle (shown in bold typeface), but I've included the whole source code of the procedure to let you know where you need to add the new code in the editor:

```
procedure TForm1.HelloButtonClick(Sender: TObject);
begin
  MessageDlg ('Hello, guys', mtInformation, [mbOK], 0);
end;
```

The code is very simple. There is only a call to a function, MessageDlg, to display a small message dialog box. The function has four parameters. You can see the details about this function by clicking on its name in the edit window and pressing F1. This brings up the Help information. Here is a summary of the description in the Help system:

- The first parameter is the string you want to display: the message.

- The second parameter is the type of message box. You can choose `mtWarn-ing`, `mtError`, `mtInformation`, or `mtConfirmation`. For each type of message, the corresponding caption is used and a proper icon is displayed at the side of the text.

- The third parameter is a set of values indicating the buttons you want to use. You can choose `mbYes`, `mbNo`, `mbOK`, `mbCancel`, or `mbHelp`. Since this is a set of values, you can have more than one of these values. Always use the proper set notation with square brackets ([ and ]) to denote the set, even if you have only one value, as in the line of the code above. (Chapter 4 discusses Pascal sets.)

- The fourth parameter is the help context, a number indicating which page of the Help system should be invoked if the user presses F1. I will usually write 0, since I don't want to include Help in the simple examples of the book.

The function also has a return value, which I've just ignored, using it as if it were a procedure. In any case, it's important to know that the function returns an identifier of the button that the user clicked to close the message box.

**NOTE**

Programmers who are not familiar with the Pascal language, particularly programmers who use C/C++, might be confused by the phrase "The function also has a return value, which I've just ignored, using it as if it were a procedure." In Pascal, there are two different keywords to define procedures and functions. The only difference between functions and procedures is that only functions have a type, or return value. Procedures have no return value, although they can have parameters passed by reference (`var` parameters), which allow a sort of return value. One enhancement over previous versions of Borland's Pascal compiler products is that Delphi allows you to ignore the return value of a function, using it as a procedure, as in the example here.

After you have written this line of code, you should be able to run the program. When you click on the button, you'll obtain the message box shown in Figure 1.8.

Every time the user clicks the left mouse button on the push button of the form, a message is displayed. What if the mouse is pressed outside that area? Nothing happens. Of course, we can add some new code to handle this event. We only need to add an OnClick event to the form itself.

To do this, move to the Events page of the Object Inspector and select the form. Then double-click at the right side of the OnClick event, and you'll end up in the

**FIGURE 1.8:**

The message box displayed when you press the Say hello button.

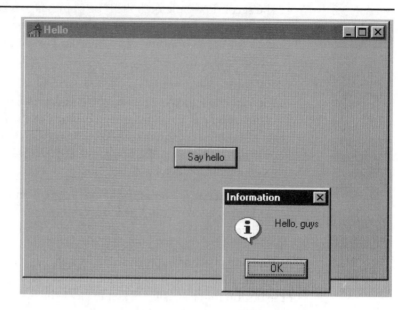

proper position in the edit window. Now add a new call to the MessageDlg function, as in the following code:

```
procedure TForm1.FormClick(Sender: TObject);
begin
  MessageDlg ('You have clicked outside of the button',
    mtWarning, [mbOK], 0);
end;
```

Notice that I've written the code on two lines, instead of one. The Pascal compiler completely ignores new lines, white spaces, tab spaces, and similar formatting characters. Program statements are separated by semicolons (;), not by starting to write code on a new line.

**WARNING**

There is one case in which Delphi doesn't completely ignore line breaks: Strings cannot extend across multiple lines. In some cases, you can split a very long string into two different strings, written on two lines, and merge them by writing one after the other.

With this new version of the program, if the user clicks on the button, the hello message is displayed (Figure 1.8), but if he or she misses the button, a warning message appears, as in Figure 1.9.

**FIGURE 1.9:**
The message displayed when you click in the form outside the button.

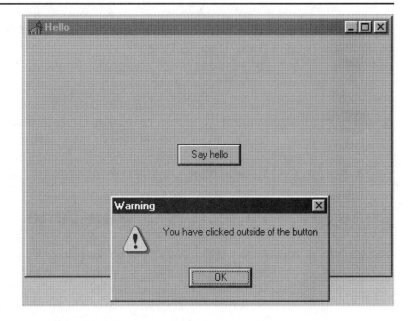

# Compiling and Running a Program

Before we make any further changes to our HELLO program, let's stop for a moment to consider what goes on when you run the application. When you click on the Run button on the toolbar or select Run ➤ Run, Delphi does the following:

1. Compiles the Pascal source code file describing the form

2. Compiles the project file

3. Builds the executable (EXE) file linking the proper libraries (as specified)

4. Runs the EXE file, usually in debug mode

The key point is that when you ask Delphi to run your application, it compiles it. As I've already mentioned, the executable file you obtain is a stand-alone program. You can easily run it from the Windows 95 Explorer or using the Run command on the Start button, and even move it to a different computer.

Because it's a compiled program, it is also extremely fast, with speed comparable to a C or C++ compiled program. Delphi compiled code runs much faster (at least 10 or 20 times faster) than the equivalent code in interpreted environments such as Visual Basic, PowerBuilder, Paradox, and dBASE.

Some users cannot believe that Delphi generates real executable code, because when you run a small program, its main window appears immediately, as in an interpreted environment. To see for yourself, try this: Open the Environment Options dialog box (using Tools ➤ Options), move to the Preferences page, and turn on the Show Compile Progress option. Now select Project ➤ Build All. You'll see a dialog box with the compilation status. You'll find that this takes just a few seconds, or even less on a fast machine.

The Pascal compiler embedded in Delphi works very quickly, in the tradition of Borland's Turbo Pascal compilers, and is really much faster than any C++ compiler for a number of technical reasons. One reason is that the language definition is much simpler. Another is that the Pascal compilers and linkers have less work to do to include libraries or other compiled source files in a program.

# Changing Properties at Run-Time

After this short digression, we are ready to finish the HELLO application, building a new version of the program, HELLO2. If you want to save the current version of the program without overwriting it, you can copy all of the source files in a new subdirectory. If you use File ➤ Save Project As, the new project will refer to (and modify) the source files of the older version.

In this book (as well as on the companion CD), you will find multiple versions for some complex examples, built step-by-step. This makes it easier to understand the various steps and to test what doesn't work well in the intermediate versions. Along this line, the current example, has two versions: HELLO and HELLO2.

NOTE
The different version names for the example refer to different subdirectories where the files are stored on the companion CD. I refer to the new example as HELLO2 because this is the name of the directory containing it, not the name of this project file or the compiled executable file, which are still named HELLO.

We now want to try to change some properties at run-time. For example, we might change the text of the HelloButton from Say hello to Say hello again after the first time a user clicks on it. (You may also need to widen the button as the caption becomes longer). This is really simple. You only need to change the code of the HelloButtonClick procedure as follows (new code is in boldface):

```
procedure TForm1.HelloButtonClick(Sender: TObject);
begin
  MessageDlg ('Hello, guys', mtInformation, [mbOK], 0);
  HelloButton.Caption := 'Say Hello Again';
end;
```

**NOTE**  The Pascal language uses the := operator to express an assignment and the = operator to test for equality. At the beginning, this can be confusing for programmers coming from other languages. For example in C and C++, the assignment operator is =, and the equality is tested with = =. After a while, you'll get used to it. In the meantime, if you happen to use = instead of :=, you'll get an error from the compiler.

A property such as Caption can be changed at run-time very easily, using an assignment statement. Figure 1.10 shows the result of this operation.

**FIGURE 1.10:**
The new caption of the button, after the change. Notice that the button is not in the middle of the form, because it has been resized—a problem we will solve soon.

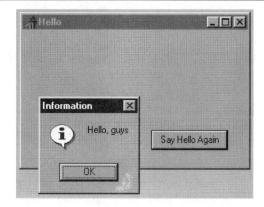

Not every property can be changed at run-time, and some can be changed only at run-time. You can easily spot this last group: They are not listed in the Object Inspector, but they appear in the Help file. Some run-time properties are defined as read-only, which means that you can access their value but cannot change it.

## Adding Code to the Program

Our program is almost finished, but we still have a problem to resolve, which will require some real coding. As I mentioned before, the button starts in the middle of the form, but will not remain there when you resize the form. This problem can be solved in two radically different ways.

One solution is to change the border of the form to a thin frame, so that the form cannot be resized at run-time. Just move to the BorderStyle property of the form, and choose bsSingle instead of bsSizeable in the combo box on the right. The result will be the form shown in Figure 1.11. As you can see in that figure, the Size command on the System menu is automatically disabled.

**FIGURE 1.11:**

The non-resizeable form with a fixed border, and its system menu with the Size command disabled.

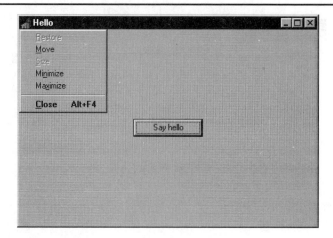

The other approach is to write some code to move the button to the center of the form each time the form is resized, and that's what we'll do next. Why have I chosen this second approach? Just to start showing you some code. You might start having the idea that programming with Delphi is just a matter of selecting options and visual elements. This is certainly a main approach, but there comes a time when you need to write code.

When you want to add some code to a program, the first question you need to ask yourself is Where? In an event-driven environment, the code is always executed in response to an event. When a form is resized, an event takes place: OnResize.

Select the form in the Object Inspector and double-click to the right of the name of this event in the Events page. A new procedure is added to the source file of the form. Now you need to type some code in the editor, as follows:

```
procedure TForm1.FormResize(Sender: TObject);
begin
  HelloButton.Top :=
    Form1.ClientHeight div 2 -
    HelloButton.Height div 2;
  HelloButton.Left :=
    Form1.ClientWidth div 2 -
    HelloButton.Width div 2;
end;
```

The meaning of this code should be clear. The Top and Left properties of the button—that is, the position of its upper-left corner—should be set considering these factors:

- The center of the frame, which is determined by dividing the height and the width of the internal area of the frame by 2. The internal area is its client area, indicated by the ClientWidth and ClientHeight properties. If you use the Height and Width properties instead, you will reference the center of the whole window, including the caption at the top border. Here, we really need the center of the internal portion of the window.

- The height and the width of the button, since the upper-left corner of the button should not be placed in the center of the form, but in the center minus half the height and half the width of the button itself.

This final version of the example works quite well, as you can see in Figure 1.12. This figure includes a couple of versions of the form, with different sizes. By the way, this figure is a real snapshot of the screen. Once you have created a Windows application, you can run several copies of it at the same time by using the Explorer (or File Manager). The Delphi environment can run only one copy of a program, instead. Why? Because when you run a program within Delphi, you really start its debugger, and it cannot debug two programs at the same time—not even two copies of the same program.

**FIGURE 1.12:**
With the last version of the program, the Hello button always remains in the center of the form.

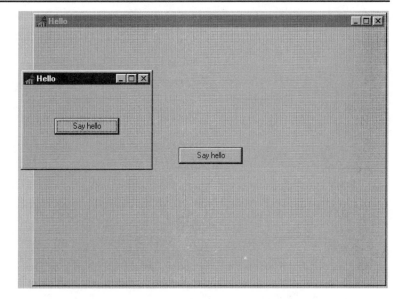

# A Two-Way Tool

In the HELLO example, we have written three small portions of code, to respond to three different events. Each portion of code was part of a different method. But where does the code we write end up? The whole source code of a form is written in a single Pascal language source file, the one we've named HELLO_F.PAS. This file evolves and grows not only when you code the response of some events, but also as you add components to the form. The properties of these components are stored together with the properties of the form in a second file, named HELLO_F.DFM.

Delphi can be defined as a two-way tool, since everything you do in the visual environment ends up in some code. Nothing is hidden away and inaccessible. You have the complete code, and although some of it might be fairly complex, you can edit everything. Of course, it is easier to use only the visual tools, at least until you are an expert Delphi programmer.

The term two-way tool means also that you are free to change the code that has been produced, and then go back to the visual tools. This is true as long as you follow some simple rules.

## Looking at the Source Code

Although you might not be able to understand everything in the source code of a program, let's take a look at what Delphi has generated during the operations we have done previously. Every action has an effect—in the Pascal code, in the code of the form, or in both.

When you start a new, blank project, the empty form has some code associated with it, as in the following listing.

```
unit Unit1;

interface

uses
  SysUtils, Windows, Messages, Classes, Graphics,
  Controls, Forms, Dialogs;

type
  TForm1 = class(TForm)
  private
    { Private declarations }
  public
    { Public declarations }
  end;

var
  Form1: TForm1;

implementation

{$R *.DFM}

end.
```

The file, named Unit1, uses a number of units and defines a new data type (a class) and a new variable (an object of that class). The class is named TForm1, and it is derived from TForm. The object is Form1, of the new type TForm1.

> Units are the modules into which a Pascal program is divided. When you start a new project, you have a program and a unit. Each time you add a form to a Delphi program, you add a new unit. Units are then compiled separately and linked into the main program. In other words, units are the Pascal code source files indicated by the PAS extension.

If you rename the files as suggested in the example, the code changes slightly, since the name of the unit must reflect the name of the file. If you name the file HELLO_F.PAS, the code begins with

```
unit Hello_f;
```

As soon as you start adding new components, the form class declaration in the source code changes. For example, when you add a button to the form, the portion of the source code defining the new data type becomes the following (the new line is in boldface):

```
type
  TForm1 = class(TForm)
    Button1: TButton;
  private
    { Private declarations }
  public
    { Public declarations }
end;
```

Now if you change the button's Name property (using the Object Inspector) to HelloButton, the code changes slightly again:

```
type
  TForm1 = class(TForm)
    HelloButton: TButton;
    private
    { Private declarations }
    public
    { Public declarations }
  end;
```

Setting properties other than the name has no effect in the source code. The properties of the form and its components are stored in a separate form description file (with a DFM extension).

Adding new event handlers has the biggest impact on the code. Each time you define a new handler for an event, a line is added to the data type definition of the form, an empty method body is added in the implementation part, and some information is stored in the form description file, too. The following listing shows the complete Pascal source code of the HELLO example (not the second version, HELLO2):

```
unit Hello_f;

interface

uses
  SysUtils, Windows, Messages, Classes, Graphics,
  Controls, Forms, Dialogs, StdCtrls;

type
  TForm1 = class(TForm)
    HelloButton: TButton;
    procedure HelloButtonClick(Sender: TObject);
    procedure FormClick(Sender: TObject);
  private
    { Private declarations }
  public
    { Public declarations }
  end;

var
  Form1: TForm1;

implementation

{$R *.DFM}

procedure TForm1.HelloButtonClick(Sender: TObject);
begin
  MessageDlg ('Hello, guys', mtInformation, [mbOK], 0);
end;

procedure TForm1.FormClick(Sender: TObject);
begin
  MessageDlg ('You have clicked outside of the button',
    mtWarning, [mbOK], 0);
end;

end.
```

It is worth noting that there is a single file for the whole code of the form, not just small fragments. Of course, this source code is only a partial description of the form. The source code determines how the form and its components react to events. The form description (the DFM file) stores the properties of the form and its components, including descriptions of the components in the form, where they are located on the form's display surface, and a host of other information about the form's state. In general, source code provides the actions of the system, and properties provide the state of the system.

# The Textual Description of the Form

As I've just mentioned, along with the PAS file containing the source code, there is another file describing the form, its properties, its components, and the properties of the components. This is the DFM file, a binary file that isn't readable with an editor. However, if you load this file in the Delphi code editor, it will be converted into a textual description. This might give the false impression that the DFM file is indeed a text file. For performance reasons, Borland has preferred to save the binary version, and has provided tools that allow for easy conversion to and from text. The simplest of these tools is the editor itself. In Figure 1.13, you can see the two representations of the file when loaded in two different editors.

**FIGURE 1.13:**

The DFM file holds a binary code that can be converted with the Delphi editor.

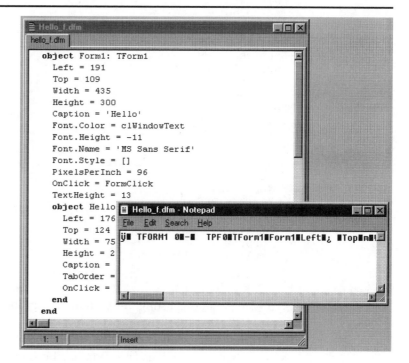

**NEW**

In Delphi 2, you can open the textual definition of a form simply by selecting the SpeedMenu of the form designer (that is, clicking on the surface of the form at design-time using the right mouse button) and selecting the View as Text command. This closes the form, eventually saving it, and opens the DFM file in the editor. You can later go back to the form using the View as Form command of the SpeedMenu in the editor window.

To understand what is stored in the DFM file, look at the next listing, which shows the textual description of the form of the first version of the HELLO example. This is exactly the code you'll see giving the View as Text command in the local menu of the form, with boldface characters added to highlight the different portions of the text. You can compare this code with the short one I used before to indicate the key features and properties of the form and its components.

```
object Form1: TForm1
  Left = 191
  Top = 109
  Width = 435
  Height = 300
  Caption = 'Hello'
  Font.Color = clWindowText
  Font.Height = -11
  Font.Name = 'MS Sans Serif'
  Font.Style = []
  PixelsPerInch = 96
  OnClick = FormClick
  TextHeight = 13
  object HelloButton: TButton
    Left = 176
    Top = 124
    Width = 75
    Height = 25
    Caption = 'Say hello'
    TabOrder = 0
    OnClick = HelloButtonClick
  end
end
```

As you can see in this listing, the textual description of a form describes a number of objects (in this case, two) at different levels. The Form1 object contains the HelloButton object, as you can infer from the indentation of the text. Each object has a number of properties and some methods connected to events (in this case, OnClick).

If you use the Delphi editor to view the textual description of a form, you are requested by the system to save the form first, to avoid having two representations of the same file you can work on. In fact, you can *edit* the textual description of the form, although this should be done with extreme care. As soon as you save the file, it will be turned back into a binary file, using a sort of compile process.

If you've made incorrect changes, this compilation will stop with an error message, and you'll need to correct the contents of your DFM file before you can reopen the form in the editor. For this reason, you shouldn't try to change the textual description of a form manually until you have a good knowledge of Delphi programming.

An expert programmer might choose to work on the text of a form for a number of reasons. For big projects, the textual description of the form is a powerful documenting tool, an important form of backup (in case someone plays with the form, you can understand what has gone wrong by comparing the two textual versions), and a good version-handling tool. For these reasons, there is also a DOS command line tool, CONVERT.EXE, which can translate forms from the compiled version to the textual description and vice versa. As we will see in the next chapter, the conversion is also applied when you cut or copy components from a form to the Clipboard.

## The Project File

In addition to the two files describing the form (PAS and DFM), there is a third file that is vital to rebuild the application. This is the Delphi project file (DPR). This file is built automatically, and you seldom need to change it, particularly for small programs. If you do need to change the behavior of a project, there are basically two ways to do it: You can use the Delphi Project Manager (see Figure 1.14) and set some project options, or you can manually edit the project file directly.

**FIGURE 1.14:**

The Delphi Project Manager allows you to add units to the project, thus changing the contents of the project source file.

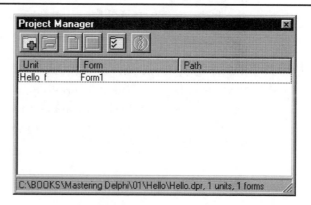

This project file is really a Pascal language source file, describing the overall structure of the program and its startup code:

```
program Hello;

uses
  Forms,
  Hello_f in 'HELLO_F.PAS' {Form1};

{$R *.RES}

begin
  Application.Initialize;
  Application.CreateForm(TForm1, Form1);
  Application.Run;
end.
```

You can see this file with the View ➤ Project Source menu command. As an alternative, you can select the Select unit from the SpeedBar (or the equivalent menu command View ➤ Units). When you use one of these commands, a dialog box with the list of the source files of the project (or a list with the forms) appears. You can choose the project file (named HELLO in the example), or any other file you are interested in seeing. Again, you should not edit this file unless you know what you are doing. You can find more details on this code in Chapter 19, where I discuss the use of the application object. Some basic information about how to manage a project without editing its source file manually is provided in Chapter 2.

# Summary

In this chapter, we have created a simple program, added a button to it, and handled some basic events, such as a click with the mouse or a resize operation. We have also seen how to name files, projects, forms, and components, and how this affects the source code of the program.

Before we can look into more complex examples, however, we need to explore the Delphi development environment and study the Object Pascal language. These are the topics of the next few chapters.

The example in this chapter should have shown you that Delphi is really easy to use. Now we'll start to show you that there are some complex elements behind the scenes. You'll see that Delphi is a very powerful tool, even though you can use it to write programs easily and quickly.

# CHAPTER
## TWO

# Highlights of the Delphi Environment

- Delphi Help

- Delphi menus and SpeedBars

- Form design tools

- The Delphi editor

- Project management

- Compiled program tools

- Delphi source files

In a visual programming tool such as Delphi, the role of the environment is certainly important, at times even more important than the programming language used by its compiler or interpreter. This is a good reason to spend some time reading the Delphi *User's Guide* manual, as well as this chapter. Even if the main features of this environment are intuitive, it is a mistake to skip the manual (or this chapter) altogether.

In this chapter, I won't discuss all of the features of Delphi or list all of its menu commands. The focus here is to give you the overall picture and help you to explore some of the environment traits that are not obvious, while suggesting some tips that may help you.

# Different Versions of Delphi

Before delving into the details of the Delphi programming environment, let's take a side step to underline two key ideas. First, there isn't a single version of Delphi 2; there are three of them:

- The basic version (the Desktop edition) has all the features required to write programs in Delphi for Windows 95 and Windows NT 3.51, including many new features not found in the first version of Delphi.

- The second level (the Developer edition) includes more database support, more documentation, and several tools aimed at the professional developer.

- The full-blown version (the Client/Server Suite) is aimed at developers building client/server applications and includes specific SQL-related tools, workgroup support, and 2 licenses for InterBase for NT.

This book will cover features present in each of these versions, although a few of them (discussed in Chapter 18) are available only in the Client/Server Suite. Some of the tools and components described in this book, however, are not available in the Desktop edition. I'll try to keep track of them in this book, but I may miss a few. If you own the Desktop edition and see the description of a feature that doesn't seem to work, consider this difference in the Delphi 2 versions. Notice, however, that since the CD-ROM includes the executable files, you can still understand how many of these features work, in case you eventually decide to upgrade your version of Delphi.

Besides having different capabilities, the menu structure also has some differences between versions. For example, the Client/Server Suite includes a version control system (PVCS Version Management from Intersolv) that adds a new pull-down menu, Workgroups, to the menu bar. Beside this, there are a number of ways to customize the Delphi environment. You can change the buttons of the SpeedBar, attach new commands to the Tools menu, hide some of the windows or elements, and resize and move all of them. I'll try to use a standard user interface (as it comes out of the box), although I have my preferences and they will probably be reflected in some of the screen shots I'll show you in this chapter and throughout the whole book.

# Asking for Help

Now we can really start our tour. The first element of the environment we'll explore is the Help system. Since I'm not going to describe 100 percent of Delphi's components, objects, and methods, you will want to complement the information provided in this book by using the reference material present in the Help files.

There are basically two ways to invoke the Help system: select the proper command in the Help pull-down menu, or choose an element of the Delphi interface or a token in the source code and press F1.

**TIP**

When you press F1, Delphi doesn't search for an exact match in the Help Search list. Instead, it tries to guess what you are asking. For example, if you press F1 when the text cursor is on the name of the Button1 component in the source code, the Delphi Help system automatically opens the description of the TButton class, since this is what you are probably looking for. This technique also works when you give the component a new name. Try naming the button *Foo*, then move the cursor to this word, press F1, and you'll still get the help for the TButton class. This means Delphi looks at the contextual meaning of the word for which you are asking help.

Note that there isn't just a single help file in Delphi. Most of the time, you'll invoke Delphi Help, but this file is complemented by an ObjectPascal Help file, the Windows API Help and the Component Writer's Help. These help files and other help files related to Delphi external tools have a common outline and a common search engine you can activate by pressing the Help Topics button while in the help system. The Windows 95 help engine dialog box that appears allows you to browse the contents of all of the help files in the group, search for a keyword in the index, or start the *find* engine. The three capabilities are available in three different pages of the Help Topics dialog box.

You can find almost everything in the Help system, but you need to know what to search for. Usually this is obvious, but at times it is not. Spending some time just playing with the Help system will probably help you understand the structure of these files and learn how to find the information you need.

The Help files provide a lot of information, both for beginner and expert programmers, but they are especially valuable as a reference tool. They list all of the methods and properties for each component, the parameters of each method or function, and similar details, which are particularly important while you are writing code. Borland distributes reference material also using Adobe Acrobat files. In this case you have the electronic version of the printed manuals that come in the Delphi box, so you can search them for a word, and you can also print the portions you are interested in (or even the whole file if you've got some spare paper).

> **NOTE**
>
> The first version of Delphi included some Interactive Tutors in addition to the help system. If you've never used Delphi, you might consider running these Tutors (if you've installed Delphi 1, of course). They will guide you through Delphi's basic features and help you understand some of the terminology of the environment.

# Delphi Menus and Commands

There are basically three ways to issue a command in the Delphi environment:

- Use the menu.
- Use the SpeedBar (or toolbar).
- Use a SpeedMenu (one of the local menus activated by pressing the right mouse button).

## Using the Menus

The Delphi menus offer many commands. I have no intention of boring you with a detailed description of the menu structure. For this type of information, you can refer to your *User's Guide* or the Help file. In the following sections, I'll present some suggestions on the use of some of the menu commands. Other suggestions will follow in the rest of the chapter. Of course, these hints will probably be more useful for beginners than for experienced users.

### The File Menu

The starting point of this analysis is the File pull-down menu. This menu is somewhat complex, because it contains commands that operate on projects and commands that operate on files. OK, I know that both are files, so this is the proper menu, but every time I open this menu, I need to think twice about what I'm doing. Some commands can be used both to operate on project and on source code files.

The commands related to projects are New, New Application, Open, Reopen, Save Project As, Save All, Close All, Add to Project, and Remove from Project. Beside these, there is also a specific Project pull-down menu. The commands related to source code files are New, New Form, New Data Module, Open, Reopen, Save, Save As, Close, and Print. Most of these commands are very intuitive, but some require a little explanation. File ➤ New is a general command, which can be used to invoke Experts; start new applications; inherit from existing forms; and create a Thread, an OLE Automation object, a DLL, a new Delphi component, and so on. I'll discuss most of these features in the next chapter.

**NEW**

Use the File ➤ Reopen menu command to open the last projects or the last source code files you have worked on. This menu command replaces the list of recently used files that was available at the end of the File menu in Delphi 1. The Reopen list is also important because the new Windows 95 File Open dialog box doesn't allow you to select from the list of most recently used files.

Another peculiar command is Print. If you are editing the source code and select this command, the printer will output this text. If you are working on a form and select Print from the File menu, the printer will produce the graphical representation of the form. This is certainly nice, but can be confusing, particularly if you are working on other Delphi windows. Fortunately, two different print options dialog boxes are displayed (see Figure 2.1), so that you can check that the operation is correct.

## The Edit Menu

The Edit menu has some typical operations, such as the Undo and Redo features, and the Cut, Copy, and Paste commands, plus some specific commands for form or editor windows. The important thing to notice is that the standard features of the Edit menu work both with text and with form components. There are also some differences worth noting. For example, when you work with the editor, the first command of this pull-down menu is Undo; when you work with the form, it becomes Undelete.

Of course, you can copy and paste some text in the editor, or you can copy and paste components in one form, or from one form to another. You can even paste components to a different parent window of the same form, such as a panel or group box.

What you might not have noticed is that you can also copy components from the form to the editor and vice versa. Delphi places components in the Clipboard along with their textual description, as you can see in Figure 2.2. You can edit this text properly and then paste it back into the form as a new component.

**FIGURE 2.1:**

The two Delphi print options dialog boxes.

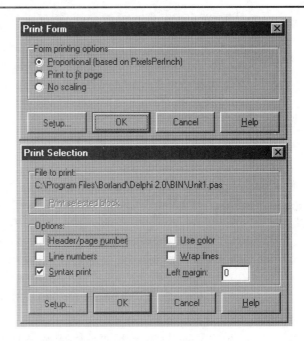

**FIGURE 2.2:**

Delphi copies the textual representation of components to the Clipboard (as you can see in the Clipboard Viewer on the right), so that they are available to any editor.

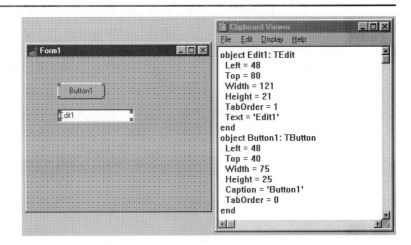

For example, if you place a button on a form, copy it, then paste it to an editor (which can be Delphi's own source code editor or any word processor), you'll get the following description:

```
object Button1: TButton
  Left = 56
  Top = 48
```

```
    Width = 161
    Height = 57
    TabOrder = 0
    Caption = 'Button1'
end
```

Now, if you change the name of the object, caption, or position, or add a new property, these changes can be copied and pasted back to a form. Here are some sample changes:

```
object MyButton: TButton
  Left = 200
  Top = 200
  Width = 180
  Height = 60
  TabOrder = 0
  Caption = 'My Button'
  Font.Name = 'Arial'
end
```

Pasting this code into the form will create a button in the specified position with the caption *My Button* in an Arial font. Figure 2.3 shows the result. If you want to make use of this technique, you need to know how to edit the textual representation of a component properly. However, during this operation, Delphi can solve some minor problems and conflicts between properties of the component. You can understand what goes on by copying the component back to the editor.

**FIGURE 2.3:**
You can paste the textual description of a component into a form.

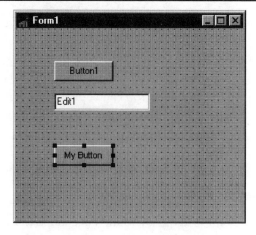

This is what you get if you copy the previous button again:

```
object Button2: TButton
  Left = 48
  Top = 144
  Width = 75
```

```
    Height = 25
    Caption = 'My Button'
    Font.Color = clWindowText
    Font.Height = -11
    Font.Name = 'Arial'
    Font.Style = []
    ParentFont = False
    TabOrder = 2
end
```

As you can see, some lines have been added automatically, to specify other properties of the font. Of course, if you write something completely wrong, such as this code:

```
object Button3: TButton
  Left = 100
  Eight = 60
end
```

Delphi will show an error indicating what has gone wrong (just a spelling error) when you paste it into the form, as you can see in Figure 2.4.

---

**FIGURE 2.4:**

An error message is displayed when you try to paste a component with a property that doesn't exist or is misspelled.

You can select several components and copy them all at once, either to another form or to a text editor. This might be useful when you need to work on a series of similar components. You can copy one to the editor, replicate it a number of times, make the proper changes, then paste the whole group into the form again.

Along with the typical commands on the Edit menu, Delphi includes a number of other commands, which are mostly related to forms. The specific operations for forms can also be accessed through the form SpeedMenu (the local menu you can invoke with the right mouse button) and will be covered later in the chapter. One command not replicated in the form local menu is Lock Controls, which is very useful to avoid an accidental change to the position of a component in a form. In fact, you might try to double-click on a component and actually end up moving it. Since there is no Undo operation on forms, protecting from similar errors by locking the controls can be really useful.

## The Search Menu

The Search menu has some standard commands, too, such as Search and Replace. Other commands are not so simple to understand. The Incremental Search command is one of them. When you select this command, instead of showing a dialog box where you can enter the text you want to find, Delphi moves to the editor. There, you can type the text you want to search for directly in the editor message area, as you can see in Figure 2.5.

**FIGURE 2.5:**

An example of using the Incremental Search command.

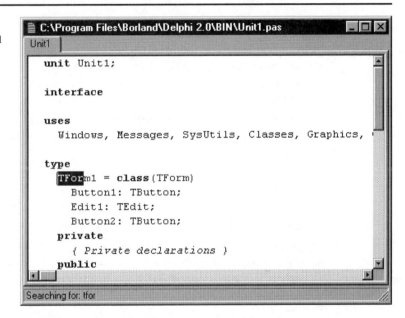

When you type the first letter, the editor will move to the first word starting with that letter. (But if your search text isn't found, the letters you typed won't even be displayed in the editor message area.) If this is not the word you are looking for, keep typing; the cursor will continue to jump to the next word that begins with those letters. Although this command might look strange at first, it is very effective and extremely fast, particularly if you are typing and invoke it with a shortcut key (Ctrl+E if you are using the standard editor shortcuts).

The Go to Line Number and Show Last Compile Error commands are quite intuitive. The Find Error command might seem strange at first. It is not used to search for a compiler error but rather to find a run-time error. When you are running a stand-alone program and you hit a very bad error, Delphi displays an internal address number (that is, the *logical* address of the compiled code). You can enter this value in the Find Error dialog box to have Delphi recompile the program, looking for the specific address. When it finds the address, Delphi shows the corresponding source code line. Many times, however, the error is not on one of the lines of your code, but in a line of library or system code: in this frequent case the Find Error command cannot locate the offending line.

The last command on the Search menu, Browse Symbol, invokes the Object Browser, a tool you can use to explore a compiled program, looking at many details. To understand the output of the Object Browser, you need an in-depth understanding of the Object Pascal language and of the Visual Components Library (VCL). For this reason, the use of the Object Browser will be discussed in Chapter 20.

## The View Menu

The View pull-down menu combines the features you usually find in View and Window menus. The Window menu is not present in Delphi, since it is not an MDI application. Most of the View commands can be used to display one of the windows of the Delphi environment, such as the Project Manager, the Breakpoints list, or the Components list. These windows are not related. Some are used during debugging; others when you are writing the code. Most of these windows will be described later in this chapter.

The commands on the second part of the View menu are important, which is why the Toggle Form/Unit, Units, and Forms commands are also available on the default SpeedBar. Toggle Form/Unit is used to move between the form you are working on and its source code. If you use a source code window big enough to hold a reasonable amount of text, you'll use this command often. As an alternative, you can place the two windows (the editor and the form) so that a portion of the one below is always visible. With this arrangement, you can click on it with the mouse to move it to the front.

The New edit window command duplicates the edit windows and its contents. It is the only way to view two files side by side in Delphi, since the editor uses tabs to show the multiple files you can load. Once you have duplicated the edit window, each one can hold different files (the two edit windows are not kept in synch).

The last two commands on the View menu can be used to hide the SpeedBar or the Components palette, although this is a good way to make Delphi look silly and uncomfortable. I know that everyone has his or her own taste, so every customizable option will make some people happy. However, working on forms without the Component palette is certainly not easy. If you remove both elements, the Delphi main window is reduced to a bare menu. (Now where is the option to hide the menus? This would reduce Delphi to a caption!)

## The Project Menu

The next pull-down menu, Project, has commands to handle a project and compile it. Add to Project and Remove from Project are two intuitive commands used to add and remove forms or Pascal source code files to a program. I recommend that you issue these commands from the Project Manager window.

The Compile command builds or updates the application executable file, checking which source files have changed. With Build All, you can ask Delphi to compile every source file of the project, even if it has not been changed since the last compilation. If you just want to know whether the syntax of the code you've written is correct, but you do not want to build the program—maybe this is still an unfinished module—you can use the Syntax Check command.

The next command, Information, displays some details about the last compilation you've made. Figure 2.6 shows the information related to the compilation of the last program presented in Chapter 1, HELLO2.

The Compile command can be used only when you have loaded a project in the editor. If no project is active and you load a Pascal source file, you cannot compile it. However, if you load the source file as if it were a project, that will do the trick. Simply select the Open Project command or button and load a .PAS file. Now you can check its syntax or compile it, building a DCU (Delphi Compiled Unit).

**FIGURE 2.6:**
The information about the compilation of HELLO2.

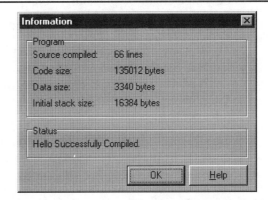

At the end comes the Options menu, used to set many project options such as compiler and linker options, application object options, and so on. When you set project options, you can check the Default box to indicate the same set of options will be used for the next new projects. We will discuss project options again in this chapter and then throughout the book when describing related topics.

## The Run Menu

The Run menu could have been named Debug as well. Most of the commands are related to debugging, including the Run command itself. As I've mentioned before, when you run a program within the Delphi environment, you execute it under the integrated debugger (unless you disable the corresponding Environment option). The Run command and the corresponding SpeedBar icon are among the most commonly used commands, since Delphi automatically recompiles a program before running it—at least if the source code has changed. Simply hit F9 as a shortcut to Run a program.

The next command, Parameters, can be used to pass some parameters on the command line to the program you are going to run. (We will see an example of its use in Chapter 19.) The remaining commands are all used during debugging, to execute the program step by step, set breakpoints, inspect the values of variables and objects, and so on. Some of these debugging commands are directly available in the editor SpeedMenu.

## The Component Menu

The commands of the Component menu can be used to write components, add them to the VCL library, or configure the library or the Components Palette. The New commands invokes the simple Component Expert. We will discuss it in more detail along with the other commands of this menu in Chapter 27, devoted to the development of Delphi components.

## The Database Menu

The Database menu collects the Delphi database related tools, from internal ones (such as the Database Form Expert) to external stand-alone programs, such as the Database Explorer. The commands on this menu depend on your edition of Delphi. The Client/Server Suite edition, of course, has more entries in this menu that the other editions.

The Database Menu is optionally followed by the Workgroups menu, available only if a Version Control system is installed in Delphi. This topic is not covered by the book.

## The Tools Menu

The Tools menu simply lists a number of external programs and tools, just to make it easier to run them. You can use the Tools command to configure and add new external tools to the pull-down. As you can see in Figure 2.7, besides simply running a program, you can pass some parameters to it. Simple parameter lists can be passed directly on the command line, while complex ones can be built using the Transfer Macros in the lower part of the Tool Properties dialog box.

**FIGURE 2.7:**
It is easy to add new applications to the Tools menu.

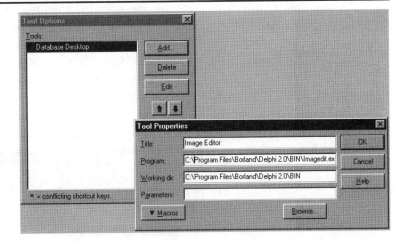

The Tools menu also includes a command to configure the Repository (discussed in the next chapter) and the Options command to configure the whole Delphi development environment (covered later in this chapter).

## The Help Menu

As often happens, our tour of the menu system ends with Help. This can be used to get information about the Delphi environment, its language, and the Windows API. As usual, this menu includes a command to display the Delphi About Box, with its (barely) hidden screens showing Delphi 2 contributors, as I mentioned in the Acknowledgment at the very beginning of the book. You can also type Alt+VERSION in the About box to see detailed version information.

# The SpeedBar

After you have used Delphi for a while, you'll realize that you frequently use only a small number of commands. Some of these commands are probably already available on the SpeedBar (Borland's name for its toolbars); some are not. If the commands you use a lot are not there, it's time to customize the SpeedBar so that it really helps you to use Delphi more efficiently.

> **TIP**
>
> An alternative to using the SpeedBar is to use shortcut keys. Although you must remember some key combinations to use them, shortcut keys let you invoke commands very quickly, particularly when you are writing code and your fingers are already on the keyboard.

You can easily resize the SpeedBar by dragging the thick line between it and the Components palette. The other operations you can do with the SpeedBar (besides removing it) are to add, remove, or replace the icons using the Configure command of the SpeedBar's own SpeedMenu. This operation invokes the SpeedBar Editor (shown in Figure 2.8), one of the Delphi tools with the best user interface, at least in my opinion.

**FIGURE 2.8:**

The SpeedBar Editor. Once it is open, you can drag icons from it to the SpeedBar.

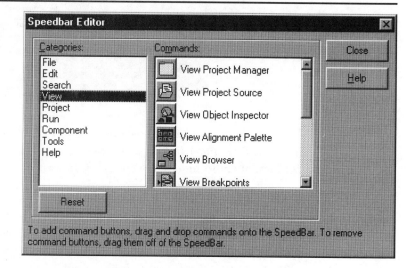

To add an icon to the SpeedBar, you simply need to find it under the proper category (corresponding to a pull-down menu), and drag it to the bar. In the same way, you can drag an icon away from the SpeedBar or simply move it to another location. During these operations, you can easily leave some space between groups of icons, to make them easier to remember and select.

# The SpeedMenus

Although Delphi has a good number of menu items, not all of the commands are available though the pull-down menus. At times, you need to use SpeedMenus (local menus) for specific windows or window areas. To activate a SpeedMenu, press the right mouse button over a certain element of the user interface, or press Alt+F10.

Even if you have other alternatives, using a SpeedMenu is usually faster because you don't need to move the mouse up to the menu bar and select two levels of menus. It's also often easier, since SpeedMenu commands are related to the current window. Figure 2.9 shows some examples of SpeedMenus.

FIGURE 2.9:

The Object Inspector, Alignment
Palette, and Code Editor
SpeedMenus.

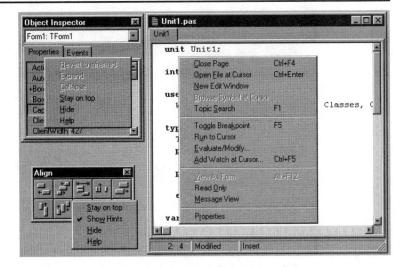

Almost every window in Delphi (with the exclusion of dialog boxes) has its own
SpeedMenu with related commands. I really suggest you try to get used to right-
clicking on windows, because this is not only important in Delphi, but also has become a standard for most applications in Windows 95. Get used to it, and add
SpeedMenus to the applications you build with Delphi, too.

# Working with Forms

The design of forms is the core of the visual development in the Delphi environment. Every component you place on a form or any property you set is stored in a
file describing the form (a DFM file) and also has some effect on the source code associated with the form (the PAS file).

When you start a new, blank project, Delphi creates an empty form, and you can
start working with it. You can also start with an existing form (using the various
templates available), or add new forms to a project. A project (an application) can
have any number of forms.

When you are working with a form, you can operate on its properties, on the properties of one of its components, or of several components at a time. To select the
form or a component, you can simply click on it or use the Object Selector (the
combo box in the Object Inspector), where you can always see the name and type
of the selected item. You can select more than one component by pressing and holding Shift while clicking on the component with the left mouse button, or by dragging a selection rectangle on the form.

**TIP**

Even when a component covers the whole surface of the form, you can still select the form with the mouse. Just press and hold Shift while you click on the selected component: this will deselect the component and select the form by default if it was the only selected component. Using the keyboard, you can press Esc to select the parent of the current component.

Once you are working on a form, the SpeedMenu has a number of useful features (some of which are also available in the Edit pull-down menu). You can use the Bring to Front and the Send to Back commands to change the relative position of components of the same kind (you can never bring a graphical component in front of a component based on a window, as we will see in Chapter 6). In an inherited form, you can use the command Revert to Inherited to restore the properties of the selected component to the values of the parent form. When you have selected more than one component, you can align or size them. Most of the options in the Alignment dialog box are also available in the Alignment palette.

From the SpeedMenu, you can also open two dialog boxes to set the tab order of the visual controls and the creation order of the nonvisual controls. You can use the Add to Repository command to add the form you are working on to a list of forms available for use in other projects. Finally, you can use the View as Text command to close the form and open its textual description in the editor. A corresponding command in the editor SpeedMenu will reverse the situation.

Along with specific SpeedMenu commands, you can set some form options by using the Tools ➤ Options command and choosing the Preferences page (see Figure 2.10). The options related to forms are listed under the Form Designer heading and refer to grid activation and size. When you activate the grid, you can use the mouse to move components on the form only at fixed positions (separated by the number of pixels of the grid size), and size them only at fixed intervals. Without a grid, you will rarely be able to align two components manually (using the mouse).

There are two alternatives to using the mouse to set the position of a component: you can either set the value for the Left and Top properties, or you can use the arrow keys while holding down Ctrl. Using the Ctrl+arrow key method is particularly useful for fine-tuning an element's position. (The Snap to Grid option works only for mouse operations.) Similarly, by pressing the arrow keys while you hold down Shift, you can fine-tune the size of a component.

Along with the commands described so far, a form's SpeedMenu offers other commands when particular components are selected. In some cases, these menu commands are an alternative to the selection of a property for a component. In some cases, they contain particularly useful commands. See Table 2.1 for a list of commands added to the SpeedMenu of a form when some of the components are

FIGURE 2.10:

The Preferences page of the
Environment Options dialog box.

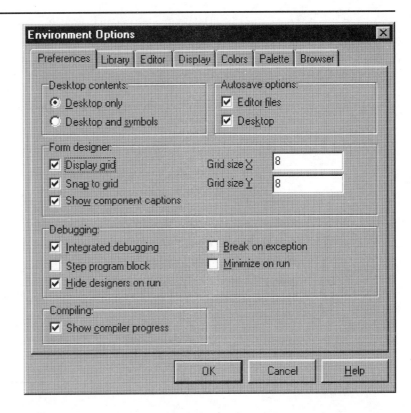

selected. Notice, however, that some of these actions are also the default action of
the component, the one automatically activated when you double-click on it in the
form editor.

## The Components Palette

When you want to add a new component to the form you are working on, you can
click on a component in one of the pages of the Components palette, then click on
the form to place the new component. On the form, you can press the left mouse
button and drag the mouse to set the position and size of the component at once,
or just click to let Delphi use a default size.

Each page of the palette has a number of components, indicated by an icon, and a
name, which appears as a "fly-by" hint (just move the mouse on the icon and wait
for a second). These names are the official names of components, and they are the
names I'll use in this book to refer to components. Actually, they are the names of
the classes defining the component, without the initial $T$ (for example, if the class
is the TButton, the name is *Button*).

**TABLE 2.1:** The Form SpeedMenu Commands Added When Some of the Delphi Components Are Selected

| Menu command | Components |
|---|---|
| Menu Designer | MainMenu, PopupMenu |
| Query Builder | Query (only if the Visual Query Builder is available) |
| Fields Editor | Table, Query, StoredProc |
| Explore | Table, Query, StoredProc, Database (only if the Database Explorer is available) |
| Define Parameters | Query, StoredProc |
| Database Editor | Database |
| Execute | BatchMove |
| Columns Editor | DBGrid |
| Edit Report | Report |
| ImageList Editor | ImageList |
| New Page | PageControl |
| Next Page | PageControl, NoteBook, TabbedNoteBook |
| Previous Page | PageControl, NoteBook, TabbedNoteBook |
| Properties | Any OCX control |

**TIP**

If you need to place a number of components of the same kind into a form, click on the Components palette while pressing Shift to activate a component. Then, every time you click on the form, Delphi adds a new component of that kind. To stop this operation, simply click on the standard selector (the arrow icon) on the left side of the Components palette.

What if you have decided to hide the Components palette? There is another way to add components to a form: select Components List from the View menu, select a component in the list or type its name in the edit window marked Search by Name, then click on the Add to Form button. This technique might be handy when you are using a mouseless computer (or laptop), or when you have installed so many components that you cannot remember where they are on the palette.

Of course, you can completely rearrange the components in the various pages of the palette, adding new elements or just moving them from page to page: select Tools ➤ Options and move to the Palette page. In this page of the dialog box, you can simply drag a component from the Components list box to the Pages list box to move that component to a different page.

It's not a good idea to move components on the palette too often. If you do, you'll probably waste time trying to locate them afterwards. Also try to avoid using too many pages (and long page names), since you'll need to scroll them if they do not fit on the screen.

## The Object Inspector

When you are designing a form, you use the Object Inspector to set the property of a component (or the form itself). Its window lists the properties (or events) of the selected element and their values in two resizable columns. An Object Selector at the top of the Object Inspector indicates the current component and its data type, and this selector can be used to change the current selection.

It is important to notice that the Object Inspector doesn't list all of the properties of a component. It includes only the properties that can be set at design-time. As mentioned in Chapter 1, other properties are accessible only at run-time. To know about all the different properties of a component, refer to the Help files.

An interesting feature of the Object Inspector is that the right column allows the correct editing for the data type of the property. Depending on the property, you will be able to insert a string or a number, choose from a list of options (indicated by a combo-box-like arrow), or invoke a specific editor (indicated by an ellipsis button). When a property allows only two values, such as True and False, you can toggle the value by double-clicking on it with the left mouse button. If there are many values available, a double-click will select the next one in the list. If you double-click a number of times, all the values of the list will appear, but it is easier to select a multiple-choice value using the small combo box. For some properties such as Color, you can either enter a value, select an element from the list, or invoke a specific editor! Other properties such as Font can be customized either by expanding their sub-properties (indicated by a plus or minus sign on the left side of the name) or by invoking an editor. In other cases, such as with string lists, the special editors are the only way to select a property.

The sub-property mechanism is available in two different cases: with sets and classes (that is, other sub-components having their own properties). We will see what a set is and how this works in Chapter 4. When you expand sub-properties, each of them has its own behavior in the Object Inspector, again depending on its data type.

You will use the Object Inspector often. It should always be visible when you are editing a form, but it can also be useful to look at the names of components and properties while you are writing code. For this reason, the Object Inspector's SpeedMenu has a Stay on Top command, which keeps the Object Inspector window in front of the Form Designer and the editor.

> **TIP**
>
> Delphi typically places the Object Inspector on the left of the screen. However if you are working on a high-resolution screen, you might move it to the right, and move the Delphi main window to the bottom of the screen, so you'll have a work area corresponding to the smaller screen real-estate of your users.

## The Alignment Palette

The last tool related to form design is the Alignment palette. You can open this palette with the View menu's Alignment Palette command. As an alternative, you can choose the components you want to align, and then issue the Align command from the SpeedMenu of the form.

The Alignment palette features a number of commands to position the various controls, center them, space them equally, and so on. To see the effect of each button, simply move the mouse over the window and look at the fly-by hints. When I'm designing complex forms, I position the Alignment palette on the far side of the screen and make sure it always stays in sight by using the Stay on Top command of its SpeedMenu.

# Writing Code

When you have designed a form in Delphi, you usually need to write some code to respond to some of its events, as we did in Chapter 1. Every time you work on an event, Delphi opens the editor with the source file related to the form. You can easily jump back and forth between the Form Designer and the editor with the related source code by pressing the Toggle Form Unit button on the SpeedBar, or by simply clicking on the corresponding window.

The Delphi editor allows you to work on several source code files at once, using a "notebook with tabs" metaphor. Each page of the notebook corresponds to a different file. You can work on units related to forms, independent units of Pascal code, and project files; open the form description files in textual format; and even work on plain text files.

**TIP**

As I've already mentioned, you can open multiple editor windows (with the View ➤ New Edit Window command or the Corresponding command of the editor SpeedMenu), each with one or more files.

When you work with the editor, you should probably expand its window so that you can see as many full lines of code as possible. A good solution is to size the editor so that it and the Object Inspector are the only windows that appear on the screen when you are writing code. By having the Object Inspector visible you can immediately see the names of the design-time properties of the components. When you are working on stand-alone units, you might also want to maximize the editor window.

There are a number of Environment Options available for the editor, mostly located in the Editor Options, Editor Display, and Editor Colors pages of the Environment Options dialog box. In the Preferences page, you can set the editor file's Autosave feature. Saving the source code files each time you run the program can save the day when your program happens to crash the whole system (something not so rare as you might think).

The other three pages of editor options can be used to set the default editor settings (choosing among different standard keystroke mappings), syntax highlighting features, and font. Most of these options are fairly simple to understand. Again, I recommend that you wait until you are better acquainted with the Delphi system before changing any of these settings.

The SpeedMenu of the editor window has many options for debugging and other options related to the editor itself, such as commands to close the current page, open the file under the cursor, view or hide the message pane below the window, and invoke the editor options discussed before.

# Managing Projects

The next important thing you'll need to be able to do in Delphi is to manage project files. In Chapter 1, we saw that you can open a project file in the editor and edit it. However, there are simpler ways to change some of the features of a project. You can use a specific Project Manager window and the options related to a project.

## The Project Manager

When a project is loaded, choose the Project Manager command from the View menu to open a project window. The window lists all of the forms and units that make up the current project. In Figure 2.11, you can see an example of such a window, related to a project with two different forms. The Project Manager's Speed-Menu allows you to perform a number of operations on the project, such as adding new or existing files, removing files, viewing a source code file or a form, and adding the project to the repository. Most of these commands are also available in the SpeedBar of this window (not the main Delphi SpeedBar).

**FIGURE 2.11:**

The Project Manager window with its SpeedMenu.

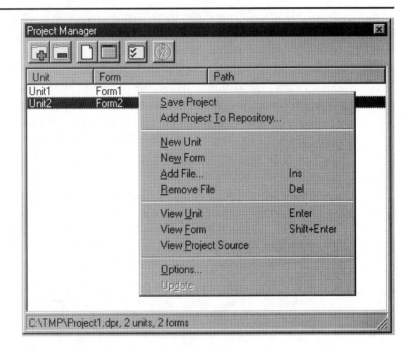

## Setting Project Options

From the Project Manager (or from the Project menu), you can invoke the Project Options. The first page of the Project Options, named Forms, lists the forms that should be created automatically at program startup (the default behavior) and the forms that are created manually by the program. You can easily move a form from one list to the other.

The next page, Application, is used to set the name of the application, set the name of its Help file, and choose the icon of the program. Other Project Options choices relate to the Delphi compiler and linker.

> There are two ways to set compiler options. One is to use the Compiler page of the Project Options, the other is to set or remove individual options in the source code with the {$X+} or {$X-} commands, where X is the option you want to set. This second approach is more flexible, since it allows you to change an option only for a specific source code file, or even for just a few lines of code.

All of the Project Options are saved automatically with the project, but in a separate file with a DOF extension. This is a text file you can easily edit. Do not delete this file if you have changed any of the default options.

# Compiling a Project

There are several ways to compile a project. If you run it (by pressing F9 or clicking on the SpeedBar icon), Delphi will compile it first. When Delphi compiles a project, it only compiles the files that have changed. If you select the Compile menu's Build All command, instead, every file is compiled, even if it has not changed. This second command is seldom used, since Delphi can usually determine which files have changed and compile them as required. Since Delphi looks at the time/date stamp of source files and intermediate files to know when they were last compiled, the Build All command might be useful when the clock of the PC doesn't work properly, when you have moved files from one computer to another, or when you change project-wide compiler options.

The project lists the source code files that are part of it, eventually with the related forms. This list is visible both in the project source and in the Project Manager, and is used to compile or rebuild a project. First, each source code file is turned into a Delphi compiled unit, a file with the same name as the Pascal source file and the DCU extension. For example, UNIT1.PAS is compiled into UNIT1.DCU.

Then the compiled units that constitute the project are merged (or linked) into the executable file together with code of the VCL library when the source code of the project itself is compiled and linked. You can better understand the compilation steps and follow what happens during this operation if you enable the Show Compiler Progress option. This option is on the Preferences page of the Environment Options dialog box, under the Compiling heading (see Figure 2.10, shown earlier). Although this slows down the compilation a little bit, the Compile window lets you see which source files are compiled each time you run the program. You can see an example of this window in Figure 2.12.

**FIGURE 2.12:**

A compiler progress window.

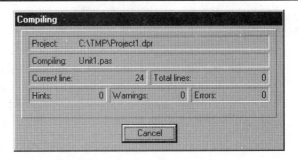

# Exploring a Compiled Program

Delphi provides a number of tools you can use to explore a compiled program, including the debugger and the Browser. The following sections provide a brief introduction to these tools, which I'll cover in detail in Chapter 20.

## The Integrated Debugger

Delphi has an integrated debugger, which has a huge number of features. However, it is also possible to buy a more powerful stand-alone debugger, called Turbo Debugger. For 90 percent of your debugging tasks, the integrated debugger works well enough. The Turbo Debugger package might be useful in special advanced cases.

You don't need to do much to use the integrated debugger. In fact, each time you run a program from Delphi, by default it is executed in the debugger. This means that you can set a breakpoint to stop the program when it reaches a set line of code.

For example, open the HELLO2 example we created in Chapter 1 and double-click on the button in the form to jump to the related code. Now set a breakpoint by clicking on the space between the left window border and the text, by choosing the Toggle Breakpoint SpeedMenu command or by pressing F5.

The editor will highlight the breakpoint as shown in Figure 2.13. Now you can run the program as usual, but each time you press the button, the debugger halts the program, showing you the corresponding line of code. You can execute this and the following lines one at a time (that is, step-by-step), look at the code of the functions called by the code, or continue running the program.

When a program is stopped, you can inspect its status in detail. You can look at the value of a variable (with the Evaluate command), set a watch on its value (to see when it changes), or even view the function calls on the stack. For example, you can set a watch on the HelloButton.Caption property, then step through the program and see when it changes. You can see this watch in Figure 2.13. I'll discuss debugging in Chapter 20.

FIGURE 2.13:

Breakpoints in source code are
clearly visible. Once the program is
stopped you can add a watch to the
value of a variable or see it change
while you step along the program.

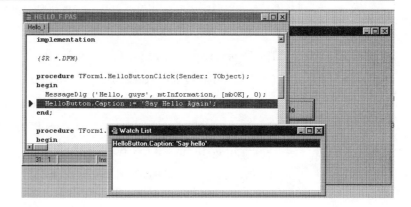

## The Object Browser

When you have compiled a program (even if you are not running or debugging it),
you can run the Object Browser to explore it. This tool allows you to see all of the
classes defined by the program (or by the units used directly and indirectly by the
program), all the global names and variables, and so on. For every class, the Object
Browser shows the list of properties, methods, and variables—both local and inherited, private and public.

But the features of the Object Browser won't mean much to you until you understand the object-oriented capabilities of the Object Pascal language used by Delphi.
We'll get to the details in Chapter 20, after we've covered the information you need
to begin to understand it properly.

# Additional Delphi Tools

Delphi provides many more tools for your programming efforts. For example, the
Menu Designer is a visual tool used to create the structure of a menu. There are also
the various Experts, used to generate the structure of an application or a new form.

Other tools are stand-alone applications related to the development of a Windows
application, such as the Image Editor and WinSight, a *spy* program that lets you see
the Windows message flow.

There are many external database tools, such as ReportSmith, the Database Desktop, and the Database Explorer (some of which are not available in the Desktop edition). A programmer can use other third-party tools to cover weak areas of Delphi.
For example, you can use a full-blown resource editor (such as Borland's Resource
Workshop), a tool to generate Help files more easily, and other technical Windows
utilities.

Here is a short list indicating where in the book I'll introduce some of the external Delphi tools:

- The Experts are covered in Chapter 3.
- The Menu Designer is described in Chapter 8.
- The Bitmap Editor is used in several chapters, starting with Chapter 10.
- Database tools are the topics of Chapters 17 and 18.
- WinSight is discussed in Chapter 21.
- Report building is described in Chapter 22.

# The Files Produced by the System

As you have seen, Delphi produces a number of files for you, and you should be aware of how it names these files. There are basically two elements that have an impact on how files are named: the names you give to a project and its forms, and the predefined extensions used by Delphi for the files you write and those generated by the system. Table 2.2 lists the extensions of the files you'll find in the directory where a Delphi project resides. The table also shows when these files are created and their importance for future compilations.

**TABLE 2.2:** The Delphi File Extensions

| Extension/File Type | Creation Time | Required to Recompile | Description |
|---|---|---|---|
| BMP, ICO/Graphical files | Development (Image Editor) | No, but they might be required at run-time | Bitmaps and icons are usually included in the code, but you won't delete them. They are used for button or list box glyphs, image components, and so on. |
| DCU/Delphi compiled unit | Compilation | No, but if the source has not changed, they speed up a compile process | These object files are the result of the compilation of a PAS file (and the corresponding form). |
| DFM/Delphi graphical form file | Development | Yes | This is the binary file with the description of the properties of a form and of the controls it contains. The file is converted to a textual format automatically when you load it in Delphi editor. |
| ~DF/Graphical form backup | Development | No | This is the backup file of the form's DFM file. |

**TABLE 2.2:** The Delphi File Extensions (continued)

| Extension/File Type | Creation Time | Required to Recompile | Description |
|---|---|---|---|
| DOF/Delphi options file | Development | Required only if special options have been set | This is a text file with the current settings for the project options. The extension was OPT in Delphi 1. |
| DPR/Delphi project file | Development | Yes | In Delphi, the project file is in Pascal source code. It lists all of the elements of a project and provides some initialization code. |
| ~DP/Project backup | Development | No | This file is a backup of the project file, generated automatically when a new version of a project file is saved. |
| DSK/Desktop settings | Development | No | This file contains information about the position of the Delphi windows, the files open in the editor, and other desktop settings, including some environment options. |
| DSM/Object Browser Data | Compilation (only if option is set) | No, used by the Browser | This file stores all the Browser information, and can be used to access this information without recompiling the project (or when you cannot recompile it because of an error). |
| EXE/Compiled executable file | Compilation | No | This is the result of your efforts: the executable file of your application. It includes all of the compiled units, resources, and forms. |
| PAS/Unit source code | Development | Yes | This file contains the source code of a Pascal unit, which can be the source code of a form or a stand-alone source file. |
| ~PA/Unit backup | Development | No | This file stores a backup copy of a PAS file of a unit. It is generated automatically by Delphi. |
| RES/Compiled resource file | Development | Yes | The binary file associated with the project and containing by default its icon. You can add other files of this type to the project. |

Most of these files are very short, including the source and backup files, the project files, the options, and the desktop file. The compiled units are slightly bigger, and the executable file is often the biggest file of the directory, unless there are files with debugging information, such as the DSM file.

The DSM file holds Browser information to allow the use of the Object Browser, even when you have changed the source code (but always after a first successful compilation). This can be particularly useful when you accidentally introduce an error in the code, preventing the compiler from building a new version of the program. DSM files, however, can easily become quite big, so you might prevent them from being created by checking Desktop Only instead of Desktop and Symbols in the Preferences page of the Environment Options dialog box. This will also slightly reduce the compile/link time.

The great advantage of Delphi over other visual programming environments is that most of the source code files are plain ASCII text files. We have already explored Pascal source code, project code, and form description files at the end of Chapter 1. Now let's take a minute to look at the structure of options and desktop files. Both these files use a structure similar to Windows INI files, where each section is indicated by a name enclosed in square brackets. For example, this is a fragment of the HELLO.DOF file of the HELLO2 example:

```
[Compiler]
A=1
B=0
...

[Linker]
MapFile=0
OutputObjs=0
MinStackSize=16384
MaxStackSize=1048576
ImageBase=4194304
...

[Directories]
OutputDir=
SearchPath=
Conditionals=

[Parameters]
RunParams=
```

**NEW**   In Delphi 2, the Option Files use the DOF extension, while in Delphi 1 they used the OPT extension. These files have different contents and are not really compatible between the two versions.

The initial part of this file (a long portion I've omitted) is a long list of compiler options. The same structure is used by the desktop files, which are usually much longer. It is worth looking at what is stored in these files to understand their role.

In short, a desktop file lists Delphi windows, indicating their position and status. For example, this is the description of the main window:

```
[MainWindow]
Create=1
Visible=1
State=0
Left=2
Top=0
Width=800
Height=97
```

These are some of the sections related to other windows:

```
[ProjectManager]
[AlignmentPalette]
[PropertyInspector]
[History_xxx]
[Closed Files]
[Modules]
[Formxxx]
[EditWindowxxx]
[Viewxxx]
[Watches]
[Breakpoints]
```

Besides environment options and windows positions, the desktop file contains a number of history lists (lists of files of a certain kind), and an indication of the current breakpoints, watches, active modules, closed modules, and forms.

# Summary

This chapter presented a short overview of the Delphi programming environment, including a number of tips and suggestions. Getting used to a new programming environment takes some time, particularly if it is a complex one. I could write a book with the details of the Delphi programming environment, but I think that describing how to actually write programs is more useful and interesting.

A good way to learn about the Delphi environment is to use the Help system. Look up information about the environment elements, windows, and commands. Spend some time just browsing through the Help files. Of course, the best way to learn how the Delphi environment works is to use it to write programs. That's what Delphi is about. Now we can move on to an introduction to one important feature of the Delphi environment we have only mentioned: the Object Repository and the Experts.

# CHAPTER

## THREE

# The Object Repository and the Experts

3

- Delphi's Object Repository

- Re-using existing applications and forms

- The Database Form Expert

- Other Delphi Experts

- Configuring the Object Repository

**W**hen you start working on a new application (or simply a new form), you have two choices. You can start from scratch with a blank application or form, or you can choose a predefined model from the Object Repository. If you decide to pick an existing model from the Object Repository, you have several alternatives. You can make a copy of an existing element (or *template*, to use the Delphi 1 name), you can inherit from an existing element, or you can use one of the available Experts. An *Expert* is a code generator. The Expert asks you a number of questions, and it uses the results to create some basic code, following standard guidelines.

In each of the cases, you start working on a project or a form that already has some code and components. Usually, the code generated by these tools can be compiled immediately, and it makes up the basic structure on which you can build your program or form.

The intention of this short chapter is to make you aware of the existence of the Object Repository and of the Experts, and of the fact that they are easy to use. We won't study the code they generate, since this will be the topic of many examples in the book. From a programming standpoint, the Experts are really useful. The pitfall is that you might be tempted to use them without trying to understand what they do. For this reason, in some examples I'll build the code manually instead of using the corresponding Expert.

# The Object Repository

In Delphi there are menu commands you can use to create a new form, a new application, a new data module, a new component, and so on. These commands are located in the File menu, and also in other pull-down menus. What happens, instead, if you select File ➤ New? Delphi opens the Object Repository.

## The Pages of the Object Repository

The Object Repository is used to create new elements of any kind: forms, applications, data modules, libraries, thread objects, components, automation objects, and more. The Object Repository dialog box has a number of pages:

- *New* allows you to create many different types of new items (as you can see in Figure 3.1). At times when you create a new item, Delphi asks you the name of a new class and few other things, in a sort of *mini-Expert*.

- Current project (actually you'll see the name of the project, such as *Project1* on this tab) allows you to inherit a form or data module from one of those included in your current project.

**FIGURE 3.1:**
The first page of the Object
Repository (indicated as *New*).

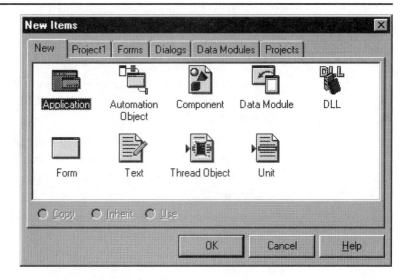

- *Forms*, *Dialogs*, and *Data Modules* allow you to create a new element of these kinds starting from an existing one or using an Expert.

- *Projects* allows you to copy the files from an existing project stored in the Repository.

In the bottom part of the Object Repository dialog box there are three radio buttons that allow you to indicate if you want to copy an existing item, inherit from it, or use it directly without making a copy. Remember that I am discussing the pages of the Object Repository as they appear in Delphi, but different editions of Delphi have more or fewer pages and items in them, and you can further customize the Repository, as we will see later on in this chapter.

**NEW**

We won't discuss form inheritance in depth until Chapter 12, but in short, it is a way to add new capabilities to an existing form without making a full copy. This way, if you make a change in the original form, the inherited form will be affected, too. I know this may not be very understandable if you've never used an object-oriented programming language (see Chapter 5 and Appendix A for an introduction to this topic and the corresponding Object Pascal capabilities).

## The New Page

The New page of the Object Repository allows you to create many new items and is often an alternative to a direct menu command. Here is a list of the elements you can create from this page (see again Figure 3.1):

- *Application* creates a new blank project (the same as the command File ➤ New Application).

- *Automation Object* creates a new OLE object after asking you to fill in a dialog box, the simple Automation Object Expert. This topic will be discussed in Chapter 25.

- *Component* creates a new Delphi component after you've completed the Component Expert. The same expert can be activated with the Component ➤ New menu command. I'll describe component creation in Chapter 27.

- *Data Module* creates a new blank data module (the same as the command File ➤ New Data Module).

- *DLL* creates a new DLL from scratch, as we will see in Chapter 28.

- *Form* creates a new blank form (the same as the command File ➤ New Form).

- *Text* opens a new ASCII text file in Delphi editor.

- *Thread Object* creates a new thread object after asking you to fill the New Thread Object dialog box. Multithreading in Windows 95 and Windows NT will be introduced in Chapter 19.

- *Unit* creates a new blank unit, a Pascal source file not connected with a form.

## The Current Project Page

From the second page, indicated by the name of the current project, you can only inherit a new form or data module from one of those already included in the current project. The content of this page depends exclusively on the units included in the current project. Simply create a couple of forms, then move again to this page and you'll see that its contents change immediately. Notice, however, that each time you perform an action, the Object Repository dialog box is automatically closed. So to make this test, you have to open it more than once.

## The Forms Page

Here is a short list of the predefined forms available in Delphi, as you can see in Figure 3.2.

- *About box* is a simple About box.

- *Database form* activates the Database Form Expert, the most important Delphi Expert, described in detail later on in this chapter. You can tell this is an expert simply because it has a light bulb glyph in the icon representing it.

**FIGURE 3.2:**

The Forms page of the repository, with form objects and Experts.

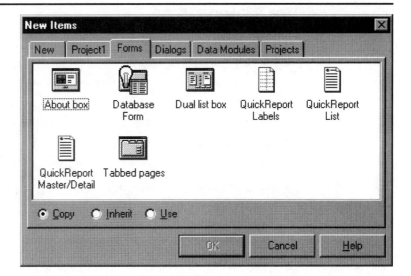

- *Dual list box* is a form with two different list boxes, allowing a user to select a number of elements and move them to the other list by pressing a button. Along with the components, this form has a good amount of non-trivial Pascal code.

- *QuickReport Labels* is a report form based on the QuickReport component. This is an add-on component which allows you to build complex reports right into a Delphi application, with no need for external run-time libraries. I'll discuss QuickReport in Chapter 22.

- *QuickReport List* is another report form with a different layout.

- *QuickReport Master/Detail* is a third report form with a more complex structure.

- *Tabbed pages* is a form based on the Windows 95 PageControl. We will discuss the use of this component in Chapter 13.

Besides the Expert, which can only be executed, you can copy the other forms into your project, inherit from them (in this case the original form will be automatically added to your project), or use them directly. When you use a form or inherit from one, notice that you'll have to take care not to make any change on the original forms in the Repository (well, unless you really want to do this…).

As we will see, it is quite simple to customize this page of the Repository adding new standard forms. You might also install new Experts in this and other pages, after you have written or bought them.

## The Dialogs Page

This page is similar to the previous one, but it lists different items:

- *Dialog Expert* is a simple Expert capable of generating different kinds of dialog boxes with one or multiple pages, as we will see later in this chapter.

- *Dialog with help* is available in two versions. One has the buttons on the right side of the form, the other in the lower portion.

- *Password dialog* is a dialog box with a simple edit box with the options required to input a password, and no code.

- *Standard dialog* is also available in two versions, with buttons in different positions.

Dialog boxes are forms with a couple of special attributes, such as a specific border, as we will see in Chapter 12.

## The Data Modules Page

You already know what a project and a form is, but what is a data module? It is a sort of form that never appears on screen at run-time and can be used to hold non-visual components. It is mostly used to define database access, as we will see in Chapter 18.

This page has only a data module at start-up, *Customer Data*. If you have several forms or applications accessing the same data tables and database queries, you can easily define new data modules and add them to the repository.

## The Projects Page

The last page contains project schemes you can use as the starting point for your own application.

- *Application Expert* is another simple expert that allows you some limited choices on the file structure and some other elements of an application.

- *MDI Application* defines the main elements of a Multiple Document Interface (MDI) program. It defines a main form for the MDI frame window, with a menu, a status bar, and a toolbar. It also defines a second form that can be used at run-time to create a number of child windows. We will explore MDI applications in Chapter 15.

- *SDI Application* defines a main form with the standard attributes of a modern user interface, including a toolbar and a status bar, and also a typical About box. We will see the details of this example when we focus on the use of toolbars and status bars in Chapter 11.

- *Win95 Logo Application* defines a sample application with most of the elements required by an application to get the Windows 95 Logo. This command basically creates an SDI application with a RichEdit component in it, and adds the code to it used to make the application *mail-enabled*.

When you select one of these projects, Delphi asks you to enter the name of an existing or a new directory, as you can see in Figure 3.3. If you indicate a new directory, Delphi will automatically create it.

**FIGURE 3.3:**

The dialog box used to select a directory for the files of the template you have chosen. Notice that you can indicate a new directory, as I've done here.

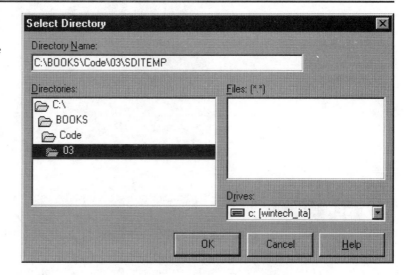

For example, create an SDI project based on the corresponding template. Now you can customize it, giving it a proper title, removing or adding new components, and writing some code. Notice, however, that some interesting components are already there, and that there is even some ready-to-use code to make those components work properly. The menu of the application, and also its toolbar, can be used to open some dialog boxes. File Open and File Save dialog boxes are wrapped up in components that are added to the form by the template; the About box is defined by the template as a second form.

In the simple SDITEMP example, I've decided to make just a few limited changes: I've entered a new title for the main form and some text for the labels for the About box (the property to use is Caption in both cases). The result is the application shown in Figure 3.4 and available on the companion CD.

FIGURE 3.4:

The output of the SDITEMP
example, built using the SDI project
template.

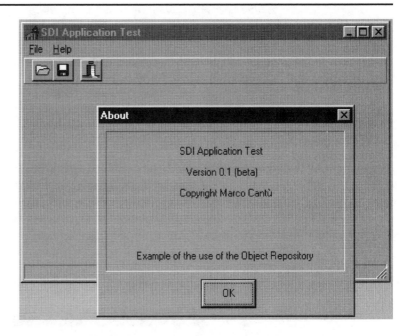

**NEW**

Delphi 1 had a CRT project template, too. It was based on a
predefined WinCrt unit, which allowed a programmer to use DOS-like
text input and output routines. This capability is available under
Windows 95 and Windows NT by creating a *console application*. This
capability is available in Delphi, too. You only need to select the
corresponding check box in the linker page of the project options.
Then you have to write a project without forms, so this is far from good
in most cases.

# Delphi Experts

Beside copying or using existing code, Delphi allows you to create a new form, application, or other code files, using an Expert. Experts allow you to enter a number of options and produce the code corresponding to your choices, using some internal schema.

The most important predefined expert is the Database Form Expert you can activate from the Database pull-down menu or from the Forms page of the Object Repository. There are also two simpler Experts, the Application Expert and the Dialog Expert. Then there are three *MiniExperts* (this is the name I like to give them) made of a dialog box with a single page and a few edit or combo boxes. These MiniExperts are the Component Expert, the Automation Object Expert, and the New Thread Object dialog box. You can also buy add-on Experts from third-party tool providers, or even write your own Experts.

## The Database Form Expert

The Database Form Expert is probably the single most interesting tool in Delphi. In this section, I'll show you a short example of its use, so that you can get an idea of its power, but I won't describe the details of what goes on. Refer to Chapter 17 for an introduction to database programming.

In this example, we'll build a database program using some of the data already available in Delphi. Note that you have to create a project first, than start the Database Form Expert. So you usually end up with two forms, unless you remove the original form from the project. The selection of the new form generated by the Expert as the main form can be accomplished using an option of the Expert itself, displayed at the end.

1. As soon as you start the Database Form Expert, you will be presented with a number of choices, which depend on the options you choose at each step. The first page, shown in Figure 3.5, lets you choose between a simple or a master detail form, and between the use of tables or queries. Leave the selections as they are by default, and move on by clicking on the Next button.

2. In the next page, shown in Figure 3.6, choose an existing database table to work on. In the Drive or Alias Name combo box, there should be a DBDEMOS alias. After you select this option, a number of Delphi demo database tables appear in the list. Choose the first, ANIMALS.DBF.

---

**FIGURE 3.5:**
The first page of the Database Form Expert.

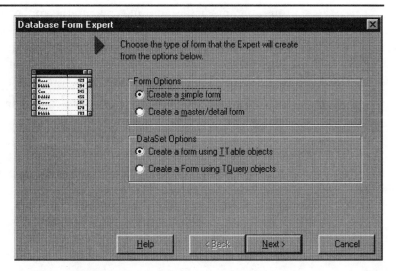

FIGURE 3.6:

The selection of a table in the Database Form Expert.

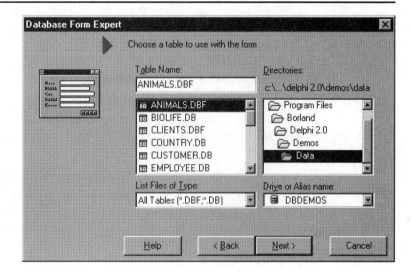

3. In the third page, you can choose the fields of the selected database table that you want to consider. To build this first example, choose all of the fields by clicking on the >> button.

4. On the next page, you can choose from various layouts. If you choose Vertical, the next page will ask you the position of the labels. The default option, Horizontal, might do.

5. Moving to the next page, we are at the end. Leave the Generate a Main Form check box and the Form Only radio button selected, and click on the Finish button.

You can immediately compile and run the application. The result is a working database application, which allows you to navigate among many records using the buttons. This specific application (the DATAEXP example) even has a graphical field, displaying a bitmap with the current animal.

The output of the generated form is usually far from adequate. In this case, the image area is too small; at other times the positioning of the editors may not be satisfactory. Of course, you can easily move and resize the various components placed on the form at design-time. To make this easier, you can select the Table component (the one in the upper-left corner of the form) and toggle its Active property to True. Then the data of the table's first record will be displayed at design-time (as you can see in Figure 3.7). This is helpful because it allows you to see an example of the length of the field's text and the size of the image.

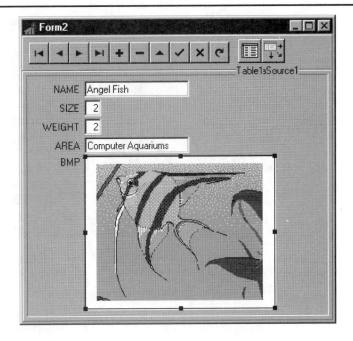

**FIGURE 3.7:**

The form of the DATAEXP example generated by the Database Form Expert, and later customized. Notice that I have activated the Table component, to be able to see data from the database table at design-time also.

Note that the Database Form Expert generates almost no code, besides a line used to open the table when the program starts. The capabilities of the resulting programs depend on the power of the database-related components available in Delphi, as we will see in Chapter 17.

## The Application Expert

Another interesting (although less powerful) code generator is the Application Expert. You can activate it from the Projects page of the Object Repository. The Application Expert allows you to create the skeleton of a number of different kinds of applications, depending on the options you select.

The first page of this Expert (see Figure 3.8) allows you to add some standard pull-down menus to the program: File, Edit, Window, and Help. If you select the File menu, the second page will ask you to enter the file extensions the program should consider. You should enter both a description of the file, such as *Text file (*.txt)*, and the extension, *txt*, and you can input several extensions, each with its own description. These values will be used by the default File Open and File Save dialog boxes that the Application Expert will add to the program if you select file support.

Then, if you have selected any of the pull-down menus, the Application Expert displays a nice visual tool you can use to build a toolbar. Unfortunately, this tool is not available by itself. You simply select one of the pull-down menus, and a number of standard buttons corresponding to the typical menu items of this pull-down menu

FIGURE 3.8:

The first page of the Application Expert.

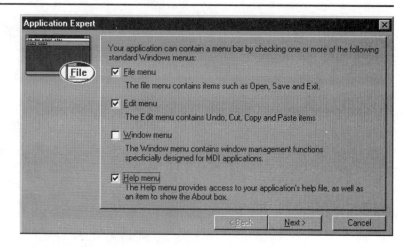

appear (but only if the menu has been selected on the first page of the Application Expert).

To add a new button, select one of them in the graphical list box on the right and press the Insert button. The new toolbar button will be added at the position of the small triangular cursor. You can move this cursor by clicking on one of the elements already added to the toolbar. Notice that the cursor also indicates the button you want to remove from the toolbar.

When the toolbar is finished, you can move to the last page (see Figure 3.9). Here you can set many more options, such as choosing MDI support, adding a status bar, and enabling hints. You can also give a name to the new application and specify a directory for the source files. The name of the application can be long, but it cannot

FIGURE 3.9:

The last page of the Application Expert, which is always displayed.

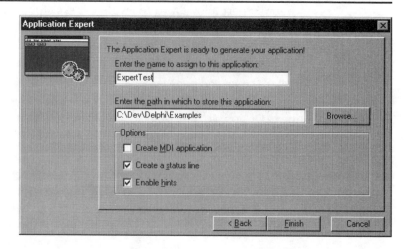

contain white spaces (it should be a valid Pascal identifier), and the directory for the application should be an existing directory. If you want to place the project files in a new directory, choose the Browse button, enter the new path, and the dialog box will prompt you if you want to create the new directory.

Although it is somewhat bare and it has room for improvement, the Delphi Application Expert can be much more useful than the predefined application templates for building the first version of an application. The biggest advantage is that you can define your own toolbar with this Expert, which allows you to choose from a number of buttons. Another advantage is that the Application Expert generates more code (and more comments) than the corresponding templates do.

The disadvantage of this Expert is that it generates an application with a single form. Its MDI support is limited, because no child form is defined, and the generated application has no About box.

## The Dialog Box Expert

Delphi's Dialog Expert is a simple Expert provided as a demo with its own source code. From the code of this Expert, in theory you should be able to learn how to build other Experts of your own. However, you can still use the Dialog Expert as a tool to build two different kinds of dialog boxes: simple dialog boxes and multiple-page dialog boxes based on the Windows 95 PageControl component (see Figure 3.10).

FIGURE 3.10:

The first page of the Dialog Expert.

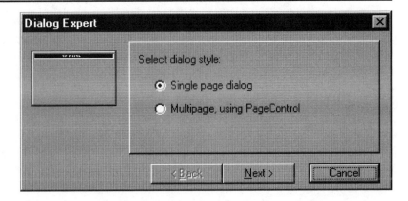

If you choose the simple dialog box, the Expert will jump to the third page, where you can choose the button layout. If you choose the multiple-page dialog box, an intermediate page will appear to let you input the text of the various tabs.

This Expert is an alternative to the corresponding form templates of the Object Repository. Its advantage is that it allows you to input the names of the PageControl tabs directly. We will explore dialog boxes in detail in Chapter 12 and the PageControl component in Chapter 13.

# Customizing the Object Repository

Since writing a new expert is far from simple, the typical way to customize the Object Repository is to add new projects, forms, and data modules. Beside this, you can also add new pages and arrange the items on some of them (not including the *New* and current project pages).

## Adding New Application Templates

Just as it is easy to use an existing template to build an application, it is also simple to add a new template to Delphi's Object Repository. When you have a working application you want to use as a starting point for further development of two or more similar programs, you can save the current status to a template, and then paste it back later on.

**NEW**

Although Borland now calls everything you can put in the Object Repository an *object*, from an object-oriented perpective this is far from true. For this reason I keep calling the schemes you can save to a disk for a later use *templates*. This is particularly true for application templates that do not relate to objects or classes in any way, and are copied to the directory of your new project. *Object Repository* sounds much better than *Browse Gallery*, but besides the capability to activate form inheritance, there is not much new in this tool.

You can add a project to the Repository by using the Project ➤ Add to Repository command, or by using the corresponding item of the local menu of the Project Manager window. As an example, the following steps describe how you can save the slightly modified version of the default SDI template (shown earlier) as a template. This example is just to demonstrate the process. (It's not a real-world example, since the code is far too simple and similar to the existing template.) Here are the required steps:

1. Open the modified SDITEMP example (or any other project you are working on).

2. Select the Project ➤ Add to Repository menu command (or the Add Project to Repository command in the SpeedMenu of the Project Manager window).

3. In the Add to Repository dialog box (see Figure 3.11), enter a title, a description for the new project template, and the name of the author. You can also choose an icon to indicate the new template or accept the default image, and choose the page of the Repository where you wish to add the project.

4. Click on OK, and the new template is added to the Delphi Object Repository.

**FIGURE 3.11:**

The Add to Repository dialog box, used to define the name and descriptions of a new application template.

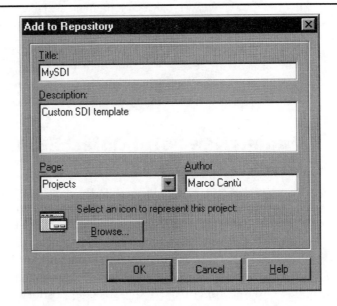

Now, each time you open the Object Repository, it will include your custom template. If you later discover that the template is not useful any more, you can remove it. You can use a project template to make a copy of an existing project so that you can continue to work on it after saving the original version.

However, there is a simpler way to accomplish this: copy the source files to a new directory and open the new project. If you do copy the source files, do *not* copy the DSK file, which indicates the position of the windows on the screen. The DSK file holds a list of files open in the editor, using an absolute path. This means that as soon as you open the new project and start working on it, you are actually editing the source code files of the older project, but you compile the files of the new version, since the project manager stores relative paths. This will certainly surprise you when the changes you make in the code or in the form seem to have no effect. Simply deleting the DSK file, or not copying it in the first place, avoids this problem.

When you start a new project, it automatically opens a blank form, too. If you want a new project and base it on one of the form objects or experts, this is not what you want. To solve this problem, you can add an *Empty Project* template to the Gallery. The steps required to accomplish this are simple. Create a new project as usual, remove its only form from the project, and add this project to the templates, naming it *Empty Project*, or something similar. When you select this project from the Object Repository, you gain two advantages. You have your project without a form, and you are asked to pick a directory for the project, where the template files will be copied. There is also a disadvantage, because you need to use the File ➤ Save Project As command to give a new name to the project.

## Adding New Form Objects to the Object Repository

Just as you can add new template projects to the Object Repository, you can also add new form objects. Simply move to the form, press the right mouse button over it, and select the Add to Repository command from the SpeedMenu. In the dialog box that appears (see Figure 3.12), you can choose which form of the current project should be added to the Repository, and set the title, description, author, page, and icon, as usual. Once you have set this element and clicked on OK, the form is added to the proper page of the Object Repository.

**FIGURE 3.12:**

Saving a form as a template, with the second Add to Repository dialog box.

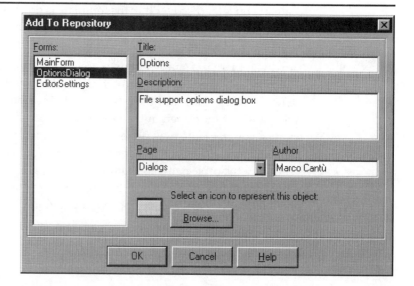

This approach is suggested if you have a complex form to make available to other applications and other programmers. Notice that they will be able to use your form as is, make a copy of it, and inherit from it. For this reason adding forms to the Repository is far more flexible than adding projects, which can only be copied as the starting point of a new application.

## The Object Repository Options

To further customize the Repository and move items to different pages (but also add new elements), you can use the Tools ➤ Repository command to open the Object Repository Options dialog box (see Figure 3.13). This dialog box is quite easy to use. Notice that it is divided in four pages, named *Form Experts*, *Form Objects* (also including Data Modules objects), *Project Experts*, *Project Templates*. These are the four group of elements stored in the repository.

You can use the three page-related buttons and the two buttons with arrows below the list of pages to arrange the structure of the Object Repository, adding new pages, renaming or deleting them, and changing their order. All these operations affect the tabs of the Object Repository itself.

An important element of the Object Repository setup is the use of defaults. You can use the New Form check box below the list of objects to indicate the form or Expert used by default when a new form is created. This relates to only one of the objects

---

**FIGURE 3.13:**

The Object Repository Options dialog box.

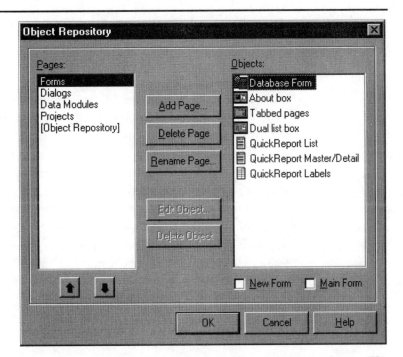

of the whole Object Repository, which is marked with a special symbol. The Main Form check box, instead, is used to indicate the form or Expert used by default when a new standard project is created. The Main form is indicated by a second special symbol.

When you select a project object, these two check boxes are replaced by a New Project check box. This can be used to mark the default project template or Project Expert Delphi uses when you issue the File ➤ New Project command. Also, the New Project is indicated by its own special symbol. If no project is selected as New Project, Delphi creates a default project based on the form marked as Main Form. If no form is marked as the main form, Delphi creates a default empty form.

**NOTE**   When you work on the Object Repository, you work with forms and modules saved in the OBJREPOS subdirectory of the Delphi main directory. When you add a new project or form, the object is saved to this directory. At the same time, if you directly use a form or any other object without copying it, then you end up having some files of your project in this directory. It is important to realize how the repository works, because if you want to modify a project or an object saved in the repository, then the best approach is to operate on the original files, without copying data back and forth to the Repository.

# Summary

In this short chapter, we have seen how you can start the development of an application not from scratch, but by using some code generated (or copied) by the system. You can use one of the predefined application templates or form objects, start the Database Form Expert, or use the other Expert for a fast start with applications, forms, and other objects.

In the rest of the book, I'll use these templates and Experts from time to time, but not very often. With the exception of the Database Form Expert, these tools let you build very simple applications, which you can often put together yourself in seconds when you are an experienced Delphi programmer.

For beginners, Experts and templates provide a quick start in code development. But you are not going to *remain* a beginner, are you? So we need to restart our exploration of Delphi from scratch, studying the Object Pascal language and exploring the use of the VCL (Visual Component Library) components. This is what we will do in the following chapters.

# CHAPTER

## FOUR

# The Pascal Language

- Predefined and user-defined data types

- Pascal string handling

- Coding style

- Conditional statements and loops

- Procedures and functions

**D**r. Nicklaus Wirth designed the Pascal language back in 1972 in Geneva, Switzerland. (That's about 300 miles from my home town, by the way.) The Pascal language, named after the French philosopher Blaise Pascal, has some distinctive characteristics. It was designed to be a learning tool, but it was found to be so powerful that it became a widespread programming language. In part, this is due to Borland and its world-famous Turbo Pascal series of compilers introduced in 1985. The Turbo Pascal compiler made the language even more popular, particularly on the PC platform, due to a proper mix of simplicity and power.

When Pascal was designed, few programming languages existed (among them FORTRAN, COBOL, and BASIC). The key idea of the new language was order, managed through a strong concept of data type. This book doesn't contain detailed material about Pascal, but this chapter should help you if you know basic programming concepts but are not sure how they are implemented in Pascal.

Even if you have already used the Pascal language, you should read this chapter. All of the examples are implemented using the Delphi environment. What you probably do not know much about is the object-oriented extensions of Object Pascal, which are available in Delphi. New Object Pascal extensions are the topic of the next chapter.

# Pascal Data Types

The original Pascal language was based on some simple notions, which have now become quite common in programming languages. The first is the notion of *data type*. The type determines the values a variable can have (and the internal representation of these values) and the operations that can be accomplished on that variable. The concept of type in Pascal is stronger than in C, where the arithmetic data types are almost interchangeable, and much stronger than in the original versions of BASIC, which had no similar concept.

Here are some sample data declarations:

```
var
  Value: Integer;
  Correct: Boolean;
  A, B: Char;
```

The var keyword can be used in several places in the code, such as at the beginning of the code for a function. After var comes a list of variable names, followed by a colon and the name of the data type. You can write more than one variable name on a single line, as in the last line of the code above.

Once you have defined a variable of a given type, you can perform on it only the operations supported by its data type. For example, you can use the Boolean value in a test and the integer value in a numerical expression. You cannot do the reverse, as is possible with the C language.

Using simple assignments, we can write the following code:

```
Value := 10;
Correct := True;
```

But the next statement is not correct, because the two variables have different data types:

```
Value := Correct;
```

If you try to compile this code, Delphi 2 issues a compiler error with this description: *Incompatible types: 'Integer' and 'Boolean'*. This is much better than the corresponding Delphi 1 error message, *Type mismatch*. Delphi 2 error messages are much more detailed, and by also enabling compiler hints and warnings, you can usually have a better understanding of errors in the code.

Usually, errors like this are programming errors, because it does not make sense to assign a True or False value to an integer. You should not blame Delphi for these errors. It only warns you that there is something wrong in the code.

Of course, it is often possible to convert the value of a variable of a type into one of a different type. In some cases, this conversion is automatic, but usually you need to call a specific system function that changes the internal representation of the data.

## Predefined Data Types

There are several predefined data types, which can be divided into three different groups: *ordinal types*, *real types*, and *strings*. We'll discuss ordinal and real types in the following sections. Strings are covered later in this chapter.

**NEW**

Delphi 2 also includes a "non-typed" data type, called a *variant*. A variant is a type without a proper type-checking. It has been introduced in the 32-bit version of Delphi to handle OLE automation. We'll see later on in this chapter how the variant concept can be used to break Pascal's strict type-checking rules.

### Ordinal Types

Ordinal types are based on a concept of order. This not only relates to the fact that you can compare two values to see which is higher, but that you can also ask for the following or preceding value of a given value or compute the lowest or highest Possible Value.

The three most important predefined ordinal types are Integer, Boolean, and Char (character). However, there are a number of other related types that have the same meaning but a different internal representation and range of values.

Here is a complete list of the ordinal types:

- Integer, Cardinal, ShortInt, SmallInt, LongInt, Byte, Word
- Boolean, ByteBool, WordBool, LongBool
- Char, ANSIChar, WideChar

The various integer types correspond to different internal representations. ShortInt, SmallInt, and LongInt represent signed numbers with various representations (see the RANGE example in the next section for the actual values); Byte and Word represent unsigned values; and Integer and Cardinal correspond to a value based on the native representation (2 bytes on a 16-bit platform, 4 bytes on a 32-bit platform) signed and unsigned, respectively.

The four Boolean types are needed for Windows programming, but Boolean is used most of the time.

The three character types are used to indicate 8-bit (ANSI) or 16-bit (Unicode) characters, and the default type. Char corresponds to ANSIChar in both the 16-bit and the 32-bit versions of Delphi, but it might be changed to the new character type in a future version.

**NOTE**

Contrary to Windows NT, Windows 95 has limited support for Unicode, the new international character set capable of representing the letters of each known alphabet. To achieve this, Unicode uses 16 bits for each character, instead of the traditional 8 bits. The VCL library is still based on ANSI characters (as is Windows 95).

## The RANGE Example

To give you an idea of the different ranges of some of the ordinal types, I've written a simple Delphi program named RANGE. You can try to rebuild it or simply run it from the companion CD. The results are shown in Figure 4.1.

The RANGE program is based on a simple form, which has six buttons (each named after an ordinal data type) and some labels for categories of information, as you can see in Figure 4.1. Some of the labels are used to hold static text, others to show the information about the type each time one of the buttons is pressed.

Every time you press one of the buttons on the right, the program updates the labels with the output. These labels are for the name of the data type, number of bytes of

**FIGURE 4.1:**
The RANGE example displays some information about ordinal data types (Integers in this screen).

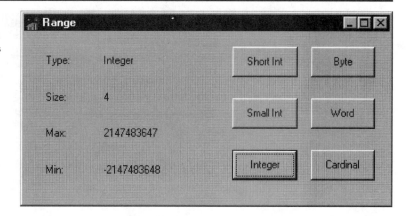

its representation, and the maximum value and minimum value the data type can store. Each button has its own OnClick event-response method, but the code used to compute the three values is slightly different from button to button. For example, here is the source code of the OnClick event for the Integer button (IntButton):

```pascal
procedure TForm1.IntButtonClick(Sender: TObject);
var
  Number: Integer;
begin
  TypeLabel.Caption := 'Integer';
  SizeLabel.Caption := IntToStr (SizeOf (Number));
  MaxLabel.Caption := IntToStr (High (Number));
  MinLabel.Caption := IntToStr (Low (Number));
end;
```

If you have some experience with Delphi programming, you can examine the source code of the program to understand how it works. For beginners, it's enough to note the use of three functions: SizeOf, High, and Low. The results of the last two functions are ordinals of the same kind (in this case, integers), and the result of SizeOf is always an integer, so they are first translated into strings using the IntToStr function, then copied to the captions of the three labels.

I won't show you the source code of the methods related to the other buttons because they are very similar to the one above. The only real difference is in the data type of the Number local variable, and in the string used to describe the type, of course. Figure 4.2 shows the result of the execution of this same program under Windows 95 after it has been recompiled with the 16-bit version of Delphi (this version is available on the CD as RANGE16). Comparing Figure 4.1 with Figure 4.2, you can see the difference between 16-bit and 32-bit integers.

The size of integers varies depending on the CPU and operating system you are using. In Windows 3.1, integers are typically two bytes wide. In Windows 95, integers are four bytes wide. For this reason, when you recompile the RANGE example, you

**FIGURE 4.2:**

The output of the 16-bit version of the RANGE example, again showing information about Integers. Compare it with the 32-bit version in Figure 4.1.

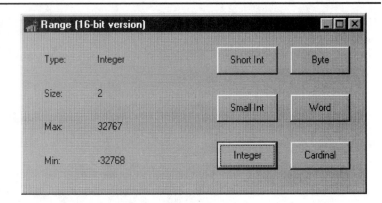

get a different output. The different representation of integers is common to all Delphi applications; however, it isn't a problem, as long as you don't make any assumptions about the size of integers. If you happen to save integers to a file using one version and retrieve them with another, though, you're going to have some trouble. In this situation, you should choose a platform-independent data type (such as LongInteger or SmallInteger). For mathematical computation or generic code, your best bet is to stick with the standard integral representation for the specific platform—that is, use Integers—because this is what the CPU likes best.

In my opinion, integers should be your first choice when handling numbers. Use a different representation only when there is a compelling reason to do so.

There are some system routines (routines defined in the Pascal language and in the Delphi system unit) working on ordinal types, as you can see in Table 4.1. C++ programmers should notice that the two versions of the Inc procedure, with one or two parameters, correspond to the ++ and += operators (the same holds for Dec).

**TABLE 4.1:** System Routines for Ordinal Types

| Routine | Purpose |
| --- | --- |
| Dec | Decrements the variable passed as parameter, by one or by the value of the eventual second parameter. |
| Inc | Increments the variable passed as parameter, by one or by the specified value. |
| Odd | Returns True if the argument is an odd number. |
| Pred | Returns the value before the argument in the order determined by the data type, the predecessor. |
| Succ | Returns the value after the argument, the successor. |
| Ord | Returns a number indicating the order of the argument within the set of values of the data type. |
| Low | Returns the lowest value in the range of the ordinal type passed as parameter. |
| High | Returns the highest value in the range of the ordinal data type. |

## Real Types

*Real types* represent floating-point numbers in various formats. The smallest storage size is given by `Single` numbers. Then there are `Real`, `Double`, and `Extended` numbers. These are all floating point data types with different precisions.

There are also two strange data types: `Comp`, which describes very big integers; and `Currency` (available only in Delphi 2), which indicates a floating point type with four decimal digits, and a 64-bit representation. As the name implies, the `Currency` data type has been added to show huge monetary values without losing the least significant digits (a common problem with floating point values). The internal representation of the `Comp` and `Currency` data types is similar to integer types, although they cannot be considered ordinal types for their huge range of values.

We cannot build a program similar to RANGE with real data types, because we cannot use the `High` and `Low` functions or the `Ord` function on real type variables. Real types represent (in theory) an infinite set of numbers; ordinal types represent a fixed set of values. For this reason, it makes sense to ask the order of the *w* character in the `char` data type, but it makes no sense at all to ask the order of 7143.1562 in the `real` data type.

Although you can indeed know whether one real number has a higher value than another, it makes no sense to ask how many real numbers exist before a given number (this is the meaning of the `Ord` function). The same discussion can be extended to other functions available only for ordinal types.

Real types are used in programs involving math formulas, and they usually have a limited role in the user interface portion of the code (the Windows side). Of course, a large number of applications involve real number math formulas. Examples are design software (CAD), image processing (ray tracing, rendering, and photo editing), image compression and decompression (JPEG and MPEG algorithms), and simulation and modeling software.

Delphi itself uses real types in the TDateTime data type. This is a floating-point type, which is the only type that has a wide enough range of values to store days, months, years, hours, minutes, and seconds, down to millisecond resolution in a single variable.

Fortunately, the existence of so many different numeric data types makes Object Pascal a complete language for those involved in mathematics. If you are interested in this aspect, you can look at the arithmetic functions provided by the Delphi in the system unit (for example, see the Delphi Help topic "Arithmetic Routines").

**NEW**

Delphi 2 also has a Math unit that defines advanced mathematical routines, covering trigonometric functions (such as the ArcCosh function), finance (such as the Interest Payment function), and statistics (such as the MeanAndStdDev procedure). There are a number of these routines, some of which sound quite strange to me, such as the MomentSkewKurtosis procedure (I'll let you find out what this is).

## Specific Windows Types

The predefined data types we have seen so far are part of the Pascal language. Delphi also includes other data types defined by Windows. These data types are not an integral part of the language, but they are part of Windows libraries.

**NOTE**

Windows types are not exactly predefined data types, since they are not directly understood by the compiler. However, they are simple data types, so I decided to discuss them here.

Among Windows data types, two simple and commonly used types are *handles* and *color references*. The names of these data types are, respectively, `THandle` and `TColorRef`. The first is just a redefinition of the `Cardinal` data type; the second is a redefinition of the `LongInt` type.

A color reference is simply a number describing a color. You can choose any kind of color by setting the amount of red, green, and blue of any TColorRef value by using the RGB function or by accessing the representation of the color directly. As we will see, in Delphi the native TColor data type is generally used instead of Windows' own TColorRef type.

Handle data types are not understandable values. In Windows, a handle is a number referring to an internal data structure of the system. For example, when you work with a window, the system gives you a *handle to the window*, or HWND. The system informs you that the window you are working with is window number 142, for example. From that point on, your application can ask the system to operate on window number 142—moving it, resizing it, reducing it to an icon, and so on.

In other words, a handle is an internal code you can use to refer to a specific element handled by the system, including windows, bitmaps, icons, memory blocks, cursors, fonts, menus, and so on. In Delphi, you seldom need to use handles directly, since they are hidden inside forms, bitmaps, and other Delphi objects. They become useful when you want to call a Windows API function that is not supported by Delphi.

**NOTE**

The size of the handle data types varies in the 16-bit and 32-bit versions of Windows. The same holds true, of course, for the different versions of Delphi. If not used with care, this might cause compatibility problems when moving applications between the two platforms. In most cases, however, the size of handles is not an issue.

# Typecasting and Type Conversions

As we have seen, you cannot assign a variable to another one of a different type. In case you need to do this, there are two choices. The first choice is *typecasting*, which uses a simple functional notation, with the name of the destination data type:

```
var
  N: Integer;
  C: Char;
  B: Boolean;
begin
  N := Integer ('X');
  C := Char (N);
  B := Boolean (0);
```

You can generally typecast between data types having the same size. It is usually safe to typecast between ordinal types, or between real types, but you can also typecast between pointer types (and also objects) as long as you know what you are doing. Casting, however, is generally a dangerous programming practice, because it allows you to access a value as if it represented something else. Since the internal representation of data types and objects generally do not match, you risk hard-to-track errors. For this reason, you should avoid typecasting, or use the safe techniques for typecasting between objects offered by run-time type methods, which we will see in the next chapter.

The second choice is to use a type-conversion routine. The routines for the various types of conversions are summarized in Table 4.2. Some of these routines work on the data types that we'll discuss in the following sections.

**TABLE 4.2:** System Routines for Type Conversion

| Routine | Purpose |
| --- | --- |
| Chr | Converts an ordinal number into a character. |
| Ord | Converts an ordinal-type value into the number indicating its order. |
| Round | Converts a real-type value into an integer-type value, rounding its value. |
| Trunc | Converts a real-type value into an integer-type value, truncating its value. |

**TABLE 4.2:** System Routines for Type Conversion (continued)

| Routine | Purpose |
| --- | --- |
| IntToStr | Converts a number into a string. |
| IntToHex | Converts an number into a string with its hexadecimal representation. |
| StrToInt | Converts a string into a number, raising an exception if the string is not correct (see Chapter 5 for a description of exceptions in Object Pascal). |
| StrToIntDef | Converts a string into a number, using a default value if the string is not correct. |
| Val | Converts a string into a number. |
| Str | Converts a number into a string, using formatting parameters. |
| StrPas | Converts a null-terminated string into a Pascal-style string. |
| StrPCopy | Converts (copies) a Pascal-style string into a null-terminated string. |
| StrPLCopy | Converts (copies) a portion of a Pascal-style string into a null-terminated string. |

## The Variant Data Type

The 32-bit version of Delphi introduces a brand new approach to handle variables, the Variant data type. As I mentioned before, this new data type was introduced to support OLE automation (a topic covered in Chapter 25), but it has a pervasive effect on the whole language. In fact, you can use variants to store any data type and perform a number of peculiar operations and type conversions. Notice that this goes against the general approach of the Pascal language and against good programming practices. Variants are checked and computed at run-time. You don't have to bother with compiler type-checking, which is generally a negative thing. On the whole, you can consider the code portions using variants more-or-less as interpreted code, because many operations cannot be resolved until run-time.

Now that I've warned you against the use of variants, it is time to look at what they can do. Basically, once you've declared a variant variable such as the following

```
var
  V: Variant;
```

you can assign to it anything:

```
V := 10;
V := 'Hello, World';
V := 45.55;
```

Once you have the variant value, you can copy it to any compatible or non-compatible data type. If you assign a value to a non-compatible data type, Delphi performs a conversion, if it can. Otherwise it issues a run-time error. In fact, variants store type information along with the data, allowing a number of run-time operations, which can be handy but are both slow and unsafe.

Consider this example (VARITEST on the companion CD), which is an extension of the code above: Place three edit boxes on a new Delphi form, add a couple of buttons, then write the following code for the OnClick event of the first button:

```
procedure TForm1.Button1Click(Sender: TObject);
var
  V: Variant;
begin
  V := 10;
  Edit1.Text := V;
  V := 'Hello, World';
  Edit2.Text := V;
  V := 45.55;
  Edit3.Text := V;
end;
```

Funny, isn't it? Besides assigning a variant holding a string to the Text property of an edit component, you can assign to the Text a variant holding an integer or a floating point number. As you can see in Figure 4.3, everything works.

**FIGURE 4.3:**
The output of the VARITEST example after the Assign button (or Button1) has been pressed.

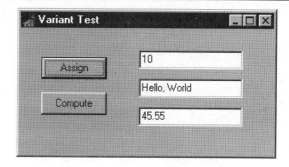

Even worse, you can use the variants to compute values, as you can see in the code related to the second button:

```
procedure TForm1.Button2Click(Sender: TObject);
var
  V: Variant;
  N: Integer;
begin
  V := Edit1.Text;
  N := Integer(V) * 2;
  V := N;
  Edit1.Text := V;
end;
```

Writing this kind of code is silly, to say the least. However, if the first edit box contains a number, everything works. If you input a string in that edit box, a run-time errors occurs (an exception is raised). Again, you can write similar code, but without a compelling reason to do so, you shouldn't use variants; stick with the traditional Pascal data types and type-checking approach. For this reason, I'll rarely use variants in the examples in the book (well, besides the OLE automation examples!).

Notice also that variants are slow, not only when you convert data types, but also when you add two variants holding an integer each. They are almost as slow as the interpreted code of Visual Basic! To compare the speed of an algorithm based on variants with that of the same code based on integers, you can look at the VARI-SPEED example on the companion CD. The speed difference is so large (almost ten times to one) that you will notice it without timing it.

# User-Defined Data Types

Along with the notion of type, one of the great ideas introduced by the Pascal language is the capability to define new data types in a program. This is something that was not commonly available in earlier programming languages. Besides using the predefined data types, programmers can define their own data types by means of *type constructors*, such as subranges, arrays, records, enumerations, pointers, and sets. The most important user-defined data type is the *class*, which I'll discuss in the next chapter.

These types can be given a name for later use or applied to a variable directly. When you give a name to a type, you must provide a specific section in the code, such as the following:

```
type
  {subrange definition:}
  Uppercase = 'A'..'Z';
  {array definition:}
  Temperatures = array [1..24] of Integer;
  {record definition:}
  Date = record
    Month: Byte;
    Day: Byte;
    Year: Integer;
  end;
  {enumerated type definition:}
  Colors = (Red, Yellow, Green, Cyan, Blue, Violet);
  {set definition:}
  Letters = set of Char;
```

Similar type definition constructs can be used directly to define a variable without an explicit type definition, as in the following code:

```
var:
  DecemberTemperature: array [1..31] of Byte;
  ColorCode: array [Red..Violet] of Word;
  Palette: set of Colors;
```

**WARNING**

In general, you should avoid using *unnamed* types as in the code above, because you cannot pass them as parameters to subroutines or declare other variables of the same type because the type compatibility rules of Pascal are based on type names, not on the actual definition of a type. Two identical types are still not compatible. Get used to defining a data type each time you need a complex variable, and you won't regret the time you spent for it.

But what do these type definitions mean? Most of you probably already know, but I'll provide some short descriptions for those of you who are not familiar with Pascal type constructs. I'll also try to underline the differences from the same constructs in other programming languages, so you might be interested in reading the following sections even if you are familiar with type definitions.

## Subranges

A *subrange type* defines a range of values within the range of another type (hence the name *subrange*). You can define a subrange of integers, from 1 to 10 or from 100 to 1000. Or you can define a subrange of characters, as in

```
type
  Uppercase = 'A'..'Z';
```

The subrange above is depicted in Figure 4.4. In the definition of a subrange, you don't need to specify the name of the base type. You just need to supply two constants of that type. Both the original type and the subrange type are ordinal types.

When you have defined a subrange, you can legally assign it a value within that range. This code is valid:

```
UppLetter := 'F';
```

But this one is not:

```
UppLetter := 'e';
```

**FIGURE 4.4:**

A representation of a subrange.

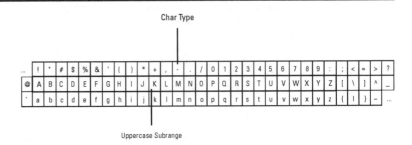

Writing this code in Delphi 2 results in a compile time error, *Constant expression violates subrange bounds*. If you write the following instead:

```
var
  UppLetter: Uppercase;
  Letter: Char;
begin
  Letter :='e';
  UppLetter := Letter;
  ...
```

Delphi will compile the code. At run-time, if you have enabled the Range Checking compiler option, you'll get a *Range check error* error message. I suggest that you turn on this compiler option (see the Compiler page of the Project Options dialog box) while you are developing a program, and then eventually disable it for the final build. This makes the programs a little faster, but a little less robustly. The same holds true for other run-time checking options, such as overflow and stack checking.

## Enumerations

*Enumerated types* constitute another user-defined ordinal type. Instead of indicating a range of an existing type, in an enumeration you list all of the possible values for the type. In other words, an enumeration is a list of values. Here are some examples:

```
type
  Colors = (Red, Yellow, Green, Cyan, Blue, Violet);
  Suit = (Club, Diamond, Heart, Spade);
```

Each value in the list has an associated *ordinality*, starting with zero. When you apply the Ord function to a value of an enumerated type, you get this zero-based value. For example, Ord (Diamonds) returns 1. Enumerations can have different internal representations. By default, Delphi uses an 8-bit representation, unless there are more than 256 different values, in which case it uses the 16-bit representation. There is also a 32-bit representation, which might be useful for compatibility with C or C++ libraries. You can actually change the default behavior, asking for a larger representation, by using the $Z compiler directive.

In Delphi, there are several properties that have an enumerated value. For example, the style of the border of a form is defined as follows:

```
type
  TFormBorderStyle = (bsNone, bsSingle, bsSizeable, bsDialog,
bsSizeToolWin, bsToolWindow);
```

When the value of a property is an enumeration, you usually can choose from the list of values displayed in the Object Inspector:

## Sets

A *set type* indicates the power set of an ordinal type, quite often an enumeration or a subrange, since the base type cannot have more than 256 possible values in its range. Each set can contain none, one, more than one, or all the values within the range of the ordinal type. Here is an example of a set. (You can also see it in Figure 4.5.)

```
type
  Letters = set of Uppercase;
```

---

**FIGURE 4.5:**

A representation of a set.

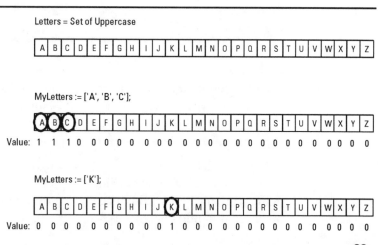

Now I can define a variable of this type and assign to it some values of the original type. To indicate some values in a set, you write a comma-separated list, enclosed within square brackets. When you have defined a variable such as

```
var
  MyLetters: Letters;
```

you can set its value with the following statements (respectively assigning several values, a single value, and an empty value):

```
MyLetters := ['A', 'B', 'C'];
MyLetters := ['K'];
MyLetters := [];
```

In Delphi, sets are often used to indicate nonexclusive flags. For example, the following two lines declare an enumeration of possible icons for the border of a window and the corresponding set:

```
type
  TBorderIcon = (biSystemMenu, biMinimize, biMaximize, biHelp);
  TBorderIcons = set of TBorderIcon;
```

In fact, a window can have none of these icons, one of them or more than one. When working with the Object Inspector, you can provide the values of a set either by writing the proper list within square brackets or by expanding the selection and toggling on and off the presence of each value.

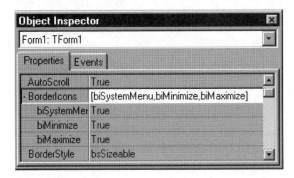

## Arrays

An *array* defines a fixed number of elements of one specific type (see Figure 4.6). For example, you can define a *group* of 24 integers with this code:

```
type
  DayTemperatures = array [1..24] of Integer;
```

In the array definition, you need to use two constants of an ordinal type to specify the valid indexes of the array. Since you specify both the upper and the lower index of the array, the indexes don't need to be zero-based, as is necessary in C/C++ and other programming languages.

**FIGURE 4.6:**

A representation of an array.

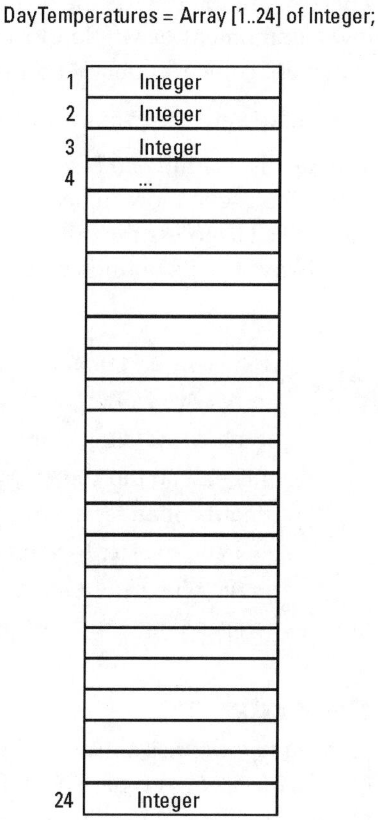

DayTemperatures = Array [1..24] of Integer;

In the former example, you can set the value of a DayTemp variable of the DayTemperatures type as follows:

```
DayTemp [1] := 34;
DayTemp [2] := 32;
...
DayTemp [24] := 36;
```

An array can have more than one dimension, as in the following examples:

```
type
  MonthTemperatures = array [1..24, 1..31] of Integer;
  YearTemperatures = array [1..24, 1..31, January..December]
    of Integer;
```

These arrays are built on the same core types. So you can declare them using the preceding data types, as in the following code:

```
type
  MonthTemps = array [1..31] of DayTemps;
  YearTemps = array [Jan..Dec] of MonthTemps;
```

This declaration inverts the order of the indexes as presented above, but it also allows assignment of whole blocks between variables. For example, the following statement copies January's temperatures to February:

```
ThisYear[Feb] := ThisYear[Jan];
```

You can also define *zero-based arrays*—arrays with the lower bound set to zero. Generally, the use of more logical bounds is an advantage, since you don't need to use the index 2 to access the third item, and so on. If you need to work on an array, you can always test its bounds by using the standard Low and High functions.

**NOTE** Using Low and High when operating on arrays is highly recommended, especially in loops, since it makes the code independent of the range of the array. Later, you can change the declared range of the array indices, and the code that uses Low and High will still work. Code that is hard-coded for an array's range would not work. Low and High make your code easier to maintain and more reliable. Incidentally, there is no run-time overhead for using Low and High. They are resolved at compile-time into constant expressions, not actual function calls.

## Records

A *record type* defines a fixed collection of elements of different types. Each element, or *field*, has its own type. The definition of a record type lists all these fields, giving each a name you'll use later to access it. Here is an example of the definition of a record type (see also Figure 4.7), a variable of that type, and the use of this variable:

```
type
  Date = record
    Year: Integer;
    Month: Byte;
    Day: Byte;
  end;
var
  BirthDay: Date;
begin
  BirthDay.Year := 1995;
  BirthDay.Month := 2;
  BirthDay.Day := 14;
```

The record type is important because it is similar to the class type, which we will discuss in the next chapter. In fact, classes and objects can be considered an extension of the record type.

Records can also have a variant part; that is, multiple fields can be mapped to the same memory area, even if they have a different data type. Alternatively, you can use these variant fields or groups of fields to access the same memory location

**FIGURE 4.7:**

A representation of a record.

```
Date = Record
  Year: Integer;
  Month: Byte;
  Day: Byte;
```

| Year : | Integer |
|---|---|
| Month: | Byte |
| Day: | Byte |

within a record, but considering those values from different perspectives. The effect you obtain is similar to that of typecasting, and this is actually the most common reason variant records were used in the past, when the Pascal language allowed no explicit typecasting. The use of variant records is not type-safe and is not a recommended programming practice, particularly for beginners.

## Pointers

A *pointer type* defines a variable that holds the memory address of yet another variable of a certain data type. So a pointer variable indirectly refers to a value, as you can see in Figure 4.8. The definition of a pointer type uses a special character, the caret (^).

```
type
  PointerToInt = ^Integer;
```

Once you have defined a pointer variable, you can assign to it the address of another variable of the same type, using the @ operator, or create a new variable on the heap with the New procedure. If a pointer has no value, you can assign nil to it. You can test whether a pointer is nil to see if it currently refers to a value. This is often used, because dereferencing an invalid pointer causes a general protection

**FIGURE 4.8:**

A representation of a pointer.

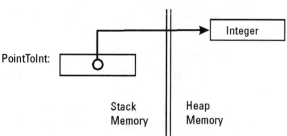

PointerToInt = ^Integer;

fault. To set the value of pointed data, just use the caret again. Here are some sample operations on pointers:

```
var
  P1, P2: ^Integer;
  N: Integer;
begin
  {initialization}
  N := 10;
  P1 := @N;
  New (P2);
  {operations}
  P1^ := 20; {actually changes the value of N}
  P2^ := P1^ * 2;
  {termination}
  Dispose (P2);
end;
```

Notice that there is also a `Pointer` data type, which indicates untyped pointers (such as void* in the C language). With an untyped pointer (or each time the size of the memory variable is not defined) you use `GetMem` instead of `New`. The fact that pointers are seldom necessary in Delphi is an interesting advantage of this environment. Understanding pointers is important for advanced programming and if you want to understand the Delphi object model, which uses pointers "behind the scenes." However, you can probably write even the most complex Delphi applications without using any *explicit* pointers at all.

**NOTE**  You use pointers often in Delphi, but behind the scenes. Every object instance is really an implicit pointer or reference to its actual data. However, this is completely transparent to the programmer, who uses object variables just like any other data type. We will see some more details about the Delphi object reference model in the next chapter.

## Files

Another Pascal-specific type constructor is the *file type*. Files are related to input/output, and they will be discussed in more detail in Chapter 23. In short, you can define a new file data type as follows:

```
type
  IntFile = file of Integer
```

Then you can open a physical file associated with this structure and write values (integers) to it or read the current values. The use of files in Pascal is quite straightforward, but in Delphi there are also some components that are capable of storing or loading their contents to or from a file. There is some serialization support and there is also database support. We will discuss these issues in Chapters 23 and 17, respectively.

# Pascal Strings

String handling is a complex issue in the Windows versions of Pascal. In fact, Pascal has one way of handling strings, while Windows has its own way, borrowed from the C language. To further confuse things, the 32-bit version of Delphi introduces support for long strings. We'll start by looking at the traditional Pascal approach.

In Pascal, the typical string type is a sequence of characters with a length counter at the beginning. Each string has a fixed size (which by default is 255), although it usually holds fewer characters. Here is an example:

```
var
  Name: string;
  Title: string [50];
```

*Name* is a string of 255 characters. *Title* holds a maximum of 50 characters. Traditional Pascal strings are limited to 255 characters, and this is a real problem.

As you can see from the use of brackets, strings are similar to arrays. In fact, a string is almost an array of characters. This is demonstrated by the fact that you can write

```
FirstChar := Name [1];
```

to access the first character of the Name string. There are a number of functions you can use to operate on strings (refer to the Delphi Help file for a full list). In particular, using Pascal strings, you can easily add two strings using the plus sign:

```
FinalString := FirstString + ' ' + SecondString;
```

This expression merges the two strings, adding a blank character (a space) between them.

## Long Pascal Strings

To overcome the limits of traditional Pascal strings, Delphi 2 introduces support for long strings. There are actually two string types:

- ShortString corresponds to typical Pascal strings, as described in the section above. These strings have a limit of 255 characters and correspond to the strings in the 16-bit version of Delphi. Each element of a short string is of type ANSIChar; that is the standard character type.

- AnsiString corresponds to the new variable length, long strings. These strings are dynamically allocated and are practically unlimited. They are also based on the ANSIChar type.

In the 32-bit version of Delphi, if you simply use the `string` data type, you get either short strings or ANSI strings, depending on the value of the new $H compiler directive. The default is $H+, which stands for long strings (`ANSIString`), and this is what is used by the components of the VCL library.

As I mentioned before, these new strings are dynamically allocated. This means that a string is actually a pointer to the real string. When you make a copy of the string, only the pointer is copied, making this operation extremely fast. But as soon as you change the contents of one of the strings referring to the same value, the string is duplicated and only the duplicated value is affected by the change. This is possible thanks to a system reference-counting mechanism, which can also free the memory when a string in memory isn't used any more (that is, when the reference count reaches zero).

The string is allocated again when you change its size, and this implies a full copy of the string when there is something else in the memory nearby and the string cannot grow in the same memory location. For this reason, you can set the maximum size of the string with the new SetLength procedure, allocating the required amount of memory:

```
SetLength (String1, 200);
```

This is seldom necessary, but can really speed up some string-related code. For example, if you have a loop that keeps adding characters to a string, it will require several memory reallocations for the string, unless you ask at the beginning for a string big enough for the largest possible case.

**NOTE**   If you allocate a very large string in Delphi 2 (that is, if you allocate a large memory block in Windows 95 or NT), the system reserves the address space for the string, but doesn't actually allocate it until it is needed. For this reason, don't be afraid to allocate a string larger than you actually need.

The only case in which you must allocate memory for the long string using SetLength is when you have to pass the string as parameter to an API function (after the proper type cast), as I'll show you later.

Another important point in favor of using long strings is that they are terminated by nulls. This means that they are fully compatible with the C language null-terminated strings used by Windows (see the next section).

All of these reasons, plus the key one—the size of the long strings—make the use of the `ANSIString` type the standard in the 32-bit version of Delphi, with the old strings available for compatibility only. Since this is the default, just use the `string` data type. Keep in mind how they are implemented, because this has some impact on the way you write good, fast code.

> **NEW**
>
> Besides the traditional Pascal string functions, Delphi 2 adds three new functions to remove the white spaces from a string: TrimLeft, TrimRight, and Trim. They remove (respectively) leading white spaces, trailing white spaces, or white spaces at both ends of the string.

## C-Like Character Arrays

As an alternative to the string type, you can use zero-based character arrays to store *null-terminated* strings. A *null-terminated* string is a sequence of characters followed by a byte set to zero (or null). Character arrays are typical of the C language, and they are used extensively by Windows API functions. Since Pascal's long strings are fully compatible with C null-terminated strings, using character arrays is useful mainly for compatibility with the 16-bit version of an application.

You declare a character array as follows

```
var
  Name: array[0..50] of Char;
```

and work with it as with any other array. However, there is a second way to use character arrays. If the language *extended syntax* is enabled (which happens by default), a zero-based character array is compatible with PChar, a pointer to a character. You might wonder why this compatibility would be necessary. The short answer is that many Windows API functions require PChar parameters, so this compatibility rule allows you to declare character arrays, eventually fill them with a value, and then pass them as parameters to these API functions.

Although many Windows functions have a PChar parameter, in most cases, declaring PChar and passing it to those functions generates a bad error. By writing such code, you end up passing a null pointer (that is, an uninitialized pointer) to the function, which will cause an error inside Windows code when the system tries to read or write the string.

In general, before passing a pointer to a Windows function, you should allocate memory for it. In the case of PChar strings, the easiest technique is to declare an array of characters instead of a pointer, and pass that array to the function. As an alternative, you can declare the pointer and dynamically allocate memory for it (with the GetMem or NewStr functions). In this case, remember to dispose the memory at the end.

# String Conversions

There are a number of functions that work on null-terminated strings, too. In particular, there are a couple of conversion functions that might come in handy. StrPas converts a null-terminated string into a short Pascal string. StrPCopy makes the reverse conversion.

If you need to convert a long Pascal string into a PChar instead, a cast is enough. To copy the caption of a form into the string (using the API function GetWindowText) and copy it into a label, you can write the following:

```
procedure TForm1.Button1Click(Sender: TObject);
var
  S1: String;
begin
  SetLength (S1, 100);
  GetWindowText (Handle, PChar (S1), Length (S1));
  Button1.Caption := S1;
end;
```

You can find this code in the LONGSTR example on the companion CD. Notice that if you write this code but fail to allocate the memory for the string with SetLength, the program will probably crash quite badly (and in Windows 95, it might as well crash the whole system).

If you are using a PChar to pass a value (and not to receive one as in the code above), the code is even simpler because there is no need to define a temporary string and initialize it. The following line of code passes the caption of a label as parameter to an API function, simply by type-casting it to PChar.

```
SetWindowText (Handle, PChar (Label1.Caption))
```

## Long Strings Conversion Blues

This compatibility and the big size of the new strings are the two key reasons to use them exclusively, unless you need to maintain compatibility with a 16-bit version of Delphi. However, there are some problems that might arise when you convert a long string to a PChar. (I suggest that inexperienced Delphi programmers skip this section, which delves into a couple of complex topics.)

Basically, after this conversion, you become *responsible* for the string and its contents, and Delphi won't help you any more. Consider the following limited change to the first program code fragment above, Button1Click:

```
procedure TForm1.Button2Click(Sender: TObject);
var
  S1: String;
begin
  SetLength (S1, 100);
 GetWindowText (Handle, PChar (S1), Length (S1));
```

```
  S1 := S1 + ' is the title';
  Button1.Caption := S1;
end;
```

This program compiles, but when you run it, you are in for a surprise: The caption of the button will have the original text of the window title, without the text of the constant string you have added to it. The problem is that when Windows writes to the string (within the `GetWindowText` call), it doesn't set the length of the long Pascal string properly. Delphi still can use this string for output and can figure out when it ends looking for the null terminator, but if you append further characters after the null terminator, they will be skipped altogether.

How can we fix this problem? The solution is to tell the system to convert the string returned by the `GetWindowText` call back to a Pascal string. However, if you write the following code:

```
S1 := String (S1);
```

the system will ignore it, because converting a data type back into itself is a useless operation. So to obtain the proper long Pascal string, you need to *recast* the string to a PChar, and let Delphi convert it back again properly to a string:

```
S1 := String (PChar (S1));
```

Actually you can skip the string conversion, because PChar to String conversions are automatic in Delphi. Here is the final code:

```
procedure TForm1.Button3Click(Sender: TObject);
var
  S1: String;
begin
  SetLength (S1, 100);
  GetWindowText (Handle, PChar (S1), Length (S1));
  S1 := String (PChar (S1));
  S1 := S1 + ' is the title';
  Button3.Caption := S1;
end;
```

You can find the three versions of the code in the LONGSTR example, which has three buttons to execute them. Notice, anyway, that if you need to access the title of a form, you can simply use the Caption property of the form object. There is no need to write all this confusing code, which was intended only to demonstrate the string conversion problems. There are practical cases when you need to call Windows API functions, and you have to consider this complex situation.

# Coding Style

Before we start to write actual Pascal language statements, it is important to highlight a couple of elements of Pascal coding style. This is the question I'm addressing: Besides the syntax rules, how do you write the code? There isn't a single answer to this question, since personal taste can dictate different styles. However, there are some principles you need to know regarding comments, uppercase, spaces, and the so-called "pretty-printing."

## Comments

In Pascal, comments are enclosed in either braces or parentheses followed by a star. Delphi 2 also accepts the C++ style comments, which can span to the end of the line:

```
{this is a comment}
(* this is another comment *)
// this is a comment up to the end of the line
```

The first form is shorter and more commonly used. The second form is often preferred in Europe because of the lack of the brace symbol on many European keyboards (including the one I currently use). Of course, one can get used to typing Alt+123 and Alt+125 to obtain the proper symbol, but having an alternative is better.

**NEW** The third form of comments has been borrowed from C++ and is available only in the new version of Delphi. Comments "up to the end of the line" are very helpful for short comments and for commenting out a line of code.

Having three different forms of comments can be helpful for making nested comments. If you want to comment out several lines of source code to disable them, and these lines contain some real comments, you cannot use the same comment identifier:

```
{  ... code
  {comment, creating problems}
  ... code }
```

With a second comment identifier, you can write the following code, which is correct:

```
{  ... code
  //this comment is OK
  ... code }
```

Note that if the open brace or parenthesis-star is followed by the dollar character ($), it becomes a compiler directive, as in

```
{$X+}
```

NOTE Actually, compiler directives are still comments. `{$X+ This is a comment}` is legal. It's both a valid directive and a comment, although "sane" programmers will probably tend to separate directives and comments.

## Use of Uppercase

Unlike in other languages, the Pascal compiler ignores the case of the characters. Therefore, the identifiers `Myname`, `MyName`, `myname`, `myName`, and `MYNAME` are all exactly equivalent. This is definitely a positive, since in case-sensitive languages, many syntax errors are caused by incorrect capitalization.

There are a couple of subtle drawbacks, however. First, you must be aware that these identifiers really are the same, so you must avoid using them as different elements. Second, you should try to be consistent in the use of uppercase letters, to improve the readability of the code.

A common approach is to capitalize only the first letter of each identifier. When an identifier is made up of several consecutive words (you cannot insert a space in an identifier), every first letter of a word should be capitalized, as in:

```
MyLongIdentifier
MyVeryLongAndAlmostStupidIdentifier
```

A consistent use of the cases isn't enforced by the compiler, but it is a good habit to get into.

## White Spaces

Other elements completely ignored by the compiler are the number of spaces, new lines, and tab spaces you add to the source code. All these elements are collectively known as *white spaces*. White spaces are used only to improve code readability; they do not affect the compilation.

Unlike BASIC, Pascal allows you to write a statement in several lines of code, splitting a long instruction on two or more lines. The drawback (at least for many BASIC programmers) of allowing statements on more than one line is that you have to remember to add a semicolon to indicate the end of a statement, or more precisely, to separate a statement from the next one. Notice that the only restriction in splitting programming statements on different lines is that you cannot have a newline character in string literals.

Again, there are no fixed rules on the use of spaces and multiple-line statements, just some rules of thumb:

- The Delphi editor has a vertical line you can place after 60 or 70 characters. If you use this line and try to avoid surpassing this limit, your source code will look better when you print it on paper. Long lines can be broken automatically at any position, even in the middle of a word, when you print them.

- When a function or procedure has several parameters, it is common practice to place the parameters on different lines.

- You can leave a line completely white (blank) before a comment or to divide a long piece of code in smaller portions. Even this simple idea can improve the readability of the code, both on screen and when you print it.

- Use white spaces to separate the parameters of a function call, and maybe even a space before the initial open parenthesis. Separate operands of an expression. I know that some programmers will disagree with these ideas, but I insist: Spaces are free; you don't pay for them. (OK, I know that they use up disk space and modem time when you upload or download a file, but they can be compressed fairly well.)

The last suggestion on the use of white spaces relates to the typical Pascal language-formatting style, known as *pretty-printing*.

## Pretty-Printing

Source-code formatting in Pascal usually follows a standard approach known as *pretty-printing*. Its rule is simple: Each time you need to write a compound statement, indent it two spaces to the right of the rest of the current statement. A compound statement inside another compound statement is indented four spaces, and so on:

```
if ... then
   statement;
if ... then
begin
   statement1;
   statement2;
end;
if ... then
begin
   if ... then
      statement1
   statement2;
end;
```

A similar indented format is often used for lists of variables or data types, as in the code fragments of this chapter, and to continue a statement from the previous line:

```
type
   Letters = set of Char;
var
   Name: string;
begin
```

```
very long source code statement going on in the
  following line, and indented two or four spaces;
```

Of course, any such convention is just a suggestion to make the code more readable to other programmers, and it is completely ignored by the compiler. I won't give you a detailed coverage of pretty-printing rules here, but I've tried to use them consistently in all of the samples and code fragments in this book. Delphi source code, manuals, and Help examples use a similar formatting style.

**NOTE**  Some programmers and authors follow different conventions for source-code formatting. For example, some insist on not using a line for a `begin` or `end` statement (mostly those coming from a C background). Packing more text in a single line, you might be able to see more lines of code in the editor window. I've never liked this approach, since I prefer to waste a line with only an open or closed parenthesis, even in C++. For readability of code, both in an editor and on paper, I tend to leave white spaces before and after operators, before the parameters of procedures, and so on. This is just my personal taste. You should follow your own habits, at least if they are not too bad!

## Syntax Highlighting

To make it easier to read and write Pascal code, the Delphi editor has a feature called *color syntax highlighting*. Depending on the meaning in Pascal of the words you type in the editor, they are displayed using different colors. By default, keywords are in bold, strings and comments are in color, and so on.

Reserved words, comments, and strings are probably the three elements that benefit most from this feature. You can see at a glance a misspelled keyword, a string not properly terminated, and the length of a multiple-line comment.

You can easily customize the syntax highlight settings using the Editor Colors page of the Environment Options dialog box (see Figure 4.9). If you work by yourself, choose the colors you like. If you work closely with other programmers, you should all agree on a standard color scheme. I find that working on a computer with a different syntax coloring than the one I am used to is really difficult.

FIGURE 4.9:

The dialog box used to set the color syntax highlighting.

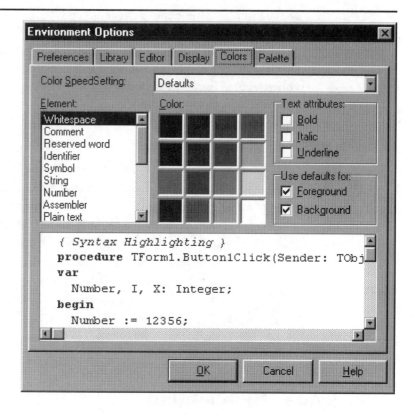

## Pascal Statements

Once you have defined some identifiers, you can use them in statements and in the expressions that are part of some statements. In Pascal, there are several different statements and expressions. Let's look at expressions and operators first.

### Expressions and Operators

There isn't a general rule for building expressions, since they mainly depend on the operators being used, and Pascal has a number of operators. There are logical, arithmetic, Boolean, relational, and set operators, plus some others. Expressions can be used to determine the value to assign to a variable, to compute the parameter of a function or procedure, or to test for a condition. Expressions can include function calls, too. Every time you are performing an operation on the value of an identifier, rather than using an identifier by itself, that is an expression.

**NOTE** Expressions are common to most programming languages. An *expression* is any valid combination of constants, variables, literal values, operators, and function results. Expressions are read-only. You can use the result of an expression but not assign a value to it. In other words, an expression can appear on the right side of an assignment, but not on the left side (that is, expressions cannot be used as l-values). Expressions can also be passed to value parameters of procedures and functions, but not to reference (`var`) parameters (which require an *l-value*).

If you have ever written a program in your life, you already know what an expression is. Here, I'll highlight specific elements of Pascal operators. You can see a list of the operators of the language, grouped by precedence, in Table 4.3.

**TABLE 4.3:** Pascal Language Operators, Grouped by Precedence

| Operator | Purpose |
| --- | --- |
| **Unary Operators (Highest Precedence)** | |
| @ | Address of (returns a pointer) |
| not | Boolean or bitwise not |
| **Multiplicative and Bitwise Operators** | |
| * | Arithmetic multiplication or set intersection |
| / | Real-type division |
| div | Integer-type division |
| mod | Modulus (the remainder of integer division) |
| as | Type-safe typecast (RTTI) |
| and | Boolean and bitwise and |
| shl | Bitwise left shift |
| shr | Bitwise right shift |
| **Additive Operators** | |
| + | Addition, set union string concatenation, positive value, or offset addition |
| – | Subtraction, set difference, negative value, or offset subtraction |
| or | Boolean or bitwise or |
| xor | Boolean or bitwise exclusive or |

**TABLE 4.3:** Pascal Language Operators, Grouped by Precedence (continued)

| Operator | Purpose |
|---|---|
| **Relational and Comparison Operators (Lowest Precedence)** | |
| = | Test if equal |
| <> | Test if not equal |
| < | Test if less than |
| > | Test if greater than |
| <= | Test if less than or equal or a subset of a set |
| >= | Test of greater or equal or superset of a set |
| in | Test if member of |
| is | Test if type compatible (RTTI) |

Notice that some of the common operators have different meanings with different data types. For example, the + operator can be used to add two numbers, concatenate two strings, make the union of two sets, and even add an offset to a PChar. However, you cannot add two characters, as is possible in C.

Another strange operator is div. In Pascal, you can divide any two numbers (real or integers) with the / operator, and you'll invariably get a real type result. If you need to divide two integers and want an integer result, use the div operator. (By the way, div is faster than /.)

## Set Operators

The set operators include

- Set union (+)
- Difference (-)
- Intersection (*)
- Set membership test (in)
- Relational operators

To add an element to a set, you can make the union of the set with another one that has only the element you need. Here's a Delphi example related to font styles:

```
Style := Style + [fsBold];
Style := Style + [fsBold, fsItalic] - [fsUnderline];
```

As an alternative, you can use the standard Include and Exclude procedures, which are much more efficient (but cannot be used with component properties of the set type, because they require an I = value parameter):

```
Include (Style, fsBold);
```

# Simple and Compound Statements

A Pascal statement is simple when it doesn't contain any other statements. Examples of simple statements are assign statements and procedure statements. Simple statements are separated by a semicolon:

```
X := Y + Z; {assignment}
Randomize; {procedure call}
```

As I mentioned in Chapter 1, assignments in Pascal use the "colon-equal" operator, something a little odd for programmers who are used to other languages. The = operator, which is used for assignments in other languages, is used to test for equality in Pascal.

**NOTE**    By using two different symbols for an assignment and an equality test, the Pascal compiler can translate source code faster, because it doesn't need to examine the context in which the operator is used to determine its meaning. The use of different operators also makes the code easier for us to read.

Usually, statements are part of a compound statement, marked by begin and end brackets. A compound statement can appear in place of a generic Pascal statement. Here is an example:

```
begin
  A := B;
  C := A * 2;
end;
```

The semicolon after the last statement before the end isn't required, as in the following:

```
begin
  A := B;
  C := A * 2
end;
```

Both versions are correct. The first version has a useless (but harmless) semicolon. This semicolon is, in fact, a null statement; that is, a statement with no code. (Notice that, at times, null statements can be used inside loops or in other particular cases.)

# Pascal Conditional Statements

A conditional statement is used to execute one or none of the statements that compose it. There are two basic flavors of conditional statements: `if` statements and `case` statements.

## If Statements

The `if` statement can be used to execute a statement only if a certain condition is met (`if-then`), or to choose between two different statements (`if-then-else`). The condition is described with a Boolean expression. We'll go through an easy Delphi example to show you how to write simple conditional statements. The example includes some components that we haven't gotten to yet, but I think you can get the basic idea. First, create a new blank application, and put two check boxes and four buttons in the form. Do not change the names of buttons or check boxes, but do double-click on each of the buttons to add an `OnClick` event handler. Here's a simple `if` statement for the first button:

```
procedure TForm1.Button1Click(Sender: TObject);
begin
  {simple if statement}
  if CheckBox1.Checked then
    ShowMessage ('CheckBox1 is checked')
end;
```

When you click the button, if the first check box has a check mark in it, the program will show a simple message in a small window (see Figure 4.10). I've used the `ShowMessage` function because it is the simplest Delphi function you can use to display a short message to the user, although the output of the `MessageDlg` function I've used in past examples is much better looking.

If you click the button and nothing happens, it means the check box was not checked. In general, it is better to make this more explicit, as with this code for the second button, which uses an `if-then-else` statement.

```
procedure TForm1.Button2Click(Sender: TObject);
begin
  {if-then-else statement}
  if CheckBox2.Checked then
    ShowMessage ('CheckBox2 is checked')
  else
    ShowMessage ('CheckBox2 is NOT checked');
end;
```

Notice that you cannot have a semicolon after the first statement and before the `else` keyword, or the compiler will issue a syntax error.

**FIGURE 4.10:**

The message displayed when the check mark is checked.

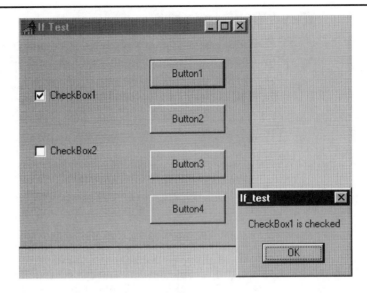

If statements can be quite complex. The condition can be turned into a series of conditions, or the if statement can nest a second if statement. The last two buttons of the IF_TEST example demonstrate these cases.

```
procedure TForm1.Button3Click(Sender: TObject);
begin
  {statement with a double condition}
  if CheckBox1.Checked and CheckBox2.Checked then
    ShowMessage ('Both check boxes are checked')
end;

procedure TForm1.Button4Click(Sender: TObject);
begin
  {compound if statement}
  if CheckBox1.Checked then
  if CheckBox2.Checked then
    ShowMessage ('CheckBox1 and 2 are checked')
  else
    ShowMessage ('Only CheckBox1 is checked')
  else
    ShowMessage (
      'Checkbox1 is not checked, who cares for Checkbox2?')
end;
```

Look at the code carefully and run the program to see if you understand everything. When you have doubts about a programming construct, writing a very simple program such as this can help you learn a lot. You can add more check boxes and increase the complexity of this small example, making any test you like.

**109**

## Case Statements

If your if statements become very complex, you can replace them with case statements. A case statement consists of an expression, used to select a value, and a list of possible values or ranges of values. These values are constants, and they must be unique and of an ordinal type. Eventually, there can be an else statement that is executed if none of the labels correspond to the value of the selector. Here are two simple examples:

```
case Number of
  1: Text := 'One';
  2: Text := 'Two';
  3: Text := 'Three';
end;
case MyChar of
  '+' := Text := 'Plus sign';
  '-' := Text := 'Minus sign';
  '0'..'9': Text := 'Number';
  'a'..'z': Text := 'Lowercase character';
  'A'..'Z': Text := 'Uppercase character';
else
  Text := 'Unknown character';
end;
```

# Pascal Loops

The Pascal language has the typical repetitive statements of most programming languages, including for, while, and repeat statements.

## For Statements

The for loop in Pascal is strictly based on a counter, which can be either increased or decreased each time the loop is executed. Here is a simple example of a for loop used to add the first ten integer numbers.

```
K := 0;
for I := 1 to 10 do
  K := K + I;
```

This same for statement could have been written using a reverse counter:

```
K := 0;
for I := 10 downto 1 do
  K := K + I;
```

The for loop in Pascal is less flexible than in C, but it is simpler and much easier to understand. If you want to test for a more complex condition, or to provide a customized counter, you need to use one of the other two repetitive statements instead of for.

# While and Repeat Statements

The difference between the while-do loop and the repeat-until loop is that the code of the repeat statement is always executed at least once. You can easily understand why by looking at a simple example:

```
while I < 100 and J < 100 do
begin
  {use I and J to compute something...}
  I := I + 1;
  J := J + 1;
end;
repeat
  {use I and J to compute something...}
  I := I + 1;
  J := J + 1;
until I < 100 and J < 100;
```

If the initial value of I or J is greater than 100, the statements inside the repeat-until loop are executed anyway.

To explore the details of loops, let's look at a small Delphi example. This example, called LOOPS, highlights the difference between a loop with a fixed counter and a loop with an almost random counter.

Start with a new blank project, place a list box and two buttons on the main form, and give the buttons a proper name ("ButtonFor" and "ButtonWhile"), removing the word *button* from the captions. Now we can add some code to the OnClick events of the two buttons. The first button has a simple for loop to display a list of numbers, as you can see in Figure 4.11.

**FIGURE 4.11:**

Each time you press the For button, the list box is filled with consecutive numbers.

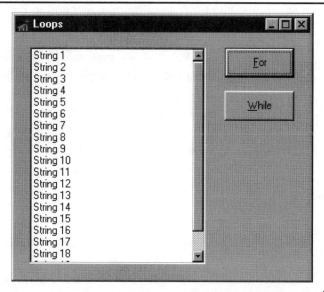

Before executing this loop, which adds a number of strings to the Items property of the list box, you need to clear the contents of the list box itself:

```pascal
procedure TForm1.ForButtonClick(Sender: TObject);
var
  I: Integer;
begin
  ListBox1.Items.Clear;
  for I := 1 to 20 do
  Listbox1.Items.Add ('String ' + IntToStr (I));
end;
```

The code associated with the second button is slightly more complex. In this case, there is a while loop based on a counter, which is increased randomly. To accomplish this, I've called the Randomize procedure, which resets the random-number generator, and the Random function with a range value of 100. The result of this function is a number between 0 and 99, chosen randomly.

```pascal
procedure TForm1.WhileButtonClick(Sender: TObject);
var
  I: Integer;
begin
  ListBox1.Items.Clear;
  Randomize;
  I := 0;
  while I < 1000 do
  begin
    I := I + Random (100);
    Listbox1.Items.Add ('Random Number: ' + IntToStr (I));
  end;
end;
```

Each time you click the second button, the numbers are different, because they depend on the random-number generator. Two examples are shown in Figure 4.12.

> **NOTE**
>
> You can alter the standard flow of a loop's execution using the Break and Continue system procedures. The first interrupts the loop; the second is used to jump directly to the loop test or counter increment, continuing with the next iteration or the loop (unless the condition is zero or the counter has reached its highest value). Two more system procedures, Exit and Halt, let you jump out of the current function of procedure or terminate the program.

**FIGURE 4.12:**

The contents of the list box of the LOOPS example changes from time to time when you press the While button.

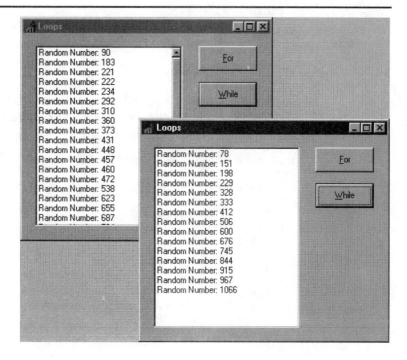

# The With Statement

The last kind of Pascal statement I'll focus on is the with statement, which is peculiar to this programming language and very useful in Delphi programming. The with statement is nothing but shorthand. When you need to refer to a record (or an object), instead of repeating its name every time, you can use a with statement. For example, for the discussion of records, I wrote this code:

```pascal
type
  Date = record
    Year: Integer;
    Month: Byte;
    Day: Byte;
  end;
var
  BirthDay: Date;
begin
  BirthDay.Year := 1995;
  BirthDay.Month := 2;
  BirthDay.Day := 14;
  ...
```

I can improve the final part of this code, using a with statement, as follows:

```pascal
begin
  with BirthDay do
```

**113**

```
begin
  Year := 1995;
  Month := 2;
  Day := 14;
end;
...
```

This approach can be used in Delphi programs to refer to components. For example, we can rewrite the final part of the last example, LOOPS, using a with statement to access the items in the list box:

```
procedure TForm1.WhileButtonClick(Sender: TObject);
var
  I: Integer;
begin
  with ListBox1.Items do
  begin
    Clear;
    Randomize;
    I := 0;
    while I < 1000 do
    begin
      I := I + Random (100);
      Add ('Random Number: ' + IntToStr (I));
    end;
  end;
end;
```

When you work with components or classes in general, the with statement allows you to save some code, particularly for nested fields. For example, suppose that you need to change the width and the color of the drawing pen for a form. You can write the following code:

```
Form1.Canvas.Pen.Width := 2;
Form1.Canvas.Pen.Color := clRed;
```

But it is certainly easier to write this code:

```
with Form1.Canvas.Pen do
begin
  Width := 2;
  Color := clRed;
end;
```

When you are writing complex code, the with statement can be effective and spares you the declaration of some temporary variables, but it has a drawback. It can make the code less readable, particularly when you are working with different objects that have similar or corresponding properties. Consider this code:

```
with Form1.Canvas.Pen do
  Width := 2;
  Color := clRed;
```

It changes the width of the pen and the color of the current object (maybe a form). In fact, the indentation above is inconsistent with the rules I've suggested. The statement changing the color should be aligned with the initial with statement.

Considering this kind of drawback, and the aim of this book, which is to show you how programs work, I've decided to use with statements sparingly, in favor of readability. However, I suggest that you do use them more often in your code, particularly if you are not a good typist.

# Pascal Procedures and Functions

Another important idea emphasized by Pascal is the concept of the *subroutine*. In Pascal, subroutines can assume two different forms: procedures and functions. The only real difference between the two constructs is that functions have a return value, while procedures don't. Here are the definitions of a procedure and two versions of the same function, using a slightly different syntax:

```
procedure Hello;
begin
  ShowMessage ('Hello world!');
end;

function Double (Value: Integer) : Integer;
begin
  Double := Value * 2;
end;

{or, as an alternative:}
function Double2 (Value: Integer) : Integer;
begin
  Result := Value * 2;
end;
```

Once these subroutines have been defined, you can call them as follows:

```
Hello;
X := Double (Y);
Hello;
Z := Double2 (X);
```

This approach is different from that of the C language, which only has functions (although some C functions do not have a return value). It is also different from the original BASIC, where you needed to use GOSUB statements. Modern BASIC dialects have introduced an approach similar to Pascal.

**NOTE**    In the last version of its Pascal compiler, Borland introduced the option of not using the return value of a function (something that was previously compulsory). Now you can freely call a function and ignore its result; that is, use a function as if it were a procedure. This is particularly useful when you call some of the functions of the Windows API.

## Reference Parameters

Both procedures and functions allow parameter passing by value and by reference. Passing a parameter by reference means that its value is not copied on the stack in the formal parameter of the subroutine (avoiding a copy often means that the program saves some time). Instead, the program refers to the original value also in the code of the subroutine. This allows the procedure or function to change the value of the parameter. Parameter passing by reference is expressed by the var keyword.

This technique is available in most programming languages. It isn't present in C, but has been introduced in C++, where you use the & operator. In Visual Basic it is based on the ByVal keyword. Here is an example:

```
procedure DoubleTheValue (var Value: Integer);
begin
  Value := Value * 2;
end;
```

In this case, the parameter is used both to pass a value to the procedure and to return a new value to the calling code.

## Constant Parameters

As an alternative to reference parameters, you can use a const parameter. Since you cannot assign a new value to a const parameter inside the routine, the compiler can optimize parameter passing, particularly for strings or big records. The compiler can choose an approach similar to reference parameters (or a const reference in C++ terms), but the behavior will remain similar to value parameters, because the original value won't be affected by the routine.

In fact, if you try to compile the following (silly) code, Delphi will issue an error:

```
function DoubleTheValue (const Value: Integer): Integer;
begin
  Value := Value * 2;      // Error
  DoubleTheValue := Value;
end;
```

# Open Array Parameters

Unlike C, a Pascal function or procedure has a set number of parameters. However, there is a way to pass a generic number of parameters to a function, using an *open array*. This is a special kind of array that has an undefined number of values, which can be handy for passing parameter. For example, this is the definition of the system `Format` function (a close relative of a `sprintf` function of the C language):

```
function Format (const Format: string; const Args: array of
const): string;
```

The second parameter is an open array, which gets an undefined number of values. In fact, you can call this function in the following ways:

```
N := 20;
S := 'Total:';
Label1.Caption := Format ('Total: %d', [N]);
Label2.Caption := Format ('Int: %d, Float: %f', [N, 12.4]);
Label3.Caption := Format ('%s %d', [S, N * 2]);
```

Notice that you can pass a parameter as either a constant value, the value of a variable, or even an expression. The `Format` function can be very handy for building complex output strings.

# Delphi 2 Calling Conventions

Delphi 2 introduces a new approach to passing parameters, known as *fastcall*: Whenever possible, up to three parameters can be passed in CPU registers, making the function call much faster.

The problem is that this is the default convention, and functions using it are not compatible with Windows: Windows API functions must be declared using the standard Pascal convention. You can actually ask Delphi to use it by placing the `stdcall` keyword after the function declaration. The fast calling convention (used by default) is indicated by the `register` keyword, instead.

There is generally no reason not to use the new fast calling convention, besides external Windows calls or the definition of Windows callback functions. I'll point out the use of this directive in the few examples of the book that require it.

There are actually two more calling conventions, `cdecl` and `pascal`, which are seldom used. You can find a summary of Delphi calling conventions in the *Calling conventions* topic under Delphi 2 help.

# What Is a Method?

If you have already worked with Delphi or read the manuals, you have probably heard the term *method*. A method is a special kind of function or procedure that is related to a data type, a *class*.

In Delphi, every time we handle an event or message, we need to define a method, which can be either a function or a procedure. For this reason, the term *method* is used to indicate functions and procedures in general, although this is not always the case. Strictly speaking, only the subroutines related to a class are methods.

We have already seen a number of methods in the examples in this and the previous chapters. Here is an empty method automatically added by Delphi to the source code of a form:

```
procedure TForm1.Button1Click(Sender: TObject);
begin
  {here goes your code}
end;
```

I will discuss methods in more detail in the next chapter when I will introduce classes.

## Forward Declarations

When you need to use an identifier (of any kind), the compiler must have already seen some sort of declaration to know what the identifier refers to. For this reason, you usually provide a full declaration before using any subroutine. However, there are cases in which this is not possible. If procedure A calls procedure B, and procedure B calls procedure A, when you start writing the code, you will need to call a subroutine the compiler still doesn't know.

If you want to declare the existence of a procedure or function with a certain name and given parameters, without providing its actual code, you can write the procedure or function followed by the forward keyword:

```
procedure Hello; forward;
```

Later on, the code should provide a full definition of the procedure, but this can be called even before it is fully defined. Here is a silly example, just to give you the idea:

```
procedure Hello; forward;

procedure DoubleHello;
begin
  Hello;
  Hello;
end;

procedure Hello;
begin
  ShowMessage ('Hello world!');
end;
```

This approach allows you to write mutual recursion: DoubleHello calls Hello, but Hello might call DoubleHello, too, provided that there is a condition to terminate this recursion.

Although a forward procedure declaration is not very common in Delphi, there is another similar case, which is much more frequent. Every time you see the declaration of a method inside a class type that was automatically generated by Delphi (as you added an event to a form or its components), this is a forward declaration, although the specific keyword is not used. Here is an excerpt of the source code of an earlier example:

```
type
  TForm1 = class(TForm)
    ListBox1: TListBox;
    Button1: TButton;
    procedure Button1Click(Sender: TObject);
    ...
  end;
```

To sum things up, when you need to call a subroutine that is still not fully defined, you can write a forward declaration, define the procedure (or method) in the type definition of a class, or place it in the interface portion of a unit. Since we have not discussed units yet, we won't go into this third approach here. You'll find more on this topic in the next chapter.

## External Declarations

Another special kind of procedure declaration is the external declaration. Originally used to link the Pascal code to external functions written in assembly language, the external directive is used in Windows programming to call functions from a DLL (a dynamic link library). In Delphi, there are a number of such declarations in the Windows unit:

```
// forward declaration
function LineTo (DC: HDC; X, Y: Integer): BOOL; stdcall;
// external declaration (instead of actual code)
function LineTo; external 'gdi32.dll' name 'LineTo';
```

This declaration means that the code of the function LineTo is stored in the GDI32.DLL dynamic library (one of the most important Windows system libraries) with the same name.

**NEW**

In the 16-bit version of Delphi, the external declaration used the name of the library without the extension, and was followed by the name directive (as in the code above) or by an alternative index directive, followed by the ordinal number of the funtion inside the DLL. The change reflects a system change in the way libraries are accessed. Notice also that the Windows unit replaces the WinProcs and WinTypes units of the 16-bit version of Delphi.

You seldom need to write similar declarations, since they are already listed in the Windows unit, which is automatically included in the uses statement at the beginning of the code for any form generated by Delphi. The only reason you might need to write this external declaration code is to call undocumented Windows functions or a custom DLL. Chapter 29 is devoted to writing and calling DLL functions.

## Procedural Types

Another strange feature of Object Pascal is the presence of procedural types. This is really an advanced language topic, which only a few Delphi programmers will use regularly. However, since we will discuss related topics in later chapters and procedural types constitute the first step in understanding events in Delphi, I've decided to devote a section to them here. If you are a novice programmer, you can skip this section for now, and come back to it when you're ready.

In the standard version of Pascal, procedures can be defined and called, period. In Borland Object Pascal extensions, there is the concept of *procedural type* (which is similar to the C language concept of *function pointer*). The declaration of a procedural type indicates the list of parameters and eventually the return type in the case of a function. For example, you can declare the type "procedure with an integer parameter" as

```
type
  IntProc = procedure (var Num: Integer);
```

Notice that the parameter can simply be an Integer. The name Num can be regarded as a comment, and has no special meaning or effect. This procedural type is compatible with procedures that have exactly the same parameters (or the same function signature, using C jargon). Here is an example:

```
procedure DoubleTheValue (var Value: Integer);
begin
  Value := Value * 2;
end;
```

In the 16-bit version of Delphi, procedures or functions must be declared using the `far` directive in order to be used as actual values of a procedural type.

You can declare variables of procedure types or pass procedures as parameters. Given the preceding type and procedure declarations, you can write this code:

```
var
  IP: IntProc;
  X: Integer;
begin
  IP := DoubleTheValue;
  X := 5;
  IP (X);
end;
```

This code has the same effect as the following shorter version:

```
var
  X: Integer;
begin
  X := 5;
  DoubleTheValue (X);
end;
```

So why use it? In some cases, being able to decide which function to call and actually calling it at a different time can be useful. It is possible to build a complex example showing this approach. However, since it might be too complex this early in the book, I prefer to let you explore a fairly simple one, named PROCTYPE. This example is more complex than those we have seen so far, to make the situation a little more realistic.

For this example, create a blank project and place two radio buttons, a push button, and two labels in the form, as shown in Figure 4.13.

**FIGURE 4.13:**
The form of the PROCTYPE example.

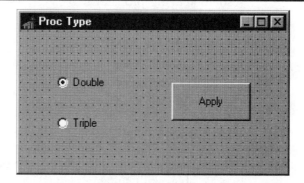

This example is based on two procedures. One procedure is used to double the value of a variable. This procedure is slightly different from the version I've already used in this section. A second procedure is to triple the value, and therefore is named `TripleTheValue`:

```
procedure TripleTheValue (var Value: Integer);
begin
  Value := Value * 3;
  ShowMessage ('Value tripled: ' + IntToStr (Value));
end;
```

Both procedures display what is going on, to let us know that they have been called. This is a simple debugging feature you can use to test whether or when a certain portion of code is executed, instead of adding a breakpoint in it.

Each time a user presses the Apply button, one of the two functions is executed, depending on the status of the radio buttons. When you have two radio buttons, only one of them can be selected at a time. This code could have been implemented by testing the value of the radio buttons inside the code for the OnClick event of the Apply push button. Instead, I've used a longer but interesting approach, to demonstrate the use of procedure types. Each time a user clicks on one of the two radio buttons, one of the procedures is stored in a variable:

```
procedure TForm1.DoubleRadioButtonClick(Sender: TObject);
begin
  IP := DoubleTheValue;
end;
```

When the user presses the push button, the stored procedure is executed:

```
procedure TForm1.ApplyButtonClick(Sender: TObject);
begin
  IP (X);
end;
```

To allow three different functions to access the IP and X variables, they cannot be declared locally (inside one of the methods) but should be visible to the whole form. A solution to this problem is to place these variables inside the form declaration:

```
TForm1 = class(TForm)
  ...
private
  { Private declarations }
  IP: IntProc;
  X: Integer;
end;
```

We will see exactly what this means in the next chapter, but for the moment, you need to modify the code generated by Delphi for the class type as indicated above, and add the definition of the procedure type we have seen before. To initialize these two variables with suitable values, we can add the OnCreate event to the form (select this event in the Object Inspector after you have activated the form). I suggest you to refer to the listing on the companion CD to study the details of the source code of this example.

# Summary

In this chapter, we have seen an overview of the basic elements of the Object Pascal language. This chapter can be considered a review of the notions of standard Pascal, plus an introduction to some advanced features.

What we have still not seen are the object-oriented capabilities of the language, which will be detailed in the next chapter. We also still have not considered the division of a program in units and other Pascal programming techniques, which we'll get to soon.

As I mentioned, this chapter was intended for people who have some programming experience, either with Pascal or another programming language. I haven't tried to explain how to use a `for` loop or write a conditional expression for an `if` statement. If these things are not clear to you, before you get started with Delphi, you should read a basic Pascal language text, or spend some time with the Delphi Help files.

This doesn't mean that you need to understand these topics perfectly. I'll show you a huge number of examples in the book, and most of them will also highlight features of the Pascal language. If you keep on reading, you will learn more about the topics we have discussed in this chapter.

# CHAPTER

## FIVE

# Object Pascal as an OOP Language

- Object Pascal classes and objects

- The Object Pascal object model

- Object instance creation

- Information hiding

- Delphi units

- The self keyword

- Class methods and method pointers

**U**sing existing data types, defining new ones, and writing code in small blocks (subroutines) are the essence of traditional Pascal programming. But modern Pascal versions allow a completely different approach: *object-oriented programming* (OOP). OOP languages are based on three fundamental concepts: classes, inheritance, and polymorphism (or late binding). These three features are available in Object Pascal, too, and will be described in the first part of this chapter.

Earlier Turbo Pascal and Borland Pascal compilers used a slightly different object-oriented extension of the Pascal language. Therefore, reading this chapter should be useful for everyone, including long-time Turbo Pascal programmers. Of course, some of the topics covered here won't be new to Pascal programmers—they serve as introductory material for the less-experienced OOP readers.

As you read this material, keep in mind that you can start to write code in Delphi without knowing all of the details of the language. For example, you don't need to understand some of OOP's advanced features, such as exception handling. As you create a new form, add new components, and handle events, most of the related code is automatically prepared for you by Delphi. But knowing the details of the language and its implementation will help you to understand precisely what goes on and to truly master Delphi. From another point of view, you don't need to understand OOP, virtual methods, or polymorphism to create a complete Delphi application. However, you do need to understand these concepts to design new components.

# Introducing Classes and Objects

*Class* and *object* are two common terms. However, since they are often misused, let's be sure that we agree on their definitions. A *class* is a user-defined data type, which has a state, a representation, and some operations or behavior. A class has some internal data and some methods, in the form of procedures or functions, and usually describes the generic characteristics and behavior of a number of very similar objects. Classes are used by the programmer to arrange the source code and by the compiler to generate the application.

An *object* is an instance of a class or, in other words, a variable of the data type defined by the class. Objects are *real* entities. When the program runs, objects take up some memory for their internal representation.

The relationship between object and class is the same as the one between variable and type. Unfortunately, in some languages or environments, this difference is not clear. To increase the confusion, earlier versions of the Borland Pascal compiler used the keyword `object` to define classes. For this reason, long-time Pascal programmers tend to use the term *object* instead of class to denote a type, and the term *object instance* to indicate the real objects.

Delphi has introduced a new object model, based on the new keyword `class`, but the older model is still available for compatibility. I'll explain some of the technical elements behind this new object model in a later section of this chapter. For the moment, however, I'll focus on the concept of class and its syntax.

To declare a new class data type in Object Pascal, use the following syntax:

```
type
  MyNewClass = class
  end;
```

Of course, this code is not very useful, because the class does not have any data or operations. We can start adding some data as follows:

```
type
  Date = class
    Month, Day, Year: Integer;
  end;
```

This declaration is similar to that of a record. In fact, we can declare an object and access its three fields with a standard notation:

```
var
  ADay: Date;
begin
  ... {something is missing here}
  ADay.Month := 7;
  ADay.Day  := 12;
  ADay.Year := 1984;
end;
```

Things start to get interesting when we put in some methods—functions or procedures—to add operations to the class:

```
type
  Date = class
    Month, Day, Year: Integer;
    procedure SetValue(m, d, y: Integer);
    function LeapYear: Boolean;
  end;
```

The function and the procedure should be supplied in the code, indicating that they are part of the Date class. To accomplish this, Object Pascal uses the dot notation again, but in a slightly different way. The syntax is `ClassName.Method`:

```
procedure Date.SetValue(m, d, y: Integer);
begin
  Month := m;
  Day := d;
  Year := y;
end;

function Date.LeapYear: Boolean;
begin
```

```
  if (Year mod 4 <> 0) then
    LeapYear := False
  else
    if (Year mod 100 <> 0) then
      LeapYear := True
    else
    if (Year mod 400 <> 0) then
      LeapYear := False
    else
      LeapYear := True;
end;
```

Once these methods have been written, they can be called as follows:

```
var
  Day: Date;
  Leap: Boolean;

begin
  ... {something is still missing here}
  Day.SetValue (10, 10, 1994);
  Leap := Day.LeapYear;
end;
```

The notation used is nothing strange, but it is powerful. We can write complex functions (such as LeapYear) and then access this value for every Date object as if it were a primitive data type. Notice that `Day.LeapYear` is a notation similar to `Day.Year`, although its meaning is completely different. The first expression stands for a direct data access, the second for a function call.

Although the code shown here is correct, it won't work as is. To use the new Object Pascal object model, we need to create an instance of an object first. This is described in the next section.

## The Delphi Object Model

The object-oriented extensions of the previous versions of the Borland Pascal language were based on the `object` keyword. In the new version, this has been replaced by the `class` keyword.

Both the `object` and `class` keywords are used to define a new data type, a new class. Both support `private`, `protected`, and `public` methods and fields (as described later in the chapter). Both allow inheritance. They are really very similar. So why did Borland introduce the new keyword? The reason is that although the code you write in the two cases is almost the same, the behavior of the compiled code is different. The new `class` keyword indicates a new object model, which we can describe as a reference model.

The basic idea is that each variable of a class type, such as Day in the code fragment above, does not hold the value of the object. Rather, it contains a reference, or a pointer, to indicate the memory location where the object has been stored. You can see a scheme of the situation in Figure 5.1.

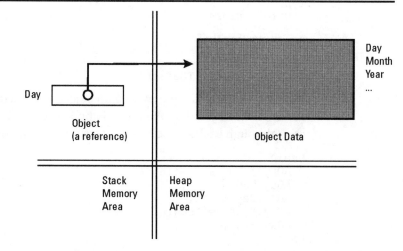

The reference object model is powerful, yet easier to use than other models. Other OOP languages use similar models, notably Eiffel. In my opinion, adopting a reference object model was one of the best design decisions of Delphi development.

The only problem with this approach is that when you declare a variable, by writing this

```
var
  Day: Date;
```

you do not create an object, only a place to keep a reference to an object—a sort of pointer. Object instances must be created manually, at least for the objects of the classes you define. Instances of the component you place on a form are built automatically.

To create an instance of an object, we can call its Create method, which is a constructor (a special procedure used to allocate memory for new objects and initialize them):

```
var
  ADay: Date;
begin
  Day := Date.Create;
  ADay.Month := 7;
  ADay.Day := 12;
  ADay.Year := 1984;
end;
```

Where does Create come from? It is a constructor of the class TObject, from which all the other classes inherit (subclassing, or inheritance, will be discussed later in this chapter). Writing this

```
type
  Date = class
```

equals writing this

```
type
  Date = class (TObject)
```

Of course, once you have created an object, you need to dispose of it. This can be accomplished by calling the Free method. The following is an example of the correct (although useless) code used to create, use, and dispose of an object:

```
begin
  ADay := Date.Create;
  ADay.Month := 7;
  ADay.Day := 12;
  ADay.Year := 1984;
  ADay.Free;
end;
```

As long as you allocate memory for an object (and free the memory when you're finished), the reference object model works without any glitches. You can assign an object to another, pass an object as parameter to a function, and perform any other operation.

# The First Delphi Example with Classes

After all this discussion, without any hands-on examples, it is time to go back to Delphi. The idea is to collect the Date class code we have written so far and write a simple program using it. This way, we can make sure that it works correctly, including the delicate point of object initialization.

The LEAPYEAR example has a simple form with two buttons, having the number of a year as a caption. Each time one of the buttons is pressed, a Date object is set and tested to see whether 1995 (or 1996) is a leap year. Here is the code of the On-Click event for one of the buttons:

```
procedure TForm1.Button1995Click(Sender: TObject);
begin
  ADay.SetValue (1, 1, 1995);
  if ADay.LeapYear then
    ShowMessage ('Leap Year')
  else
    ShowMessage ('Non Leap Year')
end;
```

The other button has a similar code, and produces the output in Figure 5.2.

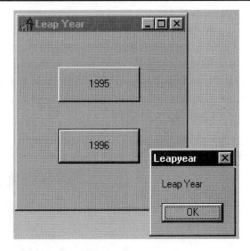

The object ADay is a new variable defined as shown here:

```
var
  Form1: TForm1;
  ADay: Date;
```

This object should be created before the button is pressed. A common approach is to use the OnCreate event of the form to create an instance of the object:

```
procedure TForm1.FormCreate(Sender: TObject);
begin
  ADay := Date.Create;
end;
```

This method is executed before a user can press the button, and even before the form and its components are displayed on the screen. The opposite holds for the OnDestroy event, which is executed after the form is hidden from view. We can use this method to free the memory used by the object:

```
procedure TForm1.FormDestroy(Sender: TObject);
begin
  ADay.Free;
end;
```

If you alter the code of this example, remember that the captions of the buttons have no direct relationship with the code. If you change the caption of the button, nothing will happen. You should also change the third parameter of the corresponding call to the SetValue procedure to try out different years.

While you are exploring the code of this example, make the following test. Comment out the code used to create an instance of the object:

```
procedure TForm1.FormCreate(Sender: TObject);
begin
  //ADay := Date.Create;
end;
```

If you recompile the project now, you won't get an error. However, when you run the program, as soon as you press one of the buttons, an exception is raised by the system (indicating that you have accessed an invalid pointer), as you can see in Figure 5.3.

**FIGURE 5.3:**

The exception error message displayed if you forget to create an instance of the object.

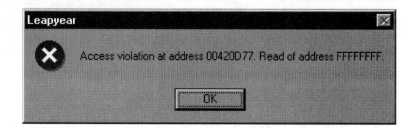

## Declaring a Constructor

To allocate the memory for the object, we call the Create method. However, before we can actually use the object, we often need to initialize it. To do this, we can add a constructor to the class. We can either provide a customized version of the Create method or define a constructor with any other name.

A constructor is a special procedure, because Delphi automatically allocates memory for the object to which you apply the constructor. Adding a constructor to the class solves any run-time error due to a missing or an incorrect initialization. These errors are usually hard to find, so you should use preventive techniques to avoid them in the first place, and one such technique is the use of constructors.

In the same way that a class can have a custom constructor, it can have a custom *destructor*, a procedure declared with the destructor keyword, which can perform some resource cleanup before an object is destroyed. Just as a constructor call allocates memory for the object, a destructor call frees the memory. Destructors are seldom redefined. Most of the time, the default Destroy destructor (inherited from TObject) is enough. Notice that instead of calling Destroy directly, a program should call Free, which calls Destroy only if the object exists—that is, if it is not nil.

To add a constructor to the Date class, write this code:

```
Date = class
  Month, Day, Year: Integer;
  constructor Init (m, d, y: Integer);
  procedure SetValue(m, d, y: Integer);
  function LeapYear: Boolean;
end;
```

I've chosen the name *Init* for the constructor, but any other name will do. The important element is the presence of the `constructor` keyword instead of the `procedure` keyword. Then we write the code of the constructor:

```
constructor Date.Init (m, d, y: Integer);
begin
  Month := m;
  Day := d;
  Year := y;
end;
```

Once this is done, we can change the initialization code of the LEAPYEAR example, to allocate memory for the ADay object and set an initial value at the same time:

```
procedure TForm1.FormCreate(Sender: TObject);
begin
  ADay := Date.Init (1, 1, 1900);
end;
```

This approach is used by the LEAP2 example, a new version of LEAPYEAR you can find on the companion disk.

# Classes and Information Hiding

A class can have any amount of data and any number of methods. However, for a good object-oriented approach, data should be hidden, or *encapsulated,* inside the class using it. When you access a date, for example, it makes no sense to change the value of the day by itself. In fact, changing the value of the day may result in an invalid date, such as February 30. Using methods to access the internal representation of an object limits the risk of generating erroneous situations, and allows the class writer to modify the internal representation in a future version.

The concept of encapsulation is quite simple: Just think of a class as a black box with a small visible portion (see Figure 5.4). The visible portion, called the *class interface,* allows other parts of a program to access and use the objects of that class. However, when you use the objects, most of their code is hidden. You seldom know which internal data the object has, and usually have no way to access it directly. Of course, you are supposed to use methods to access the data, which is shielded from unauthorized access. This is the object-oriented approach to a classical programming theory known as *information hiding.*

**FIGURE 5.4:**

A graphical representation of the information hiding of a class.

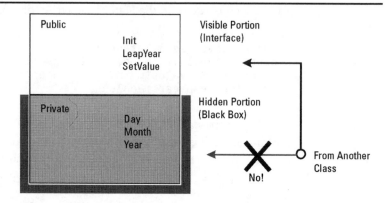

In theory, this should be nothing new for a Pascal programmer, since OOP follows the same ideas of order, type definition, and safety that are promoted by the Pascal language.

In Object Pascal, there are two different constructs involved with encapsulation, protection, and variables access: classes and units. Associated with classes are some special access-specifier keywords, which are discussed in the next section.

# Private, Protected, and Public

Object Pascal has borrowed C++'s three access specifiers: `private`, `protected`, and `public`. A fourth one, `published`, will be discussed in the next section. Another access specifier, `automated`, is used by OLE automation controls, as we will see in Chapter 16.

- The `private` keyword denotes fields and methods of a class that are not accessible outside the unit (the source code file) declaring the class. This is slightly different from C++, where the private portion of a class cannot be accessed even by other classes defined in the same module or source code file.

- The `public` specifier denotes methods and fields that are freely accessible from any other portion of the code of a program, as well as in the unit in which they are defined.

- The `protected` keyword is used to indicate partially protected methods and fields. Protected elements can be accessed by the current class and all its descendent classes, but not by users of this class (code that creates instances of this class).

Generally, the fields (the data) of a class should be private. Methods (the code) are usually public. However, this is not always the case. Methods can be private or protected if they are needed only internally to perform some computations. Fields can be public when you want an easy and direct access, and you are fairly sure that their type definition is not going to change. As an example, consider this new version of the Date class:

```
type
  Date = class
  private
    Month, Day, Year: Integer;
  public
    procedure SetValue(m, d, y: Integer);
    function LeapYear: Boolean;
    function GetText: string;
    procedure Increase;
  protected
    function DaysInMonth: Integer;
  end;
```

In this version, the fields are now declared to be private, and there are some new methods. The first, GetText, is a function that returns a string with the date. This is the only way we have to retrieve the value of the private data. We might think of adding other functions, named GetDay, GetMonth, and GetYear, which simply return the corresponding private data, but similar direct data-access functions are not always needed.

The second new method is the Increase procedure, which increases the date by one day. This is far from simple, since you need to consider the different lengths of the various months, as well as leap and non-leap years.

To simplify this (and other methods I'll add), I've written a function that returns the number of days in the current month, DaysInMonth. This function is not part of the public interface of this class. It doesn't make much sense to ask a specific Date object for the number of days in its current month without knowing which month it refers to. So, I had two choices: declare the function as private or declare it as protected. I decided to use the protected keyword because I might later define a new class that would inherit from Date and need access to this function.

## Public and Published

Along with the public, protected, and private directives, you can use a fourth one, called published, in a class declaration. A published field or method is not only available at run-time, but also at design-time. In fact, every component in the Delphi Components palette has a published interface that is used by some Delphi tools, in particular the Object Inspector. This interface is accessible through some advanced techniques.

> **NEW**
>
> There is a fifth access specifier, `automated`, which is used to define a public interface with corresponding OLE automation type information. This makes it possible to create OLE Automation Servers, as we will see in Chapter 25. The automated keyword is typically used in subclasses of the TAutoObject class.

A regular use of published fields is much more important when you write a component than when you write the code of an application. Usually, the published part of a component does not contain any fields or methods, but has a new element of the language: properties. Chapter 27 focuses on component writing and related Object Pascal language elements, but properties are introduced in the next chapter, too.

Besides the case of components, when Delphi generates a form, it places the definitions of its components and methods in the first portion of its definition, before the `public` and `private` keywords. These fields and methods of the initial portion of the class are `published`. This is the default when no special keyword is added before an element of a class.

> **NOTE**
>
> By the way, the methods assigned to any event should be published methods, and the fields corresponding to your components in the form should be published to be automatically initialized. In fact, only the published components and the published methods of your form can show up in the Object Inspector (in the list of components of the form or in the list of the available methods displayed when you select the drop-down list of an event).

# Classes and Units

Delphi applications, like most Pascal programs, make intensive use of *units*. Units, in fact, are the basis of the modularity in the language. In Delphi applications, every form has a corresponding unit behind it. The reverse is not true, however: units do not need to have forms.

The concept of unit is simple. A unit has an `interface` section declaring what is visible to other units, an `implementation` section with the real code, and other hidden declarations. Finally, the unit can have an optional `initialization` section with some startup code, to be executed when the program using this unit is loaded into memory, and an optional `finalization` section, to be executed on program termination.

**NOTE**

In previous versions of Borland Pascal language, the initialization section of a unit was marked with `begin` and `end` keywords. The `initialization` keyword was introduced in the first version of Delphi to make it easier for the environment to manage your source code. Delphi 2 adds the `finalization` keyword to provide a proper cleanup of what was allocated in the `initialization` code of that unit.

The general structure of a unit is the following (with the `interface` and `implementation` keywords in bold to highlight these two main portions of the unit):

```
unit unitName;

interface

{other units we need to refer to}
uses A, B, C;

{exported type definition}
type
  newType = TypeDefinition;

{list of exported functions and procedures}
procedure MyProc;

implementation

{all the exported functions must be coded}

procedure MyProc;
{code of procedure MyProc follows}

initialization
  {optional initialization part}

finalization
  {optional clean-up code}

end.
```

The uses clause at the beginning of the `interface` section indicates which other units we need to access in the `interface` portion of the unit. This includes the units with the definition of the data types (classes and components) we refer to in the definition of other data types, such as the components used within a form we are defining. When you need to refer to other units from the code of the routines and methods, instead, you should add a new uses clause at the beginning of the implementation portion.

All the units you refer to must be present in the project directory or in a directory in the search path. C++ programmers should notice that the uses statement doesn't correspond to an include directive. The effect of a uses statement is to read in just the interface portion of the units listed. The implementation portion of the unit is considered only when that unit is compiled.

**NEW**

> Delphi 2 introduces a new *units aliasing* technique. This means you can use the name of a unit in a uses statement and let the compiler actually refer to another unit. This alias is defined in the Directories/Conditionals page of the Project Options dialog box. In particular, Delphi 2 defines aliases for the new Windows, previously split between the WinTypes and WinProcs units and the new DBE unit. In practice, this means you can compile code that refers to old units (such as WinProcs) that do not exist any more.

The interface of the unit can declare a number of different elements, including procedures, functions, global variables, and data types. This last element is probably the most used in an object-oriented approach and in Delphi applications.

You can easily place a class in a unit, and this is probably the right thing to do. Delphi does this automatically each time you create a form. Do you remember the code generated for a new form in Chapter 1? Here is it again:

```
unit Unit1;

interface

uses
  SysUtils, Windows, Messages, Classes, Graphics, Controls,
Forms, Dialogs;

type
  TForm1 = class(TForm)
  private
    { Private declarations }
  public
    { Public declarations }
  end;

var
  Form1: TForm1;

implementation

{$R *.DFM}

end.
```

The only elements exported by this unit are the definition of a new data type, TForm1, and a global variable of this type, Form1. Notice the presence of the private and public keywords, and the inclusion of the form description file with the $R compiler directive.

Placing forms in units is certainly not the only use for units in Delphi. You can continue to have traditional units, listing functions, and procedures, and you can have units with classes that do not refer to forms or other visual elements. To create a new unit that is not related to a form, use the File ➤ New command to open the Object Repository, then select the Unit item in the New page (the File ➤ New Unit command of Delphi 1 isn't there any more). Here is the code automatically generated in this case:

```
unit Unit2;

interface

implementation

end.
```

Quite bare, isn't it? Delphi is a visual environment, so when you write nonvisual code, it cannot be of much help. To show you an example of a full-scale unit, I've further developed the Date class. Placing this class in a unit will make it available to any application, as we will investigate soon. Before we delve into this, however, we should consider some details related to class interfaces, scope, and encapsulation in units.

## The Interface of a Class

When you declare a new class type and place it in a unit, you write in the interface of the unit what is known as the *interface* of a class (that is, its declaration). The interface of a class contains the declaration of its data, its fields, and the forward declaration of its methods. The data declaration is needed to determine the size of the objects of that class. The method declaration is usually placed in the implementation portion of the unit.

Note also that it is possible to make a forward declaration of a class:

```
type
  MyClass = class;
```

You cannot really start using a class without its full declaration, but you can use this new data type as field of another class or as parameter of a method of another class. Consider this example of two related classes:

```
type
  THusband = class;
```

```
TWife = class
  Husband: THusband;
  ...
  end;

THusband = class
  Wife: TWife;
  ...
  end;
```

In other OOP languages (including C++), similar code would be illegal. In Object Pascal, it is legal, thanks to the object reference semantic. In fact, we can place a partially defined object (that is, an object of a class having only a forward reference) in another class, only because the compiler knows how much memory the object will take. In fact, every object takes up the space required for a reference or pointer. It isn't strange that in C++, writing similar code is possible only if you use explicit pointers.

## Units and Scope

In Pascal, units are the key to encapsulation and visibility (or scope), and they are probably even more important than the `private` and `public` keywords of a class. In fact, the effect of the `private` keyword is related to the scope of the unit containing the class.

The scope of an identifier (such as a variable, procedure, function, or a data type) defines the portion of the code in which the identifier is accessible. The basic rule is that an identifier is meaningful only within its scope; that is, only within the block in which it is declared. You cannot use an identifier outside its scope.

Here are some examples. If you declare a variable within the block defining a procedure, you cannot use this variable outside that procedure. The scope of the identifier spans the whole procedure, including nested blocks (unless an identifier with the same name in the nested blocks hides the outer definition).

If you declare an identifier in the implementation portion of a unit, you cannot use it outside the unit, but you can use it in any block and procedure defined within the unit. If you declare an identifier in the interface portion of the unit, its scope extends to any other unit that uses the one declaring it. Any identifier declared in the interface of a unit is indicated by the term *global*; all other identifiers are said to be *local*.

For this reason, declaring a type in the interface portion of a unit makes it accessible from the whole program. Variables of form classes are declared in the same way, so that you can refer to a form (and its public fields, methods, properties, and components) from the code of any other form.

# Encapsulating Changes

One of the key ideas of encapsulation is to reduce the number of global variables used by a program. A global variable can be accessed from every portion of a program. For this reason, a change in a global variable has effects on the whole program.

On the other hand, when you change the representation of a field of a class, you only need to change the code of some methods of that class, and nothing else. For this reason, we can say that information hiding refers to "encapsulating changes."

Let me clarify this idea with an example. In LEAPYEAR, I added a Date object to the var declarations of the unit interface. This object can be accessed from any other portion of this unit, but also from any other unit of the application, because it has been declared in the interface portion of the unit.

In our small program, this is fine. However, in a complex application, developed by several programmers, other units might use this object. In this case, changing the Date object's name or the way it is used could ruin the whole program.

To avoid this situation, I could have declared the Date object inside the class describing the new form:

```
type
  {new data type, a Date}
  Date = class
    Month, Day, Year: Integer;
    constructor Init (m, d, y: Integer);
    procedure SetValue(m, d, y: Integer);
    function LeapYear: Boolean;
  end;

  TForm1 = class(TForm)
    Button1995: TButton;
    Button1996: TButton;
    procedure FormCreate(Sender: TObject);
    procedure FormDestroy(Sender: TObject);
    procedure Button1995Click(Sender: TObject);
    procedure Button1996Click(Sender: TObject);
  private
    { Private declarations }
    ADay: Date;
  public
    { Public declarations }
  end;

var
  Form1: TForm1;
```

If I add it as a private field, the Date object won't be accessible from outside the unit, unless I provide a proper method to do so. And if I write a method, and later on I decide to change the meaning or the representation of the object, I can just change the code of the method accordingly, without any effect on the rest of the program's code.

Of course, declaring the three fields of the Date class as private will improve the encapsulation performed by the program and make it more object-oriented. To accomplish this, however, we need to add some methods to the class, to be able to access the private fields.

# A Date Unit

Throughout this chapter, we have developed a couple of examples with simple versions of a Date class. The final version of this class will have some more functions, and we will place it in a unit. This is the interface of the class, inside the interface portion of the unit:

```
unit Dates;
interface
type
  Date = class
    private
    Month, Day, Year: Integer;
  public
    constructor Init (m, d, y: Integer);
    procedure SetValue (m, d, y: Integer);
    function LeapYear: Boolean;
    procedure Increase;
    procedure Decrease;
    procedure Add (NumberOfDays: Integer);
    procedure Subtract (NumberOfDays: Integer);
    function GetText: string;
  protected
    function DaysInMonth: Integer;
  end;
```

The aim of the new methods is quite easy to understand. Increase and Decrease change the value of the date to the day after or before. Add and Subtract change the date by adding or subtracting the number of days passed as parameter, instead of a single day. For example, if the value of the current object is 3/8/1996, adding 10 days makes it 3/18/1996. GetText returns a string with the formatted date, using the Format function and some field specifiers to indicate the size of the number and to pad the number with zeros (see Delphi Help topic "Format Strings" for more details).

Listing 5.1 shows the source code of some of the member functions of this class. (You can find the full code of the unit in the companion CD as part of the VIEWDATE example used to test the class.)

## Listing 5.1: Some of the methods of the new version of the Date class.

```
function Date.DaysInMonth: Integer;
begin
  case Month of
    1, 3, 5, 7, 8, 10, 12:
      DaysInMonth := 31;
    4, 6, 9, 11:
      DaysInMonth := 30;
    2:
      if (LeapYear) then
        DaysInMonth := 29
      else
        DaysInMonth := 28;
    else
      // if the month is not correct
      DaysInMonth := 0;
  end;
end;

procedure Date.Increase;
begin
  {if this day is not the last of the month}
  if (Day < DaysInMonth) then
    Inc (Day)   {increase the value by 1}
  else
  {if it is not in December}
    if (Month < 12) then
      begin
        {Day 1 of next month}
        Inc (Month);
        Day := 1;
      end
    else
      begin
        {else it is next year New Year's Day}
        Inc (Year);
        Month := 1;
        Day := 1;
      end;
end;

function Date.GetText: string;
begin
  {format the text, converting the integers to
  strings with a fixed number of characters}
  GetText := Format ('%.2d.%.2d.%4d',
    [Month, Day, Year]);
end;

procedure Date.Add (NumberOfDays: Integer);
var
```

```
    n: Integer;
begin
  {increase the day n times}
  for n:=1 to NumberOfDays do
    Increase;
end;
```

To test this unit, we can create a new example. The new form will have a caption to display a date and four buttons, which can be used to modify the date. You can see the main form of the VIEWDATE example at run-time in Figure 5.5. Notice that to work properly, the label component has a big font, it is as wide as the form, it has the Alignment property set to taCenter, and the AutoSize property is set to False.

**FIGURE 5.5:**

The output of the VIEWDATE example at startup.

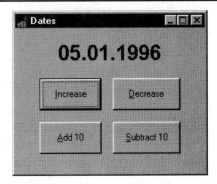

We can write the startup code of this program in the OnCreate event. In the corresponding method, we create an instance of the Date class, initialize this object, and then show its textual description in the caption of the label, as shown in Figure 5.5.

```
procedure TDateForm.FormCreate(Sender: TObject);
begin
  TheDay := Date.Init (5, 1, 1996);
  DateLabel.Caption := TheDay.GetText;
end;
```

TheDay is now a private field of the TDateForm data type. By the way, the name for the class, *TDateForm*, is automatically chosen by Delphi when we change the Name property of the form to DateForm.

When one of the four buttons is pressed, you need to apply the corresponding method to the TheDay object, then display the new value of the date in the label. Here are two examples:

```
procedure TDateForm.IncreaseButtonClick(Sender: TObject);
begin
  TheDay.Increase;
  DateLabel.Caption := TheDay.GetText;
```

```
end;

procedure TDateForm.Add10ButtonClick(Sender: TObject);
begin
  TheDay.Add(10);
  DateLabel.Caption := TheDay.GetText;
end;
```

TIP

As you can see in Figure 5.5, the four buttons of the form have the
first letter underlined, which means that those characters can be used
as shortcut keys. To obtain this effect, just add the & character in front
of the letter in the caption of the button. Pressing a shortcut key is a
quick way to change the date. When you hold down one of the four
underlined keys, the date will change rapidly.

If it still isn't clear to you how the program works, refer to its full source code on
the companion CD and try to change it. For example, you can add new buttons to
increase or decrease the date by a higher number of days. Try to add a Next Year
button—one that will also work with leap years.

## Units and Programs

A Delphi application is made of two different kinds of source code files. There are
one or more units and one program file.

The units can be considered as secondary files, which are referred to by the main
part of the application, the program. In theory, this is true. In practice, the program
file is usually an automatically generated file with a limited role. It simply needs to
start up the program running the main form. As we have already seen in Chapters
1 and 2, the code of the program file, or Delphi project file (DPR), can be edited
either manually or by using the Project Manager and some of the Project Options.

The structure of the program file is usually much simpler than the structure of the
units. For example, here is the code of the VIEWDATE program:

```
program Viewdate;

uses
  Forms,
  Date_f in 'DATE_F.PAS' {DateForm},
  Dates in 'DATES.PAS';

begin
  Application.Initialize;
  Application.CreateForm(TDateForm, DateForm);
  Application.Run;
end.
```

As you can see, there is simply a `uses` section and the main code of the application, enclosed by the `begin` and `end` keywords. The program's `uses` statement is particularly important, because it is used to manage the compilation and linking of the application.

**NEW**

In Delphi 2, the code of the project (that is, the starting point of a program), has one more line of text than it did in Delphi 1. The new line, `Application Initialize`, usually does nothing, and it is not actually necessary. The only time this is used is if the project includes a subclass of TAutoObject (which makes the application an OLE automation server)—in which case Initialize updates the system registry. There is more about this topic in Chapter 25. In general, you can remove this line (or compile Delphi 1 programs that do not have it) without any problems.

# Advanced Topics Relating to Methods and Classes

Some other advanced features are not used often in Delphi applications, but you probably should be aware of them. The structure of Delphi and of the VCL relies on some of these elements. If you are new to object-oriented programming concepts, you might want to skip this section altogether and continue with the section titled "Inheriting from Existing Types." Later, when you are more confident with the basic OOP concepts, you can return to this section.

The advanced topics relate to concept of class and its methods. We will discuss the use of `self`, the definition of class methods, and the use of method pointers.

## The Self Keyword

The `self` keyword refers to an implicit parameter automatically passed to any method when it is called. `Self` can be defined as a pointer to the current object (the current instance of the class) and is used by the language to refer to the fields of that specific object inside a method. In fact, when you declare five objects of the same class, each time you apply a method to one of the objects, the method should operate only on its own data and not affect the other objects.

Here is a method we have already encountered:

```
procedure Date.SetValue(m, d, y: Integer);
begin
  Month := m;
  Day := d;
  Year := y;
end;
```

In a method like this, Month really refers to the Month field of the current object, something you might express (those of you who know how to use pointers) as

```
Self^.Month := m;
```

If you have ever used an object-oriented programming language, you should already have encountered the concept of `self`, maybe with a different name, such as `this` in C++. `Self` is rarely used directly by programmers, but it is a fundamental language construct used by the compiler. At times, `self` is used to resolve name conflicts and to make tricky code more readable.

All you really need to know about `self` is that the presence of this hidden parameter is what makes a method different from a procedure that is not related to a class. The technical implementation of a call to a method differs from that of the call of generic subroutines. Methods have an extra hidden parameter, `self`. But since everything is behind the scenes, you do not need to know much about how `self` works.

## Class Methods and Class Data

When you add a field to a class, you really add this field to each object instance of that class. Each instance has its own independent representation (referred to by the `self` pointer). In same cases, however, it might be useful to have a field that is shared by all the objects of a class.

Other object-oriented programming languages have formal constructs to express this, such as C++'s `static`. In Object Pascal, this is not needed, because the encapsulation is always provided at the unit level. For this reason, if you simply add a variable in the implementation portion of a unit, it behaves as a class variable—a single memory location shared by all of the objects of a class.

If you need to access this value from outside the unit, you might use a method of the class. However, this forces you to apply this method to one of the instances of the class. An alternative solution is to declare a *class method*. A *class method* is a method that cannot access the data of any single object, but can be called by referring to a class rather than to a particular instance. A class method is a method related to the whole class, not its objects (*instances*). Technically, a class method is a method that does not have the `self` parameter.

Class methods are present in several object-oriented languages, and they are implemented in C++ using `static` member functions. To declare a class method in Object Pascal, you simply add the `class` keyword in front of the `function` or `procedure`:

```
type
  MyClass
    class function ClassMeanValue: Integer;
```

The use of class methods is not very common in Object Pascal, because you can obtain the same effect by adding a procedure or function to a unit declaring a class. A difference is that you can have two class methods with the same name in a complex application, but you cannot have two functions or procedures with the same name. The class methods, like any other method, are in the scope of the class. Object-oriented purists will definitely prefer the use of a class method over a procedure unrelated to a class. Class methods can also be virtual, so they can be overridden and used polymorphically (concepts which we'll discuss later in this chapter).

Class data (or unit data, to be more precise) is used to maintain general information related to the class, such as the number of objects created or a list of these objects. In these cases, class methods can return the number of objects in the class or offer a way to navigate the list of objects.

## Method Pointers

Another addition to the Object Pascal language is the method pointer. A method pointer is like a procedural type, but refers to an object method. Technically, a method pointer type implies the idea of a procedural type that has the self parameter. In other words, a method pointer stores two addresses: the address of the method body code and the address of the object instance data, which will show up as self inside the method body.

The declaration of a method pointer type is similar to that of a procedural type, except that it has the keywords of object at the end of the declaration:

```
type
  IntProceduralType = procedure (Num: Integer);
  IntMethodPointer = procedure (Num: Integer) of object;
```

When you have declared a method pointer, such as the one above, you can have a field type of this kind in an object:

```
type
  MyClass = class
    Value: Integer;
    Operation: IntMethodPointer;
  end;
```

Similar to a variable of a procedural type, this field can be assigned any other type-compatible method; that is, any other method of the same kind and with the same parameters. For example, you can declare another class having a method with the same integer parameter:

```
type
  AnotherClass = class
    X: Integer;
    procedure Add (N: Integer);
  end;
```

If you now declare a couple of objects of the two classes, such as

```
var
  MyObject: MyClass;
  AnotherObject: AnotherClass;
```

you can then make a similar assignment:

```
MyObject.Operation := AnotherObject.Add;
```

At this point, calling the method

```
MyObject.Operation;
```

you end up calling the Add method on object AnotherObject. At first glance, the goal of this overly complicated technique may not be clear, but this is one of the corner-stones of Delphi component technology. The secret is in the word *delegation*. If someone has built an object that has some method pointers, you are free to change the behavior of such prebuilt objects simply by assigning a new method to them. Does this sound familiar? It really should. When you add an OnClick event to a button, Delphi does exactly this. The button has a method pointer, named OnClick, and you can directly or indirectly assign a method of the form to it. When a user clicks on the button, this method is executed, even if you have defined it inside another class (typically, in the form).

This is the same code as above with different class, method, and parameter names, and it is a portion of the code actually used by Delphi. Here are the new declarations:

```
type
  TNotifyEvent = procedure (Sender: TObject) of object;

  MyButton = class
    FOnClick: TNotifyEvent;
  end;

  TForm1 = class (TForm)
    procedure OnButton1Click (Sender: TObject);
    Button1: MyButton;
  end;

var
  Form1: TForm1;
```

Now inside a procedure, you can write:

```
MyButton.FOnClick := Form1.OnButton1Click;
```

Although you can make this code work as it is written, you'll usually assign a new value, not directly to the method pointer but to the property wrapping it up:

```
MyButton.OnClick := Form1.OnButton1Click;
```

A property of the Events page of the Object Inspector, in fact, is nothing more than a property of a method pointer type. We will discuss this again in the next chapter.

## Class References

Another strange construct of Object Pascal is the definition of *class references*. A class reference is not an object, or a reference to an object, but a reference to the class type. A class reference is indeed a type, and you can declare variables of that type.

```
type
  MyClass = class
    ...
  end;

    MyClassRef = class of MyClass;

var
  AnObject: MyClass;
  AClassRef: MyClassRef;
```

You may wonder what class references are used for. You can use a class reference in any expression where the use of a data type is legal. Of course, there are not many, but the few cases are interesting. In general, class references allow you to manipulate a data type at run-time.

What is the use of this? Being able to manipulate a data type at run-time is a fundamental element of the Delphi environment itself. When you add a new component to a form by selecting it from the Components palette, you select a data type and create an object of that data type. Or, at least, this is what Delphi does for you behind the scenes.

To give you a better idea of how class references work, I built a simple example, named CLASSREF. The form of this example is quite simple. It just has three radio buttons in the upper portion. When you select one of these radio buttons and click on the form, you'll be able to create new components of the three types indicated by the button labels: radio buttons, push buttons, and edit boxes.

To make this program run properly, you need to change the names of the three components of the form, as you can see in the following textual description of the form.

```
object Form1: TForm1
  ActiveControl = RadioButtonRadio
  Caption = 'Component Builder'
  OnCreate = FormCreate
  OnMouseDown = FormMouseDown
  object RadioButtonRadio: TRadioButton
    Caption = 'Radio Button'
    Checked = True
    OnClick = RadioButtonRadioClick
  end
```

```
object RadioButtonButton: TRadioButton
  Caption = 'Button'
  OnClick = RadioButtonButtonClick
end
object RadioButtonEdit: TRadioButton
  Caption = 'Edit'
  OnClick = RadioButtonEditClick
end
end
```

For this program to work, the form for this example must have a class reference field. You should declare a new class reference type first:

```
type
  CRefType = class of TControl;
```

Then you can declare a two new private fields for the form:

```
private
  ClassRef: CRefType;
  Counter: Integer;
```

This field can be used to store a data type when one of the radio buttons is clicked:

```
procedure TForm1.RadioButtonRadioClick(Sender: TObject);
begin
  ClassRef := TRadioButton;
end;
```

The other two methods of the radio buttons are similar to this one, assigning the value TEdit or TButton to the ClassRef field. A similar assignment is also present in the initialization method, FormCreate.

The interesting part of the code is executed when the user clicks on the form. Instead of using the OnClick event, I've chosen the OnButtonDown event of the form to have the position of the mouse-click:

```
procedure TForm1.FormMouseDown(Sender: TObject;
  Button: TMouseButton; Shift: TShiftState; X, Y: Integer);
var
  MyObj: TControl;
  MyName: String;
begin
  MyObj := ClassRef.Create (self);
  MyObj.Visible := False;
  MyObj.Parent := self;
  MyObj.Left := X;
  MyObj.Top := Y;
  Inc (Counter);
  MyName := ClassRef.ClassName + IntToStr (Counter);
  Delete (MyName, 1, 1);
  MyObj.Name := MyName;
  MyObj.Visible := True;
end;
```

The first line of the code for this method is the key. It creates a new object of the data type stored in the class reference field:

```
MyObj := ClassRef.Create (self);
```

Now you can set the value of the Parent property, set the position of the new component, give it a name, and make it visible. Notice in particular the code used to build the name, which will also be used as the control's caption. To mimic Delphi's default naming convention, I've taken the name of the class with the expression

```
ClassRef.ClassName
```

The meaning of this method will be described in the next chapter. Then I've added a number and removed the initial letter of the string. For the first radio button, the basic string is TRadioButton, plus the *1* at the end, and minus the *T* at the beginning of the class name; that is, RadioButton1. Sound familiar?

You can see two examples of the output of this program in Figure 5.6. Notice, however, that the naming is not the same as that used by Delphi. Delphi uses a separate counter for each type of control; I've used a single counter for all of the components. If you place a radio button, a push button and an edit box in a form, their names will be RadioButton1, Button2, and Edit3.

**FIGURE 5.6:**

Two examples of the output of the CLASSREF program, in two different windows.

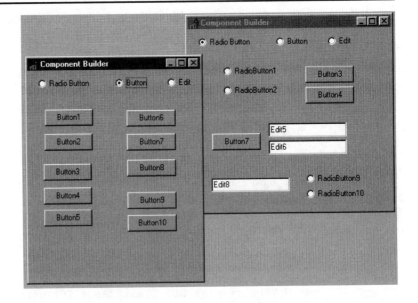

**NOTE**

Class references imply an idea similar to the concept of *meta-class* available in other programming languages. In Object Pascal, however, a class reference is not a class, but only a type pointer. Therefore, the analogy with meta-classes can be somewhat confusing. Notice also that this example actually combines class references with the call of a virtual constructor (more on virtual methods a few pages ahead), something C++ programmers are still longing for.

# Inheriting from Existing Types

It is quite common to need a slightly different version of an existing class. For example, you might need to add a new method or change an existing one slightly. You can do this easily by modifying the original code, unless you are already using the same class in another unit of your program. In that case, making changes can create problems for the other unit. You should avoid modifications that can affect other units, particularly in big applications.

A typical alternative is to make a copy of the original type definition, change its code to support the new features, and give a new name to the type. This might work, but it also might create problems, such as duplicate code and bugs. Because it results in two completely different data types, this approach cannot help you to take advantage of the similarities among different types, as we will see later.

In short, Object Pascal allows you to define a new type directly from an existing one. This technique is known as *inheritance* (or *subclassing*, or *derivation*) and is one of the fundamental elements of object-oriented programming languages. To inherit from an existing type, you only need to indicate that type at the beginning of the class declaration. This is done by Delphi each time you create a new form:

```
type
  TForm1 = class(TForm)
  end;
```

This simple definition indicates that the TForm1 class inherits all the methods, fields, and other elements of the TForm class. You can apply to an object of the TForm1 type each public method of the TForm class. If you look up TForm in the Help file, you'll see that this class has a number of methods. TForm, in turn, inherits some of its methods from another class, and so on, up to the TObject class. (For an introduction to the hierarchy of classes of Delphi, see the next chapter, which includes information about the *Visual Components Library*, or VCL.)

**NEW**

In Delphi 2, a form can be a subclass of another form you have built. This technique, known as *visual form inheritance*, is a welcome addition to the new version of Delphi. I'll discuss visual form inheritance in Chapter 12, where we look at programs with multiple forms.

As a simple example of inheritance, we can change the previous program slightly, deriving a new class and modifying one of its functions, GetText. You can find this code in the companion disk in the DATES.PAS file of the VIEWD2 example.

```
type
  NewDate = class (Date)
  public
    function GetText: string;
  end;
```

In this example, NewDate is derived from Date. It is common to say that Date is an *ancestor* class (or a *parent* class) of NewDate and that NewDate is a *descendent* class (or a *child* class) of Date. Other times, you might hear the typical C++ terms of *base* class (that is, the ancestor) and *derived* class (the descendent). Other object-oriented programming languages use different terms to denote inheritance and the classes involved. Unfortunately, there isn't a common jargon for all object-oriented languages—or better, for object-oriented *programmers*.

The new GetText function uses a constant array of month names, defined in the implementation section of the unit, to output the description of the date:

```
{definition of the month names}
const
  MonthNames: array [1..12] of string =
    ('January', 'February', 'March', 'April', 'May', 'June',
     'July', 'August', 'September', 'October', 'November', 'Decem-
ber');
```

```
{method of the descendent class}
function NewDate.GetText: string;
  GetText := Format ('%s %d, %d', [MonthNames[Month], Day, Year]);
end;
```

Note that this code works only if it is written in the same unit as the Date class, since we access private fields of the ancestor class. If we decided to place the descendent class in a new unit, we would need to either declare the three fields as protected or add three simple methods in the ancestor class to read the values of the three private fields.

Once we have defined the new class, we simply need to use this new data type to define the NewDate object and to call its constructor (the new code is in bold):

```
type
  TDateForm = class(TForm)
```

```
  ...
  private
    TheDay: NewDate;
  ...

procedure TDateForm.FormCreate(Sender: TObject);
begin
  TheDay := NewDate.Init (7, 14, 1996);
  DateLabel.Caption := TheDay.GetText;
end;
```

Without any other changes, the new VIEWD2 example will work properly. The NewDate class has inherited methods to increase the date, add a number of days, and so on. At the same time, to call the new version of the GetText method, we don't need to change the source code. Therefore, the source code of the events remains exactly the same, although its meaning changes considerably, as the new output demonstrates (see Figure 5.7).

**FIGURE 5.7:**
An example of the output of the VIEWD2 program.

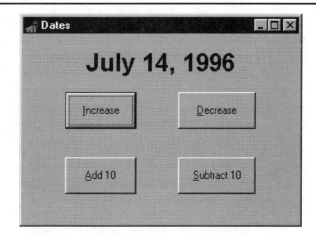

## Inheritance and Type Compatibility

Pascal is a strictly typed language. This means that you cannot assign an integer value to a Boolean variable or similar items, at least not without making a hard type cast, which can result in meaningless data. The rule is that two values are compatible only if they are of the same data type. However, there is an important exception to this rule in the case of class types. If you declare a class, such as Animal, and derive from it a new class, say Dog, you can assign an object of type Dog to a variable of type Animal. That is because a dog is an animal!

So, although this might surprise you, the following constructor calls are both legal:

```
var
  MyAnimal, MyAnimal2: Animal;
begin
  MyAnimal := Animal.Create;
  MyAnimal2 := Dog.Create;
  ...
```

As a general rule, you can use an object of a descendent class each time an object of an ancestor class is expected. However, the reverse is not legal; you cannot use an object of an ancestor class when an object of a descendent class is expected. In short

```
MyAnimal := MyDog;   // This is OK
MyDog := MyAnimal;   // This is an error!!!
```

I'll show you how you can use this feature in a complete example, ANIMALS1, which we will extend later. The two classes are defined as follows (in the ANIM.PAS unit):

```
type
  Animal = class
    public
    constructor Create;
    function GetKind: string;
    private
    Kind: string;
  end;

  Dog = class (Animal)
  public
    constructor Create;
  end;
```

The two Create functions simply set the value of kind, which is returned by the Get-Kind function:

```
constructor Animal.Create;
begin
  Kind := 'An animal';
end;

function Animal.GetKind: string;
begin
  GetKind := Kind;
end;

constructor Dog.Create;
begin
  Kind := 'A dog';
end;
```

To show an example of the use of these classes, I've built a simple form with two radio buttons, a push button, and a label with centered text and a big font (see the form in Figure 5.8).

**FIGURE 5.8:**
The ANIMALS1 form.

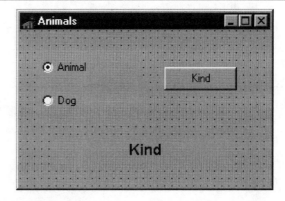

**FIGURE 5.8:**
The ANIMALS1 form.

The form has some fields, which store the values of an animal, a dog, and a generic object, MyAnimal:

```
type
  TFormAnimals = class(TForm)
    ...
  private
    MyAnimal: Animal;
    AnAnimal: Animal;
    ADog: Dog;
  end;
```

The instances of these objects are created and initialized when the form is created:

```
procedure TFormAnimals.FormCreate(Sender: TObject);
begin
  AnAnimal := Animal.Create;
  ADog := Dog.Create;
  MyAnimal := AnAnimal;
end;
```

The OnClick events handlers of the two radio buttons serve to change the object associated with the generic MyAnimal:

```
procedure TFormAnimals.DogRadioButtonClick(Sender: TObject);
begin
  MyAnimal := ADog;
end;
```

Finally, the Kind button calls the GetKind method for the current animal and displays the result in the label:

```
procedure TFormAnimals.KindButtonClick(Sender: TObject);
begin
  KindLabel.Caption := MyAnimal.GetKind;
end;
```

This is shown in Figure 5.9. Remember to destroy the two objects (ADog and AnAnimal) in the FormDestroy method.

---

**FIGURE 5.9:**

The output of the ANIMALS1 program when the Dog radio button is selected.

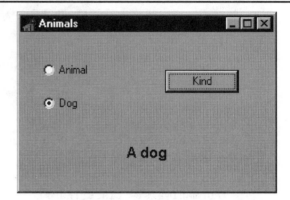

---

# Virtual and Dynamic Methods

Pascal functions and procedures are usually based on *static binding*. This means that a method call is resolved by the compiler and the linker. They replace the call with a call to the specific memory location where the function or procedure resides (which is known as the address of the function).

Object-oriented programming languages, including Object Pascal, allow the use of another form of binding, known as *dynamic binding* or *late binding*. In this case, the actual address of the method to be called is determined at run-time.

The advantage of this approach is known as *polymorphism*. Suppose that a class and its subclass (let's say Animal and Dog) both define a method, and this method has dynamic binding. Now you can apply this method to a generic variable, such as MyAnimal, which at run-time can either refer to an object of class Animal or to an object of class Dog. In this case, the actual method to call is determined at run-time, depending on the class of the current object.

The basic idea of polymorphism is that you write the call to a method, but the code actually called depends on the type of the object, which can be determined only at run-time because of the type-compatibility rule discussed in the previous section.

The following ANIMALS2 example extends ANIMALS1 and demonstrates this technique.

In the new version of the example, the Animal and the Dog classes have a new method, Verse (to get the sound made by the selected animal). This method is defined as virtual in the definition in the Animal function and is later overridden in the definition in the Dog class. This is accomplished by the use of the override and virtual keywords:

```
type
  Animal = class
    public
    constructor Create;
    function GetKind: string;
    function Verse: string; virtual;
  private
    Kind: string;
  end;

  Dog = class (Animal)
  public
    constructor Create;
    function Verse: string; override;
  end;
```

Of course, the two methods should be implemented. Here is a simple approach:

```
function Animal.Verse: string;
begin
  Verse := 'Verse of the animal';
end;

function Dog.Verse: string;
begin
  Verse := 'Arf Arf';
end;
```

Now what is the effect of this call if you write this code:

```
MyAnimal.Verse;
```

It depends. If the MyAnimal variable currently refers to an object of the Animal class, it will call the method Animal.Verse (shorthand used to indicate the Verse method of the Animal class). If it refers to an object of the Dog class, it will call the method Dog.Verse instead. This happens only because the function is virtual, and so it has dynamic binding.

The call to MyAnimal.Verse will work for an object instance of any descendent of the Animal class, even classes that are defined after or outside the scope of this method call. The compiler doesn't need to know about all the descendants in order to make the call compatible with them; only the ancestor class is needed.

In other words, this call to MyAnimal.Verse is compatible with all future Animal classes that haven't been created yet. This is the key technical reason that leads to the assumption that object-oriented programming languages favor reusability. You can write some code that uses the classes of a hierarchy without any knowledge of the actual classes of the hierarchy itself. In other words, the hierarchy—and the program—is still extensible, even when you've written thousands of lines of code using it. Of course, there is one condition: the ancestor classes of the hierarchy need to be designed very carefully.

The Delphi program used to demonstrate the use of these new classes has a form that is similar to that of the previous example. The button this time has the caption *Verse*, and a new internal name (VerseButton). The name of the label becomes Verse-Label. This code is executed by clicking on the button:

```
procedure TFormAnimals.VerseButtonClick(Sender: TObject);
begin
  VerseLabel.Caption := MyAnimal.Verse;
end;
```

In Figure 5.10, you can see an example of the output of this program. If you compare it with the previous version, you may very well say, "So what?" The output and the behavior of the two programs are similar, but something behind the scenes is really different.

**FIGURE 5.10:**
The output of ANIMALS2.

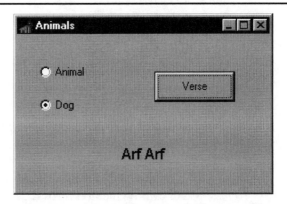

In ANIMALS1, there was a call to a function, GetKind, which simply returned the value of a field. In ANIMALS2, there is a single call, MyAnimal.Verse, that sometimes refers to a method of a class and other times refers to a method of another class. This is an interesting and powerful technique. The same compiled code calls one of two functions depending on the actual type of an object at run-time.

To appreciate this fully, consider that the two or more methods can be complex and completely different from each other. Virtual methods can also be called by other methods of the same class, and they can call other virtual or static methods.

# Overriding Virtual and Static Methods

As we have seen before, to override a virtual method in a descendent class, you need to use the override keyword. Notice, however, that this can take place only if the method was defined as virtual in the ancestor class. Otherwise, if it was a static method, there is no way to make it dynamic, other than by changing the code of the ancestor class (if this is possible).

The rules are simple: A method defined as static remains static in every subclass. A method defined as virtual remains virtual. There is no way to change this, because of the way the compiler generates the code for virtual methods.

To override a static method, you simply add a method to a subclass having the same parameters as the original one, without any further specifications. To override a virtual method, you must specify the override keyword.

```
type
  MyClass = class
    procedure One; virtual;
    procedure Two; {static method}
  end;
  MySubClass = class(MyClass)
    procedure One; override;
    procedure Two;
  end;
```

There are typically two different approaches to overriding a method. One is to replace the method of the ancestor class with a new version. The other is to add some more code to the existing method. This can be accomplished by using the inherited keyword to call the same method of the ancestor class. For example, you can write

```
procedure MySubClass.One;
begin
  {new code}
  ...
  {call older version, procedure MyClass.One}
  inherited One;
end;
```

You might wonder why you need to use the override keyword. In other languages, when you redefine a method in a subclass, you automatically override the original one. However, having a specific keyword allows the compiler to check the correspondence between the names of the methods of the ancestor class and subclass (misspelling a redefined function is a common error in other OOP languages), check that the method was virtual in the ancestor class, and so on.

# Virtual versus Dynamic Methods

In Delphi, there are basically two different ways to use *late or dynamic binding* with a method. You can declare the method as virtual, as we have seen before, or declare it as dynamic. The syntax of these two keywords is exactly the same, and the result of their use is also the same. What is different is the internal mechanism used by the compiler to implement *dynamic binding*.

Virtual methods are based on a *virtual method table* (VMT), also known as *vtable* (from the C++ jargon). A virtual method table is a collection of method addresses. For a call to a virtual method, the compiler generates code to jump to an address stored in the *nth* slot in the object's virtual method table. The compiler determines the index in the table by looking at the type of the object at run-time, often stored as a number inside the same object.

Virtual method tables allow a fast execution of the method calls. Their main drawback is that they require an entry for each virtual method for each descendent class, even if the method is not overridden in the descendent. At times, this has the effect of propagating virtual method table entries (even for methods that aren't overridden) throughout your class hierarchy. This will require a lot of memory just to store the same method address a number of times.

Dynamic method calls, on the other hand, are dispatched using a unique code indicating the method. The search for the corresponding function is generally slower than the simple one-step table lookup for virtual methods. The advantage is that dynamic method entries only propagate in descendants when the descendants override the method. For large or deep object hierarchies, using dynamic methods instead of virtual methods can result in significant memory savings, and causes just a minimal speed penalty.

From a programmer's perspective, the difference between these two approaches lies only in a different internal representation and slightly different speed or memory usage. Beside this, virtual and dynamic methods are the same.

Here is a rule of thumb: If the method is going to be overridden by nearly every descendent, make it virtual. If the method is not going to be overridden very often, but still needs late binding for flexibility, make it dynamic, especially if there will be a lot of descendent classes. If the method is going to be called a lot (such as hundreds of times per second), make it virtual. Otherwise, make it dynamic. Of course, this assumes that you have already decided the method must be late-bound. Non-virtual methods are the fastest form of method dispatch.

# Message Handlers

Some sort of dynamic method can be used to handle Windows messages, too. This can be accomplished using yet another directive, `message`, to define message-handling methods. These methods must be procedures with a single `var` parameter. They are followed by the `message` directive plus an index, which is the number of the Windows message they refer to or a corresponding mnemonic constant. For example

```
type
  TForm1 = class(TForm)
    procedure WMMinMax (var Message: TMessage);
      message WM_GETMINMAXINFO;
  end;
```

The name of the procedure and the type of the parameters are up to you, although there are a number of predefined record types for the various Windows messages. This technique can be extremely useful for long-time Windows programmers, who know all about Windows messages and API functions.

The ability to handle messages and call functions as you do when you are programming with C may horrify some programmers and delight others. But in Delphi, when writing Windows applications, you will seldom need to use message methods. When you are working with components in Delphi, most of your code will be in message methods (because components typically must work more closely with the Windows API and respond directly to Windows messages). In Chapter 9, I'll show you the example from which the code fragment above was taken.

# Abstract Methods

The `abstract` keyword is used to declare methods that will be defined only in subclasses of the current class. The abstract directive fully defines the method; it is not a forward declaration. If you try to provide a definition for the method, the compiler will complain.

In Object Pascal, you can create instances of classes that have abstract methods. However, Delphi's 32-bit compiler issues a warning message when you create an instance of a class containing abstract methods. Note that C++ uses a more strict opposite approach. In C++, you cannot create instances of abstract classes—classes that have pure virtual functions.

If you happen to call an abstract method, Delphi will issue a run-time error and terminate your application. Unlike most run-time errors, the "Call to abstract method" run-time error does not raise an exception that your program can trap. Calling an abstract method (a method which has no implementation) is considered a severe programmer error, worthy of a fatal exit.

```
type
  AbstractClass = class
    function F: Integer; virtual; abstract;
  end;
```

You might wonder why you would want to use abstract methods. The reason lies in the use of polymorphism. If class Animal has the abstract method Verse, every subclass can redefine it. The advantage is that you can now use the generic MyAnimal object to refer to each animal defined by a subclass, and invoke this method. If this method was not present in the interface of the Animal class, the call would not have been allowed by the compiler, which performs static type checking.

The next example, ANIMALS3, demonstrates the use of abstract methods and some other features of polymorphism. I've written a new version of the Anim unit, declaring three classes: Animal, Dog, and Cat. You can see the complete source code of this unit in Listing 5.2.

### Listing 5.2: The third version of the Anim unit, part of the ANIMALS3 example.

```
unit Anim;

interface

type
  Animal = class
    public
    constructor Create;
    function GetKind: string;
    function Verse: string; virtual; abstract;
    private
    Kind: string;
  end;

  Dog = class (Animal)
  public
    constructor Create;
    function Verse: string; override;
    function Eat: string; virtual;
  end;

  Cat = class (Animal)
  public
    constructor Create;
    function Verse: string; override;
    function Eat: string; virtual;
  end;
```

```
implementation

constructor Animal.Create;
begin
  Kind := 'An animal';
end;

function Animal.GetKind: string;
begin
  GetKind := Kind;
end;

constructor Dog.Create;
begin
  Kind := 'A dog';
end;

function Dog.Verse: string;
begin
  Verse := 'Arf Arf';
end;

function Dog.Eat: string;
begin
  Eat := 'A bone, please!';
end;

constructor Cat.Create;
begin
  Kind := 'A cat';
end;

function Cat.Verse: string;
begin
  Verse := 'Mieow';
end;

function Cat.Eat: string;
begin
  Eat := 'A mouse, please!';
end;

end.
```

The most interesting portion is the definition of the class Animal, which includes a virtual abstract method, Verse. It is also important to notice that each derived class overrides this definition and adds a new virtual method, Eat. What are the implications of these two different approaches? To call the Verse function, we can simply write the same code as in the previous version of the program:

```
VerseLabel.Caption := MyAnimal.Verse;
```

How can we call the Eat method? We cannot apply it to an object of the Animal class. The statement

```
VerseLabel.Caption := MyAnimal.Eat;
```

generates the compiler error "Field identifier expected."

To solve this problem, you can use RTTI to cast the Animal object to a Cat or Dog object, but without the proper cast, the program will raise an exception. We will see an example of this approach later on. Adding the method definition in the Animal class is a typical solution for the problem, and the presence of the abstract keyword favors this choice.

To test our three new classes, we can modify the form of the previous version slightly, adding a new radio button for the new kind of animal.

Along with adding the required code for the Cat class, I've made some other changes. The two previous versions of the program created an object of each type at the beginning, then assigned the existing objects to the MyAnimal variable when the user selected one of the radio buttons. Now only one object exists at a time. The form has just a private field, MyAnimal, initialized in the OnCreate method with the statement MyAnimal := Dog.Create. Each of the OnClick event handlers of the radio button removes the current object and creates a new one:

```
procedure TFormAnimals.DogRadioButtonClick(Sender: TObject)
begin
  MyAnimal.Free;
  MyAnimal := Dog.Create;
end;
```

The code of the VerseButtonClick method remains the same, still calling MyAnimal.Verse and showing the result in the caption. When you run this program, the label displays the sound of the dog or of the cat (see Figure 5.11), or you experience a bad run-time error that will stop your application (when you call the abstract method of the Animal class).

**FIGURE 5.11:**

The output of ANIMAL3, when the Cat radio button is selected.

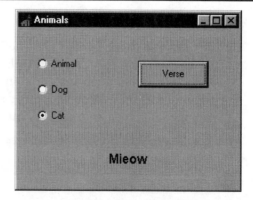

# Run-Time Type Information

The Object Pascal type-compatibility rule for descendent classes allows you to use a descendent class where an ancestor class is expected. As I mentioned earlier, the reverse is not possible. Now suppose that the Dog class has an Eat function, which is not present in the Animal class.

If the variable *MyAnimal* refers to a dog, it should be possible to call the function. But if you try, and the variable is referring to another class, the result is an error. We could cause a nasty run-time error (or worse, a subtle memory overwrite problem) by making an explicit typecast, since the compiler cannot determine if the value will be correct during execution.

To solve the problem, we can use some techniques based on RTTI. In short, each object knows its type and its inheritance, and we can ask for this information with the is operator. The parameters of is are an object and a type:

```
if MyAnimal is Dog then ...
```

The is expression evaluates as True only if the MyAnimal object is currently referring to an object of type Dog, or a type descendent from Dog. This means that if you test whether a Dog object is of type Animal, the test will succeed. In other words, this expression evaluates as True if you can safely assign the object (MyAnimal) to a variable of the data type (Dog).

Now that you know for sure that the animal is a dog, you can make a safe typecast (or type conversion). You can accomplish this direct cast by writing the following:

```
if MyAnimal is Dog then
  MyDog := Dog (MyAnimal);
```

This same operation can be accomplished directly by the second RTTI operator, as. We can write the following:

```
MyDog := MyAnimal as Dog;
Text := MyDog.Eat;
```

If we want to call the Eat function, we might also use another notation:

```
(MyAnimal as Dog).Eat;
```

The result of the expression is an object of Dog class data type, so you can apply to it any method of that class. The difference between the traditional cast and the use of the as cast is that the second one raises an exception if the type of the object is not compatible with the type you are trying to cast it to. The exception raised is EInvalidCast (exceptions will be described in the next section).

To avoid this exception, use the is operator and, if it succeeds, make a plain typecast:

```
if MyAnimal is Dog then
  (Dog (MyAnimal) ).Eat;
```

Both run-time type operators are very useful in Delphi because you often want to write generic code that can be used with a number of components of the same type or even of different types. When a component is passed as a parameter to an event-response method, a generic data type is used (TObject), so you often need to cast it back to the original component type:

```
procedure TForm1.Click(Sender: TObject);
begin
  if Sender is TButton then ...
end;
```

This is a common technique in Delphi, and I'll use it in a number of examples throughout the book. Besides its use with is and as expressions, the term RTTI refers to a number of operations you can do on any class or object, such as asking for the class name or the size of an instance. We will discuss this topic in the next chapter, where we will see the definition of the default ancestor of any class, TObject.

The two RTTI operators, is and as, are extremely powerful, and you might be considering using them as a standard programming construct. Although they are indeed powerful, you should probably limit their use to special cases.

When you need to solve a complex problem involving several classes, try using polymorphism first. Only in special cases, where polymorphism alone cannot be applied, should you try using the RTTI operators to complement it. Do not use RTTI instead of polymorphism. This is both bad programming practice and results in slower programs. RTTI, in fact, has a high negative impact on performance, since it must walk the hierarchy of classes to see if the typecast is correct. As we have seen, virtual method calls require just a memory lookup, which is much faster.

# Handling Exceptions

The last interesting feature of Object Pascal we will cover in this chapter is *exception handling*. The syntax and semantics of Object Pascal's exception handling are similar to C++. The implementation (machine code) of Pascal's exception handling is radically different (and far simpler) than C++.

The idea of exceptions is to make programs more robust by adding the capability of handling software or hardware errors. A program can survive such errors or terminate gracefully, allowing the user to save data before exiting.

There are several alternative ways to cope with errors, including extensive testing of function return codes. However, testing each time and for each function to see if something wrong has happened is boring and error-prone. Function-result error codes are problematic because each call to a subroutine must be checked for an error situation, and if such a situation exists, the current routine must be cleaned up and the error condition reported to the caller of the current routine. Each function in the call chain is responsible for passing the error information on to the next, a sort of fire brigade. If one routine in the call chain neglects to pass on the error information, your code will not be informed of errors, thus breaking down the whole process.

Exceptions solve this problem by removing the reporting mechanism, the fire brigade, from your normal code. If a particular body of code is not interested in error conditions, it doesn't need to do anything to ensure that error reporting works smoothly. Exceptions enable you to write more compact code that is less cluttered by fire brigade maintenance chores unrelated to the actual programming objective. Exceptions also allow you to separate the code that discovers an error condition from the code that reports the error condition.

Exceptions are a plus also because they define a uniform and universal (within your program) error-reporting mechanism, which is also used by Delphi. During run-time, Delphi raises exceptions when something goes wrong. If your code has been written properly, it can acknowledge the problem and try to solve it; otherwise, the exception is passed to its calling code, and so on. Eventually, if nobody handles the exception, Delphi handles it, by displaying a standard error message and trying to continue the program.

The whole mechanism is based on four keywords:

- `try` delimits the beginning of a protected block of code.

- `except` delimits the end of a protected block of code, and introduces the exception-handling statements, with this form:

  `on {exception type} do {statement}`

- `finally` indicates an optional block used to free resources allocated in the `try` block, before the exception is handled; this block is terminated by the `end` keyword.

- `raise` is the statement used to raise an exception. Most exceptions you'll encounter in your Delphi programming will be raised by the system, but you can also raise exceptions in your own code when it discovers invalid or inconsistent data at run-time. The `raise` keyword can also be used inside a handler to re-raise an exception; that is, to propagate it to the next handler.

Here is the example of a simple protected block:

```
function Divide (A, B: Integer): Integer;
begin
  try
    {the following statement is protected because it
      can generate an error if B equals 0}
    Divide := A div B;
  except
    on EDivByZero do
      Divide := 0;
end;
```

In the exception-handling statement, we catch the EDivByZero exception, which is an exception defined by Delphi. There are a number of these exceptions referring to run-time problems (such as a division by zero or a wrong dynamic cast), to Windows resource problems (such as out-of-memory errors), or to component errors (such as a wrong index). However, programmers can define their own exceptions. Simply create a new subclass of the default exception class or one of its subclasses:

```
type
  EArrayFull = class (Exception);
```

When you add a new element to your array and it is already full (probably due to an error in the logic of the program), you can raise the corresponding exception by creating an object of this class:

```
if MyArray.Full then
  raise EArrayFull.Create ('Array full');
```

This Create method has a string parameter to describe the exception. You don't need to worry about destroying the object you have created for the exception, since it will be deleted automatically by the exception handler.

> **NOTE**
>
> There is another keyword involved in exception handling, but one that is used infrequently: the at keyword. It can be used in a `raise` statement, to indicate which machine code location should be indicated as the one causing the exception. The syntax is `raise [object]` at `[location]`. For example, in the SYSUTILS.PAS source code, you can see the expression `raise OutOfMemory at ReturnAddr`. It will seem like the error was encountered in the code calling this procedure, and not in the procedure itself; that is, in the location returned by the system ReturnAddr function. This will let the run-time module think that the exception was indeed raised by the caller function. Of course, this kind of code makes sense only in special cases related to the system.

# An Example of the Use of Exceptions

The code presented in this example and the previous Divide function are part of a sample program you can experiment with to test exceptions. The program is named EXCEPT, and it is based on the simple form shown in Figure 5.12. Its form has just the buttons, each with an intuitive name and an OnClick event handler.

**FIGURE 5.12:**
The form of the EXCEPT example.

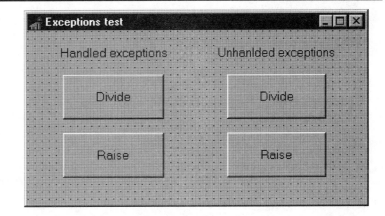

Each time a user presses one of the buttons, an exception is generated, either by making a division by zero or by an explicit `raise` statement. The two events of the two buttons on the left have the proper exception-handling code. But those on the right do not bother with handling exceptions.

**WARNING**

When you run a program in the debugger, the debugger will stop the program by default when an exception is encountered. This is certainly positive, since you'll know where the exception took place and can see the call of the handler step by step. However, this behavior will confuse the execution of this specific test program. In fact, even if the exception is properly handled by the code, the debugger will stop the program execution. Then moving step-by-step through the code, you can see how it is handled. If you just want to let the program run when the exception is properly handled, run the program from the Explorer, or temporarily disable the Break on Exception debugging feature in the Environment Options.

The first Divide button calls the Divide function, in a slightly different version than the one described earlier:

```
procedure TForm1.ButtonDivide1Click(Sender: TObject);
begin
  Divide (10, 0);
end;

{protected version of the div operator}
function Divide (A, B: Integer): Integer;
begin
  try
    {the following statement is protected because it
      can generate an error if B equals 0}
    Divide := A div B;
  except
    on EDivByZero do
    begin
      Divide := 0;
      MessageDlg ('Divide by zero corrected', mtError, [mbOK], 0);
    end;
    on E: Exception do
    begin
      Divide := 0;
      MessageDlg (E.Message, mtError, [mbOK], 0);
    end;
  end;
end;
```

This code generates an exception, which is trapped immediately. Notice that there are two different exception handlers after the same try block. You can have any number of these handlers, which are evaluated in sequence. For this reason, you need to place the broader handlers (the handlers of the ancestor exception classes) at the end.

In fact, using a hierarchy of exceptions, a handler is called also for the subclasses of the type it refers to, as any procedure will do. This is polymorphism in action again. But keep in mind that using a handler for every exception, such as the one above, is not usually a good choice. It is better to leave unknown exceptions to Delphi. The default exception handler in VCL displays the error-message text of the exception class in a message box, then resumes normal operation of the program.

Another important element is that you can use the exception object you receive in the handler. In the example above, I've written something like

```
on E: Exception do
  MessageDlg (E.Message, mtError, [mbOK], 0);
```

The object *E* of class *Exception* receives the value of the exception object passed by the raise statement. When you work with exceptions, remember this rule: You raise an exception creating an object and handle it indicating its type. This has an important benefit, because as we have seen, when you handle a type of exception, you really handle the exception of the type you specify plus each descendent type.

For this reason, Delphi defines a hierarchy of exceptions, and you can choose to handle each specific type of exception in a different way, or handle groups of them together. (Refer to the next chapter for graphs of the hierarchy of the classes Delphi defines for exceptions.)

A message box (see Figure 5.13, on the left) is displayed only because we generate it in the code, with the MessageDlg call. On the other hand, if we simply make a division by zero, Delphi will handle this exception, displaying a standard message box (see Figure 5.13, on the right).

**FIGURE 5.13:**

Two Divide buttons of the EXCEPT example raise exceptions and handle them directly (on the left) or leave them to Delphi (on the right).

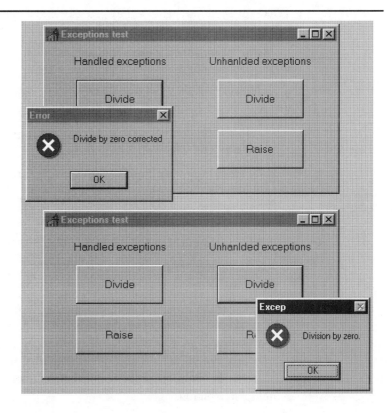

This happens when you press the second Divide button, executing the following code:

```
procedure TForm1.ButtonDivide2Click(Sender: TObject);
var
  A, B, C: Integer;
begin
```

```
  A := 10;
  B := 0;
  {generates an exception, which is not handled}
  C := A div B;
  {we have to use the result, or the optimizer will
  remove the code and the error, too}
  Caption := IntToStr (C);
end;
```

The other two buttons are even simpler. They call a function which invariably raises an exception. Again, the first button handles it, without even showing a message box to the user, and the second button doesn't seem to care. When the user presses the first Raise button, nothing seems to happen. This is exactly what is meant by handling an exception!

```
{fake procedure: the array is always full}
procedure AddToArray (N: Integer);
begin
  raise EArrayFull.Create ('Array full');
end;

procedure TForm1.ButtonRaise1Click(Sender: TObject);
begin
  try
    {this procedure raises an exception}
    AddToArray (24);
  except
    {simply ignores the exception}
    on EArrayFull do; {do nothing}
  end;
end;

procedure TForm1.ButtonRaise2Click(Sender: TObject);
begin
  {unguarded call}
  AddToArray (24);
end;
```

## Exceptions and the Stack

When you raise an exception, what happens to your function call stack? The program starts searching for a handler among the functions already on the stack. This means that the program exits from existing functions and does not execute the remaining statements.

To understand how this works, you can either use the debugger or add a number of simple message boxes in the code, to be informed when a certain source code statement is executed. In the next example, EXCEPT2, I've followed this second approach.

For example, when you press the Raise2 button in the EXCEPT form, an exception is raised and not handled, so that the final part of the code will never be executed:

```
procedure TForm1.ButtonRaise2Click(Sender: TObject);
begin
  {unguarded call}
  AddToArray (24);
  ShowMessage ('Program never gets here');
end;
```

Notice that this method calls the AddToArray procedure, which raises the exception. The final code of this procedure is not executed either:

```
procedure AddToArray (N: Integer);
begin
  raise EArrayFull.Create ('Array full');
  ShowMessage ('Program never gets here');
end;
```

If you run the EXCEPT program, you'll never see these messages, unless you comment the `raise` statement (I suggest that you do comment it, so that you can see the difference between when the exception is raised and when it is not).

**NOTE**

Technically, there are two different ways to handle exceptions in different programming languages or environments. In Object Pascal (or in C++), run-time unwinds the stack to reach a handler, and then continues with the code after the handler. Other systems use resumption instead. This means that after the handler is found, the code restarts from the exact position where the error occurred. However, this approach is not very safe, since there is a good chance that a new error will take place again in the same code. Seeing a number of system error messages in a row is something that can really bother users.

When the exception is handled, the flow starts again after the handler, and not after the code that raises the exception. Consider this modified method:

```
procedure TForm1.ButtonRaise1Click(Sender: TObject);
begin
  try
    {this procedure raises an exception}
    AddToArray (24);
    ShowMessage ('Program never gets here');
  except
    {simply ignores the exception}
    on EArrayFull do
      ShowMessage ('Handle the exception');
```

```
end;
    ShowMessage ('Exception has already been handled');
end;
```

The last ShowMessage call will be executed right after the second one, while the first is always ignored. I suggest that you run the program, change its code, and play with it. (You can find its complete source code on the companion CD, as EXCEPT2.)

## The Finally Block

There is a fourth keyword for exception handling that I've mentioned but haven't used so far: finally. A finally block is used to perform some action (usually cleanup) in the event of an exception, and in the event of normal execution. The code in the finally block will always be executed as execution leaves the associated try block, whether that departure is by normal program flow or by exception.

Consider this function:

```
function ComputeBits (A, B: Integer): Integer;
var
  Bmp: TBitmap;
begin
  try
    Bmp := TBitmap.Create;
    {compute bits ...}
    ComputeBits := A div B;
    Bmp.Free;
  except
    on EDivByZero do
    begin
      ComputeBits := 0;
      MessageDlg ('Error in ComputeBits', mtError, [mbOK], 0);
    end;
end;
```

This code is fundamentally flawed. When B is zero and the exception is raised, the statement used to free the bitmap won't be executed at all. The program jumps from the code generating the exception to the corresponding handler, skipping statements in between.

One might think of placing the resource deallocation code at the end of the function, after the try block, but if an exception is raised and not handled, the try block won't be executed. The solution to the problem is to use the finally statement:

```
function ComputeBits (A, B: Integer): Integer;
var
  Bmp: TBitmap;
  begin
  Bmp := TBitmap.Create;
  try
    {compute bits ...}
```

```
    ComputeBits := A div B;
  finally
    Bmp.Free;
  end;
end;
```

When this code is run, the Free method of the bitmap is always called, whether an exception occurs (of any sort) or not. The drawback to this version of the function is that we want to handle the exception, too. Strangely enough, this is not possible. A try block can be followed by either except or finally, but not both at the same time. The solution? Use two nested try blocks. Give the internal one a finally statement, and give the external one an except statement or vice versa, as the situation requires. Here is an example:

```
function ComputeBits (A, B: Integer): Integer;
var
  Bmp: TBitmap;
begin
  Bmp := TBitmap.Create;
  MessageDlg ('Bitmap created', mtWarning, [mbOK], 0);
  try try
    {compute bits ...}
    ComputeBits := A div B;
    MessageDlg ('Code not reached (if the exception is raised)',
      mtWarning, [mbOK], 0);
  finally
    Bmp.Free;
    MessageDlg ('Bitmap destroyed', mtWarning, [mbOK], 0);
  end;
  except
    on EDivByZero do
    begin
      {change the message and re-raise the exception}
      E.Message := 'Error in ComputeBits';
      raise;
    end;
  end;
end;
```

To demonstrate that this code works as I've described, I've written a program around this function. The new example is called EXCEPT3, and it has just two buttons (see the output in Figure 5.14, when a user clicks on the first button). Its code contains two versions of the fake ComputeBits function, one similar to the last version above and the other having only the finally block. Since the function shows a number of message boxes, you are informed of the allocation and deallocation of the bitmap, and of the flow of execution.

The *must* for a programmer is to protect blocks with the finally statement, to avoid resource or memory leaks in case an exception is raised. Handling the exception is probably less important, since Delphi can survive most of them. The difference between the two versions is that in the first one, the program customizes the

FIGURE 5.14:

The three steps of the output of the EXCEPT3 program. Notice the order of the three messages.

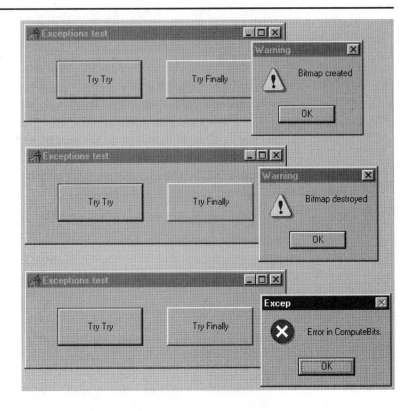

error message, using the code I've just shown. To understand this program, run it, see what it does, and try to change its behavior. As an alternative, look at Figure 5.14 above, which shows the three messages displayed when a user presses the Try Try button.

**WARNING**

If you change this code, and the new version doesn't properly free the bitmap, you might experience some memory problems or Windows resource leaks.

# Summary

In this chapter, we have discussed object-oriented programming in Object Pascal. We have considered the definition of classes, the use of methods, encapsulation, subclassing, the definition of units, run-time type information, and exception handling. Certainly this is quite a lot for a single chapter, and if you have never heard about OOP, the information presented here may be too concise.

You can refer to Appendix A for a short introduction to OOP, but I also suggest that you spend some time with a book fully devoted to this subject, one that also includes some theory. To become a fluent Delphi programmer, the ideas presented in this chapter should be enough. If they are too hard to grasp, particularly the more advanced topics, such as class references, don't let that stop you. Go on reading, and come back to this chapter later.

# CHAPTER

## SIX

# The Visual Component Library

- The Delphi hierarchy of classes

- Delphi components and objects

- An overview of Delphi properties

- Component methods and events

- Types of Delphi collections

**W**e have seen that Delphi has a number of ready-to-use, standard routines. But there is a larger and much more important set of classes. These are component classes, related to the user interface, and general-purpose classes. The use of the component classes and other classes related to Windows is the subject of the next chapters of the book. In this chapter, we'll focus on the Delphi class library. We'll discuss the structure of the Delphi hierarchy of classes, review some key concepts of their use, and look at an overview of some general-purpose classes.

The Delphi system library is called the *Visual Component Library*, or *VCL* for short, although it includes more than components. This chapter is short but delves into some intricacies of the VCL. If you would like to skip the VCL details for now, and continue with more information about the use of the Delphi components, you can go directly to the next chapter.

# The Conceptual Foundation

At the heart of Delphi is a hierarchy of classes. Since every class in the system is a subclass of the TObject data type, the whole hierarchy has a single root. This allows you to use TObject as a replacement for any data type in the system. For example, event-response methods usually have a Sender parameter of type TObject. This simply means that the sender can be of any class, since every class is derived from TObject.

The typical drawback of a similar approach is that to work on the object, you need to know its data type. One way to solve this problem is by using the *RTTI* (run-time type information) features of the language, which are represented by the is and as keywords. RTTI and the exceptions generated when a type conversion fails make it safe to use this approach to express a generic type.

Since there isn't a specific Object Pascal syntax to write *generic* classes, known also as *template* classes in C++ jargon, the use of the TObject type and RTTI is generally accepted. To be honest, I don't miss C++ templates, because Object Pascal's approach is much easier and equally as powerful. I know this is often regarded as an unsafe approach because of the required type conversions, but by using RTTI and *controlled* casts, we can avoid any problems. We will discuss generic classes later in this chapter, when we focus on some container classes of the VCL.

Since the TObject class is the "mother of all classes," let's take a quick look at its definition in the Delphi source code:

```
type
  TObject = class;
  TClass = class of TObject;
  TObject = class
    constructor Create;
```

```
    procedure Free;
    class function InitInstance(Instance: Pointer): TObject;
    procedure CleanupInstance;
    function ClassType: TClass;
    class function ClassName: ShortString;
    class function ClassNameIs(const Name: string): Boolean;
    class function ClassParent: TClass;
    class function ClassInfo: Pointer;
    class function InstanceSize: Longint;
    class function InheritsFrom(AClass: TClass): Boolean;
    procedure Dispatch(var Message);
    class function MethodAddress
      (const Name: ShortString): Pointer;
    class function MethodName(Address: Pointer): ShortString;
    function FieldAddress(const Name: ShortString): Pointer;
    procedure DefaultHandler(var Message); virtual;
    class function NewInstance: TObject; virtual;
    procedure FreeInstance; virtual;
    destructor Destroy; virtual;
  end;
```

The code above defines two data types: the class TObject and the class reference TClass. The TObject class lists a number of methods that you can use on any object, including objects that you have defined yourself (that do not contain these methods). Most of the methods of the TObject class are often used by the system, and they become particularly useful if you need to write a tool to extend the Delphi programming environment. For example, debugger and browser tools use this kind of information extensively.

Some of the TObject methods might have a role when writing generic Windows applications. For example, the ClassName method returns a string with the name of the class. You can apply this method both to an object (an instance) and to a class (a data type), because it is a class method. Suppose that you have defined a Date class and a Day object of that class. The following statements have the same effect:

```
text := Day.ClassName;
text := Date.ClassName;
```

There are occasions to use the name of a class, but it might also be useful to retrieve a class reference to the class itself or to its base class. This can be done with the ClassType and ClassParent methods. Once you have a class reference, you can use it as if it were an object; for example, to call the ClassName method.

Another method that might be useful is InstanceSize, which returns the size of an object. Although you might think that you can use the SizeOf function for this information, that function actually returns the size of an object reference—a pointer—instead of the size of the object.

To illustrate the use of some of the methods of the TObject class, and of every class in the system, I've written a small example, called OBJUSE. To rebuild it, place a button and a list box in the form of a new, blank application. Then add to the project the unit defining a Date class we have written in Chapter 5, and add a uses statement referring to it in the code of the main form of the new project. Now, when the user clicks on the button, the following code is executed:

```
procedure TForm1.ShowButtonClick(Sender: TObject);
var
  Day: Date;
begin
  {create an instance and show some information}
  Day := Date.Init (6, 1, 1995);
  ListBox1.Items.Add ('Class name: ' + Day.ClassName);
  ListBox1.Items.Add ('Parent class name: ' +
    Day.ClassParent.ClassName);
  ListBox1.Items.Add ('Instance size: ' +
    IntToStr (Day.InstanceSize));
  ListBox1.Items.Add ('Size of object: ' +
    IntToStr (SizeOf (Day)));
  {leave a blank line}
  ListBox1.Items.Add (' ');
  {show the same information about the form}
  ListBox1.Items.Add ('Class name: ' + ClassName);
  ListBox1.Items.Add ('Parent class name: ' +
    ClassParent.ClassName);
  ListBox1.Items.Add ('Instance size: ' +
    IntToStr (InstanceSize));
  ListBox1.Items.Add ('Size of object: ' +
    IntToStr (SizeOf (self)));
  {free memory}
  Day.Free;
  {disable the button, to avoid a second click}
  ShowButton.Enabled := False;
end;
```

When you run this program, the list box will contain the name of the class of the Day object, the name of its parent class, the size of its instance, and the size of the object itself, as shown in Figure 6.1.

**FIGURE 6.1:**
The output of the OBJUSE example.

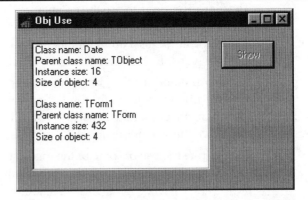

The second part of the program shows the same information for the form object. Since we are writing a method of its class, TForm1, we can call this method directly, or we can use `self` as the parameter of the SizeOf function. Notice that when you call SizeOf for an object, it always returns 4, which is not the size of the object, but of its reference.

# The VCL Hierarchy

The VCL defines a number of subclasses of TObject. Many of these classes are actually subclasses of other subclasses, forming a complex hierarchy. Unless you are interested in developing new components, you'll use only the *terminal* classes of this hierarchy—the leaf nodes of the hierarchy tree—which are fully documented in the Delphi Help system. However, if you want to have a look at the full structure of the system, you can use the ObjectBrowser (a tool discussed in detail in Chapter 20), or refer to some of the figures in the current chapter. To see some output of the Object Browser, you can look at Figure 6.2.

**FIGURE 6.2:**

An example of the output of the ObjectBrowser, showing some classes of the VCL hierarchy.

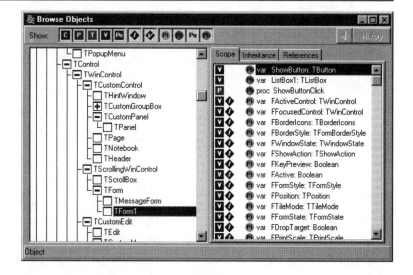

# Components

Components are the central elements of Delphi applications. When you write a program, you basically choose a number of components and define their interactions. That's all there is to most of Delphi programming.

There are different kinds of components in Delphi. Most of the components are included in the Components palette, but some of them (including TForm and TApplication) are not. Technically, components are subclasses of the TComponent class (see Figure 6.3). As such, they can be manipulated visually, as you set their properties at design-time.

We will use most of the Delphi components in the examples throughout this book. I'll try to present the components in logical groups, to cover related topics in each chapter. My logical groups only partially match the pages of the Components palette.

**FIGURE 6.3:**

The first part of the VCL hierarchy: Components.

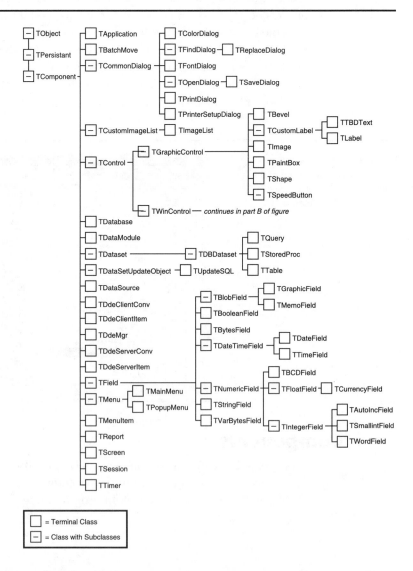

**FIGURE 6.3:**

The first part of the VCL hierarchy:
Components (continued).

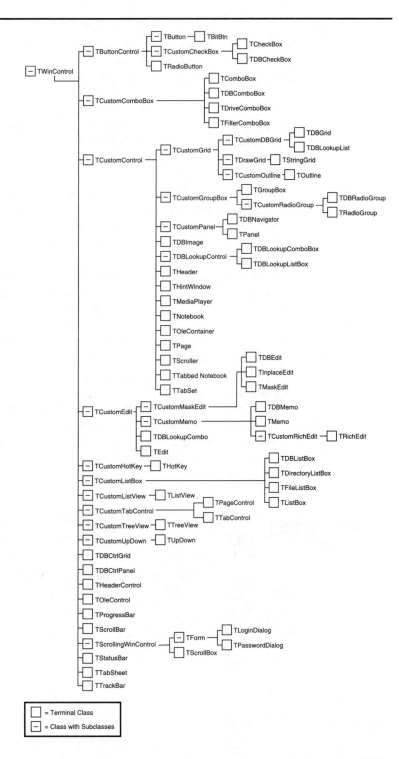

From a technical point of view, there are common names to indicate groups of components. These groups indicate components with a similar internal structure and relationship to Windows elements. These technical groups reflect each component's position in the hierarchy and its use.

*Controls* can be defined as visual components. You can place a control on a form at design-time and see how it looks, and you can see controls on the form at run-time. Controls account for most components, and the terms are often used as synonyms—although there are components that are not controls.

*Windowed controls* are visual components based on a window. From a technical point of view, this means that the controls have a windows handle. From a user perspective, windowed controls can receive the input focus and can contain other controls. This is the biggest group of components.

*Graphical controls,* or *nonwindowed controls* are visual components that are not based on a window. Therefore, they have no handle, cannot receive the focus, and cannot contain other controls. Examples of nonwindowed controls are the Label and the TSpeedButton component. There are just a few controls in this group, but they are critical to minimizing the use of system resources, particularly for components used often and in number, such as labels or toolbar buttons.

*Components* can be visual or nonvisual. *Nonvisual* components are the components that are not controls. At design-time, a nonvisual component appears on the form as a little icon. At run-time, some of these components are visible (for example, the standard dialog boxes), and others are invisible (for example, some database connections). In other words, nonvisual components are not visible themselves at run-time, but often manage something that is visual, such as a dialog box.

**NOTE**  In Delphi 2, you can use an environment option, Show Component Captions, to see the name of nonvisual components right under their icons. This helps to locate them, particularly if you have several components of the same kind on a form (all indicated by the same icon).

You can see a representation of these groups in Figure 6.4.

A graphical representation of the
groups of components.

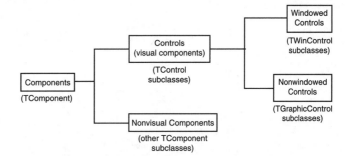

| | |
|---|---|
| **TIP** | To set the order of creation and of activation of the components on a form, you can change the creation order of nonvisual components and the tab order of windowed controls. To accomplish this, use the corresponding commands in the SpeedBar menu of the Form Designer, as I'll show you in an example in the next chapter. |

## Objects

Although the VCL is basically a collection of components, there are other classes that do not fit in this category. You can see some of these classes (only the most important ones) in the hierarchy shown in Figure 6.5.

All the noncomponent classes are often indicated by the term *objects*, although this is not a precise definition. There are mainly two uses of these classes. Generally, noncomponent classes define the data type of component properties, such as the Picture property of an image component (which is a TGraphic object) or the Items property of a list box (which is a TStrings object).

The second use of noncomponent classes is a direct use. In the Delphi code you write, you can allocate and manipulate objects of these classes. You might do this for a number of reasons, including to store a copy of the value of a property in memory and modify it while it does not relate to any component, to store a list of values, to write complex algorithms, and so on. You'll see several examples in the book that show how to use noncomponent classes directly.

There are several groups of noncomponent classes in the VCL:

- **Graphic objects:** TBitmap, TBrush, TCanvas, TFont, TGraphic, TGraphics-Object, TIcon, TMetafile, TPen, and TPicture.

- **Stream/file objects:** TBlobStream, TFileStream, THandleStream, TIniFile, TMemoryStream, TFiler, TReader, and TWriter.

- **Collections:** TList, TStrings, TStringList, and TCollection.

**FIGURE 6.5:**

The second part of the VCL hierarchy: Objects.

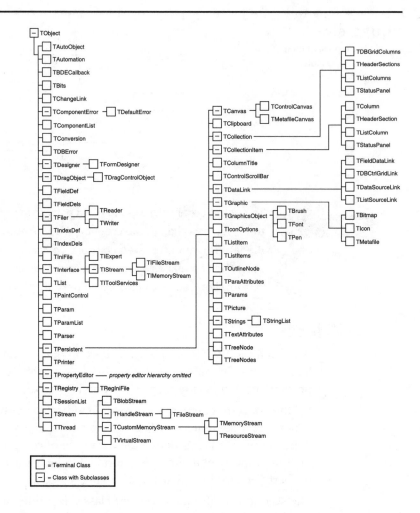

We will focus on collections in a later section of this chapter. Graphic and stream objects are described throughout the following chapters, in the discussions of the components that use them and in other sections where they are relevant.

## Exceptions

The third main part of the VCL classes is made up of the exception classes. We have already discussed exception handling in Chapter 5, so we won't repeat the details here. You can see the hierarchy of the exception classes in Figure 6.6.

**FIGURE 6.6:**

The third part of the VCL hierarchy: Exceptions.

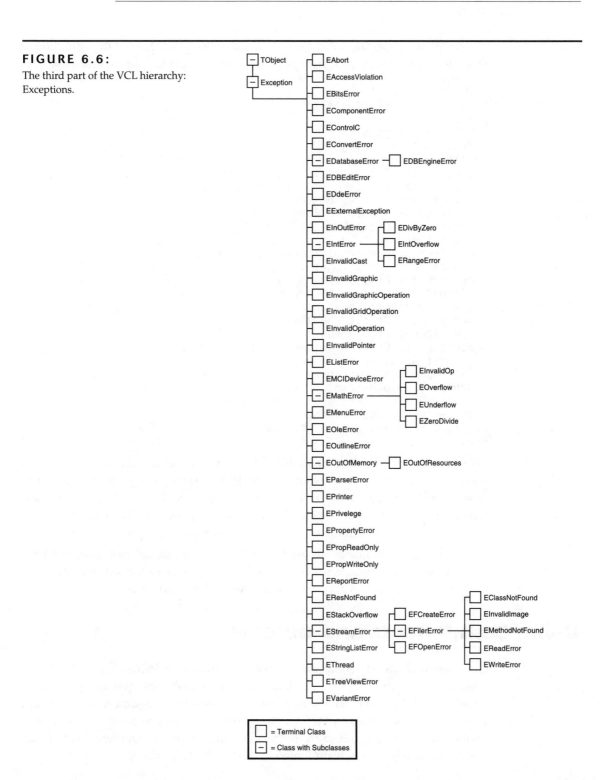

□ = Terminal Class

⊟ = Class with Subclasses

All exception classes are subclasses of the Exception class. Here is the definition of this class in Delphi 2, which is slightly different from the Delphi 1 version (particularly the help support):

```
Exception = class(TObject)
private
  FMessage: string;
  FHelpContext: Integer;
public
  constructor Create(const Msg: string);
  constructor CreateFmt(const Msg: string;
    const Args: array of const);
  constructor CreateRes(Ident: Integer);
  constructor CreateResFmt(Ident: Integer;
    const Args: array of const);
  constructor CreateHelp(const Msg: string;
    AHelpContext: Integer);
  constructor CreateFmtHelp(const Msg: string;
    const Args: array of const;
    AHelpContext: Integer);
  constructor CreateResHelp(Ident: Integer;
    AHelpContext: Integer);
  constructor CreateResFmtHelp(Ident: Integer;
    const Args: array of const;
    AHelpContext: Integer);
  property HelpContext: Integer
    read FHelpContext write FHelpContext;
  property Message: string
    read FMessage write FMessage;
end;
```

Two things are worth noticing in this definition: The various constructors, having a `string` as parameter, the resource identifier of a string, and so on; and the Message property, which can be used to access the message defined in the constructor. Other constructors define the HelpContext property, too. I will actually show you what is behind the definition of a property in a couple of pages.

To see how these elements are used, turn back to the examples of exception handling at the end of Chapter 5. More examples of the use of exceptions are presented in the rest of the book, whenever resource allocation is involved.

# Using Components and Objects

Once you have added a component to your application or defined a new object, you need to set its status and its behavior. There are a number of ways to interact with objects in Delphi, and in some cases, you can accomplish the same task in different ways. Each class defined by the VCL has some properties you can read or set, some methods you can call, and some events you can handle. An overview of these elements of the VCL classes is presented in the following sections.

Keep in mind that there are basically two ways to create an object in Delphi. You can define a new instance by adding a new component to a form, or you can create an object dynamically. We have already seen an interesting example of the definition of run-time objects in Chapter 5 (the CLASSREF example).

To recap the related information, you simply need to define an object, allocate its instance (calling the Create constructor), and set the Parent property. From this point on, you can act on the object, just as if it were defined at design-time. In any form method, you can create a new button by writing

```
MyButton := TButton.Create (self);
MyButton.Parent := self;
MyButton.Left := 100;
MyButton.Top := 200;
MyButton.Visible := True;
```

Notice that if you add a statement to define the Name property of MyButton, you cannot run this code twice. It will raise an exception, because the value of the Name property, if present, must be unique among all the components of a form. If you really want to add a name, you can use a counter to add a unique number to the name, as I've done in the CLASSREF example (in Chapter 5), and as Delphi's Form Designer does.

There are no limits to the components you can create. Every component you can use at design-time, even forms, can also be created at run-time. Well, there actually are limits, imposed by the computer memory and Windows resources, but they do not depend on Delphi and have been raised in Windows 95.

**NOTE**
Besides being a visual programming environment, Delphi allows a programmer to create the visual components. When you create a component, usually subclassing an existing one, you define its properties, methods, and events. You also need to add some code for the visual editing of your controls, such as property editors, and so on. Creating a component is not as difficult as it might seem at first, but it does require an in-depth understanding of Windows programming. Chapter 27 provides an introduction to component creation.

# Properties

Properties are class attributes that determine the status of an object, such as its position and its appearance, and also its behavior. To know the value of a property at design-time, or to change it, you can use the Object Inspector. At run-time, you can access a property by reading or writing it with some simple code. The Object

Inspector lists only the design-time properties of a component, and the run-time properties are not included. For a complete list of properties, refer to the Delphi Help files.

Usually, you can either set a property, indicating a new value, or read its current value. However, there are read-only properties, and (a few) write-only properties. Both read-only and write-only properties are usually available only at run-time.

When you write the code, you might be lead to think that properties are similar to data fields—this is not true. Every time you read the value of a property or change it, a method might be called, although some properties map directly to data fields, particularly when you read their value. To give you a better understanding, here is the definition of a property (taken from a complete example in Chapter 27):

```
property ArrowHeight: Integer
  read FArrowHeight
  write SetArrowHeight;
```

This code means that to access the value of the property ArrowHeight, the code has to read the value of the private field FArrowHeight, while to change the value it calls the method SetArrowHeight. Different combinations are possible (including also using a method to read the value or directly changing a field in the `write` directive), but the use of a method to change the value of a property is very common.

**WARNING**

It is important to realize that a method might be called when accessing a property, since some of these methods take some time to execute. They also can produce a number of side effects, often including a (slow) repainting of the component on the screen. Although property side effects are seldom documented, you should be aware that they exist, particularly when you are trying to optimize your code.

The `write` directive of a property can also be missing, making it a read-only property. Another distinction is between design-time properties and run-time properties. Design-time properties are declared in a `published` section of the class declaration and will show up in the Object Inspector. Anything that is declared in the `public` section is not available at design-time—it is run-time only. All the read-only properties are defined in the public section, because they cannot be edited in the Object Inspector, either.

To summarize, along with the properties listed in the Object Inspector (design-time), there are other properties (run-time), some of which can only be read (read-only) or can only be written (write-only). The description of each property in the Help file tells which kind of property it is. The Delphi Help system uses some icons to indicate different kinds of properties.

Note that you can usually assign a value to a property or read it, and even use properties in expressions, but you cannot always pass a property as a parameter to a procedure or method. This is because a property is not a memory location, so it cannot be used as a var parameter (or reference parameter).

Not all of the VCL classes have properties. Properties are present in components and in other subclasses of the TPersistent class, because properties usually can be streamed and saved to a file (persistency is covered in Chapter 23).

Although each component has its own set of properties, you might have already noticed that some properties are common to all of them. Table 6.1 lists some of the common properties along with short descriptions.

**TABLE 6.1:** Some Properties Available in Most Components

| Property | Available For | Description |
| --- | --- | --- |
| Align | Some controls | Determines how the control is aligned in its parent control area |
| BoundsRect | All controls | Indicates the bounding rectangle of the control (run-time only) |
| Caption | Most controls | The caption of the control |
| Component-Count | All components | The number of components owned by the current one (run-time only) |
| Component-Index | All components | Indicates the position of the component in the list of components of the owner (run-time only) |
| Components | All components | An array of the components owned by the current one (run-time only) |
| ControlCount | All controls | The number of controls that are the child of the current one (run-time only) |
| Controls | All controls | An array of controls that are the child of the current one (run-time only) |
| Color | Many objects and components | Indicates the color of the surface, of the background, or the current color |
| Ctrl3D | Most components | Determines whether the control has a three-dimensional look |
| Cursor | All controls | The cursor used when the mouse pointer is over the control |
| DragCursor | Most controls | The cursor used to indicate that the control accepts dragging |
| DragMode | Most controls | Determines the drag-and-drop behavior of the control as the starting component for a dragging operation |

**TABLE 6.1:** Some Properties Available in Most Components (continued)

| Property | Available For | Description |
| --- | --- | --- |
| Enabled | All controls and some other components | Determines whether the control is active or is inactive (or grayed) |
| Font | All controls | Determines the font of the text displayed inside the component |
| Handle | All windowed controls | The handle of the window, used by the system (run-time only) |
| Height | All controls and some other components | The vertical size of the control |
| HelpContext | All controls and the dialog box components | A context number used to call context-sensitive help automatically |
| Hint | All controls | The string used to display fly-by hints for the control |
| Left | All controls | The horizontal coordinate of the upper-left corner of the component |
| Name | All components | The unique name of the component, which can be used in the source code |
| Owner | All components | Indicates the owner component (run-time only) |
| Parent | All controls | Indicates the parent control (run-time only) |
| ParentColor | Many objects and components | Determines if the component should use its own Color property or that of the parent component |
| ParentCtl3D | Most components | Determines if the component should use its own Ctrl3D property or that of the parent component |
| ParentFont | All controls | Determines if the component should use its own Font property or that of the parent component |
| Parent-ShowHint | All controls | Determines if the component should use its own ShowHint property or that of the parent control |
| PopupMenu | All controls | Indicates the pop-up menu to use when the user clicks on the control with the left mouse button |
| ShowHint | All controls | Determines if hints are enabled |
| Showing | All controls | Determines if the control is currently showing on the screen (that is, visible) when its parent control is showing (run-time only) |
| TabOrder | All windowed controls (except TForm) | Determines the tab order in the parent control |

**TABLE 6.1:** Some Properties Available in Most Components (continued)

| Property | Available For | Description |
| --- | --- | --- |
| TabStop | All windowed controls (except TForm) | Determines if the user can tab to this control |
| Tag | All components | A long integer available to store custom data |
| Top | All controls | The vertical coordinate of the upper-left corner of the component |
| Visible | All controls and some other components | Determines if the control is visible (*see also* the Showing property) |
| Width | All controls and some other components | The horizontal size of the control |

Since there is inheritance among components, it is interesting to see in which ancestor classes the most common properties are introduced. Study the source code, and see Figure 6.7 for an overview of the properties introduced by the topmost classes of the VCL hierarchy.

We will use most of these properties in examples throughout the book. The following sections provide basic descriptions of the most common properties. I know that this is a slight violation of the rule of the book not to provide reference material directly, but to my defense, I can say that the following descriptions don't mimic the Help reference. They are intended to give you some general guidelines and hints for using the more common properties.

## The Name Property

As I've already mentioned, every component in Delphi can have a name. If you do give a component a name, the name must be unique within the owner component, generally a form. This means that an application can have two different forms that each have a component with the same name.

There are two important elements related to the Name property of the components. First, as I mentioned in Chapter 1, if you set the Name property of a control before changing its Caption property, the new name is copied to the caption. That is, if the name and the caption are identical, then changing the name will also change the caption.

Second, Delphi uses the name of the component to create the default name of the methods related to its events. If you have a Button1 component, its OnClick event is connected to a Button1Click method, unless you specify a different name. If you later change the name of the component, Delphi will modify the names of the related methods accordingly. For example, if you change the name of the button to MyButton, the method automatically becomes MyButtonClick.

**FIGURE 6.7:**

The properties introduced by the topmost classes of the VCL hierarchy, and available in all of the subclasses.

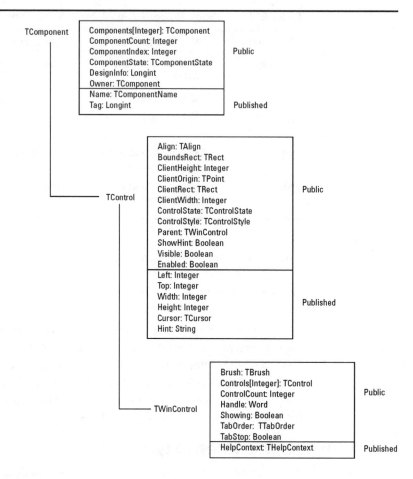

# Properties Related to Component Size and Position

Other important properties, common to most components, are those related to their size and position. The position of a component is determined by its Left and Top properties, and its size (available only for controls) is determined by the Height and Width properties.

An important feature of the position of a component, like any other coordinate in Windows, is that it always relates to the client area of its parent component (which is the component indicated by its Parent property). For a form, the client area is the surface included within its borders (but without the borders themselves). (It would have been messy to work in screen coordinates, although there are some ready-to-use methods that convert the coordinates between the form and the screen and vice versa.)

Note, however, that the same holds true for panels and other *container* components. If you place a panel in a form, and a button in a panel, the coordinates of the button relate to the panel, and not to the form. In fact, in this case, the parent component of the button is the panel.

## The Enabled, Visible, and Showing Properties

There are two basic properties you can use to let the user interact with an existing component. The simplest is the *Enabled* property. When a component is disabled (when Enabled is set to False), there is usually some visual hint to specify this state to the user. At design-time, the disabled property does not always have an effect, but at run-time, disabled components are generally grayed, as you can see in Figure 6.8.

If you want to check to see how the disabled elements behave, you can run a program used to generate the figure. It is named *DISABLED* and is available on the companion CD.

**FIGURE 6.8:**

The user interface of some common controls when they are enabled (on the left) and disabled (on the right).

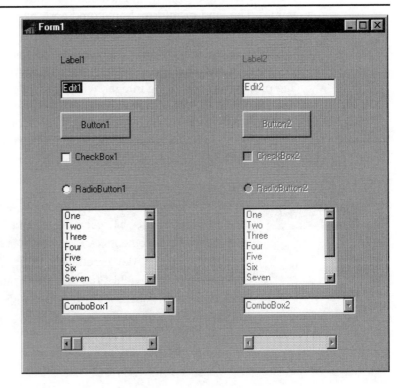

**TIP**

To disable all of the controls in the right column, you can simply select all of them (by pressing Shift while clicking on them with the mouse, or by dragging a rectangle around them) and toggle the Enabled property of all the selected components at the same time.

If you want to take a more radical approach, you can completely hide a component, either by using the corresponding Hide method or by setting its Visible property to False. Notice however, that reading the status of the Visible property does not tell you if the control is actually visible. In fact, if the container of a control is hidden, even if the control is set to Visible, you cannot see it. For this reason, there is another property, Showing, which is a run-time and read-only property. You can read the value of Showing to know if the control is really visible to the user; that is, if it is visible, its parent control is visible, the parent control of the parent control is visible, and so on.

## The Tag Property

The Tag property is a strange one, because it has no effect at all. It is merely an extra memory location, present in each component class, where you can store custom values. The kind of information stored and the way it is used are completely up to you.

It is often useful to have an extra memory location to attach information to a component, without needing to define your component class. Technically speaking, the Tag property stores a long integer, which can be a number by itself or the number of the entry of an array or list corresponding to an object. Using typecasting, in the Tag property, you can store a pointer, an object, or anything else that is four bytes wide. This allows a programmer to associate virtually anything with the component using its tag.

**NOTE**

Experienced Windows programmers might find a relationship between the Tag property of Delphi components and the extra bytes attached to windows. Both elements can be used to associate some user-defined information with a predefined structure, but the similarities end quickly. Using Delphi's Tag property is much easier than using extra bytes, and is also a lot faster than digging up the Windows extra bytes.

# Properties Related to Color and Font

Two properties often used to customize the user interface of a component are Color and Font. There are several properties related to the color. The Color property itself usually refers to the background color of the component. Also, there is the Color attribute of fonts and many other graphic elements.

Many components also have a ParentColor and a ParentFont property, indicating whether the control should use the current font and color of the parent component, usually the form. You can use these properties to change the font of each control of a form by setting only the Font property of the form itself.

Notice that when you set a font, either by entering values for the attributes of the property in the Object Inspector or by using the standard font selection dialog box, you can choose one of the fonts installed in the system. The fact that Delphi allows you to use all the fonts installed on your system has both advantages and drawbacks. The main advantage is that if you have a number of nice fonts installed, your program can use all of them. The drawback is that these fonts might not be available on the computers of the users of your application.

If your program uses a font that your user doesn't have, Windows will select some other font to use in its place. In some cases, they might see just plain fonts when running the program. At times, the program's nice output can be ruined by the font substitution. For this reason, you should probably rely only on Windows' standard fonts (System, Arial, Times New Roman, and so on). The alternative is to ship some fonts with your application.

When you set the value of a color, you have a number of options. The type of this property is TColor. This type allows you to choose a value from a series of predefined constants or to enter a value directly.

You can specify the name of a color, using one of the *clXXX* constants, to try to use the closest matching color in the system palette. These are the possible values:

| | | | |
|---|---|---|---|
| clAqua | clBlack | clBlue | clDkGray |
| clFuchsia | clGray | clGreen | clLime |
| clLtGray | clMaroon | clNavy | clOlive |
| clPurple | clRed | clSilver | clTeal |
| clWhite | clYellow | | |

As an alternative, you can use one of the colors used by Windows for system elements, such as the background of a window, a highlighted menu, the active caption, and so on. You can see a list of these values, along with a short description, in Table 6.2.

**TABLE 6.2:** Colors Used by Windows for System Elements

| Name | Applies To |
| --- | --- |
| cl3DDkShadow | Color used for the 3D dark shadow effect (not available in Delphi 1.0) |
| cl3DLight | Color used for the 3D light effect (not available in Delphi 1.0) |
| clActiveBorder | Border color of the active window |
| clActiveCaption | Color of the title bar of the active window |
| clAppWorkSpace | Color of the application work space |
| clBackground | Color of your Windows background |
| clBtnFace | Color of a button face |
| clBtnHighlight | Color of the highlighting on a button |
| clBtnShadow | Color of a shadow cast by a button |
| clBtnText | Color of the text on a button |
| clCaptionText | Color of the text on the title bar of the active window |
| clGrayText | Color of text that is dimmed |
| clHighlight | Background color of selected text |
| clHightlightText | Color of selected text |
| clInactiveBorder | Border color of inactive windows |
| clInactiveCaption | Color of the title bar of inactive windows |
| clInactiveCaptionText | Color of the text on the title bar of an inactive window |
| clInfoBk | Background color of the hint window (not available in Delphi 1.0) |
| clInfoText | Color of the text of the hint window (not available in Delphi 1.0) |
| clMenu | Background color of menus |
| clMenuText | Color of text on menus |
| clScrollBar | Color of the scroll bars (not available in Delphi 1.0) |
| clWindow | Background color of windows |
| clWindowFrame | Color of window frames |
| clWindowText | Color of text in windows |

Another option is to specify TColor as a number (a four-byte hexadecimal value) instead of using a predefined value. If you use this approach, you should know that the low three bytes of this number represent RGB color intensities for blue, green, and red, respectively. For example, $00FF0000 corresponds to a pure blue color, $0000FF00 to green, $000000FF to red, $00000000 to black, and $00FFFFFF to white. Specifying intermediate values, you can obtain any of the 16 million possible colors.

Instead of using these hexadecimal values directly, I suggest that you use the RGB function, which has three parameters ranging from 0 to 255, the first for the amount of red, the second for the amount of green, and the last for the amount of blue. Using RGB makes the programs slightly more readable than using a single hexadecimal constant.

**NOTE**  RGB is *almost* a Windows API function. It is defined by the Windows related units and not by Delphi units, but a similar function does not exist in the Windows API. In C, there is a macro that has the same name and effect, so this is a welcome addition to the Pascal interface to Windows.

The highest-order byte of the TColor type is used to indicate which palette should be searched for the closest matching color, but this is far too advanced a topic to discuss here. It is also used by sophisticated imaging programs to carry transparency information for each display element on the screen.

Regarding palettes and color matching, just notice that sometimes the color is matched by Windows using the closest available solid color, at least in video modes that use a palette. This is always the case with fonts, lines, and so on. Other times, Windows uses a dithering technique to mimic the requested color by drawing a tight pattern of pixels with the available colors. In 16-color adapters (VGA), but also at higher resolution, you often end up seeing confused patterns of pixels of different colors, and not the color you had in mind.

# Component Methods

Component methods are just like any other methods. There are procedures and functions related to an object you can call to perform the corresponding action. As I already mentioned, you can often use methods to accomplish the same effect as reading or writing a property.

Usually, the code is easier to read and to understand when you use properties. However, not all of the methods actually have corresponding properties. Most of them are procedures, which actually execute an action, instead of reading or writing a value.

Again, there are some methods available in all of the components, other methods that are shared only by controls (visual components), and so on. Table 6.3 lists some common component methods.

**TABLE 6.3:** Some Methods Available for Most Components or Controls

| Method | Available For | Description |
|---|---|---|
| BeginDrag | All controls | Starts manual dragging |
| BringToFront | All controls | Puts the component in front of all others |
| CanFocus | All controls | Determines if the control can receive the focus |
| ClientToScreen | All controls | Translates screen coordinates |
| ContainsControl | All windowed controls | Determines if a certain control is contained by the current one |
| Create | All objects and components | Creates a new instance |
| Destroy | All objects and components | Destroys the instance (if you have used Create to build the object, it is better to use the Free method instead of Destroy) |
| Dragging | All controls | Indicates if the controls are being dragged |
| EndDrag | All controls | Manually terminates dragging |
| FindComponent | All components | Returns the component in the Components array property having a given name |
| Focused | All windowed controls | Determines if the control has the focus |
| Free | All objects and components (not suggested for forms) | Deletes the instance and its associated memory (forms should use the Release method instead) |
| GetTextBuf | All controls | Retrieves the text or caption of the control |
| GetTextLen | All controls | Returns the length of the text or caption of the control |
| HandleAllocated | All controls | Returns True if the handle of the control exists |
| HandleNeeded | All controls | Creates a handle if one doesn't already exist |
| Hide | All controls | Makes the control not visible |
| InsertComponent | All components | Adds a new element to the list of owned components |
| InsertControl | All controls | Adds a new element to the list of controls that are the children of the current one |
| Invalidate | All controls | Forces a repaint of the control |
| Remove-Component | All components | Removes a component from the Components list |
| ScaleBy | All controls | Scales the control by a given percentage |
| ScreenToClient | All controls | Translates screen coordinates |
| ScrollBy | All controls | Scrolls the contents of the control |
| SendToBack | All controls | Puts the component behind all the others |

**TABLE 6.3:** Some Methods Available for Most Components or Controls (continued)

| Method | Available For | Description |
|---|---|---|
| SetBounds | All controls | Changes the position and the size of the control (faster than accessing the related properties one by one) |
| SetFocus | All controls | Gives the input focus to the control |
| SetTextBuf | All controls | Sets the control text or caption |
| Show | All controls | Makes the control visible |
| Update | All controls | Immediately repaints the control, but only if a repaint operation has been requested (that is, after a call to the Invalidate method) |

# Component Events

When a user makes an action on a component, such as clicking on it, the component generates an event. Other times, events are generated by the system, as a response to a method call or a property change on that component (or even on a different one). For example, if you set the focus on a component, the component currently having the focus loses it, triggering the corresponding event.

Technically, Delphi events are triggered when a corresponding Windows message is received, although the events do not match the messages on a one-to-one basis. Delphi events tend to be higher-level than Windows messages, as is the case in the mouse-dragging area (there are no specific mouse-dragging events in Windows).

Just as there is a set of properties common to all components, so there are some events that are available for all components. Table 6.4 provides short descriptions of these events.

**TABLE 6.4:** Some Events Available for Most Components

| Event | Available For | Description |
|---|---|---|
| OnChange | Many objects and components | Occurs when the object (or its content) changes |
| OnClick | Many controls | Occurs when the left mouse button is clicked over the component |
| OnDblClick | Many controls | Occurs when the user double-clicks with the mouse over the component |
| OnDragDrop | Many controls | Occurs when a dragging operation terminates over the component |
| OnDragOver | Many controls | Occurs when the user is dragging over the component |

**TABLE 6.4:** Some Events Available for Most Components (continued)

| Event | Available For | Description |
|---|---|---|
| OnEndDrag | Many controls | Occurs when the dragging terminates; is sent to the component that started the dragging operation |
| OnEnter | All windowed controls | Occurs when the component is activated; that is, the component receives the focus |
| OnExit | All windowed controls | Occurs when the component loses the focus |
| OnKeyDown | Many controls | Occurs when the user presses a key on the keyboard; is sent to the component with the focus |
| OnKeyPress | Many controls | Occurs when the user presses a key; is sent to the component with the focus |
| OnKeyUp | Many controls | Occurs when the user releases a key; is sent to the component with the focus |
| OnMouseDown | Many controls | Occurs when the user presses one of the mouse buttons; is generally sent to the component under the mouse cursor |
| OnMouseMove | Many controls | Occurs when the user moves the mouse over a component |
| OnMouseUp | Many controls | Occurs when the user releases one of the mouse buttons |
| OnStartDrag | Many controls | Occurs when the user starts dragging; is sent to the component originating the dragging operation |

## Delegation Is the Key

From a theoretical point of view, an event is the result of a message sent to a window, and this window (or the corresponding component) is allowed to respond to the message. Following this approach, to handle the click event of a button, we need to subclass the TButton class and add the new event handler.

In practice, creating a new class is too complex to be a reasonable solution. In Delphi, the event handler of a component usually is a method of the form that holds that component, not of the component itself. In other words, the component delegates its owner to handle its events.

## Events Are Properties

Another important concept is that events are properties. This means that you can handle an event of a component, but also assign a method to it (or check the currently assigned method). This is exactly what happens when you handle an event for a component: A new method is added to the owner form, and this method is assigned to the proper event property.

For this reason, it is possible for several events to share the same event handler, but also to change an event handler at run-time, as I mentioned in Chapter 5 (in the section titled "Method Pointers"). To use this feature, you don't need much knowledge of the language. In fact, when you select an event in the Object Inspector, you use the small combo box on the right of the event name to see a list of "compatible" methods—a list of methods having the same method pointer type. Using the Object Inspector, it is easy to select the same method for different components or different events.

**NOTE**  The Object Inspector reads the list of available compatible methods from the source code of your form class definition: If you add a new custom published method (just add it before the `public` keyword) with the same parameters of a valid event handler, it will automatically be listed in the Object Inspector when you select an event with a compatible handler.

# Using Delphi Collections

Among the various objects (that is, the noncomponent classes), an important group is *collections*. There are basically three different collection classes:

- TList defines a list of objects of any class. The list actually stores pointers to the objects. A list is far more flexible than an array, since it can be expanded and reduced at run-time.

- TStrings is an abstract class to represent all forms of string lists, regardless of what their storage implementations are. This class defines a list of strings, without providing proper storage. For this reason, TStrings objects are used only as properties of components capable of storing the strings themselves, such as a list box.

- TStringList defines a list of strings with their own storage. You can use this class to define your own lists of strings in a program.

- TCollection defines a homogenous list of objects, which are owned by the collection class. The objects should be persistent (that is, derived from TPersistent) because the whole collection is streamable (it can be saved to a file). Since the collection class owns the objects, it is responsible for deleting them.

**NOTE**
> TListbox actually uses a TStringList object when it needs to store strings while its window handle is invalid, or a TStrings object when it relates to a Windows list box control, which stores its own strings. Making all string list properties use the same abstract type allows you to copy data between different string lists, copying the actual strings between components and not just assigning string list pointers.

All these lists have a number of methods and properties. You can operate on lists using the array notation [ and ], both to read and to change elements. There are other properties, including a Count property, as well as typical access methods, such as Add, Insert, Delete, Remove, and Search methods (for example, IndexOf, First, and Last).

Notice that TStringList and TStrings objects have both a list of strings and a list of objects associated with the strings. This opens up a number of different uses for these classes. For example, you can use them for dictionaries of associated objects or to store bitmaps or other elements to be used in a list box.

The two classes of lists of strings also have some ready-to-use methods to store or load their contents to or from a text file. To iterate on a list, you can use a simple for loop based on its index, as if it were an array (or, as an alternative, use the List property). Here is how you can operate on each of the objects of type MyClass stored in AList:

```
for Index := 0 to AList.Count - 1 do
  with AList[Index] as MyClass do
  begin
    {operate on the object}
  end;
```

# The VCL Source Code

In this chapter, we have barely scratched the surface of the VCL. To learn more about the library classes—the components—just go on reading the book. Of course, you can also use the Delphi Help system, which includes a complete reference to the properties, events, and methods of every component, together with the description of the most common tasks and operations.

If you really want to delve into the details and study the implementation of the components, there is another path to explore: the VCL source code. This is included in the Developer and Client/Server Suite versions of Delphi, but is also available as a separate purchase for owners of the Delphi Desktop edition.

Delphi comes with the source code of the run-time library (RTL) and the VCL library. Only the source code of a couple of components, TTabSet and TTabbedNotebook, is not present for copyright reasons. These components are available on request to registered owners of the VCL source code package. You can peruse the VCL source code if you want to understand what goes on in detail.

However, do not take this approach to learn how to *use* components. Looking at the source code is useful for learning how to write new components and how to extend existing ones. Before you attempt this, you should be fluent in Delphi programming and in Windows programming, with a complete knowledge of the API of the environment.

If you want to spend some time browsing through Delphi source code, consider using the ObjectBrowser or the Integrated Debugger, instead of loading the files in an editor. To let these tools see the VCL source code, you need to set its path (usually C:\DELPHI\SOURCE\VCL) for the Search Path option in the Directories page of the Project Options. By rebuilding the project, it will be compiled using the source code, which takes some more time.

The advantage is that now you can use the integrated debugger to trace the execution both through your code and the VCL source code. Using the Browser, you can see where in the source code each class is defined and referenced, and open the editor on the proper file (and the right line) with a click of the left mouse button. I will discuss these tools in Chapter 20.

# Summary

As we have seen in this chapter, Delphi includes a full-scale class library that is just as complete as Borland's OWL or Microsoft's MFC C++ class libraries. Delphi VCL, of course, is much more component-oriented, and it encapsulates the behavior of the operating system in a hierarchy of higher-level classes than the C++ libraries do.

As you can tell from the length of this chapter, a great advantage of VCL and of Delphi is that you are not required to know the structure of the hierarchy of classes to use the components. You only need a clear understanding of the leaf nodes of the tree; that is, the components you are going to use. You really don't need a deeper knowledge of the VCL internals to use components; this knowledge is only necessary to write new components or modify existing ones.

Another reason that this chapter is short is that I've discussed components in general, without providing real examples. The following chapters are devoted to exploring most of the Delphi predefined components.

# PART II

## Using Components

# CHAPTER
## SEVEN

# A Tour of the Basic Components

- Clicking a button or another component

- Adding colored text to a form

- Dragging from one component to another

- Accepting input from the user

- Creating a simple editor

- Making a choice with radio buttons and list boxes

- Allowing multiple selections

- Choosing a value in a range

**A**fter an introduction to the use of the environment and an overview of the Object Pascal language and the Visual Component Library, we are ready to delve into the most important part of the book: the use of components. This is really what Delphi is about. Visual programming using components is the key feature of this development environment.

The system comes with a number of ready-to-use components. I will not describe every component in detail, examining each of its properties and methods. If you need this information, you can find it easily in the Help system. The aim of Part II of this book is to show you how to use some of the features offered by the Delphi predefined components to build applications. In fact, this chapter and those following will be based heavily on sample programs. These examples tend to be quite simple— although I've tried to make them meaningful—to focus on only a couple of features at a time. In future chapters, I'll try to show you some more complex examples.

I'll start by focusing on a number of basic components, such as buttons, labels, list boxes edit fields, and other related controls. Some of the components discussed in this chapter are present in the Standard page of the Delphi Components palette; others are in different pages. I'm not going to describe all the components of the Standard page, either. My approach will be to discuss, in each chapter, logically related components, ignoring the order suggested by the pages of the Components palette.

# Windows' Own Components

You might have asked yourself where the idea of using components for Windows programming came from. The answer is simple: Windows itself has some components, usually called controls. A *control* is technically a predefined window with a specific behavior, some properties, and some methods (although every access to the predefined components in Windows is done by sending and receiving messages). These controls were the first step in the direction of components development. The second step was probably Visual Basic controls, and the third step is the Delphi components.

Windows 3.1 has six kinds of predefined controls, generally used inside dialog boxes. They are buttons (push buttons, check boxes, and radio buttons), static labels, edit fields, list boxes, combo boxes, and scroll bars. Windows 95 adds a number of new components, such as the list view, the status bar, the spin button, the progress bar, the tab control, and others.

The standard system controls are the basic components of each Windows application, regardless of the programming language used to write it, and are very well known by every Windows user. Delphi literally wraps these Windows predefined controls in some of its basic components—including those discussed in this chapter.

# Clicking a Button

In the first chapter of this book, we built small applications based on a button. Clicking on that button caused a "Hello" message to appear on the screen. The only other operation that program performed was moving the button so that it always appeared in the middle of the form.

Now we are going to build another form with several buttons and change some of their properties at run-time; clicking a button will usually change a property of another button.

To build the BUTTONS program, I suggest you follow the instructions closely at first and then make any changes you want. Of course, you can read the description in the book and then work on the source files on the companion CD.

## The BUTTONS Example

First, open a new project and give it a name by saving it to disk. I've given the name BUTTON_F.PAS to the unit describing the form and the name BUTTONS.DPR to the project. Now you can create a number of buttons, let's say six.

**TIP**

Instead of selecting the component, dragging it to the form, and then selecting it again and repeating the operation, you can take a shortcut. Simply select the component by clicking on the Components palette while holding down Shift. The component will remain selected, as indicated by a little border around it. Now you can create a number of instances of that component.

Even if you use the grid behind the form, you might need to use the Edit ➤ Align command to arrange the buttons properly. Remember that to select all six buttons at a time, you can either drag a rectangle around them or select them in turn, holding down Shift. In this case, it's probably better to select a column of three buttons at a time and arrange them as shown in Figure 7.1.

Now that we have a form with six buttons, we can start to set their properties. First of all, we can give the form a name (ButtonsForm) and a caption (Buttons). The next step is to set the text, or *captions*, of the buttons. Usually, a button's caption describes the action performed when a user clicks on it. We want to follow this rule, adding the number of the button at the beginning of each caption. So if the first button disables button number four (which is the one on the same row), we can name it *1: Disable 4*. Following the same rule, we can create captions for the other buttons, as you can see in Figure 7.1.

FIGURE 7.1:

The six aligned buttons used to build the example.

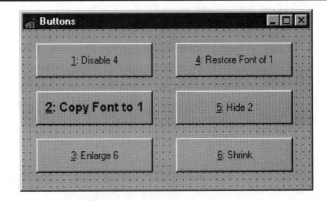

TIP

Notice that every button has an underlined shortcut key, in this case the number of the button. Simply by placing an ampersand (&) character in front of each caption, as in &1: Disable 4, we can create buttons that can be used with the keyboard. Just press a number below 7, and one of the buttons will be selected, although you won't see it pressed and released.

The final step, of course, is to write the code to provide the desired behavior. We want to handle the OnClick property of each button. The easiest code is that of Buttons 2 and 4. Button 2 copies its font (which is different from the standard font of the other buttons) to Button 1, then disables itself:

```
procedure TButtonsForm.Button2Click(Sender: TObject);
begin
  Button1.Font := Button2.Font;
  Button2.Enabled := False;
end;
```

Button 4 restores the original font of the button. Instead of copying the font directly, we can restore the font of the form, using the ParentFont of the button. The event also enables Button 2, so that it can be used again to change the font of Button 1:

```
procedure TButtonsForm.Button4Click(Sender: TObject);
begin
  Button1.ParentFont := True;
  Button2.Enabled := True;
end;
```

To implement the disable and the hide operations of Buttons 1 and 5, we might use a Boolean variable to store the current status. As an alternative, we can decide which operation to perform checking the current status of the button. The two methods use two different approaches, as you can see in the following code:

```
procedure TButtonsForm.Button1Click(Sender: TObject);
begin
  if not Button4.Enabled then
  begin
    Button4.Enabled := True;
    Button1.Caption := '&1: Disable 4';
  end
  else
  begin
    Button4.Enabled := False;
    Button1.Caption := '&1: Enable 4';
  end;
end;
procedure TButtonsForm.Button5Click(Sender: TObject);
begin
  Button2.Visible := not Button2.Visible;
  if Button2.Visible then
    Button5.Caption := '&5: Hide 2'
  else
    Button5.Caption := '&5: Show 2';
end;
```

You can see the results of this code in Figure 7.2.

---

**FIGURE 7.2:**

In the BUTTONS form, you can hide or disable some buttons, or reduce the size of one of them.

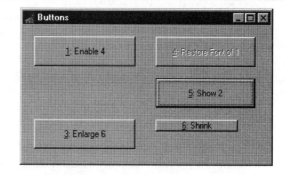

---

The last two buttons have *unconstrained* code. This means that you can shrink Button 6 so much that it will eventually disappear completely:

```
procedure TButtonsForm.Button3Click(Sender: TObject);
begin
  Button6.Height := Button6.Height + 3;
  Button6.Width := Button6.Width + 3;
end;
procedure TButtonsForm.Button6Click(Sender: TObject);
begin
  Button6.Height := Button6.Height - 3;
  Button6.Width := Button6.Width - 3;
end;
```

It would have been quite easy, in any case, to check the current size of the button and prevent its reduction or enlargement by more than a certain value.

# Clicking the Mouse on a Component

Up to now we have based the examples on the OnClick event of buttons. Almost every component has a similar click event. But what exactly is a click? And how is it related to other events, such as OnMouseDown and OnMouseUp?

First, consider the click. At first sight you might think that to generate a click, a user has to press and release the left mouse button on the control. This is certainly true, but the situation is more complex. When the user clicks the left mouse button on a button component, the component is graphically pressed, too. However, if the user moves the cursor (holding down the left mouse button) outside the button surface, this button will be released. If the user now releases the left mouse button outside the button area, no effect—no click—takes place. On the other hand, if the user places the cursor back on the button, it will be *pressed* again, and when the mouse button is released, the click will occur. If this is not clear, experiment with a button; any button in any Windows application will do.

Now to the second question. In Windows, the behavior just described is typical of buttons, although Delphi has extended it to most components, as well as to forms. In any case, the system generates more basic events—one each time a mouse button is pressed, and another each time a button is released. In Delphi, these events are called MouseDown and MouseUp.

Since the mouse has more than one button, these same events are generated when the user presses either the left mouse button or the right mouse button (or even the middle mouse button if your input device has one and the driver you have installed handles it).

Since you might want different actions to occur depending on the mouse button that has been pressed or released, these event handlers include a parameter indicating which button was pressed. These methods also include another parameter, indicating whether some special key (such as Shift or Ctrl) has been pressed and, finally, two more values indicating the $x$ and $y$ positions where the action took place. This is the method corresponding to this event for a form:

```
procedure TForm1.FormMouseDown(
  Sender: TObject;
  Button: TMouseButton;
  Shift: TShiftState;
  X, Y: Integer);
```

Most of the time, we do not need such a detailed view, and handling the mouse-click event is probably more appropriate. In Chapter 9, I'll show you a more detailed example of mouse input.

# Adding Colored Text to a Form

Now that you have played with buttons for a while, it's time to move to a new component, labels. Labels are just text, or comments, written in a form. Usually, the user doesn't interact with a label at all—or at least not directly. It doesn't make much sense to click on a label.

We use labels to provide descriptions of other components, particularly edit fields and list or combo boxes, because they have no titles. If you open a dialog box in any Windows application, you'll probably see some text. These are *static controls* (in Windows terms) or *labels* (in Delphi terms).

**NOTE** Windows implements labels as windows of the static class. Delphi, instead, implements labels as non-windowed, graphical components. This is very important since it allows you to speed up form creation and save some Windows resources.

Besides using labels for descriptions, we can use instances of this component to improve and add some color to the user interface of our application. This is what we are going to do in the next example, LABEL_CO. The basic idea of this application is to test a couple of properties of the label component at run-time. Specifically, we want to alter the color of the label, the color of its font, and the alignment of the text.

## The LABEL_CO Example

The first thing to do is to place a big label in the form and enter some text. Write something long. I suggest you set the WordWrap property to True, to have several lines of text, and the AutoSize property to False, to allow the label to be resized freely. It might also be a good idea to select a large font, to choose a color for the font, and to select a color for the label itself.

To change some of the properties of the label at run-time, we can use some buttons. We need a couple to change the colors and three more to select the alignment—left, center, or right. The resulting form is shown in Figure 7.3.

Now it's time to write some code. The click methods for the three alignment buttons are very simple. The program has to change the alignment of the label, as in

```
Label1.Alignment := taLeftJustify;
```

**219**

The form of the colored label example.

The other two methods should use the values `taCenter` and `taRightJustify` instead of `taLeftJustify`. You can find the names of these three choices in the Alignment property of the label, in the Object Inspector.

Writing some code to change the color is a little more complex. In fact, we can provide a new value for the color, maybe choosing it from a list with a series of possible values. We might solve this problem, for example, by declaring an array of colors, entering a number of values, and then selecting a different element of the array each time. However, I'll apply a different and more professional solution, which needs even less code: using the Windows standard dialog box to select a color.

## The Standard Color Dialog Box

To use the standard Color dialog box, move to the Dialogs page of the Delphi Components palette. Select the ColorDialog component and place it anywhere on the form. The position has no effect since at run-time this component is not visible inside the form. (There is a more detailed presentation of these standard dialog boxes in Chapter 12, although I'll use them often before.)

Now we can use the component, writing the following code:

```
ColorDialog1.Color := Label1.Color;
ColorDialog1.Execute;
Label1.Color := ColorDialog1.Color;
```

The three lines have the following meanings: with the first, we select the color of the label as the current color displayed by the dialog box; with the second, we run the dialog box; with the third, the color selected by the user in the dialog box is copied back to the label. You can see the dialog box in action in Figure 7.4. This dialog box can also be expanded by clicking on the Define Custom Colors button.

To change the color of the label's text, we have to write a similar piece of code, referring this time to the `Label1.Font.Color` property.

**FIGURE 7.4:**
The dialog box used to select the color of the label and its text (in this case, the user is changing the color of the text).

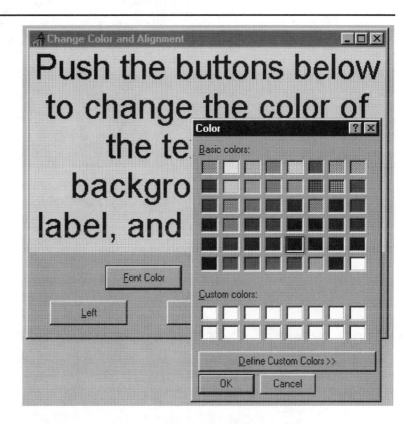

# Dragging from One Component to Another

Before I introduce you to another component, I would like to devote a section to a particular technique: *dragging*. The dragging operation is quite simple and is increasingly common in Windows. In Delphi, you usually perform this operation by pressing the mouse button on one component and releasing it on another component. When this operation occurs, you can provide some code, usually for copying a property, a value, or something else to the destination component.

As an example, consider the form in Figure 7.5. There are four color labels, with the name of each color as text, and a destination label, with some descriptive text. The

FIGURE 7.5:

The form of the DRAGGING
example.

aim of this example, named DRAGGING, is to be able to drag the color from one of the labels on the left to the big one, changing its color accordingly.

After preparing the labels by supplying the proper values for the names and caption, as well as a corresponding color, you have to enable dragging. You can do this by selecting the value dmAutomatic for the DragMode property of the four labels on the left and responding to a couple of events in the destination label.

> **NOTE**
>
> As an alternative to automatic dragging, you might choose a manual dragging approach, based on the use of the BeginDrag and EndDrag methods. This technique will be shown in the NODES example in Chapter 10. Other examples in the book will show you how to handle dragging manually, simply by providing a handler for events related to moving the mouse and pressing and releasing mouse buttons.

## The Code for the DRAGGING Example

The first event I want to consider is OnDragOver, which is called each time you are dragging and move the cursor over a component. This event indicates that the component accepts dragging. Usually, the event takes place after a determination of whether the Source component (the one that originated the dragging operation) is of a specific type:

```
procedure TDraggingForm.Label5DragOver(
  Sender, Source: TObject;
```

```
  X, Y: Integer; State: TDragState;
  var Accept: Boolean);
begin
  Accept := Source is TLabel;
end;
```

This code accepts the dragging operation, activating the corresponding cursor only if the source object is really a label object. Notice the use of the is RTTI operator.

The second method we have to write corresponds to the OnDragDrop event:

```
procedure TDraggingForm.Label5DragDrop(
  Sender, Source: TObject;  X, Y: Integer);
begin
  Label7.Color := (Source as TLabel).Color;
end;
```

To read the value of the Color property from the Source object, we need to cast this object to the proper data type, in this case TLabel. We have to perform a type conversion—technically speaking, a type downcast (a typecast from a base class to a derived class, down through the hierarchy). A type downcast is not always type safe. In fact, the idea behind this cast is that we receive the parameter Source of type TObject, which is really a label, and want to use it as a TLabel object, where TLabel is a class derived by TObject. However, in general, we face the risk of downcasting to TLabel an object that wasn't originally a label but, say, a button. When we start using the button as a label, we might have run-time errors.

In any case, using the as typecast, a type check is performed. Had the type of the Source object not been TLabel, an exception would have been raised. In this particular case, however, we haven't much to worry about. In fact, the OnDragDrop event is received only when the Accept parameter of the OnDragOver method is set to True, and we make this only if the Source object really is a TLabel.

# Accepting Input from the User

We have seen a number of ways a user can interact with the application we write using a mouse: mouse clicks, mouse dragging, and so on. However, what about the keyboard? We know that the user can use the keyboard instead of the mouse to select a button by pressing the key corresponding to the underlined letter of the caption (if any).

Aside from some particular cases, Windows can handle keyboard input directly. Defining handlers for keyboard-related events isn't a common operation, anyway. In fact, the system provides a ready-to-use control to build edit fields. Delphi has a slightly different approach, with two components, Edit and Memo.

An Edit component allows a single line of text and has some specific properties, such as one that allows only a limited number of characters or one that shows asterisks instead of the actual characters of the text (a useful technique for entering a password). A Memo component, as we will see later, can host several lines of text.

Our first example of the Edit component, named FOCUS, will stress a feature common to many controls, the focus. In Windows, it's fairly simple to determine which is the active main window: it is in front of the other windows, and the title bar is a different color (blue, by default). It is not as easy to determine which window (or component) has the *input* focus. If the user presses a key, which component is going to receive the corresponding input message? It can be the active window, but it can also be one of its controls or subwindows. Consider a form with several edit fields. Only one has the focus at a given time. You can move the focus by using Tab or by clicking with the mouse on another component.

## Handling the Input Focus

What's important for our example is that each time a component receives or loses the focus, it receives a corresponding event indicating that the user either has reached (OnEnter) or has left (OnExit) the component. So we can add some methods to the form to take control over the focus and display this information in a label or a status bar. The form has also some labels indicating the meaning of the three edit fields (First name, Last name, and Password). You can see the form used for this example in Figure 7.6. I've used a Windows 95 component, the status bar, but using a label or a panel would have had a similar effect. In fact, you can use the TStatusBar component as a single line output tool, by setting its SimplePanel property to True.

**FIGURE 7.6:**
The form of the FOCUS example.

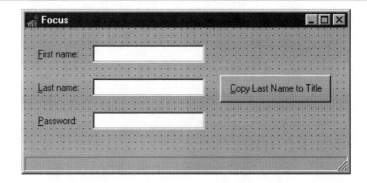

The form contains some edit boxes, as well as a button we can use to copy the text of the LastNameEdit to the form's caption. This is just a sample of how to use the text that has been entered. As you can see in the following code, it's a good idea to test whether some text has really been entered by the user or if the edit field is still empty:

```
procedure TFocusForm.CopyButtonClick(Sender: TObject);
begin
  if (LastNameEdit.Text <> '') then
    FocusForm.Caption := LastNameEdit.Text;
end;
```

Now to the most interesting part of the program. We can write a comment in the status bar each time the focus is moved to a different control, as in Figure 7.7. To accomplish this, we need four methods, one for each of the Edit components and one for the button referring to the OnEnter event. Here is the code of one of the methods (the other three event handlers are very similar):

```
procedure TFocusForm.FirstNameEditEnter(Sender: TObject);
begin
  StatusBar1.SimpleText := 'Entering the first name...';
end;
```

**FIGURE 7.7:**

One of the messages shown in the status bar when the FOCUS program is running. Notice the form's new caption.

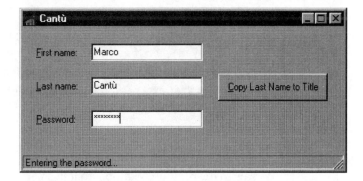

You can test this program with the mouse or use the keyboard. If you press Tab, the input focus cycles among the Edit components and the button, without involving the labels. To have a proper sequence, you can change the TabOrder property of the windowed component.

You can change this order either by entering a proper value for this property in the Object Inspector or (much better and easier) by using the Edit Tab Order dialog box, which can be called using the Tab Order command on the form's SpeedMenu. If you open this dialog box for the FOCUS example, you can see the output shown in Figure 7.8. Notice that the status bar is listed but you cannot actually move onto it using Tab.

A second way to select a component is to use a shortcut key. It is easy to place a shortcut key on the button, but how can you jump directly to an edit? It isn't

possible, but there is an indirect way. You can add the shortcut key—the ampersand (&)—to the label before the Edit component, then set the FocusControl property of the label, selecting the corresponding Edit component.

> **TIP**
>
> In Windows 95, the edit controls automatically have a local menu displayed when the user presses the right mouse button over them. Although you can easily customize such a menu in Delphi (as we will see in the next chapter) it is important to realize this is standard behavior of Windows 95.

## Entering Numbers

We saw in the previous example that it is very easy to use an Edit component to ask the user to input some text, although it must be limited to a single line. In general, it's quite common to ask the user to input a number, too. To accomplish this, you can use the MaskEdit component (in the Additional page of the Components palette) or simply use an Edit component and then convert the input string into an integer, using the standard Pascal Val procedure or the IntToStr function.

This sounds good, but what if the user types a letter when a number is expected? Of course, these conversion functions return an error code, so we can use it to test whether the user has really entered a number. The second question is, when can we perform this test? Maybe when the value of the edit box changes, when the component loses the focus, or when the user clicks a particular button, such as the OK button in a dialog box. As you'll see, not all of these techniques work well.

There is another, radically different, solution to the problem of having only numerical input in an edit box. You can look at the input stream to the edit box and stop any non-numerical input. This technique is not foolproof (a user can always paste some text into an edit box), but it works quite well and is easy to implement. Of course, you can improve it by combining it with one of the other techniques.

The next example, NUMBERS, shows just some of these techniques so you can compare them easily. Before you start working on it, however, remember that this is not the best way to handle numerical input; Delphi provides the MaskEdit component, as mentioned earlier. We will see an example of the use of this component in the following section.

First of all, build a form with five edit fields and five corresponding labels, describing when the corresponding Edit component checks the input. The form also has a button to check the contents of the first edit field.

Since the elements of this form have no particular properties, let's look directly to the code. The contents of the first edit box are checked when the button on the right is pressed. First of all, the text is converted into a number, using the Val procedure, which eventually returns an error code. Depending on the value of the code, a message is shown to the user:

```
procedure TNumbersForm.CheckButtonClick(Sender: TObject);
var
  Number, Code: Integer;
begin
  if Edit1.Text <> '' then
  begin
    val (Edit1.Text, Number, Code);
    if Code <> 0 then
    begin
      Edit1.SetFocus;
      MessageDlg ('Not a number in the first edit',
        mtError, [mbOK], 0);
    end
    else
      MessageDlg ('OK, in the first edit there is a number',
        mtInformation, [mbOK], 0);
  end;
end;
```

If an error occurs, the application moves the focus back to the edit field before showing the error message to the user, thus inviting the user to correct the value. Of course, in this case a user can ignore this suggestion and move to another edit field.

**WARNING** In the new version of Delphi, this code produces a warning message (a hint) when compiled, because the Number variable is not used after a value has been assigned to it.

The same kind of check is made on the second edit field when it loses the focus. In this case, the message is displayed automatically, but only if an error occurs (see Figure 7.9). Why bother the user if everything is fine?

The code is somewhat different from that of the first edit field; it makes no reference to the Edit2 component but always refers to the generic Sender control, making a safe typecast. To indicate the number of each button, I've used the Tag property, entering the number of the edit control. This code is a little more complex to write, but we will be able to use it again for a different component. Here is its code:

```
procedure TNumbersForm.Edit2Exit(Sender: TObject);
var
  Number, Code: Integer;
begin
  if (Sender as TEdit).Text <> '' then
  begin
    val ((Sender as TEdit).Text, Number, Code);
    if Code <> 0 then
    begin
      (Sender as TEdit).SetFocus;
      MessageDlg ('The edit field number ' +
        IntToStr ((Sender as TEdit).Tag) +
        ' does not have a valid number',
        mtError, [mbOK], 0);
    end
  end;
end;
```

**FIGURE 7.9:**

The error displayed when the second edit loses the focus and the user has entered letters.

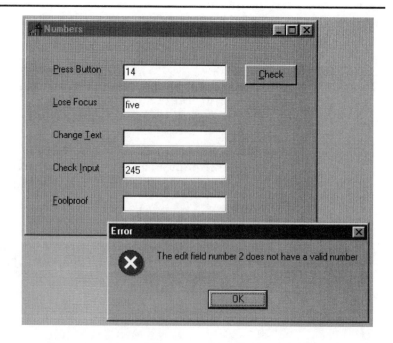

The third Edit component makes a similar test each time its content changes (using the OnChange event). Although we have checked the input on different occasions—using different events—the three functions are very similar to each other. The idea is to check the string once the user has entered it. For the fourth Edit component, instead, I want to show you a completely different technique. We are going to make a check *before* the Edit even knows that a key has been pressed.

The Edit component has an event, OnKeyPress, that corresponds to the action of the user. We can provide a method for this event and test whether the character is a number or the Backspace key (which has a numerical value of 8). If not, we change the value of the key to Null so it won't be processed by the edit control and produce a little warning sound using the MessageBeep function of the Windows API:

```
procedure TNumbersForm.Edit4KeyPress(Sender: TObject; var Key:
Char);
begin
  if not (key in ['0'..'9', #8]) then
  begin
    Key := #0;
    MessageBeep ($FFFFFFFF);
  end;
end;
```

**TIP**
> The MessageBeep function has a parameter indicating the sound you want your computer to produce. Using $FFFFFFFF or the equivalent expression Cardinal (-1), the computer produces a short beep; it doesn't use the sound card even if one is present. There are other parameters you can use, as I'll show you in Chapter 26.

The fourth Edit component accepts only numbers for input, but it is not foolproof. A user can copy some text to the Clipboard and paste it into this Edit control with the Shift+Ins key combination (but not using Ctrl+V), avoiding any check. To solve this problem, we might think of adding a check on the change of the contents, as in the third edit field, or a check on the contents when the user leaves the edit field, as in the second component. This is the reason for the fifth, Foolproof edit field: it uses the OnKeyPress event of the fourth edit field, the OnChange method of the third, and the OnExit event of the second, thus requiring no new code.

To reuse an existing method for a new event, just select the Events page of the Object Inspector, move to the component, and instead of double-clicking to the left of the event name, select the button in the combo box at the right. A list of names of old methods compatible with the current event—having the same number of parameters—will be displayed, as you can see in Figure 7.10.

**FIGURE 7.10:**

The Edit5 component uses methods already written for other components. All compatible methods are displayed when you select the small combo box button of the Object Inspector.

If you select the proper methods, the fifth component will combine the features of the third and the fourth. This is possible because I took care in writing these methods, avoiding any reference to the control to which they were related.

The technique I used was to refer to the generic Sender parameter and cast it to the proper data type, which in this case was TButton. As long as you connect a method of this kind to a component of the same kind, no problem should arise. Otherwise, you should make a number of type checks (using the is operator), which will probably make the code more complex to read. My suggestion is to share code only between controls of the same kind.

Notice also that to tell the user which edit box has incorrect text, I've added to each Edit component a value for the Tag property, as I mentioned before. Every edit box has a tag with its number, from 1 to 5.

# Sophisticated Input Schemes

In the last example, we saw how an Edit component can be customized for special input purposes. The components could really accept only numbers, but handling complex input schemes with a similar approach is not straightforward. For this reason, Borland has supplied a ready to use *masked edit component*, an edit component with an input mask stored in a string.

For example, to handle numbers of no more than five digits, we can set the Edit-Mask property to *99999* (9 stands for *non-compulsory digit*). You can refer to Delphi documentation for the meaning of the various characters and symbols in the edit mask. I suggest that you don't enter a string directly in this property, but instead always open the associated editor, which has a test window and includes sample masks for commonly used input values (see Figure 7.11).

**FIGURE 7.11:**

The editor of the EditMask property of the MaskEdit component.

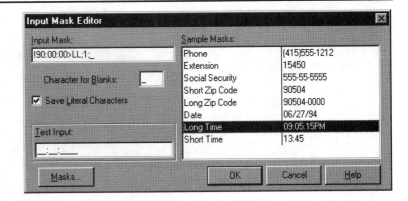

Notice that the Input Mask editor allows you to enter a mask, but it also asks you to indicate a character to be used as a place-holder for the input and to decide whether to save the literals present in the mask, together with the final string. For example, you can choose to have the parentheses around the area code of a phone number only as an input hint or to save them with the string holding the resulting number. These two entries in the Input Mask editor correspond to the last portion of the mask, made of two more fields (separated, by default, with semicolons).

For more default input masks, you can press the Masks button, which allows you to open a mask file. The predefined files hold standard codes grouped by country. For example, if you open the Italian group, you can find the taxpayer number (or *fiscal code*, which is used like social security numbers in the U.S.). This code is a complex mix of letters and numbers (including the consonants representing  name, birth date, area code, and more), as its mask demonstrates: *LLLLLL00L00L000L*. In this kind of code, *L* stands for a letter and *0* for a number. While you can look these up in the Help file, there is a summary of these codes in the following MASK1 example (in Figure 7.12).

The form of this example includes a MaskEdit and an Edit component. The edit is used to change the EditMask property of the first one at run-time. To accomplish this, I've just written a couple of lines of code to copy the text of the property into the edit box at the beginning (OnCreate event) and make the reverse action each time the plain edit box changes (Edit1Change):

```
procedure TForm1.FormCreate(Sender: TObject);
begin
  Edit1.Text := MaskEdit1.EditMask;
end;
```

```
procedure TForm1.Edit1Change(Sender: TObject);
begin
  MaskEdit1.EditMask := Edit1.Text;
end;
```

**FIGURE 7.12:**

An example of the output of the MASK1 program.

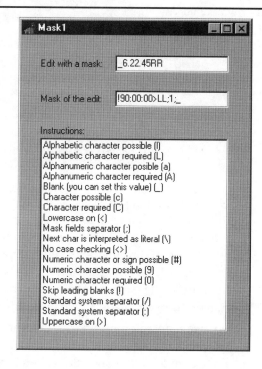

As you can see in Figure 7.12 (above), the form also has a list box with the description of the most important codes used to build the mask.

# Creating a Simple Editor

Edit components can handle a limited amount of text, and only on a single line. If you need something similar to an Edit field but more powerful, you should use the Memo component. A Memo component is like an Edit component, but it can span several lines, contain scroll bars to move though the text, and contain more text. (The idea for the Memo and its name probably come from the database world, in which a table, instead of storing some text, can refer to an external text file, usually called a memo.)

The easiest thing we can use a Memo for is as an Editor, and this is what I'm going to show you in the next example, NOTES. The idea is to implement an Editor covering all of the window (or form) containing it, to resemble Windows' own Notepad. The only other option we will implement is to give the user the option of choosing the font for the editor.

Both parts are very easy to implement. Create a new project and place in it a Memo component (from the Standard page of the Components palette). Delete its text, remove the border, and set the Alignment property to alClient, so that it will always cover the whole client area—the internal surface—of the form. Also add both scroll bars, horizontal and vertical, selecting the value ssBoth for the memo's ScrollBars property.

## The Font Dialog Box

The second portion of the program involves the font. In the same way we used the standard Color dialog box in a previous example, we can use the standard Font selection dialog box provided by Windows. Just move to the Dialogs page of the Components palette and select the FontDialog component. Place it anywhere on the form, and add the following code when the user double-clicks inside the Memo:

```
procedure TNotesForm.Memo1DblClick(Sender: TObject);
begin
  FontDialog1.Font := Memo1.Font;
  FontDialog1.Execute;
  Memo1.Font := FontDialog1.Font;
end;
```

This code copies the current font to the corresponding Dialog property so it will be selected by default. Then it executes the dialog box (see Figure 7.13). At the end, the Font property will contain the font the user selected, which the third line of the above code copies back to the Memo, activating it.

This program is more powerful than it appears at first glance. For example, it allows copy and paste operations using the keyboard—this means you can copy text from your favorite word processor—and can handle the color of the font. Why not use it to place a big and colorful message on your screen?

## Creating a Rich Editor

Although you can choose a font in the NOTES program, all of the text you have written will have the same font. Windows 95 has a new control that can handle the Rich Text Format (RTF). A new Delphi component, RichEdit, encapsulates the behavior of this standard control.

You can find an example of an editor based on the RichEdit component among the examples that ship with Delphi 2. (It is named RICHEDIT). Here, we'll only change the previous program slightly by replacing the memo with a rich edit, and allow a user to change the font of the selected portion of the text, not the whole text.

The Font dialog box for the NOTES program.

The RICHNOTE example has a RichEdit component filling its client area, too. However, the component has no double-click event, so I added a button to select the font and placed it into a panel aligned to the top of the form, making a simple toolbar. Here is the textual description of some of the properties of the three components:

```
object RichEdit1: TRichEdit
  Align = alClient
  HideScrollBars = False
  ScrollBars = ssBoth
end
object Panel1: TPanel
  Align = alTop
  object Button1: TButton
    Caption = '&Font...'
  end
end
```

Notice the caption of the button, which has an ampersand and an ellipsis at the end to indicate that pressing it will open a dialog box. When the user clicks on the button, if some text is selected, the program shows the standard Font dialog box using the default font of the RichEdit component as the initial value. At the end, the selected font is copied to the attributes of the current selection. The DefAttributes and SelAttributes properties of the RichEdit component are not of the TFont type, but they are compatible, so we can use the Assign method to copy the value:

```
procedure TForm1.Button1Click(Sender: TObject);
begin
  if RichEdit1.SelLength > 0 then
  begin
    FontDialog1.Font.Assign(RichEdit1.DefAttributes);
    if FontDialog1.Execute then
      RichEdit1.SelAttributes.Assign(FontDialog1.Font);
  end
  else
    ShowMessage ('No text selected');
end;
```

The RichEdit component has other attributes related to fonts and paragraph formatting. We will use this component in further examples of the book; however, the simple code above is enough to let users produce much more complex output than the memo component allows. You can see a funny example in Figure 7.14.

**FIGURE 7.14:**

An example of the font effects you can have using the RICHNOTE program.

# Selecting a Choice

There are two standard Windows controls that allow the user to choose different options. The first is the check box. A *check box* corresponds to an option that can be selected freely, although at times a check box can be disabled. The second control is the radio button. A *radio button* corresponds to an exclusive selection. For example, if you see two radio buttons with the labels *A* and *B*, you can select A or select B, but not both of them at the same time. The other characteristic of a multiple choice is that you *must* choose one of the selections.

If the difference between check boxes and radio buttons is still not clear, an example might help you. In Figure 7.15, you see the output of the CHOICE example. There are three check boxes to select the style Bold, Italic, or Underlined, and three radio buttons to choose a font (Times New Roman, Arial, or Courier). There is also a memo field with some text to show the effect of the user selections immediately.

**FIGURE 7.15:**
The output of the CHOICE example.

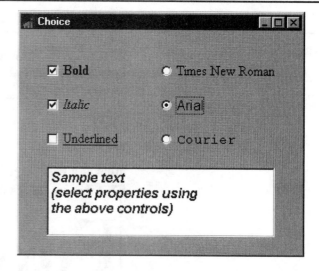

The difference between the use of the check boxes and the radio buttons should be obvious. The text might be bold and italic at the same time, but it cannot be Arial and Courier at once. A user must choose only one font (and cannot choose none) but can select each of the styles independently from the other two (including no style at all).

This program requires some simple code. In short, each time the user clicks on a check box or radio button, we have to create a corresponding action. For the text styles, we have to look at the Check property of the control and add or remove the corresponding element from the memo's Font property Style set:

```
procedure TForm1.CheckBoldClick(Sender: TObject);
begin
  if CheckBold.Checked then
    Memo1.Font.Style := Memo1.Font.Style + [fsBold]
  else
    Memo1.Font.Style := Memo1.Font.Style - [fsBold];
end;
```

The other two check boxes have similar code for their OnClick events. The basic code for the radio buttons is even simpler since you cannot deselect a radio button by clicking on it:

```
procedure TForm1.RadioTimesClick(Sender: TObject);
begin
  Memo1.Font.Name := 'Times New Roman';
end;
```

# Grouping Radio Buttons

Radio buttons represent exclusive choices. However, a form might contain several groups of radio buttons. Windows cannot determine by itself how the various radio buttons relate to each other. The solution, both in Windows and in Delphi, is to place the related radio buttons inside a container component. The standard Windows user interface uses a group box control to hold the radio buttons together, both functionally and visually. In Delphi, this control is implemented in the Group-Box component. However, Delphi has a second, similar component that can be used specifically for radio buttons: the *RadioGroup* component. A RadioGroup is a group box with some radio button clones painted inside it.

Using the radio group is probably easier than using the group box, but I'll use the more traditional approach to show you the code you can write to work with controls that have been placed inside another control. The fact that you have some controls inside another control is also a good reason *not* to follow this approach in real programs, because you end up with more windows on the screen (wasting some system resources) and with slightly slower code. Beside this, the RadioGroup component can automatically align its radio buttons, and you can easily add new choices at run-time. You can see the differences between the two approaches in the next example.

The rules for building a group box with radio buttons are very simple. Place the GroupBox component in the form, then place the radio buttons in the group box. The GroupBox component contains other controls and is one of the container components used most often, together with the Panel component. If you disable or hide the group box, all the controls inside it will be disabled or hidden.

You can continue handling the individual radio buttons, but you might as well navigate through the array of controls owned by the group box. The name of this property is Controls. Another property, ControlCount, holds the number of elements. These two properties can be accessed only at run-time.

> **NOTE**
>
> In Delphi, there are some components that are also component containers: the GroupBox, the Panel, the Windows 95 Page control, the Notebook, the TabbedNotebook and, of course, the TForm component. When you use these controls, you can add other components inside them. In this case, the container is the parent of the components (as indicated by the Parent property), while the form is their owner (as indicated by the Owner property). You can use the Controls property of a form or group box to navigate the child controls, and you can use the Components property of the form to navigate all the owned components, regardless of their parent. We already saw an example of a container component, when we placed a button in a panel to build the RICHNOTE example.

## The PHRASES Example

I spent some time figuring out an example for this section; then I had an idea. If you've ever tried to learn a foreign language, there is some chance you spent some time repeating the same silly and useless phrases over and over. Probably the most typical, when you learn English, is the infamous *The book is on the table*. The aim of this example is to create a tool to build such phrases by choosing among different available options. A look at the form in Figure 7.16 will probably make the idea clearer.

**FIGURE 7.16:**
The form of the PHRASES1 example.

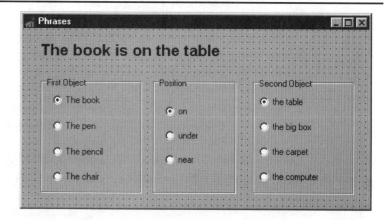

The form for this example, named PHRASES1, is quite complex. If you rebuild it, remember that you must place the GroupBox components first and the radio buttons later. After doing this, you have to enter a proper caption for each element, as you can see in Figure 7.16 (above). Although you cannot really see it from the output, the last selection is based on a radio group component, instead of a group box holding some radio buttons. In this case you create the option by entering a list of values in the Items property (a TStringList). Remember that you also need to add a label, select a large font for it, and enter text corresponding to the radio buttons that are checked at design-time. This is an important point: When you place some radio buttons in a form (or in a group box), remember to check one of the elements at design-time. One radio button in each group should always be checked, and the ItemIndex property of the radio group (indicating the current selection) should have a proper value.

Now we have to write some code so that when the user clicks on the radio buttons, the phrase changes accordingly. There are different alternatives. One is to follow the same approach as in the last example, providing a method for each button's On-Click event. Then we need to store the various portions of the phrase in some of the form's variables, change the portion corresponding to that button, and rebuild the whole phrase.

An alternative solution is to write a single method that looks at which buttons are currently checked and builds the corresponding phrase. This single method must be connected to the OnClick event of every radio button and of the RadioGroup component. This is simple to accomplish. Select each of the radio buttons on the form (clicking on each one while you hold down Shift) and enter the name of the method in the Object Inspector. Since the method used to compute the new phrase doesn't refer to a specific control, you might name it yourself, simply entering a name in the second column of the Object Inspector next to the OnClick event. Here is the code of this single complex method:

```
procedure TForm1.ChangeText(Sender: TObject);
var
  Phrase: string;
  I: integer;
begin
  {look which radio button is selected and
  add its text to the phrase}
  for I:=0 to GroupBox1.ControlCount - 1 do
    if (GroupBox1.Controls[I] as TRadioButton).Checked then
      Phrase := (GroupBox1.Controls[I] as TRadioButton).Caption;
  {add the verb and blank spaces}
  Phrase := Phrase + ' is ';
  {repeat the operation on the second group box}
  for I:=0 to GroupBox2.ControlCount - 1 do
    with GroupBox2.Controls[I] as TRadioButton do
      if Checked then
```

```
      Phrase := Phrase + Caption;
  {retrieve the radiogroup selection, and
  display the result in the label}
  Label1.Caption := Phrase + ' ' +
    RadioGroup1.Items [RadioGroup1.ItemIndex];
end;
```

The ChangeText method starts looking at which of the first group of radio buttons is selected, then moves on to adding a verb and the proper spaces between words. To determine which control in a group box is checked, the procedure scans these controls in a `for` loop. The `for` loop ranges from 0 to the number of controls minus 1, because the Controls array is zero-based, and tests whether the Checked property of the radio button is True. A cast is required to perform this operation—we cannot use the Checked property on a generic control. When the checked radio button has been found, the program simply copies its caption to the string. At this point, the `for` loop might terminate, but since only one radio button is checked at a time, it is safe to let it reach its natural end—testing all the elements. The same operation is repeated two times, but you can see that the second time a `with` statement is used to make the code shorter and simpler.

As you can see from the final portion of the method above, if you are using the RadioGroup component, the code is much simpler. This control, in fact, has an ItemIndex property indicating which radio button is selected and an Items property with a list of the text of the fake radio buttons. Overall, using a radio group is very similar to using a list box (as we will see in the next example), aside from the obvious differences in the user interface of the two components.

# A List with Many Choices

If you want to add many selections, radio buttons are not appropriate, unless you create a really big form. The usual number of radio buttons is in the range between 2 and 5 or 6. Another problem is that although you can disable a radio button, the elements of a group are usually fixed. Only when using a radio group can you have some flexibility.

When these problems occur, there is a solution: use a list box. A *list box* can host a large number of choices in a small space, because it can contain a scroll bar to show on screen only a limited portion of the whole list. Another advantage of a list box is that you can easily add new items to it or remove some of the current items. List boxes are extremely flexible and powerful.

Another important feature is that by using the ListBox component, you can choose between a single selection—a behavior similar to a group of radio buttons—and a multiple selection—similar to a group of check boxes. The next version of this example will have a multiple-selection list box.

For the moment, though, let's focus on a single-selection list box. We might use a couple of these components to change the PHRASE1 example slightly. Instead of having a number of radio buttons to select the first and second objects of the phrase, we can use two list boxes. Besides allowing us to have a larger number of items, the advantage is that we can allow the user to insert new objects in the list and prevent selection of the same object twice, to avoid a phrase such as *The book is on the book.* As you might imagine, this example is really much more complicated than the previous one and will require some fairly complex code.

## The Form for PHRASES2

As usual, the first step is to build a form (see Figure 7.17). You can start with the form from the last example and remove the two group boxes on the sides and replace them with two list boxes. The radio buttons inside the group boxes will be deleted automatically. I've also replaced the central group box with a radio group. Actually, there's not much left from the previous example!

Now, add some strings to the Items property of both list boxes. For the example to work properly, the two list boxes should have the same strings; you can copy and paste them from the editor of the Items property of one list box to the editor of the same property of the other component.

To improve the usability of the program, you might sort the strings in the list boxes, setting their Sorted property to True. Remember also to add a couple of labels above the list boxes, to describe their contents.

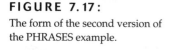

**FIGURE 7.17:**
The form of the second version of the PHRASES example.

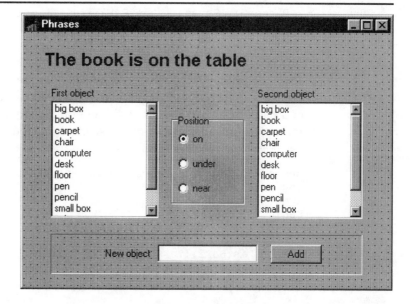

In the lower part of the form (see Figure 7.17 again), I've also added an edit field, with its label, and a button, and a bevel around them to group them visually (the bevel is just a graphical component, not a container). As we will see later, when a user presses the button, the text in the Edit control is added to both list boxes. This operation will take place only if the text of the edit box is not empty and the string is not already present in the list boxes.

## Working with the List Boxes

Once you have built this or a similar form, you can start writing some code. The first thing to do is to provide a new ChangeText procedure, connected with the OnClick event of the radio group and of the two list boxes. This procedure is simpler than in the previous version of the example. In fact, to retrieve the selected text from the list box, you only need to get the number of the item selected (stored in the run-time property ItemIndex) and then retrieve the string at the corresponding position of the Item array, as the PHRASES1 program did.

Here is the code for the procedure (which is not present on the companion CD because it is replaced by another version that I'll show you in a moment):

```
procedure TForm1.ChangeText(Sender: TObject);
var
  Phrase: String;
begin
  Phrase := 'The ';
  Phrase := Phrase + ListBox1.Items [ListBox1.ItemIndex];
  Phrase := Phrase + ' is ';
  Phrase := Phrase + RadioGroup1.Items [RadioGroup1.ItemIndex];
  Phrase := Phrase + ' the ';
  Phrase := Phrase + ListBox2.Items [ListBox2.ItemIndex];
  Label1.Caption := Phrase;
end;
```

This program, however, won't work properly because, at the beginning, no item is selected in either list box. To solve this problem, we can add a method for the form's OnCreate event. In its code, we can look for the two default strings, *book* and *table*, and select them. You should do this operation in two steps. First, you need to look for the string's index in the array of strings, with the IndexOf method. Then you can use that value as the index of the currently selected item:

```
procedure TForm1.FormCreate(Sender: TObject);
var
  N : Integer;
begin
  N := ListBox1.Items.IndexOf ('book');
  ListBox1.ItemIndex := N;
  N := ListBox2.Items.IndexOf ('table');
  ListBox2.ItemIndex := N;
end;
```

# Removing a Selected String from the Other List Box

Once this part of the program works, we have two more problems to solve: We must remove the selected string from the other list box to avoid using the same term twice in a phrase, as already described, and we must write the code for the click event on the button.

The first problem is more complex, but I'll address it immediately since the solution of the second problem will be based partially on the code already written for the first one. Our aim is to delete from a list box the item currently selected in the other list box. This is easy to code. The problem is that once the selection changes, we have to restore the previous items, or our list boxes will rapidly become empty. A good solution is to store the two currently selected strings for the two list boxes in two variables of the form, String1 and String2.

Now we have to change the code executed at startup and the code executed each time a new selection is made. In the FormCreate method, we need to store the initial value of the two strings and remove them from the other list box; the first string should be removed from the second list box, and vice versa. Since the Delete methods of the TStrings class require the index, we again have to use the IndexOf function to determine it. The code to select the string should be executed after the deletion because removing an element before the one currently selected will alter the selection. The fact is that the selection is just a number referring to a string, not the reverse, as it should probably be. By the way, this doesn't depend on Delphi implementation but on the behavior of list boxes in Windows. In Listing 7.1 you can see the final code of the PHRASES2 example.

### Listing 7.1: The final code of the PHRASES2 example.

```
unit Phrase_f;

interface

uses
  SysUtils, WinTypes, WinProcs, Messages, Classes,
  Graphics, Controls, Forms, Dialogs, StdCtrls, ExtCtrls;

type
  TForm1 = class(TForm)
    Label1: TLabel;
    ListBox1: TListBox;
    ListBox2: TListBox;
    EditNew: TEdit;
    ButtonAdd: TButton;
    RadioGroup1: TRadioGroup;
    procedure ChangeText(Sender: TObject);
    procedure FormCreate(Sender: TObject);
```

```
    procedure ButtonAddClick(Sender: TObject);
  private
    String1, String2: String;
  end;

var
  Form1: TForm1;

implementation

{$R *.DFM}

procedure TForm1.ChangeText(Sender: TObject);
var
  TmpStr: String;
begin
  {delete the selected item from the other listbox}
  if Sender is TListBox then
  begin
    TmpStr := ListBox1.Items [ListBox1.ItemIndex];
    if TmpStr <> String1 then
    begin
      ListBox2.Items.Add (String1);
      ListBox2.Items.Delete (ListBox2.Items.IndexOf (TmpStr));
      ListBox2.ItemIndex := ListBox2.Items.IndexOf (String2);
      String1 := TmpStr;
    end;
    TmpStr := ListBox2.Items [ListBox2.ItemIndex];
    if TmpStr <> String2 then
    begin
      ListBox1.Items.Add (String2);
      ListBox1.Items.Delete (ListBox1.Items.IndexOf (TmpStr));
      ListBox1.ItemIndex := ListBox1.Items.IndexOf (String1);
      String2 := TmpStr;
    end;
  end;
  {build the phrase}
  Label1.Caption := 'The ' + String1 + ' is ' +
    RadioGroup1.Items [RadioGroup1.ItemIndex] +
    ' the ' + String2;
end;

procedure TForm1.FormCreate(Sender: TObject);
var
  N : Integer;
begin
  String1 := 'book';
  String2 := 'table';
  {delete the selected string from the other
  listbox to avoid a double selection}
  ListBox2.Items.Delete (ListBox2.Items.IndexOf (String1));
  ListBox1.Items.Delete (ListBox1.Items.IndexOf (String2));
  {selects the two strings in their respective listboxes}
  N := ListBox1.Items.IndexOf (String1);
```

```
    ListBox1.ItemIndex := N;
    N := ListBox2.Items.IndexOf (String2);
    ListBox2.ItemIndex := N;
  end;

procedure TForm1.ButtonAddClick(Sender: TObject);
begin
  {if there is a string in the edit control and
    the string is not already present in one of the lists}
  if (EditNew.Text <> '') and
    (ListBox1.Items.IndexOf(EditNew.Text) < 0) and
    (ListBox2.Items.IndexOf(EditNew.Text) < 0) then
  begin
    {add the string to both listboxes}
    ListBox1.Items.Add (EditNew.Text);
    ListBox2.Items.Add (EditNew.Text);
    {re-selects the current items properly}
    ListBox1.ItemIndex := ListBox1.Items.IndexOf (String1);
    ListBox2.ItemIndex := ListBox2.Items.IndexOf (String2);
  end
  else
    MessageDlg ('The edit control is empty or contains'
      + ' a string which is already present',
      mtError, [mbOK], 0);
end;

end.
```

The final version of the code executed produces the effects shown in Figure 7.18.
Things get complicated when a new item is selected in one of the list boxes. The

**FIGURE 7.18:**
The PHRASES2 example. Notice that the string selected in one list box is not present in the other one.

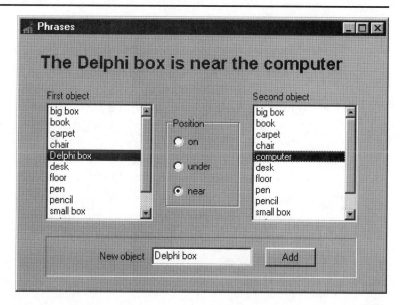

ChangeText procedure has some new code at the beginning, executed only if the click took place on one of the list boxes (remember that the code is also associated with the group box).

For each string, we have to check whether the selected item has changed and, in this case, add the previously selected string to the other list box and delete the new string from the other list box.

Here is a detailed description of the operations, referring to a new selection in the first list box (the full source code is in Listing 7.1). The procedure stores the selected element of the first list box in the temporary string TmpStr. If this is different from the older selection, String1, four operations take place:

```
if TmpStr <> String1 then
begin
  {1.} ListBox2.Items.Add (String1);
  {2.} ListBox2.Items.Delete (ListBox2.Items.IndexOf (TmpStr));
  {3.} ListBox2.ItemIndex := ListBox2.Items.IndexOf (String2);
  {4.} String1 := TmpStr;
end;
```

This is what the operations do:

1. The previously selected string, String1, is added to the other list box, List-Box2.

2. The new selection, TmpStr, is removed from the other list box.

3. The selected string of the other list box, String2, is reselected in case its position has changed because of the two preceding operations.

4. Once the two lists contain the correct elements, we can store the new value in String1 and use it later on to build the phrase.

The same happens for the other list box a few lines later. Notice that we can avoid having to access the list boxes again to build the phrase at the end of the OnChange method, since String1 and String2 already contain the values we need.

Implementing the OnClick event for the Add button is quite simple. The only precautions we have to take are to test whether there is actually some text in the edit box or if it is empty and to check whether the string is already present in one of the two list boxes. Checking only one of the list boxes will miss a correspondence between the text of the edit box and the item currently selected in the other list box.

To make this check, we can ask the new string's index; if it is not present in the list—if there is no match—the value –1 will be returned. Otherwise, the IndexOf function returns the correct index, starting with 0 for the first element. In technical terms, we can say that the function returns the *zero-based* index of the element, or the error code –1 if it is not found.

In the final part of this method's code, we need to reselect the current item of the list box since the position of the selected item might change. This happens if the new item is inserted before the one that is currently selected—that is, if it has a lower sort order.

# Allowing Multiple Selections

There is a basic choice that determines how a list box works. A list box can allow the selection of a single element or the selection of a number of elements. The actual choice is determined by the value of the list box's Multiple property. As the name implies, setting Multiple to True allows multiple selections.

There are really two different kinds of multiple selections in Windows and in Delphi list boxes; one is called *multiple selection* and the other *extended selection*. This second choice is determined by the ExtendedSelect property.

If setting up a multiple-selection list box is very simple, the problems start to appear when you have to write the code. Accessing the selected item of a single-selection list box is simple. The ItemIndex property holds the index of the selected item, and the selected string can be retrieved with a simple expression:

```
ListBox2.Items[ListBox2.ItemIndex];
```

In a multiple-selection list box, on the other hand, we do not know how many items are selected, or even whether there is any item selected. In fact, a user can click on an item to select it, drag the cursor to select a number of consecutive items in the list, or click the mouse button on an item while holding down Ctrl to toggle the selection of a single item without affecting the others. Using this last option, a user can even deselect all the items in a list box.

From a program, we can retrieve information on the currently selected items by examining the Selected array. This array of Boolean values has the same number of entries as the list box. Each entry indicates whether the corresponding item is selected, as shown in the schema of Figure 7.19.

**FIGURE 7.19:**

A schema of the relationship between the Selected and Items properties in a multiple-selection list box.

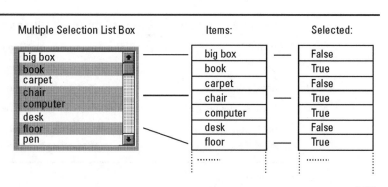

For example, to know how many items are selected in a list box, we need to scan the Selected array, usually with a `for` loop ranging from 0 to the number of items in the list minus one:

```
SelectCount := 0;
for ListItem := 0 to ListBox1.Items.Count - 1 do
  if ListBox1.Selected[ListItem] then
    Inc (SelectCount);
```

# The Third Version of PHRASES

With this information, we can build a new version of the PHRASES example, allowing a user to select several items in the first list box. The only difference between the form of this new version and that of the last one is the value of the MultiSelect property in the first list box:

```
object ListBox1: TListBox
  MultiSelect = True
end
```

In addition, the label at the top of the form has been enlarged, enabling the Word-Wrap property and disabling the AutoSize property, to accommodate longer phrases. Since the example's code is complex enough, I've removed the portion used to delete from a list box the item selected in the other list box. In the case of multiple selections, this would have been really complicated.

The main problem we face is building the different phrases correctly. The basic idea is to scan the Selected array each time and add each of the selected objects to the phrase. However, we need to place an *and* before the last object, omitting the comma if there are only two. Moreover, we need to decide between singular and plural (*is* or *are*) and provide some default text if no element is selected.

As you can see from Table 7.1 (and in Figure 7.20), building these phrases is not simple. In fact, if we store the phrase *The book and the computer*, when we need to add a third item, we must go back and change it.

**TABLE 7.1:** Possible Combinations of Phrases

| Items Selected | SelectCount | Phrase |
| --- | --- | --- |
| (none) | 0 | Nothing is… |
| book | 1 | The book is… |
| book, computer | 2 | The book and the computer are… |
| book, computer, pen | 3 | The book, the computer, and the pen are… |
| book, computer, pen, small box | 4 | The book, the computer, the pen, and the small box are… |

**FIGURE 7.20:**

An example of the output of the PHRASES3 program.

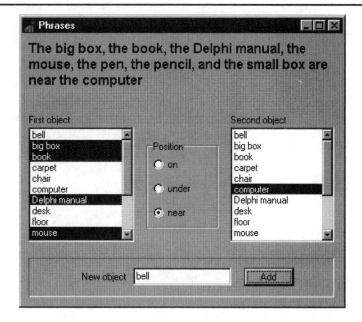

An alternative idea is to create two different phrases, one good if no other elements will be added, the other prepared to host future objects (without the *and*). In the code, the TmpStr1 string is the tentative final statement, while TmpStr2 is the temporary string used to add a further element. At the end of the loop, TmpStr1 holds the correct value.

Notice when scanning a sorted list box that the objects are always added to the resulting string in alphabetical order, not in the order in which they were selected. You can study this idea as it has been implemented in the new version of the ChangeText method, in the following code. If things are still not clear, look at Table 7.2, which describes step-by-step how the strings are built.

```
procedure TForm1.ChangeText(Sender: TObject);
var
  Phrase, TmpStr1, TmpStr2: String;
  SelectCount, ListItem: Integer;
begin
  SelectCount := 0;
  {look at each item of the multiple selection listbox}
  for ListItem := 0 to ListBox1.Items.Count - 1 do
    if ListBox1.Selected [ListItem] then
    begin
      {if the item is selected increase the count}
      Inc (SelectCount);

      if SelectCount = 1 then
      begin
```

```
      {store the string of the first selection}
      TmpStr1 := ListBox1.Items.Strings [ListItem];
      TmpStr2 := TmpStr1;
    end;

    if SelectCount = 2 then
    begin
      {add the string of the second selection}
      TmpStr1 := TmpStr1 + ' and the ' +
        ListBox1.Items.Strings [ListItem];
      TmpStr2 := TmpStr2 + ', the ' +
        ListBox1.Items.Strings [ListItem];
    end;

    if SelectCount > 2 then
    begin
      {add the string of the further selection}
      TmpStr1 := TmpStr2 + ', and the ' +
        ListBox1.Items.Strings [ListItem];
      TmpStr2 := TmpStr2 + ', the ' +
        ListBox1.Items.Strings [ListItem];
    end;
  end;

{build the first part of the phrase}
if SelectCount > 0 then
  Phrase := 'The ' + TmpStr1
else
  Phrase := 'Nothing';
if SelectCount <= 1 then
  Phrase := Phrase + ' is '
else
  Phrase := Phrase + ' are ';

{add the text of the radio button}
Phrase := Phrase +
  RadioGroup1.Items [RadioGroup1.ItemIndex];

{add the text of the second listbox}
Phrase := Phrase + ' the ' +
  ListBox2.Items [ListBox2.ItemIndex];
Label1.Caption := Phrase;
end;
```

The other procedures of the program change only slightly. The FormCreate method is simplified because we do not need to delete the selected item from the other list box. The Add method is simplified because both list boxes always have the same items and because the multiple-selection list box creates no problems if you add a new element.

An alternative solution to handle the status of multiple-selection list boxes is to look at the value of the ItemIndex property, which holds the number of the item of the list having the focus. If a user clicks on several items while holding down Ctrl, each

**TABLE 7.2:** The Process of Building the Strings Step-by-Step

| Items Selected | Steps | TmpStr1 (tentative final statement) | TmpStr2 (temporary statement) |
|---|---|---|---|
| book | 1 | book | book |
| + computer | 2 | book and the computer | book, the computer |
| + pen | 3 | book, the computer, and the pen | book, the computer, the pen |
| + small box | 4 | book, the computer, the pen, and the small box | book, the computer, the pen, the small box |

time a click event takes place, you know which of the items have been selected or deselected—you can easily determine which of the two operations took place by looking at the value of the Selected array for that index. The problem is that if the user selects a number of elements by dragging the mouse, this method won't work. You need to intercept the dragging events, and this is considerably more complex than the technique described earlier.

# Many Lists, Little Space

List boxes have a problem: they take up a lot of screen space. Another problem is that they offer a fixed selection. That is, a user can choose only among the items in the list box, and he or she cannot make a choice that was not foreseen.

You can solve both these problems by using a ComboBox control. A *combo box* is similar to an edit box, and you can often enter some text in it. It is also similar to a list box since pressing the arrow at the end of the control displays a list box below it. Even the name of the control suggests that it is a combination of two other controls, an Edit and a ListBox.

However, the behavior of a ComboBox component might change a lot, depending on the value of its Style property. Here is a short description of the various styles:

- The `csDropDown` style defines a typical combo box, which allows direct editing and displays a list box on request.

- The `csDropDownList` style defines a combo box that does not allow editing. By pressing a key, the user selects the first word starting with that letter in the list.

- The `csSimple` style defines a combo box that always displays the list box below it. This version of the control allows direct editing.

- The `csOwnerDrawFixed` and `csOwnerDrawVariable` styles define combo boxes based on an owner-draw list—that is, a list not containing simple strings but, instead, any graphics determined by the program.

If this is not clear, you can run the COMBOS example that I'll describe in a moment. As you can see in Figure 7.21 and better appreciate by testing the program, there are three combo boxes having three different styles: drop-down, drop-down list, and simple.

**FIGURE 7.21:**

The output of the COMBOS example, with the three basic types of combo boxes.

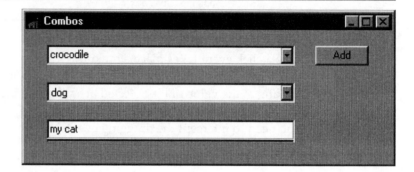

This program is very simple. Each of the combo boxes has the same basic strings—the names of more than 20 different animals.

The first combo box contains an Add button. If the user presses the button, the text entered in the combo box (if any) is added to its list, provided it is not already present. This is the code associated with the OnClick event of the button:

```
procedure TForm1.ButtonAddClick(Sender: TObject);
begin
  with ComboBox1 do
    if (Text <> '') and (Items.IndexOf (Text) < 0) then
      Items.Add (Text);
end;
```

You can use the second combo box to experiment with the automatic lookup technique. If you press a key, the first of the names in the list starting with that letter will be selected. By pressing ↑ and ↓, you can further navigate in the list without opening it. This navigation technique of using initial letters and arrows can be used with each of the combo boxes.

The third combo box is a variation of the first. Instead of adding the new element when the Add button is pressed, that action is performed when the user presses ↵. To test for this event, we can write a method for the combo box's OnKeyPress event and check whether the key is ↵, which has the numeric code 13. The remaining statements are similar to those of the button's OnClick event:

```
procedure TForm1.ComboBox3KeyPress(Sender: TObject;
  var Key: Char);
begin
  {if the user presses the Enter key}
  if key = chr (13) then
    with ComboBox3 do
      if (Text <> '') and (Items.IndexOf (Text) < 0) then
        Items.Add (Text);
end;
```

# Choosing a Value in a Range

The last basic component I want to explore in this chapter is the *scroll bar*. Scroll bars are usually associated with other components, such as list boxes and memo fields, or are associated directly with forms. Notice, however, that when a scroll bar is associated with another component, it is really a portion of that component—one of its properties—and there is little relationship to the ScrollBar component itself. Forms having a scroll bar have no ScrollBar component. A portion of their border is used to display that graphical element. Forms with scroll bars will be discussed in Chapter 13.

Direct usage of the ScrollBar component is quite rare, especially with the new track-bar component of Windows 95. However, there are cases in which it can play a role. The typical example is to allow a user to choose a numerical value in a large range (since trackbars are better for smaller ranges).

Most Windows programming books describe scroll bars using the example of selecting a color. This book makes no exception to the rule. But if you've seen one of the original Windows examples, you'll notice something very interesting: using Delphi, you can build this example in half the time and by writing a minimal amount of code.

## The Scroll Color Example

The SCROLLC example—the name stands for scroll color—has a simple form with three scroll bars and three corresponding labels, a track bar with its own label, and some shape components to show the current color. Each of the scroll bars refers to one of the three fundamental colors, which in Windows are red, green, and blue (RGB). Each of the labels displays the name of the corresponding color and the current value.

The scroll bars have a number of peculiar properties. You can use Min and Max to determine the range of possible values; Position holds the current position; and the

LargeChange and SmallChange properties indicate the increment caused by clicking on the bar or on the arrow at the end of the bar, respectively. You can see a graphical description of these properties, with the values used in the example, in Figure 7.22.

**FIGURE 7.22:**

A graphical description of some properties of a scroll bar (the values are borrowed from the SCROLLC example).

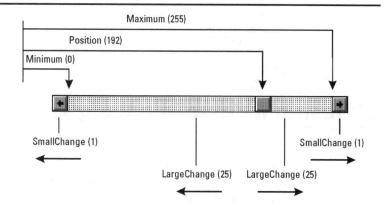

In the SCROLLC example, the value of each bar ranges from 0 to 255, the initial value is 192, and the changes are 1 and 25. The range is determined by the fact that each color is a byte, with 256 possible values. The value of 192 has been chosen for the position because with settings of 192 for red, 192 for green, and 192 for blue, you get the typical light gray, which is the default value for the color of the form and of the shapes:

```
object ScrollBarRed: TScrollBar
  LargeChange = 25
  Max = 255
  Position = 192
  OnScroll = ScrollBarRedScroll
end
```

The trackbar has similar properties (Min, Max, Position), and is used in this example to set the LargeChange property of the three scrollbars, with the following code:

```
procedure TFormScroll.TrackBar1Change(Sender: TObject);
begin
  LabelScroll.Caption := 'Scroll by ' + IntToStr(TrackBar1.Posi-
tion);
  ScrollBarGreen.LargeChange := TrackBar1.Position;
  ScrollBarRed.LargeChange := TrackBar1.Position;
  ScrollBarBlue.LargeChange := TrackBar1.Position;
end;
```

When one of the scroll bars changes (the OnScroll event), the program has to update the corresponding label and the color of the shapes. The first of them is used to show the color as it is determined by the three RGB values of the scrollbars. Assigning this color to the Color property of the brush used to fill the surface of the shape, we obtain a dithered color, an approximation of the real tint made with the colors available on the video adapter. The same color is assigned to the Color property of the pen of the second shape, resulting in the closest approximation of the requested color. Pens, in fact, do not use dithering, but rather the *closest* pure color. You can see the difference in Figure 7.23, and by running this example, although the effect might change depending on the video adapter of the computer.

**FIGURE 7.23:**

The output of the SCROLLC example.

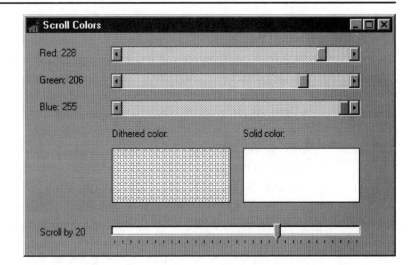

If you browse though the code of the program, notice also that there is a third shape component used to mimic the border of the second shape. The real border of this shape, in fact, is enlarged to fill its whole surface, using a wide pen. This way we use the color of the pen—the wide border—to actually fill the shape. Here is the code corresponding to one of the scroll bars:

```
procedure TFormScroll.ScrollBarRedScroll(Sender: TObject;
  ScrollCode: TScrollCode; var ScrollPos: Integer);
begin
  LabelRed.Caption := 'Red: ' + IntToStr(ScrollPos);
  Shape1.Brush.Color := RGB (ScrollBarRed.Position,
    ScrollBarGreen.Position, ScrollBarBlue.Position);
  Shape2.Pen.Color := RGB (ScrollBarRed.Position,
    ScrollBarGreen.Position, ScrollBarBlue.Position);
end;
```

You need to copy this code once for each scroll bar and correct the name of the label and its output. The second and third statements always remain the same. They are based on a Windows function, RGB, which takes three values in the range 0–255 and creates a 32-bit value with the code of the corresponding color.

It is interesting to note that the OnScroll event has three parameters: the sender, the kind of event (ScrollCode), and the final position of the thumb (ScrollPos). This type of event can be used for very precise control of the user's actions. Its value indicates whether the user is dragging the thumb (`scTrack`, `scPosition`, and `scEndScroll`), whether he or she has clicked on the arrows or on the bar in one of the two directions (`scLineUp`, `scLineDown`, `scPageUp`, and `scPageDown`), and if the user is trying to scroll out of the range (`scTop` and `scBottom`).

# Summary

In this chapter, we have started to explore some of the basic components available in Delphi. These components correspond to the standard Windows controls and some of the new Windows 95 common controls, and are extremely common in applications (with the exception of the stand-alone scroll bars).

Of course, when you start adding more advanced Delphi components to an application, you can easily build more complex and colorful user interfaces and more powerful programs.

We will explore some of the advanced components in future chapters, but the next two are devoted to specific and important topics: the use of menus and a detailed description of forms. After these two in-depth discussions, we will move back to the use of other components, including the graphical versions of list boxes, edit boxes allowing specific data entries, grids, and more.

# CHAPTER

## EIGHT

# Creating and Handling Menus

- The structure of a menu

- Checking, disabling, and modifying menus at run-time

- The Menu Designer

- Menu templates

- A custom menu check mark

- Pop-up menus

- The system menu

**T**he programs we have built so far have lacked one of the most important user-interface elements of any Windows application: the menu bar. Although our forms have a system menu, it has a very limited use. The menu bar, on the other hand, is a central element in the development of a program. The user can press buttons, drag the mouse, and select options, but usually, most of the complex tasks involve using a menu command. Consider the application you use and the number-of-menu-commands issue, including those invoked by an accelerator key, such as Ctrl+Ins or Ctrl+C, which replace the Edit ➤ Copy command in most applications.

Menus are so important that almost any real Windows application has at least one. In fact, an application can also have several menus that change at run-time (more on this later). The Borland programmers who created Delphi also considered them very important; the menu components are in the Standard page of the Components palette.

# The Structure of a Menu

Before delving into ideas and examples on the use of menus in Delphi, let me recap some general information on menus and their structure.

Usually, a menu has two levels. A menu bar, appearing below the title of the window, contains the names of the pull-down menus. Each pull-down menu contains a number of items. However, the menu structure is very flexible. It is possible to place a menu item directly in the menu bar and to place a pull-down menu inside another pull-down menu. You should always avoid the first situation because users tend to select the elements of the menu bar to explore the structure of the menu. They do not expect to issue a command this way. If, for some reason, you really need to place a command in the menu bar, at least place the standard exclamation mark after it (as you can see in Figure 8.1).

Using an exclamation mark is a standard hint, but most users have never seen it, so it's best to avoid the whole situation altogether. There is nothing negative, instead, in having a pull-down menu with a single menu item. Having a pull-down menu inside another pull-down menu, or a second-level pull-down, is far more common, and Windows in this case provides a default visual clue, a small triangular glyph at the right of the menu (see Figure 8.1 again).

Many applications use this technique, particularly in Windows 95, because the system makes a heavy use of multilevel menus (consider the Start button's Programs menu). At least keep in mind that selecting a menu item in a second-level pull-down takes more time and can become tedious. Many times, instead of having a second-level pull-down, you can simply group a number of options in the original pull-down and place two separators, one before and one after the group.

**FIGURE 8.1:**

Besides the typical two-level menu structure, a menu item can be placed in the menu bar (below) and a pull-down menu inside another pull-down (above).

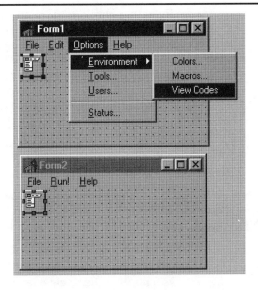

You can see a multilevel menu in Figure 8.2, or you can test it directly using the LEVELS example on the disk. Since it is a demonstration of what you should try to avoid, I won't list the structure of the menu here.

**FIGURE 8.2:**

The multilevel menu of the LEVELS example.

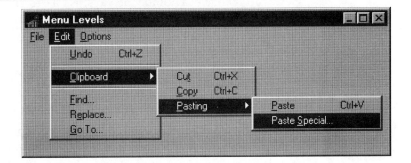

# Different Roles of Menu Items

Now let's turn our attention to menu items, regardless of their position in the menu structure. There are three fundamental kinds of menu items:

- Commands are menu items used to give a command to execute an action. They provide no special visual clue.

- State-setters are menu items used to toggle an option on and off, to change the state of a particular element. When they have two states, these commands usually have a check mark on the left when they are active. In this case, selecting the command produces the opposite action.

- Dialog items are menu items causing a dialog box to appear. The real difference between these and the other menu items is that a user should be able to explore the possible effects of the corresponding dialog box and eventually abort them by choosing the Cancel button in the dialog box. These commands should have a visual clue, consisting of three dots after the text. This is not compulsory from a technical point of view—you write the text of the menu item—but it is so common that you just cannot ignore this guideline.

**NEW**

In Windows 95, besides the traditional state-setters with a check mark, you can also have radio menu items with a bullet check mark. These menu items represent alternative selections, just as RadioButton components do, and simply checking one of them disables the other elements of the group.

# Changing Menu Items at Run-Time

It is important to notice that menu items can change at run-time. The structure of a menu can change in a number of ways, as I'll describe later in this chapter, but some important changes apply to individual items. For example, when a menu command cannot or should not be selected, it is usually grayed. In this case, the user has no way to issue that command.

Another visual change is the use of the check mark, which applications can toggle on and off easily. At times, to implement a state-setter menu item, you can change the text of the menu item altogether, which might result in an easier interface.

I'll describe what I mean with an example. Suppose an application has a List ➤ Visible command. If you select it, a list box will probably appear. Now, if you look at the menu, there should be a check mark near the item. This means that if you select the List ➤ Visible command now, the list box will disappear. When the check mark is present, the command you issue has the opposite effect of its textual description. As an alternative, you might use two different captions for the two states of the item, such as Show List and Hide List. No user will have any doubt about the effect of choosing commands like these.

The same technique can be applied to commands having three or more states, although this is rare. When the user can select more than two choices, it is better to use the new radio menu item user interface, which is becoming the standard approach.

# Editing a Menu with the Menu Designer

Delphi includes a special editor for menus, the Menu Designer. To invoke this tool, place a menu component on a form and double-click on it. Don't worry too much about the position of the menu component on the form, since it doesn't affect the result; the menu is always placed properly, below the form's caption.

**NOTE**  To be more precise, the form displays, below its caption, the menu indicated in its Menu property, which is set by default as soon as you create the first main menu component of the form. If the form has more than one main menu component, this property should be set manually and can be changed both at design-time and at run-time.

My convention is to place the icon of the menu component in the upper-left corner of the form, to make it easy to spot it, but this is only a personal convention. As you know, a number of components in Delphi provide no visual clue at design-time. They are just displayed as an icon. Of course, you won't see these icons at run-time. Some of them will correspond to certain visual elements, such as menus, but most of them won't.

The Menu Designer is really powerful: It allows you to create a menu simply by writing the text of the commands, to move the items or pull-down menus by dragging them around, and to set the properties of the items easily. It is also very flexible, allowing you to place a command directly in the menu bar (this happens each time you do not write any element in the corresponding pull-down menu) or to create second-level pull-down menus. To accomplish this, you have to select the Create Submenu command on the Menu Designer's SpeedMenu (the local menu invoked with the right mouse button).

Another very important feature available through the Menu Designer is the ability to create a menu from a template. You can easily define new templates of your own. Simply create a menu, and use the Save As Template command on the SpeedMenu to add it to the list. This makes sense particularly if you need to have a similar menu in two applications or in two different forms of the same application. This last case, however, is not common, since there are a number of techniques you can use to merge the menus of two different forms of an application. Some examples of menu merging will be described in Chapter 12 (for multiple forms) and Chapter 15 (for MDI applications).

# The Standard Structure of a Menu

If you've used Windows applications for some time, you have certainly noticed that the structure of an application's menu is not an invention of its programmers. There are a number of standard Windows guidelines describing how to arrange the commands in a menu. However, you can infer most of the rules by looking at the menu of some of the best-selling applications.

An application's menu bar should start with a File pull-down, followed by Edit, View, and some other specific commands. The final part of the sequence includes Options, Tools, and Window (only for MDI applications) and always terminates with Help. Each of these pull-down menus has a standard layout, although the actual items depend on the specific applications. The File menu, for example, usually has commands such as New, Open, Save, Save As, Print, Print Setup, and Exit.

# Menu Shortcuts

A common feature of menu items is that they contain an underlined letter, generally called a hotkey. This letter, which is often the first letter of the text, can be used to select the menu using the keyboard. Pressing Alt plus the underlined key selects the corresponding pull-down menu. By pressing Alt plus another underlined key on that menu, you issue a command.

Of course, each element of the menu bar must have a different underlined character. The same is true for the menu items on a specific pull-down menu. Obviously, menu items on different pull-down menus can have the same underlined letter; otherwise, we would end up with the ridiculous limit of about 50 menu commands (26 letters, 10 numbers, and certain other keys).

To indicate the underlined key, you simply place an ampersand (&) before it, as in &File or Save &As.... In these examples, the underlined keys would be F for File and A for Save As. You can also place the ampersand in the middle of a word.

Menu items have another standard feature: shortcut keys. When you see the shorthand description of a key or key combination beside a menu item, it means you can press those keys to give that command. Although giving menu commands with the mouse is easier, it tends to be somewhat slow, particularly for keyboard-intensive applications, since you have to move one of your hands from the keyboard to the mouse. Pressing Alt and the underlined letter might be faster, but it still requires two operations. Using a shortcut key usually involves pressing a special key and another key at the same time (such as Ctrl+C). Windows doesn't even display the corresponding pull-down menu, so this results in a faster operation.

In Delphi, associating a shortcut key with a menu item (pull-down menus cannot have a shortcut key) is easy. You need only select a value for the ShortCut property, choosing one of the standard combinations: Ctrl or Shift plus almost any key.

You might even add shortcut keys to a program without adding a real menu. For example, you can create a pop-up menu, connect it with a form, set the Visible property of all of its items to False, and add the proper shortcut keys; a user will never see the menu, but the shortcuts will work. If this is not clear, you can look at the HSHORT (hidden shortcut) example on the companion CD.

## Using the Predefined Menu Templates

To let you start developing an application's menu following the standard guidelines, Delphi contains some predefined menu templates. The templates include two different File pull-down menus, an Edit menu (including OLE commands), a Window menu, and two Help menus. There is also a complete MDI menu bar template, which has the same four menu categories.

Using these standard templates brings you some advantages. First of all, it is faster to reuse an existing menu than to build one from scratch. Second, the menu template follows the standard Windows guidelines for naming menu commands, for using the proper shortcuts, and so on. Of course, using these menus makes sense in a file-based application. But if the program you are writing doesn't handle files, has no editing capabilities, and is not MDI, you'll end up using only the template Help pull-down menu.

# Responding to Menu Commands

For MENU_ONE, the first example with menus, I've chosen the application LABEL_CO from the last chapter. You can see its original form in Figure 7.3 in Chapter 7. The new version of the form is still simpler: I've removed all the buttons and added a menu bar instead. This menu bar has three pull-down menus: the File pull-down with only the Exit option, one with the various options, and a Help menu with the About menu item. You can see the menu bar in the Menu Designer in Figure 8.3.

**FIGURE 8.3:**
The menu bar of the MENU_ONE application.

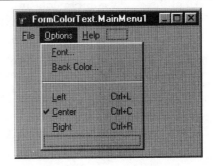

To add the separator in the Options pull-down menu, you simply insert a hyphen as the text of the command. Do not alter the Break property. Except for rare situations, the Break property will make a mess of your menu. You are better off forgetting the existence of this property.

> **NOTE**
>
> Of course, the Break property has its uses, or it would not have been added to the component. You can better understand it if I use the real name of its parameters, NewLine or NewColumn. If an item on the menu bar has the mbMenuBarBreak (or NewLine) value, this item will be displayed in a second or subsequent line. If a menu item has the mbMenuBreak (or NewColumn) value, this item will be added to a second or subsequent column of the pull-down. Neither of these things are used very often.

## The Code Generated by the Menu Designer

Once you have built this menu, take a look at the list of components displayed by the Object Inspector, or open the DFM file with the textual description of the form, which will also contain a textual description of the menu structure. There is a separate component for each menu item, one for each pull-down menu, and, surprisingly, even one for each separator.

Delphi builds the names of these components automatically when you insert the menu item's label. The rules are simple:

- Any blank or special character (including the ampersand and the hyphen) is removed.

- If there are no characters left, the letter N is added.

- A number is always added at the end of the name (1 if this is the first menu item with this name, a higher number if not).

All of these new components are listed in the Object Inspector, and you can navigate among them by opening the Menu Designer and selecting menu items. To respond to menu commands, you need to define a method for the OnClick event of each menu item. The OnClick event of the pull-down menus is used only in special cases—for example, to check whether the menu items below should be disabled. The OnClick event of the separators is useless.

Once you have defined the main menu of a form and it is displayed below the caption, you can add a new method for the OnClick event of a menu command simply by selecting it in the menu bar. If a handler is already present, Delphi will show you the corresponding portion of the source code; otherwise, a new method will be added to the form.

## The Code of the MENU_ONE Example

The code of the MENU_ONE example is very simple, and is similar to that of the earlier LABEL_CO example. Notice that the label should automatically resize itself when a user changes the dimensions of the form. For this reason, you have to set its Align property to alClient.

The two menu commands involving dialog boxes have the same code of the earlier version; they copy the current font or color to the standard dialog box, execute the dialog box, and then retrieve the final value only if the user has selected the OK button (that is, if the Execute function returns True). The other menu items can have the same code as the earlier version: the code of their OnClick event handlers simply set the Alignment property of the label.

This works fine, but the resulting application doesn't follow the standard guidelines. Each time you have a series of choices in a menu, the selected choice should have a check mark beside it. To accomplish this, you need to create two different operations. First of all, you have to place a check mark near the default choice, Center, changing the value of the menu item's Check property in the Object Inspector. Second, you should correct the code so that each time the selection changes, the check mark is properly set (as shown in Figure 8.4):

```
procedure TFormColorText.Left1Click(Sender: TObject);
begin
  Label1.Alignment := taLeftJustify;
  Left1.Checked := True;
  Center1.Checked := False;
  Right1.Checked := False;
end;
```

The other two functions are similar. You might as well copy the source code of the last three statements, paste this text twice in the other two functions, and correct the values of the three Checked properties so that each time one of them is set to True. The Help ➤ About and File ➤ Exit commands are very simple, so I won't discuss them here.

FIGURE 8.4:
The check mark in the pull-down menu of the MENU_ONE example indicates the current selection.

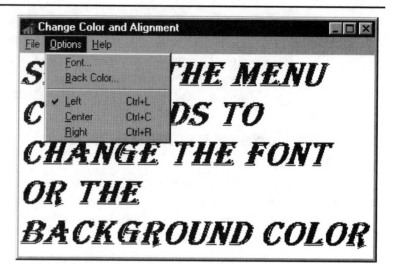

## Checking and Disabling Menus

You can perform a number of operations in Windows to change the structure of the menu at run-time. For the moment, we will focus only on changes involving single menu items.

### Changing Menu Items

Three properties are commonly used to modify a menu item. We used the Checked property in the example above to add or remove a check mark beside the menu item. The Enabled property can be used to gray a menu item so it cannot be selected by a user. The last property of this group is the Caption, the text of the menu item. By changing the text of a menu item, you indicate to the user that the program has a different status.

I'll try to show you the use of these properties with a simple example, named CHANGE because its menu changes a lot. The form of this example is shown in Figure 8.5.

As you can see, the form has two group boxes and two buttons. The first group box contains two edit boxes; the second, two check boxes. The components inside the group boxes are not really used by the example. You can use the two buttons, instead, to hide or display each of the two group boxes, together with the controls they contain.

The same action can be accomplished with two menu commands, View ➤ Edit Boxes and View ➤ Check Boxes. Each time you select one of these two menu commands or press one of the two buttons, three different actions take place. First, the

FIGURE 8.5:

The form of the CHANGE example.

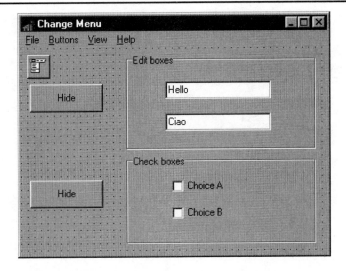

group box is either shown or hidden; second, the text of the button changes from Hide to Show or vice versa; third, a check mark is added to or removed from the corresponding menu item. Here is the code of one of the two methods, which is connected to both the menu-command click and the button click events:

```
procedure TForm1.ViewEdit1Click(Sender: TObject);
begin
  {toggle status and menu checkmark}
  GroupBox1.Visible := not GroupBox1.Visible;
  ViewEdit1.Checked := not ViewEdit1.Checked;
  {change the text of the button}
  if GroupBox1.Visible then
    Button1.Caption := 'Hide'
  else
    Button1.Caption := 'Show';
end;
```

The other two menu commands use a different approach. Instead of having a check mark, their text changes to reflect their current status. They also disable or enable the corresponding item of the View menu and the button (see Figure 8.6):

```
 procedure TForm1.ButtonsFirst1Click(Sender: TObject);
begin
  if Button1.Enabled then
  begin
    Button1.Enabled := False;
    ViewEdit1.Enabled := False;
    ButtonsFirst1.Caption := 'Enable &First';
  end
  else
  begin
    Button1.Enabled := True;
```

FIGURE 8.6:

When you disable a button, the corresponding menu item is disabled, too, regardless of the fact that it can have a check mark.

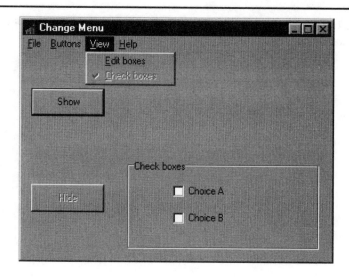

```
    ViewEdit1.Enabled := True;
    ButtonsFirst1.Caption := 'Disable &First';
  end;
end;
```

At the beginning of this section, I mentioned three common operations on a menu item: adding a check mark, disabling the command, and changing its text. In theory, there is a fourth operation: removing the menu item, or making it invisible. This is easily accomplished by changing the value of the Visible property to False.

However, I suggest you avoid this operation. If you remove a menu item, an inexperienced user of your application may lose some time trying to find it in the various pull-down menus. The user might try to remember where the item was and what exactly its name was. It is much more common to disable a menu item so the user can see where it is and realize that it is temporarily not available.

## Changing Pull-Down Menus

You can use the Visible property to change pull-down menus. You can choose between a disabled pull-down or an invisible pull-down since there are applications using both approaches, but the second choice is more common.

Study the second version of the CHANGE example, CHANGES2, which has a pull-down menu with menu items used to gray or hide other pull-down menus. In Figure 8.7, the File pull-down menu has been removed, and the View pull-down menus is disabled, as you can see by looking at the check marks next to the items on the Pulldowns menu. The four commands of this menu are associated with the

FIGURE 8.7:
The form of the CHANGE2 example at run-time, with some pull-down menus disabled or hidden.

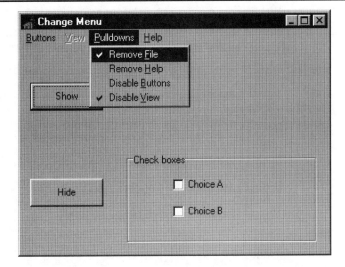

four similar methods, which operate both on other pull-downs and on the check mark of the menu item itself. Here is one of them:

```
procedure TForm1.RemoveFile1Click(Sender: TObject);
begin
  File1.Visible := not File1.Visible;
  RemoveFile1.Checked := not RemoveFile1.Checked;
end;
```

# Using Radio Menu Items

In addition to using check marks, in Windows 95 (and in Windows NT 3.51, but only if the new shell has been installed in the system) you can use radio items. This means having not only a different user interface, but also a different behavior.

In fact, if you select the RadioItem Boolean property of a MenuItem component, in Delphi, you get the new check mark for the item. But if you set this property to True for several consecutive menu items and set their GroupIndex properties to the same value, they'll both use the new mark, but they'll also behave as radio buttons. This means only one of the radio menu items in the group can be selected at a time. Instead of having to de-select all other items manually, as you did in Windows 3.1, now you simply select the proper menu item, and the rest is automatic.

To show you how to use menu items and some advanced menu handling features, I've built an example named RERADIO. The name stands for Rich Edit Radio, because the example is actually an update of the RICHEDIT example from Chapter 7. The new version of the example simply has a RichEdit component covering its whole form, and a complex menu with four pull-down menus: File, Font, Paragraph, and Help. File has a couple of simple methods used to load a file into the rich edit or to save it. The file handling capabilities of this example are quite limited, and the program doesn't ask you to save changes before closing or loading a new file. For a more complete example of file handling, you can see the NOTES2 program later in this chapter.

Here is the code of the two methods for loading and saving files:

```
procedure TForm1.Open1Click(Sender: TObject);
begin
  if OpenDialog1.Execute then
    RichEdit1.Lines.LoadFromFile (
      OpenDialog1.FileName);
end;

procedure TForm1.Saveas1Click(Sender: TObject);
begin
  if SaveDialog1.Execute then
    RichEdit1.Lines.SaveToFile (
      SaveDialog1.FileName);
end;
```

The fourth pull-down menu is the simplest. The Help ➤ About menu command shows an information box obtained with the MessageDlg function. Things are more interesting in the second and third pull-down menus. The Paragraph pull-down menu has the following structure (extracted by the textual description of its form):

```
object Paragraph1: TMenuItem
  Caption = 'Paragraph'
  object LeftAligned1: TMenuItem
    Caption = '&Left Aligned'
    Checked = True
    GroupIndex = 1
    RadioItem = True
    OnClick = RightAligned1Click
  end
  object RightAligned1: TMenuItem
    Caption = '&Right Aligned'
    GroupIndex = 1
    RadioItem = True
    OnClick = RightAligned1Click
  end
  object Centered1: TMenuItem
    Caption = '&Centered'
    GroupIndex = 1
    RadioItem = True
    OnClick = RightAligned1Click
  end
end
```

As you can see, the three menu items share the same value for the GroupIndex property, and have the RadioItem property set to True. You can see the corresponding output in Figure 8.8 (notice that you get the new check mark only at run-time, not at design time).

FIGURE 8.8:

The glyph of the new Windows 95 radio menu items, from the RERADIO example

The menu items also share the same RightAligned1Click method for their OnClick event. Here is the code of the method, which is based on the correspondence between the position of the menu items in the pull-down (indicated by their MenuIndex property) and the order of the values of the TAlignment enumeration:

```
procedure TForm1.RightAligned1Click(Sender: TObject);
begin
  RichEdit1.Paragraph.Alignment :=
    TAlignment ((Sender as TMenuItem).MenuIndex);
  (Sender as TMenuItem).Checked := True;
end;
```

First, it sets the alignment of the current paragraph (the paragraph including the selected text or the editor cursor), then it checks the current menu item—the menu item that has activated the method (the Sender object). As you can see, this code relies on some controlled type casts, based on the as keyword: this is what you have to do any time you want to write generic code (that is, to attach the same methods to events of different components).

Notice that setting the check mark for the current menu item is correct until you don't change the selection or the current line in the text. For this reason, we can handle the OnSelectionChange event of the RichEdit component, and update the menu each time:

```
procedure TForm1.RichEdit1SelectionChange(Sender: TObject);
begin
  Paragraph1.Items [Integer (
    RichEdit1.Paragraph.Alignment)].
    Checked := True;
end;
```

The Font pull-down menu is built on the same concept, but it has two groups of radio items, plus items with a standard check mark. Each group, then, uses a different approach to handle the menu item selection with a single event response method. Here is the structure of the menu, again taken from the textual description of the form. It is quite long, but I think it is important for you to understand how the menu is arranged:

```
object Font1: TMenuItem
  Caption = 'F&ont'
  object TimesRoman1: TMenuItem
    Caption = '&Times New Roman'
    Checked = True
    GroupIndex = 1
    RadioItem = True
    OnClick = TimesRoman1Click
  end
  object Courier1: TMenuItem
    Caption = '&Courier New'
    GroupIndex = 1
    RadioItem = True
    OnClick = TimesRoman1Click
  end
  object Arial1: TMenuItem
    Caption = '&Arial'
    GroupIndex = 1
    RadioItem = True
    OnClick = TimesRoman1Click
  end
  object N2: TMenuItem
    Caption = '-'
    GroupIndex = 1
  end
  object Bold1: TMenuItem
    Caption = '&Bold'
    GroupIndex = 2
    OnClick = Bold1Click
  end
  object Italic1: TMenuItem
    Caption = '&Italic'
    GroupIndex = 2
    OnClick = Italic1Click
  end
  object N3: TMenuItem
    Caption = '-'
    GroupIndex = 2
  end
  object Small1: TMenuItem
    Tag = 12
    Caption = '&Small (10)'
    GroupIndex = 3
    RadioItem = True
    OnClick = Large1Click
  end
  object Medium1: TMenuItem
    Tag = 14
    Caption = '&Medium (14)'
    Checked = True
```

```
      GroupIndex = 3
      RadioItem = True
      OnClick = Large1Click
    end
  object Large1: TMenuItem
    Tag = 18
    Caption = '&Large (18)'
    GroupIndex = 3
    RadioItem = True
    OnClick = Large1Click
  end
end
```

The code of the first group of menu items (used to select the font) is based on a simple trick: the name of the font to select corresponds to the Caption of the menu item, without the initial & character:

```
procedure TForm1.TimesRoman1Click(Sender: TObject);
var
  FontName: string;
begin
  // get the font name and remove the &
  FontName := (Sender as TMenuItem).Caption;
  Delete (FontName, 1, 1);
  // change selected text font
  if RichEdit1.SelLength > 0 then
    RichEdit1.SelAttributes.Name := FontName;
  (Sender as TMenuItem).Checked := True;
end;
```

This code acts on the current selection (using the SelAttributes property of the RichEdit1 component), as the RICHEDIT example in Chapter 7 did. Notice that you can easily extend this code by adding new menu items with the name of the font in them, preceded by the & character. Then you'll have to set the same value for the GroupIndex property (1), set the RadioItem property to True, and connect the On-Click event to the TimesRoman1Click method.

The selection of the bold and italic styles, made in two similar but separate methods, is simpler:

```
procedure TForm1.Bold1Click(Sender: TObject);
begin
  Bold1.Checked := not Bold1.Checked;
  if RichEdit1.SelLength > 0 then
    with RichEdit1.SelAttributes do
      if Bold1.Checked then
        Style := Style + [fsBold]
      else
        Style := Style - [fsBold];
end;
```

The last part of the menu has another group of radio menu items, used to set the size of the font. As you can see in the textual description of the Font pull-down menu above, they refer to a number in the caption and have the same value stored in their Tag property. This makes the code easier to write. Again, there is a single method for the three menu items, but you can add new items to this group with little effort:

```
procedure TForm1.Large1Click(Sender: TObject);
begin
  if RichEdit1.SelLength > 0 then
    RichEdit1.SelAttributes.Size :=
      (Sender as TMenuItem).Tag;
  (Sender as TMenuItem).Checked := True;
end;
```

All the commands of this menu affect the status of the current selection, setting the check boxes and radio items properly, as you can see in Figure 8.9.

**FIGURE 8.9:**

The check boxes and radio items of the Font menu of the RERADIO example indicate the status of the current selection.

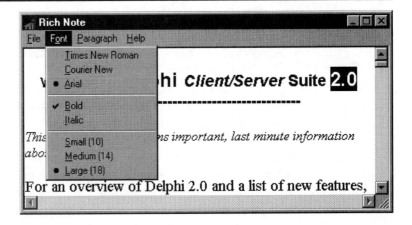

Again we have the problem of updating the status of the menu items when the selection changes. Here is the final code of the OnSelectionChange event handler of the RichEdit component, which scans some of the groups to determine which of the elements has to be checked. As in the methods above, this code has also been written so that you can easily extend it for new menu items:

```
procedure TForm1.RichEdit1SelectionChange(Sender: TObject);
var
  FontName: string;
  I: Integer;
begin
  // check the font name radio menu item
  FontName := '&' + RichEdit1.SelAttributes.Name;
  for I := 0 to 2 do
    with Font1.Items [I] do
      if FontName = Caption then
```

```
      Checked := True;
// check the bold and italic items
Italic1.Checked := fsItalic in
  RichEdit1.SelAttributes.Style;
Bold1.Checked := fsBold in
  RichEdit1.SelAttributes.Style;
// check the font size
for I := Small1.MenuIndex to
    Large1.MenuIndex do
  with Font1.Items [I] do
    if Tag = RichEdit1.SelAttributes.Size then
      Checked := True;
// check the paragraph style
Paragraph1.Items [Integer (
  RichEdit1.Paragraph.Alignment)].
  Checked := True;
end;
```

All this code makes the RERADIO program an interesting editor, but still not a complete one. We will see how to implement other menu commands (related to the simpler Memo component) before the end of this chapter.

# Changing the Menu Structure at Run-Time

The run-time changes on menu items and pull-down menus we've seen so far were all based on the direct manipulation of some properties. These components, however, also have some interesting methods, such as AppendTo, AtInsert, AtRemove, and so on, that you can use to make further changes.

The basic idea is that each object of the TMenuItem class—which Delphi uses for both menu items and pull-down menus—contains a list of menu items. Each of these items has the same structure, in a kind of recursive way. A pull-down menu has a list of submenus, and each of these submenus has a list of submenus, each with its own list of submenus.... The properties you can use to explore the structure of an existing menu are Items, which contains the actual list of menu items, and ItemsSize, which contains the number of items of the list, which is 0 for a menu item and has a positive value for a pull-down menu.

Adding new menu items (or entire pull-down menus) to a menu is fairly easy. Slightly more complex is the handling of the commands related to the new menu items. Basically, you need to have a specific message-response method in your code, and you can assign it to the new menu item by setting its OnClick property. As an alternative, you can have a single method used for several OnClick events and use its Sender parameter to determine which menu command the user issued.

If you don't like this approach, there are a couple of good alternatives. You can create a large menu with all the items you need, then hide all the items and pull-down menus you do not want at the beginning. To add a new command you need only unhide it. This solution is a follow-up on what we have done up to now. You can also create several menus, possibly with common elements, and exchange them as required. This approach is demonstrated in the next section.

> **NOTE**
>
> Besides the run-time changes on a menu's structure I've listed so far, which are all directly available in Delphi, consider that there are a number of operations you can perform on menus using the Windows API. In fact, there are several API functions referring to menus. The menu is a typical no-limit area of the system, although you should avoid the more uncommon operations. An example of the direct use of a Windows API function is described later in this chapter, in the section "Customizing the Menu Check Mark."

## Short and Long Menus

A typical example of a form having two menus is one that uses two different sets of menus (long and short) for two different kinds of users (expert and inexperienced). This technique was common in major Windows applications for some years and has since been replaced by other approaches, such as letting each user redefine the whole structure of the menu.

The idea is simple and its implementation straightforward:

1. Prepare the full menu of the application, adding a Short menu command.

2. Add this menu to the Delphi menu template.

3. Place a second MainMenu component on the form, and copy its structure from the template.

4. In the second menu, remove the items corresponding to advanced features and change the Short menu item into a Long menu item.

5. In the Menu property of the form, set the MainMenu component you want to use when the application starts, choosing one of the two available. Notice that this operation has an effect on the form at design-time, too.

6. Write the code for the Short and Long commands so that when they are selected, the menu changes.

If you follow these steps, you'll end up with an application similar to TWOMENUS (see Figure 8.10), which can change its menu at run-time. The example has two

**FIGURE 8.10:**

The long and short menus of the TWOMENUS example.

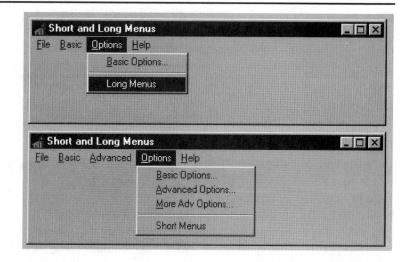

different MainMenu components, with a bunch of useless menu items, plus the Short and Long commands.

The application does nothing apart from changing the main menu when the Short Menu or Long Menu menu items are selected. Here is the code for Short Menu:

```
procedure TForm1.ShortMenus1Click(Sender: TObject);
begin
  {activate short menu}
  Form1.Menu := MainMenu2;
end;
```

## Customizing the Menu Check Mark

As I've mentioned before, there are a number of common (and less common) ways to customize a menu in Windows. In this section, I'm going to show you how you can customize the check mark used by a menu item, using two bitmaps of your own. This example, NEWCHECK, involves using bitmaps and calling a Windows API function.

First of all, I have to explain why we need two bitmaps, not just one. If you look at a menu item, it can have either a check mark or nothing. In general, however, Windows uses two different bitmaps for the checked and unchecked menu item.

I've prepared two bitmaps, of $16 \times 14$ pixels, using the Delphi Image Editor (see Figure 8.11). You can easily run this program from the Tools menu, but you can prepare the bitmaps with any other editor, including Windows' Paintbrush. The bitmaps should be stored in two BMP files in the same directory as the project.

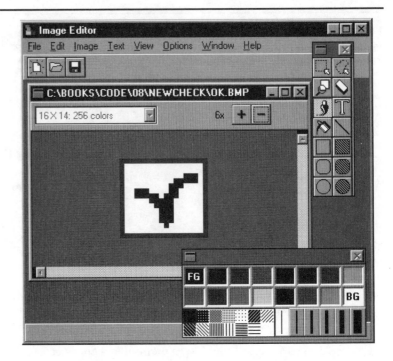

The NEWCHECK program has a very simple form (see Figure 8.12), with just two
components, a MainMenu and a label. The menu has a single command, Toggle,
which changes the text of the label from ON to OFF and changes the check
mark, too:

```
procedure TForm1.Toggle1Click(Sender: TObject);
begin
  Toggle1.Checked := not Toggle1.Checked;
  if Toggle1.Checked then
    Label1.Caption := 'ON'
```

FIGURE 8.12:

The NEWCHECK example at
run-time. Notice the new check
mark.

```
   else
     Label1.Caption := 'OFF';
end;
```

The most important portion of the code of this example is the call of the SetMenu-ItemBitmaps Windows API function. This function has a number of parameters:

```
function SetMenuItemBitmaps (Menu: HMenu;
  Position, Flags: Word;
  BitmapUnchecked, BitmapChecked: HBitmap): Bool;
```

The first parameter is the pull-down menu we refer to, the second is the position of the menu item in that pull-down menu, the third is a flag that determines how to interpret the previous parameter (Position), and the last two parameters indicate the bitmaps that should be used. Notice that this function changes the check mark bitmaps only for a specific menu item. (You can look up a detailed description of the function in the Help related to the Windows API, directly available from the Delphi Help menu or by pressing F1 after you have selected the name of the function in the code.)

Here is the code you can use in Delphi to call the function. Figure 8.10 is an example of its effect:

```
SetMenuItemBitmaps (Command1.Handle, Toggle1.Command,
  MF_BYCOMMAND, Bmp2.Handle, Bmp1.Handle);
```

This call uses two bitmap variables that are defined inside the code and the names of some components (Command1 is the name of the pull-down, and Toggle1 is the name of the menu item). The code above shows that it is usually very easy to pass the handle of an element to a Windows function—just use its Handle property.

At first I thought this function could be called when the form was created, after the two bitmaps had been loaded from the file, but I've found out that is not true. Delphi changes the default Windows behavior somewhat, forcing the application to re-associate the bitmap to the menu items each time they are displayed.

The solution I've found is to execute this call each time the pull-down menu is selected—that is, on the OnClick event of the pull-down.

The only thing left is to load the bitmaps. You need to declare two variables of the TBitmap class, create an instance of the two objects, and then load the bitmaps from the two BMP files. This is done once, when the form is created:

```
procedure TForm1.FormCreate(Sender: TObject);
begin
  Bmp1 := TBitmap.Create;
  Bmp2 := TBitmap.Create;
  Bmp1.LoadFromFile ('ok.bmp');
  Bmp2.LoadFromFile ('no.bmp');
end;
```

The two bitmaps should also be destroyed when the program terminates (using the FormDestroy method). Notice that to run this program, you need to have the two BMP files in the same directory as the executable file. The bitmaps, in fact, are loaded at run-time and are not embedded by Delphi in the EXE file.

> **NOTE**
>
> You can indeed include a bitmap in the resources of an application and in its executable file in order to be able to ship the application in a single file. This process, however, is slightly more complex, so I've decided not to use it for the moment. Later chapters (starting with Chapter 10) include examples of the use of resources to store a bitmap. Chapter 21 is devoted entirely to Windows resources.

# Changing the System Menu

In some circumstances, it is interesting to add some menu commands to the system menu itself, instead of having a menu bar. This might be useful for secondary windows, toolboxes, windows requiring a large area on the screen, and for quick and dirty applications. Adding a single menu item to the system menu is straightforward:

```
AppendMenu (GetSystemMenu (Handle, FALSE),
  MF_SEPARATOR, 0, '');
AppendMenu (GetSystemMenu (Handle, FALSE),
  MF_STRING, idSysAbout, '&About...');
```

The code fragment above adds a separator and a new item to the system menu item, accessed through the GetSystemMenu API function (which requires as parameter the handle of the window). The AppendMenu API function is a general purpose one, and can add menu items or complete pull-down menus to any menu (the menu bar, the system menu, or a pull-down). When adding a menu item, you have to specify its text and an ID, defined as

```
const
  idSysAbout = 100;
```

This code is typically executed in the OnCreate event handler. This is what I've done in the SYSMENU example, as you can see in the output of Figure 8.13. Adding a menu item to the system menu is easy, but how can we handle its selection? Selecting a menu generates a wm_Command system message. This is handled by a Delphi OnCommand handler, which activates the OnClick event of the corresponding menu item. The selection of system menu commands, instead, generates a wm_Sys-Command message, which is passed by Delphi to the default handler. Windows has usually something to do in response to a system menu command.

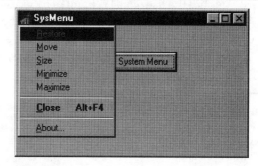

**FIGURE 8.13:**

The new item of the system menu of the SYSMENU example, added in the OnCreate event handler.

We can intercept this command and check to see whether the command identifier (passed in the wParam Windows message parameter) is our idSysAbout. Since there isn't a corresponding event in Delphi, we have to define a new message-response method to the form class:

```
public
  procedure WMSysCommand (var Msg: TMessage);
    message wm_SysCommand;
```

The code of this procedure is not very complex. We have just to check whether the command is our own and call the default handler (that is, the handler of the parent class):

```
procedure TForm1.WMSysCommand (var Msg: TMessage);
begin
  if Msg.WParam = idSysAbout then
    ShowMessage ('Mastering Delphi: SysMenu example');
  inherited;
end;
```

To build a more complex system menu, instead of adding and handling each menu item as we have just done, we can follow a different approach. Just add a MainMenu component to the form, create its structure, and write the proper event handlers. Then, reset the Menu property of the form, removing the menu bar, and write some code to add each of the items from the hidden menu to the system menu, and invoke the proper handlers when the form receives a wm_SysCommand message.

As an example, in the SYSMENU program I've added a button to copy the structure of the menu to the system menu, using generic code that doesn't depend on its structure:

```
with MainMenu1 do
  for I := 0 to Items.Count - 1 do
    AppendMenu (GetSystemMenu (self.Handle, FALSE),
      MF_POPUP, Items[I].Handle, PChar (Items[I].Caption));
```

Notice the use of self.Handle to access the handle of the form, instead of using the MainMenu1 component (because of the with statement). The flag used in this case, MF_POPUP, indicates we are adding a pop-up menu, so that the final structure of the system menu will have two levels, as you can see in Figure 8.14.

FIGURE 8.14:

The second level system menu of the SYSMENU example is the result of copying a full menu to the system menu.

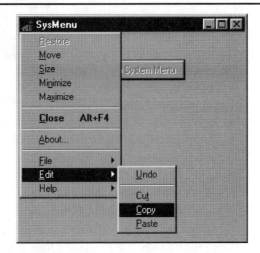

Once you have added the menu items to the system menu, you need to handle them in a smarter way. Since each menu item has its own OnClick handler, we can find the item in the menu structure using its command, then call its Click method (which invokes the OnClick handler). Here is the code I've added to the WMSysCommand method:

```
var
  Item: TMenuItem;
Item := PopupMenu1.FindItem (Msg.WParam, fkCommand);
if not (Item = nil) then
  Item.Click;
```

The wParam field of the message that is passed to the WMSysCommand procedure holds the command of the menu item being called. You can also use a simple if or case statement to handle one of the system menu's predefined menu items that have special codes for this identifier, such as sc_Close, sc_Minimize, sc_Maximize, and so on. For more information, you can see the description of the wm_SysCommand message in the Windows API Help (available in Delphi).

# The NOTES Program Menu

Now that we know how to write a complex menu, disable and check menu items, and so on, we are ready to build the menu for a full-fledged application. Do you remember the NOTES example from the last chapter? You could use it to write text and change the font, but that was all. Now we want to add a menu to it and implement a number of features, including a complex scheme to open and save text files. In fact, we want to be able to ask the user to save any modified file before opening a new one, to avoid losing any changes. Sounds like a professional application, doesn't it?

**NOTE**
You might want to apply these changes to the RERADIO example shown before, which is based on the more powerful RichEdit component. This will let you build a real editor. You can also find a similar example in the Delphi 2 sample programs (called RICHEDIT).

First of all, we need to build the menu, following the standard. The menu's structure has standard File and Edit pull-down menus, a Text menu with items to align and wrap the text, an Options menu with commands to change the color and the font and to count the characters, and the typical Help ➤ About command. In this example, we want to implement most but not all of the commands of the menu. Those referring to printing and to accessing the Clipboard will be implemented in Chapters 22 and 24, respectively.

As in the NOTES example in Chapter 5, the Memo component, which is the only visual component of the form, is aligned with the form. Some of the properties of the memo are set by corresponding menu items and are very easy to figure out. You can change the color of the background of the text, change the font (and color) of the text, align the text to the left or right, or center it. As the text alignment changes, a check mark is added to the menu beside the current selection. As you can guess, some of these commands are based on Windows system dialog boxes.

Activating the word-wrap features of the Memo component is slightly more complex. When the text beyond the visible end of a line moves automatically to a new line, the horizontal scroll bar becomes useless and is removed:

```
if Memo1.WordWrap then
begin
  Memo1.WordWrap := False;
  WordWrap1.Checked := False;
  Memo1.ScrollBars := ssBoth;
end
else
begin
  Memo1.WordWrap := True;
  WordWrap1.Checked := True;
  Memo1.ScrollBars := ssVertical;
end;
```

An interesting feature we can add to the program is a method to count the number of characters in the text and display it in a message box. The core of the method is the call to the memo's GetTextLen function. This number is extracted and formatted into the output string:

```
MessageDlg (Format (
  'The text has %d characters', [Memo1.GetTextLen]),
  mtInformation, [mbOK], 0);
```

# Loading and Saving Files

As I mentioned at the beginning of the description of the NOTES example, the most complex part is the implementation of the File pull-down menu commands. The commands are New, Open, Save, and Save As. In each case, we need to track whether the current file has changed, saving the file only if it has. We should ask the user to save the file each time he or she creates a new file, loads an existing one, or exits from the application.

To accomplish this, I've added two fields and three methods to the class describing the form of the application:

```
private
  filename: string;
  modified: Boolean;
public
  function SaveChanges: Boolean;
  function Save: Boolean;
  function SaveAs: Boolean;
```

The filename string and the modified flag are set when the form is created and changed when a new file is loaded or the user gives a new name to a file with the Save As command. The flag's value changes as soon as you type new characters in the memo (in its OnChange event handler).

When a new file is created, the program checks whether the text has been modified. If it has, it calls the SaveChanges function, which asks the user whether to save the changes, lose them, or skip the current operation:

```
procedure TNotesForm.New1Click(Sender: TObject);
begin
  if not modified or SaveChanges then
  begin
    Memo1.Text := '';
    modified := False;
    filename := '';
    NotesForm.Caption := 'Notes - [Untitled]';
  end;
end;
```

If the creation of a new file is confirmed, some simple operations take place, including using Untitled instead of the file name in the form's caption.

**NOTE**

The expression `if not modified or SaveChanges then` requires some explanation. By default, Pascal performs what is called *short-circuit evaluation* of complex conditional expressions. The idea is simple: if the expression `not modified` is true, we are sure that the whole `or` expression is going to be true. The evaluation of the second expression becomes useless. In this particular case, the second expression is a function call, and the function is called only if `modified` is True. This behavior of `or` and `and` expressions can be changed by setting a compiler option. In Delphi, this option is called Complete Boolean Eval. You can find it on the Compiler page of the Project Options dialog box.

The message box displayed by the SaveChanges function has three options (see Figure 8.15). If the user selects the Cancel button, the function returns False. If the user selects the No button, nothing happens (the file is not saved) and the function returns True, to indicate that although we haven't actually saved the file, the requested operation (such as creating a new file) can be accomplished. If the user selects the Yes button, the file is saved and the function returns True. Here is the code:

```
function TNotesForm.SaveChanges: Boolean;
var
  code: Integer;
begin
  SaveChanges := True;
  code := MessageDlg ('The document ' + filename +
    ' has changed.' + #13#13 + 'Do you want to save the changes?',
    mtConfirmation, mbYesNoCancel, 0);
  if (code = IDYES) then
```

**FIGURE 8.15:**

The message box displayed when the text of the memo has been changed and has not been saved.

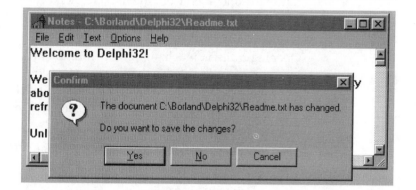

```
    SaveChanges := Save;
  if (code = IDCANCEL) then
    SaveChanges := False;
end;
```

To actually save the file, another function is invoked: Save. This method saves the file if it already has a proper file name or asks the user to enter a name, maybe using the SaveAs functions:

```
function TNotesForm.Save: Boolean;
begin
  if filename = '' then
    Save := SaveAs
  else
  begin
    modified := False;
    Memo1.Lines.SaveToFile (filename);
    Save := True;
  end;
end;

function TNotesForm.SaveAs: Boolean;
begin
  SaveDialog1.FileName := filename;
  if SaveDialog1.Execute then
  begin
    filename := SaveDialog1.FileName;
    Memo1.Lines.SaveToFile(filename);
    modified := False;
    NotesForm.Caption := 'Notes - ' + filename;
    SaveAs := True;
  end
  else
    SaveAs := False;
end;
```

I use two functions to perform the Save and SaveAs operations (and do not call the corresponding menu handler directly) because I need a way to report a request to cancel the operation from the user. To avoid code duplication, the handlers of the Save and SaveAs menu items call the two functions too, although they ignore the return value.

Opening a file is much simpler. Before loading a new file, the program checks whether the current file has changed, asking the user to save it with the SaveChanges function, as before. The Open1Click method is based on the Open-Dialog component, another default dialog box provided by Windows and supported by Delphi:

```
procedure TNotesForm.Open1Click(Sender: TObject);
begin
  if not modified or SaveChanges then
    if OpenDialog1.Execute then
```

```
begin
  filename := OpenDialog1.FileName;
  Memo1.Lines.LoadFromFile(filename);
  modified := False;
  NotesForm.Caption := 'Notes - ' + filename;
end;
end;
```

The only issue I want to discuss now is that both this and the SaveDialog component of the NotesForm have a particular value for their Filter property:

```
Text Files (*.txt)|*.txt|Pascal files (*.pas)|*.pas|
Windows ini files (*.ini)|*.ini|All files (*.*)|*.*
```

This string (which should be written on a single line) contains four pairs of substrings, separated by the ¦ symbol. Each pair has a description of the type of file that will appear in the File Open or File Save dialog box, and the filter to be applied to the files in the directory, such as *.txt.

To set the filters in Delphi, you can simply invoke the editor of this property, which displays a list with two columns (see Figure 8.16). More details on this topic will be presented in Chapter 12.

**FIGURE 8.16:**

The standard Open File dialog box in the NOTES2 program. On the left you can see the value of the Filter property in the Object Inspector and the Filters Editors.

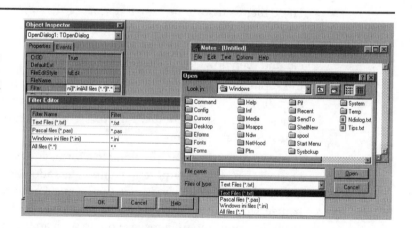

The last method of the source code of this example (available only on the companion CD) that I want to discuss refers to closing the form. The FormCloseQuery method is called each time the user tries to close the form, terminating the program. We can make this happen in various ways—by double-clicking on the system menu icon, selecting the system menu's Close command, pressing the Alt+F4 keys, or calling the Close method in the code, as in the File ➤ Exit command.

In FormCloseQuery, you can decide whether or not to actually close the application by setting the CanClose parameter, which is passed by reference. Again, if the current file has been modified, we call the SaveChanges function. This time, however, the implementation uses two different `if` statements instead of the short-circuit evaluation technique:

```
procedure TNotesForm.FormCloseQuery(Sender: TObject;
  var CanClose: Boolean);
begin
  if modified then
    if SaveChanges then
      CanClose := True
    else
      CanClose := False
  else
    CanClose := True;
end;
```

# Pop-Up Menus (and the Right Mouse Button)

In Windows 95, it is common to see applications that have special local menus you activate by clicking the right mouse button. The menu that is displayed—a pop-up menu, in Windows terms—usually depends on the position of the mouse click. These menus tend to be easy to use since they group only the few commands related to the element that is currently selected. They are also usually faster to use than full-blown menus because you don't need to move the mouse up to the menu bar and then down again to go on working.

In Delphi, there are basically two ways to display pop-up menus, using the corresponding component. You can let Delphi handle them automatically or you can choose a manual technique. I'll explore both approaches, starting with the first, which is the simplest one.

If you want to add a pop-up menu to a form, you need to perform a few simple operations. Create a PopupMenu component, add some menu items to it, and select the component as the value of the form's PopupMenu property. That's all. Of course, you should also add some handlers for the OnClick events of the local menu's various menu items, as you do with an ordinary menu.

## The LOCAL Example

To show you how to create a local menu, I've built an example that is an extension of the DRAGGING example in Chapter 7. The new example is named LOCAL1. I've added a first PopupMenu1 component to the form, and I've connected it using the PopupMenu property of the form itself. Once this is done, running the program and clicking the right mouse button on the surface of the form displays the local menu.

Then, I've added a second pop-up menu with two levels to the form, and I've attached it to the big label on the right, Label5. To connect a local menu to a specific component, you simply need to set its PopupMenu property. You can see the result in Figure 8.17. The four methods related to the first group of commands of the Colors pull-down menu just select a color (Label5.Color := clRed). The Transparent command selects the color of the parent form as the current color, setting the value of the ParentColor property to True.

The checked Alignment pull-down menu of the second pop-up in the example.

**NOTE**

The components of a form usually borrow some properties from the form. This is indicated by specific properties, such as ParentColor or ParentFont. When these properties are set to True, the current value of the component's property is ignored, and the value of the form is used instead. Usually, this is not a problem since as soon as you set a property of the component (for example, the font), the corresponding property indicating the use of the parent attribute (ParentFont) is automatically set to False.

The last command of the pull-down menu, User Defined, presents the standard Color Selection dialog box to the user. The three commands of the pop-up menu's second pull-down change the alignment of the text of the big label and add a check mark near the current selection, deselecting the other two menu items:

```
procedure TDraggingForm.Center1Click(Sender: TObject);
begin
```

```
   Label5.Alignment := taCenter;
   Left1.Checked := False;
   Center1.Checked := True;
   Right1.Checked := False;
end;
```

A pop-up menu, in fact, can use all the features of a main menu and can have checked, disabled, or hidden items, and more.

## Changing a Pop-Up Menu When It Is Activated

Why not use the same technique to display a check mark near the selected color? It is possible, but it's not a very good solution. In fact, there are six menu items to consider, and the color can also change when a user drags it from one of the labels on the left of the form. For this reason, and to have the opportunity to show you another technique, I've followed a different approach.

Each time a pop-up menu is displayed, the OnPopup event is sent to your application. In the code of the corresponding method, you can place the check mark on the current selection of the color, independently from the action used to set it:

```
procedure TDraggingForm.PopupMenu2Popup(Sender: TObject);
var
  I: Integer;
begin
  with Colors1 do
    for I := 0 to Count - 1 do
      Items[I].Checked := False;
  case Label5.Color of
    clRed: Red1.Checked := True;
    clAqua: Aqua1.Checked := True;
    clGreen: Green1.Checked := True;
    clYellow: Yellow1.Checked := True;
  else
    if Label5.ParentColor = True then
      Transparent1.Checked := True
    else
      Userdefined1.Checked := True;
  end;
end;
```

This method's code requires some explanation. At the beginning, the menu items are all unchecked by using a for loop on the Items array of the Colors1 menu. The counter of the loop starts at 0 and stops at Count –1. The advantage of this loop is that it operates on all the menu items, regardless of their number. Then the program uses a case statement to check the proper item.

**NEW** Notice that this code works only in the 32-bit version of Delphi. In the 16-bit version, a case statement cannot handle long integers (such as the color). As an alternative, you can use a series of nested `else if` statements.

# Handling Pop-Up Menus Manually

Up to now, we have seen how to use an automatic pop-up menu. As an alternative, you can set the AutoPopup property to False or not connect the pop-up menu to any component, and use the pop-up menu's Popup method to display it on the screen. This procedure requires two parameters: the x and y values of the position where the menu is going to be displayed. The problem is that you need to supply the screen coordinates of the point, not the client coordinates, which are the usual coordinates related to the form's client area.

As an example, I've taken an existing application with a menu—MENU_ONE, described at the beginning of this chapter—and added a peculiar pop-up menu. The idea is that there are two different pop-up menus, one to change the colors and the other to change the alignment of the text. Each time the user clicks the right mouse button on the caption, one of the two pop-up menus is displayed. In real applications, you'll probably have to decide which menu to display depending on the status of some variable. Here, I've followed a simple (and somewhat dumb) rule. Each time the right mouse button is clicked, the pop-up menu changes. Again, my aim is to show you how to do this in the simplest possible way, not to build complex and unmanageable examples.

The two pop-up menus are very simple, and correspond to actions already available in the main menu (and connected with the same event handlers). Actually, I've built these pop-up menus by copying the main menu to a menu template and then pasting from it. The only change I've made is to remove the shortcut keys. When the user clicks the right mouse button over the label, which takes up the whole surface of the form, a method displays one of the two menus:

```
procedure TFormColorText.Label1MouseDown(Sender: TObject;
  Button: TMouseButton; Shift: TShiftState; X, Y: Integer);
var
  ClientPoint, ScreenPoint: TPoint;
begin
  if Button = mbRight then
  begin
    ClientPoint.X := X;
    ClientPoint.Y := Y;
    ScreenPoint := ClientToScreen (ClientPoint);
    Inc (ClickCount);
```

```
    if Odd (ClickCount) then
      PopupMenu1.Popup (ScreenPoint.X, ScreenPoint.Y)
    else
      PopupMenu2.Popup (ScreenPoint.X, ScreenPoint.Y);
  end;
end;
```

In this procedure, you first have to check whether the right mouse button was clicked. The second step is to translate the coordinate of the position of the mouse click from client coordinates—the x and y parameters of the mouse events are in the client coordinate system, having their origin in the upper-left corner of the form—to screen coordinates, using the ClientToScreen method. Screen coordinates are required by the PopupMenu component's Popup method. If you look at the listing on the companion CD, you'll see I've used a slightly different version of this example to copy the current check marks to the PopupMenu2's menu items, before displaying the pop-up menu on the screen.

# Summary

In this chapter, we have seen how to create a main menu or a pop-up menu in Delphi. These are the key elements:

- When defining a menu, follow the standard guidelines for the names of the pull-down menus and of the menu items and for their ordering.

- Remember to use shortcut keys and the ampersand properly, but use them often, to allow the user to access the menu using the keyboard.

- Check menu items, disable them, and change the structure of a menu at will; Delphi and Windows offer a number of choices for changing a menu at run-time.

- Use local menus whenever possible, as most large applications do.

You can explore in other directions, as well. For example, you can create a menu dynamically (at run-time) or copy portions of a menu to another menu, as in the SYS-MENU example. We will see some further examples on the use of the menu, particularly in Chapter 12, when we will explore menu-merging techniques.

But first, in the next chapter, we will start exploring in detail a key element of Delphi programming: forms.

# CHAPTER

## NINE

# Back to the Form

- The hidden application window

- Form styles and topmost forms

- Border styles and icons

- Positioning and scaling forms

- Form creation

- Mouse input

- How to draw and paint on a form

If you've read the book up to this point, you should now be able to use Delphi's basic components and to create and use menus. So I suppose it's time to turn our attention to the central element of development in Delphi: the form. We have used forms since the first chapter, but I've never described to you in detail what you can do with a form, which properties you can use, or which methods of the TForm component are particularly interesting.

In this chapter, we'll look at some of the properties and styles of forms and at their size and position. We'll also devote some time to input and output on a form. Let me start this chapter with a general, theoretical discussion on forms and windows.

# Forms versus Windows

Do you remember the title of the first chapter of this book? It was "A Form Is a Window," and at the beginning of the text I explained that there is a sort of correspondence between the forms we create in Delphi and the Windows windows. Now it's time to look into the details of this correspondence.

In Windows, most of the elements of the user interface are windows. For this reason, in Delphi most of the components are also windows—most of them, but not all; there are some very interesting exceptions. Of course, this is not what a user perceives. To make things clearer, study the following definitions carefully. Then we can make some further observations.

- From a user standpoint, a window is a portion of the screen surrounded by a border, having a caption and usually a system menu, that can be moved on the screen, closed, and at times also minimized and maximized. Windows move on the screen or inside other windows, as in MDI applications. These user windows can be divided into two general categories: main windows and dialog boxes.

- Technically speaking, a window is an entry in an internal memory area of the Windows system, often corresponding to an element visible on the screen, that has some associated code. One of the Windows system libraries contains a list of all the windows that have been built by every application and assigns to each of them a unique number (usually known as a *handle*). Some of these windows are perceived as such by the users (see the first definition above), others have the role of controls or visual components, others are temporarily created by the system (for example, to show a pull-down menu), and still others are created by the application but remain hidden from the user.

The common denominator of all windows is that they are known by the Windows system and refer to a function for their behavior: each time an event takes place in the system, the function associated with the corresponding window is called.

**NOTE** The area of the Windows system listing all the windows that have been built is limited. Building too many windows reduces the so-called *system resources*. Windows 3.1 had a severe limit to the number of windows available in the system. In Windows 95, this limit has been greatly enlarged, and in Windows NT it doesn't even exist. Once there are too many windows in the system (counting all the controls and hidden windows, as well), you cannot create one more window, something that will block most applications. This is why, in Delphi, there are a number of non-windowed components, including labels. This approach lets you save a lot of this system memory without having to worry about or even know about it.

With these general definitions in mind, we can now move back to Delphi and try to understand the role of forms. Forms represent windows from a user standpoint and can be used to build main windows, MDI windows, and dialog boxes. Their behavior depends mostly on their code, but also on a couple of very important properties I'll discuss in a moment.

Many other components are based on windows, but only forms define windows from a user point of view. The other windowed components, or controls, can be defined as windows only according to the second, technical definition.

Take as an example the first application we built in Chapter 1, HELLO. Using the WinSight tool that comes with Delphi, you can see the list of the windows created by the application, as shown in Figure 9.1 (for more details on WinSight and the information it can deliver, see Chapter 20). These include the following windows:

- A main window, the form, with the title *Hello*. It is an overlapped window of class TForm1.

- A child window, the button inside the form, with the title *Say Hello*. This is a child window of class TButton.

- A hidden main window, the application window, entitled *Hello*. This is a pop-up window of class TApplication.

Notice that the names in brackets in WinSight, which are internal names of the system, correspond to the names of the classes of the Delphi components.

FIGURE 9.1:

The windows of the HELLO application as they appear in WinSight.

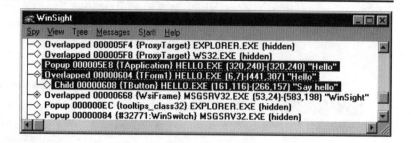

## Overlapped, Pop-Up, and Child Windows

To understand the role of the various windows of this program, we need to look at some technical elements related to the Windows environment. These are not simple concepts, but I think they are worth knowing.

Each window you create has one of three general styles that determine its behavior. These styles are overlapped, pop-up, and child. *Overlapped* windows are main windows of the application, which behave as you would probably expect. *Pop-up* windows are often used for dialog boxes and message boxes and can be considered a leftover from older versions of the system. In fact, in Windows 1.0, the windows were not overlapped but tiled, and only the pop-up windows could cover other windows. Pop-up windows are generally very similar to overlapped windows.

The third group, *child* windows, was originally used for controls inside a dialog box. You can use this style for any window that cannot move outside the client area of the parent window. The obvious extension is to use child windows to build MDI applications, but, as we will see in Chapter 12, Microsoft added a fix-up technique to allow this behavior, which is not automatic.

It is important to note that, technically speaking, only child windows can have a parent. Any other window, however, can have an owner. An *owner* is a window that has a continuous message exchange with the windows it owns—for example, when the window is reduced to an icon, when it is activated, and so on. Usually a parent is also the owner, but it forces its child to live inside its client area. The child windows don't use screen coordinates; instead, they use the client area coordinates of their parent window—they borrow pixels not from the screen to display themselves but from their parent window.

In Delphi, forms are all overlapped windows, even the dialog boxes, and the windowed components (the controls) you place inside a form are all owned by the form. However, their parent can be either the form or one of the special *container* components, such as the GroupBox or the Panel. When you place a radio button inside a group box, the group box is its parent, but the form is its owner.

What about pop-up windows? In Delphi, they are used only for the hidden application window.

## The Application Is a Window

From the analysis of the WinSight information, you might have noticed something very strange: The application is a window! When I first noticed this I was astonished, because the form works so well it appears to be the main window of the application. Instead, forms are connected to an owner, the application window. This window is hidden from sight unless you minimize the form.

What are the role and effect of this hidden main window? The role of the application object is to provide some startup code before you create any form, or even before you decide which form to create, as you can see with the View Project Source command after you've created or loaded a project. The window related to the Application object—the application window—serves to keep together all the windows of an application. The fact that all the top-level forms of a program have this hidden owner window, for example, is fundamental when the application is activated.

In fact, when the windows of your program are behind other windows, clicking on one window in your application will bring all of your application's windows to the front. In other words, the hidden application window is used to connect the different forms of the application.

The Application object, which is an instance of one of the few components not present in the Components palette, has some properties, including the name of the executable file and the title of the application. The title usually is the name of the executable file without the extension.

When you work with a form, you can see the application's title in the Windows 95 TaskBar. In Windows 3.1, the same title became visible, reducing the application to an icon. The same name appears when you scan the running application with the Alt+Tab keys.

If you don't like to have a discrepancy between the two titles, you can change the application's title at design-time, in the Application page of the Project Options dialog box. At run-time, you can copy the form's caption to the title of the application with this code:

```
Application.Title := Form1.Caption;
```

**NOTE**   The presence of the hidden application window causes some other strange behaviors in Windows 3.1. For example, Delphi applications do not tile or cascade properly. This is not an issue in Windows 95, and you can actually see that some Delphi 1.0 features were already designed with Windows 95 in mind.

The application window is hidden in most applications, but it has some interesting uses. For this reason, Chapter 19 is devoted to this topic.

# Setting Form Styles

Among the properties of a form, two of them determine the fundamental rules of its behavior: FormStyle and BorderStyle. The first of these two special properties allows you to choose between a normal SDI form—*SDI* stands for *Single Document Interface*—and one of the windows that make up an MDI application. These are the values of FormStyle:

- `fsNormal`:  The form is a normal SDI window or a dialog box.
- `fsMDIChild`:  The form is an MDI child window.
- `fsMDIForm`:  The form is an MDI parent window—that is, the frame window of the MDI application.
- `fsStayOnTop`:  The form is an SDI window, but it always remains on top of all other windows except for any that also happen to be "stay on top" windows.

Since an application following the Multiple Document Interface standard needs windows of two different kinds (frame and child), two values of the FormStyle property are involved. To build an MDI application, you can use the standard application template or look at Chapter 15, which focuses on the MDI in detail. For now, though, it might be interesting to explore the use of the `fsStayOnTop` style.

## Creating Topmost Forms

To create a topmost form (a form whose window is always on top), you need only set the FormStyle property, as indicated above. If this is the main form of an application, it will remain in front of every other application (unless other applications have the same topmost style, too). If it is a secondary form, it will remain in front of any other form of the application it belongs to. The windows of other applications are not affected, though. Before we look at an example, consider that topmost windows can be useful, but they can also be very disappointing. When a topmost window is maximized, activating another application (for example, by pressing Alt+Tab) has almost no effect. My advice is to use topmost windows sparingly, and mostly for secondary windows, such as a toolbox.

Building a topmost window is very easy. I've decided to create an example, TOP, that also allows a user to toggle the Topmost attribute on and off. The form of the example has only a menu component. When the user selects Style ➤ Stay on Top, this style is toggled, together with the check mark beside the menu item:

```
procedure TForm1.StayOnTop1Click(Sender: TObject);
begin
  if FormStyle = fsStayOnTop then
    FormStyle := fsNormal
  else
    FormStyle := fsStayOnTop;
  StayOnTop1.Checked := not StayOnTop1.Checked;
end;
```

When you run this program, you can see some flickering on the screen when the topmost style is set or removed. This occurs because Delphi has to destroy and re-create the (same) window each time you toggle the value of the Topmost property.

## Avoiding Topmost Flickering

To avoid the negative effect of topmost flickering, we can forget for a second what we know about Delphi and this form property and ask ourselves how we could have toggled the Topmost attribute using the Windows API. There are a number of possible techniques. The Topmost attribute is technically an extended Windows style (ws_ex_Topmost). For a style, we can use the SetWindowLong API function, which allows a programmer to change a number of window attributes at run-time.

A second approach is to use the SetWindowPos API function, which has seven parameters but in our case is easy to use. In fact, there are some flags we can use to toggle the Topmost property, and we can ignore most of the parameters.

To make a window into the topmost window, we can write

```
SetWindowPos (Handle, hwnd_TopMost, 0, 0, 0, 0,
  swp_NoMove or swp_NoSize);
```

> **NOTE**
>
> `SetWindowPos` is a strange function. It requires the handle of the window you want to operate on, the handle of a second window or a special flag (to set the *z-order* of window, a term indicating the relative position of windows along a z-axis coming out of the screen), two position-related parameters (x and y), two size parameters (cx and cy, the width and the height), and some flags. The strange thing is that you can use the flags to indicate which of the parameters make sense and should be used. For example, if you write `swp_NoMove`, the third and fourth parameters will be ignored (for this reason, I've just written some zeros in my code).

To get the opposite effect, removing the topmost style, simply replace `hwnd_Top-Most` with `hwnd_NoTopMost` in the function call. The new version of the example is named TOP2. Its form is the same as the previous one, aside from the fact that the Topmost property is not enabled at first. Here is the code for the new version of the StayOnTop1Click method:

```
procedure TForm1.StayOnTop1Click(Sender: TObject);
begin
  if StayOnTop1.Checked then
    SetWindowPos (Handle, hwnd_NoTopMost,
      0, 0, 0, 0, swp_NoMove or swp_NoSize)
  else
    SetWindowPos (Handle, hwnd_TopMost,
      0, 0, 0, 0, swp_NoMove or swp_NoSize);
  StayOnTop1.Checked := not StayOnTop1.Checked;
end;
```

Notice that this time I've decided to test the status of the menu item's check mark to determine the current status of the form. In fact, the FormStyle always remains normal, even when the Topmost style of the form has been set. Remember that some properties of Delphi components duplicate information available in Windows and do not retrieve it every time you access it. This is always true for properties not having a direct correspondence in the system, such as a form's style.

If you experiment with TOP and TOP2, you'll notice that the second version has no flickering at all. Although Delphi is a great environment, at times, if you know what you are doing, you can bypass undesired behavior by using a direct call to the Windows API.

With this said, you might wonder why Borland hasn't followed this approach. Well, there are a number of very good reasons. The technique based on the `SetWindow-Pos` API shown above works only in some circumstances. When your application is made up of several windows or when your topmost window opens a message box or dialog box, the system does not handle the focus and activation of the windows properly. Basically, there are problems in Windows with the ownership of topmost windows. Delphi, with its solution, bypasses these problems. For more information on this topic, look to the NormalizeTopMost and RestoreTopMost methods of the TApplication class in Delphi Help file.

To sum up, if you have just a single window, you can use the approach shown above; otherwise, I suggest you stay with the Delphi solution. Better yet, consider setting the Topmost flag at design-time and avoid toggling it whenever possible.

# The Border Style

The second basic property of a form I want to focus on is BorderStyle. This property refers to a visual element of the form, but it has a much more profound influence on the behavior of the window. The BorderStyle property of a form has six possible values, as you can see in Figure 9.2:

- `bsSizeable`: The form has a standard thick border that a user can drag to resize it. This is the default style.

- `bsDialog`: The form has a standard dialog box border, which is thick but not resizable. A form with this style behaves like a dialog box—it really *is* a dialog box.

**FIGURE 9.2:**

Sample forms with the different border styles, created by the BORDERS example.

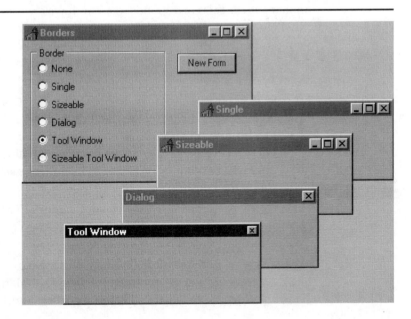

- `bsSingle:` The form has a thin border and cannot be resized; it is also known as a *fixed* border. Contrary to Windows 3.1, in Windows 95 there isn't a clear visible difference between a thin and a thick border.

- `bsToolWindow:` The form has a thin caption (with a smaller font), and only a miniature close button. This is a special style for non-resizable toolboxes.

- `bsSizeToolWin:` The form has a thin caption, as with the style above, but is also resizable.

- `bsNone:` The form has no border nor any of the traditional elements (caption, minimize and maximize buttons, system menu).

Setting the BorderStyle property at design-time produces no visible effect. There are good reasons for this. How could you resize the form with the mouse if it were turned into a dialog box? When you run the application, though, the form will have the border you requested.

Several component properties do not take effect at design-time because this would prevent you from working on them while developing the program. For example, setting its Visible property to False at design-time does not hide a component. Hidden windows, in fact, can receive no messages.

## The Effect of the BorderStyle Property

At design-time, the form is always shown with the default value of BorderStyle, `bsSizeable`. This corresponds to a Windows style known as *thick frame*. The fact is that when a main window has a thick frame around it a user can resize it by dragging its border. This is made clear by the special *resize* cursors (with the shape of a double-pointer arrow) displayed when the user moves the mouse on this thick window border.

A second important choice for this property is `fsDialog`. If you select it, the form uses as its border the typical dialog box frame—a thick frame that doesn't allow resizing. In addition to this graphical element, I would like to emphasize that if you select the `fsDialog` value, the form becomes a dialog box. This involves a number of changes. For example, the items on its system menu are different, and the form will ignore the BorderIcons property.

When are you supposed to use this kind of frame? There are two possibilities: when you are actually building a dialog box (see Chapter 12) or when you want to use a dialog box as the application's main window.

We can give four more values to the BorderStyle property. The style `bsSingle` can be used to create a main non-resizable window. Many applications based on windows with controls (such as data-entry forms) and many games use this value simply because resizing these forms make no sense. Enlarging a form to see an empty area or reducing its size to lose the visibility of some components often doesn't help a program's user (although Delphi's automatic scroll bars partially solve the last problem). The value fsNone is used only in very special situations and inside other forms. You'll never see an application with a main window with no border and caption (except as an example to show you that this makes no sense).

The last two values, bsToolWindow and bsSizeToolWin are related to the specific Windows 95 extended style WS_EX_TOOLWINDOW. This new style (not available in Windows 3.1) turns the window into a floating toolbox, with a small title font and close button. This style should not be used for the main window of an application.

# The BORDERS Example

To test the effect and behavior of the different values of the BorderStyle property, I've written a simple program. You saw its output in Figure 9.2. However, I suggest you run this example and experiment with it for a while to help you understand all the differences in the forms.

The main form of this program has a simple form, with a radio group and a button. There is also a secondary form, with no component and the Position property set to poDefaultPosOnly. This affects the initial position of the secondary form we create pressing the button (I'll discuss the Position property in full later on in this chapter).

The code of the program is very simple: when you press the button, a new form is created, depending on the selected radio button:

```
procedure TForm1.NewFormButtonClick(Sender: TObject);
var
  NewForm: TForm2;
begin
  NewForm := TForm2.Create (Application);
  NewForm.BorderStyle := TFormBorderStyle (
    BorderRadioGroup.ItemIndex);
  NewForm.Caption := BorderRadioGroup.Items[
    BorderRadioGroup.ItemIndex];
  NewForm.Show;
end;
```

This program refers to TForm2, the secondary form defined in a second unit of the program. For this reason, to compile the example you must add the following lines to the implementation section of the unit of the main form:

```
uses
  Second;
```

**TIP** Every time you have to refer to another unit of a program, place the corresponding uses statement in the implementation portion whenever possible. This speeds up the compilation process, results in cleaner code (because the units you include are separate from those included by Delphi), and never generates circular references between different units. We will discuss these topics in more detail in Chapter 12.

## The Border Icons

Another important element of a form is the presence of icons on its border. By default, a form in Windows 3.1 has in its caption a system menu, a minimize box, and a maximize box. In Windows 95 it has a small icon replacing the system menu and a close button on the far right, near the minimize and maximize buttons.

You can set different options using the BorderIcons property, a set with four possible values: biSystemMenu, biMinimize, biMaximize, and biHelp.

**NEW** The new biHelp border icon enables the "What's this?" help. When this style is included and the biMinimize and biMaximize styles are excluded, a question mark appears in the form's title bar. If you click on this question mark and then click on a form or component, Delphi activates the help about that object inside a pop-up window. (Writing a help system and associating it with a Delphi application is not covered in this book.)

Again, I've written a simple program to show you the behavior of a form with different border icons and to show you how to change this property at run-time. The form of this example is very simple: it has only a menu, with a pull-down with four menu items, one for each of the possible elements of the set of border icons.

Each time you select one of the menu commands, its check mark and the corresponding border icon are toggled. This could be accomplished by writing four methods, one for each menu command, but I've decided to use a different approach. I've written a single method, connected with the three commands, that reads the check marks on the menu items to determine the value of the BorderIcons property. This code represents a good exercise in working with sets:

```
procedure TForm1.SetIcons(Sender: TObject);
var
  BorIco: TBorderIcons;
begin
  (Sender as TMenuItem).Checked :=
    not (Sender as TMenuItem).Checked;
```

```
  if SystemMenu1.Checked then
    BorIco := [biSystemMenu]
  else
    BorIco := [];
  if MaximizeBox1.Checked then
    Include (BorIco, biMaximize);
  if MinimizeBox1.Checked then
    Include (BorIco, biMinimize);
  if Help1.Checked then
    Include (BorIco, biHelp);
  BorderIcons := BorIco;
end;
```

By running the BICONS example, you can easily set and remove the various visual elements of the form's border. You'll immediately find out that some of these elements are closely related: if you remove the system menu, all of the borders icons will disappear; if you remove either the minimize or the maximize button, it will be grayed; if you remove both these buttons, they will disappear. Notice also that in these last two cases, the corresponding items of the system menu are automatically disabled. This is the standard behavior for any Windows application. When the maximize and minimize icons have been disabled, you can activate the help button, as you can see in Figure 9.3.

**FIGURE 9.3:**
The help button displayed by the BICONS example. Notice that the system menu reflects the presence or absence of the form's minimize or maximize buttons.

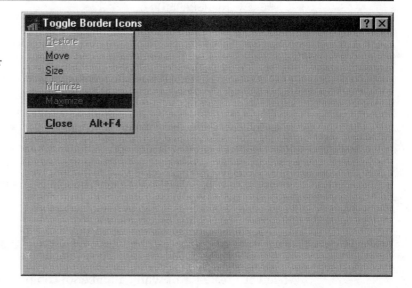

## Setting More Windows Styles

The border style and border icons are indicated by two different properties in Delphi, and they can be used to set the initial value of the corresponding user interface elements. Besides changing the user interface, we have seen that these properties affect the behavior of a window. It is important to know that these border-related properties and the FormStyle property mainly correspond to different settings in the *style* and *extended style* of a window. These two terms reflect two parameters of the CreateWindowEx API function Delphi uses to create forms.

It is important to acknowledge this, because Delphi allows you to modify these two parameters freely, overriding the CreateParams virtual method:

```
public
  procedure CreateParams (var Params: TCreateParams); override;
```

This is the only way to use some of the most peculiar window styles that are not directly available through form properties. For a list of window styles and extended styles see the API Help under the topics "CreateWindow" and "CreateWindowEx". You'll notice that the Win32 API has a number of new styles for these functions, including those related to tool windows.

To show you how to use this approach, I've written a simple example (TRANSPAR) to let you create a useless and very awkward transparent window:

```
procedure TForm1.CreateParams (var Params: TCreateParams);
begin
  inherited CreateParams (Params);
  Params.ExStyle := Params.ExStyle or
    WS_EX_TRANSPARENT;
end;
```

Notice the use of the bitwise or to add flags (styles)—bitwise logic operations are applied to each bit of a value, instead of to the value as a whole, as standard logic operations are. If you run this program, you will wonder why you need a window that cannot even paint its border properly. Well, I'm puzzled too, although I guess this can be used to place a large invisible window in front of all others, intercepting all the mouse messages. Setting window styles can be used for other reasons in Delphi. For example, you can remove the caption of a window, leaving its border. An example of a window without a caption is a splash screen, although special windows styles are more common in the definition of a new component than in a main window.

# Forms in Different Screen Resolutions

When you create forms with a number of components, it is common to make the form non-resizable to avoid having some of the components fall outside the visible portions of the form. This is not a big problem, because Delphi automatically adds scroll bars to the form so you can reach every control easily (form scrolling is one of the subjects of Chapter 13).

Be aware of this problem when you create a big form: If you build a form on a high-resolution screen, it might be bigger than the available screen size. This is a pity, and it is more common that you might expect. If you can, never build a form larger than 640 × 480 pixels.

If you have to build a bigger form and using scroll bars is not a solution, Delphi has some nice scaling features. There are two basic techniques. The form's ScaleBy method allows you to scale the form and each of its components. You can use this method at startup after you've determined the screen resolution, or it can be used in response to a specific request by the user, by means of a command you can add to the form's menu.

The PixelsPerInch and Scaled properties allow Delphi to resize an application automatically when the application is run with a different screen resolution. Of course, you can change the values of these properties manually, as described in the next section, and let the system scale the form only when you want. To make the form scale its window, be sure to also set the AutoScroll property to False. Otherwise, the contents of the form will be scaled, but the form border itself will not.

## Manual Form Scaling

Each time you want to scale a form, including its components, you can use the ScaleBy method, which has two integer parameters, a multiplier and a divisor—a fraction. You can apply the same method to a single component. For example, with the statement

```
ScaleBy (3, 4);
```

the size of the current form is divided by 4 and multiplied by 3; that is, the form is reduced to three-quarters of its original size. Generally, it is easier to use percentage values. The same statement can be written as

```
ScaleBy (75, 100);
```

When you scale a form, all the proportions are maintained, but if you go below or above certain limits, the text strings can alter their proportions slightly. Notice that if you reduce the size of a form too much, most of the components will become unusable or even disappear completely. The problem is that in Windows, components can be placed and sized only in whole pixels, while scaling almost always involves multiplying by fractional numbers. So any fractional portion of a component's origin or size will be truncated.

To avoid similar problems, you should let a user perform only a limited number of scaling operations, or re-create the form from scratch before each new scaling so round-off errors do not accumulate.

**WARNING**   If you apply the ScaleBy method to a form, the form won't actually be scaled. Only the components inside the form will change their size. As I mentioned before, to overcome this problem, you should disable the form's AutoScroll property. What is the relationship between scaling and scrolling? My guess is that if scrolling is enabled, the component can be moved outside the form's visible area without many problems; otherwise, the form is resized, too.

I've built a simple example, SCALE, to show how you can scale a form manually, responding to a request by the user. The form of this application (see Figure 9.4) has two buttons, a label, an edit box, and a component we have not yet used: the Windows 95 UpDown control. This component connects to the edit box (using its Associate property): now a user can type only numbers in the box, click on the two small arrows to increase or decrease the number in the edit box by a fixed amount (indicated by the Increment property of the UpDown component), and extract the text of the edit (Edit1.Text) or the value of the number (upDown1.Position). You can also set a range for the possible values, as you can see in the textual description of the component's key properties:

```
object UpDown1: TUpDown
  Associate = Edit1
  Min = 30
  Max = 300
  Increment = 10
  Position = 100
end
```

**FIGURE 9.4:**

The form of the SCALE example after a scaling with 50 and 200.

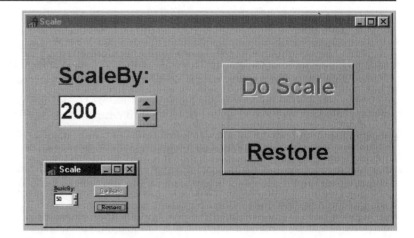

When you press the ScaleButton, the current input value is used to determine the scaling percentage of the form:

```
procedure TForm1.ScaleButtonClick(Sender: TObject);
begin
  AmountScaled := UpDown1.Position;
  ScaleBy (AmountScaled, 100);
  UpDown1.Height := Edit1.Height;
  ScaleButton.Enabled := False;
  RestoreButton.Enabled := True;
end;
```

This method stores the current input value in the form's AmountScaled private field and enables the Restore button, disabling the one that was pressed. Later on, when the user presses the Restore button, the opposite scaling takes place, by calling ScaleBy (100, AmountScaled). In both cases, I added a line of code to set the height of the UpDown comonent to the edit box it is attached to. This prevents small differences between the two.

> **TIP**
> If you want to scale the text of the form properly, including the captions of components, the items in list boxes, and so on, you should use TrueType fonts exclusively. The system font and other bitmapped fonts do not scale well. The font issue is important because the size of many components depends on that of their captions, and if the caption does not scale well, the component might not work properly. For this reason, in the SCALE example I've used an Arial font.

## Automatic Form Scaling

Instead of playing with the ScaleBy method, you can ask Delphi to do the work for you. When Delphi starts, it asks the system the screen resolution and stores the value in the PixelsPerInch property of a the Screen object, a special global object of the VCL, available in any application. At design-time, the PixelsPerInch value of the screen, which is a read-only property, is copied to any form of the application. Delphi then uses the value of PixelsPerInch, if the Scaled property is set to True, to resize the form when the application starts.

Therefore, the same application running at a different screen resolution automatically scales itself, without any specific code. You can also manually set a different value for this property at design-time so that the form automatically scales when it is executed.

**NOTE**

Both this scaling and that performed by the ScaleBy method operate on components by changing the size of the font. The size of each control (or windowed component), in fact, depends on the font it uses. For example, the value of the form's PixelsPerInch property (the design-time value) is compared to the system value (indicated by the corresponding property of the Screen object), and the result is used to change the font. However, to improve the accuracy of this code, even the final height of the text is compared to the design-time value, and its size is eventually adjusted if they do not match. It is important to note that scaling is not done according to screen size or resolution but according to font size. Even at the same screen resolution, different machines can be set up with different-sized system fonts, and therefore Delphi will activate form scaling. For example, at the 800 × 600 screen resolution, using small fonts, the PixelPerInch ratio is 96; using large fonts, it is 120.

# Setting the Form's Position and Size

If you don't set specific values for the PixelsPerInch property, you might expect your form to appear on the screen as you designed it. This is the default behavior, but you can modify it by setting some more properties.

One of them is the Position property, which indicates the initial position of the form on the screen when it is first created (and has no meaning when the form is active). Some of its choices depend on a feature of the Windows environment: using a specific flag, Windows can position new windows using a standard arrangement, which follows the cascade layout. Here are the possible values of the property:

- `poDesigned`:  The form appears in the same position and at the same size you designed it. The properties that determine this attribute are Left, Top, Height, and Width, although you usually set them by dragging the caption or the form's borders.

- `poDefault`:  Windows determines the form's position and size by using a cascade layout, ignoring the design-time attributes completely. If you run the application a number of times in a row, each time its form moves down and to the right of the screen, and if it is resizable, it is reduced from time to time. After a number of windows have been created, the original position is used again. Notice that this option works only for a main window (bsSizeable or bsFixed), not for a dialog box.

- poDefaultPosOnly: The form uses the size you determined at design-time, but Windows chooses its position on the screen, again using the same algorithm. I've used this approach in the BORDERS example, to create several secondary forms in different positions.

- poDefaultSizeOnly: The form is displayed in the design position, but Windows determines its size. The right border of the form is always near the right side of the screen, and the bottom border of the form is always near the bottom of the screen, regardless of the form's position. This value is seldom used.

- poScreenCenter: The form is always displayed in the center of the screen, with the size you set at design-time.

**WARNING**

If you do develop a Delphi application using a high-resolution video mode, be careful not to leave the Position property of your forms set to poDefault. Otherwise, if you design a form in the lower-right portion of the screen, a user running your application at a lower-resolution video mode might not be able to see the form (it might show up completely off-screen).

The second parameter that affects the initial size and position of a window is its *state*. You can use the WindowState property at design-time to display a maximized or minimized window at startup. This property, in fact, can have only three values: wsNormal, wsMinimized, and wsMaximized.

The meaning of this property is intuitive. If you set a minimized window state, it will be displayed as a minimized window (but not placed into the Windows 95 TaskBar); if you set a maximized window state, it will be displayed full-screen. Notice that if you change the default values of the border icons or set a fixed-size border for the form, it is always displayed as required by the WindowState property. In other words, if you set this property to wsMaximized, it will be displayed full-screen even if it has a dialog border, and a dialog box usually cannot be maximized.

Of course, you can maximize or minimize a window at run-time, too. Simply change the value of the WindowState property. This is exactly what happens in the example I've written, which demonstrates both the default position of a form, as determined by the system, and the use of the WindowState property at run-time.

The POSITION example has a simple form with three buttons, used to minimize, maximize, and restore the form, as you can see in Figure 9.5. When the user presses the maximize button, a simple statement is executed:

```
procedure TForm1.MaximizeButtonClick(Sender: TObject);
begin
  WindowState := wsMaximized;
end;
```

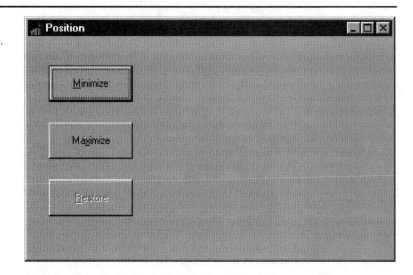

**FIGURE 9.5:**

The form of the POSITION example. Notice the status of the buttons.

The Restore button sets the property to wsNormal. Since the two buttons are exclusive, you have to disable the one that is not available. For example, if a window is maximized, pressing the maximize button again has no effect, so we can disable it. Simple? Not at all. If you disable the maximize button when it is pressed and enable it again when the Restore button is pressed, the use of the maximize button of the form's border will mess things up. We need a different approach.

Since we are in an event-based system, we should look for an event. In our example, we can use the OnResize event, which is called each time the form is resized, and this happens when we maximize, minimize, or restore it. Here is the code I've written for this event:

```
procedure TForm1.FormResize(Sender: TObject);
begin
  if WindowState = wsMaximized then
  begin
    MaximizeButton.Enabled := False;
    RestoreButton.Enabled := True;
  end
  else
  begin
    MaximizeButton.Enabled := True;
```

```
    RestoreButton.Enabled := False;
  end
end;
```

Notice that this code is executed also when the application starts, and for this reason the buttons are all enabled at design-time. What about the Minimize button? Since in a minimized form the buttons are not visible at all, changing their state would be useless. So we have no problems for the buttons states. We have a different problem, instead: Setting the WindowState property to `wsMinimized` reduces the window to an icon in Windows NT, but in Windows 95 it creates a minimized window that is not placed in the TaskBar. This is not what we are supposed to do with the main form of a program (and it *is* what pressing the minimize button on the caption does). The solution is simple: Working with the main form of a program, you have to call a method of the Application global object to minimize the form:

```
procedure TForm1.MinimizeButtonClick(Sender: TObject);
begin
  Application.Minimize;
end;
```

There is also a Restore method in the TApplication class that you can use when you need to restore a form, although most of the time the user will do this with a Windows standard operation (using the Restore system menu command, clicking on the icon in the TaskBar, and so on).

## The Size of a Form and Its Client Area

At design-time, there are two ways to set the size of a form: setting the value of the Width and Height properties or dragging its borders. At run-time, if the form has a resizable border, the user can resize it, and in any case, the program can resize it by changing the value of the two-dimensional properties.

However, if you look at a form's properties, you can see that there are two properties referring to its width and two referring to its height:

- Height is the height of the form, including the borders.
- Width is the width of the form, including the borders.
- ClientHeight is the height of the internal area of the form, excluding the borders, the caption, and the menu bar.
- ClientWidth is the width of the internal area of the form, excluding its borders.

Two of these properties refer to the client area of the form, which is its internal portion, the one gray by default. It is the area you can use to place components on the form, to create output, and to receive user input.

In Windows, it is also possible to create output and receive input from the non-client area of the form—that is, its border. Painting on the border and getting input when you click on it is really a complex issue. If you are interested in this topic, look in the Help file at the description of such Windows messages as wm_NCPaint, wm_NCCalcSize, and wm_NCHitTest and the series of non-client messages related to the mouse input, such as wm_NCLButtonDown. The difficulty of this approach is in combining your code with the default Windows behavior. Notice, however, that Delphi lets you process these low-level Windows messages without any problem, something that most visual programming environments do not allow at all.

Since you might be interested in having a certain available area, at times it makes sense to set the *client* size of a form instead of its global size. This is straightforward, since as you set one of the two client properties, the corresponding form property changes accordingly. When you modify the value of ClientHeight, the value of Height immediately changes.

## The Maximum and Minimum Size of a Form

When you choose a resizable border for a form, users can generally resize the form as they like and also maximize it to full-screen. Windows informs you that the form's size has changed with the wm_Size message, which generates the OnResize event. OnResize takes place after the size of the form has already been changed. Modifying the size again in this event (if the user has reduced or enlarged the form too much) is silly. A preventive approach is better suited to this problem.

Before I show you how to set the possible maximum and minimum sizes of a window, let me recap a couple of ideas. First of all, if you want a window of a fixed size, you should avoid a resizable border and choose instead the fixed border or the dialog one. Second, if some of the controls go out of the border and the AutoScroll property is set to True, Delphi automatically adds the scroll bars to the form so you can reach them anyway.

Nonetheless, it is often useful to set a limit on the form size, particularly the minimum size. Delphi does not include a property to set this value, but you can easily handle the proper Windows message in the form to obtain this effect.

The message we can use is wm_GetMinMaxInfo. The parameter of the corresponding method should be of the type TWMGetMinMaxInfo (the types of the message's parameters are defined in the Messages unit). This structure contains a field that is a pointer to the MinMaxInfo structure, defined in the Windows unit as

```
type
  PMinMaxInfo = ^TMinMaxInfo;
  TMinMaxInfo = record
    ptReserved: TPoint;
    ptMaxSize: TPoint;
    ptMaxPosition: TPoint;
    ptMinTrackSize: TPoint;
    ptMaxTrackSize: TPoint;
  end;
```

The fields of this structure are complex, but only because it is a very powerful tool:

- `ptReserved` is an undocumented field, reserved for Windows' internal use.

- `ptMaxSize` is a point holding, in the x field, the maximized width of the window, and in the y field, its maximized height.

- `ptMaxPosition` is a point indicating the position of the window (that is, its upper-left corner) when it is maximized.

- `ptMinTrackSize` indicates the minimum width and height of the window when a user resizes it.

- `ptMaxTrackSize` specifies the maximum width and height of the window.

When you receive this message, this structure has some default values, so you need to change only the fields you are interested in. In the MINMAX example, I've decided to fix both the minimum and the maximum *tracking* size of the window and disable its maximize button. In fact, in my opinion, letting the user maximize the window without making it full-screen (see Figure 9.6) makes sense only in a few cases. By the way, an example of one of these few cases is the Delphi main window.

The form of the MINMAX example is very simple, having no components at all. The only change you have to make from the default is to disable the `biMaximize` border icon.

To handle windows size tracking you have to add a message response procedure and write some code. In the type definition of the TForm1 class, you have to define the new procedure as

```
public
procedure GetMinMax (var MinMaxMessage: TWMGetMinMaxInfo);
  message wm_GetMinMaxInfo;
```

Notice the `message` directive, which connects the procedure directly with the Windows message. The second step is to write the code of this procedure, setting the proper values in the structure pointed to by the MinMaxInfo field of the MinMaxMessage parameter. To make it easy to access a number of fields of this structure, we can use a complex `with` statement, which uses the structure pointed to by

**FIGURE 9.6:**

The window of the MINMAX example is quite small but has the typical restore button of maximized windows.

the MinMaxInfo pointer. Inside this with statement you can easily access the various fields:

```
procedure TForm1.GetMinMax (
  var MinMaxMessage: TWMGetMinMaxInfo);
begin
  with MinMaxMessage.MinMaxInfo^ do
  begin
    ptMinTrackSize.x := 150;
    ptMinTrackSize.y := 150;
    ptMaxTrackSize.x := 300;
    ptMaxTrackSize.y := 300;
  end;
end;
```

The effect of this code is simple. A user cannot reduce the window below a certain limit or enlarge it too much. I haven't provided a figure to show this since I cannot show in a screen snapshot that the window's border cannot be moved beyond a certain position. You should run this program and test it.

# Automatic Form Creation

Up to now we have ignored the issue of form creation. We know that when the form is created, we receive the OnCreate event and can change or test some of the form's properties. But the form is invariably created. The statement responsible for this is in this project source code:

```
begin
  Application-Initialize;
```

```
  Application.CreateForm(TForm1, Form1);
  Application.Run;
end.
```

To skip the automatic form creation, you can either modify this code or, better, use the Forms page of the Project Options dialog box (see Figure 9.7). In this dialog box, you can decide whether or not the form is automatically created. If you disable the automatic creation, the project's initialization code becomes the following:

```
begin
  Applications.Initialize;
  Application.Run;
end.
```

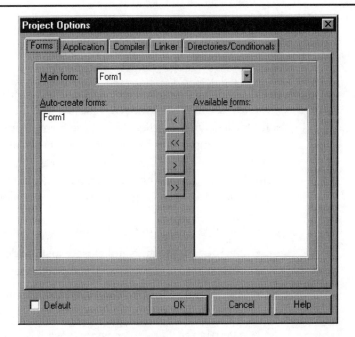

**FIGURE 9.7:**

The Forms page of the Delphi Project Options dialog box.

If you now run this program, nothing happens, and it terminates immediately because no main window is created. So, what is the effect of the call to the application's CreateForm method? It creates a new instance of the class passed as the first parameter and assigns it to the variable passed as the second parameter.

Something else happens behind the scenes. When CreateForm is called, if there is currently no main form, the current form is assigned to the application's MainForm property. For this reason, the form indicated as *Main form* in the dialog box shown in Figure 9.7 (above) corresponds to the first call to the application's CreateForm method (that is, when several forms are created at startup).

The same holds for closing a form. If you have a single form, closing the main form closes the application. If you want to perform this operation from the program's code, simply call the form's Close method.

## Closing a Form

When you close the form using the method just described or by the usual means (Alt+F4, the system menu, or the Close button), the OnCloseQuery event is called. In this event, you can ask the user to confirm the action, particularly if there is unsaved data in the form. I used this approach in the NOTES example in the preceding chapter. Just as a reminder, you can write the following code:

```
procedure TForm1.FormCloseQuery(Sender: TObject;
  var CanClose: Boolean);
begin
  if MessageDlg ('Are you sure you want to exit?',
     mtConfirmation, [mbYes, mbNo], 0) = idNo then
    CanClose := False;
end;
```

You can find this code in the simple CLOSE example, which has a form with a button to close it (you can see the result of the call of the previous method in Figure 9.8). If OnCloseQuery indicates that the form should still be closed, the OnClose event is called. This method is generally used to deallocate objects related to the form and free the corresponding memory, but it is also another chance to avoid closing the application. The method, in fact, has an Action parameter passed by reference. You can assign the following values to this parameter:

- caNone: The form is not allowed to close.

- caHide: The form is not closed, just hidden. This makes sense if there are other forms in the application; otherwise, the program terminates.

- caFree: The form is closed, freeing its memory, and the application eventually terminates if this was the main form.

- caMinimize: The form is not closed, but only minimized.

In the CLOSE example, I've written a method for the OnClose event, too. This procedure asks users once again if they really want to exit:

```
procedure TForm1.FormClose(Sender: TObject;
  var Action: TCloseAction);
begin
  if MessageDlg ('Are you REALLY SURE you want to exit?' +
     Chr(13) + '(This is your last chance to remain with us!)',
     mtConfirmation, [mbYes, mbNo], 0) = idNo then
```

**FIGURE 9.8:**

The close confirmation dialog box of the CLOSE example.

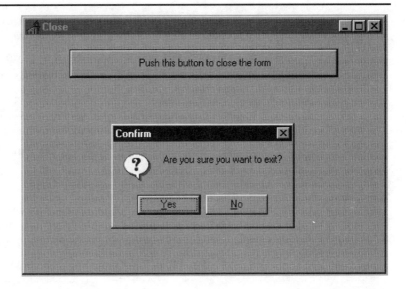

```
    Action := caNone
  else
    Action := caFree;
end;
```

I've written this second request just to demonstrate to you that there are two possible solutions to the "stop closing" problem. I don't advise ever writing something similar, since your application's users will get really angry.

When you build applications with a single main form, handling the OnClose event is not a particular problem. As you add other forms to a program, they are often created at startup by the project code and destroyed only when the program terminates. In this case, the default close action, which corresponds to hiding the form, makes sense. However, when you create forms dynamically, maybe because you need several forms of the same kind in a single program, you should also take care of deleting a form when it is closed, eventually using the caFree value as the closing action (more on this topic in the chapters dealing with multiple forms, particularly Chapters 12 and 15).

**TIP**

In the first parameter of the MessageDlg call, in the code above, I've used the Chr(13) function call to add a newline character in the string. The effect of this special character is to move the following portion of the string to a new line. If you try removing it and run the program again, the first line of the message box will be much longer than the second one, producing an unpleasant effect. As an alternative to the Char(13) expression, you can use the #13 character and concatenate it automatically in a string by writing the expression `First line'#13'Second line`.

Having discussed some special capabilities of forms, I'll now move to a very important topic: input and output. If you decide to make limited use of components, you might write complex programs as well, receiving input from the mouse (and eventually the keyboard) and drawing directly on the surface of the form.

# Getting Mouse Input

When a user presses one of the mouse buttons over a form (or over a component, by the way), Windows sends the application some messages. Delphi defines some events to write code in response to these messages. The two basic events are as follows: OnMouseDown is received when one of the mouse buttons is pressed; OnMouseUp is received when one of the buttons is released.

Another fundamental system message is related to mouse movement. The event is OnMouseMove. Although it should be easy to understand the meaning of the three messages down, up, and move, the question that might arise is, how do they relate to the OnClick event we have often used up to now?

We have often used the OnClick event for components, but it is also available for the form. Its general meaning is that the left mouse button has been pressed and released on the same window or component. However, between these two actions, the cursor might have been moved outside the area of the window or component, while the left mouse button was held down. If you press the mouse button at a certain position and then move it away and release it, no click is involved. In this case, the window receives *only* a down message, some move messages, and an up message.

Another difference is that the click event relates only to the left mouse button. Most of the mouse types connected to a Windows PC have two mouse buttons, and at times even three. Usually we refer to these buttons as the left mouse button, which is the most used; the right mouse button; and the middle mouse button.

The left mouse button is *the* mouse button. It is used to select elements on screen, to give menu commands, to click buttons, to select and move elements (*dragging*), to select and activate (usually with a double-click), and so on.

The right mouse button is used for local pop-up menus. Many applications used this approach in the past, but Windows 95 has made local menus the standard effect of clicking on the right mouse button.

The middle button is seldom used because most users either don't even have it or don't have a proper software driver. Some CAD programs use the middle button. If you want to support it, it should be optional, or else you should be ready to provide your customers with a free three-button mouse and the corresponding driver (this makes sense only if your package is expensive, of course). Keep in mind that users can customize their mouse buttons so that the left and right buttons are switched, and the middle button can be clicked once to execute a double-click. When you refer to events related to a mouse button in your code, it is not the physical button but rather its meaning that matters.

## Using Windows without a Mouse

While I am on this topic, consider the following statement: a user should always be able to use any Windows application without the mouse. This is not an option; it is a Windows programming rule. Of course, it might be easier to use an application with a mouse, but it should never be compulsory. In fact, there are users who for several reasons might not have a mouse connected to their system, such as travelers with a small laptop and no space, workers in industrial environments, and bank clerks with a number of other peripherals around.

There is another reason, already mentioned in this chapter in respect to the menu, to support the keyboard: using the mouse is nice, but it tends to be slower. If you are a touch typist, you won't use the mouse to drag a word of text; you'll use shortcut keys to copy and paste it, without moving your hands from the keyboard.

For all these reasons, you should always set up a proper tab order for a form's components, remember to add keys for buttons and menu items for keyboard selection, use shortcut keys on menu commands, and so on. An exception to this rule might be a graphics program. However, be aware that you can use a program such as Paintbrush without the mouse—although I don't recommend this experience.

## The Mouse Events

Since I'm going to build a graphics program, too, I will focus only on the use of the mouse. The first event we need to consider for the first minimal version of the

SHAPES program is OnMouseDown. The related method has a number of parameters, as shown in the following declaration:

```
procedure TShapesForm.FormMouseDown (
  Sender: TObject;
  Button: TMouseButton;
  Shift: TShiftState;
  X, Y: Integer);
```

In addition to the usual Sender parameter, there are four more:

- Button indicates which of the three mouse buttons has been pressed. Possible values are mbRight, mbLeft, and mbCenter. These are exclusive values because the purpose of this parameter is to determine which button generated the click message.

- Shift indicates which *mouse-related keys* were pressed when the event occurred. These mouse-related keys are Alt, Ctrl, and Shift, plus the mouse buttons themselves. This parameter is of a set type since several keys might be pressed at the same time. This means you should test for a condition using the in expression, not test for equality.

- *X* and *Y* indicate the coordinates of the position of the mouse, in *client area* coordinates. The origin of the x and y axes of these coordinates is the upper-left corner of the client area of the window receiving the event, not the upper-left corner of the whole window (for components, at times the client area corresponds to the surface of the whole window).

We can start writing our example, SHAPES1, with a simple MouseDown method. As you can see from the class name, the form of this example, which has no components, has been renamed ShapesForm:

```
procedure TShapesForm.FormMouseDown(
  Sender: TObject; Button: TMouseButton;
  Shift: TShiftState; X, Y: Integer);
begin
  if Button = mbLeft then
    Canvas.Ellipse (X-10, Y-10, X+10, Y+10);
end;
```

If the user presses the left mouse button, the program draws a circle on the surface of the form, using as its center the position of the mouse. To draw the circle, we have to use the Ellipse procedure since neither Windows nor Delphi has a function to draw a circle. The Ellipse method requires four parameters representing the opposite sides of the bounding rectangle, as shown in Figure 9.9.

**FIGURE 9.9:**

The bounding rectangle of an ellipse.

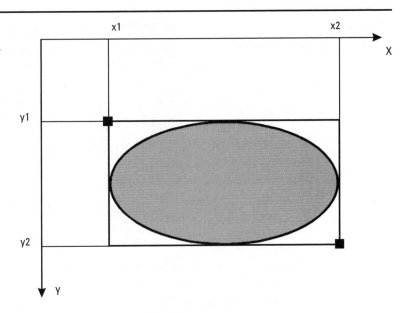

To draw on the form, we use a very special property: Canvas. A Canvas object has two distinctive features: it holds a collection of drawing tools (such as a pen, a brush, and a font) and it has a number of drawing methods, which use the current tools. More on the canvas in the next section.

Before we look into the problems of painting, let me add a couple of new features to the bare program. First of all, I want to allow the user to draw shapes of different forms depending on the keys pressed with the left mouse button. You can accomplish this by checking the value of the procedure's third parameter, corresponding to the OnMouseDown event:

```
if Button = mbLeft then
if ssShift in Shift then
    Canvas.Rectangle (X-10, Y-10, X+10, Y+10)
  else
    Canvas.Ellipse (X-10, Y-10, X+10, Y+10);
```

Now, if the user presses Shift and the left mouse button, the program draws a small square instead of a small circle (see Figure 9.10). You might further customize this example by drawing lines or rectangles with rounded corners. See the Delphi Help file for the TCanvas class for a list of the available drawing methods.

**NOTE**   Experienced Windows programmers should notice that the canvas technically represents a device context. The methods of the TCanvas class are similar to the GDI functions of the Windows API.

**FIGURE 9.10:**

The output of the SHAPES1 example.

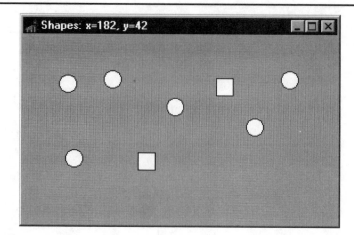

To end the first version of the SHAPES program, we can add a new feature. I want to show the position of the mouse in client-area coordinates to allow more precise drawings. As soon as the mouse moves over the form, the OnMouseMove event is sent to our program. By providing a method for this event, we can transform the $x$ and $y$ values we receive as parameters into a string and display it. Since our application has no status bar (at least for the moment) and no labels, we can use the form's caption for the output (see the title of the window in Figure 9.10, above):

```
procedure TShapesForm.FormMouseMove(Sender: TObject;
  Shift: TShiftState; X, Y: Integer);
begin
  Caption := Format ('Shapes: x=%d, y=%d', [X, Y]);
end;
```

In this code, I've used the Format system function to build a string converting several integer values. The Format function takes as parameters a string, with some placeholders indicated by the % symbol, and a list of corresponding values enclosed in square brackets. The letters and numbers following the % symbol indicate the parameter's data type and eventually some formatting information. You can find details about formatting codes in the Delphi Help file under "Format Strings".

The effect of the statement above corresponds to the following code:

```
Caption := 'Shapes: x=' + IntToStr (X) +
  ', y=' + IntToStr (Y);
```

The version I've used in the code is more efficient and uses less stack space than the statement above, based on two IntToStr calls and three different concatenations.

Now our drawing program is slightly more interesting. But the real advantage is that you can use this example to understand how the mouse works. Make this test: Run the program and resize the windows on the desktop so that the form of the

SHAPES program is behind another window and inactive, but with the title visible. Now move the mouse over the form, and you'll see that the coordinates change. This means that the MouseMove event is sent to the application even if its window is not active, and it proves what I have already mentioned: mouse messages are always directed to the window under the mouse, with only a few exceptions.

# Drawing on the Form

Using SHAPES1, you can draw a number of circles and squares on the surface of the form, as shown earlier in Figure 9.10. This looks like it works fairly well, but it doesn't. There are several related problems. If you cover your form with another window, the shapes will disappear. If you reduce the size of the form, the shapes outside the new smaller surface will disappear, too; and if you enlarge the form again, they won't reappear. (Try playing with this program to see what I mean.)

Why does this happen? It depends on Windows' default behavior. As you draw on a window, Windows does *not* store the resulting bitmap. When the window is covered, its contents are usually lost.

Why doesn't Windows store the contents of each window in a bitmap? The answer is simple: to spare memory. A color bitmap for a 300 × 400 image at 256 colors requires about 120 KB. By increasing the color count or the number of pixels, you can easily have full-screen bitmaps of about 1 MB and reach 4 MB of memory for a 1280 × 1024 resolution at 16 million colors. If storing the bitmap was the default choice, running half a dozen simple applications will require at least 8 MB of memory, if not 16 MB.

There are some techniques in both Windows and Delphi to save the contents of a form in a bitmap. In Windows, these techniques require some coding; in Delphi, they require the use of the proper components. In this chapter, focusing on forms and on direct output, I'll follow the usual Windows drawing technique, based on painting, which is the focus of the next section. In the next chapter I'll show you how to use the Image component to store the current output of a form in a bitmap.

## The Drawing Tools

For the moment, let me improve the application by playing with the drawing tools available in a canvas. Here is a list of these drawing tools (or *GDI objects*, from the Graphics Device Interface, one of the Windows system libraries) of a canvas:

- The Brush property determines the color of the enclosed surfaces. The brush is used to fill closed shapes, such as circles or rectangles. The properties of a brush are its color, its style, and eventually its bitmap.

- The Pen property determines the color and size of the lines and of the borders of the shapes. The properties of a pen are its color, its size if it is a solid line, or other styles, including a number of dotted and dashed lines (1 pixel in size).

- The Font property determines the font used to write text in the form, using the TextOut method of the canvas. A font has a name, a size, a style, a color, and so on.

Brushes, pens, fonts, forms, and most other components have a Color property, but to change the color of an element properly, you should know how Windows treats the color. In theory, Windows uses 24-bit RGB colors. This means you can use 256 different values for each of the three basic colors (red, green, and blue), obtaining an impressive number of different shades.

The reality is that you or the users of your programs might have a video adapter which cannot display such a variety of colors, although this is increasingly less frequent. In this case, Windows uses either a technique called *dithering*, which basically consists of using a number of pixels of the available colors to simulate the requested one; or it approximates the color, using the nearest one.

**NOTE**     When Windows runs with a poor video adapter, dithering takes place for the background color of a form or component and for the color of a brush. Pens and fonts, instead, use a different technique. They use only *pure* colors—that is, colors that are directly available for the currently installed video driver. If you ask for a color that is not available, instead of using dithering, Windows chooses the nearest pure color.

In terms of pens, you can read (but not change) the current pen position with the PenPos property. The pen position determines the starting point of the next line the program will draw, using the LineTo method. To change it, you can use the canvas's MoveTo method.

Other properties of the canvas affect lines and colors, too. Interesting examples are CopyMode and ScaleMode. Another property you can manipulate directly to change the output is the array of pixels, which you can use to access (read) or change (write) the color of any individual point on the surface of the form.

## Drawing Shapes

Now we want to improve the SHAPES application. We need to add a menu to choose the color of the shapes and of their borders—that is, the color of the pen and the brush, respectively—and the size of the shape and of its border.

The code needed to implement these commands is quite simple, although somewhat longer than usual. The form initializes and stores only the current radius of the circle (used also as the value of half of the side of the square—that is, the *radius of the square*) since all the other values are directly saved in properties of the canvas. To change the colors, I've used the standard Color dialog box:

```
procedure TShapesForm.PenColor1Click(Sender: TObject);
begin
  ColorDialog1.Color := Canvas.Pen.Color;
  if ColorDialog1.Execute then
    Canvas.Pen.Color := ColorDialog1.Color;
end;
```

When setting the size of the border and of the shape, I disabled the menu items to avoid negative values:

```
procedure TShapesForm.DecreasePenSize1Click(Sender: TObject);
begin
  Canvas.Pen.Width := Canvas.Pen.Width – 2;
  if Canvas.Pen.Width < 3 then
    DecreasePenSize1.Enabled := False;
end;
```

If you want, you can add similar checks to avoid too-large values. The only really strange portion of the code is the method the program uses to clear the surface of the form when the File ➤ New command is called. The code simply calls the Repaint method of the form. This method repaints the whole surface of the window, erasing its contents. The effect, of course, is that you lose any previous output since it was not stored. This program, in fact, has the same big problem of the previous version (as you can see in Figure 9.11). If you move another window over this form or reduce its size, you lose its contents. We need a way to store the contents and repaint the window on request.

**NOTE**  Curiously enough, the contents of the form are also erased if you open the Color dialog box to its maximum extent (by pressing the Define Custom Colors button) or you move this dialog box, but it remains on screen if you open only the basic version of the dialog box and don't move it. In fact, when small areas are covered (by menus, message boxes, or small dialog boxes), Windows actually saves the bitmap of the corresponding area of the form being covered. When these elements become too big, however, Windows doesn't save the surface and later asks the program to redraw the area. For Windows experts, this is the effect of the cs_SaveBits class style.

**FIGURE 9.11:**

The output of the SHAPES2 program is improved over the last version, but it is still flawed, as you can see in the right portion of the window.

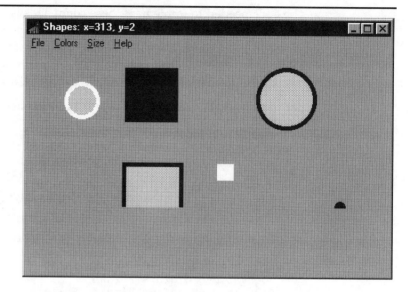

# Drawing and Painting in Windows

It's time to face the problems related to *drawing* and *painting* in Windows. What do I mean by these two terms?

- *Drawing* is what we have done up to now in the Shape application. You access the form's canvas and call some of its methods. Since the image is not saved, the form can lose part or all of its contents, as shown earlier in Figure 9.11. The output might change because the image is not saved and the application doesn't know how to redraw it.

- *Painting* is what we will do to let the application repaint its whole surface under any of the possible conditions. If we provide a method to redraw the contents of the form and this method is automatically called when a portion of the form has been hidden and needs repainting, we will be able to re-create the output properly.

Painting is the common approach in handling output in Windows, aside from particular graphics-oriented programs that store the form's whole image in a bitmap (as I'll describe in the next chapter). The approach used to implement painting has a very descriptive name: *store and paint*. In fact, when the user presses the mouse buttons or performs any other operation, we need to store the position and other elements; then, in the painting method, we use this information to actually paint the corresponding image.

Since this approach takes two steps, we must be able to execute these two operations in a row, asking the system to repaint the window—without waiting for a portion of the window to become invalid because some other window has been placed above it. You can use several methods (which can be applied to both forms and controls) to invoke repainting; the first two correspond to the Windows API functions, while the latter two have been introduced by Delphi:

- The Invalidate method informs Windows that the entire surface of the form should be repainted. The most important thing is that Invalidate does *not* enforce a painting operation immediately. Windows simply stores the request and will respond to it only after the current procedure has been completely executed and as soon as there are no other events pending in the system. Windows deliberately delays the painting operation since it is one of the most time-consuming operations. At times, with this delay, it is possible to paint the form only after a number of changes have taken place, avoiding a number of consecutive calls to the (slow) paint method.

- The Update method asks Windows to update the contents of the form, repainting it immediately. However, remember that this operation will take place only if there is an *invalid area*. This happens if the Invalidate method has just been called or as the result of an operation by the user. If there is no invalid area, a call to Update has no effect at all. For this reason, it is common to see a call to Update just after a call to Invalidate. This is exactly what is done by the two new Delphi methods, Repaint and Refresh.

- The Repaint method calls Invalidate and Update in sequence. As a result, it activates the OnPaint event immediately. There is a slightly different version of this method called Refresh. For a form the effect is the same, for components it might be slightly different.

**NOTE**  As in Delphi 1, the Help file in Delphi 2 still insists that the difference between Repaint and Refresh lies in the fact that the first method doesn't erase the surface of the form before repainting it. However, this is *not* true. The Refresh method is identical to Repaint. Contrary to what the documentation says, to avoid erasing the form's background, you need to set the `csOpaque` flag in the undocumented Control-Style property of the form (or of the component you want to use).

When you need to ask the form for a repaint operation, you should generally call Invalidate, following the standard Windows approach. This is particularly important when you need to request this operation very often, because if Windows takes too much time to update the screen, the requests for repaint can be accumulated into a simple repaint action. The wm_Paint message in Windows is a sort of low-priority message. To be more precise, if a request for repaint is pending but other messages are waiting, the other messages are handled before the system actually performs the paint action.

On the other hand, if you call Repaint several times, the screen must be repainted each time before Windows can process other messages, and since paint operations are slow, this can actually make your application less responsive. There are times, however, when you want the application to repaint a surface as quickly as possible. In these less-frequent cases, calling Repaint is the way to go.

## Painting a Single Shape

Do you remember the first version of the SHAPES example? It was the one capable of drawing simple circles and squares, with no support for color or other frills. I've implemented it again using the *store and draw* technique because I thought it was better to write a simple program with this approach than to start with a complex one.

When the user presses the left mouse button, we need to store three values: the two coordinates of the center of the shape and a Boolean indicating whether the shape is a circle or a square:

```
procedure TShapesForm.FormMouseDown(
  Sender: TObject; Button: TMouseButton;
  Shift: TShiftState; X, Y: Integer);
begin
  if Button = mbLeft then
  begin
    {store the value of the center}
    Center.X := X;
    Center.Y := Y;
    {store the kind of shape}
    if ssShift in Shift then
      Circle := False
    else
      Circle := True;
    {ask to repaint the form}
    Invalidate;
  end;
end;
```

The values are stored in the Center and Circle fields of the form (respectively a TPoint and a Boolean). At the end of the FormMouseDown method, there is a call to Invalidate, which indirectly calls FormPaint, the method associated with the On-Paint event. This procedure draws a shape, using the current values:

```
procedure TShapesForm.FormPaint(Sender: TObject);
begin
```

```
    if Circle then
      Canvas.Ellipse(Center.X-10, Center.Y-10,
        Center.X+10, Center.Y+10)
    else
      Canvas.Rectangle(Center.X-10, Center.Y-10,
        Center.X+10, Center.Y+10);
  end;
```

The values of the private fields are set at the beginning, in the FormCreate method. The coordinates of the center are set at a negative offset, so that at the beginning, the shape is not visible. In fact, the OnPaint method is also executed at startup.

As you can see by running the program, SHAPES3 allows you to draw only one shape at a time.

This last version of the SHAPES program we have built is probably the most robust. Although it is not by any means the best, you might easily paste its code with that of version 2 to allow a user to choose the colors and sizes of the single shape.

We can improve this program (or the modified version I've just suggested) by storing not only the last shape, but a number of them, and not only the position and type, but also the color, size, and all the other attributes we need to repaint them properly.

## Painting a Number of Shapes

There is a simple solution in Delphi to the problem of storing a number of elements: Use a TList object. This is what I've done in SHAPES4, which is a mix of the second and third versions of the program, plus the support for a number of shapes. In particular, the new version uses the same form and the same menu structure as the SHAPES2 example.

The program defines a custom ShapeData data type to store the attributes of a single shape:

```
ShapeData = class (TObject)
    Circle: Boolean;
    X, Y, Size, PenSize: Integer;
    PenColor, BrushColor: TColor;
  end;
```

The form has a TList object data member, named ShapesList, which is initialized in the OnCreate event:

```
ShapesList := TList.Create;
```

A new object is added to the list each time the user creates a new shape by pressing the left mouse button:

```
Shape := ShapeData.Create;
{... store the values ...}
```

```
ShapesList.Add (Shape);
Invalidate;
```

In the method corresponding to the OnPaint event, all the shapes currently stored in the list are painted:

```
procedure TShapesForm.FormPaint(Sender: TObject);
var
  I: Integer;
  CurShape: ShapeData;
begin
  for I := 0 to ShapesList.Count - 1 do
  begin
    CurShape := ShapesList.Items [I];
    with CurShape do
    begin
    Canvas.Pen.Color := PenColor;
      Canvas.Pen.Width := PenSize;
      Canvas.Brush.Color := BrushColor;
      if Circle then
      Canvas.Ellipse (X-Size, Y-Size, X+Size, Y+Size)
      else
      Canvas.Rectangle (X-Size, Y-Size, X+Size, Y+Size);
    end;
  end;
end;
```

The other methods of the ShapeForm class are simple. The program asks the user to confirm some operations, such as exiting from the program or removing all the shapes from the list (with the File ➤ New command), but you should easily understand the corresponding code.

This time, the output looks great (see Figure 9.12), and whatever happens to the window, the shapes are always repainted in the proper position.

**FIGURE 9.12:**
The output of the SHAPES4 example.

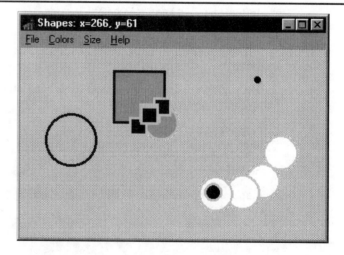

The only drawback is that when you have a number of shapes on the form, if you add a new shape, the program takes some time to redisplay them all, and the drawing tends to flicker. Instead of invalidating, erasing, and repainting the whole surface of the form, you might consider doing the same operation for only a smaller portion of it. To accomplish this, Delphi offers no specific support, but you can call a function of the Windows API, InvalidateRect:

```
procedure InvalidateRect(Wnd: HWnd;
  Rect: PRect; Erase: Bool);
```

The three parameters indicate the handle of the window (that is, the Handle property of the form), the rectangle you want to repaint, and a flag indicating whether or not you want to erase the area before repainting it. In SHAPES4, in the FormMouse-Down procedure, we can write the following code:

```
InvRect := Rect (X - Radius - Shape.PenSize,
  Y - Radius - Shape.PenSize, X + Radius + Shape.PenSize,
  Y + Radius + Shape.PenSize);
InvalidateRect (Handle, @InvRect, False);
```

This code is already present in the SHAPES4 example on the companion disk, but it is commented. You only need to uncomment it and comment or delete the Invalidate call instead. I suggest you experiment with the two versions of the example to get an idea of why calling InvalidateRect at times is really a great benefit to a slow graphical program. The key idea is that if Repaint or Invalidate is called, the surface of the form is erased, and then each shape is repainted.

Invalidating only a small portion of the window, instead, makes any flicker less noticeable, because it involves only a smaller area and because Windows can redraw it more quickly. In fact, paint operations are limited by a clipping rectangle, which usually has the size of the form but in this case is limited to the invalidated area. Windows automatically skips every output operation outside the clipping rectangle, avoiding any time-consuming video driver access.

To be more precise, I should have used the term *clipping region* instead of *clipping rectangle* because this area can have any complex form. If you want more details, you can see the description of the InvalidateRegion and CreateRegion API functions in the Windows Help file.

**TIP**
The area you invalidate with the InvalidateRect call should be big enough for the last shape, including its eventual thick border (unless the pen style is psInsideFrame). For this reason, I've added the size of the pen (as you can see in the code fragment above), although half the size of the pen would have probably been enough.

# Delphi Output Components

We have made four versions of the SHAPES example, using almost no components, aside from a standard color selection dialog box. As an alternative, we could have used two Delphi components: the PaintBox and the Shape. What are these two components for?

- You use the PaintBox component when you need to paint on a certain area of a form and that area might move on the form. For example, the PaintBox is useful for painting on a dialog box without the risk of mixing the area for the output with the area for the controls. The PaintBox might fit within other controls of a form, such as a toolbar or a status bar, and avoid any confusion or overlapping of the output. In the SHAPES example, using this component made no sense since we always worked on the whole surface of the form.

- You use the Shape component to paint shapes on the screen, exactly as we have done up to now. We could indeed use the Shape component instead of our manual output, but I really wanted to show you how to accomplish some direct output operations. Our approach was not much more complex than the one Delphi suggests. Using the Shape component would have been useful to extend the example, allowing a user to drag shapes on the screen, remove them, and work on them in a number of other ways. You can see an example of the use of the Shape component in the MDIDEMO4 example in Chapter 15.

# Summary

Since Chapter 1 we have seen that a form is a window, but until this chapter we had not explored any of a form's properties. Now we know how to handle the size and position of a form, how to resize it, how to get mouse input, and how to paint on the surface of the form. I've also mentioned the existence of two global objects, Application and Screen, which will be further explored in Chapter 19.

Other chapters in the book will describe other topics strictly related to forms. In particular, Chapters 11 through 15 cover the use of toolbars and status bars; building a dialog box and an application with multiple forms; scrolling forms; building forms with multiple pages; splitting forms; and building MDI applications. As you can see from this list, forms play a central role in Delphi programming, and we still have to explore a number of topics related to them.

Before going on to these topics, however, in the next chapter I'll show you how to use a number of other components, including the graphical components mentioned in the last section of this chapter, and many other graphical components, including buttons, list boxes, and grids. Now, who told you that you could learn Delphi programming in two days? To master Delphi, you probably need to take some more time (and to read the rest of this book!).

# CHAPTER

## TEN

# Graphical Components

- Bitmap buttons

- Animated buttons

- An image viewer

- Drawing over a bitmap

- Graphical list boxes

- The Mines game

- Font and color selection grids

10

In addition to the basic controls borrowed from Windows, Delphi sports a number of more powerful components that have a modern user interface. Some of these controls are the graphical versions of traditional components (such as graphical buttons or list boxes), others are brand-new elements; some of them are new Windows 95 common controls, others are defined by Delphi and are also available in the old version of the Borland development environment. We will start exploring some of these advanced controls in this chapter, and we will continue to look at them for several more chapters.

We saw in the last chapter that it is easy to draw on the surface of a form. The same operation is possible for other components, too. However, we have also seen that the Windows painting model is far from simple. For this reason, having ready-to-use graphical controls is a big advantage over the traditional approach. You can improve your application's user interface with a very limited effort by using graphical buttons, grids, and outlines and, at the same time, adding powerful capabilities to the application in almost no time.

# Improving the User Interface with Graphics

The user interface of old Windows applications was very different. With Windows 3.1, a number of techniques to improve the user interface became common, including toolbars, graphical buttons, graphical list boxes, and so on. The 16-bit Windows API did not directly support these elements, and they required a lot of coding. However, articles in magazines and tutorials in conferences started spreading the word, and it became much easier to find documentation on how to build one of these nice graphical windows.

Now things have changed. The new version of the operating environment, Windows 95, includes a number of improved graphical controls, ready to use. Delphi has still other graphical and complex components, including grids. I'll briefly describe some of these components and show their use in simple examples, as usual. Before we start looking at the code, however, consider that while some graphics can improve a program and make it seem more professional, too many colors and too many graphics can be counterproductive. The user interface of Windows and of the application running in this environment follow specific rules, defined by Microsoft and known as *Windows Style Guides.* Without referring to this document, you can easily understand what these rules dictate by looking at the mainstream Windows applications.

Slight differences from the rules can improve a program, but diverging too much from the standard might backfire. If one application behaves differently from the others, a user might conclude that it isn't working properly. Of course, you can write a manual to explain the details of your choices, but how many users will read your manual before they start using the program? An important point, however, is that the *standard* for a user interface is a moving target. Each time someone (read *Microsoft*) writes down the details, a new application with a new feature comes out, thus changing the standard.

Consider this example: A couple of years ago, there were no toolbars. Then some toolbars with big buttons containing text and graphics were introduced. The next standard was to have smaller buttons, and maybe several lines of them. A couple of months later, every application allowed users to change the buttons on the toolbar. More time passed, and an application without *tool tips* (the yellow *hint* messages that appear when the cursor remains for some time over a button) was considered old. Other waves are coming, including dockable toolbars (that is, toolbars you can drag to different positions on the screen), an increased use of color, and many more.

# A Bitmap in a Button

One of the simplest and most common improvements to an application's user interface is to make the buttons more colorful and, at the same time, more intuitive. Several years ago, Borland started to place bitmaps in buttons to highlight their meanings. For example, OK buttons have a green check mark on them, and Cancel buttons have a red cross. Delphi offers two kinds of graphical buttons:

- The BitBtn (bitmap button) component usually has some graphics and some text, as did the old Borland buttons. The behavior of BitBtn buttons is similar to the TButton components—that is, they implement push buttons. You can choose one of the typical Borland buttons with a corresponding return value for these buttons in a modal form or dialog box.

- The SpeedButton component allows both graphics and text, but you'll often use it with only a glyph. As the name implies, speed buttons are mainly used in toolbars. Their behavior can mimic push buttons, check boxes with an off and an on state, and even radio buttons. They also allow you to use different glyphs for the various states.

The key technical difference between the BitBtn component and the SpeedButton component is that the first is based on a Windows button, using the owner-drawn technique to paint on its surface, and the second is a graphical component, not based on a window (it has no window handle). For this reason, speed buttons make a more limited use of system resources, which is particularly important when you need many buttons. Notice also that speed buttons cannot receive the input focus (you cannot select them with the Tab key), and for this reason you should generally avoid using them in generic forms or dialog boxes. In this section, I'll focus on bitmap buttons, leaving the speed buttons for the next chapter, which is entirely devoted to SpeedBars (or toolbars) and status bars.

Once you have created an object with the BitBtn component, you can simply use the Kind property to select a default text, glyph, and return value. The available choices are the values of the TBitBtnKind enumeration:

```
TBitBtnKind = (bkCustom, bkOK, bkCancel, bkHelp, bkYes,
  bkNo, bkClose, bkAbort, bkRetry, bkIgnore, bkAll);
```

If you select a custom button, you have to supply the button's caption and its glyph; otherwise, a default glyph and caption are shown. Other properties let you arrange the position of text and graphics (Layout) and set the space between them (Spacing). Another important concept is the idea of transparent color. When you prepare a bitmap for a button or other graphical components, the color found in the lower-left corner pixel of the bitmap is considered the transparent color. For this reason, many applications and Delphi itself use bitmaps with a dark yellow background (the clOlive color), a color seldom used in the bitmap itself. This value determines which color of the glyph should be considered transparent and replaced by the button's background color. If you use this approach, the system will be able to use the default colors (light gray, dark gray, and so on) for the various states of the button, always integrating your bitmap seamlessly.

**NEW**

If you choose a bitmap with a background color that you want to use as the transparent color for a button disabled at design-time, once you enable it at run-time, you'll still see the transparent color as if it was an actual color—the color that is supposed to be replaced (the transparent color) is actually displayed as is. I'm not sure why, but a couple of programs that worked in Delphi 1 seem to have problems in Delphi 2. I had to use a gray background for the bitmaps of some of the buttons on the CARS example (the next example) to avoid a similar problem.

## A Car in a Button

To experiment with graphical buttons, we'll build a simple and almost useless example, CARS, having a number of bitmap buttons with different behaviors. The program is going to have a *two-state* button that changes its text and its image each time it is pressed. It will also have a group of three buttons, only one of which is active at a time. The last two buttons are simpler. One of them, however, has its text and its caption reversed, for symmetry, as you can see in Figure 10.1.

Besides the bitmap buttons, the form contains a label, an Image component, and a Bevel component. We have never used these two components, so I'll describe them briefly (and then move back to the example):

- You can use the Image component to display images on the background of the form, eventually behind other components. To load the bitmap for an image from a file or to store it in a new file, you simply call the LoadFromFile and SaveToFile methods of the component's Picture property. You can choose to show the image in its original size or stretch it to the size of the component. Since Image components support only click events, they can be considered almost static elements. Later in this chapter, we'll use this component again to build an image viewer.

- The Bevel component defines a 3D effect you can use to make some of the form's controls stand out or to group them. It defines *beveled* boxes, frames or lines (see its Shape property) that can be either lowered or raised, as described by the Style property. Bevels have no events at all, so their only use is to improve the user interface. As we will see in detail in the next chapter, there is another component, Panel, that is similar to a bevel but with much more functionality. Along with TPanel's extra capabilities comes additional resource overhead, so do not use a panel when a bevel is enough.

As you can see in Figure 10.1, the form of the CARS example has a number of bitmap buttons, plus a bevel in the upper-left portion, with an image and a label inside. When the Left or Right button is pressed, the image is moved to the left or right until it bounces against the form's border (or almost the border, since some pixels are left). As you can see in Figure 10.1, this is far from good since the limit should be set on the border of the bevel. This simple change is left to you as an exercise.

**FIGURE 10.1:**

The output of the CARS example. The image of the car can be moved outside of the bevel.

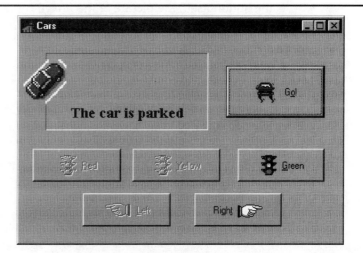

When each of the three buttons with the traffic-light bitmaps is pressed, the code simply disables the button and enables another one, following a round-robin approach: the green button follows the red button, the yellow button follows the green button, and the red button follows the yellow button. Here is one of the three methods:

```
procedure TCarsForm.RedButtonClick(Sender: TObject);
begin
  {after the red, green}
  GreenButton.Enabled := True;
  GreenButton.SetFocus;
  RedButton.Enabled := False;
end;
```

In the code above you can notice that there is a call to the SetFocus method of the GreenButton object before the RedButton is disabled. By disabling the button, it loses the focus anyway, but it will move almost randomly to other buttons, with a nasty flash effect. Instead, if the SetFocus method is called before the button is disabled, we can decide which button is going to receive the focus.

The advantage of moving the focus is that if you press the button by pressing the spacebar, you can tap the spacebar a number of times and see the active state moving from button to button, together with the focus. The same happens with the Left and Right buttons. If you press the spacebar repeatedly, the image will bounce against the border and then move back since the focus is set on the button corresponding to the opposite direction. Notice that you can also use shortcut keys (defined using the & in the button captions) to give a command. Even when you change button captions at run-time (see below) remember to set the & properly, to keep shortcuts consistent.

The example's most complex piece of code is that of the button with the car picture on it. The effect of a click on this button is to change the glyph and the caption of the button itself, the picture of the Image component, and the caption of the label below it. The code also sets the value of a private Boolean field of the form CarStopped to keep track of the current status.

To avoid loading a bitmap for the image and one for the button each time, with a statement such as

```
CarButton.Glyph.LoadFromFile ('cars2.bmp');
```

I've decided to add to the form two bitmap objects, storing the two graphical images. The form has three fields:

```
private
  CarStopped: Boolean;
  Car1Bmp, Car2Bmp: TBitmap;
```

These private fields are initialized when the form is created:

```
procedure TCarsForm.FormCreate(Sender: TObject);
begin
  {set the flag and load the two bitmaps of the car}
  CarStopped := True;
  Car1Bmp := TBitmap.Create;
  Car2Bmp := TBitmap.Create;
  Car1Bmp.LoadFromFile ('cars.bmp');
  Car2Bmp.LoadFromFile ('cars2.bmp')
end;
```

After this initialization, we can use the two bitmap objects to set a value for the image and the graphical button. Of course, there are two alternative versions, which depend on the value of the CarStopped flag. There is also a special case. If the car is not moving and the red light is on—that is, the RedButton is enabled—you cannot go. A warning message is displayed, and nothing happens. Here is the first part of the source code of the CarButton OnClick event handler:

```
procedure TCarsForm.CarButtonClick(Sender: TObject);
begin
  {a car should not start if the light is red}
  if CarStopped then
    if RedButton.Enabled then
      MessageDlg ('No turn on red, please!',
        mtWarning, [mbOK], 0)
    else
    {if was stopped and it is not red}
    begin
      {change the bitmaps and captions}
      CarButton.Glyph := Car1Bmp;
      CarButton.Caption := 'St&op';
      CarImage.Picture.Graphic := Car2Bmp;
      CarLabel.Caption := 'The car is on the road';
      CarStopped := False;
    end
  else
    {if it was moving, regardless of the lights}
    ...
```

# An Animated Bitmap in a Button

As you saw in the previous example, bitmap buttons are easy to use and can produce better-looking applications than the standard push buttons (the Button component). To further improve the visual effect of a button, we can also think of *animating* the button. There are basically two kinds of animated buttons—buttons that change their glyph slightly when they are pressed and buttons having a moving image, regardless of the current operation. I'll show you a simple example of each kind, FIRE and WORLD. Each of these examples will have a couple of slightly different versions.

## A Two-State Button

The first example, FIRE, has a very simple form, containing only a bitmap button. This button has the caption *Fire* and is connected to a glyph representing a cannon. Imagine such a button as part of a game program. As the button is pressed, the glyph changes to show a firing cannon, as you can see in Figure 10.2. As soon as the button is released, the default glyph is loaded again. In between, the program shows the user a message if that user really presses the button. In fact, a user might press the button and then move the mouse away and release it. In this case, the On-Click event doesn't take place, but the bitmap is temporarily changed anyway.

**FIGURE 10.2:**

The image displayed when the button is pressed, and the "Boom" message.

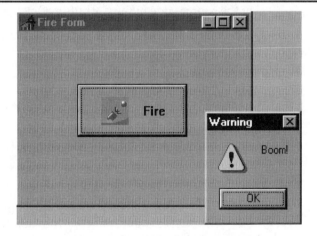

To write this program, we need to handle three of the button's events: OnMouse-Down, OnMouseUp, and OnClick. The code of the three procedures is extremely simple:

```
procedure TForm1.BitBtnFireMouseDown(Sender: TObject;
  Button: TMouseButton;
  Shift: TShiftState; X, Y: Integer);
begin
  {load firing cannon bitmap}
  if Button = mbLeft then
    BitBtnFire.Glyph.LoadFromFile ('fire2.bmp');
end;
procedure TForm1.BitBtnFireMouseUp(Sender: TObject;
  Button: TMouseButton;
  Shift: TShiftState; X, Y: Integer);
begin
  {load default cannon bitmap}
```

```
    if Button = mbLeft then
      BitBtnFire.Glyph.LoadFromFile ('fire.bmp');
end;
procedure TForm1.BitBtnFireClick(Sender: TObject);
begin
  MessageDlg ('Boom!', mtWarning, [mbOK], 0);
end;
```

When you press the left mouse button over the bitmap button, the bitmap button is pressed. If you then move the mouse cursor away from the button while holding down the mouse button, the bitmap button is released, but it doesn't get an On-MouseUp event, so the firing cannon remains there. If you later release the left mouse button outside the surface of the bitmap button, it receives the OnMouseUp event anyway.

Windows follows this rule: all mouse events are sent to the window or component behind the cursor. So how can we send a mouse event to the button if we release it outside its surface? This behavior depends on the *mouse capture*. A window can decide to capture all of the following input of the mouse, independently of the current window below the cursor. This is the default behavior of all the buttons in Windows when they are pressed. So we can state the rule above more correctly: all mouse events are sent to the window or component behind the cursor or to the window, if any, that has captured the mouse input.

**TIP**

You can capture the mouse using the Windows API SetCapture function and later stop this operation with ReleaseCapture. Capturing the mouse can be very interesting in some applications and is the basis for every dragging operation, as we will see in later chapters (Chapter 14 in particular).

## Many Images in a Bitmap

In the FIRE example, I have used a manual approach. I loaded two bitmaps and changed the value of the Glyph property when I wanted to change the image. The BitBtn component, however, can also handle a number of bitmaps automatically. You can prepare a single bitmap that contains a number of images (or glyphs) and set this number as the value of the NumGlyphs property. All sub-bitmaps must have the same size since the overall bitmap is divided into equal parts.

If you provide more than one glyph in the bitmap, they are used according to the following rules:

- The first bitmap is used for the released button, the default position.
- The second bitmap is used for the disabled button.

- The third bitmap is used when the button is clicked.

- The fourth bitmap is used when the button remains down, such as in buttons behaving as check boxes.

Usually you provide a single glyph and the others are automatically computed from it, with simple graphical changes. However, it is easy to provide a second, a third, and a fourth customized picture. If you do not provide all four bitmaps, the missing ones will be computed automatically from the first one. However, only the last or the last two bitmaps can be missing. You can't specify a normal and a pressed image without including the disabled bitmap between them.

In our example, the new version of FIRE (named FIRE2), we only need the first and third glyphs of the bitmap but are obliged to add the second bitmap, too. To see how this glyph (the second of the bitmap) can be used, I've added a check box to disable the bitmap button.

To build the new version of the program, I've prepared a bitmap of 32 × 96 pixels (see Figure 10.3) and used it for the Glyph property of the bitmap. To my surprise, the NumGlyphs property was *automatically* set to 3 since the bitmap is three times wider than it is high. Then I removed the BitBtnFireMouseDown and BitBtnFire-MouseUp methods, added the new check box, and wrote a line of code for its On-Click property:

```
procedure TForm1.CheckBox1Click(Sender: TObject);
begin
  BitBtnFire.Enabled := not BitBtnFire.Enabled;
end;
```

I've also decided to add some sound capabilities, playing a wav file when the button is pressed (with a call to the SndPlaySound function of the MMSystem unit).

---

**FIGURE 10.3:**

The bitmap with three images of the FIRE2 example, as seen in the Delphi Image Editor.

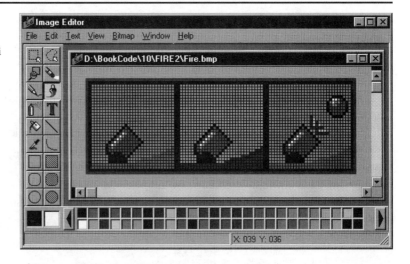

The code is very simple, so I'll skip any details about sound and multimedia and refer you to Chapter 26:

```
procedure TForm1.BitBtnFireClick(Sender: TObject);
begin
  SndPlaySound ('Boom.wav', snd_Async);
  MessageDlg ('Boom!', mtWarning, [mbOK], 0);
end;
```

When you run the program, there are two ways to change the bitmap in the button. You can disable the bitmap button by using the check box (see Figure 10.4), or you can press the button to see the cannon fire. If you compare the output of this program with Figure 10.2, showing FIRE, you will notice a remarkable difference. In the first version, the image with the firing cannon remained on the button until the message box was closed. Now the image is shown only while the button is pressed. As soon as you move outside the surface of the button or release the button after having pressed it (activating the message box), the standard glyph is displayed.

**FIGURE 10.4:**
The enabled and disabled bitmap buttons of the FIRE2 example, in two different copies of the application.

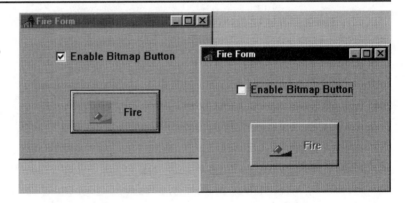

## The Rotating World

The second example of animation, WORLD, has a button featuring the earth, which slowly rotates, showing the various continents. You can see some samples in Figure 10.5, but, of course, you should run the program to see its output.

In the previous example, the image changed when the button was pressed. Now the image changes by itself, automatically. This occurs thanks to the presence of a Timer component, which receives a message at fixed time intervals. For a detailed discussion of timers and related topics, see Chapter 19.

This timer is started and stopped by pressing the bitmap button with the world image. The button has a *Start* caption, which changes to *Stop* when the timer is active.

**FIGURE 10.5:**

Some examples of the running WORLD program.

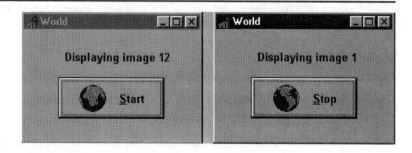

So by pressing the button, you start or stop the animation:

```
procedure TWorldForm.WorldButtonClick(Sender: TObject);
begin
  if Timer1.Enabled then
  begin
    Timer1.Enabled := False;
    WorldButton.Caption := '&Start';
  end
  else
  begin
    Timer1.Enabled := True;
    WorldButton.Caption := '&Stop';
  end;
end;
```

As you can see in Figure 10.5, a label above the button indicates which of the images is being displayed. I added the label as a debugging tool when I started writing this program, but then I decided to leave it there. You might replace it with information on time zones or something else. Each time the timer message is received, the image and label change:

```
procedure TWorldForm.Timer1Timer(Sender: TObject);
begin
  Count := (Count mod 16) + 1;
  Label1.Caption := 'Displaying image ' + IntToStr (Count);
  WorldButton.Glyph.LoadFromFile (
    'w' + IntToStr (Count) + '.bmp');
end;
```

*Count* is a field of the form that is initialized to 1 in the FormCreate method. At each timer interval, Count is increased modulus 16 and then converted into a string when it is used. The modulus operation returns the remainder of the division between integers. This means that the resulting value is always in the range 1–16. The reason for this limit is simple: I had 16 bitmaps of the earth to display. Naming the bitmap files W1.BMP, W2.BMP, and so on, makes it easy for the program to access them, building the string with the name at run-time.

# A List of Bitmaps, the Use of Resources, and a PaintBox

The WORLD program works, but it is very slow, for a couple of reasons. First of all, at each timer interval, it needs to read a file from the disk, and although a disk cache can make this faster, it is certainly not the most efficient solution. Besides reading the file from disk, the program has to create and destroy Windows bitmap objects, and this takes some time, too. The second problem is because of updating the image: When you change the button's bitmap, the component has some flickering.

To solve the first problem (and to show you a different approach to handling bitmaps), I've added a TList object, storing a list of bitmaps, to the form of the second version of the example, WORLD2. All the bitmaps are loaded when the program starts and destroyed when it terminates. At each timer interval, the program shows one of the list's bitmaps in the bitmap button. By using a list, we avoid loading a file each time we need to display a bitmap, but we still need to have all the files with the images in the directory with the executable file. A solution to this problem is to move the bitmaps from independent files to the application's resource file. This is easier to do than to explain.

*Resources* are graphical or textual data connected to a Windows program. The most important resources in Delphi include bitmaps, icons, fonts, string tables, and the images of the forms. (Note that an application's resources have nothing to do with free system resources—the two uses of the term are completely unrelated!) We will discuss resources in Chapter 21.

**NOTE** There are basically three reasons for resources in Windows applications. The first is that some of them refer to graphical elements and require proper editors; the second and more important reason is that resources are handled in memory in a special way (see Chapter 20 for more information on memory in Windows); the third is that to localize a Windows application, you usually translate the text of the resources in a different language, without changing the source code.

To use the resources instead of the bitmap files, we need first of all to copy the bitmap to the resource file. If you want to do a tedious operation, you can use the Delphi Image Editor to open the WORLD.RES file of the example and create new bitmap resources. Afterwards you can open each of the bitmap files and perform a copy-and-paste operation to the bitmap in the resource file.

As a better alternative, you can write a resource script (an RC file) listing the names of the bitmap file and the names of the corresponding resources. Just select the

File ➤ New command to open the Object Repository, then click on the Text icon in the New page. In the blank text field Delphi generates, write the following code:

```
W1   BITMAP   "W1.BMP"
W2   BITMAP   "W2.BMP"
W3   BITMAP   "W3.BMP"
...
```

Once you have prepared the RC file (I've named it WORLDBMP.RC), you can compile it into a RES file using the resource compiler included in Delphi (the BRCC32 command-line application):

```
BRCC32 WORLDBMP.RC
```

Notice that you have to use a different filename than the application default resource file. Then you have to add a compiler directive to include the new resource file:

```
{$R *.DFM}
{$R WORLDBMP.RES}
```

Once you have properly defined the resources of the application, you need to load the bitmaps from the resources. Delphi components do not support this operation directly, but you can easily accomplish it using the Windows API `LoadBitmap` function. This function requires two parameters: a handle to the application, known as HInstance, which is available in Delphi as a global variable; and a string with the name of the resource. Of course, you need to pass a PChar string, not a Pascal string, so a conversion might be required (if you decide to use Pascal strings to define the text in the first place). This is a portion of the FormCreate method:

```
ImageList := TList.Create;
for I := 1 to 16 do
begin
  Bmp := TBitmap.Create;
  StrPCopy (Name, 'W' + IntToStr (I));
  Bmp.Handle := LoadBitmap (HInstance, Name);
  ImageList.Add (Bmp);
end;
```

**NOTE**  Delphi 2 includes a new ImageList component, based on one of the Windows 95 common controls. I'll show you how to use this component in a later example, REFLIST. In this case, I'm just using a plain list of objects, called ImageList, but not based on the specific component. For the moment, I prefer to give you an idea of a list of images, building it from scratch. We will later see the difference between our approach and the real ImageList.

One problem remains to be solved. How can we obtain a smooth transition from one image of the world to the following one? I tried to work it out using the TBitBtn class, but there were many obstacles. After a while, I figured out a completely different solution. Why not paint the bitmaps in a canvas using the Draw method? Unluckily, the bitmap button's canvas is not directly available, so I added a new component, PaintBox, to the form. Again, things weren't working. You cannot place the paintbox inside the button; you can place it only inside the form. Even if you place it over the button, Delphi will connect the paintbox to the form, thus hiding it behind the button. The paintbox, in fact, is not a window. It uses its parent control—in this case, the form. The solution? Very easy, once you think about it—change the parent of the paintbox at run-time, by writing this code:

```
PaintBox1.Parent := WorldButton;
```

If you originally placed the paintbox near the upper-left corner of the form, it will appear near the upper-left corner of the button. Once the paintbox is properly set, you can simply write in the Timer1Timer method:

```
PaintBox1.Canvas.Draw (
  WorldButton.Margin + 2,
  WorldButton.Margin + 3,
  ImageList.Items[Count-1]);
```

This code copies the bitmap to the surface of the paintbox—that is, the surface of its parent component, the bitmap button. The position I've copied the bitmap to depends on the margin from the borders of the button to the bitmap, plus some border. Two more things to do are to create a proper FormDestroy method to deallocate each of the bitmaps and to synchronize the bitmap button with the image displayed in the paintbox each time the button is actually pressed (and stopped). You can see these changes in the source code of the example in the companion CD.

**NOTE**  Placing a PaintBox component in front of a button creates a problem: when you click on its surface, the button is not pressed. To improve the program, I've connected the OnClick event of the PaintBox1 component to the method used to handle the OnClick event of the button. This works, but if you click on that area, you won't see the button being pressed. To make the button behave better, we should probably dispatch any mouse operation on the PaintBox (including OnMouseDown, OnMouseMove, and OnMouseUp) to it, but this might generate further problems.

# An Image Viewer

The Image component I briefly described earlier in this chapter is usually considered to be an image viewer. In fact, you can easily load into it a bitmap file (BMP), an icon (ICO), or a Windows metafile (WMF). Bitmap and icon files are well-known formats. Windows metafiles, however, are not so common. They are a collection of graphical commands, similar to a list of GDI function calls that need to be executed to rebuild an image. Metafiles are usually referred to as *vector graphics* and are similar to the graphics file formats used for clip-art libraries.

**NOTE**
> To produce a Windows metafile, a program should call GDI functions, redirecting their output to the file. Later on, this metafile can be *played* or executed to call the corresponding functions, thus producing a graph. The advantage of metafiles is the limited amount of storage required compared to other graphical formats, and the device independence of their output.

To build a full-blown image viewer program, IMAGEV, around the Image component we need only a form with an image filling the whole client area, a simple menu, and an OpenDialog component. Surprisingly, this application requires very little coding, at least for a first basic version. The File ➤ Exit and Help ➤ About commands are simple, and the File ➤ Open command has the following code:

```
procedure TViewerForm.Open1Click(Sender: TObject);
begin
  if OpenDialog1.Execute then
  begin
    Image1.Picture.LoadFromFile (OpenDialog1.FileName);
    Caption := 'Image Viewer - ' + OpenDialog1.FileName;
  end;
end;
```

The fourth and the fifth menu commands, Options ➤ Stretch and Options ➤ Center, simply toggle the component's Stretch property (see Figure 10.6 for the result) or Center property and add a check mark to themselves:

```
procedure TViewerForm.Stretch1Click(Sender: TObject);
begin
  Image1.Stretch := not Image1.Stretch;
  Stretch1.Checked := Image1.Stretch;
end;
```

Consider in any case that when stretching an image you can change its width-to-height ratio, altering the forms, and that not all the images can be properly

FIGURE 10.6:

**FIGURE 10.6:**

The IMAGEV program displaying the regular and stretched versions of the bitmap used in the FIRE2 example.

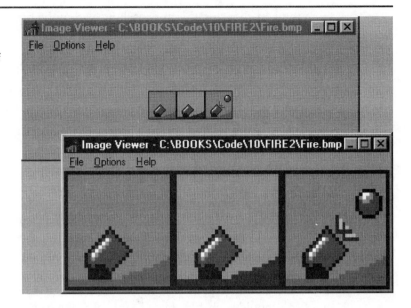

stretched. Stretching black-and-white or 256-color bitmaps doesn't always work correctly.

Besides this problem, the application has some other drawbacks. If you select a file without the proper extension, you'll get an exception error. At debug-time, this will stop the program and jump you back to the Code Editor window, but if you run the program by itself, the behavior of the exception handler provided by the system is good enough: the wrong image file is not loaded and the program can safely continue. Another problem is that if you load a large image, the viewer has no scroll bars. You can maximize the viewer window, but this might not be enough. The Image components do not handle them automatically, but the form can do it. I'll further extend this example to include scroll bars in Chapter 13.

# Drawing in a Bitmap

In the last chapter, I mentioned that by using an Image component, you can draw images directly in a bitmap. Instead of drawing on the surface of a window, you draw in a bitmap in memory; then the bitmap is copied to the surface of the window. The advantage is that instead of having to repaint the image each time an On-Paint event occurs, the component copies the bitmap back to video.

Technically, a TBitmap object has its own canvas. By drawing on this canvas, you can change the contents of the bitmap. As an alternative, you can work on the canvas of an Image component connected to the bitmap you want to change. You might think of choosing this approach instead of the typical painting approach if one or more of the following conditions are true:

- The program has to support freehand drawing or very complex graphics (such as fractal images).

- The program should be very fast in drawing a number of images.

- You and your users have a lot of RAM or are going to use only a few applications.

- You are a lazy programmer.

The last point is interesting because painting generally requires more code than drawing, although it allows more flexibility. In a graphics program, for example, if you use painting, you have to store the location and colors of each shape. On the other hand, you can easily change the color of an existing shape or move it. These operations are very difficult with the painting approach and may cause the area behind an image to be lost. If you are working on a complex graphical application, you should probably choose a mix of the two approaches. For casual graphics programmers, the choice between the two approaches involves a typical speed-versus-memory decision: painting requires less memory; storing the bitmap is faster.

## Drawing Shapes

After this general introduction about the use of the Image component to paint on a bitmap in Delphi, I'm going to show you an example. What better than a new version of the SHAPES series of examples from the last chapter? The idea is simple. I've taken version 2 of the SHAPES example, the one having colored shapes but still no support to save them—that is, with drawing but without painting. Then I placed an Image component on its form, covering the whole client area, and I redirected all the output operations to the canvas of this Image component.

In the example SHAPES5, I've also added some new menu items to save the image to a file and to load an existing bitmap. To accomplish this, I've added to the form a couple of default dialog components, OpenDialog and SaveDialog. One of the properties I had to change was the background color of the form. In fact, when you perform the first graphical operation on the image, it creates a bitmap, which has a white background by default. If the form has a gray background, each time the window is repainted, some flickering occurs. For this reason, I've chosen a white background for the form, too.

The code of this example is still quite simple, considering the number of operations and menu commands. The drawing portion is linear and very close to SHAPES2, except that the mouse events now relate to the image instead of to the form, and that the canvas of the image is used:

```
procedure TShapesForm.Image1MouseDown(Sender: TObject;
  Button: TMouseButton; Shift: TShiftState; X, Y: Integer);
begin
  {draw a form in x:y, using the current radius}
  if Button = mbLeft then
    if ssShift in Shift then
      Image1.Canvas.Rectangle (X - Radius, Y - Radius,
        X + Radius, Y + Radius)
  ...
```

To avoid overly complex file support, I decided to implement File ➤ Load and File ➤ Save As commands, and not handle Save. I've only added a Changed variable to know if an image has changed, and checked this value a number of times (before asking the user to confirm). To add full-blown file saving support, you should merge the code of this example with that of the NOTES2 example of Chapter 8.

You can look at the complete source file on the companion CD, but I'll describe here two small code excerpts, which need some comments. The first is the code of the File ➤ New menu item, which calls the FillArea method to paint a big white rectangle over the whole bitmap. In this code you can also see how the Changed variable I've just mentioned is used:

```
procedure TShapesForm.New1Click(Sender: TObject);
var
  Area: TRect;
  OldColor: TColor;
begin
  if not Changed or (MessageDlg (
    'Are you sure you want to delete the current image?',
    mtConfirmation, [mbYes, mbNo], 0) = idYes) then
  begin
    {repaint the surface, covering the whole area,
    and resetting the old brush}
    Area := Rect (0, 0, Image1.Picture.Width,
      Image1.Picture.Height);
    OldColor := Image1.Canvas.Brush.Color;
    Image1.Canvas.Brush.Color := clWhite;
    Image1.Canvas.FillRect (Area);
    Image1.Canvas.Brush.Color := OldColor;
    Changed := False;
  end
end;
```

Of course, the code has to save the original color and restore it later on. The same happens in the File Load command response method. When you load a new bitmap, in fact, the Image component creates a new canvas, with the default attributes.

For this reason, the program saves the pen's colors and size and copies them later to the new canvas:

```
PenCol := Image1.Canvas.Pen.Color;
BrushCol := Image1.Canvas.Brush.Color;
PenSize := Image1.Canvas.Pen.Width;
Image1.Picture.LoadFromFile (OpenDialog1.Filename);
Image1.Canvas.Pen.Color := PenCol;
Image1.Canvas.Brush.Color := BrushCol;
Image1.Canvas.Pen.Width := PenSize;
```

SHAPES5 is an interesting program (see Figure 10.7), with bare but working file support. The real problem is that the Image component creates a bitmap of its own size. When you increase the size of the window, the Image component is resized, but not the bitmap in memory. Therefore, you cannot draw on the right and bottom areas of the window.

**FIGURE 10.7:**

The SHAPES5 example has limited but working file support: you can load an existing bitmap, draw shapes over it, and save it to disk.

There are a number of possible solutions: Use the Windows `wm_GetMinMaxInfo` message to set the maximum size of the form (as shown in Chapter 9), use a fixed border, visually mark the *drawing area* on the screen, and so on. However, I've decided to leave the program as is since it does its job of demonstrating how to draw in a bitmap well enough. The second reason is that this is already the fifth version of the SHAPES program. It seems better to move to another topic and to a different example.

# Graphical Lists

It has become common to see Windows applications with graphical list boxes, particularly lists of files. To draw in a standard list box in Windows 3.1, you had to declare it as owner-drawn and provide some painting code. Windows 95 introduces some new common controls, such as ListView and TreeView, which can display graphical lists and hierarchical information. In Delphi, you can still have an owner-drawn list box, but you'll generally use the Windows 95 common controls. As an alternative there are also some native Delphi components, such as the Outline, the FileListBox, and the DirectoryListBox components.

If you use the common controls in your application, users will already know how to interact with them, and they will regard the user interface of your program as a very modern one. TreeView and ListView are the two key components of Windows 95 Explorer, and you can assume that many users will be familiar with them. The drawback of the common controls is that you won't be able to recompile your application with the 16-bit version of Delphi and run it on old versions of Windows. Using instead a component such as Outline, your application will be portable between the two versions of Delphi and between 16-bit and 32-bit versions of Windows (provided you recompile it with the two versions of Delphi). Having said this, I'll show you a simple comparative example of the use of a TreeView and an Outline, then a couple of more advanced examples, and then focus on the ListView component. The examples presented here tend to be quite simple: I'll use these components to build more complex examples in later chapters.

## The Outline of the Book

First, I'll use the Outline component, demonstrating its various features. The Outline allows you to add a bitmap before the text of the list items and to build a graphical hierarchy of items. To create a simple list of elements, you only need to add them to the Lines property and provide a specific bitmap in the PictureLeaf property.

The use of the outline makes particular sense when you have hierarchical information to display. I've taken as an example the table of contents of the last edition of this book, and I've built the BOOKOUT example with it. Due to publishing time constraints, the example cannot be built around this edition of the book.

**WARNING**    When I started writing the example, my intention was to call it OUTLINE. However, had I done so, the Pascal compiler would not have been able to refer properly to the Outline unit of the system since it is *hidden* by the program file. The moral of this story is that you should avoid duplicate identifiers in general, but especially unit and module names.

Before looking at the example, let me describe some of the properties and styles of the Outline component. The Lines property has the textual version of the contents of the control, and you can access it at design-time. The Items property has the same information, but in more hierarchical structure, and is accessible only at run-time. When you enter the text of the outline or read it from a text file, notice that you can leave either a space or a tab in front of an item's text to indicate its level of indentation. To work on this list of strings at design-time you can open the String Editor connected to the property and eventually load a text file from it.

> **TIP**   When you are using the Delphi String List Editor, by pressing Tab you move the focus to one of the buttons below instead of entering a tab in the text. To enter a tab in front of an item, use Ctrl+Tab instead of pressing only Tab.

Once you have defined the outline's text, you can set its style. The OutlineStyle property has six possible values:

- osPictureText defines an outline with the open picture for the expanded nodes, the closed picture for the collapsed nodes, or the leaf picture for the items without further sub-items.

- osTreePictureText defines an outline with open and closed pictures, also having some lines to highlight the tree of items and the different indentation levels.

- osPlusMinusText defines an outline having only the plus and minus pictures.

- osPlusMinusPictureText defines an outline with both open and closed pictures, and plus and minus pictures.

- osText  defines an outline having only text, with no glyphs.

- osTreeText defines an outline having only the graphical tree and the text, with no bitmaps.

You can see the effect of these properties by running the BOOKOUT example. Each of these versions of the outline shows the text with the proper indentation. A second relevant property is Options, which you can use to define the presence of a tree root (ooDrawTreeRoot), choose the activation of a focus rectangle (ooDrawFocusRect), or stretch the standard bitmaps (ooStretchBitmap) to fit in the size of the item, which depends on the height of the component's font. If you don't set the oo-StretchBitmap option, the bitmaps are displayed as they are, eventually cutting out a portion or leaving some border around them. When you select a big font or big bitmaps, this option can come in handy. These properties can be changed at run-time using the BOOKOUT example, as you can see in the output of Figure 10.8.

Having seen the main elements of an Outline component, we can write an example to see how it can be used. As I've already mentioned, the BOOKOUT example will

**FIGURE 10.8:**

The BOOKOUT program allows you to configure many properties of an outline, as you can see comparing the two examples here.

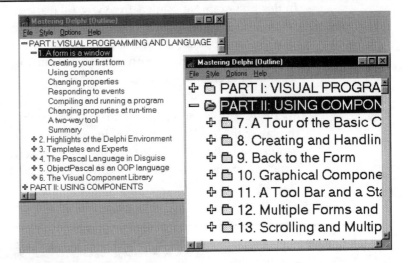

allow you to test the different styles of the outline, which can be activated by means of the application's menu.

The simple form of the BOOKOUT example contains an outline that fills the form's whole client area, and a menu. The code of the application is simple, too. It contains only commands to toggle on and off some styles of the outline, with the proper check marks beside the selected menu items.

The menu items of the Style menu are mutually exclusive. This means that when you select and check an item, all the other items should be unchecked. For this reason, I've added a RemoveStyleChecks private method to the form, which is called every time one of this menu's commands is selected, and removes all check marks from the group.

## A Tree of Chapters

Now we can try to build a similar example, using the TreeView component instead of the Outline component. Unluckily there isn't a direct way to load the text into a component, so we'll have to write this code by ourselves. The TreeView has a flexible user interface (with support for editing and dragging elements), but also a more standard one, because it is the Explorer user interface. There are a number of properties and various ways to customize the bitmap of each line, or of each kind of line. The TreeView, in fact, is connected with a TImageList component. This allows a programmer to associate a number of bitmaps with the TreeView, and to set an index for each node or item.

In this first example using a TreeView, I'll just build a program very similar to the last one, BOOKOUT, called CHAPTREE. This example is based on a form with a TreeView component aligned to the whole client area, and a menu with some commands corresponding to properties you can toggle on and off. There is also a command to change the font.

The problem, in this example, is to find a way to load the information in the TreeView. This component is not based on a string list and has no string list editor to play with. The Items property has a specific editor (see Figure 10.9), which you can use to build the structure of the data. Since it makes no sense to rebuild the structure of the book with this editor, I've decided to load it in the TreeView at startup.

**FIGURE 10.9:**

The TreeView Items property editor.

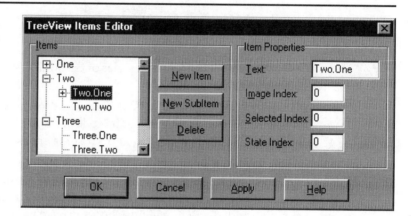

The Items property of this new component has many member functions you can use to alter the hierarchy of strings. For example, we can build a two-level tree with the following lines:

```
var
  Node: TTreeNode;
begin
  Node := TreeView1.Items.Add (nil, 'First level');
  TreeView1.Items.AddChild (Node, 'Second level');
```

Using these two methods (Add and AddChild) we can build a complex structure at run-time. But how do we load the information? Instead of accessing a file directly (which isn't that difficult in itself) I decided to create a memo component at run-time, load a text file with the saved form of the outline from the previous example, and parse it. Basically, the program counts the number of tabulators (character number 9), and adds a new item to the tree at the proper level. If there are no tabulators, the new item is connected to the root; otherwise, it is connected with the last item of the previous level. Sound complex? The code actually isn't too convoluted:

```
procedure TForm1.FormCreate(Sender: TObject);
var
  Node, Node1, Node2: TTreeNode;
  Memo: TMemo;
  I: Integer;
begin
  Memo := TMemo.Create (self);
  Memo.Parent := self;
  Memo.Width := 1000;
  Memo.Lines.LoadFromFile ('toc.txt');
  for I := 0 to Memo.Lines.Count - 1 do
    if Memo.Lines[I][1] <> #9 then
      Node := TreeView1.Items.Add (nil, Trim(Memo.Lines[I]))
    else if Memo.Lines[I][2] <> #9 then
      Node1 := TreeView1.Items.AddChild (Node,
        Trim (Memo.Lines[I]))
    else if Memo.Lines[I][3] <> #9 then
      Node2 := TreeView1.Items.AddChild (Node1,
        Trim (Memo.Lines[I]))
    else if Memo.Lines[I][4] <> #9 then
      TreeView1.Items.AddChild (Node2, Trim (Memo.Lines[I]));
  Memo.Free;
end;
```

As you can see, I've used the Trim function to remove white spaces and tabulators from the strings. You can see the result of running this code in Figure 10.10. Notice that this component allows direct editing of the text of each node or leaf of the tree.

**FIGURE 10.10:**
The output of the CHAPTREE example.

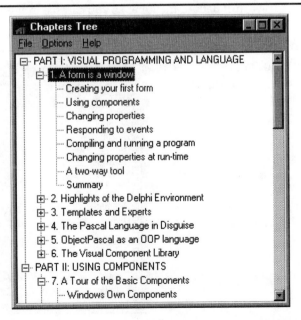

# The Nodes of the Outline

As we have seen for the TreeView, there is also a list of objects (of type TOutlineNode) at the core of the Outline component. Each of these objects has some text, possibly some data, and a bunch of other properties. For example, Level indicates the level of indentation of an item, and FullPath indicates the name, including all the parent items. If you plan advanced use of the Outline component, study the class of the nodes in detail. Instead of boring you with a list of all the operations you can do on an outline, I will show you a slightly more advanced example of the use of this component.

The example, named NODES, is a kind of geography test. The main form of the program (see Figure 10.11) has two graphical list boxes. The list on the left contains a number of countries, states, and country organizations (such as the European Community or NAFTA). Of course, this is not a full list: if you live in a state or country that is not present, please add it to the list. The list on the right contains just two entries, America and Europe (again, you can expand this by adding more continents). The aim of the program is to drag items from the left outline to the proper position in the hierarchy on the right. To accomplish this, you need to select an element in the left outline and drag it over the parent node in the right outline. For example, you can select Brazil and drag it over South America.

Other elements should be dragged to a lower level. For example, England should be placed under United Kingdom, which should go under European Community, which should be under Europe. When you have done this, you can get information on an item by pressing the Info button below the list. This information includes the full path of the item, as you can see in Figure 10.12.

**FIGURE 10.11:**

The aim of the NODES program is to drag items properly to the hierarchy on the right.

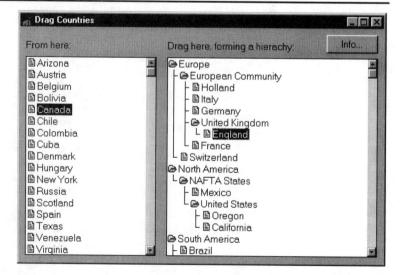

FIGURE 10.12:

The information about the England
item, including its full path.

If we want to build the example, the form is quite simple: just two Outline components, two labels, and a button. The two outlines have no special attributes. I've
only removed the root node and added the text of the items. Notice that automatic
dragging has not been enabled—I decided to use manual dragging instead.

> **TIP**
>
> If you select automatic dragging for a list box or similar component,
> your code should handle the selection of elements. To allow a user to
> both select items and drag them, you have to use manual dragging,
> calling the BeginDrag method and passing to it the False parameter. In
> this case, dragging is not started immediately, and a click properly
> selects a new item.

Handling the dragging manually is easy. When the user presses the left mouse
button over the first outline component (if it is not empty), the program calls the
BeginDrag method:

```
procedure TForm1.Outline1MouseDown(
  Sender: TObject; Button: TMouseButton;
  Shift: TShiftState; X, Y: Integer);
begin
  if (Outline1.ItemCount > 0) and (Button = mbLeft) then
    OutLine1.BeginDrag (False);
end;
```

As soon as the button is released, the program automatically calls the EndDrag
method of the first outline. The second outline component defines a simple handler
for the OnDragOver event, and performs the real work in the OnDragDrop event:

```
procedure TForm1.Outline2DragDrop(Sender, Source: TObject; X, Y:
Integer);
var
  Current: Integer;
begin
  Current := Outline2.GetItem (X, Y);
  Outline2.AddChild (Current, Outline1.
    Lines[Outline1.SelectedItem - 1]);
```

```
    Outline2.Items [Current].Expanded := True;
    Outline1.Delete (Outline1.SelectedItem);
end;
```

This last method, the heart of the program, is quite complex. When the user drags a new element, the program first determines the item of the destination outline on which the element was dropped, using the GetItem function and the coordinates passed by the event. Then the program selects this item as the outline's current item—that is, the item that will be affected by the following call to the AddChild method. The –1 is needed because the Lines array is zero-based, while the items are numbered starting from 1. It is possible to extract the text of the item directly from the Lines array only because the items of the source list have no indentation. The Lines value for an indented item, in fact, might have a tab character at the beginning. Windows displays this as a vertical line (in this case calling the Trim function can do the trick). After the element is copied to the destination outline, it should be deleted from the source outline, and its new parent node should be expanded to show the new element.

The only other complex method is the one that computes the string to display as information about the item (see again Figure 10.12). This string includes the item's full path, its level, and whether it is an intermediate node:

```
Node := Outline2.Items [Outline2.SelectedItem];
Text := Format ('Item: %s'#13'Level: %d',
  [Node.FullPath, Node.Level]);
if Node.HasItems then
  Text := Text + #13'* Has sub-items';
if Node.Expanded then
  Text := Text + ' and is expanded';
MessageDlg (Text, mtInformation, [mbOK], 0);
```

## A Graphical List

When you use a TreeView component, besides creating a structure, you can also provide bitmaps for each node and leaf of the structure. Actually, you can provide bitmaps both indicating the status of the element (for example, the selected item) and describing the contents of the item in a graphical way. Consider again the Windows Explorer application: the tree of directories in the left pane has glyphs to indicate open or closed folders (the status of the item), but it also has special bitmaps for the recycle bin, the system itself, the network, and so on.

Instead of showing you an example of a graphical TreeView, I prefer to use another component: the ListView, another powerful Windows 95 common control. What the two components have in common is the way they connect bitmaps to the items, although the ListView component is more complex because it connects a small and a large bitmap to each item of the list.

How do we connect the images to a list or tree? We need to use a specific component, TImageList. An image list is a sort of interface to a bitmap having various subimages, each corresponding to an item in the image list. If you have a number of bitmaps ready, you can place an ImageList component in a form and activate the Image List Editor using the local menu of the component. As you can see in Figure 10.13, this special editor allows you to add many bitmaps to the ImageList, defining some of their properties.

**FIGURE 10.13:**

The ImageList Editor allows you to create a list, adding bitmaps of the same size to it.

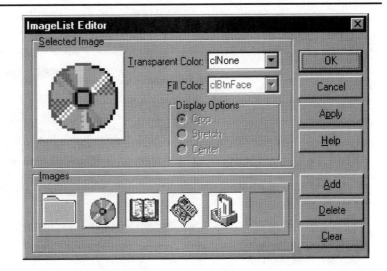

Before you use the Image List Editor, however, I suggest that you set the height and width of the bitmaps in the list, using the two properties with those names in the ImageList (this is a nonvisual component, so it doesn't use size-related properties itself). I've used this approach to build the ImageList1 component of the REFLIST example, after setting the width and height to 32. This image list, in fact, is used for the LargeImages property of a list view component. To define the SmallImages property, I've used an alternative approach: I've created a single big bitmap (16 × 80 pixels) with all the images inside. Then I've added the bitmap to a resource file, and I've written some code to load it all at once (not one image at a time):

```
procedure TForm1.FormCreate(Sender: TObject);
var
  ImageList2: TImageList;
begin
  ImageList2 := TImageList.Create (self);
  ImageList2.ResourceLoad(rtBitmap,
    'SmallImages', clOlive);
  ListView1.SmallImages := ImageList2;
```

```
    ListView1.Arrange (arDefault);
end
```

After the definition of the two image lists, I've added some items to the list using the complex editor of the Items property. You can define items and so-called sub-items, which are displayed only in the detailed view (when you set the vsReport value of the ViewStyle property). For each item, you can indicate the index of a sub-image in the image lists; this image (in the small or large version) will be used in conjunction with the list item. In Figure 10.14, you can see an example of the use of the Items property editor, with the values I've provided for my RefList example, a list of references to books, magazines, CD-ROMs, and similar resources.

**FIGURE 10.14:**

The Items property editor of the ListView component.

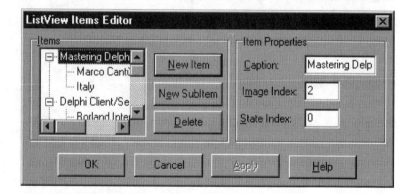

Since I've added some sub-items to the list, I also need to edit their captions and the size of the columns used to display them. The Columns property of the ListView has a specific editor for this. When the definition of the properties of the List-View component is completed, you can write some code both to toggle between different views and to make some other standard operations on the component. You can refer to the REFLIST example on the CD for the details, but setting the Items and Columns properties at design-time and assigning the proper image lists at run-time is all we need to do to have a working list view. You can see some examples of its output in Figure 10.15.

In the REFLIST example, you can easily change the style of the list view component using the View menu. This menu has four radio menu items, each setting one of the four possible values of the ViewStyle property of the component. Here is one of the four OnClick event handlers (the other three are very similar):

```
procedure TForm1.LargeIcons1Click(Sender: TObject);
begin
  ListView1.ViewStyle := vsIcon;
  LargeIcons1.Checked := True;
end;
```

**FIGURE 10.15:**

Different examples of the output of a ListView component, obtained by changing the ViewStyle property.

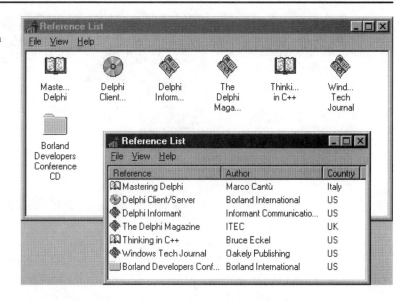

# Building Grids

Another interesting group of Delphi graphical components is represented by grids. The system contains different grid components: a grid of strings, one of images, database-related grids, and a grid of colors. The first two kinds of grids are particularly useful since they allow you to represent a lot of information and let the user navigate it. Of course, grids are extremely important in database programming, as we will see in Chapters 17 and 18, which are devoted to databases and client-server programming, respectively.

The DrawGrid and StringGrid components are closely related. In fact, the TString-Grid class is a subclass of TDrawGrid. What is the use of these grids? Basically, you can store some values, either in the strings related to the StringGrid or in other data structures, and then display each of the values, using specific criteria. While grids of strings can almost be used as they are since they already provide even editing capabilities, the grids of generic objects usually require more coding.

Grids, in fact, define display organization, not storage. The only grid that stores the data it displays is the StringGrid. All other grids are just viewers, not containers.

The basic structure of a grid includes some fixed columns and rows (as you can see in Figure 10.16), which indicate the non-scrollable region of the grid. Grids are among the most complex components available in Delphi, as indicated by the high number of properties and methods they have. There is a plethora of options and properties for grids, controlling both their appearance and their behavior.

**FIGURE 10.16:**

When you place a new grid component on a form, it contains a fixed row and a fixed column by default.

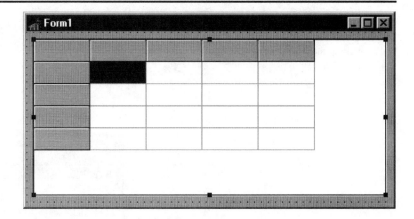

Regarding the user interface, the grid can have lines of different sizes, or it can even have no lines. You can set the size of each column or row independently of the others because the RowSize, ColWidth, and RowHeight properties are arrays. Regarding user actions, you can let the user resize the columns and the rows (goColSizing and goRowSizing), drag entire columns and rows to a new position (goRowMoving and goColumnMoving), select automatic editing, and allow range selections. Since users can perform a number of operations on grids with the proper options, there are also a number of events related to grids, such as OnColumnMoved, OnDrawCell, or OnSetEditText.

The most important event is probably OnDrawCell. In response to this event, a program has to paint a certain cell of the grid. Only string grids can automatically display their contents. The DrawGrid, in fact, doesn't have support for storing data. It is simply a tool for arranging a portion of the screen to display information in a regular format. It is a simple tool but, at the same time, a powerful one. Methods like CellRect, which returns the rectangle corresponding to the area of a cell, or MouseToCell, which returns the cell in a specific location, are a joy to use, considering that they handle resizable rows and columns and scrollable grids.

What can you use a grid for? Building a spreadsheet is probably the first idea that comes to mind, but Delphi already includes an OCX component with spreadsheet capabilities. I've decided to use the two grids to build two examples, presented in the next two sections. The StringGrid is used in a program that shows the fonts installed in the system, and the DrawGrid in a program that emulates the Minesweeper game. Yes, a game: Delphi is good for games, too (although the game I've built is not very efficient during screen redrawing). The fact that you can build Windows games in Delphi should not be underestimated, even if your business is completely different. Games and other entertainment programs, in fact, demand more in terms of system and development tools than any other category of software, databases included. So being good for games means that Delphi is a very good development environment. After the Minesweeper clone comes a simple example of the use of another, completely different grid, the ColorGrid.

# A Grid of Fonts

If you place a StringGrid component on a form and set its options properly, you have a full working editor of strings arranged in a grid, with no programming at all. To make the example more interesting, I've decided to draw each cell of the grid with a different font, varying both its size and its type. You can see the result of this program, FONTGRID, in Figure 10.17.

The form of this program is very simple. You need only place a grid component on a form, align it with the client area, set a few properties and options, and let the program do the rest. The number of columns and rows and their size, in fact, are computed at run-time. The important properties you need to set are DefaultDrawing, which should be False to let us paint the grid as we like, and Options. As usually happens in Delphi, the simpler the form is, the more complex the code, at least when you are building a non-trivial application. This example follows that rule, although it has only two methods, one to initialize the grid at startup and the other to draw the items. The editing, in fact, has not been customized and takes place using the system font. The first of the two methods is FormCreate. At the beginning, this method uses the global Screen object to access the fonts installed in the system.

The grid has a column for each font, plus a fixed column with numbers representing font sizes. The name of each column is copied from the Screen object to the first row of each column (which has a zero index):

```
StringGrid1.ColCount := Screen.Fonts.Count + 1;
...
StringGrid1.Cells [I, 0] :=   Screen.Fonts.Strings [I-1];
```

The width of each column is computed by evaluating the space occupied by the custom string of text *AaBbYyZz*, using the font of the column (written in the first row, Cells [I, 0]) and the biggest size used by the program (32). To compute the space required by the text, you can apply the TextWidth and TextHeight methods to a canvas with the proper font selected:

```
StringGrid1.Canvas.Font.Name :=
  StringGrid1.Cells [I, 0];
StringGrid1.Canvas.Font.Size := 32;
StringGrid1.ColWidths [I] :=
  StringGrid1.Canvas.TextWidth ('AaBbYyZz');
```

The rows, instead, are always 26 and have an increasing height, computed with the approximate formula $15 + I \times 2$. In fact, computing the highest text means checking the height of the text in each column, certainly too complex an operation for this example. The approximate formula works well enough, as you can see in Figure 10.17, and by running the program. In the first cell of each row, the program writes the size of the font, which corresponds to the number of the line plus seven:

```
StringGrid1.Cells [0, I] := IntToStr (I+7);
StringGrid1.RowHeights [I] := 15 + I*2;
```

The last operation is to store the test string *AaBbYyZz* in each non-fixed cell of the grid. To accomplish this, the program uses a nested for loop. Expect to use nested for loops often when working with grids:

```
for I := 1 to 25 do
  for J := 1 to StringGrid1.ColCount do
    StringGrid1.Cells [J, I] := 'AaBbYyZz'
```

Now we can study the second method, StringGrid1DrawCell, which corresponds to the grid's OnDrawCell event. This method has a number of parameters:

```
procedure TForm1.StringGrid1DrawCell(Sender: TObject;
  Col, Row: Longint; Rect: TRect; State: TGridDrawState);
```

Col and Row refer to the cell we are currently painting; Rect is the area of the cell we are going to paint; State is the state of the cell, a set of three flags, which can be active at the same time: gdSelected (the cell is selected), gdFocused (the cell has the input focus), and gdFixed (the cell is in the fixed area, which usually has a different background color). Knowing the state of the cell is important because this usually affects its output. The DrawCell method paints the text of the corresponding element of the grid, with the font used by the column and the size used for the row. The font's name is retrieved by the first row of the same column:

```
StringGrid1.Canvas.Font.Name :=
    StringGrid1.Cells [Col, 0];
```

The size is calculated with this statement:

```
StringGrid1.Canvas.Font.Size := Row + 7;
```

The fixed columns use some default values, instead. Having set the font and its size, the program selects a color for the background for the possible states of the cell: selected, fixed, or normal (that is, no special style). The value of the style's gdFocused flag is used a few lines later to draw the typical focus rectangle—a rectangle with a thin dotted line:

```
if gdSelected in State then
  StringGrid1.Canvas.Brush.Color := clHighlight
else if gdFixed in State then
  StringGrid1.Canvas.Brush.Color := clBtnFace
else
  StringGrid1.Canvas.Brush.Color := clWindow;
```

When everything is set up, the program can perform some real output, drawing the text and eventually drawing the focus rectangle:

```
StringGrid1.Canvas.TextRect (Rect, Rect.Left, Rect.Top,
    StringGrid1.Cells [Col, Row]);
if gdFocused in State then
    StringGrid1.Canvas.DrawFocusRect (Rect);
```

**TIP**　To draw the text in the grid's cell, I've used the TextRect method of the canvas instead of the more common TextOut method. The reason is that TextRect clips the output to the given rectangle, preventing drawing outside this area. This is particularly important in the case of grids because the output of a cell should not cross its borders. Since we are painting on the canvas of the whole grid, when we are drawing a cell, we can end up corrupting the contents of neighboring cells, too.

As a final observation, remember that when you decide to draw the contents of a grid's cell (or that of an item of an owner-drawn list, by the way), you should not only draw the default image, you should also provide a different output for the selected item, properly draw the focus, and so on.

## Mines in a Grid

The StringGrid component uses the Cells array to store the values of the elements and also has an Objects property to store custom data for each cell. The DrawGrid component, instead, doesn't have a predefined storage. For this reason, in the next example, I'm going to define a two-dimensional array to store the value of the grid's cells, or better, of the playing field.

As I mentioned before, the MINES example is a clone of the Minesweeper application. If you have never played this game, I suggest you try it and read its rules in the Help file since I'll give only a basic description. When the program starts, it displays an empty field where there are some hidden mines. By clicking the left mouse button, you test whether or not there is a mine in that position of the grid. If you find a mine, it explodes, and the game is over. You have lost.

If there is no mine, the program indicates in the cell the number of mines in the eight other cells surrounding it. Knowing the number of mines near the cell, you have a good hint for the following turn. To help you further on, when a cell has zero mines in the surrounding area, the number of mines for these cells is automatically displayed, and if one of them has zero surrounding mines, the process is repeated. So if you are lucky, with a single click you might uncover a good number of mines (see Figure 10.18).

When you think you have found a mine, simply click on the cell with the right mouse button, positioning a flag. The program ignores whether or not the flag is in the proper position; it is only a hint for your future attempts. If you later change your mind, you can again click the right mouse button on the cell to remove the flag. When you have placed a flag on each of the mines, you have won, and the game terminates.

Those are the rules of the game. Now we have to implement it, using a DrawGrid as a starting point. In this example, the grid is fixed and cannot be resized or modified in any way at run-time. In fact, it has square cells of $30 \times 30$ pixels, which will be used to display bitmaps of the same size.

The code of this program is complex, and it is not easy to find a starting point to describe it. For this reason, I've added more comments than usual to the source code on the companion CD so you can browse through it to understand what it does. Nonetheless, I'll describe its most important element, highlighting the key methods and algorithms used and trying to follow its logical flow. If you can, I

**FIGURE 10.18:**

The MINES program after a single
lucky click. A group of cells with no
mines is displayed at once.

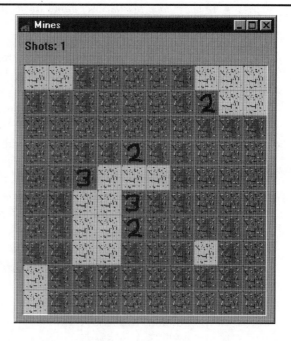

suggest you follow this description after you've printed the listing of the example, or with its source code on a monitor nearby.

First of all, the program's data is stored in two arrays (declared as private fields of the form):

```
Display: array [0 .. NItems - 1, 0 .. NItems -1] of Boolean;
Map: array [0 .. NItems - 1, 0 .. NItems -1] of Char;
```

The first is an array of Boolean values that indicates whether the items should be displayed or remain hidden. Notice that the number of rows and columns of this array is NItems. You can freely change this constant, but you should resize the grid accordingly. The second array, Map, holds the positions of the mines and flags and the numbers of the surrounding mines. It uses character codes instead of a proper enumeration data type, for the advantage of using the digits 0–8 to indicate the number of mines around the cell. Here is a list of the codes:

- *'M': Mine* indicates the position of a mine that the user still has not found.

- *'K': Known mine* indicates the position of a mine already found by the user and having a flag.

- *'W': Wrong mine* indicates a position where the user has set a flag but where there is no mine.

- *From '0' to '8': Number of mines* indicates the number of mines in the surrounding cells.

The first method I'll explore is FormCreate, executed at startup. This method initializes a number of fields of the form class, fills the two arrays with default values (using two nested `for` loops), and then sets the mines in the grid. For the number of times defined in a constant (that is, the number of mines), the program adds a new mine in a random position. However, if there was already a mine, the loop should be executed once more since the final number of mines in the Map array should equal the requested one. If not, the program will never terminate since it tests when the number of mines found equals the number of mines added to the grid. The following is the code of the loop, which can be executed more than NMines times, thanks to the use of the MinesToPlace integer variable, which is increased when we try to place a mine over an existing one:

```
Randomize;
{place 'NMines' non-overlapping mines}
MinesToPlace := NMines;
for I := 1 to MinesToPlace do
begin
  X := Random (NItems);
  Y := Random (NItems);
  {if there isn't a mine}
  if not (Map [X, Y] = 'M') then
    {add a mine}
    Map [X, Y] := 'M'
  else
    {else, repeat the loop once more}
    Inc (MinesToPlace);
end;
```

The last portion of the initialization code is the computation of the number of surrounding mines for each cell not having a mine in itself. This is accomplished by calling the ComputeMines procedure for each cell. The code of this function is fairly complex since it has to consider the special cases of the mines near a border of the grid. The effect of this call is to store in the Map array the character with the number of mines.

The next logical procedure is DrawGrid1MouseUp, called when the mouse button is released over a cell (there were some problems with the focus using the mouse-down event, so I decided on the mouse-up event). This method first computes the cell on which the mouse has been clicked, with a call to the grid's MouseToCell method. Then there are three alternative portions of code: a small one when the game has ended, and the other two for the two mouse buttons.

When the left mouse button is pressed, the program checks whether there is a mine (hidden or not), and in this case it displays a message and terminates the program with an explosion (see Figure 10.19).

**FIGURE 10.19:**
Ouch! You have stepped on a mine.

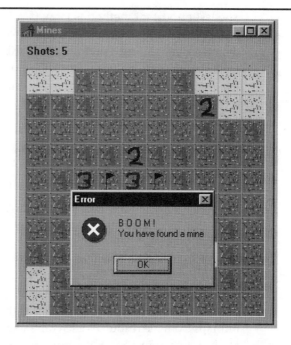

If there is no mine, the program sets the Display value for the cell to True, and if there is a 0, it starts the FloodZeros procedure. This method displays the eight items near a visible cell having a value of 0, repeating the operation over and over if one of the surrounding cells also has a value of 0. This recursive call is complex because you have to provide a way to terminate it. If there are two cells near each other and both having a value of 0, each one is in the surrounding area of the other one, so they might continue forever to ask the other cell to display itself and its surrounding cells. Again, the code is complex; you can either study it or skip it altogether since the focus of this book is on Delphi programming, not on writing complex algorithms in Object Pascal.

If the right mouse button was pressed, the program changes the status of a cell from *M* (Hidden mine) to *K* (Known mine) and vice versa, or from a number to *W* (Wrong mine) and vice versa. When all the mines have been found, the program terminates with a congratulations message.

A very important piece of code is at the end of the OnMouseUp event response method. Each time the user clicks on a cell and its contents change, that cell should be repainted. If you ask to repaint the whole grid, the program will be slower. For this reason, I've used the Windows API function InvalidateRect, as I already did once before in Chapter 9:

```
MyRect := DrawGrid1.CellRect (Col, Row);
InvalidateRect (DrawGrid1.Handle, @MyRect, False);
```

The last important method is DrawGrid1DrawCell. We already used this painting procedure in the last example, so you should remember that it is called for each cell that needs repainting. Fundamentally, this method extracts the code corresponding to the cell, which shows a corresponding bitmap, loaded from a file. Once again, I've prepared a bitmap for each of the images in a new resource file, included in the form's code with this directive:

```
{$R BITMAPS.RES}
```

The reason is that when using resources, the code tends to be faster than when using separate files, and again, we end up with a single executable file to distribute. The bitmaps have names corresponding to the code in the grid, with a character (*M*) in front since the *0 name would have been invalid. The bitmaps can be loaded and drawn in the cell with this code:*

```
StrPCopy (Name, 'M' + Code);
Bmp.Handle := LoadBitmap (HInstance, Name);
DrawGrid1.Canvas.Draw (Rect.Left, Rect.Top, Bmp);
```

Of course, this takes place only if the cell is visible, if Display is True. Otherwise, a default undefined bitmap is displayed (the bitmap name is UNDEF). Loading the bitmaps from the resources each time seems slow, so the program could have stored all the bitmaps in a list in memory, as I did in the WORLD2 example earlier in this chapter. However, this time, I've decided to use a different, although slightly less efficient, approach: a cache. This makes sense because we already use resources instead of files to speed up things.

The bitmap cache of MINES is small since it has just one element, but its presence speeds up the program considerably. The program stores the last bitmap it has used and its code; then, each time it has to draw a new item, if the code is the same, it uses the cached bitmap. Here is the new version of the code above:

```
if not (Code = LastBmp) then
begin
  StrPCopy (Name, 'M' + Code);
  Bmp.Handle := LoadBitmap (HInstance, Name);
  LastBmp := Code;
end;
DrawGrid1.Canvas.Draw (Rect.Left, Rect.Top, Bmp);
```

Increasing the size of this cache will certainly improve its speed. You can consider a list of bitmaps as a big cache, but this is probably useless since some bitmaps (those with high numbers) are seldom used. As you can see, some improvements can be made to speed up the program. At the same time, much can be done to improve its user interface. You could add a menu, allowing a user to start a new match (currently you have to restart the program) and change the number of mines and the size of the grid. If you have understood this version of the program, I think you'll be able to improve it considerably.

## Choosing Colors

The last example on grids is much simpler than the previous ones. It uses the ColorGrid, a component of the Samples page of the Components palette. This component doesn't have much in common with the other grids, and its use is straightforward. A ColorGrid has a number of cells, each with a color, and uses the left and right mouse clicks to select two colors, namely a foreground color with the left mouse button and a background color with the right mouse button. Two properties, ForegroundIndex and BackgroundIndex, hold the values of the current colors, which the user automatically changes by clicking, but only if they are active.

The only other peculiar property is the GridOrdering, which indicates the structure of the grid—the number of lines and rows. Since the color grid always has 16 colors, you can choose a vertical or horizontal line, two lines of 8 colors, or a 4 × 4 square grid.

I've built a simple example, COL_GRID, which has a grid and a text label, using the colors indicated in the grid (see Figure 10.20). Its source code is just two lines. Each time a user clicks on the grid, the two colors are copied to the label:

```
procedure TForm1.ColorGrid1Change(Sender: TObject);
begin
  Label1.Color := ColorGrid1.BackgroundColor;
  Label1.Font.Color := ColorGrid1.ForegroundColor;
end;
```

**FIGURE 10.20:**
The COL_GRID example at run-time.

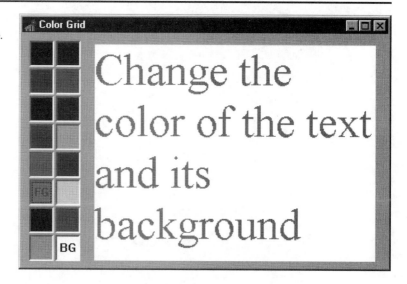

# Summary

In this chapter, we have explored a number of different Delphi components, including outlines, grids, bitmap buttons, and some Windows 95 common controls, such as the TreeView and the ListView. Of course, there are other components of this kind, including those of the Sample pages of the Components palette. You can also create or buy new components and add them to Delphi. We will explore this topic briefly at the end of the book. What is important is that when components are well documented, using them is usually fairly simple. There is nothing to understand, aside from the meanings of the properties and methods. What is required of a great Delphi programmer is a good knowledge of the basics and some imagination in mixing different components on a form to build an application.

It is just with such imagination that Delphi programmers can easily build complex toolbars and status bars out of the existing components, as we will do in the next chapter. And it is with our imagination that we will be able to build splitters (in Chapter 14) or figure out strange uses for the PageControl and the Notebook components (in Chapter 13). These are some of the topics of the next chapters, after we have examined the foundations for applications with multiple forms and dialog boxes (in Chapter 12).

# CHAPTER

## ELEVEN

# A Toolbar and a Status Bar

- How to use a TPanel to build a toolbar

- Toolbar buttons

- A combo box in a toolbar

- How to drag a toolbar around the form

- The StatusBar component

- Hints and the status bar

**O**ne of the distinctive features of many Windows applications is the presence of a toolbar at the top of the window and a status bar at its bottom. The toolbar might have a variety of names, such as SpeedBar or control bar, depending on the application's producer. Some of these names are also trademarks, although I find this really strange.

Whatever name you give it, a toolbar usually contains a number of small buttons you can press with a mouse click to give commands or to toggle options on and off. At times, a toolbar can also contain a combo box, an edit box, or some other control. The toolbars of the last generation of big applications usually can be moved to the left or right of the window, or even taken away and used as a *toolbox*, a small floating window with an array of buttons.

A status bar, instead, usually has one or more areas with a textual description of the current status of the program. You might have an area for coordinates; to show the selected font; or to display hints on what to do next, error messages, and so on. What should go in a status bar really depends on the application.

# Grouping Controls with Panels

To create a toolbar or status bar in Delphi, you can use the Panel component, adding a number of buttons or other panels inside it, or you can use the specific StatusBar component. A panel can be considered a tool to divide the client area of a frame into different portions and to group other components.

Although a panel can have its own text, it rarely does. Instead, panels can make good use of their three-dimensional aspect to improve the look of the application. In this respect, a panel is similar to a bevel, although this last component has a less important role and much less functionality. From a graphical point of view, a panel can be described as a *double-bevel* since it has two elements of this kind you can play with (see the properties BevelInner and BevelOuter). Combined with the different values for the BevelWidth, this allows for a variety of effects, as you can see by playing with these properties or running the PAN_BORD example you can find on the companion CD. Usually, when you create a panel, you place it in a particular area of the form, changing the value of the Align property. For a typical toolbar, use the value alTop, while the StatusBar component is automatically aligned to the bottom (alBottom). You might also choose vertical panels, although they are less common. Besides other common properties, the Panel component can handle hints; Hint and ShowHints are the two most relevant properties. *Hints* are short messages displayed near the cursor when the user moves the mouse over a toolbar button; they will be discussed later in this chapter. Of course, a form can have several toolbars and change the active one easily. In this case, a good suggestion is to define a variable in the form referring to the current toolbar so you can easily access its properties.

Hints are available not only in panels. Every form can have hints for some or all of the components it contains. We will see an example of a plain form with hints later in this chapter.

# Building a Toolbar

To build a typical toolbar, you simply need to place a panel at the top of the frame and place a number of SpeedButton components in it. A *speed button* is similar to a bitmap button, a component described in the last chapter. Like bitmap buttons, speed buttons can have a caption and a glyph, although usually they have only the graphical element.

The main difference is in the behavior. Bitmap buttons are like push buttons (that is, the Button component) and are mainly used inside dialog boxes. Speed buttons can behave like push buttons, check boxes, or radio buttons, and they can have different bitmaps for various situations. However, there are also important technical differences between SpeedButtons and bitmap buttons. The first is a graphical component, has no window handle (thus consuming no windows resources), cannot receive the input focus, has no tab order, and is faster to create and paint.

If you simply select the SpeedButton component and place an instance in the panel—the toolbar—you end up with a graphical push button. You can select a bitmap for it or type in a caption, although the first solution is more common. A toolbar's push buttons tend to be quite small, around 20 × 20 pixels. You cannot usually write much text in such a limited space. A glyph, on the other hand, can be meaningful even if it is small. Consider, in any case, that 20 × 20-pixel glyphs on a high-resolution screen can be quite small.

## A Simple Toolbar

Once you have added a speed button, you might simply write some code for its On-Click event. This is the default operation you obtain by double-clicking on it in the form. In the TOOLBAR example, I've prepared a musical note glyph and added the following code to the button:

```
procedure TToolbarForm.SpeedButtonNoteClick(Sender: TObject);
begin
  MessageBeep (0);
end;
```

Now we can add a group of speed buttons that will work like radio buttons. Just place some more speed buttons on the panel, select all of them, and give their GroupIndex properties the same value. All the buttons having the same GroupIndex become mutually exclusive selections, similar to radio buttons. One of these buttons should always be selected, so remember to set the Down property to True for one of them at design-time or as soon as the program starts.

As an alternative, you can have mutually exclusive buttons that can all be *up*. This means you can click on the selected button and deselect it. You can choose this behavior by setting the AllowAllUp property for all the buttons of the group to True (the default is False). In this case, of course, at startup the buttons can all be in the up position.

As an example of the two approaches, you can add two different groups of speed buttons to the panel (or toolbar). In the TOOLBAR example (see the form in Figure 11.1), I've added three exclusive buttons to determine the alignment of a label's text and three more buttons to determine its style. The idea is that one of the alignment buttons should always be selected since the text must always have an alignment. The methods corresponding to the three OnClick events of these buttons have the following structure:

```
procedure TToolbarForm.SpeedButtonLeftClick(Sender: TObject);
begin
  Label1.Alignment := taLeftJustify;
end;
```

**FIGURE 11.1:**

The form of the TOOLBAR example.

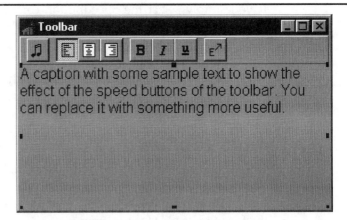

On the other hand, the three style speed buttons (those of the second group) can all be off since the text can be *normal*. This use of the styles is far from perfect since they are not usually considered exclusive selections—you can have **bold italic** text, but I've decided to part from the common behavior for this example.

The problem in this portion of the code is that you cannot simply select the style when the button is pressed. You also have to deselect it, resetting the normal style, when the button is released. In the methods responding to the click events of these speed buttons, we have to write something similar to this code:

```
procedure TToolbarForm.SpeedButtonBoldClick(Sender: TObject);
begin
  if SpeedButtonBold.Down then
    Label1.Font.Style := [fsBold]
  else
    Label1.Font.Style := [];
end;
```

I could have used three different speed buttons behaving as check boxes instead of this second group of buttons since the three attributes are not really exclusive. But how do you add a speed button that works as a check box to the toolbar? Is there a special property? If you look at the properties of the SpeedButton component, you'll find nothing. In fact, the solution is already at hand: A check box is a group with only one item that allows all the buttons to be deselected.

In practice, you accomplish this by adding a new speed button, giving it a specific value for the GroupIndex property (different from the indexes of the other groups), and choosing True for the AllowAllUp property. That's all you need to have a fully working check box. The code corresponding to this last speed button is simple:

```
procedure TToolbarForm.SpeedButtonBigClick(Sender: TObject);
begin
  if SpeedButtonBig.Down then
    Label1.Font.Size := 24
  else
    Label1.Font.Size := 12;
end;
```

As you press this button, it remains down (see Figure 11.2); when you press it again, it is released. I suggest you test the example to check the behavior of the various buttons and groups of buttons.

**FIGURE 11.2:**

The last speed button behaves like a check box.

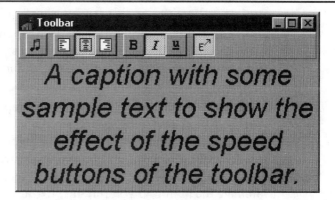

383

# Enabling and Disabling Toolbar Buttons

This simple example has more or less standard behavior. Every button has its own glyph, which is used both for selected and deselected check boxes or radio buttons. However, each speed button can have a number of different glyphs (that is, different bitmaps) without requiring you to change the bitmap manually. We saw the differences between these two approaches in the two versions of the FIRE example in the last chapter.

To make some tests on this topic, I've prepared a second version of the toolbar example, TOOLBAR2. In this example, I've added a menu with some menu items that can be used to disable some of the speed buttons or even hide the whole toolbar. The Toolbar pull-down menu contains a command to hide the whole toolbar. It calls the following method:

```
procedure TToolbarForm.Visible1Click(Sender: TObject);
begin
  {hide or display the toolbar, setting the menu item check mark}
  Panel1.Visible := not Panel1.Visible;
  Visible1.Checked := not Visible1.Checked;
end;
```

This code toggles the value of two Boolean properties, one to accomplish the required action and the second to add or remove the check mark beside the menu item. Two similar statements are also present in the commands used to disable or enable specific speed buttons:

```
procedure TToolbarForm.DisableSound1Click(Sender: TObject);
begin
  {disable or enable button and set menu check mark}
  SpeedButtonNote.Enabled := not SpeedButtonNote.Enabled;
  DisableSound1.Checked := not DisableSound1.Checked;
end;
```

When you disable one of these speed buttons, Delphi automatically paints a "grayed" version of the bitmap you have supplied (actually the color of the "grayed" item depends on the Desktop properties), as you can see by comparing Figure 11.3 with one of the figures of the previous version of the example (such as Figure 11.2).

In this example, Delphi generates three versions of the bitmaps: normal, pressed, and disabled. However, I've decided to supply a custom version of the glyphs of the last button, preparing the bitmap shown in Figure 11.4, with four different portions. For this button, I just needed two glyphs, one for the normal button and one for the pressed button, but I had to provide two more glyphs for the other states because the Stay Down glyph is the fourth. By preparing more glyphs, I was able to animate the button. If you run the program and press the button, the bitmap will

**FIGURE 11.3:**

The output of the TOOLBAR2 example, with some disabled toolbar buttons, and a different bitmap for the last button.

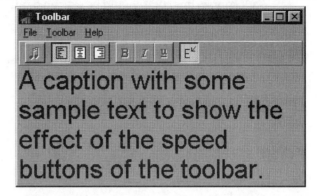

**FIGURE 11.4:**

The bitmap used for the last speed button of the toolbar in the TOOLBAR2 example.

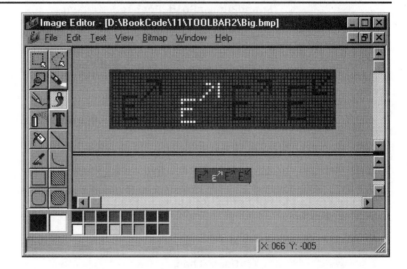

change immediately and will later change again, after the click event (see again Figure 11.3).

This program is nice, but a minor problem shows up. If you select one of the three font style buttons, disable them using the corresponding menu command, and enable them again, the button that was originally pressed will be repainted as if it were up (not down). The problem is in the transition between the disabled and the down state. Everything works (the button is really pressed), but the wrong image is displayed on the screen. To correct this problem, you might force an update of the button glyph by toggling it up and down:

```
SpeedButtonBold.Down := False;
SpeedButtonBold.Down := True;
```

Of course, this code should be executed only if the button is currently selected. You should write the same code for the other two buttons and add it to the form's DisableStyles1Click method:

```
procedure TToolbarForm.DisableStyles1Click(Sender: TObject);
begin
  {disable or enable buttons and set menu text properly}
  if SpeedButtonBold.Enabled then
  begin
    SpeedButtonBold.Enabled := False;
    SpeedButtonItalic.Enabled := False;
    SpeedButtonUnderline.Enabled := False;
    DisableStyles1.Checked := True;
  end
  else
  begin
    SpeedButtonBold.Enabled := True;
    SpeedButtonItalic.Enabled := True;
    SpeedButtonUnderline.Enabled := True;

    {FIX: toggle the down button to repaint
    it with the proper attributes}
    with SpeedButtonItalic do
      if Down then
      begin
        Down := False;
        Down := True;
      end;
    with SpeedButtonBold do
      if Down then
      begin
        Down := False;
        Down := True;
      end;
    with SpeedButtonUnderline do
      if Down then
      begin
        Down := False;
        Down := True;
      end;

    DisableStyles1.Checked := False;
  end;
```

The same problem is present in the *check box* SpeedButtonBig, and I haven't fixed it to let you see that it doesn't work. This problem also shows up in the future versions of these examples (such as TOOLBAR3, COMBOBAR, and DRAGTOOL), but I've decided not to correct it in every example because it is a minor glitch, and because I always hope that Borland will fix it.

**NOTE**

In the TOOLBAR example, I've used grayscale bitmaps, but you can make intensive use of color in speed buttons. In the last year, this has become common in all major applications. Actually, too much color can be confusing, and having no speed buttons is probably better than having confusing ones, but I wouldn't like living in a gray world. Maybe those who suggest avoiding colors in toolbar buttons are the types who have a closet full of gray suits.

## Adding Hints to the Toolbar

Another element becoming quite common in toolbars is the *hint*, also called *balloon help*—some text that briefly describes the speed button that is currently under the cursor. This text is usually displayed in a yellow box after the mouse cursor has remained steady over a button for a set amount of time. To add hints to an application's toolbar, simply set the ShowHints property of the panel used as the toolbar to True. You can also change the default value of the HintColor and HintPause properties of the Application global object and, optionally, add a specific text for the hint of the toolbar itself (Hint property).

The toolbar itself, however, usually has no hint. It only shows the hints of the buttons or other elements it contains. In this example, TOOLBAR3, I've added a proper value for the Hint property of the various speed buttons. Without writing any code, the new version of the programs works very well and makes the example look much more professional (see Figure 11.5). However, we can still do something to improve the program. The last button has a hint, *Expand*, which is appropriate only when the button is not pressed. When it is down, the hint should become *Shrink* or something similar. We can accomplish this by adding two lines of code to the SpeedButtonBigClick method, to change the hint each time its status changes:

```
procedure TToolbarForm.SpeedButtonBigClick(Sender: TObject);
begin
  if SpeedButtonBig.Down then
  begin
    Label1.Font.Size := 24;
    SpeedButtonBig.Hint := 'Shrink';
  end
  else
  begin
    Label1.Font.Size := 12;
    SpeedButtonBig.Hint := 'Expand';
  end;
end;
```

As you have seen, there was almost no coding involved in adding the hints. I've added some code only to support *context-sensitive hints,* hints with text that changes depending on the status of the speed button.

FIGURE 11.5:

The output of the TOOLBAR3
example, with the fly-by hints.

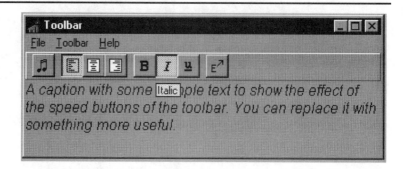

# Adding Hints to a Form

As we have added hints to an application's toolbar, we can add hints to forms, or to the components of a form, without the need to add a panel. I'll show you a simple example of adding fly-by hints to an existing program, PHRASES3. The new version, PHRASES4, shows hints when you move over the components contained by the form, as you can see in Figure 11.6.

As you can see in the figure and if you run the program, the hints are usually displayed below the component, which is okay for the buttons of a toolbar but not always the best solution for the components of a form. If you add a hint to the form

FIGURE 11.6:

The output of the PHRASES4
example, with a hint.

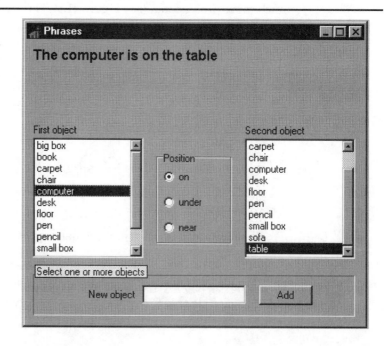

itself, it will be displayed below the window. If you add it to the label at the top, it will be shown far away from its text because the surface of the label, at least at the beginning, has enough space to show three lines. The only way to display hints near the mouse position, and not below the current component, is to customize hints, something possible but not very simple to do. The next section provides a simple peek into the topic.

## Customizing Hints

We have seen that it is easy to add hint support to a toolbar or a form. It is also easy to customize the way hints are displayed. The simplest thing you can do is change the value of the HintColor and HintPause properties of the Application object. The first defines the background color of the hint window, usually yellow, and the second the amount of time the cursor should remain on a component before hints are displayed.

To obtain more control over their display, you can customize hints even further by assigning a method to the application's OnShowHint event. You cannot do this with the Object Inspector since the Application object doesn't show up in the list. Instead, you need to add a new method to the form manually and then assign it to the OnHint property of the Application object at startup (for example, when the form is created).

The method you have to define has some interesting parameters, such as a string with the text of the hint, a Boolean flag for its activation, and further information:

```
TShowHintEvent = procedure (
  var HintStr: string;
  var CanShow: Boolean;
  var HintInfo: THintInfo) of object;
```

Each of the parameters is passed by reference, so you have a chance to change it. The last parameter is a structure, with the indication of the control, the position of the hint, its color, and other information:

```
THintInfo = record
  HintControl: TControl;
  HintPos: TPoint;
  HintMaxWidth: Integer;
  HintColor: TColor;
  CursorRect: TRect;
  CursorPos: TPoint;
end;
```

Again, you can modify the values of this structure, for example, to change the position of the hint window before it is displayed.

# Adding Features to a Toolbar

The TOOLBAR example we built in three steps contained a standard toolbar, although it had buttons with different behaviors, changing bitmaps, and hints. We can extend this example in two directions. The first is to add some new features to the toolbar panel, such as a combo box, a pop-up menu, and so on. The second is to implement a *dockable* or *draggable* toolbar—a toolbar you can position on any side of the form at run-time.

## A Combo Box in a Toolbar

The first extension of TOOLBAR3 is the COMBOBAR example, which has a combo box in its toolbar. There are a number of common applications using combo boxes in toolbars to show lists of styles, fonts, font sizes, and so on. Our program is along the same lines, but it follows a slightly different approach: it uses a combo box to let the user choose a font and a spin edit box for setting the font size. You can see an example of this program's form at run-time in Figure 11.7.

**FIGURE 11.7:**

The COMBOBAR example at run-time.

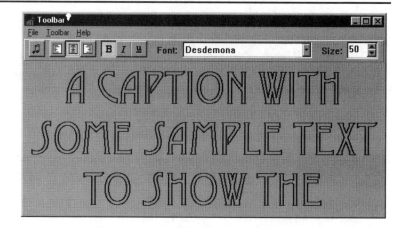

The form of this example is similar to that of the previous version, TOOLBAR3. I've removed the size speed button and added a combo box and a spin edit control, each with its own label. The two new components and their labels have a proper message in the Hint property. Having removed the size button, I had to delete the menu item used to disable it, delete its code, and delete the code related to the click on the button itself. The form has another component, a pop-up menu, connected with the panel and having almost the same menu commands as the menu bar's Toolbar pull-down. To make this new pop-up menu work without much effort, I simply connected the OnClick events of its items with the methods of the corresponding items of the main menu, using the Object Inspector.

The original methods associated with these commands add and remove the check marks only from the items of the Toolbar pull-down, not from the items of the pop-up menu. I could have changed these methods to operate also on the items of the pop-up menu, but I decided to follow a different approach. When the pop-up menu is going to be displayed, I copy to its items the current check marks of the corresponding items of the main menu:

```
procedure TToolbarForm.PopupMenu1Popup(Sender: TObject);
begin
  DisableSound2.Checked := DisableSound1.Checked;
  DisableStyles2.Checked := DisableStyles1.Checked;
end;
```

The rest of the new code of the example refers to the new components placed on the toolbar. The combo box is filled when the application starts, copying once more the names of the current fonts from the Screen object (as happened in the FONTGRID example in Chapter 10):

```
procedure TToolbarForm.FormCreate(Sender: TObject);
var
  I: Integer;
begin
  for I := 1 to Screen.Fonts.Count do
    {copy the name of the font in the combo box}
    ComboBox1.Items.Add (Screen.Fonts.Strings [I-1]);
  {select the current font}
  ComboBox1.ItemIndex :=
    ComboBox1.Items.IndexOf (Label1.Font.Name);
end;
```

Notice the last statement of the method, used to select the current font of the label into the combo box. When a new element of the combo box is selected, the reverse action takes place: The text of the current item of the combo box is copied to the name of the label's font:

```
procedure TToolbarForm.ComboBox1Change(Sender: TObject);
begin
  Label1.Font.Name :=
    ComboBox1.Items [ComboBox1.ItemIndex];
end;
```

Something similar takes place for the spin edit control. You can access the current value of the spin edit by using its Value property and copy it to the Size field of the label's Font property. You might think this a safe operation to do each time the contents of the spin edit box change, since its limits have been set to 8 and 72 (using the MinValue and MaxValue properties). This is not true. The limits of a spin edit control affect only the scrolling operations, but a user can type in a new value, which has no limit, aside from the fact that this edit box accepts only two input characters (as indicated by its MaxLength property).

Even worse, when the user replaces the current text with something else, for a moment there will be no text in the control, and if you access the Value property while the spin edit box has no text, an exception occurs. In fact, the code behind the Value property tries to convert the current text to a number, but if there is no text, it fails. The solution? We should test whether the spin edit box really has some text before we can safely access its value:

```
procedure TToolbarForm.SpinEdit1Change(Sender: TObject);
begin
  if not (SpinEdit1.Text = '') then
    Label1.Font.Size := SpinEdit1.Value;
end;
```

If you consider only the toolbar of this example (not the rest of the form), it seems almost a professional application. You can mix this code with that of an example, such as NOTES2 in Chapter 8, or even better, with a RichEdit component to obtain a nice editor. In this case you'll need to change the status of the buttons on the toolbar each time the user selects new text in the RichEdit, matching the attributes of the selected text. I'm not going to show you how to write this example, because it is already available among the demo program shipping with Delphi (see the RICHEDIT example in Delphi DEMOS directory). I suggest you open and study that program.

## A Toolbar You Can Drag

Another improvement to the TOOLBAR3 example is to allow the user to drag the toolbar to a different area of the screen. Some Windows applications have toolbars that can be placed only below the menu or at the bottom of the window, others allow vertical bars, and some even have the choice of turning the toolbar into a toolbox—that is, a small floating window. In the following example, DRAGTOOL, I'm going to explore all of these choices.

To accomplish this, the panel used as the toolbar should support automatic dragging, and the label should accept dragging. So first of all, set the DragMode property of Panel1 to dmAutomatic, and then add an OnDragOver event method to the label covering the form, setting the Accept reference parameter to True. To indicate the possible positions of the toolbar, I used the TAlign data type defined by the VCL as follows:

```
TAlign = (alNone, alTop, alBottom,
  alLeft, alRight, alClient);
```

The value alNone will be used to indicate the toolbox (no toolbar). This data type is the return value of a GetBarPos function, which returns the different code depending on the value of the X and Y parameters, which represent form coordinates:

```
function TToolbarForm.GetBarPos (X, Y: Integer): TAlign;
begin
```

```
    if X < DragSize then
      GetBarPos := alLeft
    else if Y < DragSize then
      GetBarPos := alTop
    else if X > ClientWidth - DragSize then
      GetBarPos := alRight
    else if Y > ClientHeight - DragSize then
      GetBarPos := alBottom
    else
      GetBarPos := alNone;
end;
```

In this code, DragSize is a constant defined by the program that should be less than the height (or width) of the toolbar. Once the dragging ends, we have to move the toolbar to the new position. This is the interesting part of the program, but it is probably easier than you might imagine.

Let me start with a simple case. What is the code you have to write to move the toolbar from the top to the bottom of the form? You should change only the value of the Align property of the panel:

```
Panel1.Align := alBottom;
```

Notice that we can simply ignore the form's other components only because there is a label aligned with the client area; that is, it covers the whole area of the form, excluding the rectangle taken up by the toolbar. To restore Panel1 to the top, the reverse action is required. When you move the toolbar to another location (see Figure 11.8), a similar action should be performed, using the return value of the GetBarPos function directly:

```
ReqPos := GetBarPos (X + Label1.Left, Y + Label1.Top);
Panel1.Align := ReqPos;
```

**FIGURE 11.8:**

In the DRAGTOOL example, a user can drag the toolbar to a side of the form.

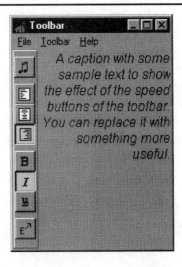

In turning the panel into a vertical one, the problem is not in the panel itself but in the speed buttons it hosts. We need to move each of the buttons to a new location or they won't be visible, aside from the first one. Again, this seems more complex than it is.

To move a button from the horizontal bar to the vertical bar, you can simply exchange its Top coordinate with its Left coordinate. If you think about it a bit, you should understand why. Luckily, to move the buttons back to a horizontal bar, we only have to perform exactly the same operation again. Here is the code of the RotateSpeedbar procedure:

```
procedure TToolbarForm.RotateSpeedbar;
var
  I, X, Y: Integer;
begin
  for I := 0 to Panel1.ControlCount - 1 do
  begin
    {reverse X and Y}
    X := Panel1.Controls [I].Top;
    Y := Panel1.Controls [I].Left;
    Panel1.Controls [I].Top := Y;
    Panel1.Controls [I].Left := X;
  end;
end;
```

The method inverts the $X$ and $Y$ values for each of the controls of the bar, scanning the Controls array ControlCount times. Of course, this code works well only for *square* controls. If you have a combo box on the toolbar, it will fail. When should you call this method? Only when the old and the new toolbar are one vertical and the other horizontal, or vice versa:

```
if ( (ReqPos in [alTop, alBottom]) and
    (BarPos in [alLeft, alRight]) ) or
    ( (ReqPos in [alLeft, alRight]) and
    (BarPos in [alTop, alBottom]) ) then
  RotateSpeedbar;
```

In this if test, BarPos is the current position of the toolbar. With this code, we can now move the SpeedBar to each of the four sides of the form. The last thing we have to do is to turn the toolbar into a toolbox, as you can see in Figure 11.9. To accomplish this, I've added a second form to the project, named it *ToolBox*, and set its BorderStyle to bsToolWindow and its FormStyle to fsStayOnTop.

At first I thought I could have copied the speed buttons from the panel to the other window, but then I realized that keeping their attributes in sync would have been a nightmare. So I decide to leave the toolbox form empty and copy the speed buttons into it when they are needed. If the dragging operation terminates in the central portion of the form, I show the toolbox, hide the toolbar, eventually rotate the speed buttons if they are vertical, and then call the MoveButtons method. The code

The toolbox of the DRAGTOOL example.

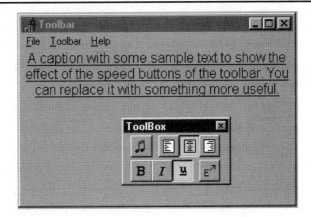

also sets a private Boolean field of the form, BoxOn, to True, to indicate that the toolbox is visible. Here is the code:

```
if ReqPos = alNone then
begin
  ToolBox.Show;
  Panel1.Visible := False;
  BoxOn := True;
  if BarPos in [alLeft, alRight] then
    RotateSpeedbar;
  {move buttons to the toolbox}
  MoveButtons (ToolBox);
end
```

MoveButtons makes two different actions: First it moves the button to the TWin-Control passed as parameter, then it places the speed buttons on two lines, or moves them back to one line (I'm going to use this same method also to restore the position of the speed buttons):

```
procedure TToolbarForm.MoveButtons (Win: TWinControl);
var
  I, J: Integer;
begin
  {move the speed buttons to a new parent component}
  for I := 0 to ComponentCount - 1 do
    if Components [I] is TSpeedButton then
      TSpeedButton (Components [I]).Parent := Win;
  if Win = ToolBox then
  begin
    {place the buttons on two lines}
    for J := 0 to Win.ControlCount - 1 do
      if Win.Controls [J].Left > 110 then
      begin
        Win.Controls [J].Left := Win.Controls [J].Left - 112;
        Win.Controls [J].Top := 30;
      end;
```

```
    end
  else
  begin
    {place back the buttons on one line}
    for J := 0 to Win.ControlCount - 1 do
      if Win.Controls [J].Top = 30 then
      begin
        Win.Controls [J].Left := Win.Controls [J].Left + 112;
        Win.Controls [J].Top := 2;
      end;
  end
end;
```

Once the toolbox is visible, you cannot drag it into a side of the form to turn it into a toolbar. If you don't want the toolbox anymore just close it, and the toolbar will be displayed again in its former position. The code to accomplish this is in the On-Close event of the toolbox:

```
procedure TToolBox.FormClose(Sender: TObject; var Action:
TCloseAction);
begin
  ToolbarForm.Panel1.Visible := True;
  ToolbarForm.BoxOn := False;
  ToolbarForm.MoveButtons (ToolbarForm.Panel1);
  if ToolbarForm.BarPos in [alLeft, alRight] then
    ToolbarForm.RotateSpeedbar;
end;
```

# Creating a Status Bar

Building a status bar is even simpler than building a toolbar. In fact, Delphi includes a specific StatusBar component, based on a specific Windows 95 control. Although you can use a Panel component, place it on the form, usually aligned at the bottom, and define a proper three-dimensional effect, I suggest you rely on the StatusBar component. This component can be used almost as a panel when its SimplePanel property is set to True. In this case you can use the SimpleText property to output some text. The real advantage of this component, however, is that it allows you to define a number of sub-panels by simply activating the editor of its Panels property, as you can see in Figure 11.10. Each sub-panel has its own graphical attributes, customizable using the editor. Another feature of the status bar component is the "size grip" area added to the lower-right corner of the bar, which is useful to resize the form itself. This is a typical element of the Windows 95 user interface.

There are a number of uses for a status bar. The most common is to display information about the menu item currently selected by the user. Besides this, a status bar often displays status information about the status of a program (hence the name).

**FIGURE 11.10:**

The StatusBar Panels Editor.

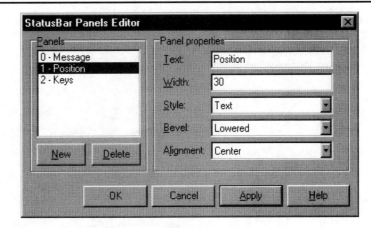

For example, you might display the position of the cursor in a graphical application, the current line of text in a word processor, the status of the lock keys, the time and date, or other information.

## Menu Hints in the Status Bar

The first example, STATUS1, has a status bar capable of displaying the description of the current menu item and the status of the Caps Lock key. The form has a main menu, of course, and when the user moves to the menu to select an element, the program displays a description of the current command in the status bar, as you can see in Figure 11.11.

To obtain this effect, you need to take two steps. First, input a string as a Hint property of each item or pull-down of the main menu. Second, write some code to handle the application's OnHint event. You need to add a new method to the form manually and then assign it to the OnHint property of the Application object at startup (for example, when the form is created):

```
procedure TForm1.FormCreate(Sender: TObject);
begin
  Application.OnHint := ShowHint;
end;
```

In the form's interface, you can add the following definition:

```
procedure ShowHint(Sender: TObject);
```

This procedure copies the current value of the application's Hint property, which temporarily contains a copy of the hint of the selected item to the status bar:

```
procedure TForm1.ShowHint(Sender: TObject);
begin
  StatusBar1.Panels[0].Text := Application.Hint;
end;
```

**FIGURE 11.11:**

The simple status bar of the STATUS1 example displays a description of the current menu item.

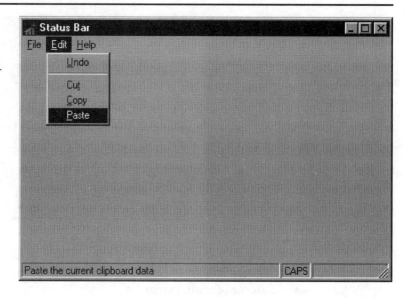

This is all you need to do to display a hint indicating the effect of a menu in the status bar. To display the status of the Caps Lock key, or of any other key, you have to call the GetKeyState API function, which returns a state number. If the low-order bit of this number is set (that is, if the number is odd), then the key is pressed. When do we check this state? We can do it every time the user presses a key on the form, or we can add a timer and make the check every second. This second approach has an advantage, because the user might press the Caps Lock key while working with a different application and this should be indicated on the status bar of our program, too. However, using a timer makes the response to pressing the key quite slow. So I've decided to execute the following statements in both cases, also adding a timer to the STATUS1 example:

```
if Odd (GetKeyState (VK_CAPITAL)) then
  StatusBar1.Panels[1].Text := 'CAPS'
else
  StatusBar1.Panels[1].Text := '';
```

## Speed Button Hints in the Status Bar

We can easily extend this application by adding a toolbar to it and providing a way to display a description of the speed buttons when the mouse moves over them. As you should remember, the Hint property of the speed buttons is already used to display the yellow fly-by hints near the buttons. How can we use the same property for two different strings? Strangely enough, this problem has a direct solution: write a simple string divided in two portions by a separator, the ¦ character.

For example, you might enter the following as the value of the Hint property:

```
Help|Activate the help of the application
```

The first portion of the string, *Help*, is used by fly-by hints, the second portion by the status bar. This takes place automatically when you have written the code described in the first version of the status bar.

**NOTE**  When the hint for a control is made up of two strings, you can use the GetShortHint and GetLongHint methods to extract the first (short) and second (long) substrings from the string you pass as a parameter, which is usually the value of the Hint property.

For example, in STATUS2, I copied the form of STATUS1 and its code; then I pasted the toolbar of an older application. I've also removed the sub-panels of the status bar, and set its SimplePanel property to True. Then I've changed the code of the ShowHint method as follows:

```
StatusBar1.SimpleText := Application.Hint;
```

Then I've set the value of the Hint property of the graphical buttons, and without changing the code I've been able to show both hints at once, as you can see in Figure 11.12. Aside from showing hints and status messages, the STATUS2 example doesn't work at all, so do not even try to use it, except for testing the hints.

**FIGURE 11.12:**
The output of STATUS2, with speed buttons having both a fly-by hint and a status bar description.

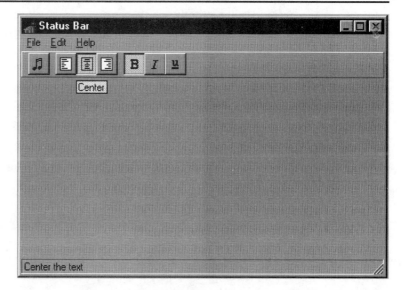

**TIP**

To build the example above, I copied a group of components from one application to another. This is quite simple, as I mentioned in Chapter 2. Open the source example, select a number of components (in this case, the panel and some of the speed buttons it contains), copy them to the Clipboard, and then move to the destination form and paste them in.

# Summary

In this chapter, we have examined a specific topic: the definition of a toolbar and a status bar for simple SDI applications. We have seen that although there are predefined components for these elements in Delphi, it is easy to build them using the Panel component. Actually, there is a different approach for building a toolbar or a status bar in Delphi, using the Application Expert or one of the Application templates. When these projects are generated, the application's main form has both a working toolbar and a working status bar.

You can consider this chapter the first step toward professional applications. We will take other steps in the following chapters, but our programs now are similar to some best-selling Windows applications, which may be very important for our own clients.

Now that the elements of the main form of our programs are properly set up, we can consider adding secondary forms and dialog boxes. This is the topic of the next chapter, although we already saw how simple it is to add a second form to a program to build a toolbox.

# CHAPTER

## TWELVE

# Multiple Forms and Dialog Boxes

- Modal and modeless forms

- How to merge form menus

- Modal and modeless dialog boxes

- Predefined dialog boxes

- Extensible dialog boxes

- Visual form inheritance

**12**

**U**p to this point, the programs in this book have been made up of a single form. Although it is possible to build fully functional applications with one form and a number of components, it is far more common to have more than one form. Usually, applications have a main window, some floating toolboxes or palettes, and a number of dialog boxes that can be invoked though menu commands or command buttons. More complex applications might have an MDI structure—a frame window with a number of child windows inside its client area. The development of MDI applications will be discussed in Chapter 15. This chapter focuses on applications having more than one form or having dialog boxes.

Dialog boxes are not a new subject. We have already used a number of default dialog boxes to select colors, fonts, and files, and we've used some message boxes, obtained with the MessageDlg function. In this chapter, you will see how you can define your own dialog boxes.

# Dialog Boxes versus Forms

Before presenting examples of applications with multiple forms and applications with user-defined dialog boxes, let me begin with a general description of these two alternatives and their differences.

We have already seen a correspondence between forms in Delphi and Windows as perceived by the user (see the definitions in the section "Forms versus Windows" in Chapter 9). Since dialog boxes are a particular kind of window, you expect dialog boxes in Delphi to be based on forms, too. This is indeed the case. Once we have added a second form to a program, we can display it as a form or as a dialog box. Something slightly different might take place behind the scenes in Delphi and in Windows, but it won't matter to us.

When you write a program, there is really no big difference between a dialog box and a second form, aside from the border and other user-interface elements you can customize.

What users usually associate with the idea of a dialog box is the concept of a modal window. A *modal window* is a window that takes the focus and must be closed before users move back to the main window. This is true for message boxes and usually for dialog boxes, as well. However, you can also have nonmodal—or *modeless*—dialog boxes. So if you think that dialog boxes are just modal forms, you are on the right track, but your description is not precise. In Delphi (as in Windows), you can have modeless dialog boxes and modal forms.

We have to consider two different elements:

- The form's border and its user interface determine whether it looks like a dialog box.

- The use of two different functions (Show or ShowModal) to display the second form determines its behavior (modeless or modal).

By combining these two elements, we can build any kind of secondary form. This is what we will do in this chapter.

# Adding a Second Form to a Program

Now we are ready to dive into an example. We will add a second form to an application to experiment with modeless forms. I won't show you how to create a modal form now, simply because this is what dialog boxes are for.

The example, PHONES, is simple: The main form (Form1) has a list of phone numbers; the secondary form (Form2) has a list of e-mail addresses. (Of course, to build this program, I've just invented a list of names and nonexistent phone numbers and e-mail addresses. Any resemblance to existing people or references is unintentional.)

**NOTE**  To add a second form to an application, you simply click on the New Form button on the Delphi toolbar or use the File ➤ New Form menu command. As an alternative you can select File ➤ New, move to the Forms or Dialogs page, and choose one of the available form templates or the form Expert. In most of the examples in this chapter, we will start with a blank main form and one or more blank secondary forms.

You can see the two forms in Figure 12.1. If you have two forms in a project, you can use the Select Form or the Select Unit button of the toolbar to navigate through them at design-time.

You can also choose which form is the main one and which forms should be automatically created at startup using the Forms page of the Project Options dialog box (see Figure 12.2).

Once you have prepared the two forms, you need to add some code to the program to make them work properly. In both forms, I've added a button. In the first form, the button is used to show the second window, and in the second form, it is used to close itself. In fact, you can close the second form and continue with the first one. The opposite is not possible: as soon as you close the main form of a Delphi application, the program terminates.

**FIGURE 12.1:**

The two forms of the PHONES example at run-time.

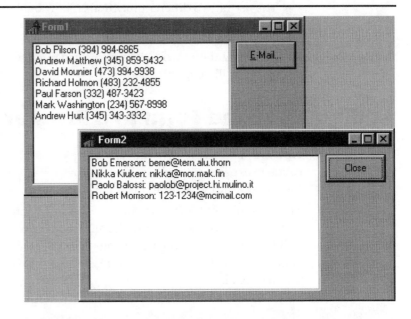

**FIGURE 12.2:**

The Forms options of the PHONES project.

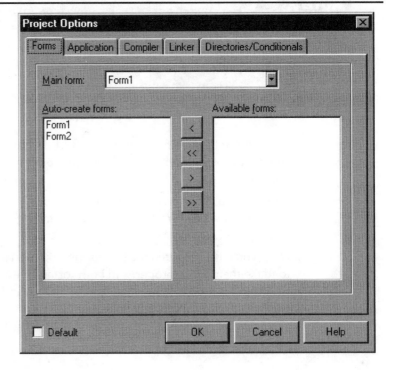

To run the second form when the user presses Button1, you should write this simple code:

```
procedure TForm1.Button1Click(Sender: TObject);
begin
  Form2.Show;
end;
```

If you use the Show function, the second form will be displayed as modeless, so you can move back to the first one while the second is still visible. Notice that the code simply displays the form; it doesn't create it. In fact, the form is created by the project file, as indicated in the Forms page of the Project Options dialog box. If you look at the project file's code, you can see that both forms are included (*used*) and that both are created, using the application's CreateForm method. The first form being created becomes the application's main form:

```
program Phones;

uses
  Forms,
  Unit1 in 'UNIT1.PAS' {Form1},
  Unit2 in 'UNIT2.PAS' {Form2};

begin
  Application.Initialize;
  Application.CreateForm(TForm1, Form1);
  Application.CreateForm(TForm2, Form2);
  Application.Run;
end.
```

If you now compile this application, Delphi will issue an error message, but it will also ask you to fix the problem, as you can see in Figure 12.3. To compile the code of the first form, in fact, you need to include the unit containing the second form (in this case, Unit2) with a `uses` statement, possibly in the implementation portion. As an alternative, you can select the first form and issue the File ➤ Use Unit menu command.

**FIGURE 12.3:**

The request from the compiler to add the proper **uses** statement to the code of the main form.

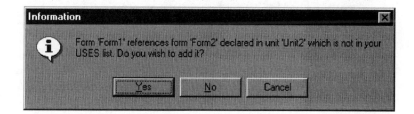

Information

Form 'Form1' references form 'Form2' declared in unit 'Unit2' which is not in your USES list. Do you wish to add it?

| Yes | No | Cancel |

To close the second form, you might use its system menu or click on the Close button, calling the following method:

```
procedure TForm2.CloseButtonClick(Sender: TObject);
begin
  Close;
end;
```

By running this code, Delphi does not close the secondary form, but instead simply hides it. This is what we need, since we want to be able to display the secondary form again without having to re-create it. In other cases, you need to override the OnClose event and actually destroy the form, to avoid having too many forms in memory at the same time.

# Modal and Modeless Forms

As you saw in the previous section, adding a second form to a program (and a third, and so on) is really simple, so let's try something more complex. I would like to expand this example into a generic one allowing a user to open a number of modal or modeless forms. The main form of the MODES program has two buttons, used to create modal and modeless forms. Once you have added two new forms to the project—I've named them ModalForm and ModelessForm—you can write the following methods, corresponding to the two OnClick events of the two buttons, which create a new form on the fly:

```
procedure TMainAppForm.ModalButtonClick(Sender: TObject);
var
  Modal: TModalForm;
begin
  Modal := TModalForm.Create (Application);
  Modal.ShowModal;
  Modal.Free;
end;

procedure TMainAppForm.ModelessButtonClick(Sender: TObject);
var
  NonModal: TModelessForm;
begin
  NonModal := TModelessForm.Create (Application);
  NonModal.Show;
end;
```

When the modal form is created and executed by means of ShowModal, it remains active until you close it. This means that the call to the ShowModal function does not return until the form is closed. During this time, the application's main form remains *disabled*. You cannot click the two buttons or interact with the form in any way. Once the modal form has been closed, the ShowModal function terminates and the code deletes the object from memory.

The behavior of the modeless form is different. The Show procedure—notice that this is a procedure, while ShowModal is a function—returns immediately. Of course, we cannot delete the object from memory since the corresponding window is currently on the screen (for this reason, the form will free itself when it is closed). We can, instead, press the Modeless button again to create a second modeless form, then a third form, a fourth, and so on. There is practically no limit.

The main form can display secondary forms. What can you do with these forms? They both have a Close button, as you can see in Figure 12.4. The two Close buttons are connected with a simple method that calls the Close procedure. The modal form has also a second button, to create another *nested* modal form. The OnClick method for this button has the same code of the ModalButtonClick of the main form.

**FIGURE 12.4:**

The modal and modeless forms of the MODES program at run-time.

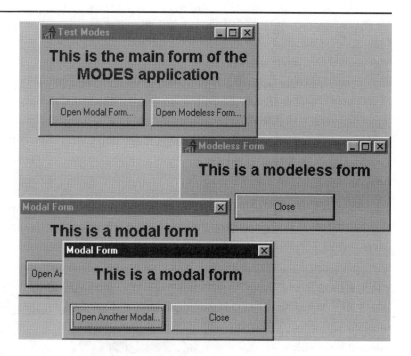

An important element of this program is that each time you create a form object in your code, you can remove the code that Delphi automatically generates to define an object for the form (in the interface section, after the var keyword) and initialize it in the project source file. To remove the automatic form creation, you can easily use the Forms page of the Project Options dialog box, already shown in Figure 12.2.

## Two Forms, Two Menus

Now we can go back to our PHONES example and try to add a menu to the forms, building PHONES2. The easiest thing to do is to add a menu to each of the forms. To show that this approach works with both a modal and a modeless form, I've added to the older version of the program the code to create the second form as either modal or modeless, using the two menu items of the EMail Form pull-down menu. To show the form, you need only apply either the ShowModal or Show method to it. In fact, the forms of this program are both created by the project's code at startup. When the program shows the second form as modal, the main form's menu is automatically disabled, together with the form itself. When the form is displayed as modeless, you should disable its menu manually. Since there is only one form, trying to show it twice won't be a good choice.

```
procedure TForm1.ShowModeless1Click(Sender: TObject);
begin
  ShowModal1.Enabled := False;
  ShowModeless1.Enabled := False;
  Form1.CloseModeless1.Enabled := True;
  Form2.Show;
end;
```

When the form is displayed, the first two items of the EMail Form pull-down menu are disabled and the third is enabled (it was disabled at design-time), as shown in Figure 12.5.

Notice that in the figure, the menu items have different colors because the first is currently selected (although it is grayed). When you select this last menu item, the modeless form is closed, calling its Close method. So what happens to the menu items? Shouldn't we re-enable them when the Close Modeless menu item is called? We might do so, but the program won't work properly. In fact, there are a number of ways to close the second modeless form, including the Close command of its own

**FIGURE 12.5:**

The disabled menu items of the main form of the PHONES2 example, when the second is executed as modeless.

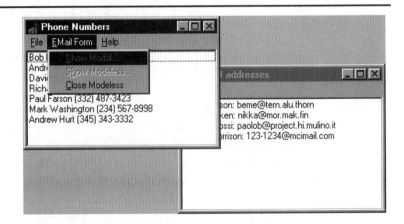

menu. Instead of repeating the code to enable the menu items in a number of places, you can write it in the second form's OnClose event:

```
procedure TForm2.FormClose(Sender: TObject;
  var Action: TCloseAction);
begin
  Form1.ShowModal1.Enabled := True;
  Form1.ShowModeless1.Enabled := True;
  Form1.CloseModeless1.Enabled := False;
end;
```

Notice that this method of the second form refers to the first one; that is, it needs access to some properties of the TForm1 class. For this reason, the second form should use the first one. In this case, the uses statements *must* be in the implementation section of the unit. Otherwise the program would cause a circular reference between the two units, with each unit referring to the other one in its interface portion. If the two units refer to each other, but the uses statements are in the implementation portion, there is no problem, because the other unit will be considered only when the first one is compiled, and not when it is included in another unit.

This example demonstrates that on the whole, handling modal forms is usually easier than handling modeless forms, since you do not need to change the behavior of the main window. In fact, the user cannot interact with the main form when the modal form is open, and you don't need to keep track of the open or closed forms, as you do with modeless forms.

# Merging Form Menus

In the preceding version of the PHONES program, each of the two forms had its own menu bar. Delphi, however, supports a technique to merge the menu bars of two or more forms automatically. This is the idea: The application's main window has a menu bar, as usual. The other forms have a menu bar with the AutoMerge property enabled, so their menu bar won't be displayed in the form, but will instead be merged with the one from the main window.

These are the rules for menu merging: Each pull-down menu has a GroupIndex property. When menu bars are merged, the pull-down menus are arranged as follows:

- If two elements of the different menu bars have the same GroupIndex, those of the original menu are removed.

- Elements are ordered for ascending GroupIndex values.

For example, in Figure 12.6, you can see how the menus of the two forms of the PHONES3 example are merged. The pull-down menus of the main form have indexes 0, 1, and 2. The only pull-down of the second form has an index 1, so it

**FIGURE 12.6:**

The two menu bars of the PHONES3 example and how they are merged.

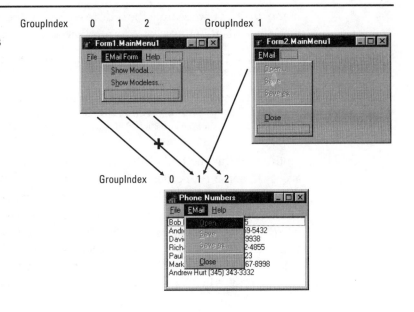

replaces the pull-down with the corresponding index of the main form's menu. Consider, however, that menu merging makes sense only for modeless forms. If you display the second form as modal, you cannot access the main window's menu bar, so Delphi doesn't perform any merging.

Using menu merging is extremely simple, at least at first glance. If you open PHONES2 again, set the AutoMerge property of the second form's main menu to True, and set proper values for the GroupIndex properties, as indicated in the following list, the program will almost work:

| Form | Pull-Down Menu | GroupIndex |
|------|----------------|------------|
| Form1 | File | 0 |
| | EMail Form | 1 |
| | Help | 2 |
| Form2 | EMail | 1 |

In fact there is still a problem: when the form is displayed as modal, its menu is not accessible. We can solve the first problem easily by adding a statement to set the value of the AutoMerge property of the second form's menu dynamically.

However, instead of simply setting this property, I want to use a more radical and dynamic approach, to show you one more example of dynamic form creation. What I want to do is to create and destroy the secondary form each time it should be shown or hidden. This requires a number of simple changes in the source code.

First of all, you need to disable automatic form creation using the Forms page of the Project Options dialog box. To show the form as modal, we have to create it, set its properties, and later destroy it:

```
procedure TForm1.ShowModal1Click(Sender: TObject);
begin
  Form2 := TForm2.Create (Self);
  Form2.MainMenu1.AutoMerge := False;
  Form2.ShowModal;
  Form2.Free;
end;
```

The approach used for the modeless activation is slightly different. The form is created but not destroyed:

```
procedure TForm1.ShowModeless1Click(Sender: TObject);
begin
  Form2 := TForm2.Create (Self);
  Form2.MainMenu1.AutoMerge := True;
  Form2.Show;
end;
```

Notice that from the previous version, I've removed the code used to disable some menu items, since the whole pull-down menu is completely hidden. For this reason, I've also removed the last item, Close.

The modeless form is destroyed when it is closed if you set the Action parameter of the OnClose event to caFree:

```
procedure TForm2.FormClose(Sender: TObject;
  var Action: TCloseAction);
begin
  Action := caFree;
end;
```

The rest of the code is the same as in PHONES2, although there isn't much left after the changes we have made.

# Creating a Dialog Box

I stated earlier in this chapter that a dialog box is not very different from other forms. There is a very simple trick to building a dialog box instead of a form. Just select the bsDialog value for the form's BorderStyle property. With this simple change, the interface of the form becomes dialog box-like, with the proper system menu (but no system icon in Windows 95), and no minimize or maximize boxes. Of course, such a form has the typical dialog box thick border, which is nonresizable (see the BORDERS example in Chapter 9 for a comparison of the border styles).

Once you have built a dialog box form, you can display it as a modal or modeless window using the two usual show methods (the procedure Show and the function ShowModal). Modal dialog boxes, however, are more common than modeless ones. This is exactly the reverse of forms: modal forms should generally be avoided since a user won't expect them. See the following list for the complete schema of the various combinations of styles:

| Window Type | Modal | Modeless |
| --- | --- | --- |
| Form | Never | Usual, in SDI applications |
| Dialog box | Most common kind of secondary form | Used, but not very common |

Keep in mind that this list lacks an important element, the use of MDI forms, which will be discussed in Chapter 15. As we will see, using the MDI was the most common way to have several forms in an application, although Windows 95 and OLE document-oriented approaches tend to favor an SDI approach instead. Delphi itself is a good example of an SDI application. In both cases, MDI and SDI, having a second modeless form can be very useful for holding palettes or special toolboxes. Sometimes, an alternative to the use of a second form is to build multipage forms, a new kind of user interface that is spreading rapidly among Windows applications. You can do this easily using Delphi's Notebook and PageControl components, as we'll see in Chapter 13.

## Modal Dialog Boxes

Since modal dialog boxes are more common than modeless ones, I'll concentrate on them first. As an example, we'll build a typical options dialog box. The main form of this example, named DIALOG1, has two labels, and you can use the dialog box to hide or show them. You can see the main form and the dialog box at run-time in Figure 12.7.

The dialog box also has two standard bitmap buttons, with the default glyphs for OK and Cancel. Using these default buttons is usually a good idea because you can set a single property (Kind) instead of a number of them (including the text, the glyph, the return value, and others). As a consequence, and an important one, you get a standard user interface. The code of this application is quite simple. After you have included the unit describing the dialog box form in the code of the main form, you can simply call ShowModal to display the dialog box. This is not very useful, by itself. In fact, we do not respond to any actions the user might have taken in the dialog box. Here is a better alternative:

```
procedure TForm1.ConfigureButtonClick(Sender: TObject);
begin
```

FIGURE 12.7:
The main form and the dialog box of
the DIALOG1 example.

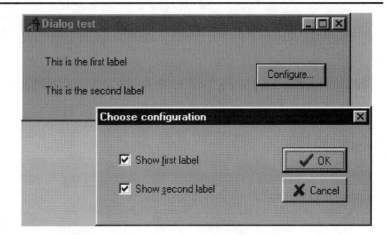

```
  ConfigureDialog.ShowModal;
  Label1.Visible := ConfigureDialog.CheckBox1.Checked;
  Label2.Visible := ConfigureDialog.CheckBox2.Checked;
end;
```

Each time the dialog box is executed, the status of the two check boxes is used to
determine which of the labels should be visible. However, this code has at least one
bad bug. If the user terminates the dialog box by pressing the Cancel button, the
values are considered, anyway. So we need to make the two assignments only if the
return value of the ShowModal function (that is, the modal result) is mrOk:

```
procedure TForm1.ConfigureButtonClick(Sender: TObject);
begin
  if ConfigureDialog.ShowModal = mrOk then
  begin
    Label1.Visible := ConfigureDialog.CheckBox1.Checked;
    Label2.Visible := ConfigureDialog.CheckBox2.Checked;
  end;
end;
```

However, something is still wrong. If you open the dialog box, set some options,
and press Cancel, the new values are not considered; but the next time you open
the dialog box, you'll see the options you set before pressing the Cancel button,
not the currently active options. As a final step, we need to set up the dialog box
properly each time it is executed. Here is the final code of the DIALOG1 example:

```
procedure TForm1.ConfigureButtonClick(Sender: TObject);
begin
  {copy current values to the dialog box}
  ConfigureDialog.CheckBox1.Checked := Label1.Visible;
  ConfigureDialog.CheckBox2.Checked := Label2.Visible;

  if ConfigureDialog.ShowModal = mrOk then
  begin
```

```
  {copy new dialog box values in the main form only if OK}
  Label1.Visible := ConfigureDialog.CheckBox1.Checked;
  Label2.Visible := ConfigureDialog.CheckBox2.Checked;
  end;
end;
```

This is one of the approaches you can follow when you run a modal dialog box. These are the steps:

1. Set the initial values each time you run the dialog box.

2. Show the dialog box.

3. If the OK button has been pressed, copy the new values back to the form.

Of course, this is not the only possible technique. As an alternative, you can set up the values of the dialog box only the first time, store the current values each time you run it, and reset the values to the current ones when the user quits the dialog box with the Cancel button. In our example, we could have written

```
procedure TForm1.ConfigureButtonClick(Sender: TObject);
var
  old1, old2: Boolean;
begin
  {store the old values of the dialog box}
  old1 := ConfigureDialog.CheckBox1.Checked;
  old2 := ConfigureDialog.CheckBox2.Checked;

  if (ConfigureDialog.ShowModal = mrOk) then
  begin
    {set the new values in the form}
    Label1.Visible := ConfigureDialog.CheckBox1.Checked;
    Label2.Visible := ConfigureDialog.CheckBox2.Checked;
  end
  else
  begin
    {restore the old values of the dialog box}
    ConfigureDialog.CheckBox1.Checked := old1;
    ConfigureDialog.CheckBox2.Checked := old2;
  end;
end;
```

The advantage here is that the code that saves and restores the old values can be moved into the code of the dialog box. This is useful if there are several places in the code where you can show the same dialog box. In this case, the code to set up and even show the dialog box can be written in a custom method of the dialog box form, and the OnClick method of the dialog box's OK button should copy the proper final values to some fields or components of the main form. This is a change of perspective: instead of having a main form accessing values and properties of the dialog box, we can have a dialog box getting and setting values from and to the main form directly.

## Closing a Dialog Box

What happens when the user clicks on OK or Cancel? The code should close the dialog box, returning the proper value to the application. You can indicate the return value by setting the ModalResult property of the button the user clicks to terminate the dialog box. As a side effect, when you assign a value to this property of the form, the modal dialog box is automatically closed.

Notice that the ModalResult value becomes exactly the return value of the Show-Modal method that was used to show the modal dialog box. So that we don't need to code this by hand, each button component, including bitmap buttons, has a ModalResult property. If you do not handle a button's OnClick event, it automatically uses its ModalResult value to set the corresponding property of its parent form.

# A Modeless Dialog Box

The second example of dialog boxes shows a more complex modal dialog box that uses the standard approach, as well as a modeless dialog box. The main form of the DIALOG2 example has five labels with names (see Figure 12.8). If the user clicks on a name, its color turns to red; if the user double-clicks on it, the program displays a modal dialog box with a list of names to choose from. If the user clicks on the Style button, a modeless dialog box appears, allowing the user to change the font style of the main form's labels.

**FIGURE 12.8:**

The three forms (a main form and two dialog boxes) of the DIALOG2 example at run-time.

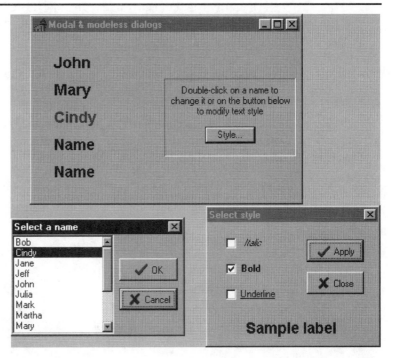

On the whole, this program is based on three forms: a main form and two dialog boxes. The five labels of the main form are connected to two methods, one for the OnClick event and the second for the OnDoubleClick event. The first method turns the last label a user has clicked on to red, resetting all the others to black. Notice that a single method is associated with each of the labels:

```
procedure TForm1.LabelClick(Sender: TObject);
begin
  {set the color of all the labels to black}
  Label1.Font.Color := clBlack;
  Label2.Font.Color := clBlack;
  Label3.Font.Color := clBlack;
  Label4.Font.Color := clBlack;
  Label5.Font.Color := clBlack;
  {set the color of the clicked label to red}
  (Sender as TLabel).Font.Color := clRed;
end;
```

The second method common to all of the labels, and related to the OnDoubleClick event, shows the modal dialog box after the user selects the label's current caption in the list box of the dialog itself. If the user closes the dialog box by clicking on OK and an item of the list is selected, the selection is copied back to the label's caption:

```
procedure TForm1.LabelDoubleClick(Sender: TObject);
begin
  with ListDial.Listbox1 do
  begin
    {select the current name in the list box}
    ItemIndex := Items.IndexOf ((Sender as TLabel).Caption);
    {show the modal dialog box, checking the return value}
    if (ListDial.ShowModal = mrOk)
        and (ItemIndex >= 0) then
      {copy the selected item to the label}
      (Sender as TLabel).Caption := Items [ItemIndex];
end;
```

Notice that all the code used to customize the modal dialog box is in the Label-DoubleClick method of the main form. The form of this dialog box has no added code.

When you write generic code in a method connected to components of the same kind, there is no need to test that the Sender is a component of that kind (if `Sender is TLabel then`). In fact, Sender is always a label. And if by any chance it is not, you'll get a run-time error when the as statement is executed. This means that our assumption (that the method is connected to components of the same kind) is wrong, and we'll be grateful to see the error, and correct the program. Leaving out one test speeds up the program too, because RTTI operations can be quite slow.

The modeless dialog box, instead, has a lot of coding behind it. The main form simply runs it when the Style button is clicked (notice that the button caption ends with three dots to indicate that when it is pressed, the program will open a dialog box):

```
procedure TForm1.StyleButtonClick(Sender: TObject);
begin
  {run modeless dialog}
  StyleDial.Show;
end;
```

You can see the dialog box running in Figure 12.8 above. Notice the names of the two buttons, Apply and Close, which usually replace the OK and Cancel buttons in a modeless dialog box. At times, you can find a Cancel button that works as a Close button, but the OK button in a modeless dialog box usually has no meaning at all. Instead, there might be one or more buttons that perform specific actions on the main window, such as Apply, Change Style, Replace, Delete, and so on.

If the user clicks on one of the check boxes of this modeless dialog box, the style of the sample label's text at the bottom changes accordingly. You accomplish this by adding or removing the specific flag to or from the set indicating the style, as in the following:

```
procedure TStyleDial.ItalicCheckBoxClick(Sender: TObject);
begin
  if ItalicCheckBox.Checked then
    LabelSample.Font.Style :=
      LabelSample.Font.Style + [fsItalic]
  else
    LabelSample.Font.Style :=
      LabelSample.Font.Style - [fsItalic];
end;
```

When the user selects the Apply button, the program copies the style of the sample label to each of the form's labels, rather than checking the values of the check boxes:

```
Form1.Label1.Font.Style := LabelSample.Font.Style;
Form1.Label2.Font.Style := LabelSample.Font.Style;
...
```

Notice that when the user clicks on the Apply button, the dialog box is not closed. Only the Close button has this effect. Consider also that this dialog box needs no initialization code because the form is not destroyed, and its components maintain their status each time the dialog box is displayed.

# Using Predefined Dialog Boxes

Besides building your own dialog boxes, Delphi allows you to use some default dialog boxes of different kinds. Some are predefined by Windows, others are simple dialog boxes (such as message boxes) displayed by a Delphi method. Delphi also includes template forms and form experts you can use to create dialog boxes. These were already covered in Chapter 3, and don't require advanced information to be used, so I won't discuss them in detail in this chapter.

## Windows Common Dialogs

The Delphi Components palette contains a page of dialog boxes. Each of these dialog boxes—known as *Windows common dialogs*—is defined in the library COMMDLG.DLL, which first appeared in Windows 3.1. I have already used some of these dialog boxes in several examples in the previous chapters, so you are probably already familiar with them. Basically, you need to put the corresponding component on a form, set some of its properties, run the dialog box (with the Execute method), and retrieve the properties that have been set while running it.

Here we will build a kind of test program, COMMDLG1, to highlight some of the features of the common dialog boxes. In fact, by setting some of the properties and options, you can obtain very different versions of the same dialog box, altering its behavior and its user interface more than you might expect.

The program can display each of the common dialog boxes, although some of them have no real effect (such as the Print dialog box). Some of the properties of the controls are set at design-time, other properties are set at run-time, so we can experiment with different values without having to declare multiple objects. The only common dialog box for which there are two copies is the Font dialog box, to allow one of the two copies to have an associated OnApply event. A Font dialog box with the Apply button behaves almost like a modeless dialog box, but it isn't. The Find and Replace dialog boxes are truly modeless, though.

You can see the choices this program offers by running it and using each of its menu items. I recommend that you spend some time looking at its source code on the companion CD. I'll just highlight a couple of interesting points. The first is the use of the Apply button in the second Font dialog box (see Figure 12.9). This is the code associated with this button:

```
procedure TCommDlgForm.FontDialog2Apply(
    Sender: TObject; Wnd: Word);
begin
  Memo1.Font := FontDialog2.Font;
end;
```

Notice that there is no flag to add the Apply button to the dialog box; you need only specify a handler for this event, as I've done above. Consider also that the button is part of the dialog box, but its event handler is written in the program's main form. This is really useful since we can change the behavior of the dialog box without having to customize the component.

Another interesting behavior is that of the Color selection dialog box. You can open only the basic portion of the dialog box and let the user expand it by clicking on a button; display it already fully open; or open only the first part, preventing the user from expanding it.

**FIGURE 12.9:**

The Font selection dialog box with the Apply button.

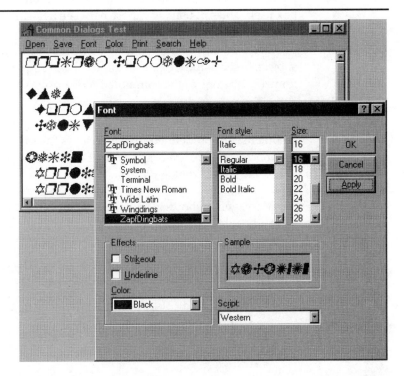

The Open dialog box has a strange feature, too. If you run it using the third menu item, you can select multiple files; then the program asks you to confirm the open operation for each of them. Of course, having a single memo as a viewer, at the end of the operation you'll see only the last file opened. Finally, notice that I've implemented a limited version of the Find and Replace methods. These methods are connected to the buttons of the two dialog boxes, as in the case of the Apply button in the Font dialog box. The FindDialog1Find method looks for a match (using the Pos system function) in the text of the memo. To be more precise, it searches the text of the memo that follows the current selection.

**NEW**

To write a similar code with Delphi 1.0, you had to scan each line of the memo (since the Pos function worked only on Pascal strings of up to 255 characters. In Delphi 2, we can simply treat the full text of the memo as a single long Pascal string.

The Find operation for the Replace dialog box is so similar that I could simply call it after an assignment. The best solution would probably have been to write a single Find method to be called to implement the code of the Replace routine, as well. Other variations in the behavior of these dialog boxes include the presence of a Help button, of optional check boxes, and even of optional portions of the dialog box itself. You can usually choose between a normal and 3D effect, ask users to confirm their choice (particularly in the file-related dialog boxes), and so on. Since I'm probably already boring you, I'll stop here. However, I suggest you explore this subject, first by studying the details of the example and then by adding further customized versions of the common dialog boxes.

## Message Boxes Parade

Another set of predefined dialog boxes is the group of Delphi message boxes and input boxes. There are basically six Delphi procedures and functions you can use to display simple dialog boxes:

- MessageDlg shows a customizable message box, with one or more buttons and usually a bitmap. We have used this message box quite often in the past examples.

- MessageDlgPos is similar to MessageDlg. The difference is that the message box is displayed in a given position, not in the center of the screen.

- ShowMessage displays a simpler message box, with the application name as the caption, and just an OK button.

- ShowMessagePos is the same, aside from the fact that you indicate the position of the message box.

- InputBox asks the user to input a string. You provide the caption, the query, and a default string.

- InputQuery asks the user to input a string. The only difference between this and InputBox is in the syntax. Input Query has a Boolean return value that indicates whether the user has clicked on OK or Cancel.

The first two message boxes are more complex and have a higher number of parameters, including a set of buttons, the type of message box, a help context code (useful if there is a Help button), and eventually the position. The MessageDlg and MessageDlgPos functions can display different types of message boxes, depending on the value of the second parameter, of type TMsgDlgType, which can assume these values: `mtWarning`, `mtError`, `mtInformation`, `mtConfirmation`, `mtCustom`. Each type of message box has its own glyph (a yellow exclamation point, a red stop sign, a blue *i*, a green question mark, or no bitmap, respectively).

To let you see the various choices of message boxes available in Delphi, I've written another sample program, with a similar approach to the preceding COMMDLG1 example. In this example, MBPARADE, you have a high number of choices (radio buttons, check boxes, edit boxes, and spin edit controls) to set before you press one of the buttons that displays a message box. You can get an idea of the program by looking at its form in Figure 12.10.

For a MessageDlg box, you can choose the style of the message box, its buttons (also adding the Help button), and the message. The two positional functions also use the values of the two spin edit controls. What's interesting is that if you choose a custom type and only the OK button, the MessageDlg box degrades to a ShowMessage box.

The input boxes use only the values in the three edit boxes in the second half of the form. Aside from the fact that the code used to execute them is different, their output is exactly the same (see Figure 12.10 again):

```
// sample InputBox call
EditValue.Text := InputBox (EditCaption.Text,
  EditPrompt.Text, EditValue.Text);

// sample InputQuery call
Text := EditValue.Text;
if InputQuery (EditCaption.Text, EditPrompt.Text, Text) then
  EditValue.Text := Text;
```

**FIGURE 12.10:**

The main form of the MBPARADE example, with an InputQuery message box open.

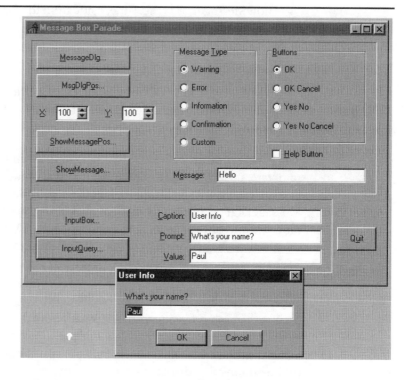

Having said this, I think you can easily understand the rest of the source code by looking at the code of the example. What's more important, however, is to run it, so that you can have a fast overview of the effect of the parameters of the various functions.

**TIP**

Although Delphi message boxes are graphically superior to the default Windows message boxes, you can always choose between the two. To display a message box, you can use the Windows API MessageBox function, which has parameters similar to the Delphi MessageDlg function. An advantage of the system message boxes is that you can use them to simulate system errors, using specific styles. The real value of the typical system error message box is that it can always be executed, even when Windows has such limited memory it cannot create a normal message box.

# A Dialog Box as a Main Window

When the aim of the main form of an application is to contain a number of components, you might want to disable the default resizing feature, selecting the `bsFixed` value for the form's BorderStyle property. An interesting alternative to a fixed-size main form is a dialog box. The use of a dialog box as the main window of an application is quite common, particularly for simple programs. Using Delphi, it's easy to create such a dialog box. You only need to set the BorderStyle property of the main (or only) form of the application to `bsDialog`.

Notice that in Windows 3.1, a dialog box couldn't paint its menu bar properly. The effect was that using a dialog box as main window, you could have no menu. In Windows 95 (and Windows NT) this bug has been removed, so that now adding a menu to a dialog box is as simple as adding it to any other window. In Windows 95, however, there is another reason to avoid using a dialog box as main menu: setting the `bsDialog` style will cause the form to have no icon in its upper-left corner. This is quite negative, and should be a good reason *not* to use a dialog box as main window. Another reason is that in Windows 95, the border of a dialog box is not very different from that of a resizable or fixed form. As a result, you can use a form with a fixed size, which will look very similar to a dialog box, but will still have the proper system icon.

# Extensible Dialog Boxes

Some dialog boxes display a number of components to the user. At times, you can divide them into logical pages, which Delphi supports through the TabControl and Notebook components (discussed in Chapter 13). At other times, some of the dialog box controls can be temporarily hidden to help first-time users of an application.

There are basically two approaches for displaying advanced information only when the user asks for it: build a secondary dialog box, displayed when the user presses a button with an Advanced label on it, or increase the size of the dialog box to host new controls when the user presses a More button.

The second approach is certainly more interesting but requires a little more care. I'll use it to extend the first example on dialog boxes (DIALOG1) and build the MORE example. First of all, we need to extend the dialog box with new controls: a More button (see Figure 12.11) and a whole new portion of the form with two new check boxes labeled *italic* and *bold* and used to change the style of the font of the text of the main form. Once you have added the new controls, you need to resize the dialog box so that the new elements are outside its visible surface.

Now we need to add some code to the application to handle the two new check boxes and to resize the form when a user clicks on the More button. To prepare the

**FIGURE 12.11:**

The dialog box of the MORE example at design-time. Some of the components are invisible because they are beyond the border.

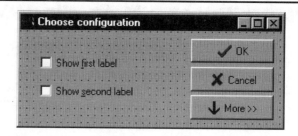

resize effect, we need a couple of fields in the form (named OldHeight and New-Height) to store the two different heights of the form. We can set up their values when the form is first created:

```
procedure TConfigureDialog.FormCreate(Sender: TObject);
begin
  OldHeight := Height;
  NewHeight := 210;
end;
```

I've determined the value 210 simply by stretching the dialog box at design-time to enclose all of the hidden components and looking at the Height property of the form. The real dialog box resizing takes place when the More button is pressed. Here is a first version:

```
procedure TConfigureDialog.BitBtn3Click(Sender: TObject);
begin
  BitBtn3.Enabled := False;
  BoldCheckBox.Enabled := True;
  ItalicCheckBox.Enabled := True;
  Height := NewHeight;
end;
```

The result it produces is shown in Figure 12.12. If you want a more spectacular effect, you might increase the height a pixel at a time instead of setting the final value at once. If you write a `for` loop, increase the height, and repaint the form each time to make the new controls appear, you get a nice effect, only a little slower. Of course, you could increase the speed by changing the way the loop counter is increased. The last line of the BitBtn3Click method above becomes

```
for I := Height to NewHeight do
begin
  Height := I;
  Update;
end;
```

Each time the dialog box is activated (OnFormActivate event), we reset its height, disable the hidden components (to avoid letting the user move to them using Tab), and enable the More button. This code is required so that each time the dialog box is displayed it starts in the default *small* configuration.

**FIGURE 12.12:**
The dialog box of the MORE example, once it has been resized.

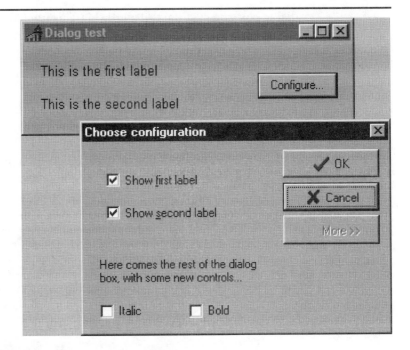

# Special About Boxes

Windows applications usually have an About box, where you can see information such as the version of the product, a copyright notice, and so on. The simplest way to build an About box is to use the MessageDlg function. In this case, you can show only a limited amount of text and no special graphics.

Therefore, the usual method for creating an About box is to use a simple dialog box, such as the one generated with one of the Delphi default templates. I say *simple* because when you have designed the form with a logo and so on, you seldom need much code. Some code might be required to display system information, such as the version of Windows or the amount of free memory, or some user information, such as the registered user name.

## Using the System About Box

A strange alternative is to use the standard dialog box of many Windows applications. If you select the About box of the Explorer or any application that comes with Windows, you can see that they all use the same dialog box. This is a system dialog box that was already present in Windows 3.1, although it was not documented. In the Win32 API and in Delphi 2, the use of this dialog box is partially documented: you can use the ShellAbout function of the ShellApi unit to display the system dialog box and customize it a little bit. This function is called in the SHABOUT example when the user presses the only button of the main form:

```
ShellAbout (Handle,
    'About ShellAbout Test#makes funny programs like',
    'Portions Copyright 1996 Marco Cantù', 0);
```

The first part of the second parameter is used as the title of the system About box, while the second part is displayed between standard (and fixed) lines of text. The effect is quite funny, as you can see in Figure 12.13. I do not think this is really useful, because the text of the dialog box will be plagued by the presence of the Microsoft name, something you won't like to have in your own application.

FIGURE 12.13:

The standard About box displayed by the SHABOUT program.

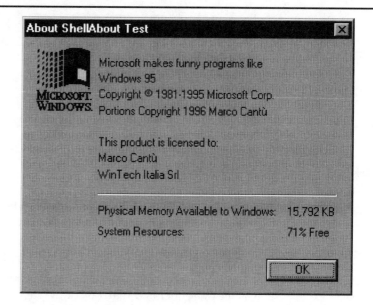

## Building a Custom Hidden Screen

It looks like we'll just have to build our own About box. While we do it, we can add a hidden credit screen, such as Delphi and many other applications have. You might want to add a hidden credit screen for a number of reasons. If you work in a big company, this might be your way to prove that you worked on that project, which might help you in finding a new job (but only if the project was successful). At times, a hidden About box can be fun to see, and they sometimes also provide a good occasion for making jokes about your competitors. Another more serious reason is that a hidden credit screen can be used to demonstrate who wrote the program, as a sort of legal copyright.

I've written a simple example, showing how you might implement a hidden screen. As you can see in Figure 12.14, the dialog box has a Panel component with two Label components inside its surface. The panel might contain any number of components to display graphics and text. Some of the strings might even be computed at run-time. The only added feature required to show the hidden credits is a Paintbox component covering part of the form.

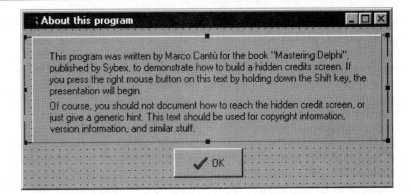

When the user makes a specific complex action (in this case, a click on the upper label with the right mouse button while holding down Shift), the panel is hidden and something appears on the screen. A simple solution is to have some text painted on the surface of the form—that is, on its canvas:

```
if (Button = mbRight) and (ssShift in Shift) then
begin
  Panel1.Visible := False;
  PaintBox1.Canvas.Font.Name := 'Arial';
  PaintBox1.Canvas.Font.Size := 20;
  PaintBox1.Canvas.TextOut (40, 50, 'Author: Marco Cantù');
  PaintBox1.Canvas.TextOut (40, 100, 'Version 1.0');
end;
```

To build a more spectacular hidden screen, we might scroll some text in a for loop, as I've done in the CREDITS example.

Now that I've suggested this idea to you, don't spend so much time preparing astounding hidden credit screens that you neglect writing the rest of the code for your applications. Although you can save some time by programming with Delphi, you can probably think of better ways to use that time!

Consider another aspect of the preceding example. We have written some code to draw on the surface of a dialog box. Although it is not very common, dialog boxes can have graphical output and respond to mouse input the same as any other form. In fact, a dialog box *is a form*.

# Visual Form Inheritance

One of the most important innovations of Delphi 2 is *visual form inheritance*. I've decided to discuss this topic in the current chapter because it is the first time we write projects with multiple forms. You could also inherit one form class from another in Delphi 1.0, but it was not possible to add a new component to the inherited form at design-time. Now this is extremely simple to do, but what is the advantage to having form inheritance?

Well, this mostly depends on the kind of application you are building. If it has a number of forms, some of which are very similar to each other or simply include common elements, then you can place the common components and the common event handlers in the base form and add the specific behavior and components to the subclasses. For example, you can prepare a standard parent form with a toolbar, a logo, default sizing and closing code, and the handlers of some Windows messages, and use it as the parent class for each of the forms of an application.

Another reason for visual form inheritance is that you can use it to customize an application for different clients, without duplicating any code: just inherit the specific versions for a client from the standard forms. The same approach can be used to localize an application in a different language: simply inherit the local version of each form, translating the captions of the components. You can also try placing some data access components in a base form, but it is often better to *use* a secondary form, or a Data Module, with the database components, than to inherit from it.

Remember that the main advantage of visual inheritance is that you can later change the original form and automatically update all the derived forms. This is the typical advantage of inheritance in object-oriented programming languages. But there is a side effect: polymorphism. You can add a virtual method in a base form and override it in a subclassed form. Then you can refer to both forms and call this method for each of them.

## Inheriting from a Base Form

The rules governing visual form inheritance are quite simple, once you have a clear idea of what inheritance is. Basically, a subclass form has the same components as the parent form, plus some new components, and you can change the properties of the inherited components. If you change a property of a component in the inherited form, any modification in the parent class will have no effect. However, you can re-synchronize the two values by using the Revert to Inherited local menu command of the Object Inspector. The same thing is accomplished by setting the two properties to the same value and recompiling the code. An alternative technique is to open the textual description of the inherited form and remove the line that changes the value of the property (we will look at the structure of this file in a second). Besides inheriting components, you inherit all the methods of the base form, including the event handlers. You can add new handlers in the inherited form, and also override existing handlers.

To describe how visual form inheritance works, I've built a very simple example, called VFI. I'll describe step-by-step how to build it. First, start a new project, and add four buttons to its main form. Then select File ➤ New and choose the page with the name of the project in the New Items dialog box (see Figure 12.15). Here you can choose the form from which you want to inherit. The new form has the same four buttons. Here is the textual description of the new form:

```
inherited Form2: TForm2
  Caption = 'Form2'
end
```

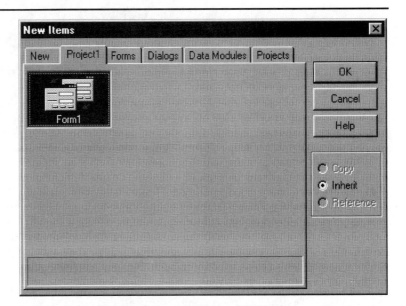

**FIGURE 12.15:**

The New Items dialog box allows you to create an inherited form.

Notice the presence of the `inherited` keyword, and the fact that the form indeed has some components, although they are defined in the base class form. If you move the form and add the caption of one of the buttons, the textual description will change accordingly:

```
inherited Form2: TForm2
  Left = 313
  Top = 202
  Caption = 'Form2'
  inherited Button2: TButton
```

```
      Caption = 'Beep...'
    end
end
```

Only the properties with a different value are listed (and by removing these properties from the textual description of the inherited form, you can reset them to the value of the base form, as I mentioned before). I've actually changed the captions of most buttons, as you can see in Figure 12.16.

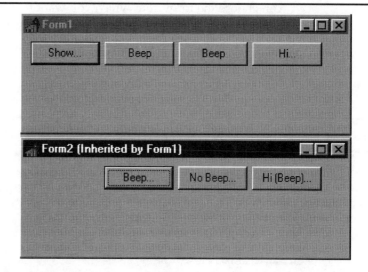

**FIGURE 12.16:**

The two forms of the VFI example at run-time.

Each of the buttons of the first form has an OnClick handler, with simple code. The first button shows the inherited form, calling its Show method; the second and the third buttons call MessageBeep (0); and the last button displays a simple message calling ShowMessage ('Hi'). What happens in the inherited form? The first thing I'd like to do is to remove the first button, since the secondary form is already visible. However, you cannot delete a component from an inherited form. An alternative solution is to leave the component there, but set its Visible property to False. The button will still be there, but not visible (as you can guess from Figure 12.16).

The other three buttons will be visible, but with different handlers. This is simple to accomplish. If you select the OnClick event of a button in the inherited form (by double-clicking on it), you'll get an empty method slightly different from the default one:

```
procedure TForm2.Button2Click(Sender: TObject);
begin
  inherited;
end;
```

The `inherited` keyword stands for a call to the corresponding handler of the base form. Notice that this keyword is always added, even if the handler is not defined in the parent class (and this is reasonable, because it might be defined later) but also if the component is not present in the parent class (which doesn't seem like a great idea to me).

It is very simple to execute the code of the base form, and make some other operations:

```
procedure TForm2.Button2Click(Sender: TObject);
begin
  inherited;
  ShowMessage ('Hi');
end;
```

This is not the only choice. An alternative approach is to write a brand-new handler and not execute the code of the base class, as I've done for the third button of the VFI example:

```
procedure TForm2.Button3Click(Sender: TObject);
begin
  ShowMessage ('Hi');
end;
```

Another choice includes calling a base class method after some custom code has been executed, or eventually conditionally calling it, and calling the handler of a different event of the base class, as I've done for the fourth button:

```
procedure TForm2.Button4Click(Sender: TObject);
begin
  inherited Button3Click (Sender);
  inherited;
end;
```

Probably, this won't be very common, but you must be fully aware that you can do it. Of course, you can consider each method of the base form as a method of your form, and call it freely. This example allows you to explore some features of visual form inheritance, but it doesn't demonstrate its true power. This is possible only in a complex real-world example, something I'm not going to show you. There is something else I want to show you here: *visual form polymorphism*.

# Polymorphic Forms

The problem is simple. If you add an event handler to a form, then change it in an inherited form, there is no way to refer to the two methods using a common variable of the base class, because the event handlers use static binding by default.

Confusing? Here is an example. Suppose you want to build a bitmap viewer form and a text viewer form in the same program. The two forms have similar elements, a similar toolbar, a similar menu, an OpenDialog component, and different components to view the actual data. So you can decide to build a base class form containing the common elements and inherit the two forms from it. You can see the three forms at design-time in Figure 12.17.

**FIGURE 12.17:**

The base form and the two inherited forms of the POLIFORM example at design-time.

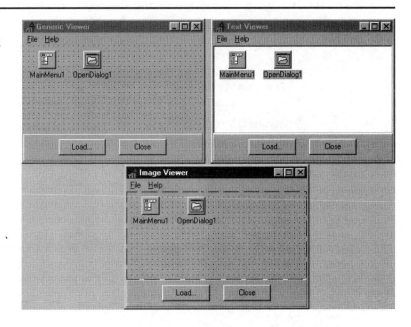

The main form has some common code, too. The Close button and the File ➤ Close command call the Close method of the form. The Help ➤ About command shows a message box. The Load button of the base form has the following code:

```
procedure TViewerForm.ButtonLoadClick(Sender: TObject);
begin
  ShowMessage ('Error: File loading code missing');
end;
```

The File ➤ Load command, instead, calls another method:

```
procedure TViewerForm.Load1Click(Sender: TObject);
begin
  LoadFile;
end;
```

This method is defined in the TViewerForm class as

```
public
    procedure LoadFile; virtual; abstract;
```

Being an abstract method, we will need to redefine it (and override it) in the inherited forms:

```
type
TImageViewerForm = class(TViewerForm)
  Image1: TImage;
  procedure ButtonLoadClick(Sender: TObject);
public
  procedure LoadFile; override;
end;
```

The code of this LoadFile method simply uses the OpenDialog1 component to ask the user to select an input file, and loads it into the image. The other inherited class has similar code. The project has one more form, a main form with two buttons, used to reload the files in each of the viewer forms. The main form is the only form created at run-time by the project. The generic viewer form is never created: it is only a generic base class, containing common code and components of the two subclasses. The forms of the two subclasses are created in the OnCreate event handler of the main form:

```
FormList [1] :=
  TTextViewerForm.Create (Application);
FormList [2] :=
  TImageViewerForm.Create (Application);
```

See Figure 12.18 for the resulting forms (with text and image already loaded in the viewers). FormList is a polymorphic array of forms, declared in the TMainForm class as

```
private
  FormList: array [1..2] of TViewerForm;
```

**FIGURE 12.18:**
The POLIFORM example at
run-time.

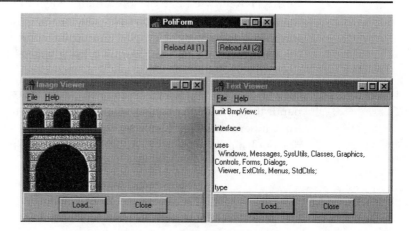

Notice that to make this declaration in the class, you need to add the Viewer unit in the uses clause of the interface portion. The array of forms is used to load a new file in each viewer form when one of the two buttons is pressed. The two handlers use two different approaches:

```
procedure TMainForm.ReloadButton1Click(Sender: TObject);
var
  I: Integer;
begin
  for I := 1 to 2 do
    FormList[I].ButtonLoadClick (self);
end;
procedure TMainForm.ReloadButton2Click(Sender: TObject);
var
  I: Integer;
begin
  for I := 1 to 2 do
    FormList[I].LoadFile;
end;
```

The second button calls a virtual method, and it will work without any problem. The first button calls an event handler and will always reach the generic TForm-View class (displaying the error message of its ButtonLoadClick method). This happens because the method is static, not virtual. Is there a way to make this approach work? Sure: Declare the ButtonLoadClick method of the TFormView class as virtual, and declare it as override in each of the inherited form classes. Simple, isn't it? This trick really works, as you can see in the full source code of the POLIFORM example on the companion CD.

# Summary

In this chapter, we have explored many ways to build applications having more than one form. We have seen how you can create a secondary modal or modeless form or a dialog box. The most important point to remember is that in Delphi, dialog boxes are just plain forms with a special border and a couple of other attributes—nothing more.

Besides the basic examples, we have delved into some advanced topics, such as dynamically building a number of forms, creating hidden screens, and using visual form inheritance. Another enhancement, the use of the increasingly widespread notebook metaphor, will be one of the topics of the next chapter. Another important topic in Chapter 13 is form scrolling.

# CHAPTER

## THIRTEEN

# Scrolling and Multipage Forms

- Scroll bar handling

- Scrolling and form coordinates

- Windows 95 PageControl and TabControl

- Borland-style notebooks with tabs

- Tabs without a notebook

- A notebook without tabs

13

In the beginning, the user interface of Windows applications was very simple. Over the years, the most widespread applications and the system itself introduced new features and elements to improve it. For example, to improve ease of use, toolbars and status bars were added. Another leading idea has been to mimic common metaphors, based on tools we use every day; one such idea was to imitate the behavior of a notebook with tabs to move among the various pages or areas. Delphi has a number of these elements. Tabs are used in Options dialog boxes, in the editor, in the Object Inspector, and in the Components palette.

Many applications have similar approaches in their dialog boxes. Some applications, including leading spreadsheets, even use the notebook metaphor for their main windows. The use of notebooks and tabs has become so important that Microsoft has added direct system support for them in Windows 95.

But before delving into notebooks and multipage forms, we will discuss a simpler but effective technique to use when you need to cram several components into a form: scrolling.

# When Forms Are Too Big

When you build a simple application, a single form might hold all of the components you need. As the application grows, you need to squeeze in the components, increase the size of the form, or add new forms. If you reduce the space occupied by the components, you might add some capability to resize them at run-time, eventually splitting the form in different areas. If you choose to increase the size of the form, you might use scroll bars to let the user move around in a form that is bigger than the screen.

Finally, if you choose to add a new form, there are basically three approaches:

- Create secondary forms and dialog boxes, as described in Chapter 12.

- Use Windows 95 PageControl or Delphi's Notebook component to create forms with multiple pages, as described in this chapter.

- Follow the typical Windows MDI approach, which will be the focus of Chapter 14.

Multipage forms have been introduced in dialog boxes in several Windows applications. Of course, there are several versions of this approach. Microsoft WinWord 2.0 used a graphical list box to select a page. Quattro Pro for Windows used lateral tabs to change the page of its dialog boxes, and it introduced the notebook metaphor for its main window to build a three-dimensional spreadsheet. The latest generation of Microsoft applications has introduced a new kind of notebook approach for dialog boxes, with tabs above the pages. This has become a standard in Windows 95, although the user interface of Windows 95 TabControl is slightly different than its past incarnations.

Delphi 2 has both a TabControl and a PageControl component, based on Windows 95 common controls, and a custom Notebook component, which can be combined with a custom Tab component to build a notebook with tabs. The Notebook component, however, can also be used in conjunction with other elements, as we will see later in this chapter.

# Scrolling a Form

Adding a scroll bar to a form is simple. In fact, there is nothing to do. If you place a number of components in a big form, then reduce its size, a scroll bar will be added to the form automatically, as long as you haven't changed the value of the AutoScroll property, which by default is set to True.

Along with AutoScroll, forms have two properties, HorzScrollBar and VertScrollBar, which can be used to set several properties of the two TFormScrollBar objects associated with the form. The Visible property indicates whether the scroll bar is present, the Position property determines the initial status of the scroll thumb, and the Increment property gives the effect of a click on one of the arrows at the ends of the scroll bar. The most important property, however, is Range.

The Range property of a scroll bar determines the virtual size of the form in one direction, not the actual range of values of the scroll bar. At first, this might be somewhat confusing. Here is an example to clarify how the Range property works. Suppose that you need a form with a number of components, and so the form needs to be 1000 pixels wide. We can use this value to set the virtual range of the form, changing the range of the horizontal scroll bar. See Figure 13.1 for an illustration of the virtual size of a form implied by the range of a scroll bar. If the width of the client area of the form is smaller than 1000 pixels, a scroll bar will appear. Now you can

**FIGURE 13.1:**

A representation of the virtual size of a form implied by the range of a scroll bar.

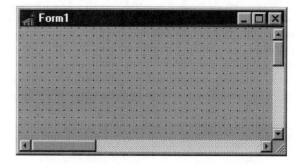

start using it at design-time to add new components in the "hidden" portion of the form.

The Position property of the scroll bar ranges from 0 to 1000 minus the current size of the client area. In fact, if the client area of the form is 300 pixels wide, you can scroll 700 pixels to see the far end of the form (the thousandth pixel).

## The Scroll Testing Example

I've built an example, SCROLL1, which has a virtual form of 1000 pixels. To accomplish this, I've simply set the range of the horizontal scroll bar to 1000:

```
Width = 458
HorzScrollBar.Range = 1000
```

The form of this example has been filled with a number of useless list boxes, and I could have obtained the same scroll bar range by placing the right-most list box so that its position (Left) plus its size (Width) would equal 1000.

The interesting part of the example is the presence of a toolbox window displaying the status of the form and of its horizontal scroll bar. This second form has four labels, two with fixed text and two with the actual output. Besides this, the Status form has a bsToolWindow border style and is a top-most window. You should also set its Visible property to True, to have its window automatically displayed at startup. There isn't much code in this program. The aim of the program is to update the values in the toolbox each time the form is resized or scrolled (as you can see in Figure 13.2).

The first part is extremely simple. You can handle the OnResize event of the form, and simply copy a couple of values to the two labels. Notice that the labels are part of another form, so you need to prefix them with the name of the form instance, Status:

```
procedure TForm1.FormResize(Sender: TObject);
begin
  Status.Label3.Caption := IntToStr(ClientWidth);
  Status.Label4.Caption := IntToStr(HorzScrollBar.Position);
end;
```

If we wanted to change the output each time the user scrolls the contents of the form, we could not use a Delphi event-handler, because there isn't an OnScroll event for forms (although there is one for stand-alone ScrollBar components). Not having this event makes sense, because Delphi forms handle scroll bars automatically in a powerful way. In comparison, in Windows, scroll bars are extremely low-level elements, requiring a lot of coding. Handling the scroll event makes sense only in special cases, such as in the program I'm building, which is a sort of exploration program.

**FIGURE 13.2:**
The output of the SCROLL1 example.

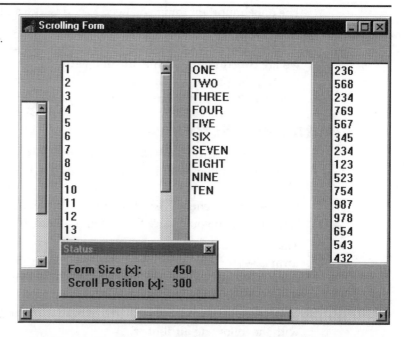

> **NOTE**
>
> What I really like in Delphi is that handling a Windows message that is not supported by the environment requires only one more line of code. I know that we have already seen this technique in earlier chapters, and that I have already told you how much I like this feature, but I've never seen something so nice in any other visual environment.

Here is the code we need to write. First, add a method declaration to the class, related to the Windows horizontal scroll message (wm_HScroll):

```
type
  TForm1 = class(TForm)
    ...
  public
    procedure FormScroll (var ScrollData: TWMScroll);
      message wm_HScroll;
  end;
```

Then write the code of this procedure, which is similar to the code of FormResize:

```
procedure TForm1.FormScroll (var ScrollData: TWMScroll);
begin
  inherited;
  Status.Label3.Caption := IntToStr(ClientWidth);
  Status.Label4.Caption := IntToStr(HorzScrollBar.Position);
end;
```

The only important thing you need to add is the call to `inherited`, which activates the method related to the same message in the base class form. Notice that the `inherited` keyword in Windows message handlers calls the method of the base class we are overriding, which is the one with the same Windows message associated (even if the procedure name is different). Of course, without this default call, the form won't have its default scrolling behavior; that is, it won't scroll at all.

## Automatic Scrolling

The use of the scroll bar's Range property can seem strange until you start to use it consistently. When you think twice about it, you'll start to understand the advantages of this approach. First of all, the scroll bar is automatically removed from the form when the client area of the form is big enough to accommodate the virtual size, and when you reduce the size of the form, the scroll bar is added again.

This feature becomes particularly interesting when the AutoScroll property of the form is set to True. In this case, the extreme positions of the right-most and lower controls are automatically copied into the Range properties of the form's two scroll bars. Automatic scrolling works well in Delphi. In the last example, the virtual size of the form would be set to the right border of the last list box. This was defined with the following attributes:

```
object ListBox6: TListBox
  Left = 832
  Width = 145
```

Therefore, the horizontal virtual size of the form would be 977 (which is the sum of the two above values). This number is automatically copied into the Range field of the HScrollBar property of the form, unless you change it manually to have a bigger form (as I've done for SCROLL1, setting it to 100 to leave some space between the last list box and the border of the form). You can see this value in the Object Inspector, or make the following test: Run the program, size the form as you like, and move the scroll thumb to the right-most position. When you add the size of the form and the position of the thumb, you'll always get 1000, the virtual coordinate of the right-most pixel of the form, whatever the size.

## Scrolling an Image

An advantage of the way automatic scrolling works in Delphi is that if the size of a single big component contained in a form changes, scroll bars are added or removed automatically. A good example is the use of the Image component. If you load a new picture in the component and its AutoSize property is set to True, the component automatically sizes itself, and the form eventually adds or removes the scroll bars.

An example will probably help clarify how image scrolling works. Do you remember the image viewer we built in Chapter 10? Its form showed a bitmap loaded from a file, either stretching it to fit the size of the form or leaving it in its original size. The problem is that when the original size is too big to fit in the form, part of the bitmap remains hidden. The solution to this problem is simple. We can set the AutoSize property of the Image component to True and disable its alignment with the client area (which is in contrast with the other property, since both can affect the size of the component). You should also set a small initial size for the image. You don't need to make any adjustments when you load a new bitmap, because the size of the Image component is automatically set for you by the system. Simply write the following code:

```
procedure TViewerForm.Open1Click(Sender: TObject);
begin
  if OpenDialog1.Execute then
    Image1.Picture.LoadFromFile (OpenDialog1.FileName);
end;
```

You can see in Figure 13.3 that scroll bars are actually added to the form. The figure shows two different copies of the program. The difference between the copy of the program on the left and the one on the right is that the first has an image smaller than its client area, so no scroll bars were added. When you load a larger image in the program, two scroll bars will automatically appear, as in the example on the right in Figure 13.3.

Some more coding is required to disable the scroll bars and change the alignment of the image when the Stretch menu command is selected, and to restore them when this feature is disabled. Again, we do not act directly on the scroll bars themselves, but simply change the alignment of the panel, its Stretch property, and eventually manually calculate the new size using the size of picture currently loaded

**FIGURE 13.3:**

In the IMAGEV2 example, the scroll bars are added automatically to the form when the whole bitmap cannot fit into the client area of the form displayed.

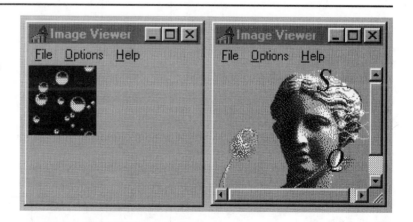

(this code mimics the effect of the AutoSize property, which works only when a new file is loaded):

```
procedure TViewerForm.Stretch1Click(Sender: TObject);
begin
  Image1.Stretch := not Image1.Stretch;
  Stretch1.Checked := Image1.Stretch;
  if Image1.Stretch then
    Image1.Align := alClient
  else
  begin
    Image1.Align := alNone;
    Image1.Height := Image1.Picture.Height;
    Image1.Width := Image1.Picture.Width;
  end;
end;
```

## Scrolling and Form Coordinates

As we have seen in the examples in the two previous sections, forms can automatically scroll their components. But what happens if you paint directly on the surface of the form? Some problems arise, but their solution is at hand. Suppose that we want to draw some lines on the virtual surface of a form, as shown in Figure 13.4. Since you probably do not own a monitor capable of displaying 2000 pixels on each

**FIGURE 13.4:**

The lines to draw on the virtual surface of the form.

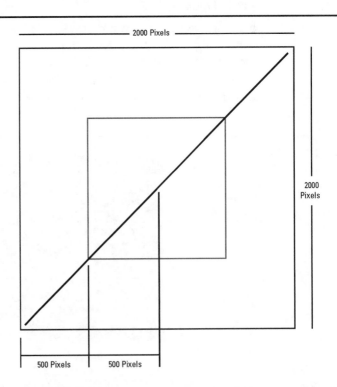

axis, you can create a smaller form, add two scroll bars, and set their Range properly, as I've done in the SCROLL2 example. Here is the textual description of the form:

```
object Form1: TForm1
  Caption = 'Form1'
  HorzScrollBar.Range = 2000
  VertScrollBar.Range = 2000
  ClientHeight = 336
  ClientWidth = 472
  OnPaint = FormPaint
end
```

If we simply draw the lines using the virtual coordinates of the form, the image won't display properly. In fact, in the OnPaint response method, we need to compute the virtual coordinates ourselves. Fortunately, this is easy, since we know that the $x$ and $y$ virtual coordinate of the upper-left corner of the client area corresponds to the current positions of the two scroll bars:

```
procedure TForm1.FormPaint(Sender: TObject);
var
  X1, Y1: Integer;
begin
  X1 := HorzScrollBar.Position;
  Y1 := VertScrollBar.Position;
  {draw a yellow line}
  Canvas.Pen.Width := 30;
  Canvas.Pen.Color := clYellow;
  Canvas.MoveTo (30-X1, 30-Y1);
  Canvas.LineTo (1970-X1, 1970-Y1);
  {draw a blue line}
  Canvas.Pen.Color := clNavy;
  Canvas.MoveTo (30-X1, 1970-Y1);
  Canvas.LineTo (1970-X1, 30-Y1);
  {draw a fuchsia square}
  Canvas.Pen.Color := clFuchsia;
  Canvas.Brush.Style := bsClear;
  Canvas.Rectangle (500-X1, 500-Y1, 1500-X1, 1500-Y1);
end;
```

You can see an example of the output of the program in Figure 13.5. Try using the program and changing the drawing functions, but remember to always use coordinates relative to the virtual origin of the form by subtracting the virtual coordinates X1 and Y1 (which refer to the scroll bar position).

You might also try to use plain coordinates to see what happens. You'll find that the output of the program is not correct—it won't scroll, and the same image will always remain in the same position, regardless of scrolling operations.

**FIGURE 13.5:**
An example of the output of the
SCROLL2 example.

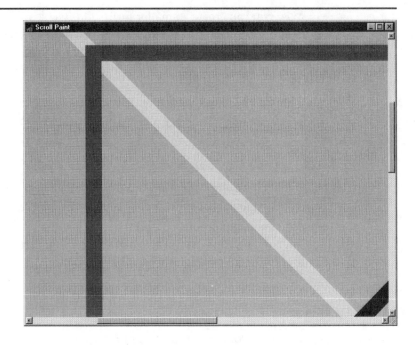

# Building Notebooks with Delphi

There are three different ways to build a notebook with a tab to change the current page. The first is to use the Windows 95 PageControl component, the second is to use a Notebook component together with a TabSet component, and the third is to use the TabbedNotebook component, which is still available in Delphi 2 for compatibility purposes only.

The main difference between the three approaches is in the user interfaces of these components, as you can see in the figures in the following sections. In general, since the PageControl and TabControl are based on a Windows common control, you should probably use these two component unless you have compatibility problems or some other special reason not to do so. Technically speaking, TTabControl is built around the Windows 95 tab control, providing little else than the capability to show its own tabs. The TPageControl is based on a tab control plus some panels (tab sheets), and provides more capabilities.

If you only need a tab, without the notebook or pages, you can use the TabControl or TabSet component. If you need the Pages without the tabs, you can use the Page-Control (hiding the tabs) or use the Notebook component by itself.

# TabControl, PageControl, and TabSheets

There are three components used to handle pages and tabs in Windows 95, which are represented in Delphi by the TabControl and PageControl components, and by the TabSheet component used inside a PageControl. The TabControl is used to build stand-alone tabs (not connected with pages; I'll use it later in a specific example). The PageControl component, instead, is used to build an application or a dialog box using the common multipage or notebook metaphor.

As usual, instead of providing you a list of properties and methods of the PageControl component, I've built an example which stretches its capabilities and allows you to change its behavior at run-time. The example, PAGES, has a PageControl with three pages. To rebuild it, you can simply place the control on a new form, then select it and use the local menu to add new pages or tab sheets. Each TabSheet object has its own Caption, which is displayed as tab. You can use the same local menu to change pages, but you can also do this by clicking on the tab directly (and then clicking back on the surface of the form to select the TabSheet). You can see the local menu of the PageControl component in Figure 13.6, together with the first page. This page holds a list box and a small caption, and shares two buttons with the other pages.

If you place a component on a page, it is available only in that page. How can you have the same component (in this case, two bitmap buttons) in each of the pages, without duplicating it? Simply place the component on the form, outside of the

---

**FIGURE 13.6:**

The first sheet of the PageControl of the PAGES example, with its local menu.

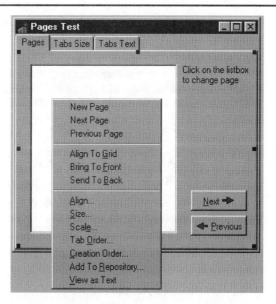

PageControl (or before aligning it to the client area) and then move it in front of the pages, calling the Bring to Front command of the form's local menu. The two buttons I've placed in each page can be used to move back and forth between the pages and are an alternative to using the tabs. Here is the code associated with one of them:

```
procedure TForm1.BitBtnNextClick(Sender: TObject);
begin
  PageControl1.SelectNextPage (True);
end;
```

The other button calls the same procedure, passing False as parameter to select the previous page. Notice that there is no need to check whether we are in the first or last page, because SelectNextPage considers the last page to also be the one before the first, and will move you directly between those two pages.

Now that we have defined the use of the common component, we can focus back on the first page. It has a list box, which at run-time will hold the name of the tabs. If a user clicks on an item of this list box, the current page changes. This is the third method available to change pages (after tabs and buttons). The list box is filled using the FormCreate method, copying the caption of each page (the Page property stores a list of TabSheet objects):

```
for I := 0 to PageControl1.PageCount -1 do
  ListBox1.Items.Add (
    PageControl1.Pages [I].Caption);
```

When you click on the page, you have to re-scan the list to find a match. In fact, there is no direct way to choose a page without knowing the specific TabSheet object you want:

```
procedure TForm1.ListBox1Click(Sender: TObject);
var
  I: Integer;
begin
  for I := 0 to PageControl1.PageCount -1 do
    if PageControl1.Pages [I].Caption =
        ListBox1.Items [ListBox1.ItemIndex] then
      PageControl1.ActivePage :=
        PageControl1.Pages [I];
end;
```

The second page hosts two edit boxes (connected with two UpDown components), and two check boxes, as you can see in Figure 13.7. The user can input a number (or choose it by clicking on the up and down buttons with the mouse or pressing ↑ or ↓ while the corresponding edit box has the focus) and check the boxes, then press the Apply button to make the changes:

```
procedure TForm1.BitBtnApplyClick(Sender: TObject);
begin
```

**FIGURE 13.7:**

The second page of the example can be used to size and position the tabs: Here you can see large tabs on multiple thin lines.

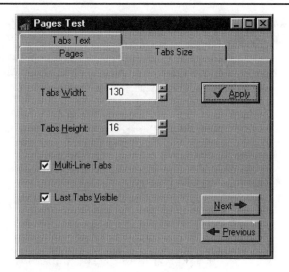

```
  {set tabs width, height, and lines}
  PageControl1.TabWidth := StrToInt (EditWidth.Text);
  PageControl1.TabHeight := StrToInt (EditHeight.Text);
  PageControl1.MultiLine := CheckBoxMultiLine.Checked;
  {show or hide the last tab}
  TabSheet3.TabVisible := CheckBoxVisible.Checked;
end;
```

With this code we can change the width and height of each tab (remember that *0* means the size is computed automatically from the space taken by each string), and choose to have either multiple lines of tabs or two small arrows to scroll the tab area. You can also hide the last tab on the PageControl, which corresponds to the Tab-Sheet3 component.

If you hide one of the tabs by setting the TabVisible option of the tab sheet property to False, you cannot reach that tab by clicking on the Next and Previous buttons, based on the SelectNextPage method. Instead, you should use the FindNextPage function, as shown below in this new version of the OnClick event handle of the NextButton component:

```
procedure TForm1.BitBtnNextClick(Sender: TObject);
begin
  PageControl1.ActivePage :=
    PageControl1.FindNextPage (
      PageControl1.ActivePage, True, False);
end;
```

WARNING

Notice that when you change the height of the tabs of a PageControl or set multiple lines at run-time, every component in the page is moved downwards, and might even slip out of the visible area. At the same time, if you have components that are not children of the PageControl although they are placed in front of it (as with the two bitmap button in the PAGES example), they will not move and might hide other components of a specific page.

The last page has a memo component again with the names of the pages (added in the FormCreate method). You can edit the names of the pages and press the Change button to change the text of the tabs, but only if the number of strings matches the number of tabs:

```
if Memo1.Lines.Count <> PageControl1.PageCount then
  MessageDlg ('One line per tab, please', mtError, [mbOK], 0)
else
  for I := 0 to PageControl1.PageCount −1 do
    PageControl1.Pages [I].Caption := Memo1.Lines [I];
```

Another feature we might add to the example is a way to add new pages at run-time and to place some components inside them. We might also add a pull-down menu listing the pages, to offer a fourth technique to change pages.

TIP

Whenever you write a form based on a PageControl or notebook, remember that the first page displayed at run-time is the page you were in before the code was compiled. This means that if you are working on page 3, then compile and run the program, it will start with page 3, not with page 1. A common way to solve this problem is to add a line of code in the FormCreate method to set the PageControl or notebook to the first page. This way, the current page at design-time doesn't determine the initial page at run-time.

## A Notebook with a Tab Set

The standard approach to build a notebook with tabs in Delphi 1.0 was to use the two separate components, the Notebook and the TabSet. This might still be a useful approach, because it is very flexible and because it is highly compatible between the 16-bit and the 32-bit versions of Delphi. A program using the PageControl, in fact, cannot be recompiled in Delphi 1.0. To describe the Notebook and TabSet components in detail, I've written an example similar to the previous one and named it TAB1.

To create this form, you can place a Notebook component on the form, then place a TabSet component on the form, align the TabSet to the bottom of the form (al-Bottom), and align the Notebook with the client area (alClient). Now you can name the pages of the notebook by selecting the Pages property and entering some values in the corresponding editor. The next step is to prepare the tabs by entering some strings for the Tabs property. It might be a good idea to use the same names for the pages of the notebook and for the tabs of the TabSet component. However, the names you use for the TabSet component are not particularly important, since they are not visible. The important thing is that the tabs themselves must have meaningful names, because they are visible to the user.

To connect the notebook to the tab set, you need to write at least one line of code in response to the OnChange event of the TabSet component:

```
procedure TForm1.TabSet1Change(Sender: TObject;
  NewTab: Integer; var AllowChange: Boolean);
begin
  Notebook1.PageIndex := NewTab;
end;
```

**WARNING**
In the OnChange response method, you should use the NewTab parameter and *not* the current index of the tab, because this field contains the older value, the one before the click took place. In fact, the OnChange method can even be used to prohibit the page change by setting the AllowChange parameter, which is passed by reference, to False.

As an alternative, you can activate the pages by using their names (the ActivePage property of the notebook) instead of their index (the PageIndex property). This works only if the names of the pages match those of the tabs:

```
procedure TForm1.TabSet1Change(Sender: TObject;
  NewTab: Integer; var AllowChange: Boolean);
begin
  Notebook1.ActivePage := TabSet1.Tabs [NewTab];
end;
```

To make this program interesting, we need to add some components to the various pages. At design-time, you can work on the various pages of the notebook by changing the value of its PageIndex property; you can't just click on the tabs as with the PageControl component. As soon as you enter a new value for the PageIndex or the ActivePage property in the Object Inspector, the visible page of the notebook changes accordingly. A better alternative is to select the notebook in the Form Designer, and activate the SpeedMenu, which has commands to move to the next or previous page.

Now that we know how to change the active page at design-time, what's in the pages of this example? Again, I decided to fill the pages with some controls we can use to change the properties of these two components. The first page—would you guess it?—holds a list box with the names of the pages, filled when the form is created with the names of the pages of the notebook. This time the code is simpler, because both components are based on a StringList:

```
ListBox1.Items := Notebook1.Pages;
```

To change between pages, when the user clicks on an item in the list box, we can write a simpler code, too. As we change the active page of the notebook, we must only remember to select the proper tab as well, since the page and tab index synchronization is not automatic:

```
Notebook1.PageIndex := ListBox1.ItemIndex;
TabSet1.TabIndex := ListBox1.ItemIndex;
```

The second page has two radio buttons to activate or disable the dithering effect of the background of the TabSet control. You can see the code of these and other methods of this example in the source code on the companion CD-ROM. The third page contains a ColorGrid component you can use to select the background color of the form, used also for the notebook. Therefore, it might be a good idea to use it for the background of the tab set and for the active tab, too. The important idea is that to provide the proper three-dimensional effect, the color of the active tab should always match the color of the notebook, so that it seems like an extension of its surface (see Figure 13.8). The second color, the foreground color, is used for the inactive tabs.

The fourth page allows a user to change the text of the tabs (but not of the memo pages). It contains a memo field, which is initialized as usual in the FormCreate method. If you write longer and more descriptive names for the pages, the TabSet component is capable of adding two "mini" scroll buttons to move among the tabs

**FIGURE 13.8:**

An example of the new colors and the dithering effect you can set for the notebook and the tab of the TAB1 example.

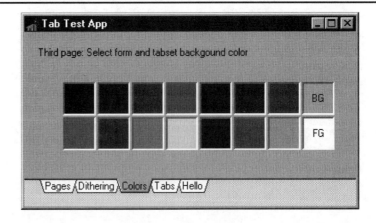

when they do not fit into the width of the Tab control, working similarly to the PageControl tabs.

This example and the PAGES example highlight two interesting points:

- You are not limited to the use of tabs to change the page of a PageControl or notebook. The list box on the first page that we have used for this purpose could be placed on one side and used as a page selector, as we will do in the next section.

- It is quite simple to edit the text of the tabs. An instructive example in this direction is Quattro Pro for Windows, which allows users to customize the text of the tabs used to change the active page of the spreadsheet and to refer to that new text in formulas.

## Changing the Page of a Notebook

The example we have just finished can be further extended in a number of directions, particularly in providing alternative ways to change the page of the notebook. The same could be said for the PAGES example. However, when you use the standard Windows 95 component, it is not as important to examine many other techniques to change the page as it is when you are using a less-standard user interface. This is particularly important because a notebook can easily be used without tabs, building a completely custom user interface.

The technique we'll try first is to add a list box similar to the one on the first page of the notebook, and to make it always visible in the window. Then all you need to do is click on this list box to change to another page. The second addition will be a menu to select the page.

To build the TAB2 example, we can add a new list box on the left or right side of the form. To accomplish this, we need to resize the various components, disable their top alignment, and choose a fixed border for the frame so that it cannot be resized. You can see an example of the final form in Figure 13.9.

At program startup, we can initialize the new list box with the same text as the labels of the TabSet component.

We can handle the click on an element of the new list box (ListBox2) by writing a code fragment similar to the one used for the first list box. Copying and pasting might be the way to go, but remember to change the list box numbers. Even better, we can write a single version of the code to act with both list boxes, and connect it with the click event of both of them:

```
procedure TForm1.ListBox1Click(Sender: TObject);
{works with both list boxes}
begin
```

```
    Notebook1.PageIndex := (Sender as TListBox).ItemIndex;
    TabSet1.TabIndex := (Sender as TListBox).ItemIndex;
end;
```

**FIGURE 13.9:**

The TAB2 program shows the selected page both in the tab, in the list box on the left, and with a check mark in the Page pull-down menu.

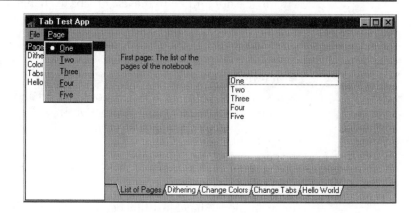

With this code, when the list box selection changes, we select a new page and activate the proper tab.

The second technique introduced in TAB2 is to add a pull-down menu to select the various pages. The OnClick event for each menu item is associated with a single function, MenuPage, which is based on a simple trick: The name of each menu item corresponds to the name of a page of the notebook. This simplifies the code quite a bit:

```
procedure TForm1.MenuPage(Sender: TObject);
begin
  Notebook1.ActivePage := (Sender as TMenuItem).Name;
  TabSet1.TabIndex := Notebook1.PageIndex;
  ListBox2.ItemIndex := Notebook1.PageIndex;
  CheckCurrentPage;
end;
```

This approach also makes the program easily extensible, because you don't need to write new code or change it when new pages and the corresponding menu items are added. Only the first statement above contains real code. The other two are needed to change the list box and tab selections according to the new page (using the number). The last statement invokes a procedure I've defined, named Check-CurrentPage. This method places a check mark on the menu item corresponding to the currently selected page, as already shown in Figure 13.9. It removes the check mark from every menu item, then enables the one corresponding to the current page with a case statement:

```
procedure TForm1.CheckCurrentPage;
var
  I: Integer;
begin
  One.Checked := False;
  Two.Checked := False;
  Three.Checked := False;
  Four.Checked := False;
  Five.Checked := False;
  case Notebook1.PageIndex of
    0: One.Checked := True;
    1: Two.Checked := True;
    2: Three.Checked := True;
    3: Four.Checked := True;
    4: Five.Checked := True;
  end;
end;
```

The code is placed in a stand-alone procedure because we need to call it each time the active page changes. The CheckCurrentPage method is called at the end of the methods ListBox1Click, TabSet1Change, and FormCreate.

To write a better CheckCurrentPages procedure and to improve the user interface, you can use radio menu items for the Pages pull-down menu and remove the five lines above used to deselect each possible item. Actually, you can also remove the case statement, considering that the number of the active page corresponds to the number of the menu item you have to select. Here is the final code you'll find in the example on the companion CD (together with the earlier versions, commented):

```
procedure TForm1.CheckCurrentPage;
begin
  Page1.Items [NoteBook1.PageIndex].
    Checked := True;
end;
```

This new way is actually much simpler, and the user interface of the example is now based on radio menu buttons, as required by Windows 95 (but not by Windows NT).

Of course, you will seldom need three different ways to select the page of a notebook, as I've included in the TAB2 example, but a couple of choices might be useful to satisfy the tastes of different users. The aim of this example was to show you some alternatives you can apply also to the PageControl component (in particular the selection of page using a pull-down menu).

# Tabbed Notebooks

A third alternative to the use of the PageControl and the TabSet and Notebook components is the use of the TabbedNotebook component. This component has a user interface quite similar to the Windows 95 PageControl, but it was also available in the 16-bit version of Delphi, so it can be used for Windows 3.1 applications, too.

The example I've built to show the use of the TabbedNotebook, named SIMTAB, is similar to—although somewhat simpler than—the PAGES and TAB1 examples shown earlier. As you can see in Figure 13.10, the first page of this multipage form has a list box with the names of the pages. There is also a Close button, which should be present on every page of the notebook. Again, I've placed the button on the form, not on the notebook, and then I've moved it over the notebook.

I've placed the button in the bottom-center of the form, and I've selected a non-resizable dialog border for the form.

The other pages of the notebook in the SIMTAB example allow you to change the font of the tab captions and the number of tabs per row. The last two pages are almost empty.

**FIGURE 13.10:**
The first page of the SIMTAB example.

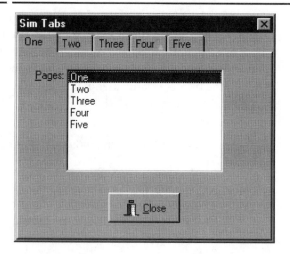

The code of this example is fairly simple. In fact, the TabbedNotebook component handles page changing automatically, as the PageControl. This means that we don't need to change the active page each time the user clicks on a tab, as is the case in the TAB1 and TAB2 examples. Again, however, we can implement more than one technique to change the page. As a recurring example, we can fill the list box of the first page with the names of the pages, and then move to another page when the user clicks on the corresponding element in the list box.

To change the page in the tabbed notebook, we can set the name of the page or its index, as with the other multipage components. Since the list box has a zero-based ItemIndex property, indicating the selected item, we can simply write the following code:

```
TabbedNotebook1.PageIndex := ListBoxPages.ItemIndex;
```

The other two pages of the notebook can be used to change the font and arrangement of the tabs. To change the font when the user clicks on the corresponding button, you can simply use a FontDialog component, and use the selected value to change the font of the tabs:

```
if FontDialog1.Execute then
  TabbedNotebook1.TabFont := FontDialog1.Font;
```

The program also changes the Caption of a test label to show the name of the current font, and an example of how the font will look.

For the last operation—changing the number of tabs per row—I've simply added a SpinEdit component and a button. The code is simple. When the user clicks the button, the value of the SpinEdit component is used as the new number of tabs per row:

```
TabbedNotebook1.TabsPerRow := SpinEdit1.Value;
```

**WARNING**
Unfortunately, this code does not work as documented—changing the TabsPerRow property has no effect on the tabs! I've decided to leave the wrong code in the example anyway for two reasons: first, there is no obvious way to fix it, not even by inheriting a new component from the TTabbedNotebook class; and second, I hope Borland will fix it in a future update, although I was hoping the same for the final release of Delphi 2.

# Notebooks without Tabs and Tabs without Notebooks

The interface of the PageControl is getting quite common, and the Notebook and TabSet components naturally fit with each other. However, using the two components together is not the only choice. As the title of this section suggests, you can write applications with tabs but without a multipage component, or with notebooks but without any sort of tabs or list to select the page from. Here are some examples, some of which will be fully implemented in the following sections.

The TabControl (or TabSet) alone can be used in a multipage editor (such as the editor in Delphi), in a multipage bitmap viewer, to select a disk drive in a file viewer, in a three-dimensional spreadsheet, or to select a form in a multiple-form program. Delphi uses tabs to select pages in the Component palette, too.

A notebook can be used without tabs if you replace it with a list box or a menu (as shown in the TAB2 example). As an alternative, you can use a TreeView component instead of a list, obtaining an effect similar to a multipage explorer. Another alternative to the use of a tab is to add buttons to navigate through the notebook, as partially demonstrated by the PAGES example. There are basically two ways to use buttons for navigation:

- Add a row of buttons with commands such as First, Next, Previous, and Last, similar to database navigation commands. A special case of this is the development of Experts or Wizards. The form of these applications is made with a notebook and usually has a button to move to the next page, and one to go back to the previous page. Typically it is possible to move to the following page only after you have selected some options. The order of the pages (and even their presence) might depend on your past selections.

- Add specific buttons in the various pages of the notebook to move to other relevant pages. This solution is similar to the use of hyperlinks, and you can use specific portions of the text or of an image instead of push buttons to launch the move.

## A Presentation in a Notebook

Our first example is a notebook without a tab, called NOTEONLY. It has both a row of buttons at the bottom and some buttons in the pages to give specific navigation commands. The four buttons in the row at the bottom of the form are placed on a panel, so that the notebook can take up the rest of the client area of the form. Probably the best way to understand this example is to run it. It is a presentation about traveling in Italy (I thought it might be interesting to many people around the world, although I've written just minimal information about the places).

Each page usually has a button to move to the next step, as you can see in Figure 13.11, but at times you have two or more choices. There is nothing else besides buttons, and their code is quite simple. Usually, when you select a button, a new page of the notebook is chosen. Some more coding is required to disable the useless buttons of the panel. For example, after a user clicks on the First button, you should disable the first two buttons (since the user is already at the first page and there are no previous pages) and enable the other two buttons in case they had been disabled.

**FIGURE 13.11:**

A couple of pages of the NOTEONLY example, featuring a simple presentation about Italy.

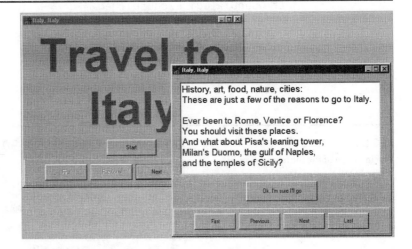

Slightly more complex is the case of the Next and the Previous buttons. You should check whether the notebook has reached the first or the last page, and disable or enable the various buttons accordingly. The real problem here is that we also need to enable and disable some of the buttons on the button row when the navigational buttons of the various pages of the notebook are clicked, to avoid inconsistent behavior.

## An Image Viewer with Tabs

Now that we've gone through an example of a notebook without tabs, we are ready to explore the opposite situation: a tab that is not attached to a notebook. Often, you'll find another component connected to a tab. For example, you might attach a tab set to a panel, an image, one of the various kinds of grids, or other types of components. In our next example, TABONLY, we want to display a bitmap in an Image component. The image that appears depends on the selection in the tab above it (see Figure 13.12 for an example of the running program). This is a simple example. The form has a TabControl component aligned to the whole client area, and an Image component inside the TabControl and covering its client area. The other two components are a main menu and a File Open dialog box that allows multiple selections.

At the beginning, the TabControl has only a fake tab, describing the situation (*No file selected*). When the user selects File ➤ Open, the dialog box is displayed. The user can select a number of files, and the array of strings with the names of the files (the Files property of the OpenDialog1 component) is used as the text for the tabs (the Tabs property of TabControl1):

```
procedure TForm1.Open1Click(Sender: TObject);
begin
```

```
  if OpenDialog1.Execute then
  begin
    TabControl1.Tabs := OpenDialog1.Files;
    TabControl1.TabIndex := 0;
    TabControl1Change (TabControl1);
  end;
end;
```

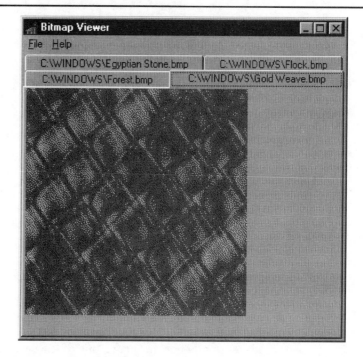

**FIGURE 13.12:**

The interface of the bitmap viewer in the TABONLY example.

After we display the new tabs, we have to update the image so that it matches the first tab. To accomplish this the program calls the method connected with the On-Change event of the TabControl, which loads the file corresponding to the current tab in the image component:

```
procedure TForm1.TabControl1Change(Sender: TObject);
begin
  Image1.Picture.LoadFromFile (
    TabControl1.Tabs [TabControl1.TabIndex]);
end;
```

This example works, but not very well. One of the problems is related to the fact that displaying the whole path makes the tabs very big, so that they will take up a lot of screen space (because I've set the Multiline property of the TabControl to True). To correct this problem, the program defines a set of hidden temporary strings, so that the path name can be removed from the tabs. Another problem is that if you select a file that doesn't contain a bitmap, an error will occur. However, the program will warn the user with a standard exception, ignore the file, and continue its execution.

The last problem involves usability. This program is not very suitable for browsing the hard disk looking for a bitmap, because you need to execute the OpenDialog over and over again. A better idea is to have a list of directories directly on the form and allow the user to browse through it. This is easy to do in Delphi, since there is a DirectoryListBox component readily available. By using some advanced system components and only a few lines of code, we can build a full-fledged image browser. In doing this, I've converted the program to use Delphi's own TabSet component instead of the Windows 95 TabControl.

## An Image Browser with Tabs

To build the TABONLY2 example—the image browser—place in a new form a DriveComboBox with a DirectoryListBox below it, as shown in Figure 13.13. On the right of the form, place an Image with a TabSet below it. I've also added a Bevel component behind them, to improve the user interface.

**FIGURE 13.13:**

The bitmap viewer of the TABONLY2 example.

The idea of this program is that as the user selects a new directory, the tabs should immediately display the names of bitmap files of that directory. First, we need to connect the combo box with the names of the drives and with the directory list box, so that each change in the combo box is reflected in the other component. This can be easily done by setting the DirList property of the DriveComboBox. The second step is to load the names of the bitmap files in the tabs each time the selection in the directory list box changes. We might do this manually, by accessing DOS functions, or we can use another component to solve the problem. The latter solution is more Delphi-oriented, and also much easier, so I've chosen to follow it.

Just place a FileListBox component on the form, and reduce its size so that it will be invisible, place it behind another component, or simply set its Visible property to False. Then change the value of the Mask property of the file list box to *.bmp. Now add a method for the OnChange event of the directory list box, and write the following code:

```
procedure TForm1.DirectoryListBox1Change(Sender: TObject);
begin
  with FileListBox1 do
    if Items.Count = 0 then
    begin
      TabSet1.Tabs.Clear;
      Image1.Visible := False;
      TabSet1.Tabs.Add ('None');
    end
    else
    begin
      Image1.Visible := True;
      TabSet1.Tabs := FileListBox1.Items;
    end;
end;
```

Using this method, each time the user selects a new directory (or a new disk), the directory shown in the file list box changes. Then, if there are some items in this directory, the array of strings is copied to the tab set. As an alternative, the *None* string is added to an empty tab set, and the image with the old bitmap is temporarily hidden. When the tabs display the names of the files, we can use a statement very similar to that of the TABONLY example to load the corresponding bitmap in the picture of the Image component:

```
procedure TForm1.TabSet1Change(Sender: TObject; NewTab: Integer;
  var AllowChange: Boolean);
begin
  if TabSet1.Tabs [NewTab] <> 'None' then
    Image1.Picture.LoadFromFile (TabSet1.Tabs [NewTab]);
end;
```

## A Multipage Toolbar

The last example of this chapter defines a notebook with tabs used to build a multipage toolbar. Building a multipage toolbar, in general, is easy. You only need to place a number of speed buttons in the pages of a PageControl or a notebook. You can see an example of such a toolbar running the MULTIBAR example, which is based on a Notebook and a TabSet component. I decided not to enter the text for the tabs of the TabSet component, but to simply copy the names of the pages into the tabs of the notebook at run-time:

```
procedure TForm1.FormCreate(Sender: TObject);
begin
  TabSet1.Tabs := Notebook1.Pages;
end;
```

Of course, to make the tabs work properly, you should also connect them to the notebook as usual:

```
procedure TForm1.TabSet1Change(Sender: TObject;
  NewTab: Integer; var AllowChange: Boolean);
begin
  Notebook1.PageIndex := NewTab;
end;
```

Notice that the tabs of this example mimic the names of possible pull-down menus. A better solution might be to provide two or three toolbars corresponding to different environment situations (file editing, folder handling, other tools, and so on). The program might automatically change the toolbar page when you change the context, but the user is still free to select a different page of the toolbar. Having a multipage toolbar, such as the Delphi components palette, might be a better alternative than having many toolbars using up all of the screen real estate, as many applications do.

**NOTE** I've borrowed all of the bitmaps for the examples in this chapter from the Delphi Image Library, a collection of graphic files usually available in the Delphi 2.0 Images directory and in the C:\DELPHI\IMAGES directory and its subdirectories.

A problem in building a similar example is that you need to manually select the bitmap for each of the buttons, which can be extremely boring. A solution is to give names to the buttons, so that they can later load a bitmap having the same name at run-time. If you follow this approach, another improvement might come from storing the bitmaps as resources inside the executable file, instead of as external BMP files.

# Summary

In this chapter, we have seen how Delphi handles form scrolling, and how you can work with it. We have seen how to paint on a scrolling surface and how to track scrolling operations by the user. In the second part, we focused on other techniques you can use to increase the number of components you can display on a form, using various forms of multiple-page components. We have seen how to use the new Windows 95 PageControl and TabControl components, and how you can connect a TabSet to a Notebook component.

Delphi components are very flexible. Rather than sticking with a fixed design, you can choose from the many options available. You'll see this theme continued in the next chapter, which is devoted to form splitting and the various ways you can arrange and resize components in a form at run-time. A third approach to building complex applications is MDI. This will be the topic of Chapter 15.

# CHAPTER

## FOURTEEN

# Splitting Windows

- A splitter implemented with Headers

- A splitter based on a Panel

- A splitter line that moves on drag termination

- Direct mouse splitting

- A File Manager clone with a preview pane

**A**n interesting user interface feature that is becoming common is the splitter, an element you can drag to resize or move some components in a window. The most typical example is the Windows 95 Explorer splitter (quite similar to the Windows 3.1 File Manager's splitter), which separates the directories tree from the files list box. Another interesting example of the use of splitters is in SideKick for Windows, which uses a number of elements in a form instead of an MDI approach.

I decided to focus a whole chapter on this topic, because this is a significant feature of the user interface of many applications, and it involves some interesting programming problems. At the same time, this is a good occasion to start presenting a fairly complex application, which would have required a lot of time to program without Delphi. As our last example in this chapter, we'll build a customized version of good old File Manager, which, of course, will use a splitter.

# Form Splitting Techniques

There are several ways to implement splitters in Delphi, although there is no specific support for them. You can use the following techniques to split forms; that is, to let the user resize some of the components, while the others are arranged automatically:

- A HeaderControl or a Header component can be used to size components horizontally in a form. The header handles the sizing operations, the mouse, the cursor, and other details automatically, so most of the work is already done. For this reason, it is quite common in Delphi to use a header to implement splitting.

- Any component, but usually a Panel or a GroupBox, can be placed between two other elements that can be resized. Using Delphi's dragging support, this component can be moved, and the change can affect the relative position of other components.

- You can use a component that supports dragging inside itself. For example, the StringGrid and DrawGrid components allow dragging. Using a grid is probably the simplest and most powerful approach to splitting. The drawback is that grids are also the most expensive, in terms of the amount of code you have to write to customize them.

- You can handle mouse-dragging operations manually, particularly on the form itself. Just leave a blank area between different components, and check when the user drags through this area.

Each of these three approaches will be demonstrated using the same example: a form with three list boxes containing names of animals. The list boxes will support font changing with a mouse double-click.

# Splitting with a Header

The Windows 95 HeaderControl is the most common technique used to implement a vertical splitter. As an alternative (for compatibility with Windows 3.1), you can use Delphi's own Header component. I'll write this program using the new HeaderControl first, then show you the differences in the implementation of the Header component.

## Using the HeaderControl Component

If you place a HeaderControl component on a form, it will be automatically aligned with the top of the form. Then you can add the three list boxes to the rest of the client area of the form. The first list box can be aligned on the left, but you cannot align the second and third list box this way, too. In fact, the sections of the header can be dragged outside the visible area, and alignment attributes create problems for components outside of the visible area. We will be able to use this auto-alignment approach in the next version, based on the old Header component, but this time, I'll align the components using some code.

First, we need to fill the list boxes and define the sections of the header, using the specific editor of the Sections property. As you can see in Figure 14.1, this property editor allows you to change various settings besides the names of the sections. You can set the alignment of the text; the current, minimum, and maximum size of the header; and so on. Setting the limit values is really a powerful tool, which allows

**FIGURE 14.1:**
The editor of the Sections property of the HeaderControl component.

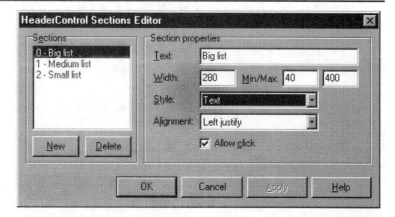

us to avoid handling this problem at run-time. The only problem is with the last section of the header. We want the third list box to fill up the client area, if possible, but the header usually has some empty space after the last section.

To reduce the impact of this problem, I've made the last header very big (see Figure 14.2). Here are the values (taken from the textual description of the form):

```
object HeaderControl1: THeaderControl
    Sections = <
      item
        MaxWidth = 400
        MinWidth = 40
        Text = 'Big list'
        Width = 280
      end
      item
        MaxWidth = 400
        MinWidth = 40
        Text = 'Medium list'
        Width = 180
      end
      item
        MaxWidth = 1000
        MinWidth = 40
        Text = 'Small list'
        Width = 1000
      end>
    OnSectionClick = HeaderControl1SectionClick
    OnSectionResize = HeaderControl1SectionResize
  end
```

**FIGURE 14.2:**

The output of the SPLIT1 example.

As you can see in the listing above, I've decided to handle two events: OnSection-Resize and OnSectionClick. In the first handler, I simply resize the three list boxes according to the width of the three sections:

```
procedure TForm1.HeaderControl1SectionResize(
  HeaderControl: THeaderControl;
  Section: THeaderSection);
begin
  ListBox1.Width := HeaderControl1.Sections[0].Width;
  ListBox2.Left := ListBox1.Width;
  ListBox2.Width := HeaderControl1.Sections[1].Width;
  ListBox3.Left := ListBox2.Width + ListBox2.Left;
  ListBox3.Width := Form1.Width -
    HeaderControl1.Sections[0].Width -
    HeaderControl1.Sections[1].Width;
end;
```

**NOTE** I've written `Form1.Width` instead of accessing the property directly, because the handler of the OnSectionTrack event of the THeaderControl component (called while the user is dragging the separators) has Width as one of its parameters. This parameter hides the corresponding property of the form.

Along with this event, we need to handle the resizing of the form, using the following code (remember that the first list box is automatically aligned):

```
procedure TForm1.FormResize(Sender: TObject);
begin
  ListBox2.Height := ListBox1.Height;
  ListBox3.Height := ListBox1.Height;
  HeaderControl1SectionResize(HeaderControl1,
    HeaderControl1.Sections [0]);
end;
```

After setting the height of the list boxes, this method simply calls the previous one, passing casual parameters. The second method, the click on the section, is used to sort the contents of the corresponding list box. The problem is, how do you know which section was clicked? The best way I've figured out (but there might be a better one) is to compare the section object passed as parameters with the section objects of the Sections list property of the HeaderControl:

```
procedure TForm1.HeaderControl1SectionClick(HeaderControl: THeaderControl;
  Section: THeaderSection);
begin
  if Section = HeaderControl1.Sections[0] then
    ListBox1.Sorted := True;
  if Section = HeaderControl1.Sections[1] then
```

```
      ListBox2.Sorted := True;
  if Section = HeaderControl1.Sections[2] then
      ListBox3.Sorted := True;
end;
```

The last method simply executes the FontDialog1 component and sets the font of the list box on which you have double-clicked. The same code is used for the three list boxes:

```
procedure TForm1.ListBoxDblClick(Sender: TObject);
begin
  with Sender as TListbox do
  begin
    FontDialog1.Font := Font;
    if FontDialog1.Execute then
      Font := FontDialog1.Font;
  end;
end;
```

## Using the Header Component

As an alternative to the new header, and for compatibility with the 16-bit version of Delphi, you can use the Header component. I'll demonstrate this in the example below, which is named OLDHEAD. You can replace the HeaderControl with the other header, and this time you can align the second list box to the left, and the third list box with the client area. Again, we can use the Sections property of the header, but this time it is a plain StringList. You can set the initial size of the headers by dragging the separator with the right mouse button at design-time.

Again, we need to resize the list boxes each time the user resizes one of the sections of the header. The header has two methods for this: OnSized is called when the user has terminated the dragging operation; OnSizing is called several times during the operation, once for each mouse movement.

The OnSized method has an AWidth parameter, indicating the width of the section being resized, and an ASection parameter, which indicates the number of the section the user is acting on (the section to the left of the separator being dragged). Since we have aligned the list boxes, we need only write the following code:

```
procedure TForm1.Header1Sized(Sender: TObject;
  ASection, AWidth: Integer);
begin
  if ASection = 0 then
    ListBox1.Width := AWidth;
  if ASection = 1 then
    ListBox2.Width := AWidth;
end;
```

# Setting a Maximum and Minimum Size

By writing this code, we've made the header work as a splitter, but with two limitations: the list boxes are resized only when the user ends the sizing operation, and they can be reduced or enlarged to any size, or even be made to disappear or make other sections disappear.

The first problem could be solved by simply copying the above code into the On-Sizing event-response method. However, I've decided not to do this, because if you resize the list boxes too frequently, their repainting operation will cause some flickering on the screen. You might even end up dragging empty list boxes, because the system doesn't have time to repaint them during the dragging.

To solve the second problem and make sure that the user cannot make the sections in the header too small, we can write this code for the OnSizing event:

```
procedure TForm1.Header1Sizing(Sender: TObject;
  ASection, AWidth: Integer);
begin
  if AWidth < 40 then
    Header1.SectionWidth [ASection] := 40;
end;
```

This code almost works. However, it causes some flickering on the screen, since the header is trying to reduce the size of the section and your code is enlarging it to 40 pixels. The real problem is that the component repaints the screen before you have a choice to check its size, and eventually change it.

To solve this problem, we can use a technique that is not elegant, but works quite well. When the user tries to make the section too small, we can call the Windows API function `ReleaseCapture`, which terminates mouse dragging. Since this forced termination skips the sending of the OnSized event, the code should mimic this event:

```
procedure TForm1.Header1Sizing(Sender: TObject;
  ASection, AWidth: Integer);
begin
  if AWidth < 40 then
  begin
    Header1.SectionWidth [ASection] := 40;
    ReleaseCapture;
    Header1Sized (Sender, ASection, 40);
  end;
end;
```

You can add similar code to prevent the user from making the sections too big. The code required for this is more complex, because we need to compute the maximum size each time, considering the size of the form and of the other two list boxes:

```
if ASection = 0 then
  MaxWidth := ClientWidth - 40 - Header1.SectionWidth [1]
else
  MaxWidth := ClientWidth - 40 - Header1.SectionWidth [0];
if AWidth > MaxWidth then
begin
  Header1.SectionWidth [ASection] := MaxWidth;
  ReleaseCapture;
  Header1Sized (Sender, ASection, MaxWidth);
end;
```

You can find the full listing on the companion CD. Notice that the output of this example is very similar to the last one, already shown in Figure 14.2

## A Header behind the Scenes

Our next version of the SPLIT example will allow the user to drag the separator between list boxes. This can be accomplished in various ways. The first one we'll explore is using a Header component once again, but this time the header will be placed "behind the scenes." Figure 14.3 shows the output of the SPLIT2 example. To rebuild it, place a header on the form and align it with the whole client area. Next, add three list boxes as before, placing them approximately over the three sections of the header. However, do not align the three list boxes. The position of the list boxes is not particularly relevant, since we will change it when the application

**FIGURE 14.3:**

The output of the SPLIT2 example, with a header behind the list boxes, but still usable.

starts. The three list boxes cover all of the header's surface except for its separators, so a user can still drag the sections.

> **NOTE**
>
> If the separator is placed in the middle of the borders of the two adjacent list boxes, it has a three-dimensional effect and doesn't look like a split bar. The separator will look better if it is aligned with one of the borders of the list boxes, or at least placed very close to one of the borders, so that the separator itself is barely visible.

Now we simply need to move the list boxes so that the separators always remain visible. I've written this code in a specific method, which is called when the form is created, when the header has been resized (OnSized), and eventually also during the dragging operation (OnSizing):

```
procedure TForm1.ResizeListBoxes;
begin
  ListBox1.Width := Header1.SectionWidth [0] - 1;
  ListBox2.Left := Header1.SectionWidth [0] + 3;
  ListBox2.Width := Header1.SectionWidth [1] - 4;
  ListBox3.Left := Header1.SectionWidth [0] +
    Header1.SectionWidth [1] + 3;
  ListBox3.Width := ClientWidth - ListBox3.Left;
end;
```

This code leaves one pixel between the border of the list box on the left and the separator, and three pixels between the border of the list box on the right and the separator, so that the separator looks more like a split bar.

The Header1Sizing method is similar to the previous version, and it might call the ResizeListBoxes procedure each time, so that the list boxes are immediately aligned. Although this can cause the negative blinking effect I've described before, if you don't resize the list boxes each time, the user has no indication of the dragging operation, other than the cursor. In the previous version, a user could see the new position of the header sections.

# Splitting with Panels

In our next example, the splitter is based on a Panel component. Although it uses a different approach, the output and the behavior of the resulting program, SPLIT3, is similar to those of the last version, SPLIT2. To build this third version, place the three list boxes on the form, and then add two thin vertical panels in between (see Figure 14.4). Now align every component, except the third list box, to the left. The third list box, as you can probably guess, is aligned with the client area. Note that

**FIGURE 14.4:**

The form of the SPLIT3 example at design-time. Notice the panels between the list boxes.

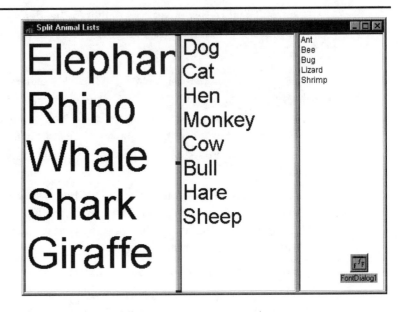

you should set the alignment of the components in the proper order, starting from the first list box, moving on to the first panel, then the second list box, the second panel, and finally the third list box.

This time, there isn't the automatic resizing support offered by the header. Therefore, we need to solve the problem by using the automatic dragging features of any Delphi component. The two panels of this example support automatic dragging—their DragMode property is set to dmAutomatic—and they have the special *horizontal-splitting* cursor (crHSplit) for both the standard and the custom cursor. The three list boxes use the same cursor for dragging, too.

Each panel accepts the dragging of the panel or panels near its borders, and immediately provides the proper resizing of the list boxes (again causing some repainting problems). As a further enhancement, each list box cannot become less than 40 pixels wide. For example, only the first panel can be dragged over the first list box, and the cursor horizontal coordinate (X) cannot be less than 40 pixels:

```
procedure TForm1.ListBox1DragOver(Sender, Source: TObject;
  X, Y: Integer; State: TDragState; var Accept: Boolean);
begin
if (Source = Panel1) and (X > 40) then
  begin
    Accept := True;
    ListBox1.Width := X;
  end
  else
    Accept := False;
end;
```

Notice the equality test between the Source parameter and the Panel1 component. When the same panel is dragged over itself (that is, the user is not moving it), Accept should be set to True again, to set the drag cursor instead of the no-drag cursor:

```
procedure TForm1.PanelDragOver(Sender, Source: TObject;
  X, Y: Integer; State: TDragState; var Accept: Boolean);
begin
  if Source = Sender then
    Accept := True
  else
    Accept := False;
end;
```

This time, the program tests whether the component that originated dragging (Source) is the same one that is receiving the drag event (Sender). If this is the case, we are dragging a panel onto itself, and not over another panel. Because we have written the method with this generic code (without references to specific panels), we can use it for both panels.

The first panel can also be dragged onto the second list box. In this case, we should still resize the first list box, enlarging it, but check that the third one doesn't shrink below a certain limit:

```
procedure TForm1.ListBox2DragOver(Sender, Source: TObject;
  X, Y: Integer;
  State: TDragState; var Accept: Boolean);
begin
  if (Source = Panel1) and (ListBox3.Width > 40) then
  begin
    Accept := True;
    ListBox1.Width := ListBox1.Width + X;
  end
  ...
```

Now X is relative to the second list box, so we can use it as an increment for the size of the first one. The maximum-width test performed by this code is far from perfect, since it checks to see if the third list box was big enough, not if it still will be more than 40 pixels after the current mouse-move message. The code could test whether the future size of the third list box will be big enough, but in this example, this is probably not necessary. If we end up with a list box that is 30 pixels wide, it isn't a big problem. We could easily fix this by increasing the value we test for (such as using 45 instead of 40, considering an average of 5 pixels for each mouse move message).

**NOTE**

Actually, no one can say what the movement of the mouse is between two consecutive mouse-move messages. The system cannot send a message for each movement of a single pixel, unless you move the mouse really slowly. The move messages are discrete, not continuous. Their generation depends on system timers and similar hardware-related parameters, but they are added to a message queue. For this reason, an application receives mouse-move messages at a rate that depends on the total workload of the system. The idea of an average of 5 pixels per movement is almost a random guess.

The same ListBox2DragOver should also test to see if the second panel is being dragged over the second list box, checking that the list box is not reduced too much. Also, the third list box has an OnDragOver handler, related to the second panel. I suggest you study the final code for this example, which is available on the companion CD.

## Drawing a Split Line

In the two preceding examples, we moved or resized the list boxes during the dragging operation, and not at the end. The advantage of this approach is that the user always has a clear picture of what is going on. The disadvantage is that the contents of the list boxes must be repainted several times, often with a nasty flickering, and if you resize the list boxes quite fast, the program will delay the window update, showing you large gray areas.

If you have ever used a splitter in a big application (see the Explorer or File Manager as examples), you have probably dragged a big line indicating the final position of the splitter, without actually moving the components until the end of the dragging operation. This is the approach we'll take in the next version of our example, SPLIT4.

To add a splitter line, we could draw a thick gray line on the list box in the current horizontal position. The problem is that we will need to delete that gray splitter line as soon as the splitter is moved. To accomplish this, the program needs to remember where the line was and be able to restore the previous contents of the list box (its text). A solution is to draw a line using the pmNot pen mode, which reverses the current output. This is useful because, by reversing the output twice, we can easily restore the original drawing. To obtain this effect, for each list box, write the following initialization code:

```
ListBox1.Canvas.Pen.Width := 5;
ListBox1.Canvas.Pen.Mode := pmNot;
```

The form of SPLIT4, shown in Figure 14.5, has the same components as the previous version, but a more complex source code.

**FIGURE 14.5:**

The line splitter of the SPLIT4 example.

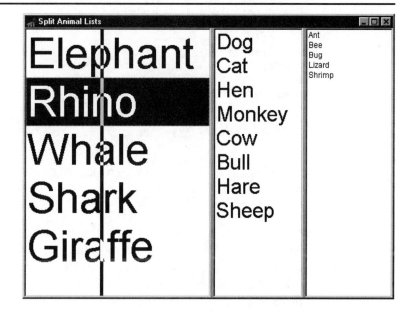

**FIGURE 14.5:**

The line splitter of the SPLIT4 example.

First, notice that I've written two custom methods. The DrawDragLine method is used to draw the new line and eventually delete the old one. The other method, DeleteDragLine, is used to delete the current line when dragging ends. To draw or delete a line, these functions use the MoveTo and LineTo methods of the canvas of the current list box (passed as parameter) or of the old list box. Here is the code of the two methods:

```
procedure TForm1.DrawDragLine (List: TListBox;
  X: Integer; State: TDragState);
begin
  {if there is currently a line...}
  if OldList <> nil then
  begin
    {delete the previous line, re-drawing onto it}
    OldList.Canvas.MoveTo (OldX, 0);
    OldList.Canvas.LineTo (OldX, ClientHeight);
  end;
  {if the user is not leaving the list box, draw the new line
  and store the older values}
  if not (State = dsDragLeave) then
  begin
    List.Canvas.MoveTo (X, 0);
    List.Canvas.LineTo (X, ClientHeight);
```

```
    OldX := X;
    OldList := List;
  end
  else
  {if the user is leaving the list box, then do *not* draw
  and set old values to nil/invalid}
  begin
    OldX := -10;
    OldList := nil
  end;
end;
procedure TForm1.DeleteDragLine (List: TListBox);
begin
  {delete the old line and reset the invalid position}
  if OldList <> nil then
  begin
    OldList.Canvas.MoveTo (OldX, 0);
    OldList.Canvas.LineTo (OldX, ClientHeight);
    OldX := -10;
    OldList := nil;
  end;
end;
```

Notice that the line-drawing procedure tests the value of the State parameter passed by the dragging event, checked for with dsDragLeave. If the mouse cursor is leaving the list box, then the line is not drawn, and the OldList and OldX private fields of the form are set to nil and a random negative value, respectively. Another important part of the SPLIT4 example is the test to see if the OldList object is currently storing a list box or if it is nil. This test is done before any call to a method of the object. If you don't do this, you risk accessing an undefined object, which will raise an exception.

In the code of the three OnDragOver events, you can see something similar to the code in the SPLIT3 example. We check to see if the list box should accept dragging from the current panel (except for ListBox2, which can accept input from both), and then we also test whether the current position is within the permitted range. When the splitter is in the range, the program calls the line drawing (or even better, *moving*) method. When the splitter goes out of the proper area, the program removes the last line, calling DeleteDragLine.

As usual, to test if the position is valid, we check whether X is less than 40 or whether the last list box has enough space. To make this last check, however, we need to compute the size of the third list box, since it doesn't change continuously during the dragging operation as in the other examples. The simplest way to compute whether the third list box is large enough is to test whether the increase in width (X) will leave it at more than 40 pixels, as you can see in the full listing on the companion CD. Here is a simpler case:

```
procedure TForm1.ListBox1DragOver(Sender, Source: TObject;
  X, Y: Integer; State: TDragState; var Accept: Boolean);
```

```
begin
  Accept := False;
  if Source = Panel1 then
    if X > 40 then
    begin
      Accept := True;
      DrawDragLine (ListBox1, X, State);
    end
    else
      DeleteDragLine (ListBox1);
end;
```

The new width of the list box being dragged is set only when the dragging operation ends, as in the following code:

```
procedure TForm1.ListBox1DragDrop(Sender, Source: TObject;
  X, Y: Integer);
begin
  DeleteDragLine (ListBox1);
  ListBox1.Width := X;
end;
```

As you can see, there is no test of any sort, since dropping can take place only if dragging is allowed. However, in the OnDragDrop method of the second list box, we need to consider which panel originated the dragging:

```
if Source = Panel1 then
  ListBox1.Width := ListBox1.Width + X
else
  ListBox2.Width := X;
```

Although the code of this example is more complex, and it took me some time to devise the whole schema, the effect is worth the effort. A particular challenge was handling the case of two consecutive dragging operations on two different list boxes (which takes place only after a fast mouse movement). To handle this situation, I've introduced the idea of the OldList object.

# Direct Mouse Splitting

The fifth and final version of this same splitting example is less Delphi-oriented and more Windows-oriented. It uses no components other than the list boxes. Without panels or headers, and without the mouse-dragging support offered by Delphi (which is not available in forms), the form must receive and handle mouse events directly. The other disadvantage of this approach is that we need to leave some space between the list boxes, to allow the user to operate on the form, and we lose the automatic alignment features. The advantage is that we have a very precise control, although, in this example, I haven't taken advantage of it to implement a splitter line, as in SPLIT4.

**NOTE**

I decided not to include a sixth version that uses the direct mouse splitting method and implements a splitter line, because five implementations of the same example are boring enough. However, it's important to study the advantages and disadvantages of solving a problem in different ways, and you might want to try this approach on your own.

So here we are with three list boxes and a form. You don't see much of the form, just two small vertical areas we will use as a splitter, as shown in Figure 14.6. The form uses the crHSplit cursor as standard cursor. The SPLIT5 version of the form is not much different from the previous one, although now you can see the background of the form between the list boxes. To make Figure 14.6 more understandable, I've temporarily resized the second list box, to show the form behind it.

When the user presses the left mouse button on the form (that is, on one of the two vertical lines), the program starts some dragging code, which continues until the user releases the mouse button. During this period of time, any mouse movement has the effect of moving the list boxes, simulating a corresponding movement in the splitter area. Before we discuss the code of this example, however, let's take a moment for an overview of implementing dragging and capturing the mouse input.

**FIGURE 14.6:**

The form of the SPLIT5 version at design-time.

# Dragging the Mouse

As we discussed in Chapter 9, in Windows, there are three basic groups of mouse messages: those related to pressing a button, those related to releasing the button, and those related to moving the mouse. Delphi components also add the concept of the left-button click. But there is no concept of dragging. So how can you implement it, and how has Borland implemented it in Delphi? The idea behind dragging is quite simple. The program receives a sequence of button-down, mouse-move, and button-up messages. When the button is pressed, dragging begins, although the real actions take place only when the user moves the mouse (without releasing the mouse button) and when dragging terminates (when the button-up message arrives).

The problem with this basic approach is that since a window usually receives mouse events only when the mouse is over its client area, we cannot build a reliable program. For example, what if the mouse button is pressed, the mouse is moved onto another window, and then the button is released? The second window will receive the button-up message.

There are two solutions to this problem. One (seldom used) is mouse clipping. Using a Windows API function (namely ClipCursor), you can force the mouse not to leave a certain area of the screen. When you move it outside the specified area, it stumbles against an invisible barrier.

The second (more common) solution is to capture the mouse. When a window captures the mouse, all the subsequent mouse input is sent to that window, as we have already seen in Chapter 10 (commenting the FIRE example). This is the approach we will use for the SPLIT5 example.

# The Dragging Code

The code of SPLIT5 is built around three methods: FormMouseDown, FormMouse-Move, and FormMouseUp. Pressing the left mouse button over the form (that is, over a splitter) starts the process, setting a couple of Boolean fields of the form, named Dragging and FirstSplit. The first variable is used to indicate that dragging is in action, and this variable will be used by the other two methods. The second variable indicates which of the two splitters the user is currently dragging (True indicates the first one; False the second).

```
procedure TForm1.FormMouseDown(Sender: TObject;
  Button: TMouseButton; Shift: TShiftState; X, Y: Integer);
begin
  if Button = mbLeft then
  begin
    Dragging := True;
    SetCapture (Handle);
    if (X <= ListBox2.Left) then
```

```
        FirstSplit := True
      else
        FirstSplit := False;
    end;
end;
```

The most important action of this method is the call to the `SetCapture` API function. When dragging is active, as indicated by the corresponding variable (Dragging), and the user moves the mouse, the program performs a number of actions, but the idea is simple: resize the list boxes, unless we are out of range:

```
procedure TForm1.FormMouseMove(Sender: TObject;
  Shift: TShiftState; X, Y: Integer);
begin
  if Dragging then
    if FirstSplit then
      if (X > 40) and
         (X < ClientWidth - ListBox3.Width - 40) then
        begin
          ListBox1.Width := X - 2;
          ListBox2.Left := X + 2;
          ListBox2.Width := ListBox3.Left - ListBox2.Left - 4;
        end
      else {out of range}
        begin
          Dragging := False;
          ReleaseCapture;
        end
    else
      {similar code for the second split}
      ...
end;
```

Notice that this time X is expressed in form coordinates, not the coordinate of the list box over which we are dragging the splitter. If we are within the range, the list boxes are moved and arranged properly. In this example, when the first splitter is dragged, the first list box is enlarged and the second is reduced by a corresponding amount. The third list box is not involved. The behavior is different from the previous example, which emulated the behavior of the Header component. Remember also that some space (4 pixels) should be left free between the list boxes to implement the splitter.

If we move out of the range, the dragging operation terminates, calling the `ReleaseCapture` API function, and setting the value of the Dragging field to False. The same thing happens when the mouse button is released:

```
procedure TForm1.FormMouseUp(Sender: TObject;
  Button: TMouseButton; Shift: TShiftState; X, Y: Integer);
begin
  if Dragging then
    begin
      ReleaseCapture;
```

```
      Dragging := False;
    end;
end;
```

# A Custom File Manager

Now that we have explored dragging techniques in some detail, we can use these techniques to build a complex example. Our final example in this chapter is a File Manager clone that has a preview window for the most common file formats. We will build this File Manager in two steps, working first on the form and on limited file handling capabilities, and then developing the preview window in the second version of the example.

This File Manager won't have all the features we would like included, and it will probably be less usable than the Delphi examples already available with the product. However, you might want to merge the code presented here with some of the code of other File Manager clones, or even better, an Explorer clone, building your own customized version. The key focus of this example is in the preview capabilities, which will be added only in the second version.

## Components Used in the File Manager

As you might guess, the FILEMAN1 example uses all the Delphi file-, disk-, and directory-related components of the System page of the Components palette. There are four of these components:

- DirectoryListBox is a graphical and hierarchical list box, an outline of the directory tree of a certain drive.

- FileListBox is a graphical list box of the files of a certain directory, which match certain properties.

- DriveComboBox is a graphical combo box listing all of the disk drives installed in the system.

- FilterComboBox is a combo box listing the file filters indicated in the Filters property.

You can see all of these components in the form of the FILEMAN1 example in Figure 14.7. One of the most interesting features of these components is that they can be connected using some properties, so that they will automatically work together.

Here is a list of the connections:

- The drive combo box has a DirList property that lets you indicate a connected directory list box. When the current drive changes, the value of the Drive property is copied to the corresponding property of the directory outline.

- The directory list box has a FileList property that lets you indicate a connected file list box, so that the Directory properties of the two components are synchronized. The same list box can also be connected to a label using the DirLabel property. Such a label automatically displays the path of the current directory. You can see a label of this kind in the status bar of the FILE-MAN1 form (see Figure 14.7), which is actually a panel, and not a proper status bar component, because I needed a label inside it.

- The file list box can be connected to an edit box with the FileEdit property, so that a user can enter the name of a file to select it. (I haven't used this connection in our example here.)

- The filter combo box has a FileList property that lets you indicate the connected file list box. When a new filter is selected, the component notifies the file list box of the new value, setting its Mask property.

You make these connections either at design-time or in the code at program startup. I suggest that you make them at design-time, so that the components immediately display live data, as in Figure 14.7.

**FIGURE 14.7:**

The form of the FILEMAN1 example at design-time. Notice that the file components already display live data.

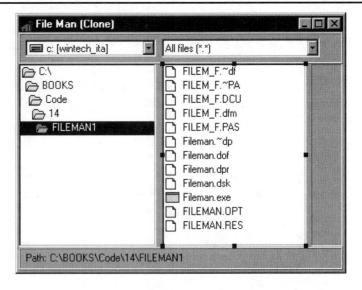

Before reviewing the code, which implements dragging and a few other techniques, let's take a look at some of the important properties of the file list box and filter combo box components. The files actually listed by the file list box depend on two properties: Mask, connected to the filter combo box; and FileType, which indicates the type of files being displayed. The FileType property has a value of the TFileType set, which can be used to indicate whether the list box includes files with the read-only, hidden, archive, or system attributes, and whether it should include the volume name and the sub-directories, shown in square brackets.

In this example, I've used a set with the following value:

```
[ftReadOnly,ftArchive,ftNormal]
```

Removing directory names was particularly important, since a user might be tempted to double-click on them to change the current directory (something you would need to implement in the code). The filter combo box has a Filter property. An important feature of this property, and of the corresponding properties of the standard OpenDialog and SaveDialog components, is that you can specify a file type with multiple extensions, as you can see in Figure 14.8.

**FIGURE 14.8:**

The Filter property editor for the FilterComboBox of the FILEMAN1 example.

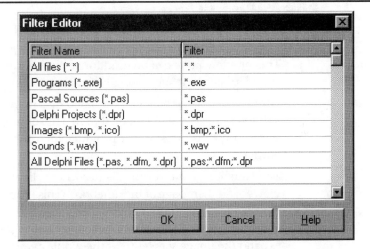

As I've mentioned before, most of this program's code has to do with resizing the components on the form. The code used to accomplish this is similar to the code of the SPLIT5 example. The only differences are that this example includes the status bar and the toolbar, and that the window can be resized (the examples in the SPLIT series use a fixed border). Notice that the toolbar and the status bar are two panels I've named SpeedBar and StatusBar. This makes the code more readable, since it avoids using identifiers such as Panel2, which let the reader wonder what the panel is for and where it is located in the form. You can see the code I've added to handle form resizing properly in the listing on the companion CD.

What is the final aim of this version of the example? If the user double-clicks on an executable file in the file list box, that program is executed. This is done with a few lines of code using the FileListBox1DblClick method. The current file is used as parameter of the WinExec API function, but only if the file extension, retrieved with the ExtractFileExt Delphi function, is .exe. Otherwise, the name of the file is shown in a message box:

```
procedure TForm1.FileListBox1DblClick(Sender: TObject);
var
  FileExt: string;
begin
  FileExt := ExtractFileExt(FileListBox1.Filename);
  if FileExt = '.exe' then
    WinExec (PChar (FileListBox1.Filename), sw_ShowNormal)
  else
    ShowMessage (FileListBox1.Filename);
end;
```

## Adding a Preview Pane to the File Manager

On the right side of the form in the FILEMAN1 example there is a useless panel. It is a placeholder for the preview pane we are going to build now, in FILEMAN2. This preview pane can be used for several different types of files: image, text, and sound, plus a hint suggesting how to run the executable programs.

For this reason, the panel is populated by a number of viewer components, each on a different page of a notebook that fills the entire surface of the panel. The panel itself is almost useless; it just provides the proper three-dimensional effect for the borders.

The Notebook component fills the whole client area of the panel, and most of the viewers fill their page of the notebook. This is an advantage because when the form is resized, these components will be adjusted automatically. As an alternative, I could have added some buttons to the various pages, such as a button to shrink or expand the image viewer to fit the whole available area.

The notebook has five pages with descriptive names. These names are not important, because there isn't a tab set attached. The program changes the page depending on the extension of the current file, when the selection in the file list box changes. Here are the names and a short description of the pages:

- *Image* contains an Image component, used to view bitmap files and icon files (see Figure 14.9).

**FIGURE 14.9:**
The FILEMAN2 example with the Image page of the preview notebook active.

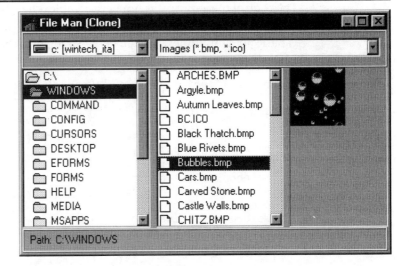

- Text contains a Memo component, used to view any kind of text file, including Windows ini files, Delphi source files, and even old versions of the Delphi source files.

- Sound contains a MediaPlayer component, used to play sound files (wav and mid), and a label with some instructions.

- Exe contains only a label, suggesting that the user double-click on the file in the list box. A button with the same effect—running the file—could be added.

- None is an empty page, used when the file extension is not recognized.

Using a notebook for the preview pane makes this program easily upgradable with new pages that handle other file formats.

> **TIP**
>
> When you work with the form of this program, there are a number of invisible components. For example, if the text page of the notebook is active, the Memo component hides both the notebook and the panel. In this case, the use of the Esc key to navigate the components becomes extremely useful. Each time you press Esc, the component containing the current one will be activated, so you can easily move from the memo to the notebook, from the notebook to the panel, and from the panel to the form.

The code of this example is not very complex. It is the same as the code for the previous version, plus a new method, FileListBox1Change. The code of this procedure is basically a multiple if-then-else statement, checking for the correspondence of the file extension with the predefined values:

```
procedure TForm1.FileListBox1Change(Sender: TObject);
var
  FileExt: string;
begin
  FileExt := LowerCase (ExtractFileExt(
    FileListBox1.Filename));
  if FileExt = '.exe' then
    Notebook1.ActivePage := 'Exe'
  else if (FileExt = '.bmp') or (FileExt = '.ico') then
  begin
    Notebook1.ActivePage := 'Image';
    ImagePreview.Picture.LoadFromFile (FileListBox1.Filename);
  end
  else if (FileExt = '.txt') or (FileExt = '.pas') or
    (FileExt = '.ini') or (FileExt = '.dpr') or
    (FileExt = '.bat') or (FileExt = '.dsk') or
    (FileExt = '.rc') or (FileExt = '.~pa') or
    (FileExt = '.~dp') or (FileExt = '.dof') then
  begin
    Notebook1.ActivePage := 'Text';
    MemoPreview.Lines.LoadFromFile (FileListBox1.Filename);
  end
  else if (FileExt = '.wav') or (FileExt = '.mid') or
    (FileExt = '.avi') then
  begin
    Notebook1.ActivePage := 'Sound';
    MediaPreview.Filename := FileListBox1.Filename;
    MediaPreview.Open;
  end
  else
    Notebook1.ActivePage := 'None'
end;
```

Each of the branches of this compound statement activates one of the pages of the notebook, indicating its name, and most branches also load a file.

The only difference is in the code for the sound files, which just after loading a file calls the Open method to activate it. By the way, I've referred to "sound" files, but, as you can see in the code, video files (avi) are supported too. You only need to have the proper drivers installed. The text viewer is the one that can be used with the most file extensions, but you could also add some more:

- *.txt*, for text files. I have not added other document formats, because in most cases, their content is unreadable. You might add another page with a RichEdit component, and handle the *.rtf* extension.

- *.pas*, for Pascal source code files.

- *.ini*, for Windows ini files.

- *.dpr*, for Delphi project files, which are text files with Pascal source code (see Figure 14.10 for an example).

- *.bat*, for DOS batch files. You could add an option to run these files.

- *.dsk*, for Delphi desktop information files, which are text files.

- *.dof*, for Delphi options files, which are actually ini files in disguise.

- *.rc*, for Windows resource files, found in some of the Delphi libraries and source code.

- *.~pa*, for the backup versions of Delphi Pascal files.

- *.~dp*, for the backup versions of Delphi project files.

**FIGURE 14.10:**

A Delphi project file loaded in the viewer of the FILEMAN2 example.

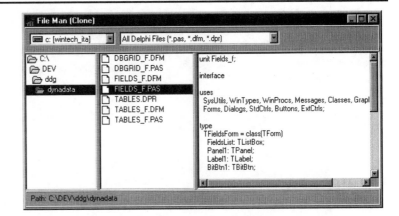

The preview pane of this example can be useful for browsing through a series of files, even if they have different extensions. Of course, it can handle only the basic formats. Supporting other formats requires coding, and doesn't come for free as in the cases we have seen. The only real drawback of this immediate preview approach is that long files take a while to load, and if you select an unwanted file, you must wait until it is loaded. This mainly depends on Windows, an operating environment with very limited concurrency. When you are loading a file in Windows, you need to wait until the end of the operation to regain control. A solution might be to check the file size, and for big files, display a warning and wait for a specific action by the user to load the file in the preview pane.

# Summary

In this chapter, we have explored several techniques to implement form splitting. These techniques include the use of the HeaderControl and Header components, some panels placed between other components, and direct handling of the mouse messages.

Now that you have seen the use of multiple windows, dialog boxes, notebooks, and scrolling, the next step in the development of complex applications is the Windows MDI approach, described in the next chapter. A component we have just mentioned in this chapter is the MediaPlayer. I'll come back to it and provide some more details in Chapter 26.

# FIFTEEN

# Creating MDI Applications

- Frame and child windows

- The Window menu

- MDI with multiple child windows

- A child window with a bouncing square

- The MDI Application template

**S**o far, we've covered how to handle simple Delphi applications that have a single main form, as well as more complex applications that have a number of different forms and dialog boxes. We have also seen that scrolling, splitting, and layering (that is, using notebooks) are techniques you can use to display a lot of information and components in a single form.

Besides using dialog boxes, or secondary forms, and squeezing components into a form, there is a third approach that is common in Windows applications: *MDI* (*Multiple Document Interface*). MDI applications are made up of a number of forms that appear inside a single main form. In this chapter, we'll start with some general and technical information about MDI development in Windows. Then we'll build an MDI program in Delphi step by step. We'll also explore using Delphi's MDI Application template to generate the initial code of an MDI application.

# MDI in Windows: A Technical Overview

In the early days of Windows, each application was made up of a number of different windows floating around the screen. This was with the second version of the environment, since the first version of the Microsoft operating system could only *tile* its windows, not overlap them. A few years later, Microsoft introduced a technique to have a full-blown window (we might call it a *form*) living inside another window, usually called the *frame*. This model is known as Multiple Document Interface (or MDI) because an application generally uses a *child window* for each document. If you use Windows Notepad, you can open only one text document, because Notepad isn't an MDI application. But with your favorite word processor, you can probably open a number of different documents, each in its own child window, because it is an MDI application. All these windows referring to the documents are usually held by a *frame*, or *application*, window. Although it is quite common to think of MDI as a technique for allowing users to work on a number of documents or files at the same time, this is not always the case.

In Windows 3.1, the Program Manager and File Manager, for example, used MDI to display system information, not documents. Other applications use MDI to display various views of the same data in different windows.

**NOTE**

When Windows 3.0 was released, Microsoft really stressed the use of MDI. By the time Windows 3.1 came out, Microsoft had acknowledged that the implementation of MDI was flawed, and that many users were not comfortable with the interface. With the advent of different approaches to the user interface, and particularly with the release of Windows 95, MDI is becoming less common. For example, the Explorer is an SDI (*Single Document Interface*) application. However, MDI won't disappear too quickly, because there are simply too many applications following this approach, and the interface has become familiar to many users.

This section provides a short overview of MDI, in technical Windows terms. Just forget Delphi for a moment, and I'll try to give you an idea of what MDI really is (not what an MDI application looks like). If you've never built an MDI application and you want a quick start, you might consider skipping this section, at least the first time you read the book.

You know that the idea behind MDI is to have a child window similar to a main window, but placed inside another window. What you might not know is that to make this work, Windows requires a complex structure. If you simply place a window inside another one as a child window, a lot of strange things happen. If you don't believe me, try running the CHILD example. Figure 15.1 shows the output of this application. When you run this program, you'll find that things are funny

**FIGURE 15.1:**
The output of the CHILD application. It looks like an MDI application, but doesn't work like one.

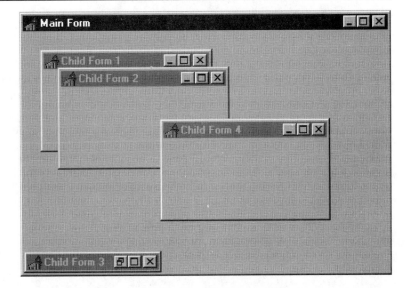

when you try to work with the windows. Notice that the active child window does not have an active title bar. Clicking inside the client area of the child window doesn't activate it. Maximizing a child window has a weird effect.

This example defines two forms: a main form and a child form. When the user clicks in the main form, a new child form is created, with the following code:

```
procedure TMainForm.FormClick(Sender: TObject);
var
  NewForm: TChildForm;
begin
  {increase the child window counter}
  Inc (Counter);
  {create a new form and define it as child of the current form}
  NewForm := TChildForm.Create (self);
  NewForm.Parent := self;
  {add the number to the caption, and move it slightly}
  NewForm.Caption := NewForm.Caption + ' ' + IntToStr (Counter);
  NewForm.Left := Counter * 20;
  NewForm.Top := Counter * 20;
  {show the form}
  NewForm.Show;
end;
```

In this procedure, Counter is an integer, a private field of the form, and TChildForm is the data type of the form defined in a second unit, CHILD_F.PAS. This second form is a plain default form, without any special properties, as is the main form. The Counter value is used to give a different name to each form, and to make sure that they won't all be placed in the same position. But the key element of the program is the line NewForm.Parent := self, which assigns to the Parent property of the new form the main form, self. This makes the new form a child of the main window.

As you can see, this program seems like an MDI application, but it is not. Some of its problems are that the active child doesn't have an active title bar, the child windows are moved to the front only if you select their borders, and the child windows are not maximized properly. Note that this strange behavior is not Delphi's fault. It is the default (although wrong) Windows behavior. This misbehaving application can be corrected by handling a number of Windows messages to make it resemble the default behavior, but there is an easier solution: use the MDI approach. MDI was introduced to fix just these kinds of problems.

Although the MDI structure is not simple, it gives programmers a number of benefits automatically. For example, Windows handles a list of the child windows in one of the pull-down menus of the application, and there are specific Delphi methods that activate the corresponding MDI functionality, to tile or cascade the child windows. The following is the technical structure of an MDI application in Windows:

- The main window of the application acts as a frame, or a container. This window requires a proper menu structure and some specific coding (at least when programming with the API).

- A special window, known as the *MDI client,* covers the whole client area of the frame window, providing some special capabilities. For example, the MDI client handles the list of child windows. Although this might seem strange at first, this MDI client is one of the Windows predefined components, just like an edit box or a list box. The MDI client window does not have the typical elements of the interface of a window, such as a caption or border, but it is visible. In fact, you can change the standard system color of the MDI work area (called "Application Background") in the Appearance page of the Display Properties dialog box of Windows 95.

- A number of child windows, of the same kind or of different kinds. These child windows are not placed in the frame window directly, but each is defined as a child of the MDI client window, which in turn is a child of the frame window. (We might say that the child windows are the nephews of the frame, but this might confuse the matter instead of clearing it up.)

When you program using the Windows API, some work is usually required to build and maintain this structure, and other coding is needed to handle the menu properly. As you'll see in this chapter, these tasks become much easier with Delphi.

# Frame and Child Windows in Delphi

Delphi makes the development of MDI applications easy, even without considering the MDI application template. You only need to build at least two forms, one with the FormStyle property set to `fsMDIForm`, and the other with the same property set to `fsMDIChild`. That's all, almost.

## A First Delphi MDI Demo

Once the two forms have these two values for the Style property, which is set by default to `fsNormal`, you need to provide a way to create one or more child windows. This can be done by adding a menu with a New menu item and writing the following code:

```
procedure TMainForm.New1Click(Sender: TObject);
var
  ChildForm: TChildForm;
```

```
begin
  ChildForm := TChildForm.Create (Application);
  ChildForm.Show;
end;
```

> **NOTE**
>
> When you create a new form you can pass either `Application` or the parent form (`self`) as parameter of the Create constructor. Most of the time, a program will work fine in both cases, but there are some differences. The parameter you pass indicates the owner of the form, the one that will destroy the form when it is closed. In some cases this relationship also affects the behavior of the windows (for example when you minimize one), particularly in an application with many forms.

In the above code, I've named the two forms MainForm and ChildForm. Since you refer to the TChildForm class, the unit defining it should be included in this source code. In the MDIDEMO1 example, this second file is simply CHILD.PAS.

To create an even better program, you can name the pull-down menu containing this item Window, and use it as value of the WindowMenu property of the form. Of course, you can choose any other name for the menu item, but *Window* is standard. With these simple operations, which might require less than a minute, I have built the first MDI demo program.

To make this program work properly, we need to take a few more steps. First, notice that only the first form (the main form) should be created automatically at startup. You can set this in the Forms page of the Project Options dialog box. Then, we can add a number to the title of any child window when it is created:

```
procedure TMainForm.New1Click(Sender: TObject);
var
  ChildForm: TChildForm;
begin
  WindowMenu := Window1;
  Inc (Counter);
  ChildForm := TChildForm.Create (self);
  ChildForm.Caption := ChildForm.Caption + ' ' +
    IntToStr (Counter);
  ChildForm.Show;
end;
```

This first version of the MDIDEMO application performs some of the common tasks of MDI applications. Figure 15.2 shows an example of this program's output. You can open a number of child windows, minimize or maximize each of them, close them, and use the Window pull-down menu to navigate among them.

**FIGURE 15.2:**

An example of the output of the
MDIDEMO1 program.

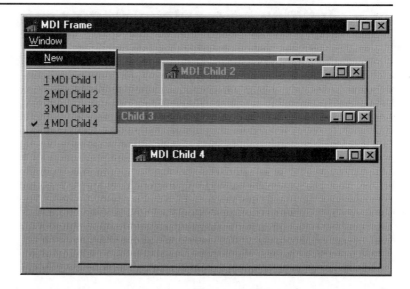

As you can see in Figure 15.2, Delphi has already added the list of child windows, using their names, in the Window menu. If you create more than nine child windows, a More Windows menu item is added to the pull-down menu; when you select this menu item, you'll see a dialog box (provided by Windows, not part of your program) with a complete list of the child windows.

Now suppose that we want to close some of these child windows, to unclutter the client area of our program. Double-click on the system menu box of some of the child windows and they are minimized! What is happening here? Remember that when you close a window, you generally hide it from view. The closed forms in Delphi still exist, although they are not visible. In the case of child windows, simply hiding them won't work, because the MDI Window menu and the list of windows will still list existing child windows, even if they are hidden. For this reason, Delphi simply minimizes the MDI child windows when you try to close them. To solve this problem, we need to delete the child windows when they are closed, as we will do in the next version of this example.

MDIDEMO1 has another problem: its Window pull-down menu is somewhat bare. We should add some commands to tile or cascade the child windows, and to arrange their icons. This is standard in any Windows MDI application, and it is simple to implement in Delphi.

# Building a Complete Window Menu

Our first task is to define a better menu structure for the example. Here you can see the typical structure of this menu, taken from the textual description of the main form of the MDIDEMO2 example:

```
object Window1: TMenuItem
  Caption = '&Window'
  object Cascade1: TMenuItem
    Caption = '&Cascade'
  end
  object Tile1: TMenuItem
    Caption = '&Tile'
  end
  object ArrangeIcons1: TMenuItem
    Caption = '&Arrange Icons'
  end
end
```

To handle the menu commands, we can use some of the predefined methods that are available in forms that have the fsMDIForm value for the FormStyle property:

- The Cascade method cascades the open MDI child windows. The child forms are arranged starting from the upper-left corner of the client area of the frame windows, and moving toward the lower-left corner. The windows overlap each other. Iconized child windows are also arranged (see Arrange-Icons below).

- The Tile procedure tiles the open MDI child windows. The child forms are arranged so that they do not overlap. The client area of the frame windows is divided into equal portions for the different windows, so that they can all be shown on the screen, no matter how many windows there are. Figure 15.3 shows an example of five child windows tiled on the screen. Iconized child windows are also arranged. The default behavior is horizontal tiling, although if you have several child windows, they will be arranged in several columns. This default can be changed by using the TileMode property.

- The TileMode property determines how the Tile procedure should work. The only two choices are tbHorizontal, for horizontal tiling, and tbVertical, for vertical tiling. Some applications use two different menu commands for the two tiling modes; other applications check whether the Shift key is pressed when the user selects the only Tile menu command.

- The ArrangeIcons procedure arranges all the iconized child windows, starting from the lower-left corner of the client area of the frame window, and moving to the upper-right corner. Open forms are not moved.

**FIGURE 15.3:**

An example of child window tiling in MDIDEMO2.

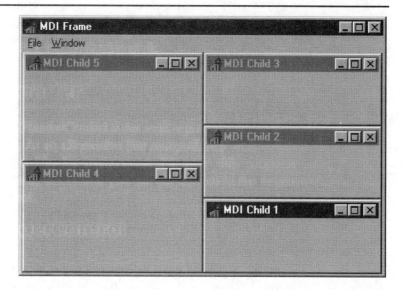

These procedures and properties are useful for handling the Window menu of an MDI application. For example you can write the following code:

```
procedure TMainForm.Cascade1Click(Sender: TObject);
begin
  Cascade;
end;
```

The other menu command handlers of the program are simple, too. There are also some other interesting methods and properties related strictly to MDI in Delphi:

- ActiveMDIChild is a run-time and read-only property of the MDI frame form, and holds the active child window. The value can be changed by the user of the program by selecting a new child window or by the program using the Next and Previous procedures.

- The Next procedure activates the child window following the active one in the internal order.

- The Previous procedure activates the child window preceding the active one in the internal order.

- The ClientHandle property holds the Windows handle of the MDI client window, which covers the client area of the main form.

- The MDIChildCount property stores the current number of child windows.

- The MDIChildren property is an array of child windows. You can use this and the MDIChildCount property to cycle among all of the child windows, for example using a `for` loop. This can be useful for finding a particular child window, or to operate on each of them.

Note that the internal order of the child windows is the reverse order of activation. This means that the last child window that has been selected is the active window (the first in the internal list), the second-to-last child window that has been selected is the second, and the first child window that has been selected is the last. This order determines how the windows are arranged on the screen. The first window in the list is the one above all others, while the last window is below all others, and probably hidden away. You can imagine an axis (the Z axis) coming out of the screen towards you. The active window has a higher value for the Z coordinate, and thus covers other windows. For this reason, the Windows ordering schema is known as the *Z-order*.

To make the list of child windows work properly, we need to add a few lines of code to the OnClose event of the child window, as mentioned earlier:

```
procedure TChildForm.FormClose(Sender: TObject;
  var Action: TCloseAction);
begin
  Action := caFree;
end;
```

Up to now, we have focused on the frame window, but the form used for the child windows has no components and very little code. The frame window usually doesn't change much in the different MDI examples (besides having a toolbar, a status bar, and similar enhancements). Usually, most of the code goes in the child forms. Now it's time to look into a real example of using child windows.

## Building a Child Window

In the last two examples, we have seen how to build the structure of an MDI application in Delphi, focusing on the frame window. Thus, we've obtained a program with the typical MDI behavior, but no real functionality. What can we do with the child form? The answer is anything we can do with a form. We can add a number of components, build editors, add graphics programs, and so on. Any of the programs we have built up to now could be turned into an MDI application (although this wouldn't make much sense for some of them).

Our first example is an MDI version of a simple graphical program (similar to the second version of the SHAPE program we built in Chapter 9), named MDIDEMO3. This program can display a circle in the position where the user clicked one of the mouse buttons. Figure 15.4 shows an example of the output of the MDIDEMO3 example. The program includes a Circle menu, which allows the user to change the

**FIGURE 15.4:**

The output of the MDIDEMO3 example, with a child window that displays circles and a flexible menu bar. Notice the different menu bars at startup and when a child window has been created.

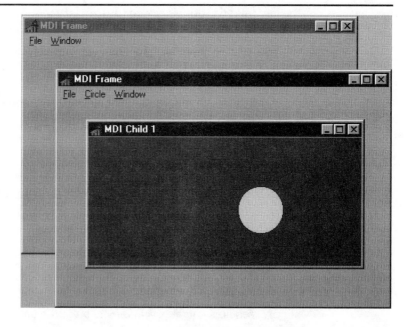

color of the surface of the circle, as well as the color and size of its border. What is interesting here is that to program the child form, we do not need to consider the existence of other forms or of the frame window. We simply write the code of the form, and that's all. The only special care required is for the menus of the two forms.

If we prepare a main menu for the child form, once this is displayed on the screen, it replaces the main menu of the frame window. An MDI child window, in fact, cannot have a menu of its own. But the fact that a child window can't have any menus should not bother you, because this is the standard behavior of MDI applications. You can use the menu bar of the frame window to display the menus of the child window. Even better, you can merge the menu bar of the frame window and that of the child form. For example, in this program, the menu of the child form can be placed between the frame window's File and Window pull-down menus. You can accomplish this by using the following group index values:

- File pull-down menu, main form: 1

- Help pull-down menu, main form: 3

- Circle pull-down menu, child form: 2

Using these settings for the menu group indexes, the menu bar of the frame window will have either two or three pull-down menus. At startup, the menu bar has two menus. As soon as you create a child window, there are three menus, and when the last child window is closed (destroyed), the Circle pull-down menu disappears. You can see this in Figure 15.4, but you should also spend some time testing this behavior by running the program.

The source code of the main form is the same as for the previous version of the program. The code of the child window has been only slightly changed from Chapter 9. If you look at the source code (on the companion CD), it is interesting to notice how the menu commands of the running program pertain to the two forms, and that in the source code, each form handles its own commands, regardless of the existence of other elements.

The data of the child form, particularly the values of the center of the circle, must be declared using some fields of the form, and not other variables declared inside the unit. In fact, we need specific memory location to store the center of the circle for each child window.

> **NOTE**
>
> Storing the child form's data is simple to implement in Delphi, but not in Windows programming using the API. Traditional Windows code requires complex schemes to store the data of the child windows of an MDI application. I'll spare you the details, but I thought you should be aware of this great advantage of object-oriented programming in a not truly object-oriented operating system and user interface.

# MDI Applications with Different Child Windows

A common approach in complex MDI applications is to include child windows of different kinds (that is, based on different child forms). We can extend the previous example to highlight some problems you may encounter with this approach. For this example, we need to build a new child form. Any form would do, but I wanted to use this example to show you something new: limited multitasking. Therefore, I decided to use a form that contains a bouncing square.

## Adding a Bouncing Shape

The square, a Shape component, moves around the client area of the form at fixed time intervals, using a Timer component, and bounces on the edges of the form, changing its direction. This turning process is determined by a fairly complex (compared with most of the examples in this book) algorithm. The idea is that the square has its own position and is associated with a Dir (direction) value—another member of the form class—which can assume one of the following values:

```
type
  Directions = (up_right, down_right, down_left, up_left);
```

When the time period elapses, the square is moved in the corresponding direction:

```
procedure TBounceChildForm.Timer1Timer(Sender: TObject);
begin
  case Dir of
    up_right: begin
      Shape1.Left := Shape1.Left + 3;
      Shape1.Top := Shape1.Top - 3;
    end;
    down_right: begin
      Shape1.Left := Shape1.Left + 3;
      Shape1.Top := Shape1.Top + 3;
    end;
    ...
  end;
end;
```

This accounts for the movement. The real problem is to make the square bounce on the edges of the form. In short, each time the square reaches an edge, we must change its direction. To determine when the shape has reached an edge, you can check its top and right values against zero and the bottom and right values against the size of the client area. The bottom and right values are not directly available, but you can compute them by adding the height of the shape to its top value (or the width to the left value):

```
if Shape1.Top <= 0 then ...
if Shape1.Top + Shape1.Height >= ClientHeight then ...
if Shape1.Left <= 0 then ...
if Shape1.Left + Shape1.Width >= ClientWidth ...
```

You might try making these checks at the end of the code in order to increase the current values, but that would not work. In fact, to make the square move gracefully, you should choose a good (and more complex) pattern. For example, suppose that we want each turn to be at 90 degrees, so that the square doesn't bounce back in the same direction as its approach, as illustrated in Figure 15.5.

**FIGURE 15.5:**

The proper path of the Shape object, which should turn 90 degrees each time it bounces against a border.

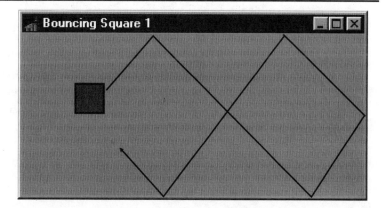

The idea is that if the form is itself a square, the shape should always move clockwise, or always counterclockwise, depending on the initial direction. If the form is a rectangle, the two kinds of turns alternate, as you can see in Figure 15.5. (Of course, you can see this behavior in action by running the MDIDEMO4 program, but if you can't reach your computer right now, the static figure will give you the general idea.) To obtain this behavior, we need to write some code to change the current direction in each of the different branches of the case statement mentioned before. In fact, the next direction of the square when it has reached a border of the form depends on the current direction. Here is a portion of the code of the OnTimer response function (the complete code is available on the CD):

```
case Dir of
  up_right:
  begin
    {move the shape}
    Shape1.Left := Shape1.Left + 3;
    Shape1.Top := Shape1.Top - 3;
    {if it has reached one of the borders,
    make it turn properly}
    if Shape1.Top <= 0 then
      Dir := down_right;
    if Shape1.Left + Shape1.Width >= ClientWidth then
      Dir := up_left;
  end;
  ...
```

# The Menu Bar of the New Child Form

Like any child form, the one in our example will have its own menu bar, which is merged with the menu bar of the frame window. The menu structure is quite simple, although it has two different pull-down menus. The first menu, Square, has two commands to change the color of the square or to retrieve its position.

The code to respond to these menu commands is quite simple. Since we use the color selection dialog box for only one color (the color used to fill the square), we don't need to store it in a separate variable. Of course, we need to initialize this value, along with the starting direction, in the FormCreate method. The GetPosition method is similar to the one of the other child form.

The second menu, Movements, has two commands to start or stop the movement of the shape. This can be accomplished easily by enabling or disabling the timer. Besides this, each of the two procedures disables the corresponding command, and enables the opposite one (it makes no sense to start a moving shape, or stop one that has already been stopped).

## Changing the Main Form

Now that the bouncing square form is complete, we need to integrate it into the MDI application. The main form must provide a menu command to create a child form of this new kind and to check the group indexes of the pull-down menus. I've slightly changed the structure of the menu of this form. The File pull-down menu here has a second New menu item, which is used to create a child window of the new kind. The code uses the same child window counter of the other form. As an alternative, you could use two different counters for the two kinds of child windows.

As soon as a form of this kind is displayed on the screen, its menu bar is automatically merged with the main menu bar. When you select a child form of one of the two kinds, the menu bar changes accordingly. Once all the child windows are closed, the original menu bar of the main form is reset. By using the proper menu group indexes, everything is accomplished automatically by Delphi, as you can see in the two windows shown in Figure 15.6.

**FIGURE 15.6:**

The menu bar at the MDIDEMO4 application changes automatically to reflect the currently selected child window.

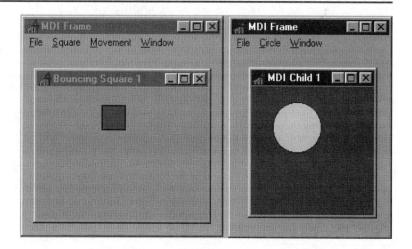

I've added a few other new menu items in the main form. One menu choice is used to close every child window, a second tiles the child windows horizontally instead of vertically, and another shows some statistics about them. The methods connected to these menu items use some specific MDI properties of the form, such as the TileMode property, the MDIChildCount property, and the MDIChildren array. Two of these methods are quite interesting, because they show how to take an action on each of the child windows. For example, the CloseAll1Click procedure has the following code:

```
Total := MDIChildCount - 1;
for I := 0 to Total do
  MDIChildren [0].Close;
```

To close every child window, you can't refer to the child window by number. Instead, you should always calculate the first one. In fact, as you close windows, their forms are deleted (because they have the Action parameter of the FormClose method set to caFree) and the structure of the array changes immediately.

Another example is in the method related to the Count command. In this procedure, the array is scanned to count the number of child windows of each kind. This is accomplished using the is RTTI operator:

```
for I := 0 to MDIChildCount - 1 do
  if MDIChildren [I] is TBounceChildForm then
    Inc (NBounce)
  else
    Inc (NCircle);
```

Once these values are computed, they are shown on the screen with the MessageDlg function, as you can see in Figure 15.7.

**FIGURE 15.7:**

The output of the Count menu command of the MDIDEMO4 example, indicating the number of child windows of each kind.

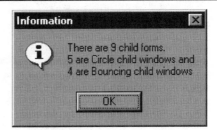

# A Fast Start with MDI

In this chapter, we have built some MDI applications in Delphi from scratch. Taking this approach allowed us to learn the details of MDI in Windows and of Delphi's support for this approach. However, the "from-scratch" approach is not the best way to go when you need to build a real MDI application. Delphi provides an MDI Application template, and you can also use one of the Experts to build the initial code of an MDI application quickly. We'll look at the framework each of these tools produces, and then see how to build an application starting with the code generated by Delphi.

To use the MDI Application template, just issue the File ➤ New command in the Delphi environment, choose the Projects page, and then MDI Application. Select a directory for the project, and Delphi will copy the files you need for a simple MDI application, with a toolbar, a status bar, and a menu, into that directory (I've reported the generated files in the MDITEMP directory of the current chapter, together with the generated executable file, for your convenience).

The form generated by the template contains standard elements: a main menu, a Panel used as toolbar, a StatusBar component, and some system dialog boxes.

The source code of the form has some interesting elements. I suggest you generate the code and study it with some care. First, notice the code of the FormCreate method:

```
procedure TMainForm.FormCreate(Sender: TObject);
begin
  Application.OnHint := ShowHint;
  Screen.OnActiveFormChange := UpdateMenuItems;
end;
```

The first statement activates the hints at the application level, as we have seen in Chapter 11. It works together with the ShowHint procedure, which displays the hints in the StatusBar component. The second statement of the FormCreate method is something new. What is the Screen object? What is this OnActiveFormChange event? You might remember that I've used the Screen global object in a couple of programs in earlier chapters. This object provides access to the list of fonts installed in the system. The Screen object handles a lot of information related to the output of the application, including the available fonts and a list of the forms in the application. We will see some more details about the TScreen class in Chapter 19. For the moment, it is enough to know that the OnActivateFormChange event takes place each time the active form of the application changes.

The OnActivateFormChange event refers to the active form or window of the application, not the active application. In other words, this event is not activated when the user changes the active window among all of the Windows applications that are running; the event is activated when the user changes the active form within the current application. It is an application-wide event, not a system-wide one. To execute some code when the active Windows application changes, you can use the OnActivate event of the Application object. Do not confuse this with the OnActivate event of a form, which takes place when the form itself becomes active. You can use the OnActivateFormChange event of the Screen object instead of the OnActivate event of each of the different forms, obtaining a similar effect.

As with events of the Application object, events of the Screen object must be set in the code. Notice that this operation is canceled, setting the event to nil, inside the FormDestroy method. By the way, the effect of the UpdateMenuItems procedure is to enable or disable some of the menu items when there are no more child windows.

Another interesting part of the source code generated by Delphi is the way file opening is handled. There is a CreateMDIChild method, responsible for creating a new child form and giving it a title, using the value of its parameter:

```
Child := TMDIChild.Create(Application);
Child.Caption := Name;
```

This method is called by the procedure related to both the New and Open commands on the File menu:

```
procedure TMainForm.FileOpenItemClick(Sender: TObject);
begin
  if OpenDialog.Execute then
    CreateMDIChild(OpenDialog.FileName);
end;
```

The files are not automatically opened: only the file name is used! You might extend this by merging into this program the code of the NOTES example we have built throughout the book, that of an example using the RichEdit component (there is one among Delphi own examples), or that of an image viewer example. This is really not too difficult to do, but is not fully in the spirit of Windows 95. In this environment, you should try to open a specific window—run a copy of the program—for each file you are working on.

# Summary

There are many things we could do to further explore MDI support in Windows, but I think that this chapter is enough for an overview. In particular, I've decided not to show you more MDI examples, because this kind of model is being de-emphasized in Windows 95. With this chapter, we have concluded the specific study of multiple-form applications, which we started in Chapter 12 when we explored secondary forms (modal and modeless) and dialog boxes. We have also seen some examples of notebook-based applications, the use of form-splitting techniques, and in this chapter, MDI.

In some cases, each of these techniques are valid solutions, so you will need to decide which approach to use. I've given equal coverage to each of these techniques, although I have my preferences: few secondary forms, more dialog boxes, a little MDI if it is needed, and notebooks whenever possible. Now we can go back to components, namely OCX components, and then move to one of the hottest topics in Delphi programming: building database applications.

# CHAPTER

# SIXTEEN

# Using OLE Controls

- Differences between OLE Controls and Delphi components

- Using OLE Controls in Delphi

- Installing an OLE Control in Delphi

**M**icrosoft's Visual Basic was the first program-development environment to introduce the idea of supplying software components to the mass market. The concept of reusable software components is older than Visual Basic, and it relates to the theories of object-oriented programming. However, OOP languages never delivered the reusability they promised, probably more because of marketing and standardization problems than for any other reasons. Although Visual Basic does not fully exploit object-oriented programming, it applies the concept of a component through the definition of a standard way to build and distribute new controls that developers can integrate into the environment. The first standard promoted by Visual Basic was the VBX standard, a 16-bit standard fully available in the 16-bit version of Delphi. Moving to the 32-bit platforms, Microsoft has replaced the VBX standard with the more powerful (and more open) OLE controls (OCXs for short) standard.

Delphi takes a further step with its own components: it allows you to build components in a truly OOP way. Delphi components have inheritance, something that is missing in both Visual Basic and OLE controls. Delphi's encapsulation of OLE controls even allows you to inherit a new Delphi component from an existing OCX, adding new properties or capabilities. This short chapter shows how OLE controls can be used in Delphi.

**NOTE**   The reason this chapter is short is that we are focusing on using OLE Controls, not creating them, and although some versions of Delphi include the trial versions of some OCXs, writing many examples of using components simply highlights the capabilities of the specific component, not of Delphi itself. Although the chapter is short, this topic is really a very important one, and this is the reason I've devoted a specific chapter to it.

We'll begin with a definition of an OCX, followed by a discussion of the differences between Delphi components and OLE controls. Then we'll look at some simple examples that use the OLE controls included in the Delphi package.

# What Is an OLE Control?

From a general perspective, an OLE control is not very different from a Windows, Delphi, or Visual Basic control. A control is always a window, with its associated code defining its behavior. The key difference between various families of controls is the interaction between the control and the rest of the application, the interface of the control. Typical Windows controls use a message-based interface, VBX controls use properties and events, OLE automation objects use properties and methods, and OLE controls use properties, methods, and events. This is also the case for Delphi's own components.

Using OLE jargon, an OLE control is a "compound document object which is implemented as an in-process server DLL, and supports OLE automation, visual editing, and inside-out activation." So now you know everything—or did this definition confuse you, too? I'll rephrase this definition with my own words.

An OLE control uses the same approach as OLE objects, which are the objects you can insert into a document, such as a graph embedded into the document written with a word processor. *Embedding* means that the data is actually inside the document, so the data of an OCX is stored by the application using it, the OLE control container (for example, Delphi and our applications). Some OLE container applications can indeed include OLE controls, although they cannot use all of the capabilities of an OCX. (By the way, I'll discuss building OLE containers using Delphi in Chapter 25.)

A difference between a generic OLE server and an OLE control is that servers can be implemented in three different ways:

- as stand-alone applications (for example, Microsoft Excel)

- as out-of-process servers—that is, executables files that cannot be run by themselves, but can only be invoked by a server (for example, Microsoft Graph, and other similar applications)

- as in-process servers, such as DLLs loaded into the same memory space of the program using them

OLE controls can only be implemented using the last technique, which is fortunately the fastest.

Furthermore, OLE controls are OLE automation servers (also discussed in Chapter 25). This means you can access properties of these objects and call some methods. The OLE automation interface lacks events, which are added by the OLE control interface. This makes the OCX interface specification similar to that of Delphi components.

You can see an OLE control in the application that is using it and interact with it directly in the container application window, and not in a separate window: this is the meaning of the term *visual editing*, or *in-place activation*. A single click activates the control, rather than a double-click, and the control is active whenever it is visible (which is what the term *inside-out activation* means).

As I've mentioned before, an OCX has properties, methods, and events. Properties can be state identifiers, but they also activate methods (particularly for OCX controls that are *updated* VBX controls, because in a VBX there was no other way to activate a method other than setting a property), and they can refer to aggregate values, arrays, sub-objects, and so on. Properties can also be dynamic (or read-only, to use the Delphi term). Properties are divided into different groups: stock properties that most controls need to implement; ambient properties that offer information about the container (something similar to the ParentXxx properties of Delphi); extended properties managed by the container, such as the position of the object; and custom properties, which can be anything. It is not very important to know these differences, since we are focusing on using OLE components in Delphi, not writing them.

Events and methods are...well, events and methods. *Events* relate to a mouse click, a key press, the activation of a component, or specific user actions. *Methods* are functions and procedures related to the control. There is no major difference between events and methods in OLE and Delphi terms.

## OLE Controls versus Delphi Components

Before I show you how to use OLE components in Delphi, let's go over some of the technical differences between the two kinds of controls. OLE controls are DLL-based (DLLs will be discussed in Chapter 28). This means that when you use them, you need to distribute their code (the OCX file) along with the application using them. In Delphi, the code of the components is statically linked to the executable file. This single file contains everything. Someone might claim that having a separate file is better, because it allows you to share code among different applications, as DLLs usually do. This is true. If two applications use the same control, you need only one copy of it on the hard disk and a single copy in memory. The drawback, however, is that if the two programs have to use two different versions of the OLE control, a number of compatibility problems might arise.

Another advantage of the Delphi approach is that it tends to be slightly faster (although the executable files tend to be bigger in comparison). You will also have fewer problems building an installation program. The other difference relates to licensees of OCX and Delphi components. When you distribute an OCX file, you might need to pay a royalty. More commonly, you are allowed to distribute a slightly different version of the OCX, or are prohibited from distributing a separate license file. There are a number of solutions to this problem that you could consider, but I won't discuss them in this book. The point I want to make is that there are no such problems in Delphi. Components are embedded in the final application, and there is no way to use them for further development without having the original files.

Now, what is the drawback of using Delphi components? The real problem is that there are fewer Delphi components than OCXs, although there are a number of powerful Delphi components, and if you use several development environments, you might want to buy one of the components and use it in each of them (since Delphi components will only work in Delphi, but OCXs will work in many environments). You can only do this with a standard component. However, if you develop mainly or only in Delphi and find two similar components, I suggest you buy the Delphi one, because it will be more integrated with the environment and easier to use for a Delphi programmer. The native Delphi component will probably be better documented (from the Pascal perspective), and it will take advantage of Delphi and Object Pascal features not available in the general OLE interface, which is typically based on C.

# OLE Controls in Delphi

Delphi comes with some pre-installed OLE controls, and you can buy and install more third-party OCXs easily. Actually, the OCXs included in Delphi have been made by third parties, not by Borland. For the reasons mentioned above (i.e., I don't know which OLE Controls you are going to use, which version of Delphi you have, and which bundled OCXs), I will describe how OLE Controls work in general and show you a only couple of very simple examples.

## Installing a New OLE Control

Although I've made my point about which type of controls I consider easier to use, we still must deal with the reality that you may need to use other kinds. There are many OLE controls that provide valuable capabilities not available in Delphi native components, at least for the time being.

This means that you may need to install new OLE controls in Delphi to make them visible to the system. Here is an overview of the installation process:

1. Select Components ➤ Install in the Delphi menu. This opens the Install Components dialog box (see Figure 16.1). To install new Delphi components (as we will do in Chapter 27), you can click on the Add button. For OLE Controls, click on the OCX button.

2. In the Import OLE Control dialog box (also shown in Figure 16.1), you can see a list of OLE components registered in Delphi. You can press the Register button to add new OCX files, usually found in the WINDOW\SYSTEM directory.

3. The lower part of the Import OLE Controls dialog box allows you to specify a file name for the Object Pascal interface to the OLE control. You can also see (or edit) the class name and choose a page on the Components Palette for the new component. Clicking on OK generates the Pascal interface for the OLE control.

**FIGURE 16.1:**

The dialog boxes used to install new components and new OLE controls in Delphi.

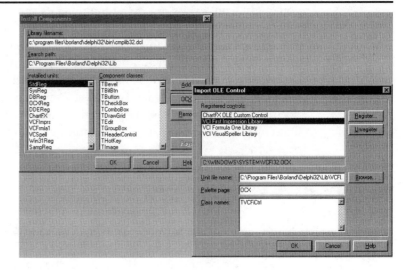

4. Once you have closed the Import OLE Controls dialog box, you can close the Install Components dialog box, and Delphi will rebuild its component library (the VCL) immediately, adding the new OLE control. Of course, this takes some time.

5. When the operation is complete, move to the Components palette, and you'll see the new component. Place it in a new form, and you are ready to use it (assuming you know how or have some documentation).

The Object Pascal source code file that resulted from the installation contains a definition of the class that wraps the OLE control. This class defines the same properties of the control itself, as well as some properties that are shared by every Delphi component. In fact, the new class is inherited from the generic TOLEControl class. Here are a few selected lines of the interface definition of the ChartFX OLE control included in Delphi:

```
TChartFX = class(TOleControl)
public
  procedure Refresh; stdcall;
  property Value[index: Smallint]: Double
    read Get_Value write Set_Value;
  property Const_[index: Smallint]: Double
    read Get_Const_ write Set_Const_;
  property Color[index: Smallint]: TColor
    read Get_Color write Set_Color;
published
  property Visible;
  property ThisSerie: Smallint index 1
    read GetSmallintProp write SetSmallintProp
    stored False;
```

```
property AutoInvalidate: TOleBool index 3
  read GetOleBoolProp write SetOleBoolProp
  stored False;
// here comes an event
property OnLButtonDblClk: TChartFXLButtonDblClk
  read FOnLButtonDblClk write FOnLButtonDblClk;
```

This code has the definition of a method of the OCX (Refresh), indicated by the `stdcall` keyword because it has to use the standard Windows calling convention. It shows the Delphi properties inherited by the base class (such as Visible) and public and published properties defined by the component. You can see that they have a different definition from standard Delphi properties, including an index referring to the number of the property in the OCX file.

Notice that Delphi tries to keep the original names of the properties, but this is not always possible. At the beginning of the Pascal files generated during the installation of the components (such as the one above), you'll find a *Conversion log* indicating which names Delphi has to change. For example, in this file we can find the line:

```
Array property TChartFX.Const renamed to Const_: Identifier is a
reserved word.
```

This is the reason for the underscore after the name in the code fragment above.

If you are planning to use OLE controls, follow the procedure outlined here to install them. Then you can study the Object Pascal source code file for the control to see how it is defined. What you won't find in the Pascal code, however, is a list of constant values. C uses constants or defines where Pascal uses enumerations, so you'll have to write your own definitions, or else use plain numbers.

# The TOLEControl Class

For each new OLE control you install, Delphi defines a new ObjectPascal class, derived from the TOLEControl class of the VCL. What is this class for? It encapsulates the basic behavior of OLE Controls, defining all the code needed by its subclasses to access properties and other information (in a number of protected methods). The class has also some public methods and properties, including the following:

```
TOleControl = class(TWinControl)
  ...
public
  procedure BrowseProperties;
  function GetEnumPropDesc(DispID: Integer): TEnumPropDesc;
  procedure SetBounds(ALeft, ATop,
    AWidth, AHeight: Integer); override;
  property OleObject: Variant read GetOleObject;
end;
```

Notice that you can access the internal OLE object, getting a `variant` value. This allows you direct access to the control object, but makes the code more complex, slower, and more difficult to write. So most of the time, using the Delphi interface of the control is better than a direct access.

The key portion of the class is the following private definition: `FOleObject: IOleObject`. This is how the OleControl class encapsulates the OLE Object. Notice the use of *I* in the class name to indicate the code is using an OLE Interface class. In fact, the IOLEObject class is a subclass of IUnknown, the fundamental OLE interface class. As you might have already understood, the interface classes form a hierarchy separate from the rest of the VCL.

The OLE interfaces are defined in the OLE2 and OLECTL unit, two collections of the Pascal version of the OLE interfaces defined by Microsoft. That's enough for the moment. We will discuss some of these topics again in Chapter 25, which is devoted to OLE containers and OLE automation.

# Using OLE Controls

To place one of Delphi's pre-installed OLE controls into a form, simply drag it there, as you would to place any other component. You can set its properties, handle its events, and work with it almost exactly as you work with other Delphi components. However, there are some important differences in the use of OLE controls.

The first thing you'll notice is that OLE controls use numbers for enumeration-based properties, as I've just mentioned. Actually, if you look at the textual description of the form, you'll see a single entry (ControlData) with the hexadecimal values corresponding to all of the components properties. Here is an example of the VCSpeller OCX:

```
object VCSpeller1: TVCSpeller
  Left = 376
  Top = 8
  Width = 23
  Height = 23
  ControlData = {
    0000020001010100005E7E00000A0001000C616D65726963616E2E767464
    DC050000000000000001C0C0C0000000000C767370656C6C65722E686C70
    0C767370656C6C65722E686C70000080}
end
```

Although this isn't easy to interpret, it demonstrates that OCXs are really embedded objects. Their data is stored in the application containing the control. This value is the result of some simple settings on the OCX control, as you can see in the SPELLNOTE example. You can set these values with the Object Inspector, or use the custom properties editor of the whole OLE control, which is available via the Properties command of the Form SpeedMenu (right mouse click) when the component is selected in the form, or by double-clicking on the component. In Figure 16.2, you can see both the Object Inspector and the VisualSpeller Control Properties.

**FIGURE 16.2:**

Two ways to set the properties of an OLE control: the Object Inspector or the specific properties editor.

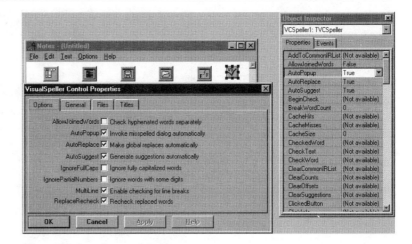

As I've mentioned before, I've used this spelling component in the SPELLNOTE example. This is a very simple example: I've taken the NOTE2 example from Chapter 8, added a menu item to activate the spelling, placed the VCSpeller component on the form, and this is almost enough. In fact, the code to spell-check our text file is incredibly simple:

```
procedure TNotesForm.Spelltext1Click(Sender: TObject);
begin
  VCSpeller1.CheckText := Memo1.Text;
  if VCSpeller1.ResultCode = 0 then
    // no error occurred
    Memo1.Text := VCSpeller1.Text;
end;
```

When you run this program and select Options ➤ Spell, the OCX control will display a dialog box, which allows you to perform standard (but powerful) spell-checking operations. You can see the program running in Figure 16.3. Although the example is far from good (it should use a RichEdit component, have a toolbar, and so on), it demonstrates how simple it is to use third-party components to create powerful applications. Now you have no more excuses not to have a spelling checker in your program!

## Building a Chart

Delphi includes two different charting OLE controls: ChartFX by Software FX and VCFirstImpression by Visual Controls (makers of the VCSpeller and VCFormula-One OLE Controls, also included in Delphi). These are powerful components (although the version you find in Delphi has reduced capabilities), and I've chosen one of them just to show you how it works. In general you'll find some difficulties because the Help file of OCX components is mainly geared toward Visual Basic

FIGURE 16.3:

The VCSpeller OLE control in action.

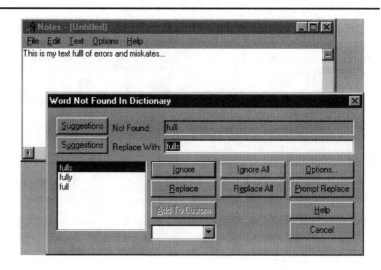

programmers and might have some documentation of the C++ interface (intended for Visual C++ or Borland C++ programmers, and simple to do because OLE Controls are typically developed in C++). It is quite difficult to find Delphi versions of the examples and Help files, but fortunately it is becoming more common. Before I show you this example, consider also that there are many third-party Delphi charting components available.

To demonstrate how the First Impression charting OLE component can be used, I've built another simple program, called CHART. There is a chart in the top portion of the screen, with a string grid below it (see Figure 16.4). A push button labeled *Update* is used to copy the numeric values of the string grid to the chart. Both the chart and grid components are based on the same 5 × 4 matrix structure, and you can choose a chart type by using the combo box in the bottom-right corner of the form.

The chart object has a number of properties and a number of editors and Wizards to set the initial values. Actually, when you double-click on the component, a menu appears containing a list of categories of properties and some tools you can use to define the key elements of the OLE component. The Wizards let you set the key properties, but then you can set the details using all the other commands.

The second important component of the CHART example is the string grid, which has standard options, including editing capabilities. To set the grid to accept only numbers, you need to handle its OnGetEditMaskEvent, supplying a mask for numbers only, as shown in the following code:

```
procedure TForm1.StringGrid1GetEditMask(Sender: TObject; ACol,
  ARow: Longint; var Value: string);
begin
  Value := '!09';
end;
```

**FIGURE 16.4:**

The form of the Chart example at design-time, with the properties menu of this graphical OLE control.

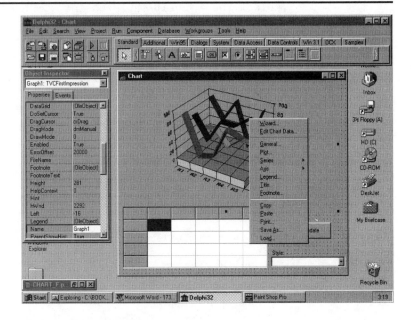

This allows you to input one or two numbers (the first number is required and the second is optional). When the form is created, the program fills the grid with random values and stores descriptive names into its fixed row and column, as you can see in the output shown in Figure 16.5. In the same OnCreate method, the grid's elements are copied to the chart by calling the UpdateButtonClick method (that is, by simulating a click on the button). At the end, the current type of graph is selected in the combo box:

```
procedure TForm1.FormCreate(Sender: TObject);
var
  I, J: Integer;
begin
  with StringGrid1 do
  begin
    {fills the fixed column and row}
    for I := 1 to 5 do
      Cells [I, 0] := Format ('R%d:', [I]);
    for J := 1 to 4 do
      Cells [0, J] := Format ('C%d:', [J]);
    {fills the grid with random values}
    Randomize;
    for I := 1 to 5 do
      for J := 1 to 4 do
        Cells [I, J] := IntToStr (Random (100));
  end;
  {update the chart}
  UpdateButtonClick (self);
```

```
  {select the initial style in the combo box}
  ComboBox1.ItemIndex := Graph1.ChartType;
end;
```

An advantage of having the fixed portions of the grid is that the real values start from column and row one, and the graph component uses one-based indexes, too. The grid has a zero-based index, but the fixed row and column make it simpler to handle the correspondence between the indexes of the grid and those of the graph component. The UpdateButtonClick method is probably the core of the example. To copy the data to the chart OLE control, you need to set the value of the Row and Column properties, then set the Data value:

```
procedure TForm1.UpdateButtonClick(Sender: TObject);
var
  I, J: Integer;
begin
  for I := 1 to 5 do
  begin
    Graph1.Row := I;
    for J := 1 to 4 do
    begin
      Graph1.Column := J;
      Graph1.Data := StringGrid1.Cells [I, J];
    end;
  end;
end;
```

**FIGURE 16.5:**

The output of the CHART example at startup depends on the random values of the grid. Here I've changed the type of graph.

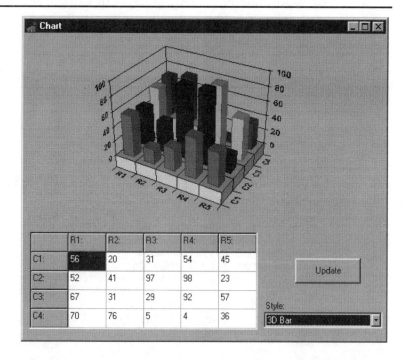

Notice that the chart requires string data, which is not such a big deal since we do have string data in the grid. The final method of the example is called when the user selects a new type of graph in the combo box:

```
procedure TForm1.ComboBox1Change(Sender: TObject);
begin
  Graph1.ChartType := ComboBox1.ItemIndex;
end;
```

The only thing you have to be concerned with is to list the names of the graph in the combo box in the same order they appear in the documentation, since we use their numeric code, not a constant or string literal. With this limited code, we have built a program that can show a variety of graphs, based on the data the user inputs. Consider building this program without the support of a component, and you will realize the worth of add-in components besides those provided by Borland. This same component can display other advanced types of graphs, but only if you buy the full-blown version.

Having said this, I want to stress again that if you have the choice of using a Delphi component instead of OLE controls, you'll find better-integrated and easier-to-use components, which will probably have the same number of capabilities. You can refer to the companion CD-ROM for some samples or demo versions of Delphi components, including charting components.

# But What about Writing OLE Controls in Delphi?

We can easily use OLE Controls in Delphi, but what about writing them without having to use C++? Microsoft, in fact, distributes the OLE Control Development Kit (OLE CDK) as a Visual C++ add-on, since it is based on the Microsoft Foundation Class (MFC) library, but we would certainly like to use Delphi to build OLE Controls.

Technically this is possible, since many OLE interfaces are already defined, and others can be translated. The problem is that it is quite complex without specific tools and Experts. Borland might deliver such a tool in the future, but it is not available right now. However, there is a good chance that you'll be able to use tools for OCX creation in Delphi that are made by third-party companies.

# Summary

In this short chapter, we have focused our attention on a single topic: Delphi's compatibility with OLE controls. You now know the differences between OLE controls and Delphi components, and I've highlighted the advantages of Delphi's approach and the more widespread availability of OLE controls.

I'll come back to the topic of Delphi components (showing how to build them) in Chapter 27. And I'll be back on other aspects of OLE technology in Chapter 25. But in Chapter 17, we are in for one of the key features of Delphi: database support.

# CHAPTER

## SEVENTEEN

17

# Building Database Applications

- Delphi's database components

- Manual database application construction

- The new DBGrid and the Multi Record Object

- The use of the Database Form Expert

- Query and table field manipulation

- Forms with more than one database table

**D**atabase support is one of the key features of the Delphi programming environment. Many programmers spend most of their time writing data-access code, and this should be the most robust portion of a database application. This chapter provides just an overview of Delphi's extensive support for database programming. You can create even very complex database applications, starting from a blank form or one generated by Delphi's Database Form Expert.

What you won't find here is a discussion of the theory of database design. I'm assuming that you already know the fundamentals of database design and have already designed the structure of a database. I won't delve into database-specific problems; my goal is to help you understand how Delphi supports this kind of programming.

We'll begin with an explanation of how data access works in Delphi, and then review the database components that are available in Delphi. Then we'll move on to some basic examples to see how the components work. After this, we'll delve into some more advanced features, such as getting information about the tables at run-time, creating new tables from Delphi code, using graphics fields, and building forms with more than one table.

> **NOTE**
>
> Besides accessing data in local databases, the Delphi Client/Server Suite edition can be used to connect to SQL databases on server computers. This topic will be covered in the next chapter, together with other advanced topics related to Delphi database architecture, such as the Data Modules.

# Data, Files, Databases, and Tables

On a computer, permanent data is always stored in files. This is also true for database data. There are several techniques you can use to accomplish this storage. The two most common approaches are to store a whole database in what appears to the file system as a single file, or to store each table, index, and any other elements of the database in a separate file. In the latter approach, the concept of *database* is not so precise, and a database can be seen as a collection of files, often stored in a single directory.

Delphi can use both approaches; or more precisely, it uses a custom approach that works well with both underlying structures. You always refer to a database with its name or an *alias*, which is a sort of a nickname of a database, but this reference can be to a database file or to a directory containing files with tables. It just depends on the data format you are using. But Delphi is not tied to a specific data format. It can use dBASE or Paradox tables, and access SQL (Structured Query Language) server databases or databases in other formats via the Microsoft ODBC (Open Database Connectivity) standard.

Delphi database applications do not have direct access to the data sources they reference. Delphi interfaces with the Borland Database Engine (BDE), which does have direct access to a number of data sources, including dBASE, Paradox, and ASCII tables (using the appropriate drivers).

The BDE can also interface with Borland's SQL Links, which allows access to a number of local and remote SQL servers. The local server available is InterBase for Windows; remote servers include Oracle, Sybase, Informix, and InterBase. If you need to access a different database or data format, the BDE can interface with ODBC drivers. Although ODBC can provide access to data sources, this is usually the least efficient method. Use ODBC only as a last choice. See Figure 17.1 for an illustration of how database access works in Delphi.

The fact that Delphi doesn't support direct data access basically means that you will need to install the BDE along with your applications on your clients' computers. This is not difficult, since Delphi includes a freely distributable BDE installation program. Just remember, without the BDE, your Delphi database applications won't work.

**FIGURE 17.1:**

The overall picture of data access in Delphi.

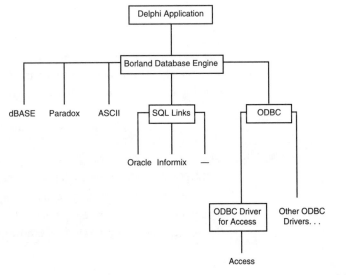

# What Is a Table?

In general, we can use the term *database* to refer to a collection of tables. But what exactly is a table? Although most of you probably know the answer, I'll recap the basic information for the database newcomers.

A table in a database can be compared to a file of records in Pascal. A table has many records, or *rows*, and many columns, one for each field of the record. You can see the structure of a table, with its key elements labeled, in Figure 17.2. Notice that in a table there are the concepts of *current record* (the record a user is operating in) and *current field* (the active field of the current record).

---

**FIGURE 17.2:**

The schema of a database table. The table has been loaded in the Database Explorer.

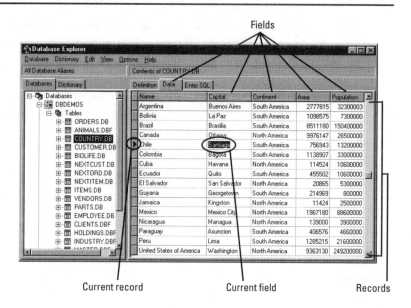

The structure of a table can be clearly seen when you load it in a table viewer program, such as the Database Desktop or the Database Explorer included in Delphi. This last is the tool I used to create the image in Figure 17.2.

> **NOTE**
>
> The sample table shown in Figure 17.2, COUNTRY.DB, is part of the Delphi examples (in the directory DEMOS\DATA, also indicated by the DBDEMOS alias, set up by Delphi during the installation). Many of my examples will use this Delphi database. This way, instead of needing to build new ones, you already have these files available. In some examples, however, I'll show you how to build tables from scratch.

Above the table you can see the names of the various fields, such as Name, Capital, Continent, and so on. Below this are the actual values of these fields in the various rows of the table. You can also see that there are visual hints indicating the current record and the current field.

## Operations on Database Data

Once you have a database table, you can perform a number of actions, such as edit values, insert new records, and delete existing records. You can also perform operations on a window that contains a copy of some of the database data, then later copy that data back into the database. You'll see these two different steps in the code of many of the database application examples.

The problem of synchronizing the values seen by the user with the real data is complicated by the fact that several users might be accessing a database at the same time from different computers on a network. To avoid conflicts, databases have some form of locking to prevent two users from changing the same database data at the same time. However, you seldom need to deal with this issue directly. The BDE and the databases you connect to shield you from most of the details of database handling and data processing.

Delphi offers a uniform view of database access, but you must be aware of the fact that not all databases support the same features.

**NEW**

In the 32-bit version of the BDE, all databases have the concept of transaction (a single atomic, indivisible operation on data) and of transaction rollback (the process of ignoring a transaction and returning to the preceding situation). This is a feature of SQL server databases that is now also available for Paradox and dBASE tables.

# Delphi Database Components

Delphi includes a number of components related to databases. The Data Access page of the Components palette contains components used to interact with databases. Most of them are nonvisual components, since they encapsulate database connections, tables, queries, and similar elements. Fortunately, Delphi also provides a number of predefined components you can use to view and edit database data. In the Data Controls page, there are visual components used to view and edit the data in a form. These controls are called *data-aware* components.

To access a database in Delphi, you generally need a data source, described by the DataSource component. The DataSource component, however, does not indicate the data directly; it refers either to a table, to the result of a query, or to a stored procedure. Therefore, you also need a Table, Query, or StoredProc component in the form, as you can see in the scheme shown in Figure 17.3. What this figure does not show is that the DataSource component can be connected to either a table or a query, but not both at the same time. Multiple data-aware components are usually connected to a single data source.

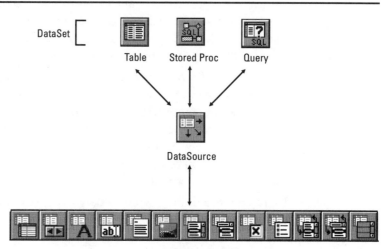

**FIGURE 17.3:**

The role of the DataSource component is to connect multiple data-aware controls with one data set.

As soon as you have placed a Table or Query component on the form, you can use the DataSet property of the DataSource component to refer to it. For this property, the Object Inspector lists the available data set of the current form, or of other forms connected with the current one (using the File ➤ Uses Form command). In other words, a database application must provide a DataSource component and one of the data set components, in one of its forms.

> **NOTE**
>
> By *data set component*, I mean either a TTable, a TQuery, or a TStoredProc object, which are all subclasses of the TDataSet class.

## Tables and Queries

The simplest way to specify data access in Delphi is to use the Table component. A Table object simply refers to a database table. When you use a Table component, you need to indicate the name of the database you want to use in its DatabaseName property. You can enter the name itself, an alias, or the path of the directory with the table files. The Object Inspector lists the available names, which depend on the aliases installed in the BDE.

You also need to indicate a proper value in the TableName property. Again this can be an internal name or the name of the file holding the table. The Object Inspector lists the available tables of the current database (or directory), so you should generally select the Database property first, and the Table property soon afterwards.

Two other relevant properties of the Table component are ReadOnly, used to prevent any changes in the data, and Exclusive, used to forbid concurrent access to a networked table from several applications at the same time. There are also properties related to indexes and master tables. We will focus on these last properties again at the end of this chapter, in the MASTDET example.

A second data set available in Delphi is the Query component. A query is usually more complex than a table, because it requires a SQL language string. However, you can customize a query using SQL more easily than you can customize a table (as long as you know at least the basic elements of SQL, of course).

**NOTE**    SQL is a standard language for writing database queries and generally interacting with a database. If you are not fluent in SQL, you can refer to Appendix B for a minimal description of its basic commands. If you remember at least the key elements, however, you can probably read the simple SQL examples in this book without worrying too much about the details. The Client/Server Suite of Delphi includes a specific tool to create SQL queries, called the Visual Query Builder, which is discussed in Chapter 18.

The Query component has a DatabaseName property as the Table component, but it does not have a TableName property. The table is indicated inside the SQL statement, stored in the SQL property. As we will see in an example later in this chapter, this SQL statement can also include parameters, specified with the Parameters property. You can set the SQL statement both at design-time, by opening the SQL string editor, or at run-time. For example, you can write a simple SQL statement like this:

```
select * from Country
```

where Country is the name of a table, and the star symbol (*) indicates that you want to use all of the fields in the table. If you are fluent in SQL, you might use the Query component more often, but the efficiency of a table or a query varies depending on the database you are using. The Table component tends to be faster on local tables, while the Query component tends to be faster on SQL servers, although this is not always the case.

In a simple example, you can use either a Table or Query component to achieve the same effects. In general, tables tend to be used to browse through most of the fields of a table. Queries are generally used when you have particularly complex restrictive clauses, and when you want the database server (and not the client, the Delphi application) to elaborate the data.

Queries are also often used to join two or more tables and see the result as if it were a single table stored in the database. While a Table component refers to a current table of the database, a SQL statement (and therefore a Query component) produces a table as its result. This allows you to browse through a table that is not in the database, but is the result of a join, a selection, or other computations. Of course, these computations take time. Complex operations, such as table joins, might take quite a while.

The third data set component is StoredProc, which refers to local procedures of a SQL server database. You can run these procedures and get the results in the form of a database table. Stored procedures can only be used with SQL servers, and won't be covered in the book.

When you operate on a data set in Delphi (such as a table or a query), you can work in different states, indicated by a specific State property, which can assume several different values:

- dsBrowse indicates that the data set is in normal browse mode, used to look at the data and scan the records.

- dsEdit indicates that the data set is in edit mode. A data set enters this state when the program calls the Edit method or the DataSource has the AutoEdit property set to True, and the user starts editing a data-aware component, such as a DBGrid or DBEdit. When the changed record is posted, the data set exits the dsEdit state.

- dsInsert indicates that a new record is being added to the data set. Again, this might happen when calling the Insert method, moving to the last line of a DBGrid, or using the corresponding command of the DBNavigator component.

- dsInactive is the state of a closed data set.

- dsSetKey indicates that we are preparing a search on the data set. This is the state between a call to the SetKey method and a call to the GotoKey or GotoNearest methods (see the SEARCH example later in this chapter).

- dsCalcFields is the state of a data set while a field calculation (a call to an OnCalcFields event handler) is taking place.

In simple examples, the transitions between these states are handled automatically, but it is important to understand them because there are many events referring to the state transitions. Most of these events have two versions, Before and After. You can execute some code before the standard operation takes place or after it has been done. For example, the BeforePost and AfterPost events of a data set are called before and after a record is updated in the data set. There is also a generic On-StateChange event in the DataSource component.

## Other Data-Access Components

Along with the Table, Query, StoredProc, and DataSource, there are some other components in the Data Access page of the Components palette:

- The Database component is used for transaction control, security, and connection control. It is generally used only to connect to remote databases in client/server applications.

- The Session component provides global control over database connections for an application, including a list of existing databases and aliases and an event to customize database log-in.

- The BatchMove component is used to make batch operations, such as copying, appending, updating, or deleting values, on one or more databases.

- The new UpdateSQL component allows you to use the cached updates support, available in Delphi 2, with a read-only data set. In practice, you can write some SQL statements to perform the various update operations on the data set, even when using a read-only query. This component is used as the value of the UpdateObject property of tables or queries.

- The Report component is an interface to Borland's ReportSmith application.

These can be considered advanced database components, and some of them are meaningless in a local environment. We will use some of these components in this chapter and the next one, but we won't focus on them in great detail.

## Delphi Data-Aware Components

We have seen how it is possible to connect a data source to a database, using either a table or query, but we still do not know how to show the data. For this purpose, Delphi provides many components that resemble the usual Windows controls, but are data-aware. For example, the DBEdit component is similar to the Edit component, and the DBCheckBox component corresponds to the CheckBox component.

You can find all of these components in the Data Controls page of the Delphi Components palette:

- DBGrid is a grid capable of displaying a whole table at once. It allows scrolling and navigation, and you can edit the grid's contents.

- DBNavigator is a collection of buttons used to navigate and perform actions on the database.

- DBLabel displays the contents of a field that cannot be modified.

- DBEdit lets the user edit a field (change the current value).

- DBMemo lets the user see and modify a large text field, eventually stored in a memo or BLOB (which stands for Binary Large OBject) field.

- DBImage shows a picture stored in a BLOB field.

- DBListBox and DBComboBox let the user select a single value from a specified set. If this set is extracted from another database table or is the result of another query, you should use the DBLookupListBox or DbLookupComboBox components instead. These components replace the DBLookupList and DBLookupCombo of Delphi 1, still available in the Win 3.1 page of the Components Palette.

- DBCheckBox can be used to show and toggle an option, corresponding to the evaluation of a function.

- DBRadioGroup provides a series of choices, with a number of exclusive selection radio buttons, similar to the ListBox or ComboBox component.

- DBCtrlGrid is a multi-record grid, which can host a number of other data-aware controls. These controls are duplicated for each record of the data set.

All of these components are connected to a data source using the corresponding property, DataSource. Many of them refer to a specific field of the data source, as indicated by the DataField property. Once you select the DataSource property, the DataField property will have a list of values available in the drop-down combo box of the Object Inspector. Other than these and a few other specific properties, the properties of the Data Controls page components are similar to those of the corresponding standard controls. Note however, that the DBEdit component is more like the MaskEdit component than the Edit component.

Although we haven't seen many details of the use of the components, this brief overview is enough for the moment. Now let's turn to the job of building database applications. First, we'll see how to create such an application by hand, and then later we'll try using the Database Form Expert.

# Building Database Applications by Hand

Now that we know the role of Delphi's various database components, we are ready to start building an application, or actually, a series of simple examples. We will use both tables and queries, and we'll also use a number of data-aware controls. The first example shows the simplest approach, with the use of a DBGrid component.

## A Grid of Countries

Our first database example, called HANDGRID, uses the table shown earlier in Figure 17.2, which lists American countries with their capitals and population. To make things simple, we can use a grid to display all of the data in the table. To begin, on a new form, place a Table, DataSource, and DBGrid component. This last component can be aligned with the whole client area. To connect the three elements to each other and with the proper database table, use DataSource1 as the value of the DataSource property for the DBGrid component, use Table1 as the value of the DataSet property for the DataSource component, and use DBDEMOS as the value of the DatabaseName property and COUNTRY.DB as the value of the TableName property for the Table component.

If you set the Active property of the table to True, the data will appear in the form at design-time (this technique is usually called *live-data* design). When a grid displays live data, you can even use its scroll bars to navigate through the records and view the other fields also at design-time, as you can see in Figure 17.4.

**FIGURE 17.4:**

The form of the HANDGRID example with live data at design-time.

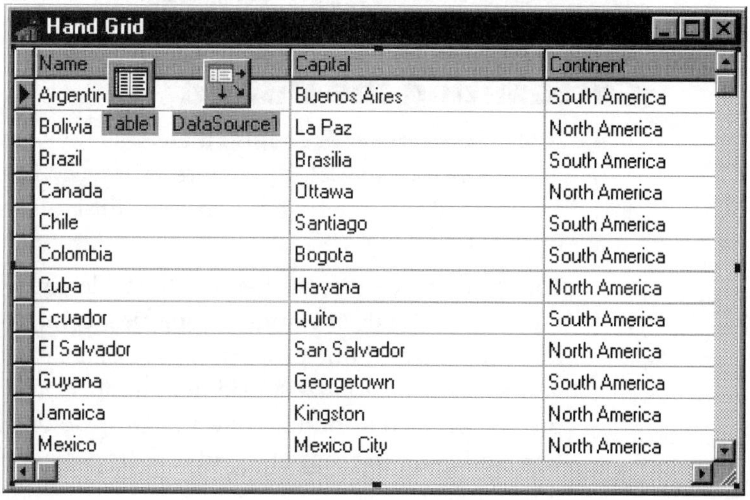

| Name | Capital | Continent |
|------|---------|-----------|
| Argentin | Buenos Aires | South America |
| Bolivia | La Paz | North America |
| Brazil | Brasilia | South America |
| Canada | Ottawa | North America |
| Chile | Santiago | South America |
| Colombia | Bogota | South America |
| Cuba | Havana | North America |
| Ecuador | Quito | South America |
| El Salvador | San Salvador | North America |
| Guyana | Georgetown | South America |
| Jamaica | Kingston | North America |
| Mexico | Mexico City | North America |

**NEW**

In Figure 17.4 you can also see the captions of the Table1 and DataSource1 components. They are very useful when you have several similar components. To enable the captions, use the Show component captions checkbox in the Preferences page of the Environment Options. This is a new capability of Delphi 2.

Now we can run the program, and it will show the same data we could already see at design-time. The difference now is that we can also edit the values, writing new text in each of the cells. This is possible because the DBGrid component's Options property includes the flag `dgEditing` and the ReadOnly property is set to False. You are working directly on the database data, so if you make a change, it will become permanent.

Besides changing the current values of a record, this program also allows you to insert or append new records. To insert a new row in a given position, press the Insert key with the cursor positioned there. To append a new record at the end, just move the cursor below the last element of the grid (go to the last record and press ↓). You can also press Ctrl+Del to delete the current record, after you confirm the action. Try to use this program for a while (maybe after making a backup copy of the original database), and test how it works when you toggle the various flags of the Options property of the grid on and off.

What about the code of the program? There is none. The Pascal file contains only the usual declarations of the objects used by the form, automatically added by Delphi. So we have an application with no code at all, which can be used to perform a relevant number of operations on a table. This is really a nice side of Delphi database programming.

## Customizing the DBGrid

In the first version of Delphi, there was no simple way to customize the output of the DBGrid. In Delphi 2, there is an easy-to-use yet very powerful property: Columns. This property has a custom editor with a number of capabilities (see Figure 17.5).

You can easily choose the fields of the table you want to see in the grid as columns, then set a number of column properties (color, font, width, alignment, and so on) for each field and title properties such as the caption, font, and colors. This allows you to easily customize a grid in a number of ways. Some of the more advanced properties, such as ButtonStyle and DropDownRows, can be used to provide custom editors for the cells of a grid or a drop-down list (we will see how at the end of this chapter).

FIGURE 17.5:

The DBGrid Columns Editor.

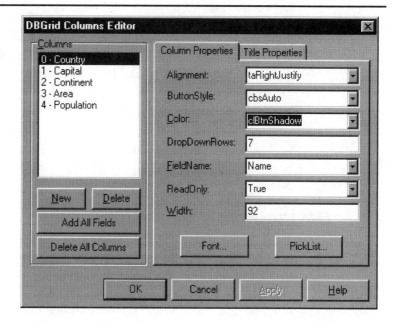

In the HANDGRID2 example, I've taken the grid from the HANDGRID example, changed the caption of the first column and the font of the first and third. I've also chosen a dark gray background and a white font color for the first column. You can see the result in Figure 17.6.

FIGURE 17.6:

The output of the HANDGRID2 example.

Notice that once you have defined the Columns property of the DBGrid, you can size the columns at design-time simply by dragging the lines separating them. The same capability is optionally available at run-time, and can be set along with many others using the Options property of the grid.

There are many more things you can do to customize grids, and we'll explore some of them in the rest of this chapter. Keep in mind that the DBGrid component has been much improved in Delphi 2, but there are also some third-party data grid components that are very flexible.

## Navigating through Countries

The HANDGRID2 example works well, but we want to try using other controls, such as edit boxes, and we want to see specific information rather than all the data in our database. The next example, called NAVIG1, is similar to the previous one, but it uses some DBEdit components and a couple of traditional labels, along with the table and the data source. We also need to add a brand new component, the DBNavigator. Figure 17.7 shows the form of the NAVIG1 example.

**FIGURE 17.7:**
The two DBEdit and the DBNavigator components of the NAVIG1 example, with live data.

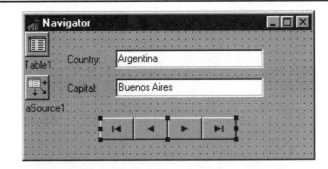

You can use the standard Windows Copy and Paste commands to copy components such as the Table and DataSet components, with all their properties, from one form to another or from one example to another. In this case, the trick is really helpful, because you can copy the two components along with their database connections and all their other properties.

Again, we need to connect the three data-aware controls to the data source and also indicate a specific field for each of the two edit boxes (Name and Capital are the fields for this example). If you have already connected the data source to the table and the edit boxes to the data source, you can simply select a field in the list displayed by the Object Inspector for the DataField property. When this connection is made, the values of the first record's fields appear automatically in the two edit boxes (see Figure 17.7). I've also set the ReadOnly property of the two edit boxes to True, so that a user cannot change the current data.

Another step we can take is to disable some of the buttons of the DBNavigator control, by removing some of the elements of the VisibleButtons set. The meanings of the buttons are shown in Table 17.1.

**TABLE 17.1 :** The meanings of the buttons of the DBNavigator control.

| Button | Meaning |
| --- | --- |
| nbFirst | Go to the first record |
| nbPrior | Go to the previous record |
| nbNext | Go to the next record |
| nbLast | Go to the last record |
| nbInsert | Insert a new blank record in the current position |
| nbDelete | Delete the current record |
| nbEdit | Allow the editing of the current record |
| nbPost | Post (store) the changes that occurred in the current edit action |
| nbCancel | Cancel the changes in the current edit action |

You can see the graphical representation of the various buttons of the navigator, along with the descriptions of their actions, in Figure 17.8. The glyphs of some of these buttons are not very intuitive, but they feature automatic fly-over hints, so that a user can see the function of a button just by moving the mouse over it.

**FIGURE 17.8 :**

The meaning of the buttons of the DBNavigator component.

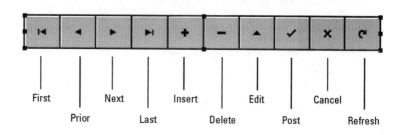

> **TIP**
>
> Of course, you can turn off the ShowHint property to disable the fly-over hints of the navigator. As a better alternative, you can provide a customized description for their text, using the Hints string list. This can be useful when you need to translate an application into another language (or to write it directly in another language, as I often do). The strings you insert are used for the buttons in order: the first string is used for the first button, the second for the second, and so on. If some buttons are not visible, you can provide empty strings (just a blank space), as place-holders.

In the NAVIG1 program, I've used only the first four buttons. You can run it and test whether it works properly. Try changing some of the properties of the navigator and of the two edit boxes. For example, you might disable the ReadOnly property to allow changes. You can also add new data-aware edit boxes for the other fields of the table.

Notice that when the program is running at the beginning or when you jump to the first or to the last record of the table, two of the navigator's buttons will be disabled automatically. However, if you move step-by-step to the first or last record, the buttons are disabled only when you try to move beyond those records. The navigator only realizes at this point that there are no more records in that direction. The same happens when you use the DBGrid's vertical scrollbar.

## Using a Query

In the first two examples, we have used a Table component, and we have browsed through all of the records in the table. For our next example, called NAVIG2, we'll remove the Table component and add a Query component instead. We can connect the query to the usual DBDEMO database alias and enter the text of a simple SQL statement. As we have already seen, we can select all of the fields of all of the records in the table by writing the following code:

```
select * from Country
```

When this query has been entered, you can activate the Query component, setting the Active property to True, and the values of the fields of the first record should appear again in the edit boxes. Of course, this happens only if the SQL statement you have inserted is correct. Otherwise, Delphi will issue an error message, and the query won't be activated.

> **NOTE** If you want to change the current SQL statement of a query at design-time or at run-time, you need to set the Active property of the component to False first, then change the value, and then set it to True again, reactivating the connection between the data-aware components and the data. Otherwise, you will see no effect (other than an error message!).

Of course, this example won't be particularly interesting. Why use the Query component instead of the Table component if this is all we want? We can take advantage of the new component by adding some radio buttons to select different queries at run-time. I decided to add four radio buttons—that is, four different options.

The first button is used to select the default SQL statement, and it is checked at startup. The second and third buttons can be used to choose only the records that have a specific value, either North America or South America, for their Continent field. To accomplish this, we need to add a where clause to the SQL statement, as we will see shortly. The last radio button allows a user to enter the text of the where statement, writing a custom condition in the edit box next to the radio button (for a description of the where clause in SQL you can refer to Appendix B).

Letting a user type in a statement is slightly dangerous, since entering the wrong text can cause an error. But Delphi is robust enough to withstand this risk, thanks to its exception handling. For the first time in this chapter, we need to write some code. The code is necessary to change the value of the SQL property of the Query component when a new radio button is checked. Each time we do this operation, we must remember to call the Close and Open methods of the Query component, or to set the value of the Active property to False and True. Here is the code associated with the first radio button:

```
procedure TNavigator.RadioButton1Click(Sender: TObject);
begin
  Query1.Close;
  Query1.Sql.Clear;
  Query1.Sql.Add('select * from Country');
  Query1.Open;
end;
```

Notice that the SQL property is not a string, but has a TStrings type. This can be used to build very long queries (the text limit for an array of strings is high) and to define different portions of the query in different places of the code and merge them. I've chosen to follow a more traditional approach, with a query made of a single line of text. The second and third radio buttons share the same code, which uses the caption to build the text of the SQL statement:

```
procedure TNavigator.RadioButton2Click(Sender: TObject);
begin
  Query1.Active := False;
  Query1.Sql.Clear;
  Query1.Sql.Add('select * from Country where Continent = ''' +
    (Sender as TRadioButton).Caption + '''');
  Query1.Active := True;
end;
```

This code defines a SQL statement by adding several substrings. Notice that we need to use double single-quotation marks (that is, two consecutive single quotation marks) to indicate a quotation mark within a Pascal string. For this reason, in the code above, we happen to have triple and even quadruple quotation marks. In this last case, the four quotation marks in a row, we simply need a string containing a quotation mark, therefore the two external quotation marks indicate the beginning and end of the string, and the two enclosed quotation marks denote the single quotation mark we really need.

For the last radio button, the code is simpler, since we only need to merge the default statement with the text of the edit box:

```
procedure TNavigator.RadioButton4Click(Sender: TObject);
begin
  Query1.Active := False;
  if (Edit1.Text <> '') then
  begin
    Query1.Sql.Clear;
    Query1.Sql.Add('select * from Country where ' + Edit1.Text);
  end;
  Query1.Active := True;
end;
```

This code is executed any time the edit box is not empty, based on the assumption that the text is a correct SQL statement (the program doesn't check this assumption). To further improve the program, the last radio button is automatically disabled each time the edit box has no text. This check takes place in the OnChange event of the Edit component :

```
procedure TNavigator.Edit1Change(Sender: TObject);
begin
  RadioButton4.Enabled := Edit1.Text <> '';
end;
```

When you run this program, you can choose any of the four buttons and see immediately the effect on the current record. Notice that the navigator works on the resulting table of the query, so that it correctly considers Canada to be the first North American country in alphabetic order. The Custom edit box can be used in a number of different ways. Figure 17.9 shows two different examples of its use. One example shows a single country of the database selected, and the other shows a population range. If you write something meaningless, or just make a small syntax error, the program will stop with an error message.

**FIGURE 17.9:**

Two copies of the NAVIG2 example with a custom where clause. On the left is the selection of a single country. On the right is all those having a large population.

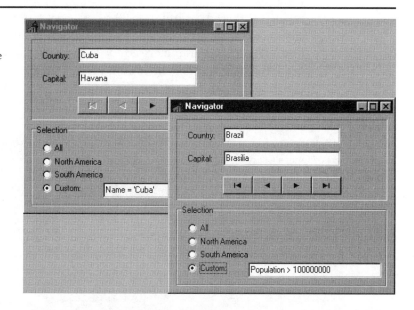

> **NOTE**
>
> As an alternative to the use of where SQL statements, you can set a range of records you want to consider. The range should be based on an indexed field, and of course is not terribly flexible. A powerful alternative is to filter a data set. Simply set the Filtered property of a Table or Query to True, and the program will call the OnFilterRecord event of the data set component to determine which records to show. We will see an example of filtering in the next chapter.

## A Query with Parameters

The last version of our navigator example demonstrates the use of query parameters. All of the queries in the previous version were very similar. Instead of building a new query each time, we can write a query with a parameter, and simply change the value of the parameter.

If we decide to choose North American or South American countries, for example, we can write the following statement:

```
select * from Country where Continent = :Continent
```

In this SQL clause, :Continent is a parameter. We can set its data type and startup value, using the special editor of the Params property of the Query component. You can access this editor from the Object Inspector or through the Define Parameters command on the form's SpeedMenu when the Query component is selected in the form. When the Parameters editor is open, as shown in Figure 17.10, you see a list of the parameters defined in the SQL statement of the Query component. For each of these parameters, you can set a data type and provide an initial value.

**FIGURE 17.10:**

The Parameters editor of a Query component.

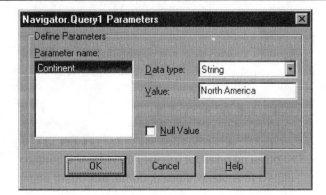

Using this approach makes the new version of this example extremely simple. Its form is a reduced version of the previous example's form, with only two radio buttons. Its most significant code is the response method for the OnClick event of both radio buttons. Here is its code:

```
procedure TNavigator.RadioButton2Click(Sender: TObject);
begin
  Query1.Active := False;
  Query1.Params[0].AsString :=
    (Sender as TRadioButton).Caption;
  Query1.Active := True;
end;
```

This method copies the caption of the radio button to the first parameter of the query. The first parameter is number 0, since the Params array is zero-based, and you should access its value as a string. This AsString property is common to parameter and field arrays of the database components. As we will see in more detail later in the chapter, these are arrays of elements that can have different data types, so one of the *As* conversion properties is always required.

We can add a second method to this program to take advantage of a specific feature of parameterized queries. To react faster to a change in the parameters, these queries can be optimized, or *prepared*. Simply call the Prepare method before the program first opens the query. In our example, NAVIG3, we have to set the Active property of the Query to False at design-time, then write the following OnCreate handler for the form:

```
procedure TNavigator.FormCreate(Sender: TObject);
begin
  Query1.Prepare;
  Query1.Open;
end;
```

**NOTE**  Prepared parameterized queries are very important when you work on a big table, and even more so when you work with a SQL server. In fact, to optimize complex queries, many databases create temporary indexes. Instead of creating an index each time you open it, a prepared query can set up this optimization only once at the beginning, then saving a lot of time when a parameter changes.

# Using the Database Form Expert

We have been able to build some simple examples by placing database components on the main form of the application and then connecting them. Often, this operation requires some time. For this reason, Delphi has a Database Form Expert tool, which provides a fast start in the development of a database application. You had a brief introduction to this tool in Chapter 3, which provided an overview of Delphi's Repository. Now we are ready to use it.

Just to gain some confidence in using this tool, we can try to rebuild the first example in this chapter, HANDGRID, using the Expert. The new example is named EXPGRID. Create a new, blank project, and start the Database Form Expert. In the Expert, select a simple form based on a table, choose the COUNTRY.DB table in the DBDEMOS database, select all the fields, and choose a grid. One of these steps is shown in Figure 17.11. Now you can generate the code, remove the older blank form from the project (probably Form1), compile the program, give proper names to the files, and run it. This program is similar to the one we built before, but this time the process was much simpler and faster.

The Expert is even faster when your form is based on labels and edit fields, instead of on a single grid. In this case, placing all of the components on the form, aligning them, and so on, requires more time. But when you use the Database Form Expert, you can simply choose a vertical or a horizontal layout. If you use a vertical

**FIGURE 17.11 :**

The second step of building the new version of the grid of countries using the Database Form Expert.

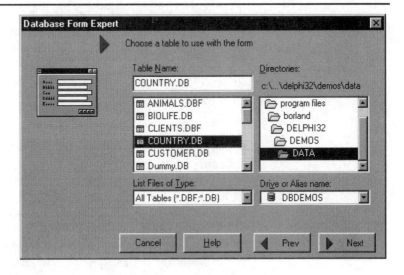

layout, you can decide if you want to place the label above or on the left of the corresponding edit field. We will use this approach in an example later in this chapter.

Before we use the Expert to build new examples, let's take a moment to study the code that it has generated for us. The form of the EXPGRID program has six components, as you can see by opening the project on the companion CD or generating a new one on the fly.

There is a table, connected with the data, a data source associated with the table, a navigator (hosted by two nested panels), and a grid aligned to the remaining area. The two panels are used to place the navigator near the right border of the form, but not too close to the border (not aligned to the right).

The code generated for this example is simple. The only predefined method corresponds to the OnCreate event of the form; it is used to activate the table:

```
procedure TForm2.FormCreate(Sender: TObject);
begin
  Table1.Open;
end;
```

# Accessing the Fields of a Table or Query

Before we try to build more attractive examples, which include support for images, there are few more technical elements we should explore. Up to now, we have included all of the fields in the source database tables. You probably noticed that the Database Form Expert lets you choose the fields you want to use. Suppose that we have already built an example. How could we remove a field? How can we add new fields, such as calculated fields? In trying to solve these problems, we face a more general question: how do we access the values—the fields—of the current record from a program? How can we change them, without a direct editing action by the user?

The answer to all of these questions lies in the concept of *field*. Field components (instances of class TField) are nonvisual components that are fundamental for each Delphi database application. Data-aware components are directly connected to these Field objects, which correspond to database fields.

In the examples we have built up to now, TField components were automatically created by Delphi at run-time. This happens each time a DataSet component is active. These fields are stored in the Fields property of tables and queries, which is an array of fields. We can access these values in our program by number or by name:

```
Table1.Fields[0].AsString
Table1.FieldByName('Name').AsString
```

As an alternative, the Field components can be created at design-time, using the Fields Editor. In this case, you can set a number of properties for these fields. These properties affect the behavior of the data-aware components using them, both for visualization and for editing. When you define new fields at design-time, they are listed in the Object Inspector, just like any other component.

As an example, we can access the Fields editor of the table we generated in the last example. To open the editor for the fields in a table, select the Table object on the form, activate its SpeedMenu, and choose the Fields Editor command. An empty Fields Editor appears. Now you have to activate the SpeedMenu of this editor, to access to its capabilities. The simplest operation you can do is to select the Add command, which allows you to add any other fields in the database table to the list of fields. Figure 17.12 shows the Add Fields dialog box, which lists all the fields that are still available. These are the database table fields that are not already present in the list of fields in the editor.

The Define command of the Fields editor lets you define new calculated fields. (The dialog box that appears when you select this command will be shown in Figure 17.13 later in this chapter. In this dialog box, you can enter a descriptive field name, which might include blank spaces. Delphi generates an internal name—the name of the component—that you can further customize. Next, select a data type for the field. If this is a calculated field, not just a copy of a field redefined to use a new data type, check the Calculated box.

**FIGURE 17.12:**

The Fields editor with the Add Fields dialog box.

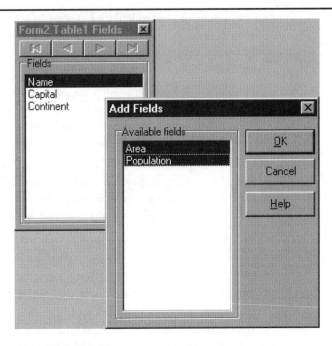

A TField component has both a Name property and a FieldName property. The Name property is the usual component name. The FieldName property is the name of the column in the database table, or the name you define for the calculated field. It can be more descriptive and allows blank spaces. The name of the TField component is copied to the DisplayLabel property (which can be changed later) and is used, among other things, to search a field.

All of the fields that you add or define are included in the Fields editor list, which has a nice dragging capability to change the order of the fields. This is particularly important when you define a grid, which arranges its columns using this order. The list of fields indicates the elements that are available to the data-enabled controls (and in our case, those that are displayed in the grid), and for which there is also a declaration of a TField component (or a component of a subclass of TField) in the form. You can later use this object to access the data of the field, to change several properties, and to compute the calculated fields in the OnCalcFields event of the table.

A great feature of the Fields Editor in Delphi 2 is that you can drag fields from this editor to the surface of a form and generate a proper data-aware component (such as a DBEdit, a DBMemo, or a DBImage). This is a very fast way to generate custom forms, and I suggest you try it out if you've never used it before.

## The TField Components

Before we look at an example, let's go over the use of the TField component, one of the few components not directly available in Delphi's Components palette. The importance of this component should not be underestimated. Although it is often used behind the scenes, its role in database applications is fundamental. Even if you do not define specific objects of this kind, you can always access the fields of a table or a query using their Fields property, an array of TField objects. When you use this approach, and also when you handle a Field object directly, you can use a series of As properties to handle the current field value using a specific data type:

```
AsBoolean: Boolean;
AsDateTime: TDateTime;
AsFloat: Double;
AsInteger: LongInt;
AsString: string;
```

This code can be used to assign or read the value of the field. As an alternative, you can use the Value property directly. This property is defined as a Variant, because its type depends on the field type.

Most of the other properties of the TField component, such as Alignment, Display-Label, DisplayWidth, and Visible, reflect elements of the field's user interface and are used in particular with the DBGrid component, since there is no other way to customize the columns of this grid. The subclasses of TField are shown in Table 17.2.

**TABLE 17.2:** The subclasses of TField.

| Subclass | Definition |
|----------|------------|
| TStringField | Text data of a fixed length (it may be up to 255 characters, but it depends on the database type) |
| TIntegerField | Whole numbers in the range of long integers (32 bits) |
| TSmallIntField | Whole numbers in the range of integers (16 bits) |
| TWordField | Whole positive numbers in the range of words or unsigned integers (16 bits) |
| TFloatField | Real floating-point numbers |

**TABLE 17.2:** The subclasses of TField (continued).

| Subclass | Definition |
| --- | --- |
| TCurrencyField | Currency values, with the same range of real numbers |
| TBCDField | Real numbers, with a fixed number of digits after the decimal point |
| TBooleanField | Field with Boolean value |
| TDateTimeField | Field with date and time value |
| TDateField | Field with date value |
| TTimeField | Field with time value |
| TBlobField | Field with binary data and no size limit (BLOB stands for *Binary Large OBject*) |
| TBytesField | Field with arbitrary data and no size limit |
| TVarBytesField | Field with arbitrary data, up to 64K characters |
| TMemoField | Text of arbitrary length |
| TGraphicField | Graphic of arbitrary length |

The availability of any particular field type depends on the database type or SQL server. For example, InterBase doesn't support BCD, so you'll never get a BCDField for a table on the InterBase server. The range and precision of floating-point fields and the size of decimal fields also vary among SQL servers.

## An Example of a Calculated Field

After this introduction to the use of TField objects, it is time to build a simple example. We can start from the last example we built, EXPGRID, and add a calculated field. The Countries database table we are accessing has both the population and the area of each country, so we can use this data to compute the population density.

To build the new application, named CALC, select the Table component in the form and open the Fields editor (using the form's SpeedMenu). In this editor, choose the Add command, and select some of the fields (I've decided to include them all). Now select the Define command and enter a proper name and data type (TFloatField) for the new calculated field, as you can see in Figure 17.13.

Of course, we also need to provide a way to calculate the new field. This is accomplished in the OnCalcFields event of the Table component, which has the following code:

```
procedure TForm2.Table1CalcFields(DataSet: TDataSet);
begin
  Table1PopulationDensity.Value :=
    Table1Population.Value / Table1Area.Value;
end;
```

**FIGURE 17.13:**

The definition of a calculated field in the CALC example.

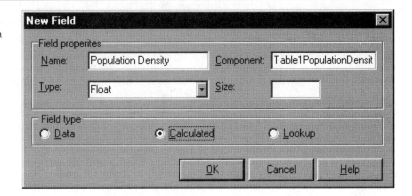

We can write this code, accessing the fields directly, because when you use the Fields editor, some components related to the fields are automatically added to the form:

```
Table1PopulationDensity: TFloatField;
Table1Area: TFloatField;
Table1Name: TStringField;
```

Each time you add or remove fields in the Fields editor, you can see the effect of your action immediately in the grid present in the form. Of course, you won't see the values of a calculated field at design-time, because they are available only at run-time, since they result from the execution of compiled Pascal code.

Since we have defined some components for the fields, we can use them to customize some of the visual elements of the grid. For example, set a display format, adding a comma to separate thousands, writing the string ###,###,### for the DisplayFormat property of some field components. This change has an immediate effect on the grid at design-time.

**NOTE**
The display format I've just mentioned uses the locale information in the WIN.INI file to format the output. The comma is in the format string, but it tells the format code to substitute the proper Thousand-Separator character for the display string. For this reason, the output of the program will automatically adapt itself to different Windows configurations when used outside the United States. On computers that have an Italian configuration, for example, the comma is replaced by a period.

After working on the table components and the fields, I've customized the DBGrid using its Columns property editor. I've set the Population Density column to read-only and set its ButtonStyle property to `cbsEllipsis`, to provide a custom editor. When you set this value, a small button with an ellipsis is displayed when the user tries to edit the grid cell. Pressing the button invokes the OnEditButtonClick event of the DBGrid:

```
MessageDlg ('To change the population density,'#13 +
    'edit the Population or the Area',
    mtInformation, [mbOK], 0);
```

Actually, I haven't provided a real editor, but rather a simple message describing the situation, as you can see in Figure 17.14, where you can note the values of the calculated fields. To create an editor, you might build a secondary form to handle special data entries.

**FIGURE 17.14:**

The output of the CALC example: notice the Population Density calculated column, the ellipsis button, and the message displayed when you select it.

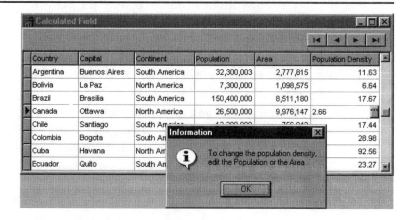

A second column I've customized is Continent. For this field, I want to offer a closed selection, with just two alternatives. To accomplish this, simply click on the PickList button and enter the names of the continents you want to support, then set the number of values (there are just a few) in the DropDownRows property. Without any further change, when you try editing the values in this column, a drop-down list is displayed, as you can see in Figure 17.15.

You can see the final values of the items of the Columns property in the corresponding editor or in the textual description of the form (where this TCollection object is marked by angle brackets). Here is a small portion of the file:

```
Columns = <
  item
    FieldName = 'Name'
  end
  ...
  item
    DropDownRows = 3
```

```
FieldName = 'Continent'
PickList.Strings = (
  'North America'
  'South America')
Width = 87
end
...
item
  ButtonStyle = cbsEllipsis
  FieldName = 'Population Density'
  ReadOnly = True
end>
```

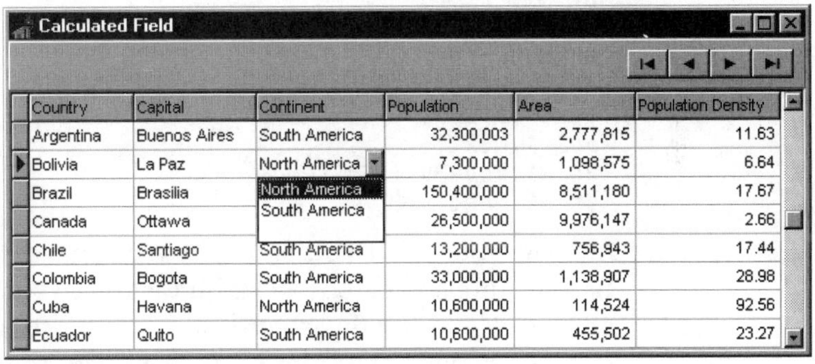

**FIGURE 17.15:**

The drop-down list defined by setting the PickList of a DBGrid's column.

# Using Fields to Manipulate a Table

The TField components you define, or the elements of the Fields array built automatically by Delphi, can be used to access data and manipulate a table at run-time, through the program. We have seen only a limited example of direct data access; in the previous example, we used the value of two fields to calculate a third one. Now we will build some simple examples that will allow us to use the fields to search elements in a table, operate on the values, and access information about the tables of a database. There are many more possible uses of fields in a table, but this should give you an idea of what can be done.

## Looking for Records in a Table

For this example and the following ones, we need a new form, connected to EMPLOYEE.DB, another of the sample Delphi tables. To prepare the form, which has a number of edit fields, you can use the Database Form Expert or drag the fields from the Fields Editor and add the corresponding labels.

If you generate the form with the Database Expert, first get rid of the DBNavigator in the toolbar, because I want to experiment with some manual table navigation.

Instead of the Delphi default component, we can add a group of six navigational buttons, using the SpeedButton component. The two buttons on the side (marked << and >>) are used to move to the first or last record in the table, and the two in the middle (marked < and >) move to the next or previous record. The other two buttons, indicated by a –5 and +5 caption, are used to move 5 records backward or forward. (I chose the amount of 5 arbitrarily.)

Since there are several SpeedButtons, and we'll add more, I've given each of them a meaningful name, such as SpeedButtonFirst or SpeedButtonNext. Each of these buttons has some code associated with its OnClick event. Basically, these six methods call some navigational procedures of the Table component. Here are the six calls, extracted from the source code of the example, and in the same order as the buttons:

```
Table1.First;
Table1.MoveBy (-5);
Table1.Prior;
Table1.Next;
Table1.MoveBy (5);
Table1.Last;
```

Moving around in a table is simple. What makes the code complex is handling the Enabled property of the toolbar buttons. Each button used to move toward the end of the table (the last three buttons) should be disabled when we reach the end. The opposite should happen for the three buttons used to move toward the beginning.

We can test whether we have reached either extreme of the table by using the BOF (Beginning Of File) and EOF (End Of File) properties of the table. The problem is that there are a number of ways to reach the end of the table and to leave it. For this reason, I've written some procedures to enable and disable the two groups of buttons. Here is one of them:

```
procedure TSearchForm.EnableNextButtons;
begin
  SpeedButtonLast.Enabled := True;
  SpeedButtonNext.Enabled := True;
  SpeedButtonMoveOn.Enabled := True;
end;
```

This procedure is called when the end of file is reached. Here is a procedure that can take place when we click on the Next button:

```
procedure TSearchForm.SpeedButtonNextClick(Sender: TObject);
begin
  Table1.Next;
  EnablePriorButtons;
  if Table1.EOF then
    DisableNextButtons;
end;
```

With this code, we always enable the first three buttons (there isn't much time penalty if they were already enabled) and disable the last three if the EOF property is True.

Once the navigation SpeedButtons are set, we can improve this example by adding search capabilities. We want to be able to enter a name in an edit box and jump to the corresponding record. This is the reason for the name of the example itself, SEARCH.

Before continuing with the discussion of the example, take a look at its final form in Figure 17.16. Notice in particular the structure of the scroll box inside the panel, which contains the data-aware edit boxes. These components were built by the Database Form Expert, and they work very well, since you can freely resize the form without any problems. When the form becomes too small, scroll bars will appear automatically in the area holding the edit boxes.

**FIGURE 17.16:**

An example of a best-match search in the SEARCH example.

The searching capabilities are activated by the two new SpeedButtons and the related edit window. The first button is used for an exact match, and the second for a nearest search. In both cases, we want to compare the text in the edit box with the Last Name fields of the Employee table. The Table component has methods to accomplish this, such as GotoKey, FindKey, GotoNearest, and FindNearest, but this component can make searches only on indexed fields.

For this reason you need to set the IndexFieldNames property of the Table component to the proper value (in this case you can directly select the string Last-Name;FirstName in the drop-down list). Were the index not defined, you should have had to add a secondary index using the Database Desktop or the Database Explorer. You can use this last tool to see the indexes currently available for a table.

When the index is properly set, we can make the actual search. The simplest approach is the use of the FindNearest method for the approximate search and the FindKey method to look for an exact match:

```
procedure TSearchForm.SpeedButtonGoNearClick(Sender: TObject);
begin
  Table1.FindNearest ([EditName.Text]);
  EnableAllButtons;
end;

procedure TSearchForm.SpeedButtonGotoClick(Sender: TObject);
begin
  if not Table1.FindKey ([EditName.Text]) then
    MessageDlg ('Name not found', mtError, [mbOk], 0)
  else
    EnableAllButtons;
end;
```

Both find methods use as parameters an array of constants matching the indexes. In our case, we pass only the value for the first field of the index, so the other fields will not be considered. This code is simple, but it is important to understand how it works by looking at the full version of the code—the code that is actually executed by the table component when you call FindNearest or FindKey. The simplest of the two is the best-guess search of the GotoNearest speed button:

```
procedure TSearchForm.SpeedButtonGoNearClick(Sender: TObject);
begin
  Table1.SetKey;
  Table1.FieldByName('LastName').AsString := EditName.Text;
  Table1.GotoNearest;
  EnableAllButtons;
end;
```

As you can see in this code, each search on a table is done in three steps:

1. Start up the search state of the table.

2. Set a value for a field. In this example, I've set the value of the LastName field, using it as a string. I've used the FieldByName method instead of a direct access (Table.Fields[1]), because the code is more readable, and I was sure to avoid errors.

3. When the search fields are set, you can actually start the process, moving the record pointer to the requested position.

You can see an example of the effect of this search in Figure 17.16 above. In the code there is also one statement to enable all of the navigational buttons of the toolbar.

The code used to call the other search method, using an exact match algorithm, is similar. The differences are in these two statements:

```
procedure TSearchForm.SpeedButtonGotoClick(Sender: TObject);
begin
  Table1.SetKey;
  Table1.FieldByName('LastName').AsString := EditName.Text;
  Table1.KeyFieldCount := 1;
  if not Table1.GotoKey then
    MessageDlg ('Name not found', mtError, [mbOK], 0)
  else
    EnableAllButtons;
end;
```

As I've mentioned before, this code requires a proper index for the table, as suggested by the value set to the KeyFieldCount property, indicating I want to use just the first of the two fields which contribute to the index. The second difference is that the GotoNearest procedure always succeeds, moving the cursor to the closest match (a closest match always exist, even if it is not very close). On the other hand, the GotoKey method fails if no exact match is available, and you can check the return value of this function, and eventually warn the user of the error.

This same error was displayed in the first version of the code, based on the FindKey method, which does nothing different from this second version, behind the scenes. The only real difference is that it is much simpler for the programmer to do a search with FindKey. However, it is important to understand how the two find methods work behind the scenes, because when they do not work as expected, you should probably use the longer version. In the SEARCH example on the companion CD, you'll find both versions of the code.

## Changing the Data and Computing New Values

So far in our examples, the user can view the current contents of a database table and manually edit the data or insert new records. Now we will see how we can change some data in the table through the program code. The idea behind this example is quite simple. The Employee table we have been using has a Salary field. A manager of the company could indeed browse through the table and change the salary of a single employee. But what if the manager wants to give a 10 percent salary increase (or decrease) to everyone?

This is the aim of the TOTAL example, which is an extension of the previous program. The toolbar of this new example has two more buttons and a SpinEdit component.

There are few other minor changes from the previous example. I opened the Fields editor of the table and removed the Table1Salary field, which was defined as a TFloatField. Then I selected the New Field command and added the same field, with the same name, but using the TCurrencyField data type. This is not a calculated field; it's simply a field converted into a new (but equivalent) data type. The reason for this change is that the output of the program changes.

Now we can turn our attention to the code of this new program. First, let's look at the code of the total button, which is the one with the dollar signs ($$) on it. This button lets you calculate the sum of the salaries of all the employees, then edit some of the values and compute a new total. Basically, we need to scan the table, reading the value of the Table1Salary field for each record:

```
Total := 0;
Table1.First;
while not Table1.EOF do
begin
  Total := Total + Table1Salary.Value;
  Table1.Next;
end;
MessageDlg ('Sum of new salaries is ' +
  Format ('%m', [Total]), mtInformation, [mbOK], 0);
```

This code works, as you can see from the output in Figure 17.17, but it has a number of problems. One problem is that the record pointer is moved to the last record. To avoid this problem, we need to store the current position of the record pointer in the table, and reset it at the end. This can be accomplished using bookmarks. We need to declare a variable of the TBookmark data type, and initialize it while getting the current position from the table:

```
var
  Bookmark: TBookmark;
begin
  Bookmark := Table1.GetBookmark;
```

At the end of the code, we can restore the position and delete the bookmark with the following two statements:

```
Table1.GotoBookmark (Bookmark);
Table1.FreeBookmark (Bookmark);
```

Another side effect of the program is that, although we will reset the record pointer to the initial position, we might see the record moving while the algorithm elaborates the data. This can be avoided by disabling the controls connected with the table during browsing. The table has a DisableControls method we can call before the while loop starts and an EnableControls method we can call at the end, after the record pointer is restored.

**FIGURE 17.17:**

The output of the TOTAL program, showing the total salaries of the employees.

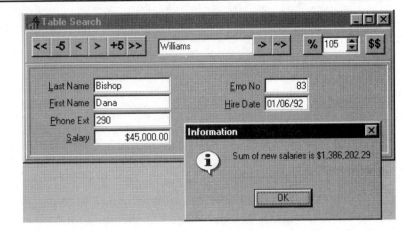

Finally, we face some dangers from errors in reading the table data, particularly if the program is reading the data from a server using a network (although this is not the current case). If any problem occurs while retrieving the data, an exception takes place, the controls remain disabled, and the program cannot resume its normal behavior. So, we should use a try-finally block. Including these three changes, this is the resulting code:

```
procedure TSearchForm.SpeedButtonTotalClick(Sender: TObject);
var
  Bookmark: TBookmark;
  Total: Real;
begin
  Bookmark := Table1.GetBookmark;
  Table1.DisableControls;
  Total := 0;
  try
    Table1.First;
    while not Table1.EOF do
    begin
      Total := Total + Table1Salary.Value;
      Table1.Next;
    end;
  finally
    Table1.GotoBookmark (Bookmark);
    Table1.FreeBookmark (Bookmark);
    Table1.EnableControls;
  end;
  MessageDlg ('Sum of new salaries is ' +
    Format ('%m', [Total]), mtInformation, [mbOK], 0);
end;
```

I've written this code to show you an example of a loop to browse the contents of a table, but it would be faster to use a SQL query to sum (or batch modify) the data (see Appendix B for an example). SQL statements can be used to query and update local tables, which is usually faster than bringing the data all the way back into the application. When you use a SQL server, the advantage of a SQL call to compute the total is even greater.

The code of the method connected to the OnClick event of the % SpeedButton is similar to the one we have just seen. This method also scans the table, computing the total of the salaries. It sets a bookmark, uses a try-finally block, and disables the controls, too.

Although there are just two more statements, there is a key difference between the two. When you increase the salary, you actually change the data of the table. The two key statements are within the while loop:

```
while not Table1.EOF do
begin
  Table1.Edit;
  Table1Salary.Value := Round (Table1Salary.Value *
    SpinEdit1.Value) / 100;
  Total := Total + Table1Salary.Value;
  Table1.Next;
end;
```

The first statement brings the table into edit mode, so that changes to the fields have an immediate effect. The second statement computes the new salary by multiplying the old one by the value of the SpinEdit component (by default, 105), and dividing it by 100. That's a five percent increase, although the values are rounded to the nearest dollar. With this program, you can change salaries by any amount—even double the salary of each employee—with the click of a button. Note that when you do this, you permanently alter the contents of the table. There is no way to restore it at the end, other than trying to make the reverse operation, which is not always easy, due to the rounding of the values and the approximation of floating-point computations.

If this table is stored on a database that supports transactions, however, you might start a transaction before the update loop, run through all the updates, then commit the transaction. That would guarantee that either all the salaries get updated or none do. Of course, after the changes are committed, you can't undo them, unless you use the approximate method just described.

# Exploring the Tables of a Database

In each of the examples in this chapter, we have always accessed a database table by setting its name at design-time. But what if you do not know which table your program is going to be connected to? At first, you might think that if you do not know the details of the database at design-time, you won't be able to create forms and operate on the table. This is not true. Setting everything at design-time is certainly easier. Changing almost everything at run-time requires you to write some more code. This is what I've done in the next example, called TABLES, which demonstrates how to access the list of databases available to the BDE, how to access the list of the tables for each database, and how to select which fields to view from a specific table.

## Choosing a Database and a Table at Run-Time

The first part of the program for this example is quite simple. I've prepared a form with two list boxes. When the program starts, it copies the names of the databases in the first list box, using the following code:

```
procedure TMainForm.FormCreate(Sender: TObject);
var
  DBNames: TStringList;
begin
  DBNames := TStringList.Create;
  Session.GetDatabaseNames (DBNames);
  ListBox1.Items := DBNames;
end;
```

As an alternative you can directly assign the value to the items of the list box:

```
procedure TMainForm.FormCreate(Sender: TObject);
begin
  Session.GetDatabaseNames (ListBox1.Items);
end;
```

The key element is the call to the GetDatabaseNames procedure of the Session global object. An object of class TSession is automatically defined and initialized by each Delphi database application (even if you don't define one), and to access its methods you only need to include the DB unit in your code.

The first version of this procedure fills the string list object you pass to it as parameter, so you need to create it first. After the call, you can copy all of the strings to a list box at once. The alternative, as you saw above, is to pass the list box items as parameter to the GetDatabaseNames function.

When you click on one of the database names in the first list box, the second one is filled with the names of the available tables. This time, the code is based on another method of the TSession class, GetTableNames, which has as parameters the name of a database, a filter string, two Boolean values indicating whether to include the table file extensions (for local tables only) and whether to include system tables in the list (for SQL databases only), and a list of strings that will be filled with the names of the tables. Here is the code the program executes when the user double-clicks on an item in the first list box:

```
procedure TMainForm.ListBox1DblClick(Sender: TObject);
var
  CurrentDB: string;
begin
  CurrentDB := ListBox1.Items [ListBox1.ItemIndex];
  Session.GetTableNames (CurrentDB, '', True, False, List-
Box2.Items);
end;
```

You can see the effect of this code in Figure 17.18. As you have seen, the key for this kind of operation is the global Session object, which holds information about the current database activity. If you connect your application to several different databases at the same time, you might consider adding more TSession instances to the program, adding the proper database components, and connecting them together.

**FIGURE 17.18:**

When you double-click on a database name in the TABLES example, the second list box shows the available tables.

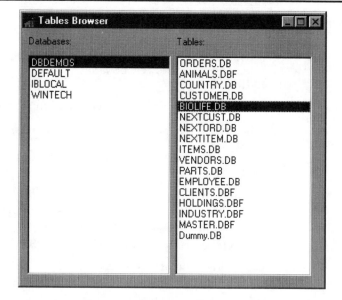

## A Table Viewer

The next step in the program is to view the contents of one of the tables the program has listed. To accomplish this, we need to define a second form, based on a DBGrid component. Using a grid, we can easily view all of the fields in a database without needing to create a number of controls at run-time. To avoid cluttering the main form, and to build a more flexible program, I've place the DBGrid component in a second form. The basic idea is that each time the user double-clicks on one of the table names in the second list box of the main form, a new secondary form is created, showing the data in the table. A new form is created each time the user views a table's data, so we need to disable the automatic definition of a form at program startup. Keep in mind that this creation is controlled by some of the code of the project files. However, you can change it through the Project Options dialog box. Select the Forms page, and remove the GridForm from the Autocreate forms list.

The advantage of not having a single global object for the second form is that we can create a number of them at run-time. These forms are modeless, which means that we can return to the main form and open another grid without closing the first one.

When the user double-clicks on the second list box in the main form, the code creates a TGridForm object, connects the Table1 component of this form to the proper database and table, and shows the form:

```
procedure TMainForm.ListBox2DblClick(Sender: TObject);
var
  CurrentDB, CurrentTable: string;
  GridForm: TGridForm;
begin
  CurrentDB := ListBox1.Items [ListBox1.ItemIndex];
  CurrentTable := ListBox2.Items [ListBox2.ItemIndex];
  GridForm := TGridForm.Create (self);
  {connect the table component to the selected
  table and activate it}
  GridForm.Table1.DatabaseName := CurrentDB;
  GridForm.Table1.TableName := CurrentTable;
  try
    GridForm.Table1.Open;
    {set the title and call a custom
    initialization method, then show the form}
    GridForm.Caption := Format ('Table: %s - %s',
      [CurrentDB, CurrentTable]);
    GridForm.FillFieldsCombo;
    GridForm.Show;
  except on Exception do
    GridForm.Close;
  end;
end;
```

This code displays a new form showing the table data, as you can see in Figure 17.19, where two forms of this kind are visible at the same time. Notice that the code above simply creates the form and never destroys it. It is the responsibility of a form to delete itself, in its OnClose method:

```
procedure TGridForm.FormClose(Sender: TObject;
  var Action: TCloseAction);
begin
  Action := caFree;
end;
```

**FIGURE 17.19:**

The TABLES example can be used to open two (or more) table viewers based on a grid.

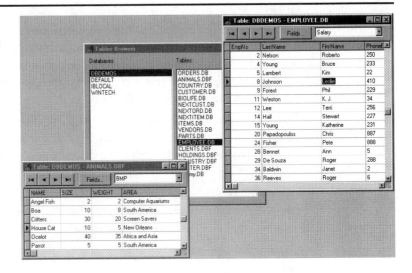

At the end of this procedure, the program sets the caption of the form using the name of the table and database, and it also calls a custom method of the form, called FillFieldsCombo. As we will see in a while, this method simply fills a combo box with the names of the fields of the table (this is the reason for the name). Basically, this is an initialization method of the form called when it is created.

However, this code can't go in the OnCreate event of the form, because the form is created before its Table1 component is properly set up. Instead of trying to find the best event to use (OnShow and OnActivate were two good choices), I've just written a custom method called from the main form. The fact that Windows is event-driven should not compel you to write event-response methods only. At times, good old-fashioned methods—not connected to any event or Windows messages, but directly called from another portion of the code—work better and are easier to understand (and debug).

This moves our attention to the code of the DBGrid form. Here is the code of the custom FillFieldsCombo method:

```
procedure TGridForm.FillFieldsCombo;
var
  I: Integer;
begin
  for I := 0 to Table1.FieldCount - 1 do
    ComboBox1.Items.Add (Table1.Fields[I].FieldName);
end;
```

In this procedure, we see how it is possible to access the third element of a database program. After a list of databases and a list of tables within a database, this code lists the fields of a table, storing them in the combo box I've placed in the toolbar of this form.

Besides accessing the fields definition using the Fields array of a data set, you can use the FieldDefs array, which contains only the field definition, not the data. FieldDefs allows you to access the field definition even if the table is still closed (although you should call the Update method of the FieldDefs to read in the data). This property allows you also to define the structure of a table, as we will see in the following CREATEG example.

What is the purpose of this combo box? Each time a user selects an element, the corresponding field is either shown or hidden depending on its current state:

```
procedure TGridForm.ComboBox1Change(Sender: TObject);
begin
  {toggle the visibility of the field}
  Table1.FieldByName (ComboBox1.Text).Visible :=
    not Table1.FieldByName (ComboBox1.Text).Visible;
end;
```

Notice the use of the FieldByName method to retrieve the field using the current selection of the combo box, and the use of the Visible property. Once a field becomes not visible, it is immediately removed from the grid associated with the table. Therefore, by simply setting this property, the grid changes automatically. You might also consider allowing the user to customize the grid further, by giving access to some values of the Columns property at run-time.

## A Field Editor

The combo box we have placed in the toolbar of the GridForm works, but if you need to select several fields in a big table, it is slow and error-prone. As an alternative, I've created a small fields editor form. This is the third form of the TABLES example, named FieldsForm. This form is displayed as a modal form, so we can use a single global object every time. The new form has no code of its own. When the Fields button of the grid form's toolbar is clicked, the multiple selection list box of the FieldsForm (which is the only relevant component) is filled with the names of the fields of the Table1 component. At the same time, the code selects the list box items corresponding to visible fields, as you can see in Figure 17.20.

The user can toggle the selection of each item in this list box while the modal form is active. When it is closed, the other form retrieves the values of the selected items,

FIGURE 17.20:

The list box can be used to select the
table fields to show in the grid.

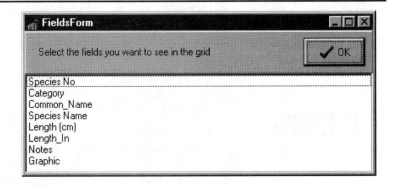

and sets the Visible property of the fields accordingly. Here is the complete code of
this method:

```
procedure TGridForm.SpeedButton1Click(Sender: TObject);
var
  I: Integer;
begin
  for I := 0 to Table1.FieldCount - 1 do
  begin
    FieldsForm.FieldsList.Items.Add (
      Table1.Fields[I].FieldName);
    if Table1.Fields[I].Visible then
      FieldsForm.FieldsList.Selected [I] := True;
  end;
  FieldsForm.ShowModal;
  for I := 0 to Table1.FieldCount - 1 do
    Table1.Fields[I].Visible :=
      FieldsForm.FieldsList.Selected [I];
  FieldsForm.FieldsList.Clear;
end;
```

This code ends the description of this complex example, which uses three forms. We
have seen that you can write database applications that do most of the work at run-
time, although this approach is slightly more complex. Realize that there are many
other things we could have done. I've just chosen the basic activities to avoid making the program too complex.

## An Outline for a Table Browser

After writing this program, I've come up with an alternative user interface, not
based on a TreeView component but more similar to the interface of the Database
Explorer included in Delphi. The program has almost the same code and capabilities as the previous version, but the database list box is replaced by a database
combo box, and the DBGrid is added directly to the main form, instead of to a separate form. You can see the output of this program in Figure 17.21.

**FIGURE 17.21:**

The output of the TABLES2 program, which integrates the DBGrid in the main form.

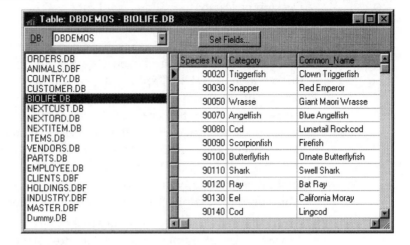

As soon as you select a table, the grid is shown (it is hidden when no form is visible, to avoid displaying an empty grid). This is the code of the OnClick event of the list box:

```
procedure TMainForm.ListBox1Click(Sender: TObject);
begin
  DBGrid1.Visible := False;
  Table1.Close;
  Table1.DatabaseName := ComboBox1.Text;
  Table1.Tablename :=
    Listbox1.Items [Listbox1.ItemIndex];
  Table1.Open;
  Caption := Format ('Table: %s - %s',
    [Table1.DatabaseName,
    Table1.Tablename]);
  DBGrid1.Visible := True;
end;
```

# Creating a Graphical Table

When you start a new project, you should sit down first and design the structure of the database tables used by your application. This is not an easy task. Also, in moderately complex programs, a flaw in the database design can lead to incredible problems. If your previous database programming experience is limited, you should consider reading a book on this topic before you start writing a complex database-access application with Delphi.

Once you have developed your database, you need to create the tables. There are basically two choices. The simplest method is to use the stand-alone Database

Desktop or Database Explorer applications. The other approach is to write some code in Delphi to create the tables.

To use the Database Explorer, simply run it, choose a database, select the New SpeedMenu command, and choose a table type in the dialog box that follows. At this point, the Database Explorer displays a Create Table dialog box, in which you can specify the various fields of the table. For each field, you should enter a name, a type, a size, and whether it is a key field (a required field that has an index connected to it). You can even use the Database Explorer to input some values into the table. This makes sense if the table has a number of initial values. If not, an empty table might do. It should be obvious, but when you build a table and create a Delphi application using it, you cannot ship your application without the proper tables, which need to be copied to the proper directories of the other computer.

As an alternative, you can do the same things using the Database Desktop tool, which is a sort of simple version of Paradox. With this tool, you can define a new table, indicating the names and types of the fields, as you can with the Database Explorer. Again, you can define indexes, input values to a new table, and so on. These two tools, the Database Explorer and the Database Desktop really have many features in common.

Now suppose that the structure of our table is simple, and that we want to allow the user to create a number of tables of the same kind (or of a similar type). We can use a Delphi application and create tables in its code. This is the aim of the next example, which uses a graphic field for the first time in the book. It is also the first example that uses the Clipboard, a topic discussed in detail in Chapter 24.

> **NOTE**
>
> Graphic, memo, and BLOB fields in Delphi are handled exactly like other fields. Just connect the proper editor or viewer, and most of the work is done behind the scenes by the system. I assume that you have already seen the Delphi graphical example, which shows fish. If not, try to build the DEMOS\DB\FISHFACT example that ships with the package and see how it works.

The name of this example is CREATEG, where *G* stands for graphics. Its goal is to allow a user to capture images on the screen and store them in a database table. Note that this table will probably become quite big after a while, so if you have limited disk space, beware of using the program. Each time you run CREATEG, it asks you if you want to create a new table or use an existing one. If you want to create a new table, you should provide a table name that doesn't exist so that you won't override existing, valuable data. If you load an existing table, you must use a table with the proper fields: a textual description of the image, the date and time it was saved, and the image itself.

When a suitable table has been created or selected, the program displays its main form, as shown in Figure 17.22. You can now capture an image on the screen, copying it to the Clipboard. This step is not performed by the program. You can just press the PrintScreen key or Alt+PrintScreen combination to capture the bitmap of the whole screen or the bitmap of the current active window. Or use another program or technique to copy a bitmap to the Clipboard.

**FIGURE 17.22:**

The main form of the CREATEG example at run-time. Notice that image stretching is disabled.

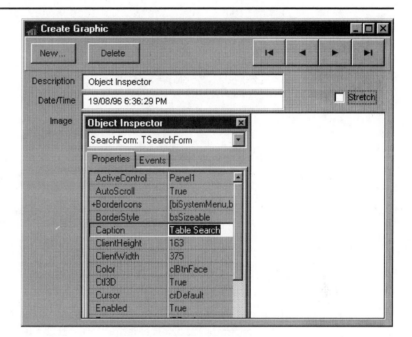

After the image has been copied to the Clipboard, click on the New button, and the program will ask you for a description of the image, take the system time, copy the bitmap from the Clipboard, and insert the new record in the table. If something went wrong, you can use the Delete button to remove the current record. Of course, you can always browse through the records of the table (which are sorted by description). Finally, you can use the check box to stretch the image or view it (or a portion of it) in the default scale.

Of course, there are many ways to improve this program, such as by making the screen capture automatic or by checking the contents of the Clipboard. However, the features it does have demonstrate the concepts, and the example is already complex enough.

## The Form and Its Startup Code

Let's begin by taking a look at the main form of this program, which has two Table components. We are going to use the second table, which is not connected to a Data-Source component, inside a search algorithm. When the program starts, it displays a simple message dialog box, as shown in Figure 17.23. This lets the user choose between creating a new form or using an existing one. The message dialog box, displayed in the FormCreate method before the main form becomes visible, has three choices:

```
Code := MessageDlg ('Do you want to create a new table?'
  + Chr(13) + '(choose No to load an existing table' +
  'Cancel to quit)',
  mtConfirmation, mbYesNoCancel, 0);
if Code = idYes then
  CreateNewTable
else if Code = idNo then
  LoadTable
else
  Application.Terminate;
```

**FIGURE 17.23:**

The message dialog box shown at program startup.

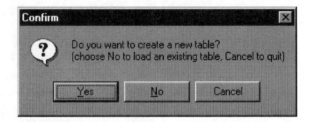

If the user selects the Yes button, the program creates a new table. If the user selects No, the program loads an existing table. If the user selects Cancel, the application terminates. The bulk of the initialization code is in the two custom methods, CreateNewTable and LoadTable.

## Creating a New Table

To create a new table in Delphi, you can call the CreateTable method of a Table component. However, before you do this, you need to set some properties of this component. You must specify a database name, a table name, the names and types of the fields, and the name of an index.

The database name is set to the DBDEMOS alias at design-time. You can change it, but if you do, you need to replace this string with the new one in several places in the source code. The table name is requested from the user, with the InputQuery function. When the user has entered a name, we need to verify whether a table with the same name already exists. In fact, the CreateTable method of the TTable class eventually overrides a table that has the same name as the new one. How do we check if the name is already in use? We can call a method of the Session global object, as we did in the last example. Here is the first part of the code of this method:

```
procedure TGraphForm.CreateNewTable;
var
  TableName: string;
  TbNames: TStringList;
begin
  {request the name of the new table from the user}
  TableName := '';
  if InputQuery ('New Table', 'Enter a new table name:',
    TableName) then
  begin
    {if the table already exists in the DBDEMOS database,
    do not overwrite it}
    TbNames := TStringList.Create;
    Session.GetTableNames ('DBDEMOS', '', False, False, TbNames);
    if TbNames.IndexOf (TableName) >= 0 then
      raise EMyDatabaseError.Create ('Table already exists');
```

The IndexOf method of the string list returns the index of the string, or −1 if the string does not exist. If the string exists, the program raises an exception to stop further execution of this method. EMyDatabaseError is a new exception class I've defined in the code of this program as follows:

```
type
  EMyDatabaseError =
    class (EDatabaseError)
  end;
```

This kind of exception is checked in the OnCreate method of the form. If an error occurs in one of the two possible procedures, CreateNewTable or LoadTable, the program shows an error message and restarts the custom initialization code, asking again for the user to choose between a new or an existing table. Here is the final complete code of Form Create method:

```
procedure TGraphForm.FormCreate(Sender: TObject);
var
  Code: Word;
begin
  try
    Code := MessageDlg ('Do you want to create a new table?' +
      #13'(choose No to load an existing table, Cancel to quit)',
      mtConfirmation, mbYesNoCancel, 0);
    if Code = idYes then
      CreateNewTable
    else if Code = idNo then
      LoadTable
    else
      Application.Terminate;
```

```
except
  on E: EMyDatabaseError do
  begin
    ShowMessage (E.Message);
    FormCreate (self);
  end;
end;
end;
```

If the table does not exist, the program can create it. First it has to store the name of the table in the Table1 component, and also set the TableType property with the value ttParadox (or any other table type). The next step, which is the most complex one, is to define the three fields of the table. We need to use the FieldDefs property (the list of field definitions) of the Table component, and call the Add method three times. The Add method adds a new field to the structure of the table, and another Add method of the IndexDefs property is used to define a primary index. Here is the second part of the CreateNewTable method:

```
Table1.TableName := TableName;
Table1.TableType := ttParadox;
with Table1.FieldDefs do
begin
  Clear;
  Add ('Description', ftString, 50, True);
  Add ('Time', ftDateTime, 0, False);
  Add ('Graphics', ftGraphic, 0, False);
end;
Table1.IndexDefs.Clear;
Table1.IndexDefs.Add('DescrIndex', 'Description',
  [ixPrimary, ixUnique]);
Table1.CreateTable;
Table1.Open;
```

As you can see in the last two lines above, after the program has set up the attributes of the table, it can create it, calling the CreateTable method and then it can open the table. Since the data source and the other data-aware components are already connected, once the table is open, we can start working with it.

If you still have questions about how this program works, you can refer to the full source code of the example on the companion CD.

## Choosing a Table with the Proper Fields

The second time you run the program, since you have already built a table with the proper fields, you can load it instead of creating a new one. The loading code is handled by the LoadTable method. This code starts by filling the list box in a dialog box with the names of the available tables.

I thought that simply accessing the dialog box components as usual was enough, but when I tried, I invariably got an error. What's wrong? The problem is that the code we are writing is initialization code, part of the OnCreate method of the main form. If you remember, the code of the typical project file of a Delphi program calls the CreateForm procedure a number of times (once for each form created at startup). One of the effects of the call of this method is that the OnCreate method takes place.

For this reason, during the OnCreate event of the main form, the dialog box form has still not been created. Accessing one of its components results in a run-time error. The compiler knows nothing about the order of execution of the events and of the initialization code. To solve the problem, simply disable the automatic creation of TablesForm in the Project Options dialog box (Forms page), and then manually create the form before accessing any components in it. Now we can move to the core of this procedure. The code retrieves the list of database tables with another call to the GetTableNames of the Session global object, but instead of copying the whole string list to the list box, it performs a test on each item. Basically the program assigns the name of each table to the Table2 component, then checks its FieldDefs property (after updating it). Here is the first part of the procedure:

```
procedure TGraphForm.LoadTable;
var
  TbNames: TStringList;
  I: Integer;
  Found: Boolean;
begin
  TablesForm := TTablesForm.Create (Application);
  Found := False;
  TbNames := TStringList.Create;
  Session.GetTableNames ('DBDEMOS', '', True, False, TbNames);
  for I := 0 to TbNames.Count - 1 do
  begin
    Table2.TableName := TbNames [I];
    Table2.FieldDefs.Update;
    if (Table2.FieldDefs.Count = 3) and
      (CompareText (Table2.FieldDefs[0].Name, 'Description') = 0)
      and (CompareText (Table2.FieldDefs[1].Name, 'Time') = 0) and
      (CompareText (Table2.FieldDefs[2].Name, 'Graphics') = 0) then
    begin
      {table fields match: add the table to the list}
      TablesForm.Listbox1.Items.Add (Table2.TableName);
      Found := True;
    end;
  end;
```

When a table passes the test, it is added to the list box in the dialog box, and a proper flag is set (Found). The dialog box is displayed on the screen, as shown in Figure 17.24. When the dialog box is closed (by clicking on OK), the list box item selected by the user is copied to the name of Table1, the table connected with the visual components of the main form. If no table passes the test, an exception is raised. Here is the second part of the LoadTable method:

```
if Found then
begin
  TablesForm.ListBox1.ItemIndex := 0;
  if TablesForm.ShowModal = idOK then
  begin
    Table1.TableName := TablesForm.ListBox1.Items [
      TablesForm.ListBox1.ItemIndex];
    Table1.Open;
  end
  else
    Application.Terminate;
end
else
  {no proper table was found}
  raise EMyDatabaseError.Create (
    'No table with the proper structure');
```

**FIGURE 17.24:**

The TablesForm dialog box allows a user to choose from only the tables that have the proper fields.

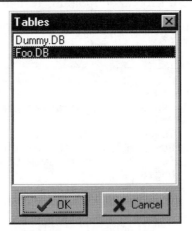

## Adding or Removing Records

Most of the program code was in the initialization portion. Once a table is open, we can simply insert new records. This happens when the user clicks on the New button in the main form of the program. The code of this button's OnClick method is quite simple. The procedure asks the user to enter a description (which must be unique), then creates a new record at the end of the table:

```
procedure TGraphForm.NewSpeedButtonClick(Sender: TObject);
var
  Descr: string;
```

```
begin
  if InputQuery ('New record', 'Enter the description:', Descr)
then
  begin
    Table1.Last;
    Table1.Insert;
    EditDescription.Text := Descr;
    EditDate.Text := DateTimeToStr (Now);
    DBIMage.PasteFromClipboard;
    Table1.Post;
  end;
end;
```

Notice that the values are copied to the data-aware components, and not directly to the fields. In this case, we can use the PasteFromClipboard method to fill the DBImage component with the bitmap currently in the Clipboard. The other two methods of the main form, one to delete the current record and the other to stretch the image, are very simple:

```
procedure TGraphForm.DeleteSpeedButtonClick(Sender: TObject);
begin
  if MessageDlg ('Are you sure you want to delete the current
  record?',
      mtConfirmation, [mbYes, mbNo], 0) = idYes then
    Table1.Delete;
end;

procedure TGraphForm.CheckBox1Click(Sender: TObject);
begin
  DBImage.Stretch := CheckBox1.Checked;
end;
```

# A Multi-Record Grid

Up until now we have seen that you can either use a grid to display a number of records of a database table or build a form with specific data-aware components for the various fields. In this case, however, we access the records one by one. There is a third alternative: use a multi-record object (a DBCtrlGrid), which allows you to place many data-aware components in a small area of a form and automatically duplicates these controls for a number of records.

Here is what we can do to rebuild the MULTI1 example. Create a new blank form, place a Table component and a DataSource component in it, and connect them to the COUNTRY.DB table. Now place a DBCtrlGrid on the form, set its size and the number of rows and columns, and place two edit components connected with the Name and Capital fields of the table. To place these DBEdit components, you can also open the Fields Editor and drag the two fields to the control grid. At design-time you simply work on the active portion of the grid (see Figure 17.25, on the right), and at run-time you can see these controls replicated a number of times (see Figure 17.25, on the left).

---

**FIGURE 17.25:**

The DBCtrlGrid of the MULTI1 example at design-time (on the right) and at run-time (on the left).

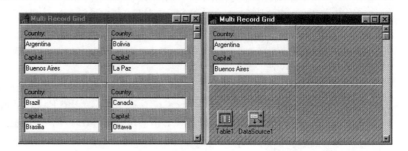

---

Here are the most important properties of the DBCtrlGrid object of this example:

```
object DBCtrlGrid1: TDBCtrlGrid
  ColCount = 2
  DataSource = DataSource1
  PanelHeight = 104
  PanelWidth = 158
  RowCount = 2
  object Label1: TLabel ...
  object Label2: TLabel ...
  object DBEdit1: TDBEdit ...
  object DBEdit2: TDBEdit ...
end
```

Actually, you can simply set the number of columns and rows. Then each time you resize the control, the width and height of each panel are set accordingly. What is not available is a way to align the grid automatically to the client area of the form.

## Moving Control Grid Panels

To improve the last example, we might resize the grid using the FormResize method. We could simply write the following code (in the MULTI2 example):

```
procedure TForm1.FormResize(Sender: TObject);
begin
  DBCtrlGrid1.Height := ClientHeight - Panel1.Height;
  DBCtrlGrid1.Width := ClientWidth;
end;
```

This works, but it is not what I want. I'd like to increase the number of panels, not enlarge them. To accomplish this we can define a minimum height for the panels and compute how many panels can fit in the available area each time the form is resized. For example, in MULTI2, I've added one more statement to the FormResize method above, which now becomes:

```
procedure TForm1.FormResize(Sender: TObject);
begin
  DBCtrlGrid1.RowCount :=
    (ClientHeight - Panel1.Height) div 100;
  DBCtrlGrid1.Height := ClientHeight - Panel1.Height;
  DBCtrlGrid1.Width := ClientWidth;
end;
```

Instead of doing the same for the columns of the control grid component, I've added a TrackBar component to a panel (the height of this toolbar panel was already considered in the code above). When the position of the trackbar changes (the range is from 2 to 10), the program sets the number of columns of the control grid and resizes it. In fact, if you simply set the number of columns, they'll be of the same width as before. Here is the code of the handler of the OnChange event of the trackbar:

```
procedure TForm1.TrackBar1Change(Sender: TObject);
begin
  LabelCols.Caption := Format (
    '%d Columns', [TrackBar1.Position]);
  DBCtrlGrid1.ColCount := TrackBar1.Position;
  DBCtrlGrid1.Width := ClientWidth;
end;
```

This code and the FormResize method above allow you to change the configuration of the control grid at run-time in a number of ways. You can see an example of a crammed version of the form in Figure 17.26.

# Building a Master Detail Form with the Expert

When you run the Database Form Expert, it asks you if you want to create a form based on a single table or a master detail form. A master detail form involves two tables, with a one-to-many join. You can define this behavior by using a proper SQL statement, or with some properties of the Table component. Either way, you can let the Expert generate the code for you. This is exactly what you'll see in the next example.

Since we're using the sample tables available in Delphi, there are not many choices for building a master detail form. Our example will use the Customer and Order tables, which are also used by some Delphi sample programs.

**FIGURE 17.26:**

The output of the MULTI2 example, with an excessive number of columns.

Here are the steps to build the MASTDET example:

1. Start a new project and run the Database Form Expert.

2. In the first page of the Expert, choose a master detail form and TTable objects.

3. Choose CUSTOMER.DB from DBDEMOS as the master table. Choose some of the fields, and select the horizontal or vertical layout.

4. As the detail table, select ORDERS.DB. Choose some of the fields from this table, and select the default grid layout.

5. You are now on the most important page of the Database Form Expert, shown in Figure 17.27. Select the CustNo index, then select the same field in the two lists of fields.

6. Click on the Add button to define a join.

7. Generate the form (as the main form), without using the data module, and the program is finished. You can run it immediately to see its effect.

**FIGURE 17.27:**

The most important page of the Database Form Expert, for a master detail application, lets you join two tables.

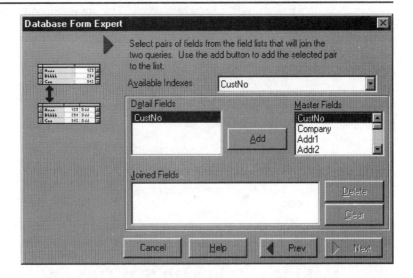

In Figure 17.28 you can see an example of the output of this program (MASTDET) at run-time. In the figure, I've increased the size of the form and moved some of the components, but the form's behavior is exactly the same as the one generated by the Expert. Each time you select a new customer, the grid below displays only the orders pertaining to that customer.

**FIGURE 17.28:**

The form of MASTDET example, an Expert-generated program, at run-time.

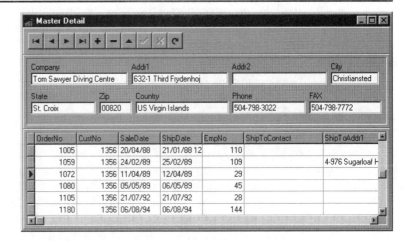

How does this program work? The answer is very simple. If you look at the properties of the two Table components in the Object Inspector, you can see the following values:

```
object Table1: TTable
  DatabaseName = 'DBDEMOS'
  TableName = 'customer.db'
end
object Table2: TTable
  DatabaseName = 'DBDEMOS'
  TableName = 'orders.db'
  IndexFieldNames = 'CustNo'
  MasterFields = 'CustNo'
  MasterSource = DataSource1
end
```

The second table has a master source (the data source connected with the first table), and relates to a specific field, which provides the cross-reference.

## Making a Join with SQL Queries

The previous example used two tables to build the master detail form, because this is exactly what we asked. As an alternative, you can define this type of join using a SQL statement. This is easy, since once again, the Database Form Expert can generate the code for us. Simply run the Expert once more, this time selecting a TQuery instead of a TForm.

For this example, I've joined the ORDERS.DB table with ITEMS.DB table, which describes each item in each order. The two tables can be joined using the OrderNo field. When you generate the code, the program, named ORDERS, behaves exactly like the previous one. This time, however the trick is in the SQL statements of the second query object:

```
Select
  items."OrderNo",
  items."ItemNo",
  items."PartNo",
  items."Qty"
From items
Where
  "items"."OrderNo" =: "OrderNo"
```

As you can see, this SQL statement uses a parameter, :OrderNo. This parameter is connected directly to the first query, because the DataSource property of Query2 is set to DataSource1, which is connected to Query1. In other words, the second query is considered as a data control connected to the first data source. Each time the current record in the first data source changes, the Query2 component is updated, just like any other component connected to DataSource1. The field used for the connection, in this case, is the field having the same name as the query parameter.

# Providing a Closed Selection in a Combo Box

The form of the ORDERS example generated with the Database Form Expert can be improved (you won't find the original version on the companion CD, only the customized one). In the customized version, I've moved some of the editor boxes and labels to place them in two columns, and moved some other elements, but in particular, I've solved a problem that this table had.

In the original version, when you view the records or enter new data, you need to work with the customer number, which is not the most natural way. However, in the database, the names of the customers are stored in a different table, to avoid duplicating the customer data for each order of the same customer. To get around working with customer numbers, I placed a new component in the form, a DBLookupComboBox control. This component can be connected to two data sources at the same time, one with the actual data and a second with the display data. Basically, we want to connect it with the CustNo value of DataSource1, the master query, but let it show the information extracted from another table, CUSTOMER.DB.

To accomplish this, I removed the DBEdit component connected to the customer number and replaced it with a DBLookupComboBox component and a DBText component. DBText is a sort of label, or text that can't be edited. Then I added a new data source (DataSource3) connected to a table (Table1), which relates to the CUSTOMER.DB file. You can see the output of the form in Figure 17.29. For the program to work, you need to set several properties of the DBLookupComboBox1 component. Here is a list of the relevant values:

```
object DBLookupComboBox1: TDBLookupComboBox
  DataField = 'CustNo'
  DataSource = DataSource1
  KeyField = 'CustNo'
  ListField = 'Company'
  ListSource = DataSource3
end
```

The first two properties determine the main connection, as usual. The other three properties determine the secondary source (ListSource), the field used for the join (KeyField), and the information to display (ListField). Contrary to what happened in Delphi 1 with the LookupDisplay property of the DBLookupCombo component, the ListField property accepts only one field.

**FIGURE 17.29:**

The output of the ORDERS example.

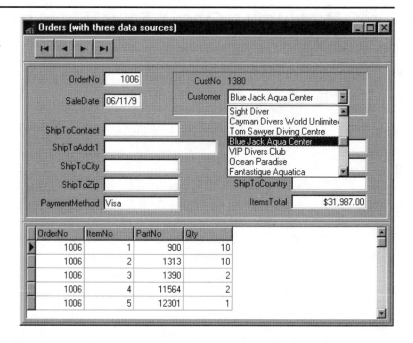

TIP

**TIP** If you set the index of the table connected with the DBLookupComboBox to the Company field, the drop-down list will show the companies in alphabetical order, and not following the customer number order. This is what I've done in the example.

What about the code of this program? Well, there is none. Everything works just by setting the correct properties. The three joined data sources do not need custom code.

## A Lookup in a Grid

As I've placed a lookup field in a form (using the DBLookupComboBox component), I can add a drop-down lookup list in a DBGrid component. We have already seen in the CALC example how to provide a drop-down list in a field of the DBGrid by customizing the Columns property providing a closed selection (pressing the PickList button in the Columns editor). However, to customize the grid by adding a lookup list, which refers to a secondary data source, we need to follow a completely different approach. In fact, we have to define a lookup field using the Fields Editor.

As an example, I've taken the MASTDET form just described and turned it into the MASTDET2 example. In the grid in the lower portion of this form of the original version there was the code of the employee who took the order. Why not show the name, instead, and let a user choose it from the list of employees using a drop-down list?

To accomplish this, I added a Table and DataSource component, referring to the EMPLOYEE.DB database table. Then I've opened the Fields Editor for the second table, the one with the orders, and I've added all the fields. I've selected the EmpNo field, and set its Visible property to False, to remove it from the grid (we cannot remove it altogether because it is used to build the cross reference with the corresponding field of the Employee table).

Now it is time to define the lookup field. If you've followed the preceding steps, you can issue the New Fields command in the local menu of the Fields Editor, and define the new Field in the following dialog box, as you can see in Figure 17.30. Simply enter a name (such as Employee) and check the Lookup radio button. Once this is done, select the field in the Object Inspector and set its lookup properties as follows:

```
object Table2Employee: TStringField
  FieldName = 'Employee'
  Lookup = True
  LookupDataSet = Table3
  KeyFields = 'EmpNo'
  LookupKeyFields = 'EmpNo'
  LookupResultField = 'LastName'
end
```

This is all that is needed to make the drop-down list work (see Figure 17.31) and to view the value of the cross-references field at design-time, too. Notice that there is no need to customize the Columns property of the grid, because the drop-down button and the value of seven rows are taken by default. This doesn't mean you cannot use this property to further customize these and other visual elements of the grid.

**FIGURE 17.30:**

The dialog box used to define a new lookup field.

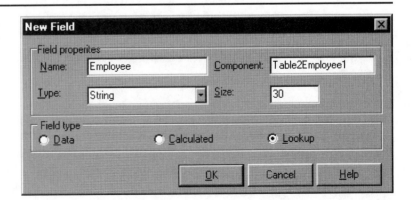

**FIGURE 17.31:**

The output of the MASTDET2 example, with the drop-down list inside the grid displaying values taken from another database table.

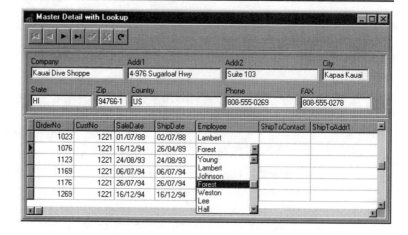

# Summary

In this chapter, we have seen a number of examples of the use of database access from Delphi programs. We have reviewed the basics of navigating in a table, entering new values, finding values, and using the grid and navigator components. In the last part of the chapter, we explored some more advanced features, such as building tables at run-time and creating table viewers at run-time to let the user select the fields he or she wants to see. We have seen an example of the use of a graphics field, and some examples of joins.

Is this all there is to say about Delphi database programming? Not at all. Delphi database support is very extensive and complete. The purpose of this chapter was to give you an idea of what you can do. What you don't find in this chapter is a discussion of database design principles, and I deliberately didn't attempt to design a full-scale database. Database design can be the subject of another book by itself (and, of course, there are many books on this topic that you can refer to).

What I'll focus on in the next chapter (still devoted to databases) is a more general picture, with some key elements of client/server programming, other Delphi tools as the Visual Query Builder, a discussion of the Data Modules, the Repository, and other new features of Delphi 2.

# CHAPTER

## EIGHTEEN

# Client/Server and Advanced Database Applications

18

- The local InterBase server

- Remote SQL server access

- The Visual Query Builder

- Table joins with the Visual Query Builder

- The Data Modules

- Table Ranges and Filters

- Using the Data Dictionary

In Chapter 17, we went through a number of examples of developing database applications. All of those examples accessed data stored in dBASE or Paradox tables; that is, in the usual files. This is certainly good enough for a simple program, but if you need your application to be robust and safe, you might think of moving your data to a SQL server. (See Appendix B for a short overview of SQL.)

The SQL server can reside on a server computer connected to a network, or it can be on the same local machine you are using to develop your programs. Delphi includes the local Windows version of Borland's SQL server, InterBase.

In this chapter, we will explore some of the details of using a SQL server. If you do not own the Client/Server Suite edition of Delphi, you might be tempted to skip this chapter. However, some of the tools described here (such as the local InterBase server) are available in every Delphi box. The second part of the chapter covers other advanced database features, most of which are introduced in Delphi 2 for the first time, such as the data modules and the data dictionary. These features do not strictly relate to client/server development, although they provide interesting benefits in that area.

# Accessing a SQL Server

The local SQL server can be used both as a target platform and as a development platform. When you use it as a target platform, you end up installing a copy of the InterBase server, along with your program and the BDE libraries your program needs. If you own the Client/Server Suite edition of Delphi, you can deploy the local InterBase engine without paying further royalties to Borland.

**NOTE**

Realize that the local InterBase server is a single-user implementation, not a full-scale multi-user SQL server. Local InterBase is useful for deploying applications that need to run on stand-alone machines (not networked), without giving up the advantages of SQL queries or writing a separate version of the application to use local tables. Borland also sells full-scale versions of InterBase, which your Delphi programs that are based on the local version can use without any changes.

Often, it is more important to use the local InterBase only as a development platform. Instead of developing the application right on a network, you can build it on a local machine, and then simply change the destination database at the end. This might also be the intermediate step between a local version using files (a prototype of your program) and a fully developed client/server version (your final application).

Developing a Delphi application that accesses a remote server is really not much different from developing a Delphi application that accesses local tables. Once the server database has been set up, and you have defined the proper tables, you use the remote server almost seamlessly from within the development environment. There are, however, some differences. For example, generally, the user must log in to access the database. Another key element of SQL servers is the presence of a more powerful transaction control (since the 32-bit version of the Borland Database Engine includes only a simple transaction control for Paradox and dBASE tables). Other features include the execution of stored procedures and increased efficiency in using queries rather than tables. Indexing and optimization techniques might even depend on the specific SQL server.

Some of the issues related to all these differences can be handled by using some of Delphi's database components. For example, the Database and Session components allow you to customize the database log-in procedure and to determine how a transaction should interact with another simultaneous transaction accessing the same tables (transaction-isolation level). Although you are not required to have these two components in your Delphi applications, using them might increase the control you have over the server environment.

Another specific SQL server component is the TStoredProc component. This allows a program to execute a procedure present on the server database, eventually passing some parameters and retrieving a return value. A third useful component for database manipulation is TBatchMove, which allows a program to copy, append, or delete groups of records or an entire table from two different databases. The interesting element is that one of these databases can be a local table and the other a SQL server.

## A First InterBase Application

Now let's get to work and build a simple Delphi application using the local InterBase engine. We'll create this program using the Database Form Expert, to make it clear that you can use this approach in developing a client/server application. (Everything we have seen in the previous chapter really works as I've described for SQL servers.)

To build this program, create a new Delphi project, then choose Database ➤ Form Expert. Select a simple form based on a query. Move to the next page and choose the IBLOCAL alias. At this point, The InterBase local server will prompt you with a log-in dialog box. If you have not worked with the local InterBase server before, the log-in name you should type will be **SYSDBA**. Enter the default password, **masterkey**, and you are ready to go on using the Database Form Expert as usual. For example, to rebuild the CURRENCY program, you should choose the Country table as the one to access.

Notice, in this case, that tables are not files. The pseudo List Files of Type combo box just lets you choose between User Tables or All Tables, including system tables. Continue with the Expert, selecting the only two fields in this table and a layout (I chose vertical, with labels on top). Then generate the form.

Customize the form as you like. I activated the table editing (by setting the RequestLive property of the Query component to True), moved some of the components on the screen, and resized the form. I also gave it a new name and caption. An example of the output of the program, named CURRENCY and included on the companion CD, is shown in Figure 18.1.

**FIGURE 18.1:**

The CURRENCY program at run-time (now, what is the last currency rate of my poor liras?). Notice the log-on dialog box, requiring a user to type in the proper password, before the main form of the program is displayed.

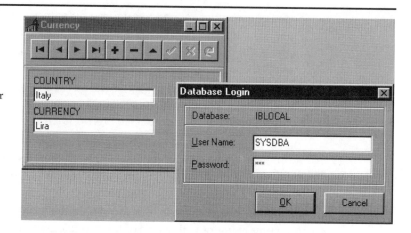

Each time you run this program, it requests your user name and password (see Figure 18.1 again). To skip this, you can add a database component to the form and set the corresponding properties. As an alternative, you might handle the OnLogin event of this component and enter some values in the LoginParams property. Either way allows you to bypass the log-in prompt, but is that what you really want to do?

Keep in mind that having a log-in prompt is one of the key features of database security. You might consider skipping it while you're developing your program, but you'll usually want to require the end users to log in before using the application. In this example, I used a local SQL database, installed on the same computer I used to develop the Delphi application. This is not the only choice. I could have developed a real client/server application, following the same steps but using a remote server, connected to my computer via a network.

## Accessing a SQL Server

The only real difference between using a local database and accessing a SQL server is that you need the Client/Server Suite version of Delphi, with its SQL Links.

Actually, you can access most SQL servers though ODBC, but this is far from the best choice if efficiency is an issue. SQL Links is basically an extension of the Borland Database Engine. As explained in Chapter 17 (and illustrated in Figure 17.1), the BDE can access some data sources, such as Paradox and dBASE tables, directly, or it can interface with ODBC (Open Database Connectivity) drivers or SQL Links.

Since there are a number of layers, you need to take several steps to install and configure everything. You can install the BDE with Delphi or separately, and it can be configured using the BDE Configuration utility. With the configuration utility, you can define aliases, install new ODBC drivers, and set parameters used to connect to the various databases.

The second layer is SQL Links, which also can be configured with the BDE Configuration Utility. After this layer there is the network, which requires the installation of a proper network protocol. The last step is to configure the SQL server.

## InterBase Server Tools

Delphi includes applications that can be used to set up, configure, and maintain both the local InterBase engine and remote servers. Here, I'll briefly describe these tools. For a full description of their capabilities, refer to the Borland documentation, which is quite extensive in this area.

### Server Manager

The Server Manager can be used for administering InterBase local or remote databases and servers. With Server Manager, you can manage database security (authorize new users, change user passwords, and remove user authorizations), back up a database, perform maintenance tasks, and execute other related operations. Figure 18.2 shows an example of using the Server Manager to add a user.

### Windows ISQL

The Windows InterBase ISQL (Interactive SQL) application can be used to execute a SQL statement on a local or remote InterBase server. You can start ISQL, connect to an existing local or remote database, and enter a SQL statement. For example, you could connect to the IBLOCAL alias, and enter this statement:

```
select First_Name, Last_Name from employee
  where Job_Code = "Eng"
```

This SQL command outputs the first and last name of all the employees in the Engineering (*Eng*) department, as you can see in Figure 18.3.

Windows ISQL can be used to view the contents of a database, but its real role is in database setup and maintenance. You can define new tables, add indexes, write procedures (the stored procedures), and so on. This is all done using InterBase SQL, so it is probably not for the casual user.

**FIGURE 18.2:**

The InterBase Server Manager tool, while adding a new user (me!).

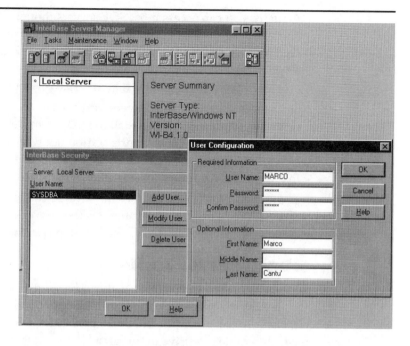

**FIGURE 18.3:**

The result of the execution of a SQL statement in the Windows ISQL application.

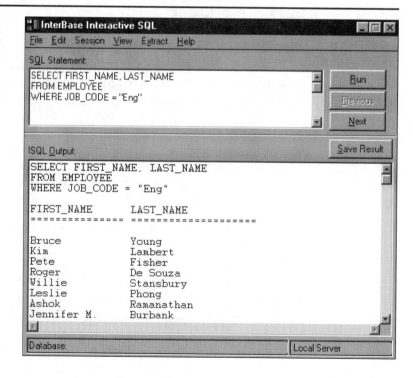

> **NOTE**
>
> Note that the SQL language recognized by InterBase is much wider than the language features I discuss in Appendix B and the standard SQL you can use with the BDE. Any SQL server usually implements some specific advanced capabilities not included in the SQL standard.

## Database Explorer and Database Desktop

Another tool you can use with local and remote InterBase servers is the Database Explorer application. It offers the easiest way to navigate through existing tables or databases, as well as to insert and delete records and modify existing values. Along with the new Database Explorer there is the Database Desktop (already available in Delphi 1). Both can be considered as table viewers and configuration tools, while the Server Manager and Windows ISQL can be considered database configuration and definition tools. These tools are not all distinct: you can run a SQL query over an InterBase database using Windows ISQL, the Database Explorer, and the Database Desktop (not to count the Visual Query Builder). For instance, with the Database Explorer you can execute a SQL statement similar to the one I used before in the Windows ISQL example (Figure 18.3). This example of the use of the Database Explorer is shown in Figure 18.4.

**FIGURE 18.4:**

The result of a SQL query on employees using the Database Explorer.

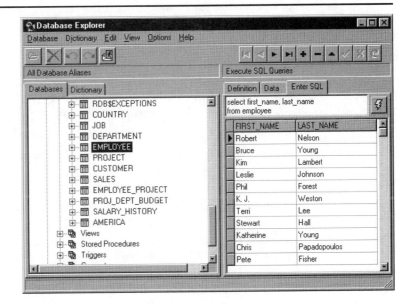

By simply selecting the Data and SQL tabs, you can see all of the data or select just some fields or records. For more information about the Database Explorer and the InterBase server tools, refer to the Borland online documentation and manuals. Now we will continue with some examples using Delphi—and some code.

# Upsizing an Existing Program

The development of a new Delphi database application using a server is similar to the development of an application based on local files. So, what is involved in upsizing an application? It takes very little to make it work. To take advantage of all the SQL server's features, including transaction processing, it takes just a little more work. In this section, we'll see what is involved in moving an existing Delphi database application based on a local table to the local InterBase server. This is usually a first step in its move to a remote SQL server. The second step is much simpler.

As an example, let's go through the steps for upsizing the CALC example presented in Chapter 17. The new version will include a viewer of the COUNTRY.DB table with a calculated field, and it will be connected to the local InterBase server. To upsize the program, proceed in two steps:

1. Copy the tables manually or write a program to copy the table from a Paradox file to an InterBase database.

2. Update the program to have it use the new table.

## Copying a Table

There are basically two ways to copy a Paradox table to a SQL server. One is to use one of the interactive tools, such as the Database Explorer. The other method is to write a program in Delphi, based on the TBatchMove component. I've chosen the second approach. To build the MOVECOUN (for Move Country) example, place two Table components, a BatchMove, and a Button in a form.

The first table should be connected with the original Paradox table (COUNTRY.DB) and we can immediately open it (set its Active property to True). The second table should relate to the target database, indicating the name of the new table. I could not choose *Country* as the target name, because there is already a table with this name in the IBLOCAL database. I decided to use *Americas*, because there are only American countries in that table. Once each table is properly set up, use them for the Source and Destination properties of the BatchMove component.

The last step is to choose a proper value for the Move property of the BatchMove component. The default is batAppend, which appends records to an existing destination table. But you can set any of the following values:

- batUpdate, which updates only matching records.
- batAppendUpdate, which does both operations (appends and updates).
- batCopy, which creates the destination table, copying the source table "as is."
- batDelete, which deletes matching records.

The batCopy parameter is what we are looking for. Set it, select the BatchMove component, activate the form's SpeedMenu, and choose the Execute command. Delphi will create the new table (after asking for log-in information, since the destination table relates to an InterBase database). We have done it, without even compiling the program! As an alternative, we can write one line of code for the OnClick event of the button:

```
BatchMove1.Execute;
```

This is certainly nice, but I would like to show you some more details. For this reason, I used the default batAppend mode in the program and created the table in the code. This approach is only slightly more complex. Before you call the CreateTable method of the Table2 component, you need to copy the structure of the first table to Table2. Here is the complete code:

```
procedure TForm1.ButtonMoveClick(Sender: TObject);
begin
  ButtonMove.Enabled := False;
  Table2.FieldDefs := Table1.FieldDefs;
  Table2.IndexDefs.Assign (Table1.IndexDefs);
  Table2.CreateTable;
  Table2.Open;
  BatchMove1.Execute;
end;
```

In the beginning, the button is disabled, so that the user can make only one copy each time the program is executed. Run the program, click on the button, and fill in the log-in dialog box. Now you are ready for the second step of the upsizing process.

**WARNING** When you run the MOVECOUN program, you might notice that the SQL operation is quite slow. The program will show a special SQL hourglass, but the screen might not be repainted properly for a while.

## Porting the Application

Now that the table has been moved to the InterBase local server, we can turn our attention to improving the CALC application. I've named the new version CALC2.

Open the old application (or a copy), select the Table component, set its Active property to False, and then choose the IBLOCAL database and the Americas table (which should appear in the list of available tables in the Object Inspector). Activate the table again, and the live data is back. But now we are accessing a SQL server. When you run the program, the new calculated field will appear, exactly as it did in the previous version. The example works, and it is so simple that performance is not a concern.

The next version of the example, CALC3, uses a Query instead of a Table component. Simply remove the table and add a query. Connect the data source with the query and write the proper SQL statement. Since we are exploring the development of client/server applications, we will try using another tool included in this version of Delphi: the Visual Query Builder. If you do not have this tool, you can enter the resulting SQL statement in the corresponding property of the Query component.

## Using the Visual Query Builder

Running the Visual Query Builder is simple: just select the Query component and activate the local SpeedMenu of the Form Designer by pressing the right mouse button (on the form). Select the Query Builder menu item and fill in the log-in fields, choosing a database and entering a password. In the dialog box that follows, choose only the Americas table. Then close the dialog box. Now we are ready to work.

As you can see in Figure 18.5, the Visual Query Builder has a lower area where you build the resulting query and an upper area for the tables you are using. The buttons on the toolbar of the Visual Query Builder are used to create a new query, open an existing one or save it, set some options, select more tables, add calculated columns, show the text or the result of the query, and accept or cancel it.

To define a query, for example, you can drag some fields from one of the tables in the upper portion to the bottom part, adding them to the result. In the lower part of the window you can set the sort order of the table resulting from the query, filter the records, and set a number of other advanced features. As we will see in an example later in this chapter, when you have more than one table loaded in the Visual Query Builder, you can also join them graphically.

Another thing you can do is to define calculated fields directly in the query. Click on the Expression button in the toolbar. In the Expression dialog box, give the expression a name (I chose Density), double-click on the Population field, then on the division sign (/), and then on the Area field.

**FIGURE 18.5:**

The main screen of the Visual Query Builder, with one table and some of its fields selected.

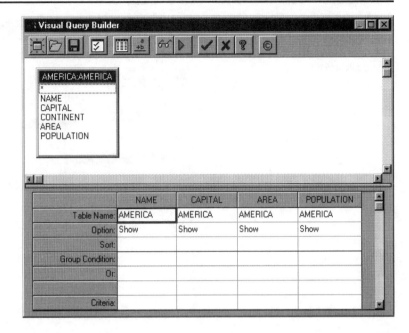

The expression appears in the Expression box at the bottom of the dialog box, as shown in Figure 18.6. If it's correct, you can eventually save the text of the query to a file, and then save the query itself into the SQL property of the table simply by clicking on the Close button. A new field will be added to the resulting table of the query. Now you can click on the Execute button to see the result, and the calculated field will be there as if it were an original field of the table.

You can also look at the code of the SQL query, which is now the following:

```
select America.Name , America.Capital ,
  America.Area , America.Population ,
  ( America.Population / America.Area ) as Density
from America America
order by
  America.Name
```

Click on the SpeedButton with the check mark, and the text of the query will be copied back to the Query component in the form. Now activate it, and you'll see the fields of the form in the grid, including the calculated field, at design-time.

There is still a minor problem, however. The division calculation we have written in the SQL query expression results in a floating-point number with several decimal places. In the expression used to calculate the field in the earlier versions, we called the Round function, which is not available in SQL.

**FIGURE 18.6:**

The Expression dialog box of the Visual Query Builder can be used to define calculated fields.

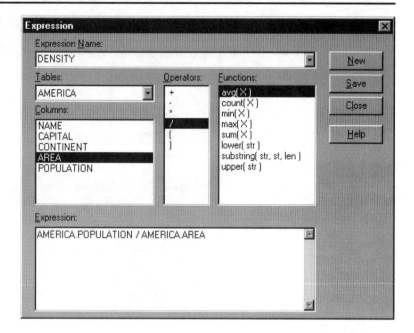

The problem is that the default grid is not wide enough to accommodate the most significant digits, and the values displayed on the screen seem to be wrong. To solve the problem, we simply need to define the fields for the query and set the proper format string for the DisplayFormat property. Indicate the thousands separators for the area and the population (with the value ###,###,###) and then set the number of decimal digits for the population density (with the value ###.###). Then you can size the grid columns properly, as you can see in Figure 18.7.

## From Porting to Upsizing

In the CALC3 example, we have obtained two interesting advantages. The first and most evident advantage is that now we can display a calculated field at run-time. This is possible because we do not need compiled Pascal code to make this computation; the server does it, while processing a SQL statement.

This is a key point. We have actually moved some computation from the client application to the server. This means that you can move computations from the client computer to the server computer, which can usually handle the huge amount of data involved in big queries more quickly and efficiently. Although we are currently running both the client and the server code on the same computer, this doesn't modify the general perspective. This is what real client/server programming means: distribute the workload of an application between a client computer

FIGURE 18.7:

The CALC3 form with the SQL calculated field at design-time.

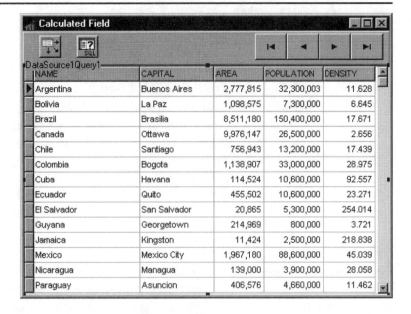

and a server computer. The client should be primarily involved in the user interface, and the server in data processing.

As a consequence of this approach, I would expect this application to run slightly faster than the previous version, although in such a simple case, there probably isn't much difference.

I think this is one of the points that marks the difference between changing an application so that it can connect to a remote database, and upsizing an application, taking advantage of a client/server platform. There are other elements in the picture as well. The SQL server can be used to improve robustness and data consistency and to speed up the access from multiple users at the same time, just to mention a few ideas. On the whole, moving your data and making the application work with the remote server is just the first step, although a very important one, of the process.

# Joining Tables with the Visual Query Builder

In the last section, we saw that owners of the Delphi Client/Server Suite can take advantage of a special tool, the Visual Query Builder. We have used it to create a SQL query with a calculated field. Now we will explore another feature of this tool, which is the ability to define table joins graphically.

# A Join with Three Tables

The form of the project, named SQLJOIN, includes only three items: a TQuery component, a data source, and a grid aligned to the client area. Basically, we want to display some information about the employees involved in each project, using the data stored in the IBLOCAL database.

The database contains an Employee_Project table, which seems to be exactly what we need. However, this table contains project codes and employee codes. To have some readable information, we need to join this table with the Project table, which contains a description of each project, and the Employee table, which stores information about each employee. Using the Visual Query Builder, we can express these two joins simply by selecting the three tables and dragging a field onto the corresponding field of the other table. Next, choose some fields for the output. You can see the query I've built with this tool in Figure 18.8.

**FIGURE 18.8:**

The query of the SQLJOIN example in the Visual Query Builder.

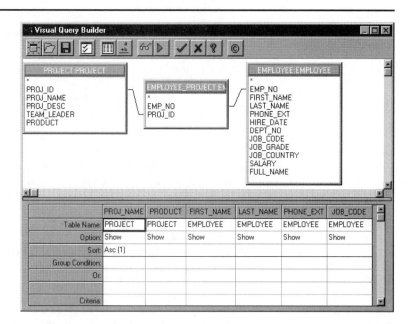

Here are the SQL statements corresponding to this graphical query:

```
select
  Project.Proj_Name , Project.Product ,
  Employee.Last_Name , Employee.First_Name ,
  Employee.Phone_Ext , Employee.Job_Code
from
  Employee Employee , Project Project ,
  Employee_Project Employee_Project
```

```
where
  ( Employee_Project.Emp_No = Employee.Emp_No )
  and
  ( Project.Proj_Id = Employee_Project.Proj_Id )
order by
  Project.Proj_Name
```

In the output, we use fields from only two tables. The third table is just used to perform two joins with corresponding codes in the other tables.

> **WARNING**
>
> When you have built a query with the Visual Query Builder, you can indeed see its text in the SQL property of the corresponding TQuery object. However, if you make any change there, you cannot access the query structure in the visual tool any more. To avoid this risk, I suggest that you always save the query to a file before you exit from the Visual Query Builder, so that you can restore the structure later.

In the output of this program, but also in the table at design-time, you can see the reason for the structure of the database, which divides the project information between several tables. You can see that there are employees working on several projects at the same time.

Following the standard database design rules (also called *normalization* rules), no information should be duplicated. For this reason, we cannot store employee data in the project-related tables. At the same time, we cannot store project information in the Employee_Project table, since a project appears several times. The only theoretically sound approach is to divide the data into three tables, as is done in this database.

> **NOTE**
>
> If you do not know what I mean by database normalization rules, you should study some database design before delving into the development of complex database applications—with Delphi or any other tool. There are many books devoted to this topic, including books on database theory for university courses. They might be difficult to understand at first, but usually provide in-depth information.

## A Join with More Tables

This program is already an interesting example of joining three tables, but there is still some information that is not set properly. For example, the resulting table uses job codes instead of the full job name. We could also add other information that is available in other tables. The improved version (called SQLJOIN2) uses an overly complex SQL statement, built with the Visual Query Builder, as you can see in Figure 18.9.

**FIGURE 18.9:**

The query of the SQLJOIN2 example in the Visual Query Builder.

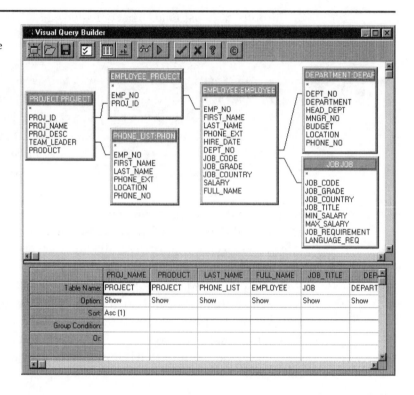

In the query of the SQLJOIN2 example, there is some more information and some more joins. I've added the full job title, replacing the short version, by joining the Job table; the department name by joining the Department table; and the team leader name by joining a second table with employee information, named Phone_List. This is the resulting SQL statement:

```
select distinct
  Project.Proj_Name , Project.Product ,
  Phone_List.Last_Name , Employee.Full_Name ,
  Job.Job_Title , Department.Department
from
  Department Department ,
  Employee_Project Employee_Project ,
  Employee Employee , Project Project ,
  Phone_List Phone_List , Job Job
where
  ( Employee.Job_Code = Job.Job_Code ) and
```

```
      ( Employee.Dept_No = Department.Dept_No ) and
      ( Employee_Project.Emp_No = Employee.Emp_No ) and
      ( Project.Proj_Id = Employee_Project.Proj_Id ) and
      ( Project.Team_Leader = Phone_List.Emp_No )
order by
    Project.Proj_Name
```

The distinct keyword in this statement prevents duplicated records from appearing in the resulting table. Notice that I did not use the Employee table for both the names of the people involved in the project and for the name of the project leader. In fact, this cannot be done directly with the Visual Query Builder. SQL, however, supports such a selection using a *subquery*, which is a query whose result is used in the main query.

As an alternative, I could have done two different queries, merging the two results in the Delphi program using data-aware components. A different solution to this problem, in fact, involves building a master detail query, with master data about the project and detail data about the list of employees working on it. This involves moving back some of the computation to the client side and having two queries instead of one, but it has some real advantages.

Returning to our SQLJOIN2 example, there is one thing we absolutely must fix. The names of the columns are not easy to understand, particularly the first name column, which stores the name of the team leader. To solve the problem, simply use the ColumnAttrib property of the DBGrid or add the components for all of the fields of the query, using the Fields editor, and change their DisplayLabel property. You can see the result of this operation in Figure 18.10. The details are so simple that I haven't listed them here (you can find the source code on the companion CD, which includes the complete form definition).

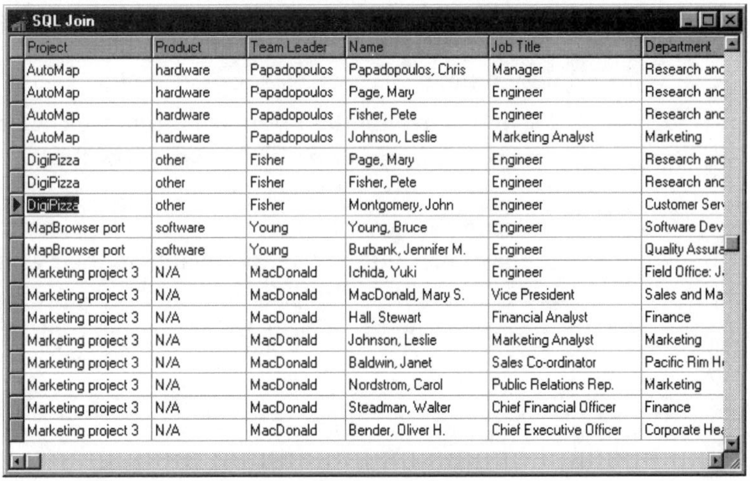

**FIGURE 18.10:**

The form of the SQLJOIN2 example, at run-time.

| Project | Product | Team Leader | Name | Job Title | Department |
|---------|---------|-------------|------|-----------|------------|
| AutoMap | hardware | Papadopoulos | Papadopoulos, Chris | Manager | Research and |
| AutoMap | hardware | Papadopoulos | Page, Mary | Engineer | Research and |
| AutoMap | hardware | Papadopoulos | Fisher, Pete | Engineer | Research and |
| AutoMap | hardware | Papadopoulos | Johnson, Leslie | Marketing Analyst | Marketing |
| DigiPizza | other | Fisher | Page, Mary | Engineer | Research and |
| DigiPizza | other | Fisher | Fisher, Pete | Engineer | Research and |
| DigiPizza | other | Fisher | Montgomery, John | Engineer | Customer Serv |
| MapBrowser port | software | Young | Young, Bruce | Engineer | Software Dev |
| MapBrowser port | software | Young | Burbank, Jennifer M. | Engineer | Quality Assura |
| Marketing project 3 | N/A | MacDonald | Ichida, Yuki | Engineer | Field Office: J |
| Marketing project 3 | N/A | MacDonald | MacDonald, Mary S. | Vice President | Sales and Ma |
| Marketing project 3 | N/A | MacDonald | Hall, Stewart | Financial Analyst | Finance |
| Marketing project 3 | N/A | MacDonald | Johnson, Leslie | Marketing Analyst | Marketing |
| Marketing project 3 | N/A | MacDonald | Baldwin, Janet | Sales Co-ordinator | Pacific Rim He |
| Marketing project 3 | N/A | MacDonald | Nordstrom, Carol | Public Relations Rep. | Marketing |
| Marketing project 3 | N/A | MacDonald | Steadman, Walter | Chief Financial Officer | Finance |
| Marketing project 3 | N/A | MacDonald | Bender, Oliver H. | Chief Executive Officer | Corporate Hea |

# From a Two-Tier to a Three-Tier Architecture

Client/server programming is a very interesting form of application partitioning, where you split the code and workload between two different logical levels, and generally, also, between two different computers. On one side, you have the database data, and on the other side you have the Delphi program accessing it. In the last few years, another approach has been developed to partition applications better, the *three-tier* approach. On one side you have the data, on another side you have the user interface, and on a third side you have some rules and criteria governing how data is accessed and modified by a program.

> **NOTE**
>
> The three-tier approach is a comprehensive technique for client/server development, and I won't discuss its details and advantages here; I'll merely outline its key points. A full discussion of database development in general is beyond the scope of this book.

We can consider the data access components (Table, Query, Data Access, and so on) as part of this third, intermediate level. These non-visual components do not pertain to the user interface, but can be used to set fields properties, add calculated fields, check the new data being posted to the tables, and so on. Using these components, we can implement some of the rules of our data access, although other rules are imposed by the database itself. In the Delphi programs we have built so far, these visual components were intertwined with the data access components, following the typical two-tier approach. All the data-related components were on a single form, and all their code was in the methods of the corresponding form class. What we can do is place the data-access components on a separate form from the data controls, then refer from one form to the other (using File ➤ Use Unit). This way we can connect the data-aware controls to the proper tables or queries at design-time.

The problem with this approach is that we need to create the forms containing the data access components and never show them. The Delphi alternative to this hidden form is to use the data modules (which can be described as *a sort of hidden forms containing non-visual components*). The data modules can hold both the data access components and the method related to their events, thus separating the database access from the user interface portion of the program. In Delphi 2, data modules can constitute a building block for three-tier applications.

## Creating a Data Module

To create a new data module, simply create a new default application, then add a data module to it by selecting File ➤ New a second time. The data module will appear on the screen as an empty white window, where you can add components as usual. There are two key differences: First, you cannot add a control to a data module; second, the data module window is only a design-time representation of a components container, as you can see in Figure 18.11.

FIGURE 18.11:

A data module containing nonvisual components of different kinds.

The TDataModule class derives directly from TContainer, so it is completely unrelated to the Windows concept of a window. The limited similarity between a form and a data module is obvious if you note that the last class has just few properties and events. For this reason, an interesting way to consider data modules is to think of them as *components and method containers in memory*.

What do data modules and forms have in common? What makes them look so similar for a Delphi developer? Like forms, data modules relate to specific Object Pascal units for their definition and to forms definition files (DFM) that list the components included in the module and their properties. The structure of the Delphi unit for a data module is very similar to that of a form. The key difference is in the parent class:

```
type
  TDataModule2 = class(TDataModule)
```

Another thing forms and data modules have in common is that they can both be created when the application starts or later. In fact, they are even listed in the Forms page of the Project Options.

> **TIP**
>
> You might think that data modules relate only to the development of database applications. This is certainly the most common case, but you can take advantage of separate code modules for other purposes, too. An example is handling system components, such as DDE components. Each time some nonvisual components do not strictly relate to a form or can be used in multiple forms, you can use secondary data modules. At times this is an alternative to visual form inheritance, in particular when you want to mimic multiple inheritance (that is, to add different capabilities implemented in various modules to a form).

# A Data Module for Multiple Views

A typical example of the use of a data module is to provide different views to the same data and to keep the views in sync. This is what I've done in the TWOVIEWS example. Later on, I'll extend this example by adding some sort of data rules and some filtering capabilities to the program.

In the TWOVIEWS example, I've created two forms and a data module. Then, I've placed a table related to the CUSTOMER.DB file of the DBDEMOS database and the data source. The data module of this application is very simple; here is its textual definition:

```
object DataModule2: TDataModule2
  object Table1: TTable
    Active = True
    DatabaseName = 'DBDEMOS'
    TableName = 'CUSTOMER.DB'
  object DataSource1: TDataSource
    DataSet = Table1
  end
end
```

Then I've built a toolbar for the main form of the program, using a panel aligned to the top, a speed button, and a DBNavigator. The speed button has a proper glyph and is used to show the secondary form. The rest of the form is filled with a DBGrid. After using the data module from the form, you can set the data access property of both the DBNavigator and the DBGrid to DataModule2.DataSource1.

**WARNING**

> Before you use another unit in a form, you should properly name the unit to which you want to refer. In fact if you use a unit (for example, Unit2), and then rename it when you first save the file, the connection will be lost, and you'll need to manually replace all the references to the renamed unit, even if Delphi built those uses statements automatically, or with the File ➤ Use Unit command.

Then I've moved to the second view, which is based on a form with many DBEdit components, one for each field of the database table except the last. Instead of placing a number of DBEdit components and connecting each of them, you can select the table component in the data module, open the fields editor, add all the fields, select all of them except the last, and then drag the selected fields to the secondary form. With this simple operation, Delphi will arrange all the proper DBEdit components on the form at once. Now add some labels describing the fields, and we are done. I've actually set the Visible property of the secondary form to True, so that it becomes immediately visible when the program starts, as you can see in Figure 18.12.

**FIGURE 18.12:**

The TWOVIEWS program at run-time, with the two synchronized forms referring to the same data.

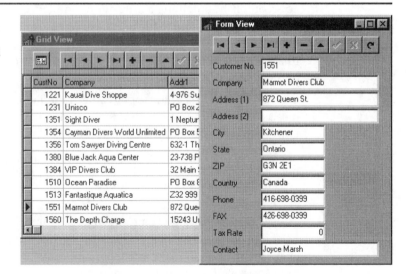

If you display both forms, they are kept in synch. Using one of the two navigators affects both forms. In fact the navigator is connected to neither of them: it relates to the data source in the data module, and the visual components of both forms are affected by any change in the common data access components. Edit one form, and the other will be updated as soon as you accept the changes. Add a new record, and the action will take place on both forms.

Notice that you can also navigate though the records at design-time. While you scroll the grid, the data in the secondary form will change, allowing you, for example, to size the DBEdits so that any of the current records fields is too long to fit in the available space.

# Setting Fields Properties and Initial Values

Using a data module to keep two forms in synch can be handy and is quite simple. We want to add some more capabilities to the program related to the data itself, not the specific viewer. For example, in the data module we can edit the properties of the fields, using a special value for the EditMask properties of the Table1Phone and Table1FAX TField components. This customization will affect the output and the editing of these fields in both forms at the same time.

To accomplish something a little more complex, we can introduce a rule in the table, or at least a suggestion to the users. We want to automatically provide a new unique value for the customer number and make it the current highest value plus one for this field. I've accomplished this by adding some code to the data module in a second version of the program, TWOVIEW2.

Basically, I want to set the proper value of the Table1CustNo field each time the user inserts or appends a new record to the table. To accomplish this you can handle the OnNewRecord event of the table as follows:

```
procedure TDataModule2.Table1NewRecord(DataSet: TDataSet);
begin
  Table1CustNo.Value := Max + 1;
end;
```

The question is, how do I compute the Max value? I can simply browse the table, as we did in the last chapter and check for the highest value of the CustNo field. However, I cannot do this in the event handler above, because this will put the table back in tsBrowse mode from the tsInsert mode. An alternative is to compute the highest value again each time the user inserts a new record, using the OnBeforeInsert event:

```
procedure TDataModule2.Table1BeforeInsert(DataSet: TDataSet);
begin
  ComputeMax;
end;
```

This ComputeMax procedure simply scans the table looking for the maximum value. Here is the structure of the code (which actually handles exceptions with a try-finally block, uses a bookmark, and disables/enables controls, too):

```
procedure TDataModule2.ComputeMax;
begin
  Max := 0;
  Table1.First;
  while not Table1.EOF do
  begin
    if Table1CustNo.AsInteger > Max then
      Max := Table1CustNo.AsInteger;
    Table1.Next;
  end;
end;
```

You can see the complete version of the code of this procedure on the companion CD, in the TWOVIEW2 example. By adding some methods to the data module, we move toward the structure of a three-tier application. This code, in fact, is completely independent from the user interface (the two views). The code of this example is very simple, and is meant to show you this important idea.

## Standard Tables Filtering

Now I want to add to the application some possibilities to filter the records in both views (again using the data module). The simplest filtering capability in Delphi tables is to set a range of values for an indexed field. For example, I've ordered the table of the TWOVIEW2 example using the ByCompany secondary index (just select this value for the IndexName property). Then I've chosen all fields between two values supplied by the user by writing the following:

```
Table1.SetRange (['Abacus'], ['Custom']);
```

As an alternative you can set key values as in the GotoKey method, calling the SetRangeStart, SetRangeEnd, and ApplyRange methods in sequence. Usually it is much simpler to call SetRange and pass it two arrays of values, with the same number of items (and the same order) on the fields in the current index. When you want to stop applying the range, simply call the CancelRange method.

Actually, in the TWOVIEW2 program I haven't indicated a fixed range of values, as suggested above, but added a new dialog box to ask the user for the initial and final value of the range. I could have used the toolbar of the main form, instead of a dialog box, but I wanted again to relate the code used to set the range to the data module itself, not a specific form used to view the data. In practice, I've prepared a form with a checkbox and two edit controls, and added a new custom method to the data modules, with the following code:

```
procedure TDataModule2.ChooseRange;
begin
  with FormRange do
    if ShowModal = mrOK then
      if CheckBoxRange.Checked then
        Table1.SetRange ([Edit1.Text], [Edit2.Text])
      else
        Table1.CancelRange;
end;
```

This means a data module has no visual components, but can rely on specific forms or dialog boxes to provide some direct input output capabilities. Each form can now call this method as it happens with a click on the new Range button of the toolbar of the main form:

```
procedure TForm1.RangeSpeedButtonClick(Sender: TObject);
begin
  DataModule2.ChooseRange;
end;
```

You can see the effect of setting a custom filter, along with the new dialog box, in Figure 18.13. Adding this dialog box is another way to customize the interaction between data and forms, working on the data access layer in between. Although I've added some user interface capabilities to the data module, notice that this dialog box doesn't show any database data, but only some visualization options. For this reason we can reasonably say it belongs to the data module, the third tier.

**FIGURE 18.13:**

The dialog box used to set a range on the table, and the result of this operation on the grid.

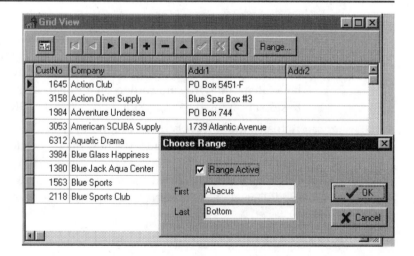

# Custom Table Filtering

Besides giving the table component a range of values to work on, in Delphi 2 you can set a custom filtering algorithm. Simply set the Filtering property of the Table component to True, and for each record the OnFilterRecord event will be called. In the method connected with this event, you can set a custom filter of your choice. Here is an example:

```
procedure TDataModule2.Table1FilterRecord(
  DataSet: TDataSet;
  var Accept: Boolean);
begin
  if (Table1Country.Value = 'US') or
      (Table1Country.Value = 'US Virgin Islands') or
      (Table1State.Value = 'Jamaica') then
    Accept := True
  else
    Accept := False;
end;
```

Again, we have connected this filtering rule to the data module, and it will effect each of the two views. Besides writing a fixed rule, as in the case above, we can allow the user to build his or her own rule, using the range dialog box for this further customization of the data module. This is what I've done in the TWOVIEW3 example (which includes also the code above, commented out).

The new dialog box has another check box and two list boxes (see Figure 18.14), filled with the names of the countries and the states when the form is created:

```
procedure TFormRange.FormCreate(Sender: TObject);
begin
  with DataModule2 do
  begin
    Table1.First;
    while not Table1.EOF do
    begin
      // add unique values
      if ListBoxCountries.Items.
          IndexOf (Table1Country.AsString) < 0 then
        ListBoxCountries.Items.Add (Table1Country.AsString);
      if ListBoxStates.Items.
          IndexOf (Table1State.AsString) < 0 then
        ListBoxStates.Items.Add (Table1State.AsString);
      Table1.Next;
    end;
    // reset the table
    Table1.First;
  end;
end;
```

This code checks to see whether the value of the current record is already present in the list box. If it is not, the value is added to the proper list box. These two lists

FIGURE 18.14:

The new dialog box of the
TWOVIEW3 example, with
advanced filtering capabilities.

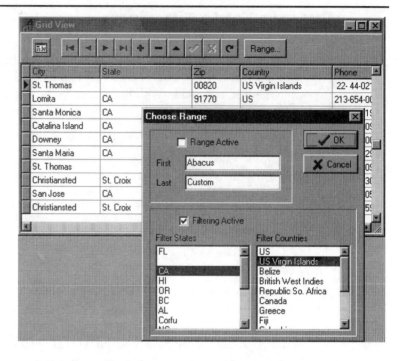

should be updated each time a new record is added to the database table, or whenever an existing record changes. I've omitted this capability, but it should be quite simple for you to implement it by handling the AfterPost event of the table and writing two lines of code similar to the body of the while loop above.

Once the program has filled the list boxes, they are displayed along with the range options. The custom ChooseRange method of the data module should show the dialog box again, check the range, set the filters, and refresh the table. This is necessary because if table filtering was already active but the rules change, Delphi will not automatically recompute the current active records. Here is the new version of the code of this method:

```
procedure TDataModule2.ChooseRange;
begin
  with FormRange do
    if ShowModal = mrOK then
    begin
      if CheckBoxRange.Checked then
        Table1.SetRange ([Edit1.Text], [Edit2.Text])
      else
        Table1.CancelRange;
      Table1.Filtered := CheckBoxFiltering.Checked;
      Table1.Refresh;
    end;
end;
```

The most important piece of code, however, is the handler of the OnFilterRecord events, which now checks to see if the country or state of the current record is one of the selected items of the two list boxes (which allow multiple selection, but not extended selection). Here is the code:

```
procedure TDataModule2.Table1FilterRecord(
  DataSet: TDataSet;
  var Accept: Boolean);
begin
  with FormRange.ListBoxCountries do
    if Selected [Items.IndexOf (Table1Country.AsString)] then
      Accept := True
    else
      Accept := False;
  with FormRange.ListBoxStates do
    if Selected [Items.IndexOf (Table1State.AsString)] then
      Accept := True;
end;
```

Notice that in the second `if` statement, the value of `Accept` should be added to the previous one with an or statement. Actually, I can simply set it to True regardless of the previous value (since an or with True always returns True), or let it maintain its current value (since an or with False keeps the existing value).

# Custom Filtering and Client/Server Development

If you browse the code of the last example, you'll see that the program interacts with the database data a lot. There are methods scanning the values of a table, looking for the highest value or for the distinct strings. There is also some filtering code written in ObjectPascal. As we have seen, most of this code is not directly connected with the user interface but logically belongs to a separate data module. This might look like a correct three-tier approach, but it can also be a bad client/server approach.

In fact, by basing this code heavily on data modules, we have loaded the client application with further computation, leaving the server with little to do (well, we used a Paradox table, so this made sense, but I'm trying to discuss a more general case here). If the table were a SQL Server table with a large amount of data in it, our program wouldn't have been very efficient. In such a case we should still use the data module, but we would try to add several queries (executed by the server) replacing our data-related methods (computed by the client).

For example, we might add to TWOVIEW3 example queries computing the highest customer number, getting all the distinct states and countries names, and write a complex where statement to filter the records or choose a range. I'm not going to write this new version of the program, but you might consider it a more complete three-tier approach, where the computational load of the intermediate tier is on the server as much as possible. Writing stored procedure on the server is the next step of this approach.

As a conclusion, consider that Delphi 2 lets you identify the three tiers (the data view, the intermediate rules, and the actual data access) but provides little help in partitioning such an application between the client (ObjectPascal code) and the server (SQL code). This is up to you and your experience, because it is not always easy to determine the best solution from an architectural point of view and yet try to make it work as fast as possible.

# Delphi Data Dictionary

It is very common to use fields with a similar layout (for example, the same display mask) in a single application or in different applications. If you use integer numbers, decimal numbers, percent values, phone and fax numbers (possibly the same number with different extensions) and other standard fields, it is extremely tedious to set each one of them from scratch. For this reason, Delphi 2 includes a Data Dictionary. This is a sort of database that stores the properties of fields. You can define the properties of these standard fields using the Dictionary, or you can simply copy them from existing fields (of course, you can also use the existing entries in the Dictionary without further work).

In a client/server environment (with several Delphi programmers), the Data Dictionary can reside on a remote server for additional sharing of information.

> **NOTE** Notice that the default Data Dictionary is implemented using a Paradox table, but you can define a new one based on a SQL server table.

## The Data Dictionary and the Fields Editor

Most of the operations involving the Data Dictionary take place in the fields editor of a table or query component. The local menu of the Fields Editor, in fact, has five commands related to the use of the Data Dictionary (see Figure 18.15).

**FIGURE 18.15:**

The local menu of the Fields Editor, with the menu commands used to interact with the Data Dictionary.

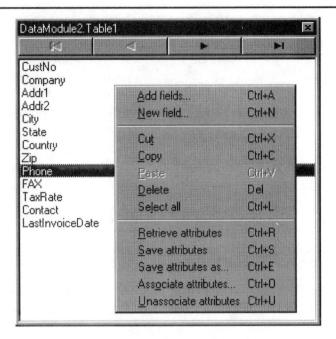

Here is what they do (I've listed them in a more logical order):

| Attribute | Usage |
|---|---|
| Associate Attributes | This command is used to associate an attribute set with a given field. In practice, you can select one of the attribute sets from the Dictionary to use with the current field. When you associate a field with an attribute set from the Data Dictionary, the attributes will actually be copied to the properties of the field. |
| Unassociate Attributes | This command is the reverse of the Associate attributes operation. It breaks the association between the field and the attribute set. |
| Retrieve Attributes | This command is used to get the current values from the related attribute set. This can be used only while the field is associated with an attribute set. You can think of this as a loading command. |

| Attribute | Usage |
|---|---|
| Save Attributes | This command is the reverse of the Retrieve attributes operation. It copies the values of the properties of the current field to the associated attribute set. If no attribute set is associated, it will prompt you for a new name, as does the Save Attributes As command below. |
| Save Attributes As | This command is used to associate the field with a new attribute set, for which you have to provide a name in the dialog box that appears. |

These commands should be quite intuitive, and I suggest that you use the Data Dictionary to learn how to use them. You'll get used to the Dictionary quickly.

Defining associations between attribute types and field names: this makes it very simple to use the proper attributes set for another field that has the same name as an existing one. All the "Phone" fields are automatically associated with a specific attribute set (such as the predefined USPhones entry in the Data Dictionary).

**TIP**

I suggest that you write down the five shortcut keys related to these five commands of the local menu on a small card and keep the card by your computer. If you memorize the shortcut keys, you'll be able to use the Data Dictionary much faster.

## What's in an Attribute Set?

In the previous section, I mentioned the term *attribute set* several times. An *attribute set* is an entry (a *record*) of the Data Dictionary. An attribute set refers to several properties of a TField object, but also includes other general properties.

Many of the properties of the attribute set correspond to properties of the various TField subclasses; these should be quite simple to understand. Here is a list of the properties:

- Alignment
- BlobType
- Currency
- DisplayFormat
- DisplayLabel
- DisplayValues

- DisplayWidth

- EditFormat

- EditMask

- MaxValue

- MinValue

- Precision

- ReadOnly

- Required

- Transliterate

- Visible

Of course, if you set a property as Precision (a value used only for floating point numbers), then associate the attribute set with a TStringField, the value will be ignored.

A few other values of the attribute set define the general behavior of a field, and are used to determine how to create a new field object for a given field of a table or query:

| Attribute | Usage |
|---|---|
| TField Class | Indicates the type of field (the TField subclass) to create when a field is added to a data set. |
| TControl Class | Determines the type of data-aware component Delphi will create when you drag a field from the Fields Editor to a form. If no value is provided, Delphi will use a standard approach, which depends on the type of the field object. |
| Based On | This is a value you are asked to provide when you save an attribute set with a new name. It indicates another attribute set upon which the current one is based. This means that if you make a change to an attribute of the original set and this attribute is not overridden by the current set, the change will affect the current set, too. The analogy that comes to mind to explain this is that of the styles for word processing program, which can be based on other similar styles. Of course, this resembles a sort of inheritance, too. |

## Exploring the Data Dictionary

You can easily define a new attributes set by saving the attributes of a current field from the Fields Editor, as I've mentioned before. However, you can also define new attribute sets, or simply view them using the Database Explorer. Simply open this tool, select the Dictionary tab above the left pane, and you'll see the Default Data Dictionary (DefaultDD), based on the BDESDD Paradox table. If you've added new Data Dictionaries, you'll see them all. Under the Dictionary entry, you'll find two subtrees, Databases and Attribute Sets, as you can see in Figure 18.16.

Under Attribute Sets, you'll find a list of these sets, each one with the values of its properties. There are also lists of database tables using each set and of the other attribute sets based on the sets. You can also use the Database Explorer to create new attribute sets or modify them.

The associations between fields of the database tables and the attribute sets can also be seen and modified by exploring the second subtree, Databases. Once you have selected a field of a table, a combo box will allow you to associate it with one of the available attribute sets in the Data Dictionary.

On the whole, when you are starting a new project and you have planned its database tables, I suggest that you start setting up some attribute sets and their associations before starting to work in Delphi. If your plan is not so well defined, though, you should simply use the Fields Editor to build up your Data Dictionary along with your tables, and then use the Explorer to revise the current situation and to document it.

**FIGURE 18.16:**

The Data Dictionary, as you can see it in the Database Explorer.

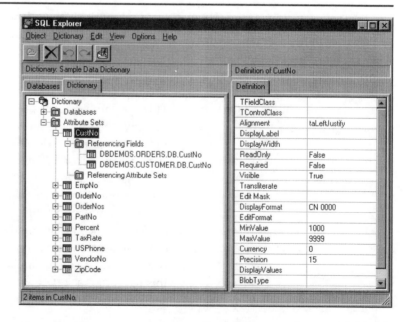

# Summary

Client/server programming has been a very hot topic for some time now, and terms such as *downsizing*, *upsizing*, and *rightsizing* are becoming increasingly common (whatever they mean, since I've noticed that to different people, these terms mean different things). Among these, however, *three-tier* is probably latest buzzword. Again, people use it for different things, and I've tried to show you how it relates to Delphi and the data modules, but also how Delphi architecture can lead to an improper use of the term.

In this chapter, we have just seen a few things, scratching the surface of the problems and showing some practical examples. I hope this was enough to make you curious about client/server application development. There is really a lot of work (and a lot of money) involved in this area of programming, which bridges personal computers and bigger machines in a way that has not been possible in the past. Most of the topics I've mentioned probably required more in-depth study, but this was well beyond the scope of a Delphi programming book.

Although it does not contain many more tools than the standard edition, Delphi Client/Server Suite has everything you need to build robust applications for enterprise environments. Furthermore, it contains a lot more licensing and redistribution rights than other editions of Delphi.

With this chapter, the database-specific portion of the book ends, although we will examine another database-related tool, ReportSmith, in Chapter 22. In that chapter, we will add report-printing capability to some of the examples developed in this and the previous chapter. For the moment, we will return to Windows programming, and look into some advanced topics.

# PART III

## Advanced Delphi Programming

# CHAPTER
## NINETEEN

# Discovering the Application Structure

- The role of the Application object

- Programs without components

- Windows command-line parameters

- A graphical clock application

- Background processing and multithreading

- Uses of the Screen object

- Windows INI files and the Registry

**W**e have seen that Delphi applications are made up of one or more forms. Everything involves forms and components placed inside forms. However, if you just look at the source code of any project file, another element appears: the Application object.

This is a global object, which has a role like the director in an orchestra; but at the same time, it is also a window. The Application object was introduced in Chapter 9. This chapter explores the possible uses of this global object, and of another global object we have already used, the Screen object. In exploring the roles of these objects, many related ideas will emerge, including a broad discussion of Windows messages, timers, background computing, and multitasking. I'll also discuss the use of INI files, the registry, and more.

During this exploration, we will examine another interesting topic: programming without components. It is possible to build a Delphi application without using components. The central focus of the programs we have built up to now has always been a component placed inside the form, and these components have always received the user input and provided some output. In this chapter, I'll show you something completely different.

# Using the Application Object

When you create a new, blank application, Delphi generates some code for the project file:

```
program Project1;

uses
  Forms,
  Unit1 in 'UNIT1.PAS' {Form1};
{$R *.RES}
begin
  Application.Initialize;
  Application.CreateForm(TForm1, Form1);
  Application.Run;
end.
```

This code uses the global object, Application, of class TApplication, defined by the VCL. This object is indeed a component, although you cannot set its properties using the Object Inspector. But this is not a real problem, since the application has only a few properties. These properties include the name of the executable file, the title of the application (by default, the name of the executable file without the extension), and a few events. You can set some of the properties of the global Application object using the Application page of the Project Options dialog box.

We can start understanding the role of the Application object by looking at an example. Create a new application, compile it (saving the files with the default names, UNIT1.PAS and PROJECT1.DPR), and run it. An empty window titled *Form1* appears on the screen, and the corresponding TaskBar icon is named Project1, which is the name of the application's main window. Behind the scenes, Delphi creates a window for the application object and a second window, the main window, which the application window owns. In fact, the application window has zero height and width, and therefore is not visible (although it is not hidden, because that would affect its behavior).

You can perform two additional tests. You can see the name of the main window in the new Windows 95 Tasks application (TASKMAN.EXE in the WINDOWS directory), as shown in Figure 19.1, on the upper-right portion. In this window, the program is listed as Form1. Now, invoke the Windows 95 Close Program window by pressing Ctrl+Alt+Del. As you can see in the bottom part of Figure 19.1, this window displays a list of the running applications, or processes, and displays the name Project1 for our new Delphi application.

**FIGURE 19.1:**

Windows 95 has both a Tasks application that lists the main window and a Close Program window that displays the list of tasks or processes.

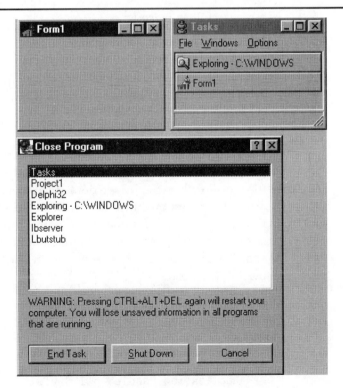

When you're running Delphi itself, Windows 95 displays Delphi's application name in the TaskBar, but it displays the name of the main form in the Tasks window and in the switch window that appears when you press the Alt+Tab. Obviously, Delphi behaves in the same way as the applications it generates (because Delphi was built with Delphi itself). When Delphi's main window (the window that contains the menu bar) is visible, you see the name of the project window's caption. However, when you look at the TaskBar, the name of the project is missing. This is possible because the TaskBar displays the caption of the application window instead of displaying the caption of the main window. It is not easy to determine whether this is an advantage or a disadvantage. To inexperienced users, seeing two different names can be confusing. However, the application name has the advantage of remaining fixed, while the caption of a program usually changes to reflect the name of the current file or other dynamic information.

You probably should use the initial name of the main form as the name of the application, or make sure that the application and form name synchronized. To accomplish this, you may need to change the title of the application each time the caption of the main form changes. Since Application object is global, it can be accessed by any unit. As soon as you change the caption of the main form, you can write the following code:

```
Application.Title := Caption;
```

You can also write this code at startup (in the OnCreate event of the main form). As an alternative, you can set the initial application name in the Application page of the Project Options dialog box, together with some other Application object properties.

## Showing the Application Window

There is no better proof that there is indeed a window for the Application object than to show it. Actually, we don't need to show it—we need to resize it and set a couple of window attributes, such as the presence of a caption and a border. Delphi provides no facilities to accomplish this directly, so we need to perform this work by using Windows API functions to modify the window indicated by the Application.Handle. For example, in the SHOWAPP program I've written the following code:

```
procedure TForm1.Button1Click(Sender: TObject);
var
  OldStyle: Integer;
begin
  // add border and caption to the app window
  OldStyle := GetWindowLong (
    Application.Handle, gwl_Style);
  SetWindowLong (Application.Handle, gwl_Style,
    OldStyle or ws_ThickFrame or ws_Caption);
```

```
// set the size of the app window
SetWindowPos (Application.Handle,
  0, 0, 0, 200, 100,
  swp_NoMove or swp_NoZOrder);
end;
```

The two `GetWindowLong` and `SetWindowLong` API functions are used to access to system information related to the window. In this case, we are using the `gwl_Style` parameter to read or write the styles of the window, which include its border, title, system menu, border icons, and so on. The code above gets the current styles and adds (using an `or` statement) a standard border and a caption to the form. You seldom need to use these low-level API functions in Delphi, because there are properties of the TForm class that have the same effect. We need this code here because the application window is not a form.

By executing this code, the project window appears as you can see in Figure 19.2. I suggest that you play with this program a little bit. Although there's no need to implement something like this in your own programs, running this program will reveal the relationship between the application window and the main window of a Delphi program. This is a very important starting point if you want to study the internal structure of Delphi applications.

**FIGURE 19.2:**

The hidden application window revealed by the SHOWAPP program.

# Checking for Multiple Instances of an Application

Probably one of the most common changes in the source code of the project file is to add a check for the existence of a previous *instance* of the application. Windows 3.1 programmers probably know that you can test the value of a system parameter, known as `HPrevInstance`. This is one of the parameters of a standard `WinMain` function, the entry point of traditional Windows programs written in C. Unfortunately, in Windows NT and Windows 95 this parameter is always 0 (for a 32-bit application).

In any case, Delphi programmers can use four global variables to retrieve the value of the WinMain parameters:

- HInstance holds an internal Windows value referring to the current instance of an application.

- HPrevInst (in Windows 3.1) holds the HInstance value of the previous running instance of the application, or zero for the first copy. Under Windows 95 or Windows NT, this value is always zero.

- CmdLine contains the command-line parameters passed to the application, such as the name of a file.

- CmdShow (in Windows 3.1) contains a display code indicating whether the main window of the application should be minimized or maximized at startup. Under Windows 95 a fixed value is passed each time, and you have to call a system function to get the real display code.

These four parameters can be important because they help make your application work seamlessly in the Windows environment.

## Testing to See if Another Instance Is Running

If you want to run a single instance of an application, the initialization code of the project source file might be written as follows:

```
var
  Hwnd: THandle;
begin
  Hwnd := FindWindow ('TForm1', 'One Copy');
  if Hwnd = 0 then
  begin
    Application.Initialize;
    Application.CreateForm(TForm1, Form1);
    Application.Run;
  end
end.
```

The FindWindow API function requires two parameters: the name of the window class (the name used to register the form's window type, or WNDCLASS, in the system) and the caption of the window for which you are looking. You are free to omit one of these two parameters, supplying only one. In a Delphi application, the name of the WNDCLASS is the same as the Object Pascal name for the class of the form (for example, *TForm1*). The result of the FindWindow function is a handle to the window, or zero if a matching window was not found.

With the above code, the user can start a new instance of the application only if there isn't already a previous instance. If a previous instance exists, nothing happens. Unfortunately, if you run this program from within the Delphi IDE, a window with that caption and class already exists: the design-time form. Thus, the program won't start even once. (However, it will run if you close the form and its corresponding source file, or if you close the project and run the program from the Explorer.)

## Activating the Previous Instance

To improve this program, you can warn the user that this is the second instance, and then activate the main form of the previous instance of the program. This is the behavior of many Windows programs, from several small applications included in the system to some big commercial applications, and it's what I've added to the ONECOPY1 example.

To activate the window of the previous instance of the application, you cannot use the SetActiveWindow API function, which was commonly used in Windows 3.1 programs. Instead, you should use the new SetForegroundWindow function, which also works for windows owned by other processes. So you can write an else branch for the if statement above:

```
var
  Hwnd: THandle;
begin
  Hwnd := FindWindow ('TForm1', 'One Copy');
  if Hwnd = 0 then
  begin
    Application.Initialize;
    Application.CreateForm(TForm1, Form1);
    Application.Run;
  end
  else
  begin
    MessageDlg ('You cannot run a second copy of the
      application!' +
      Chr(13) + 'The form of the older copy will be
        displayed',
      mtInformation, [mbOK], 0);
    SetForegroundWindow (Hwnd);
  end
end.
```

To compile this code, you should add the Dialogs and Windows units to the uses clause of the project source. Again, you might have problems running this program from inside the Delphi IDE.

The ONECOPY1 example is a bare program that has a main form with only a single big label. You can see it running in Figure 19.3, where a second instance has been

**FIGURE 19.3:**
The output of the first and second instances of the ONECOPY1 example. When you click on OK, the first instance is activated again.

launched. When you click on OK in the message box, the first instance is activated and the second terminates its execution.

If you want a program that behaves in the same way as many Windows applications, simply remove the message and activate the older instance directly.

Notice, however, that the program works only if the main window of the previous instance of the application has not been minimized. When the application is minimized, in fact, the form window is hidden and the activation code has no effect. You could use other functions to show the hidden form, but this creates far more problems than it solves. In fact, you might even end up with the form window and the minimized application window on the screen at the same time (as we saw in the SHOWAPP program).

After trying a number of ways, I've found a solution that is not elegant, but it works. Although this technique is far from perfect, I've decided to include it in the book because it shows you how to define and respond to user-defined Windows messages.

## Handling User-Defined Windows Messages

In the ONECOPY2 program, we need to ask the form of another application, the previous instance, to activate itself, even if it is not visible. This can be done by sending a user-defined Windows message to the form—a message that the form can handle in a method we write. We can test whether the form is minimized and then post a new user-defined message to the old window. The following code replaces the last code fragment in ONECOPY2:

```
begin
  Hwnd := FindWindow ('TForm1', 'One Copy');
```

```
    if Hwnd = 0 then
    begin
      Application.Initialize;
      Application.CreateForm(TForm1, Form1);
      Application.Run;
    end
    else
    begin
      if (not IsWindowVisible (Hwnd)) then
        PostMessage (Hwnd, wm_User, 0, 0);
      SetForegroundWindow (Hwnd);
    end
end.
```

The `PostMessage` API function sends a message to the message queue of the application owning the destination window, indicated as the first parameter (messages are always sent to windows). In the code of the form, you can add a special handling function related to this message:

```
type
  TForm1 = class(TForm)
    Label1: TLabel;
  public
    procedure WMUser (var msg: TMessage); message wm_User;
  end;
```

Now we can write the code of this method, which is simple:

```
procedure TForm1.WMUser (var msg: TMessage);
begin
  Application.Restore;
end;
```

Again, if you run this program from the Delphi IDE, it might not work properly, since the `FindWindow` call may return the handle of the form displayed by the Delphi Form Designer, which is usually hidden when the program runs. To test this program, do not merely close this form design window (or hide it), but instead close the corresponding source code file or the entire project and run the resulting program by itself. I'll show you a better version of the program, which does not have this problem, in the next section.

## Searching the Windows List

As I just mentioned, the `FindWindow` API function used in the last example is not always reliable. For example, it cannot discriminate between the form of the previous instance of the application and the form used at design-time in the Delphi environment. To make some improvements, I've written a third version of the example, ONECOPY3, which uses a different approach.

When you want to search for a specific main window of the system, you can use the `EnumWindows` API functions. Enumeration functions are quite peculiar in

Windows, because they usually require another function as a parameter. To be more precise, they require a pointer to a function, or a *procedural type variable* in Object Pascal terms. The idea is that this function is applied to each element of the list (in this case, the list of main windows), until the list ends or the function returns True.

We can replace the initial portion of the program (calling FindWindow) with the new code. Here is the final version of the initialization code of the project:

```
var
  OldHwnd: THandle;
begin
  OldHwnd := 0;
  EnumWindows (@EnumWndProc, Longint (@OldHwnd));
  if OldHwnd = 0 then
  begin
    Application.Initialize;
    Application.CreateForm(TForm1, Form1);
    Application.Run;
  end
  else
  begin
    if (not IsWindowVisible (OldHwnd)) then
      PostMessage (OldHwnd, wm_User, 0, 0);
    SetForegroundWindow (OldHwnd);
  end;
end.
```

In this statement, OldWnd is a window handle, passed by address, where we will store the result of our search. EnumWndProc is a function I have written. This function checks the name of each window's class, looking for the string *TForm1*. When this is found, the procedure retrieves the module file name (that is, the name of the executable file of the application) of the current program and of the program owning the matching form. If the module names correspond, too, we can be quite sure that we have found a previous instance of the same program. Here is the full source code of the enumeration function:

```
type
  PHWND = ^HWND;
function EnumWndProc (Hwnd: THandle;
  FoundWnd: PHWND): Bool; export; stdcall;
var
  ClassName, ModuleName, WinModuleName: string;
  WinInstance: THandle;
begin
  Result := True;
  SetLength (ClassName, 100);
  GetClassName (Hwnd, PChar (ClassName), Length (ClassName));
  ClassName := PChar (ClassName);
  if AnsiCompareText (ClassName, 'TForm1') = 0 then
  begin
    SetLength (ModuleName, 200);
```

```
    SetLength (WinModuleName, 200);
    GetModuleFileName ( HInstance,
      PChar (ModuleName), Length (ModuleName));
    WinInstance := GetWindowLong (Hwnd, gwl_hInstance);
    GetModuleFileName ( WinInstance,
      PChar (WinModuleName), Length (WinModuleName));
    if AnsiCompareText (ModuleName, WinModuleName) = 0 then
    begin
      FoundWnd^ := Hwnd;
      Result := False;
    end;
  end;
end;
```

Notice that we must define the function as export and stdcall, because it is passed as a pointer to another function, and then called by the system. Windows can call directly only functions we mark as export in the Pascal code, and cannot understand the default fastcall Delphi calling convention.

# Programming without Components

As I mentioned at the beginning of this chapter, programming with components is not the only choice of a Delphi developer. In this environment, components certainly have a central role, but it is possible to write Delphi applications without any components except forms. (Well, you can also write programs without forms, but this is a very special case.) Which kind of applications can you write without using components? Windows applications were traditionally written using straight C code, and it is possible to write applications using a similar low-level approach in Delphi, too.

In fact, my last question was not phrased properly. It should be, "Which kind of applications are easier to write without using components?" I think the answer is that very few applications are easier to write without components and without a visual environment. Both small and large applications benefit from a component approach. Of course, the predefined Delphi components are better suited for some kinds of programs, but by adding the proper custom components to the environment, you can write any type of complex program.

Even if the programs you write have a bare user interface or no user interface at all, like a screen saver or device driver, you can still benefit from some of the objects of the environment, such as streams or lists.

Although you can write Delphi applications without components—ignore the VCL and Delphi visual environment and write C-like code calling API functions—it doesn't make much sense. Even so, we will begin with a couple of short examples, just to show you in practice that this can be done.

> **NOTE**
>
> Another occasion when you are not going to use components, or at least not many, is when you are *writing* a component. This topic is crucial to the development of powerful Delphi applications and is the subject of Chapter 27.

## The Smallest Delphi Program?

As you have seen in the previous examples, you can add some code directly to the project file of an application. Projects can be manipulated in Delphi either by using the Project Manager and setting Project Options (the recommended way) or by changing the source code of the project file by hand (the "hacker" way).

It is possible to write any kind of code in the initialization section of the project. Instead of creating a form and running an application, you can produce a beep, display a message box, or run another program. The advantage is that if you do not use forms and the Application object, then the size of the executable code shrinks incredibly because the VCL library is not included.

Of course, such programs have a very limited use. They can be defined as the smallest programs you can compile with Delphi, but I don't consider them to be true Delphi programs (this is the reason for the question mark in the title of this section). They are just small Object Pascal Windows applications that have been written and compiled using the Delphi environment.

This is probably the shortest program you can build with Delphi (called BEEP on the companion CD):

```
program Beep;

uses
  Windows;

begin
  MessageBeep (0);
end.
```

The size of the executable file? Just a few Kbytes, compared to the typical hundreds of Kbytes of a simple Delphi executable file. Is it useful? Hardly. It just produces a beep and terminates. If you don't have a sound board installed, you can try setting different values, as we have seen in the past (see a full description of the Message-Beep API function in Chapter 26). To create a small program like this, you should remove every form from a project, using the Project Manager window, and change the default uses statement, as shown in the short BEEP program above.

# Reading the Command Line

The smallest program that is actually meaningful is a simple example that uses Windows command-line parameters. Although users seldom specify command-line parameters in a graphical user interface environment, the Windows command-line parameters are important to the system. For example, once you have defined an association between a file extension and an application, you can simply run a program by selecting an associated file. If you double-click on a bitmap file (with the BMP extension), Paintbrush will generally start and load the bitmap file automatically. In practice, when you double-click on a file that has an association, it runs the corresponding Windows program (for example, PaintBrush), and passes the selected file as a command-line parameter. It is up to the program to open the file passed as a parameter, and a well-behaved Windows application should do so.

The following example, called STRPARAM (for string parameters), demonstrates the use of the command line (or a string command). This statement shows the text of the command line:

```
ShowMessage (CmdLine);
```

If you run it, you'll see that in Windows 95 (and Windows NT) the command line includes the full path of the executable file as first parameter, followed by any other command line parameters. The program path name is enclosed within double quotation marks (" "). To remove the path name and extract just the parameters, we can scan the string locating the second double quotation mark character, as in the following code (which displays a standard message in case no other parameters are present):

```
var
  Params: PChar;
begin
  Params := StrScan (CmdLine, '"') + 1;
  Params := StrScan (Params, '"') + 2;
  if StrLen (Params) > 0 then
    ShowMessage (Params)
  else
    ShowMessage ('No command line');
end.
```

Although the code above shows how to access the CmdLine string and manipulate it, this is not the best way to write similar code. Delphi, in fact, includes two functions to handle the command line parameters: ParamCount and ParamStr. The first returns the number of parameters; the second returns the parameter in a given position. Parameters including spaces can be used if they are delimited by double quotes, as with long file names or the path of a program. Notice that you can use this expression:

```
ParamStr(0)
```

to retrieve the full path of the current program. Here is how we can correct the code above, using these functions:

```
begin
  if ParamCount > 0 then
    ShowMessage (ParamStr (1))
  else
    ShowMessage ('No command line');
end.
```

Certainly, this code is much simpler. In the source code of the STRPARAM example, you'll find each of the versions of the code. You can test this program in several ways. If you run it by itself, without a command-line parameter, the "No command line" message is displayed. To provide a command-line parameter during debugging, you can use the Parameters option on Delphi's Run menu.

Another technique is to open Windows 95's Explorer, locate the directory that contains the executable file of the program, and drag another file over the executable file. The Explorer will start the program using the name of the dropped file as command-line parameter. Figure 19.4 shows both the Explorer and the corresponding output.

**FIGURE 19.4:**
You can provide a command-line parameter to the STRPARAM example by dropping a file over the executable file in the Windows 95 Explorer.

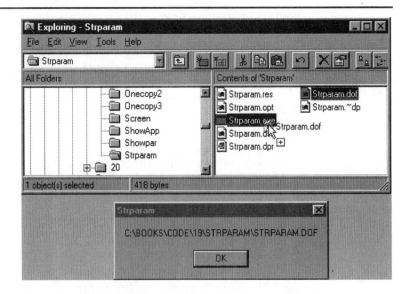

## Using the Command Show Parameter

When you start a Windows application, you can actually pass two different parameters: the command-line string and an integer code. This is quite evident from the parameters of the `WinExec` API function, which is the simplest way to run an application (an alternative is the more complex `ShellExecute` function):

```
function WinExec(CmdLine: PChar; CmdShow: Word): Word;
```

Under Windows 3.1, the application being executed should use the CmdShow parameter to display itself normally, minimized, maximized, and so on. You can see the list of values for this *show parameter* in the description of the `ShowWindow` function in the Windows API Help file included in Delphi. However, in Windows 95 the value of this parameter is always `sw_ShowDefault`.

In Windows 95, the most common way to set an application's display property is through the Properties of a shortcut (in the Explorer or on the desktop), as you can see in Figure 19.5. If you try passing the Minimized value to a standard Delphi application, nothing happens. If you try passing the Maximized value, the form is shown maximized, but only for less than a second, just long enough for you to notice the strange behavior.

To retrieve the value set with the Shortcut properties shown in Figure 19.5 you need to call another API function, `GetStartupInfo`. This fills the `TStartupInfo` structure with information about the main window of the program at startup, including the `wShowWindow` field for which we are looking.

**FIGURE 19.5:**

The Program Item Properties dialog box of Windows Program Manager can be used to run a program minimized.

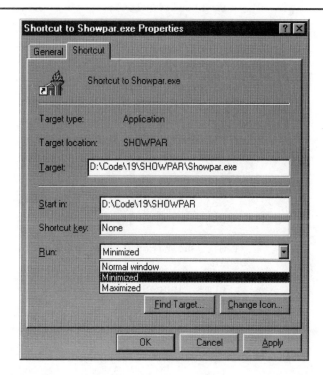

Now we are ready to build our next example, SHOWPAR. Create a new, blank project, with a generic blank form (do not remove the main form, as we did in the two previous examples). Then write the following code in the project source file:

```
program Showpar;

uses
  Forms, Windows, SysUtils, Messages,
  Show_f in 'SHOW_F.PAS' {Form1};

{$R *.RES}

type
  TTenStrings = array [0..10] of string [20];

const
  SwShowNames: TTenStrings = (
    'sw_Hide',
    'sw_ShowNormal',
    'sw_ShowMinimized',
    'sw_ShowMaximized',
    'sw_ShowNoActivate',
    'sw_Show',
    'sw_Minimize',
    'sw_ShowMinNoActive',
    'sw_ShowNA',
    'sw_Restore',
    'sw_ShowDefault');

var
  SI: TStartupInfo;

begin
  Application.Initialize;
  Application.CreateForm(TForm1, Form1);

  GetStartupInfo (SI);
  if SI.wShowWindow = sw_ShowMinNoActive then
  begin
    {minimize the main window}
    // Form1.WindowState := wsMinimized;
    PostMessage (Form1.Handle, wm_SysCommand,
      sc_Minimize, 0);
    Beep;
  end;
  if SI.wShowWindow = sw_ShowMaximized then
  begin
    {maximize the main window}
    Form1.WindowState := wsMaximized;
    Beep;
  end;
```

```
  // set the caption
  Form1.Caption := 'Command Show = ' +
    SwShowNames [CmdShow] + ' - ' +
    SwShowNames [SI.wShowWindow];
  Application.Run;
end.
```

This program is quite simple. When the value of SI.wShowWindow is sw_ShowMin-NoActive, it beeps to notify the user and minimizes the application (actually its main form).

In this code you cannot call Application.Minimize (the standard call to minimize an application at run-time) because the startup code has still not been completely executed. The alternative could be to use the wsMinimized value for the WindowState property of the form. This works, but in Windows 95 it shows the form minimized; that is, as a small rectangle above the task bar. This is far from nice, but it is how Delphi and Windows 95 show minimized forms.

The only alternative I've found is the call to the PostMessage function you see in the code above. This mimics the selection of the minimize command on the system menu, posting a message to the form. Since this message is posted (see next section for more details), it will be executed after the startup code is done. The final result is correct, but the form is first displayed as normal, then minimized. I've tried in a number of ways, but this is the best solution I've found without changing the VCL source code.

It is easier to maximize the application, because setting the wsMaximized value of the WindowState property works as documented. The other feature of the program is that it shows the value of the CmdShow parameter and of the wShowWindow field of the TStartupInfo structure in the caption of the form. To display the name of the constant instead of a numeric code, I've defined a constant array of strings storing all of the parameter names. With this enhancement, you can use this program to see which value is passed to the application each time it is executed by a shell program, such as the Explorer, by a shortcut on the desktop, or by one of the third-party shells available for the Windows environment.

# Events, Messages, and Multitasking in Windows

To understand how Windows applications work, we need to spend a minute discussing how multitasking is supported in this environment. We also need to understand the role of timers (and the Timer component) and of background (or *idle*) computing. Then we will move on to Windows 95 multithreading and support for this feature in Delphi applications.

In short, we need to delve deeper into the event-driven structure of Windows and in its multitasking support. I won't discuss this topic in detail, since this is a book about *Delphi* programming, but I will provide an overview for the readers who have limited experience in Windows programming or who are not familiar with the new capabilities of Windows 95.

# Event-Driven Programming

The basic idea behind event-driven programming is that specific events determine the flow of the application. A program spends most of its time waiting for events and provides code to respond to several of them (not all of them, since a program usually ignores events that don't interest it). For example, when a user clicks one of the mouse buttons, an event occurs. A message describing this event is sent to the window currently under the mouse cursor. The program code that responds to events for that window will receive the event, process it, and respond accordingly. When the code finished responding to this event, the program returns to a waiting state.

As this explanation shows, events are serialized; each event is handled only after the previous one is completed. When an application is executing event-response code (that is, it is not waiting for an event), other events for that application have to wait in a message queue reserved for that application. In the 16-bit versions of Windows, there was limited multitasking capability, based on the fact that each application took turns responding to its own messages. When an application had responded to a message and returned to a waiting state, it became last in the list of programs waiting to handle additional messages. In Windows 3.1, there was no way to stop an application from executing a complex event handler, and other applications simply had to wait.

Event handling and the message queues are still the core of Windows 95 and Windows NT, but in these 32-bit versions of the environment, after a fixed amount of time has elapsed, the system interrupts the current application and immediately gives control to the next one in the list. Only after each application has had a turn is the first resumed. What these operating systems implement is a form of preemptive multitasking, a feature sorely lacking in Windows 3.1.

For this reason, Windows 3.1 applications used many techniques to divide an algorithm into smaller chunks and execute them one at a time. These techniques include using timers and performing background (or idle computing), and are still useful. Therefore I'll describe them in the following sections.

By the way, in Win32, just as in Windows 3.1, if an application has responded to its events and is waiting for its turn to process messages, it has no chance to regain control until it receives another message. This is one reason timers continue to exist (besides 16-bit compatibility). One final note—when you think about events, remember that input events (using the mouse or the keyboard) account for only a small percentage of the total message flow in a Windows application. Most of the messages are the system's internal messages or messages exchanged between different controls and windows. Even a familiar input operation such as clicking a mouse button can result in a huge number of messages, most of which are internal Windows messages.

You can test this yourself by using the WinSight utility included in Delphi. In WinSight, choose to view the Message Trace, and select the messages for all of the windows. Select Start, and then perform some normal operations with the mouse. You'll see hundreds of messages in a few minutes. Of course, WinSight causes Windows to run much slower then usual, because of its monitoring. At normal speed, the flow of messages is even faster than you'll see when you run WinSight.

## Windows Message Delivery

Before looking at some real examples, there is another key element of message handling to consider. Windows has two different ways to send a message to a window:

- The `PostMessage` API function, which is used to place a message in the application's message queue. The message will be handled only when the application has a chance to access its message queue (that is, when it receives control from the system), and only after earlier messages have been processed. This is an asynchronous model, since you do not know when the message will actually be received. This API function was used in the ONECOPY2 example earlier in this chapter.

- The `SendMessage` API function, which is used to execute message-handler code immediately. `SendMessage` bypasses the application's message queue and sends the message directly to a target window or control. This is a synchronous model. This function even has a return value, which is passed back by the code handling the message.

The difference between these two ways of sending messages is similar to that between mailing a letter, which will reach its destination sooner or later, and sending a fax, which goes immediately to the recipient. Although you will rarely need to use this low-level code in Delphi, you might wonder which one you should use if you do need to write this type of code.

The advantage of using `SendMessage` is obvious: it provides more control over the system. However, you should generally use `PostMessage` for a very simple reason: when the messages are posted to the queue, each running application has a better chance to receive control, which makes the entire system behave more smoothly.

# Building a Clock with a Timer

A good example of the problems that arise in an event-driven environment is creating a clock program. A clock should automatically update its output as time passes. A traditional approach might be to check the current time continuously, reading the value stored in the system clock. Although such a program would probably work well, it would consume a lot of CPU time, depleting the amount of processing power available to other applications.

An alternative is to read the system clock approximately once each second, and then return the control to the system as soon as possible. But how can the application be awakened when each second has elapsed? This is a typical duty for a timer. In Delphi, a Timer component receives an OnTimer event each time a fixed interval has elapsed.

## Behind the Timers: The Clock

Before continuing with the clock program example, let's take a moment to detail some of the aspects of timer behavior in Windows (we have already used this component, but without examining its behavior). Timers are based on an interrupt, driven by the system clock, and timer messages are generated exactly at the specified rate.

The problem is that timer messages, like other messages, are posted to a window and are added to the message queue of the application owning the window. This implies that timer messages may not be delivered to the application at the proper rate. If another program takes control of the CPU for a while (for example, during a file-loading operation), timer messages are still generated, but they do not reach the program and it regains the control of the system.

In this situation, a second problem arises. Since timer messages can be very frequent (theoretically, each millisecond; in practice, once each 60 milliseconds at most), they don't accumulate in the message queue. If a second timer message reaches the queue and a previous similar message is still there, the two are merged in a single message. This means that an application cannot accurately count the number of timer messages received to determine how much time has elapsed. The result is that when you receive a timer message, you know for sure that some time has elapsed, but you do not know how much time.

How can we use a timer to build a clock? Simply place a Timer and a Panel component in a form. Set the timer interval to 1000 milliseconds (that is, a second), select a suitable font for the panel caption, and align the panel with the client area of the form. After you have built this form, simply write the following code to respond to the OnTimer event of the Timer component:

```
procedure TForm1.Timer1Timer(Sender: TObject);
begin
  Panel1.Caption := TimeToStr (Time);
end;
```

The Time function returns a TDateTime object with the current time, which is converted into a string by the TimeToStr function. You can see the result of this code in Figure 19.6.

**FIGURE 19.6:**

The output of the CLOCK1 example.

The output of this program depends on the time-to-string translation performed by the TimeToStr function. This function relies on some constants (remember that you can change them, they are not real constants) defined in the SysUtils unit:

```
TimeSeparator: Char;
TimeAMString: string;
TimePMString: string;
ShortTimeFormat: string;
LongTimeFormat: string;
```

The names of these constants are intuitive, so I'll spare you a detailed description. The values of these constants are loaded from the WIN.INI file and depend on the international version of Windows. For a simple test, open the Windows Control Panel, choose Regional Settings, and select a country different from your own (or move to the Time page and change some values there). Accept the new setting, then run the CLOCK1 example again. You'll find that it automatically adapts its output to the new time format.

As you have seen in this example (and as you probably could guess), timers can be used to write time-dependent applications. In Windows, however, you'll need a timer each time an application needs to monitor a value. A good example is the MEM program presented in Chapter 20.

**NOTE** Another use of the timers we have seen is to produce animation, as in the WORLD example presented in Chapter 10. However, timers are not the best solution for an animation application, because they have unreliable intervals, as we've just discussed. For animation, it is much better to use one of the techniques discussed later in this chapter.

At times, a good alternative to timers is idle computing. We'll investigate this idea a little later in the chapter, after some further refinement of the CLOCK example.

## A Full-Scale Graphical Clock

Now that the basic idea is in place, we can think about expanding the CLOCK example by adding a number of new features. Digital clocks are not my favorite. What about an analog one, with good-looking clock hands? I know that Windows comes with a clock program, so there is really no need to make a new one. But everyone has his or her own favorite clock style, and there are dozens of Windows clock applications available. So here comes yet another clock for Windows.

The foundation of the new example is the clock program we have already built. The form we need for the clock with hands is even simpler. It has just a timer, and no panel. Most of the code goes inside the form's OnPaint response method. Since we need to draw three different clock hands, we can add a generic procedure to the TForm1 operation. I've called this procedure DrawHand and given it five parameters:

```
procedure DrawHand (XCenter, YCenter, Radius,
    BackRadius: Integer; Angle: Real);
```

The first two parameters represent the x and y coordinates of the center of the clock; then there is the size of the clock hands (that is, the radius of the clock circle), and the radius to extend the hand on the opposite side of the center. The last parameter is the current angle of the hand.

The roles of these five parameters are illustrated graphically in Figure 19.7.

The only way I could work with the analog representation of the clock hands was by using trigonometric functions (cosine and sine). To make things more complex, instead of starting from the center, the hand can extend in the opposite direction, as you can see in the output shown in Figure 19.8. Here is the full source code of the DrawHand function:

```
procedure TForm1.DrawHand (XCenter, YCenter,
  Radius, BackRadius: Integer; Angle: Real);
begin
  Canvas.MoveTo (
    XCenter - Round (BackRadius * Cos (Angle)),
    YCenter - Round (BackRadius * Sin (Angle)));
  Canvas.LineTo (
```

**FIGURE 19.7:**

A graphical representation of the output of the DrawHand method of the CLOCK2 example.

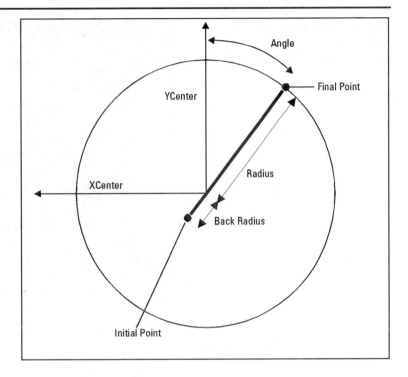

```
     XCenter + Round (Radius * Cos (Angle)),
     YCenter + Round (Radius * Sin (Angle)));
end;
```

In the FormPaint procedure, the program calculates the center of the form and the radius of the clock, then draws the three clock hands after computing their angle. To accomplish this, it uses Hour, Minute, and Second, which are three private fields I've added to the form. Their value is computed in the OnTimer response function, using the DecodeTime method defined in the Delphi system unit. The OnTimer response procedure then calls the Refresh method to update the image on the screen. Here is the code of the two methods:

```
procedure TForm1.Timer1Timer(Sender: TObject);
var
  HSec: Word;   {temporary value, not used}
begin
  {get the system time}
  DecodeTime (Time, Hour, Minute, Second, HSec);
  Refresh;
end;

procedure TForm1.FormPaint(Sender: TObject);
var
  Angle: Real;
```

The output of the CLOCK2 program. Notice that the second hand extends on the other side of the center.

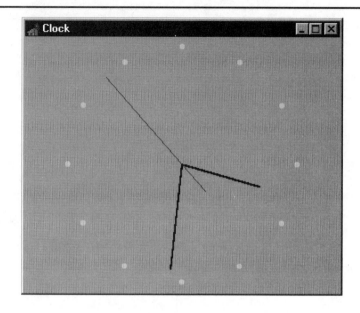

```
  I, X, Y, Size: Integer;
begin
  {compute the middle of the form}
  XCenter := ClientWidth div 2;
  YCenter := ClientHeight div 2;
  if XCenter > YCenter then
    Radius := YCenter - 10
  else
    Radius := XCenter - 10;

  {0. Draw the hour marks}
  {Yellow pen and yellow brush, using default raster mode}
  Canvas.Pen.Color := clYellow;
  Canvas.Brush.Color := clYellow;
  Size := Radius div 50 + 1;

  for I := 0 to 11 do
  begin
    Angle := 2 * Pi * (I + 9) / 12;
    X := XCenter - Round (Radius * Cos (Angle));
    Y := YCenter - Round (Radius * Sin (Angle));
    Canvas.Ellipse (X - Size, Y - Size, X + Size, Y + Size);
  end;

  {1. Draw the minutes hand}
  {Blue thick pen}
  Canvas.Pen.Width := 2;
  Canvas.Pen.Color := clBlue;
  Angle := 2 * Pi * (Minute+45) / 60;
  DrawHand (XCenter, YCenter,
```

```
      Radius * 90 div 100, 0, Angle);

  {2. Draw the hours hand: Percentage of minutes
  added to hour to move the hand smoothly}
  {Same pen as the minutes hand}
  Angle := 2 * Pi * (Hour + 9 + Minute / 60) / 12;
  DrawHand (XCenter, YCenter,
    Radius * 70 div 100, 0, Angle);

  {3. Draw the seconds hand: Red thin pen}
  Canvas.Pen.Width := 1;
  Canvas.Pen.Color := clRed;
  Angle := 2 * Pi * (Second+45) / 60;
  DrawHand (XCenter, YCenter, Radius,
    Radius * 30 div 100, Angle);
end;
```

As you can see above, the FormPaint procedure first computes the center of the form and determines the Radius (another private field of the form) of the clock. It then draws each hand, using some complex code that requires in-depth explanation. First, it sets the color and size of the clock hand (changing the properties of the Pen selected in the Canvas). Then, it computes the angle. The complex formulas then convert the numbers from 1 to 60 (for minutes and seconds) into angles in radians (hence the use of Pi). During this conversion, we also set the origin of the angle properly, adding three-quarters of a turn (45 minutes).

The code used to draw the hour hand is slightly more complex. To make the hour hand move more smoothly, in fact, the program can add to the hour the elapsed percentage of the next hour (that is, add the current number of minutes divided by 60). The initial portion of the painting method also draws tick marks corresponding to the hour positions to improve the readability of the clock. The program computes the position of these marks in a for loop, again based on the sine and cosine functions.

There are two more interesting elements in the program. A call to the Refresh procedure is required each time the form is resized, to repaint the whole form, moving the clock to the center of the screen, and computing a new radius for the clock. The other curious element is a call to the Timer1Timer method in the OnCreate event:

```
procedure TForm1.FormCreate(Sender: TObject);
begin
  Timer1Timer (self);
end;
```

This call is used to paint the clock on the form as soon as it is displayed to the screen.

# Painting the Seconds Hand with Raster Operations

The CLOCK2 program works, but it is far from satisfactory. The clock image is not steady; it flickers a lot. In fact, each second, the whole surface of the form is erased, then repainted again from scratch. This might seem the only possible behavior, since the second hand should move, but it is not. Instead of deleting the whole image, we can delete only the old second hand, then repaint it.

The problem now is how to delete the line. You might think of painting a new line with the background color, but this would not work, because you might also delete part of the other two clock hands or part of the hour marks.

## Windows Raster Modes

The solution lies in Windows *raster operations* modes, indicated in Delphi by the Mode property of the pen (we used this approach in Chapter 14 for the splitter line example, SPLIT4). Raster operations modes allow you to indicate the behavior of pens (and, in part, also brushes) during drawing functions. These are some examples of raster operations modes:

- pmBlack draws black lines regardless of the pen color you select.
- pmNot reverses the color of the current pixels on the screen, again ignoring the pen color.
- pmCopy is the default mode to copy the color of the pen to the screen.

The output of a number of these modes depends both on the color of the current pixels of the screen and the color of the pen. You can merge the colors, merge the colors inverting one of them, use a color to mask the other, xor the two colors, and perform many, many more operations with the different modes.

The raster operations mode we need to draw the second hand of the clock example is pmNotXor. Its result is the inverted color of the exclusive or performed between the two colors. The key feature of this drawing mode is that if you draw the same line twice, it disappears. Also, you can draw in color. This is exactly what we were looking for, since we can use it to delete the old line before drawing a new one.

> **NOTE**
>
> Don't feel bad if you don't quite understand what is going on with the pmNotXor mode, including how to xor two colors. I have some problems understanding how colored pixels are merged and "xored," too. Our main concern, however, is the *result* of using this mode.

## The New Version of the Graphical Clock

How can we change the CLOCK2 program (building CLOCK3)? First of all, each time the timer message arrives, we can store the old value of the seconds and of the minutes in two new private fields of the form: OldMinute and OldSecond. If the value of the minutes has not changed, we use the value of the seconds to delete the old hand and draw the new one:

```
procedure TForm1.Timer1Timer(Sender: TObject);
var
  HSec: Word;   {temporary value, not used}
begin
  {store the old values and get the system time}
  OldMinute := Minute;
  OldSecond := Second;
  DecodeTime (Time, Hour, Minute, Second, HSec);
  {If minutes haven't changed, move the seconds hand
  else redraw the whole clock}
  if Minute = OldMinute then
    DrawSecond
  else
    Refresh;
end;
```

The DrawSecond procedure draws two lines corresponding to the old and the new position of the hand:

```
procedure TForm1.DrawSecond;
var
  Angle, OldAngle: Real;
begin
  {delete the old line, drawing over it again}
  OldAngle := 2 * Pi * (OldSecond+45) / 60;
  DrawHand (XCenter, YCenter, Radius,
    Radius * 30 div 100, OldAngle);

  {draw the new line}
  Angle := 2 * Pi * (Second+45) / 60;
  DrawHand (XCenter, YCenter, Radius,
    Radius * 30 div 100, Angle);
end;
```

For this code to work properly, you need to set the pmNotXor raster mode. However, you can avoid doing this each time the second hand is drawn by placing it at the end of the painting code. Here is the final portion of this procedure (extracted from the source code of the CLOCK3 example) with the relevant changes:

```
{3. Draw the seconds hand}
{Red thin pen, with 'not xor' raster mode}
Canvas.Pen.Width := 1;
Canvas.Pen.Color := clRed;
```

```
Canvas.Pen.Mode := pmNotXor;
Angle := 2 * Pi * (Second+45) / 60;
DrawHand (XCenter, YCenter, Radius,
  Radius * 30 div 100, Angle);
```

Avoiding a repetitive call improves the speed of the program. The output of the new version, called CLOCK3, is actually very similar to that of the previous one. But if you look carefully at it, you can see that where the clock hands are overlapped, the raster mode combines the colors of the two hands. This is something hard to see when reproduced in a black-and-white book, so I suggest you run the two programs and compare their output on the screen.

# Idle Computing and Multitasking

An alternative to using timers in a Windows application is to implement some form of background computing. For example, suppose that you need to implement a time-consuming algorithm. If you write the algorithm as a response to an event, your application will be stopped completely during all the time it takes to process that algorithm. To let the user know that something is being processed, you can display the hourglass cursor, but this is not a real solution.

One solution is to split the algorithm into smaller pieces, and execute each of them in turn, letting the application respond to pending messages in between processing the pieces. A more radical solution is to use the multithreading capabilities of Windows 95 and NT, starting a separate thread to compute an algorithm, and letting the application process incoming messages as well and *at the same time*.

We will look into some techniques used to implement background computing in a single thread first. These techniques were necessary in Windows 3.1, and can still be useful in Win32 applications. Later on we will explore Delphi's multithreading support and its advantages over background processing, including some synchronization techniques and the capability to set thread priorities.

## Background Processing

There are actually several ways to implement background computing, as you'll see in the next example. These are the two most common solutions:

- Call the `Application.ProcessMessages` function each time, so that a waiting message can be processed.

- Execute each step of the program when the Application object receives the OnIdle event.

These two approaches, which are related to the Application object, let the program get more or less system time, depending on the current activity. The difference between calling ProcessMessages and using OnIdle events is that by calling Process-Messages your code will receive more processing time than it does by using the OnIdle approach. Calling ProcessMessages is a way to let the system perform other operations while your program is computing; using the OnIdle event is a way to let your application perform tasks when the system doesn't have more important things to do.

A third, but less common (and more complex) way to implement background processing is to post a user-defined message to yourself at the end of each step in your background process:

```
PostMessage (Handle, wm_User, 0, 0);
```

You'll get your message later, so you can execute the next step, then post another message to yourself, continuing until the background processing is done.

# Computing Prime Numbers the Dumb Way

To demonstrate some of these choices, I've written an example named BACKPROC (for *background processing*). The form of this program has four buttons used to start processing with four techniques, four progress bars to report the advances of the algorithm, and four labels to display the results. Above these, there is a SpinEdit control used to set the number of iterations of the algorithm. When you click on one of the four buttons, an algorithm is started to compute how many prime numbers there are below the value indicated by the SpinEdit control. In practice, the value of SpinEdit1 can be used to slow down or speed up the execution on fast or slow computers.

There are a number of very intelligent algorithms you can use to efficiently compute prime numbers. I've used none of them, since I needed something slow to demonstrate background computing. For this reason, I've written a simple function to compute prime numbers, which divides a given number by 2, 3, 4, and so on up to the value before the number itself.

**NOTE**     At this point in the description of my prime number function, some of you will already be horrified. In fact, I could have stopped at a value corresponding to the square root of the number. I know it, but I wrote it like this anyway. There's no need to send me e-mail messages telling me how to correct this, because I already know this is the worst algorithm I could find.

The function looks at the remainder of each integral division, using the mod operator, and if this is zero, the number is not a prime number. When this happens, it stops the loop and returns False:

```
function IsPrime (N: LongInt): Boolean;
var
  Test: LongInt;
begin
  IsPrime := True;
  for Test := 2 to N - 1 do
  begin
    if (N mod Test) = 0 then
    begin
      IsPrime := False;
      break; {jump out of the for loop}
    end;
  end;
end;
```

With this function, we can compute the prime numbers below a certain value with a simple loop:

```
for Number := 2 to Max do
  if IsPrime (Number) then
    Inc (NPrimes);
```

At the end of the loop, the NPrimes variable contains the result. It's simple, but not efficient. This same algorithm is used four times, with some changes in the code of the for loop just shown.

## The Hourglass Approach

The first button, labeled *Hourglass*, uses the simplest approach. It computes the algorithm, taking the time required without explicitly releasing control back to the system. As a friendly move, it shows the hourglass cursor and updates the progress gauge continuously. Figure 19.9 shows the output of the BACKCOMP example when the Hourglass button is chosen.

**FIGURE 19.9:**

The output of the BACKCOMP example when the first button is clicked.

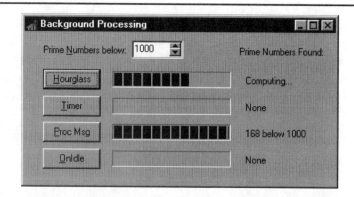

To show the hourglass, this program uses a property of the global Screen object, Cursor, setting it to crHourglass. You should be careful to reset the normal cursor at the end, and do it in the finally portion of a try-finally block. This approach ensures that the cursor is reset properly, even if an exception is raised in the code.

Two other operations are accomplished before starting the actual algorithm. The label at the right is changed to *Computing*, and the value of the SpinEdit control is copied to the Max variable. This value will be used a number of times in the following code, so the program reads its value once and stores it. Besides making the code more efficient, this is required by subsequent versions, which allow the user to perform other operations (including changing the spin edit box value) while the algorithm is being processed. Here is the full code of this first version:

```
procedure TForm1.HourButtonClick(Sender: TObject);
var
  Number, NPrimes, Max: LongInt;
begin
  Screen.Cursor := crHourglass;
  try
    NPrimes := 0;
    Max := SpinEdit1.Value;
    HourLabel.Caption := 'Computing...';
    for Number := 2 to Max do
    begin
      if IsPrime (Number) then
        Inc (NPrimes);
      ProgressBar1.Position := Number * 100 div Max;
    end;
    HourLabel.Caption := IntToStr (NPrimes) +
      ' below ' + IntToStr (Max);
  finally
    Screen.Cursor := crDefault;
  end;
end;
```

Each time the loop is executed, the value of the progress bar is updated.

This is probably one of the statements slowing down the algorithm, particularly when its effect is to repaint the control. At the end of the execution, the result is copied to the label on the right. I've provided the code of this version mainly to let you know how I changed it in the other versions. The problem with this version is that when you press the Hourglass button, the application will not respond to other messages until the algorithm is done. Contrary to what happened in Windows 3.1, however, you can work on other applications while this application is computing. However, if you hide the form of BACKPROC behind another window and then you move it in front again, it won't be repainted properly until the algorithm is done and it has a chance to process additional messages.

## Background Processing with Timers

The Timer button in the BACKPROC example starts the worst form of background processing. The use of timers makes this code very slow compared with the other solutions. To make good use of a timer, I've "unfolded" the for loop, using one of its cycles for each timer event. The procedure handling the OnClick event of the button simply sets the initial value of some private variables of the form (I needed to move these variables to the form scope because two different methods need to access them). After this is done, the timer is activated (notice that it is not active at design-time):

```
procedure TForm1.TimerButtonClick(Sender: TObject);
begin
  TimerNPrimes := 0;
  TimerMax := SpinEdit1.Value;
  TimerNumber := 2;
  Timer1.Enabled := True;
  ProgressBar2.Position := 0;
  TimerLabel.Caption := 'Computing...';
end;
```

The real code is in the Timer1Timer method. The for loop is replaced by a plain if statement and a call to the Inc (increase) system procedure:

```
procedure TForm1.Timer1Timer(Sender: TObject);
begin
  if TimerNumber < TimerMax then
  begin
    if IsPrime (TimerNumber) then
      Inc (TimerNPrimes);
    Inc (TimerNumber);
  end
  else
  begin
    Timer1.Enabled := False;
    TimerLabel.Caption := IntToStr (TimerNPrimes) +
      ' below ' + IntToStr (TimerMax);
    MessageBeep (0)
  end;
  ProgressBar2.Position := TimerNumber * 100 div TimerMax;
end;
```

You can compare this code with the original version of the algorithm, based on a for loop and shown in the previous section. The rest of the code is easy to understand. No change is made to the cursor, of course, and a simple beep is issued to notify the user at the end.

Notice that while the program is working, the Timer button is not disabled, so the user can restart the algorithm. The user can also click on the Hourglass button, starting the first version of the algorithm, which temporarily stops the timer-based code (as well as any other code of this application).

## Processing Messages in the Background

A much simpler and better solution is to let the application (and the whole system in Windows 3.1) process other messages in the background while we are computing the prime numbers. This is much simpler because it basically requires adding a single statement to the original version of the algorithm: a call to the ProcessMessages method of the Application object.

This statement is added inside the `for` loop, so that each time, other events for this application have a chance to be handled:

```
for Number := 2 to Max do
begin
  if IsPrime (Number) then
    Inc (NPrimes);
  ProgressBar3.Position := Number * 100 div Max;
  Application.ProcessMessages;
end;
```

This makes the execution smooth. You can do anything on this form, without any real problems—just more slowly. To summarize the code so far, if you click on the Hourglass button, everything within the application stops until processing is complete. If you start the Timer version, the computation will be much slower, but the application will respond to other messages. The higher-priority ProcessMessages version finishes more quickly, and still doesn't halt the application. Also notice that you can restart the ProcessMessages version before it is done (the preceding computation is stopped waiting for the new one to finish).

I suggest that you run the example program and test each method yourself. This will help you to understand the differences between these approaches to Windows 3.1-style multitasking.

Note that you can restart the Timer version while the program is processing it, but it discards the previous results and starts over again. The ProcessMessages version, on the other hand, spawns a second computation loop, and restarting it may cause some problems. The biggest problem is that each time you start or *re-enter* this function, a sizable chunk of the stack is used. Starting several computations at the same time may use up all of the program's stack space, something that Windows doesn't like at all (it can bring the system to a complete stop).

As a general-purpose programming technique, code that uses ProcessMessages must protect against re-entrancy to avoid this kind of stack problem. The best solution is to display a modal status dialog box, so that the main application window (and all its menus) is disabled. In the example program, I've just disabled the corresponding button, to let you start up other versions of the algorithm while this one is running.

## Idle-Time Computing

The solution provided by the bottom button in the BACKPROC example is the only version which really does true processing in background, by grabbing idle time from the whole system. As in the Timer version, the OnIdle method splits the code into two portions. When the OnIdle button is clicked, some initialization code is executed, including setting the OnIdle event handler of the Application object:

```
procedure TForm1.IdleButtonClick(Sender: TObject);
begin
  IdleNPrimes := 0;
  IdleMax := SpinEdit1.Value;
  IdleNumber := 2;
  Application.OnIdle := IdleProc;
  ProgressBar4.Position := 0;
  IdleLabel.Caption := 'Computing...';
end;
```

Again, this code uses some variables declared in the scope of the form (as private fields), and again it uses a test and an increment instead of a for loop. Here is the code of the IdleProc method:

```
procedure TForm1.IdleProc (Sender: TObject; var Done: Boolean);
begin
  if IdleNumber < IdleMax then
  begin
    if IsPrime (IdleNumber) then
      Inc (IdleNPrimes);
    Inc (IdleNumber);
    Done := False;
  end
  else
  begin
    IdleLabel.Caption := IntToStr (IdleNPrimes) +
      ' below ' + IntToStr (IdleMax);
    Done := True;
    MessageBeep (0);
    Application.OnIdle := nil;
  end;
  ProgressBar4.Position := IdleNumber * 100 div IdleMax;
end;
```

The second parameter, Done, is used to tell the system if further idle-time processing is required or if the algorithm is finished. For this reason, I've set Done to False in the main code and to True at the end. When the algorithm terminates, I also disable the event-handler, to avoid receiving additional idle messages when they are not needed.

Notice that in this case, we have very limited control over the execution of our code. We do not know how much time it will take. If nothing else is happening on the computer, this version of the code is as fast as the original one; but if you do other operations, such as executing the version based on the call to the ProcessMessages method, it almost stops.

There is no clear winner among these techniques. For real background computing, OnIdle is the right choice. If you just want the application to respond to other events, even while your program is working hard, use ProcessMessages instead. Using timers is a compromise of the benefits of these two. In contrast, if you want to build a real multithreading application, you must use the threading capability of the Win32 platforms, and the specific Delphi support for this feature.

# Multithreading in Delphi

Windows 95 and Windows NT allow us to let two procedures or methods execute at the same time (well, a slice of time for each, of course) and let our program control them. Before we look to the implementation of multithreading, we should ask ourselves, "What is the reason for having several threads of execution inside a given program?" First, consider some of the disadvantages to multithreading:

- Multithreading makes a program run slower, unless you have multiple CPUs and the operating system can split the threads among processors.

- Multithreading programs synchronize access to resources and memory, which makes the program more complex to write.

Fortunately, multithreading also has some advantages. You can run a thread in the background, letting the user continue to operate. You can make one thread run faster than others by adjusting its priority. You can regulate the resource access of different threads. You can assign local storage to each thread, and you can also spawn multiple threads of the same type.

## The TThread Class

Windows provides a series of API calls to control threads (the key one is CreateThread), but I don't want to discuss them. This is because Delphi 2 provides a TThread class that will let us control threads well enough. Consider, anyway, that you never use the TThread class directly, because it is an abstract class—a class with a virtual abstract method. To use threads, you always subclass TThread, although it is important to focus on the features of this base class.

The TThread class has a constructor with a single parameter that lets you choose whether to start the thread immediately or simply create it:

```
constructor Create(CreateSuspended: Boolean);
```

There are also some public synchronization methods:

```
procedure Resume;
procedure Suspend;
function Terminate: Integer;
function WaitFor: Integer;
```

The published properties include Priority, Suspended, and two read-only low-level values (Handle and ThreadID). The priority level is defined via an enumerated type:

```
TThreadPriority = (tpIdle, tpLowest, tpLower, tpNormal, tpHigher,
  tpHighest, tpTimeCritical);
```

Besides the public interface of the class, it is important to focus on its protected interface, which includes two key methods for your thread subclasses:

```
procedure Execute; virtual; abstract;
procedure Synchronize(Method: TThreadMethod);
```

The Execute method, declared as a virtual abstract procedure, must be redefined by each thread class. It contains the main code of the thread, the code you would typically place in a *thread function* when using the Windows API to control threads directly. The Synchronize method is fundamental to avoid concurrent access to VCL components and anything in the user interface. The VCL code executes the main thread of the program, and this protected approach allows you to avoid re-entrancy problems (errors from re-entering a function before a previous call is completed). The only parameter of this method is a method that accepts no parameters, typically a method of the same thread class.

## A First Example

As a first simple example, I've built a program that uses a thread to paint on the surface of an Image component (the example is called THDEMO1). The thread class, TPainterThread, overrides the Execute method and defines a new Paint method. The Paint method is used to access VCL objects, so it is called only from within the Synchronize method. Since the Paint method cannot accept parameters directly and still be a compatible method for the Synchronize method, the class requires some private data to pass parameters to the Paint method. Here is the class declaration:

```
type
  TPainterThread = class(TThread)
  private
    X, Y: Integer;
  protected
    procedure Execute; override;
    procedure Paint;
  end;
```

The Paint method marks four pixels of the image component of the form in red:

```
procedure TPainterThread.Paint;
begin
  Form1.Image1.Canvas.Pixels [X,   Y  ] := clRed;
  Form1.Image1.Canvas.Pixels [X,   Y+1] := clRed;
  Form1.Image1.Canvas.Pixels [X+1, Y  ] := clRed;
  Form1.Image1.Canvas.Pixels [X+1, Y+1] := clRed;
end;
```

The main function of the thread, Execute, randomly updates a pixel by calling the Paint method indirectly via the Synchronize method:

```
procedure TPainterThread.Execute;
begin
  Randomize;
  repeat
    X := Random (250);
    Y := Random (250);
    Synchronize (Paint);
  until Terminated;
end;
```

You can see the result of this code in Figure 19.10.

**FIGURE 19.10:**

The output of the THDEMO1: the image component is updated by a thread.

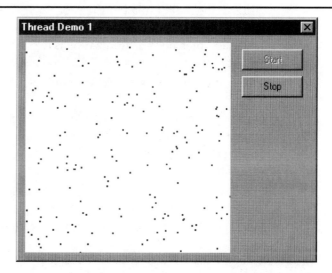

As you can see in the previous listing above, the thread runs until it is terminated. On the main form, there is a button used to start the thread. By passing *False* to the Create constructor, the thread starts immediately:

```
procedure TForm1.Button1Click(Sender: TObject);
begin
```

```
    Button1.Enabled := False;
    Button2.Enabled := True;
    PT := TPainterThread.Create (False);  // start
  end;
```

PT is a private TPainterThread field of the form class. The first button creates the thread and starts it. The second button stops the thread and frees it. Calling Suspend sets the Terminated flag of the thread to True, and then waits for a call to Resume or for the termination of the thread:

```
procedure TForm1.Button2Click(Sender: TObject);
begin
  PT.Suspend;
  PT.Free;
  Button1.Enabled := True;
  Button2.Enabled := False;
end;
```

In this example, when the next execution of the loop is completed, the thread actually ends, the Suspend method returns, and the thread object is destroyed.

## Synchronization Alternatives

You must use the Synchronize call only when your thread needs to modify something in the user interface. In fact, the main form of a Delphi programs runs in a thread, the main thread of the process. If another thread does background operations, such as file transfer or number crunching, with no need to update the user interface, then no synchronization is needed. When you need to update the user interface instead, you can call Synchronize (which might slow down the program a lot, if many threads are doing lengthy output operations) or use one of the following two alternatives.

First, the thread can update some data structure, which the main thread scans from time to time (perhaps using a timer). You have to take care at read/write collisions, trying to avoid letting them occur, but you can often solve these problems without a real lock.

As a second alternative, you can use traditional Windows-based multitasking: the thread can post a message to the main window, asking for an update, and even delivering values. Keep in mind that you cannot use SendMessage to do this.

# Setting Threads Priorities

The second example is an extension of the previous one, but starts several threads at the same time, allowing users to change their priorities with some track bars. Here is the new version of the *TPainterThread* class:

```
type
  TPainterThread = class(TThread)
  private
```

```
    X, Y, Color, ImaNum: Integer;
  protected
    procedure Execute; override;
    procedure Paint;
  public
    constructor Create (Col: TColor; ImageNum: Integer);
  end;
```

I've added a constructor to the class to pass some initial values to the thread. As an alternative, I could have made these variables public fields of the thread class to allow the program to manipulate them directly. Here is the code of the constructor:

```
constructor TPainterThread.Create
  (Col: TColor; ImageNum: Integer);
begin
  Color := Col;
  ImaNum := ImageNum;
  inherited Create (True);
end;
```

The constructor initializes the private data, then calls the constructor of the base class, creating the thread in a suspended state. The new Paint function uses one of the image components of the form, as indicated by the image number (ImaNum) passed as parameter to the constructor:

```
procedure TPainterThread.Paint;
begin
  Form1.Images[ImaNum].Canvas.Pixels [X, Y] := Color;
end;
```

This code works because the form declares an array of Image components, as we will see in a while. The Execute method of the thread simply scans each line, setting each pixel in the given color:

```
procedure TPainterThread.Execute;
var
  X1: Integer;
begin
  repeat
    // scan the lines...
    X1 := X + 1;
    X := X1 mod 105;
    Y := Y + X1 div 105;
    Synchronize (Paint);
  until Terminated;
end;
```

The main form of the example has four image components, four check boxes, and four track bars (as you can see from the output of THDEMO2 in Figure 19.11). The class of the main form has some local data, too.

```
type
  TForm1 = class(TForm)
    // components...
  private
    PT: array [1..4] of TPainterThread;
  public
    Images: array [1..4] of TImage;
  end;
```

**FIGURE 19.11:**

The output of THDEMO2, with four image components updated concurrently by four threads.

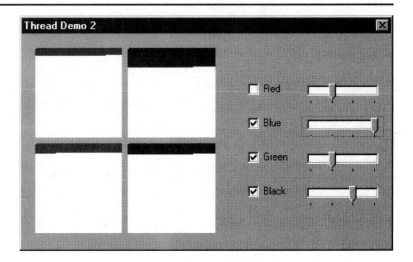

These two arrays are initialized when the form is created:

```
procedure TForm1.FormCreate(Sender: TObject);
begin
  PT [1] := TPainterThread.Create (clRed, 1);
  PT [2] := TPainterThread.Create (clBlue, 2);
  PT [3] := TPainterThread.Create (clGreen, 3);
  PT [4] := TPainterThread.Create (ClBlack, 4);
  Images [1] := Image1;
  Images [2] := Image2;
  Images [3] := Image3;
  Images [4] := Image4;
end;
```

Notice that the program creates the four threads as suspended. They are started when the corresponding check box is checked and suspended again when the check box is cleared:

```
procedure TForm1.CheckBox1Click(Sender: TObject);
begin
  if (Sender as TCheckbox).Checked then
    PT [(Sender as TCheckbox).Tag].Resume
  else
    PT [(Sender as TCheckbox).Tag].Suspend;
end;
```

To use this message response method for each check box, I've set the value of the Tag property of each one to the number of the corresponding thread. The same technique is used with the track bars, which set the current priority of the thread:

```
procedure TForm1.TrackBar1Change(Sender: TObject);
begin
  PT [(Sender as TTrackBar).Tag].Priority :=
    TThreadPriority ((Sender as TTrackBar).Position);
end;
```

To set the priority, I simply scale the current Position of the track bar to the corresponding TThreadPriority enumeration value. Then I use the resulting value to set the priority of the thread corresponding to the Tag of the current track bar.

This program is quite instructive, because you can alter thread priorities and see the effect on screen. When the priorities are too high (with two threads having the maximum value), the VCL synchronization calls almost block the whole program, because each thread performs frequent screen updates.

## Synchronizing Threads

There are many techniques to synchronize threads, including semaphores and mutexes. Here I want to discuss only the simplest one: let one thread wait until another thread is done. This is accomplished using the WaitFor method. Here is the portion of an example, in which a program starts a thread, then waits for its result:

```
Comp := TMyThread.Create (True);
// initialize the thread...
Comp.Resume;
Comp.WaitFor;
// look for final values...
Comp.Free;
```

**WARNING**  This code is quite simple to write, but remember you cannot write this code as part of the main thread (for example, in a normal message response function) if the secondary thread has to synchronize with it. If you are waiting in the thread connected to the main form for another thread to finish, and the secondary thread is waiting to access the user interface (hence waiting for the main thread to finish its current job) the program will enter a deadlock!

To avoid this problem, you can synchronize two threads. A first thread creates a secondary thread, and waits for it to end, without interfering with the main form's thread. Here is the full source code of the Execute method of a thread, which starts a secondary thread and waits for it to complete (this is actually an excerpt of the source code of the THDEMO3 example). Actually, this code is repeated a number of times, once for each value in a range:

```
procedure TPainterThread.Execute;
var
  Comp: TComputeThread;
  I: Integer;
begin
  for I := First to Last do
  begin
    Comp := TComputeThread.Create (True);
    X := I;
    Comp.Max := X;
    Comp.Resume;
    Comp.WaitFor;
    Y := Comp.NPrimes;
    Synchronize (Paint);
    Comp.Free;
  end;
  MessageBeep (Cardinal (-1)); // done
end;
```

When the Paint method is called by the Synchronize method, it simply uses the X and Y values (two private fields of the thread class) to build a graph, as you can see in Figure 19.12. The secondary thread uses the code we used earlier in this chapter to compute the prime numbers below the given value (Max).

This example is not very intelligent, because by using a direct function call, the program would have been much faster. However, I decided to leave it in the text because it shows a simple example of thread synchronization using the WaitFor method.

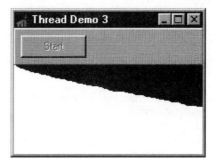

**FIGURE 19.12:**
The output of the THDEMO3 example, a graph of the number of prime numbers below a certain value.

## A Final Multithreading Example

To show you another example of synchronization with multiple threads, I've built a character-counting program, THDEMO4. The program computes how many copies of the four characters specified in an edit box are present inside the text of a Memo component (you can actually load the text from any file, as long as you do so before starting the computation). The program looks for each of the four characters at the same time, using multiple threads spawned by the main thread. To improve the output, each thread shows its status in a progress bar, as you can see in Figure 19.13.

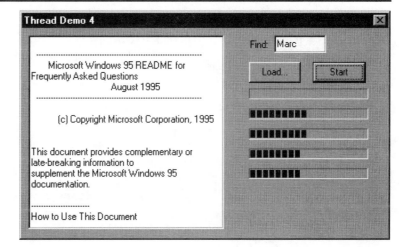

**FIGURE 19.13:**
In the THDEMO4 example, each thread outputs its status in a progress bar.

The actual engine of the program is the TFindThread class, which contains the LookFor field to hold the character we are searching for, and a Progress field to store the value of the progress bar and update its status. The result of the computation is placed in the Found field, accessible from the outside:

```
type
  TFindThread = class(TThread)
  protected
    NumLine: Integer;
    procedure Execute; override;
    procedure ShowLine;
  public
    Found: Integer;
    LookFor: Char;
    Progress: TProgressBar;
  end;
```

The private NumLine field, instead, is used to pass data to the ShowLine procedure, which updates the progress bar:

```
procedure TFindThread.ShowLine;
begin
  Progress.Position := NumLine + 1;
end;
```

As usual, the core of the thread is in its Execute method, which scans the lines of the memo, looking for the given character. Notice that we can freely access the properties of the memo without synchronization, since this operation doesn't affect the output of the program:

```
procedure TFindThread.Execute;
var
  I, J: Integer;
  Line: string;
begin
  Found := 0;
  with Form1.Memo1 do
    for I := 0 to Lines.Count - 1 do
    begin
      Line := Lines [I];
      for J := 1 to Length (Line) do
        if Line [J] = LookFor then
          Inc (Found);
      NumLine := I;
      Synchronize (ShowLine);
    end;
end;
```

This thread is activated by a primary thread of the TMultiFind class . Here is its declaration:

```
type
  TMultiFind = class(TThread)
```

```
  protected
    ProgressPos: Integer;
    procedure Execute; override;
    procedure Show;
    procedure ShowLine;
  public
    LookFor, Output: String;
    Progresses: array [1..5] of TProgressBar;
  end;
```

This thread class looks for the characters of the LookFor string (there must be four characters for the program to work correctly), using four FindThread objects:

```
procedure TMultiFind.Execute;
var
  Finders: array [1..4] of TFindThread;
  I: Integer;
begin
  for I := 1 to 4 do
  begin
    Finders[I] := TFindThread.Create (True);
    Finders[I].LookFor := LookFor[I];
    Finders[I].Progress := Progresses [I+1];
    Finders[I].Resume;
  end;
```

Then it waits for the four threads to complete, using another progress bar to display its own status:

```
  // wait the threads to end...
  ProgressPos := 0;
  for I := 1 to 4 do
  begin
    Finders[I].WaitFor;
    Inc (ProgressPos);
    Synchronize (ShowLine);
  end;
  Output := 'Found: ';
  for I := 1 to 4 do
    Output := Output + Format ('%d %s, ',
      [Finders[I].Found, LookFor[I]]);
  Synchronize (Show);

  // delete threads
  for I := 1 to 4 do
    Finders[I].Free;
end;
```

At the end, it shows the result. Here are the two synchronized methods:

```
procedure TMultiFind.ShowLine;
begin
  Progresses[1].Position := ProgressPos;
end;
```

```
procedure TMultiFind.Show;
begin
  ShowMessage (Output);
end;
```

It is important to keep these methods as simple as possible since while they are executing, other threads cannot access the user interface of the program.

The program I've written to test these threads is quite simple. As we have seen in Figure 19.13, it has a memo where you can load a file and an edit box containing four characters. The number of these characters is checked when the user exits the edit box:

```
procedure TForm1.Edit1Exit(Sender: TObject);
begin
  if Length (Edit1.Text) <> 4 then
  begin
    Edit1.SetFocus;
    ShowMessage ('The edit box requires four characters');
  end;
end;
```

The start button, as the name implies, starts the thread, which in turn spawns the secondary threads:

```
procedure TForm1.Button1Click(Sender: TObject);
var
  I: Integer;
begin
  if Assigned (MainThread) then
    MainThread.Free;
  MainThread := TMultiFind.Create (True);
  MainThread.Progresses [1] := ProgressBar1;
  MainThread.Progresses [2] := ProgressBar2;
  MainThread.Progresses [3] := ProgressBar3;
  MainThread.Progresses [4] := ProgressBar4;
  MainThread.Progresses [5] := ProgressBar5;
  MainThread.Progresses [1].Max := 4;
  for I := 2 to 5 do
    MainThread.Progresses[I].Max := Memo1.Lines.Count;
  for I := 1 to 5 do
    MainThread.Progresses[I].Position := 0;

  MainThread.LookFor := Edit1.Text;
  MainThread.Resume;
end;
```

Notice that we cannot delete the thread at the end of the method, because we cannot call WaitFor on it without creating a deadlock. From my experience, take care when writing threads under Windows 95, because such a deadlock can freeze the whole system, leaving you with nothing else to do but reach for the reset button.

At the same time, to keep the operating system stable, we must remember to delete the thread, either before creating a second one (as at the beginning of the code above), or when the program terminates. This is also the reason we need to declare the thread object as a private field of the form, and not as a local variable of the method starting it.

# Using the Screen Object

We have explored some of the properties and events of the Application global object. However, there are other documented global objects. One of them is the Screen object. The class of the Screen object, TScreen, can be used to access some information about the screen itself and about the current form of the application. This object also has a list of the available fonts we have already used in some examples (such as FONTGRID in Chapter 10).

> **NOTE** Other global objects are Printer and Clipboard, which will be discussed in Chapters 22 and 24.

## Getting Screen Information

Our next example shows some of the operations you can do with the Screen object. Create a form with some labels and two list boxes. The first list box is used to provide a list of fonts installed in the system, and the second dynamically shows the forms of this application. Both list boxes are filled using array properties of the Screen object. However, maintaining the second list box is more complex because it must be updated each time a new form is created, an existing form is destroyed, or the active form of the program changes. Note that the forms the Screen object references are the forms of the application, not the windows of the entire system. To see how this works, you can create a number of secondary forms by clicking on the button labeled *New*:

```
procedure TMainForm.NewButtonClick(Sender: TObject);
var
  NewForm: TSecondForm;
begin
  {create a new form, set its caption, and run it}
  NewForm := TSecondForm.Create (self);
  Inc (Counter);
  NewForm.Caption := 'Second ' + IntToStr (Counter);
  NewForm.Show;
end;
```

This is just standard code. One of the key portions of the program where I access Screen information is the OnCreate event handler of the form:

```
procedure TMainForm.FormCreate(Sender: TObject);
begin
  {compute screen size}
  ScreenLabel.Caption := ScreenLabel.Caption + ' ' +
    IntToStr (Screen.Width) + 'x' + IntToStr (Screen.Height);
  {display fonts and forms data}
  FontsLabel.Caption := 'Fonts: ' + IntToStr (Screen.Fonts.Count);
  FontsListBox.Items := Screen.Fonts;
  FillFormsList (self);
  {set the secondary forms counter to 0}
  Counter := 0;
  {activate an event handler of the screen object}
  Screen.OnActiveFormChange := FillFormsList;
end;
```

## Handling the Forms List

As you can see above, the OnCreate response method fills the list boxes and computes the size of the screen. The code used to fill the Forms list box is inside a second procedure, FillFormsList, which is also installed as an event handler of the OnActiveFormChange event of the Screen object:

```
procedure TMainForm.FillFormsList (Sender: TObject);
var
  I: Integer;
begin
  FormsLabel.Caption := 'Forms: ' + IntToStr (Screen.FormCount);
  FormsListBox.Clear;
  {write class name and form title to the list box}
  for I := 0 to Screen.FormCount - 1 do
    FormsListBox.Items.Add (Screen.Forms[I].ClassName +
      ' - ' + Screen.Forms[I].Caption);
  ActiveLabel.Caption := 'Active Form : ' +
    Screen.ActiveForm.Caption;
end;
```

**WARNING**   It is very important that you remove the handler of the OnActiveFormChange event before exiting the application; that is, before the main form is destroyed. Otherwise, the code will be executed when no list box exists, and you'll get a system error. To accomplish this, handle the OnClose event of the main form and write this statement: `Screen.OnActiveFormChange := nil.`

The FillFormsList method fills the list box and sets a value for the two labels above it, which show the number of forms and the name of the current one. When you click on the New button, the program creates an instance of the secondary form, gives it a new title, and displays it. The Forms list box is updated automatically because of the handler we have installed. Figure 19.14 shows the output of this program when some secondary windows have been created.

**FIGURE 19.14:**

The output of the SCREEN example with a number of secondary forms.

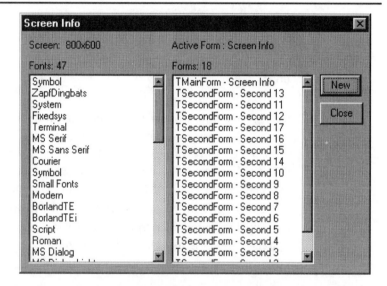

The secondary forms each have a Close button you can select to remove them. The code handles the OnClose event, setting the Action parameter to caFree, so that the form is actually destroyed when it is closed. However, this code does not work. Windows moves the focus to a new active form before destroying the old one, so that the list will still contain the name of the form we have closed.

The first idea I had to solve this problem was to call the FillFormsList method directly from the secondary form. This doesn't work, however, because when you make the call, the secondary form still exists. The solution is to use a more Windows-oriented approach: post a message. Since the posted message is queued and not handled immediately, if we send it at the last possible moment of life of the secondary form, the main form will receive it when the other form is destroyed.

The trick is to post the message in the OnDestroy event handler of the secondary form. To accomplish this, we need to refer to the MainForm object, by adding a proper uses statement in the implementation portion of this unit. I've posted a wm_User message, which is handled by a specific message method of the main form, defined in the TMainForm class as shown here:

```
public
  procedure ChildClosed (var Message: TMessage);
    message wm_User;
```

Here is the code of this method:

```
procedure TMainForm.ChildClosed (var Message: TMessage);
begin
  FillFormsList (self);
end;
```

The problem here is that if you close the main window before closing the secondary forms, the main form exists, but its code cannot be executed anymore. To avoid another system error (a General Protection Fault), you need to post the message only if the main form is not closing. But how do you know that? One way is to add a flag to the TMainForm class and change its value when the main form is closing, so that you can test the flag from the code of the secondary window.

This is a good solution—so good that the VCL provides something similar. There is a barely documented ComponentState property, a set which includes a csDestroying flag when the form is closing. Therefore, we can write the following code:

```
procedure TSecondForm.FormDestroy(Sender: TObject);
begin
  if not (csDestroying in MainForm.ComponentState) then
    PostMessage (MainForm.Handle, wm_User, 0, 0);
end;
```

With this code, the second list box always lists all of the forms in the application. Note that you need to disable the automatic creation of the secondary form by using the Forms page of the Project Options dialog box.

The last functionality I've added to the program is a simple feature. When you click on an item in the list box, the corresponding form is activated, using the BringToFront method:

```
procedure TMainForm.FormsListBoxClick(Sender: TObject);
begin
  Screen.Forms [FormsListBox.ItemIndex].BringToFront;
end;
```

Nice—well, almost nice. If you click on the list box of an inactive form, the main form is activated first, and the list box is rearranged, so you might end up selecting a different form then you are expecting. If you experiment with the program, you'll soon realize what I mean. This minor glitch in the program is an example of the risks you face when you dynamically update some information and let the user work on that element at exactly the same time.

# Saving Status Information

If you want to save information about the status of an application in order to restore it the next time the program is executed, you could use a file and store the data in any format you like. Windows, however, has explicit support for storing initialization information. In previous versions of Windows, the standard approach was to create an initialization file, indicated by the INI extension. In Windows 95 (and in Windows NT) you can still use INI files, but Microsoft recommends the use of the System Registry instead.

In Windows 95, it is important to understand both techniques, because system information is frequently stored in the registry *and* in the good old WIN.INI and SYSTEM.INI files. I don't want to discuss the advantages and disadvantages of the two approaches here, but only let you know they exist and are easily available within Delphi. For this reason, I've decided to build a program capable of saving the position of its main window and restoring it the next time it is executed. The first example uses an INI file, and the second uses the Registry.

## Using Windows INI Files

Delphi provides a class you can use to manipulate INI files, TIniFile. Once you have created an object of this class and connected it to a file, you can read and write information to it. To create the object, you need to call the constructor that passes the name of the file to it, as in the following code:

```
IniFile := TIniFile.Create ('ini_one.ini');
```

There are two choices for the location of the INI file. The first option is to store it in the application's directory, providing the full path to the Create constructor. However, if the program is moved to a new directory, it might have problems. The other, more common, solution is to store all the INI files in the Windows directory, the directory used to install Windows. This is the default when you provide only a file name, as in the statement above.

**NOTE** If you want to follow the other approach, you can use ParamStr to get the path of the executable file of the application. However, using the Windows directory is generally a better method. I had to use this approach, for example, to let you run my sample program from a read-only device, a CD-ROM.

The access to an INI file requires some explanation. These files are divided into sections, indicated by a name enclosed in square brackets. Each section can contain a number of statements of three possible kinds: strings, integers, or Boolean. If you are not aware of the structure of an INI file, you can load it in a text editor, such as Windows Notepad.

There are three methods of the TIniFile class to read each kind of data:

- ReadBool
- ReadInteger
- ReadString

There are also three methods to write the data:

- WriteBool
- WriteInteger
- WriteString

Other methods allow you to read in a whole section or to erase it. In the reading methods, you can specify a default value to be used if the corresponding entry doesn't exist in the INI file.

Our next example, INI_ONE, uses an INI file to store the location, the size, and the status of the main form of the application. (The status is the value of the Window-State property: normal, maximized, or minimized.) The only real problem in this example is that the value of this property is not always updated properly by the system, so we need to introduce another test to confirm whether the form was minimized.

The form of the INI_ONE example is just a plain, blank form, without any components. The program handles two events: OnCreate, to create the INI file and read the initial values, and OnClose, to save the status (if the user confirms this operation). Here is the code of these two methods:

```
procedure TForm1.FormCreate(Sender: TObject);
var
  Status: Integer;
begin
  IniFile := TIniFile.Create ('ini_one.ini');
  {try to read a value and test if it exists}
  Status := IniFile.ReadInteger ('MainForm','Status', 0);
  if Status <> 0 then
  begin
    {read position and size using current values as default}
    Top := IniFile.ReadInteger ('MainForm','Top', Top);
    Left := IniFile.ReadInteger ('MainForm','Left', Left);
```

```
      Width := IniFile.ReadInteger ('MainForm','Width', Width);
      Height := IniFile.ReadInteger ('MainForm','Height', Height);

      {set the minimized or maximized status}
      case Status of
        1: WindowState := wsNormal;
        // 2: WindowState := wsMinimized;
        // Better use the following as in the SHOWPAR example:
        2: PostMessage (Form1.Handle,
          wm_SysCommand, sc_Minimize, 0);
        3: WindowState := wsMaximized;
      end;
  end;
end;

procedure TForm1.FormClose(Sender: TObject;
  var Action: TCloseAction);
var
  Status: Integer;
begin
  if MessageDlg ('Save the current status of the form?',
    mtConfirmation, [mbYes, mbNo], 0) = IdYes then
  begin
    case WindowState of
      wsNormal: begin
        {save position and size only if the state is normal}
        IniFile.WriteInteger ('MainForm','Top', Top);
        IniFile.WriteInteger ('MainForm','Left', Left);
        IniFile.WriteInteger ('MainForm','Width', Width);
        IniFile.WriteInteger ('MainForm','Height', Height);
        Status := 1;
      end;
      wsMinimized: Status := 2;   {useless: this value is not set!}
      wsMaximized: Status := 3;
    end;
    {check if the window is minimized, that is, if the form
    is hidden and not active}
    if not Active then
      Status := 2;
    {write status information}
    IniFile.WriteInteger ('MainForm','Status', Status);
  end;
  {in any case destroy the IniFile object}
  IniFile.Destroy;
end;
```

This code uses a field named IniFile of type TIniFile, which I've added to the private section to the TForm1 class. I didn't include a figure showing the program's output, because showing you an empty form or an icon is not particularly helpful. Instead, you should simply run the program a number of times to investigate its behavior, resizing and repositioning its window each time. What I can provide is an example of an INI file generated by the program:

```
[MainForm]
Top=359
Left=567
Width=217
Height=201
Status=1
```

> Regarding INI files, remember that Delphi uses them quite often, even if they are disguised with different names. For example, the DSK and DOF files are structured as INI file.

## Using the Registry

Now we can write a similar program using the system registry instead of plain INI files. However, before we do so, I want to spend just a little time discussing the role and the structure of the registry.

In short, the registry is a hierarchical database of information about the computer, the software installed, and the preferences of the users of the computer. Windows has a set of API functions to interact with the registry: you basically need to open a key and then work with subkeys, but you must be aware of the structure and the details of the registry. The Windows 95 registry is based on six top-level keys, as you can see in Figure 19.15.

**FIGURE 19.15:**

The six top-level keys of Windows 95 registry, as you can see them in the Registration Editor.

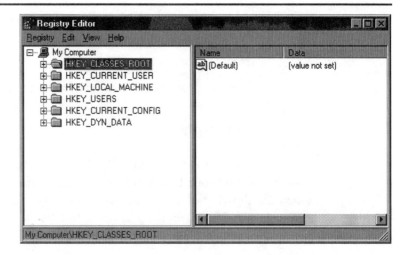

I cannot discuss the role of each part of the registry in detail here. I recommend that you refer to specific Microsoft documentation (such as the Windows 95 or NT Resource Kit) to get the details of the organization of the registry and information about where to add your own keys. The importance of the registry should not be underestimated. This tool is very important for the system hardware configuration, Control Panel settings, OLE servers information, and even statistics about the machine. To study the structure of the registry and examine the current values of the keys, you can use the REGEDIT program (available in each version of Windows, but usually not present by default among the items on the Start menu or the Program Manager icons).

> **WARNING**
>
> You can also use REGEDIT to edit the values in the registry, but you'd do better to avoid changing anything unless you are sure about what you are doing. If you damage the registry, you'll probably have to reinstall Windows from scratch.

In Delphi, there are basically two approaches to the use of the registry, indicated by two new VCL classes: TRegistry and TRegIniFile. The first class provides a generic encapsulation of the registry API, while the latter uses the same interface (methods and properties) of the TIniFile class, simply saving the data in the registry instead of using the files. This class is the natural choice for the registry version of the last program, since by using it we won't have to make many changes in the source code. This is a real advantage if you have exiting code based on INI files. Here are the three changes you have to make to the INI_ONE program:

1. Use TRegIniFile instead of TIniFile as the class of the IniFile object:

   ```
   private
     IniFile: TRegIniFile;
   ```

2. Create a new TRegIniFile object, instead of a TIniFile object, when the form is created:

   ```
   procedure TForm1.FormCreate(Sender: TObject);
   var
     Status: Integer;
   begin
     IniFile := TRegIniFile.Create ('ini_one.ini');
     ...
   ```

3. In the uses statement of the interface portion of the unit, replace the Inifiles unit with the Registry unit:

```
uses
    SysUtils, Windows, Messages, Classes, Graphics, Controls,
    Forms, Dialogs, Registry;
```

Easy, isn't it? With these simple changes, I've built the REGISTR example, which has exactly the same capabilities as the INI_ONE example, but saves its data to the registry instead. Actually, when using the TRegIniFile class, Delphi adds a new subkey with the name of the INI file under the HKEY_CURRENT_USER key. We can see the effect of this code by exploring the registry with the REGEDIT application. I've done so and shown the result in Figure 19.16.

**FIGURE 19.16:**

Using the REGISTR program, you add new entries to the registration database, as you can see with REGEDIT.

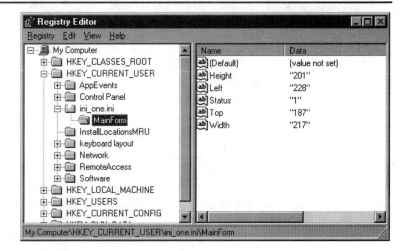

The TRegIniFile class is actually a subclass of the more generic TRegistry class, which has a number of methods very similar to registry API functions. These functions are not very simple to use at first, so I suggest that you stay with the simpler TRegIniFile in the beginning. To use the TRegistry class, in general you need to open a key first, then access its data, including its values and its subkeys.

To show you the basic capabilities of the TRegistry class, I've built a very simple registry viewer application. This program can actually show the structure of the registry and list the values of the keys, without showing the actual data connected with the values. It has just a few of the capabilities of the Registration Editor included in Windows, but I think it is an interesting example anyway.

The REGVIEW program is based on a form with two combo boxes and two list boxes. When the application starts, the TRegistry object is created:

```
procedure TForm1.FormCreate(Sender: TObject);
begin
  Reg := TRegistry.Create;
  Reg.OpenKey ('\', False);
  UpdateAll;
  // select the current root
  ComboKey.ItemIndex := 1;
end;
```

This code opens the root item (indicated by the backslash character) of the default key, then updates the user interface. At the end, it selects the current root in first combo box (more on this later). The UpdateAll method simply copies the current path to the caption of the form and fills the two list boxes with the subkeys and the values of the current key (as you can see in Figure 19.17):

```
procedure TForm1.UpdateAll;
begin
  Caption := Reg.CurrentPath;
  if Reg.HasSubKeys then
    Reg.GetKeyNames(ListSub.Items)
  else
    ListSub.Clear;
  Reg.GetValueNames(ListValues.Items);
end;
```

**FIGURE 19.17:**

The output of the REGVIEW example, showing keys and values of the registry.

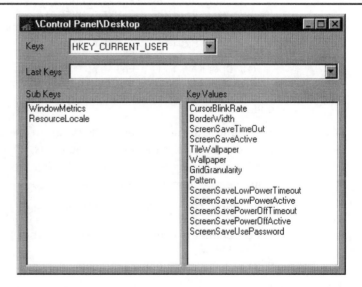

When you select an item from the first list box (ListSub), the program jumps to the selected subkey. To accomplish this, simply write the following code:

```
procedure TForm1.ListSubClick(Sender: TObject);
var
  NewKey: string;
begin
  NewKey := ListSub.Items [ListSub.ItemIndex];
  Reg.OpenKey (NewKey, False);
  UpdateAll;
end;
```

This is enough to navigate the full tree. The two combo boxes add some more capabilities to the program. The first lists the possible root keys for Windows 95:

```
HKEY_CLASSES_ROOT
HKEY_CURRENT_USER
HKEY_LOCAL_MACHINE
HKEY_USERS
HKEY_CURRENT_CONFIG
HKEY_DYN_DATA
```

When the selection changes, the corresponding contents are selected as root key of the TRegistry object:

```
procedure TForm1.ComboKeyChange(Sender: TObject);
begin
  case ComboKey.ItemIndex of
    0: Reg.RootKey := HKEY_CLASSES_ROOT;
    1: Reg.RootKey := HKEY_CURRENT_USER;
    2: Reg.RootKey := HKEY_LOCAL_MACHINE;
    3: Reg.RootKey := HKEY_USERS;
    4: Reg.RootKey := HKEY_CURRENT_CONFIG;
    5: Reg.RootKey := HKEY_DYN_DATA;
  end;
  Reg.OpenKey ('\', False);
  UpdateAll;
  ComboLast.Items.Clear;
end;
```

After setting the new root key, the program opens its root item, updates the user interface, and empties the second combo box, which stores the last selected items and can be used to traverse the tree and move up and down, without having to start from the root item each time. This is the code:

```
procedure TForm1.ComboLastChange(Sender: TObject);
begin
  Reg.OpenKey (ComboLast.Text, False);
  UpdateAll;
end;
```

This code is simple, but the code needed to update the list of the items of this combo box is quite complicated. Besides checking if a path is already present, we have to add a new backslash in front of any path that doesn't have it at the beginning. The problem here is that the method above produces a correct effect, but doesn't set the CurrentPath property of the Reg object properly. To make further selections from that path (once it is added to the list), we need to correct it first. Considering all these issues, here is the final version of the ListSubClick method:

```
procedure TForm1.ListSubClick(Sender: TObject);
var
  NewKey, OldPath: string;
begin
  // save the current path (eventually adding a \)
  // only if not already there
  OldPath := Reg.CurrentPath;
  if OldPath < '\' then
    OldPath := '\' + OldPath;
  if ComboLast.Items.IndexOf (OldPath) < 0 then
    ComboLast.Items.Add (OldPath);
  // get the selection
  NewKey := ListSub.Items [ListSub.ItemIndex];
  Reg.OpenKey (NewKey, False);
  UpdateAll;
end;
```

You can see a sample of the items added to the combo box in Figure 19.18. Notice that I've decided to keep them sorted to make it easier to locate them.

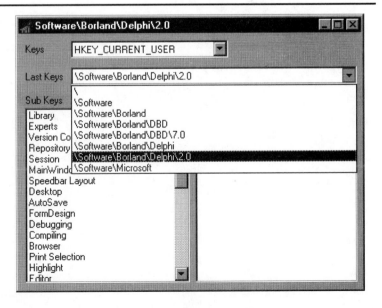

# Summary

In this chapter, we have seen some of the features of the Application global object. We've discussed multitasking, timers, and idle computing. We've also discussed the use of the parameters passed from the system to the WinMain function, which are stored in other Delphi global variables. It was also interesting to write very small programs, without any components.

These examples have demonstrated that you can use Delphi to delve into the intricacies of Windows programming, using very low-level features of the system. For more details, you can refer to Windows programming books, and then apply the information to Delphi programming.

The ability to use all the capabilities of Windows is a great feature of Delphi. At times, I must admit, using straight C code for some low-level tasks seems simpler, mainly because the presence of the hidden window for the application creates some confusing situations. However, I've still found nothing I could do in C programming that I cannot do in Delphi, and this is unusual in a visual programming environment.

We have learned about the Application object, but we have still not explored the whole structure of an application. The next two chapters, which cover topics such as memory and resources, will complete the picture.

# CHAPTER

## TWENTY

# Exploring the Behavior of a Program

- Delphi's integrated debugger

- The Object Browser

- Windows message flow

- Windows memory handling

- Monitoring free memory

**O**nce you compile a program in Delphi and run it, you may think you're finished, but not all of your problems may be solved. Programs can have run-time errors, or they may not work as you planned. When this happens, you will need to discover what has gone wrong and how to correct it. Fortunately, many options and tools are available for exploring the behavior of a Windows application.

Delphi includes an integrated debugger and the Object Browser to let you monitor the result of a compilation process in two different ways. But along with knowing how to use Delphi's tools, in order to understand what happens in a program, you should also know how it uses memory and how Windows uses the system memory.

This chapter provides an overview of all these topics, demonstrating the key ideas with simple examples. As I've said before, if you want to delve into the details of Windows, you can refer to any of the many good books on the subject. Here you will find only an overview of the ideas every good Delphi programmer should know (at least in my opinion).

The first part of the chapter covers Delphi's debugger and Browser tools. These sections are not tutorials that describe how to activate every feature of these tools; they are technical presentations. The second part of this chapter deals with the key elements of Windows 95 memory handling and internal structure and describes the memory image of a Delphi application.

# Debugging with the Debugger

As I've mentioned a number of times, each time you run a program from the Delphi environment, it is executed in the debugger. This happens unless you have disabled the Integrated Debugger option in the Preferences page of the Environment Options dialog box.

When the program is running in the debugger, clicking on the Pause button on the SpeedBar stops the execution. After you stop it, clicking on the Step Over button executes the program step by step. (Or you can start program execution step by step from the beginning, instead of running it.)

Consider, however, that Windows applications are message-driven, so there is no way to execute the application code step by step from the beginning to the end, as you can with a DOS application. For this reason, the most common way to debug a Delphi application, or any other Windows application, is to set some breakpoints in the portions of the code you want to explore.

## Debug Information

To debug a Delphi program, you must add debug information to your compiled code. This is not a problem, because it is Delphi's default behavior. You can turn debug information generation on or off in the Delphi compiled units (DCU files) through the Project Options dialog box. As shown in Figure 20.1, the Compiler page includes a Debugging section with three check boxes:

- *Debug Information* puts information in the compiled unit that maps compiled code addresses to source code line numbers. This increases the size of the DCU file but does not affect the size or speed of the executable program.

- *Local Symbols* adds the identifiers defined in the implementation part of a unit and in its methods.

- *Symbol Info* adds the line numbers of all declarations of and references to symbols in a module, to allow the Object Browser to display them.

The integrated debugger uses these debug information items. They do not end up in the executable file unless you set the corresponding linker option (in the Linker page of the Project Options dialog box), Include TDW Debug Info. Adding debug information in the executable file has two drawbacks: it increases the size of your program, and it also allows someone armed with a debugger to understand how your program was written. You should add debug information to your executable file only if you plan to use an external debugger, such as Borland's Turbo Debugger for Windows (TDW). Do not add debug information to the executable file if you

**FIGURE 20.1:**

Use the Compiler page of the Project Options dialog box to include debug information in a compiled unit.

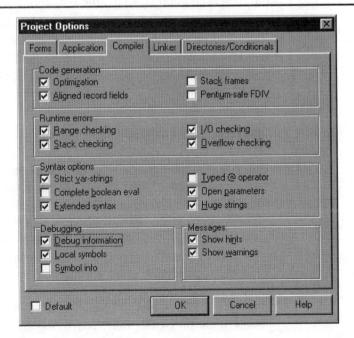

plan to use only the integrated debugger, and remember to remove the debug information from the executable file that you ship. This might seem obvious, but there are commercial products on the market that actually still contain debug information!

On the whole, debugging a Delphi program is not simple. Delphi applications, like all Windows applications, are event-driven. This means that all the procedures and functions are not executed in a predetermined sequence. After the initialization code is executed, the program stops waiting for messages. From that point, everything else happens as a response to an event. To debug a Delphi application, you will often need to place a breakpoint in each handler you want to monitor.

## Setting Breakpoints

There are a number of ways to set breakpoints in Delphi. The simplest method is to click to the left of the code in the editor window (between the text and the border of the window). As soon as you click, an icon appears near the code, and the line is shown in a different color.

However, you cannot set a breakpoint in every line of the source code. Basically, a breakpoint is valid if some code is executed on that line. This excludes comments, procedure and variable declarations, special lines (such as `implementation` and compiler directive lines), and some other cases. Although you can set a breakpoint in an invalid location, when you run the program, Delphi lets you know that it is not correct and marks the invalid breakpoint with a different icon and color.

By the way, since Delphi uses an optimizing compiler, it may remove some of the compiled code generated by *unreachable* lines of source code in your program (by *unreachable* line, I mean a line of code that will never be executed, or is completely useless, as in the example below). If you set a breakpoint on one of those lines, the compiler might flag it as an invalid breakpoint. Here is a small portion of the next example:

```
Limit := 3;
Limit := X1;
```

The code generated by the first line is removed by the optimizing compiler, so setting a breakpoint on it has no effect at all. In fact, if you set the breakpoint before it and then execute the program step by step, the debugger will skip this line, since it doesn't exist in the optimized version of the compiled code. Except for special cases such as this, once the program execution has reached a line with the breakpoint, the program stops. One common use of breakpoints is simply to let you know that a particular event handler has been executed. When you have doubts about the flow of a program's execution because you are not sure when each handler is invoked, you can add a breakpoint at the beginning of each method, as suggested in the BREAKP example. This example draws a series of lines around the border of the form. A button in the middle of the form allows you to move the lines toward the center, but not over the button. Here is the code of this simple program:

```
procedure TForm1.FormPaint(Sender: TObject);
begin
  {set a breakpoint on the next line}
  Canvas.MoveTo (X1, Y1);
  Canvas.LineTo (X2, Y1);
  Canvas.LineTo (X2, Y2);
  Canvas.LineTo (X1, Y2);
  Canvas.LineTo (X1, Y1);
end;

procedure TForm1.Button1Click(Sender: TObject);
var
  Limit: Integer;
begin
  {set a breakpoint on the next line}
  X1 := X1 + 5;
  Y1 := Y1 + 5;
  X2 := X2 - 5;
  Y2 := Y2 - 5;
  {dummy code: try setting
  a breakpoint on next line}
  Limit := 3;
  Limit := X1;
  {is the line over the button?}
  if X1 >= Button1.Left then
  begin
    Button1.Enabled := False;
    X1 := Button1.Left;
  end;
  if Y1 >= Button1.Top then
  begin
    Button1.Enabled := False;
    Y1 := Button1.Top;
  end;

  Invalidate;
end;
procedure TForm1.FormResize(Sender: TObject);
begin
  {set a breakpoint on the next line}
  Button1.Enabled := True;
  X1 := 10;
  Y1 := 10;
  X2 := ClientWidth - 10;
  Y2 := ClientHeight - 10;
  Invalidate;
end;
```

When you have set a number of breakpoints (in the lines following the comments), you can use the Breakpoints command on the View menu to open the Breakpoint List window, which is shown in Figure 20.2.

**FIGURE 20.2:**

The Breakpoint List window, with its local menu.

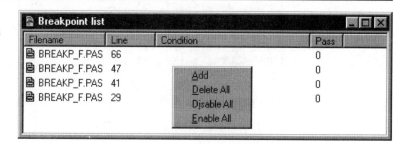

As one of the headings at the top of the Breakpoint List window suggests, you can add a condition to a breakpoint, so that the program halts only when a given condition is met. You'll see an example with a conditional breakpoint a little later in this chapter.

Once the program has stopped, you can continue executing it using the Run command. As I've mentioned before, an alternative is to execute the program step by step. The Step Over button on Delphi's SpeedBar allows you to see the execution of statements one after the other. The Trace Into button allows you to trace the methods that are called (that is, to execute the code of the subroutines step by step, and to execute the code of the subroutines called by the subroutines, and so on).

The current line of execution is highlighted with a different color, so that you can see what your program is doing. With this color (and a small arrow-shaped icon), Delphi indicates the line that is about to be executed. The effect of the *execution point* (the highlighted line) is accomplished as soon as you execute another step.

Note that when you trace subroutines and reach code that exists in a different unit, this file is automatically loaded in the editor. While you're tracing a program, you can see the subroutine calls currently on the stack with the Call Stack command on Delphi's View menu. By adding a breakpoint in the OnClick event of a button and looking at the stack when the program stops, you get the information shown in Figure 20.3.

The Call Stack window shows the names of the methods on the stack and their memory addresses. It is particularly useful when you're tracing a series of nested calls.

**FIGURE 20.3:**

The Call stack window when a
button is clicked.

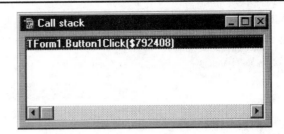

## Inspecting Values

When a program is stopped in the debugger, you can inspect the value of any identifier (variables, objects, components, properties, and so on) that's accessible from that location in the program (that is, only if the identifier is in the current scope). There are basically two ways to accomplish this: use the Evaluate/Modify dialog box or add a watch to the Watch List window.

As the name suggests, the Evaluate/Modify dialog box is a double-duty tool. You can use it to inspect the value of a given identifier or expression, or to change the value of a variable. The easiest way to open this dialog box is to select the variable in the code editor, and then choose the Evaluate/Modify command from the editor's SpeedMenu. If you want to select a long expression, copy it from the editor and paste it in the dialog box, since long selections are not automatically used.

For example, by setting a breakpoint in the OnResize handler of the BREAKP example and stepping through the code, you can evaluate and actually change the value of X1, as shown in Figure 20.4. In this dialog box, you can enter complex expressions, as long as there are no function calls involved. You can also enter the name of a constant (such as the color value clYellow) and see the corresponding numeric value.

When you want to test the value of a variable over and over, using this dialog box becomes too slow. As an alternative, you can set a *watch* (an entry in a list of variables you're interested in monitoring) for any variable, property, or component. For example, you might set a watch for each of the values used in the BREAKP example's Button1Click method, which is called each time the user clicks on the button. I've added a number of watches to see the value of the most relevant variables and properties involved in this method, as you can see in Figure 20.5.

You can set watches by using the Add Watch at Cursor command on the editor's SpeedMenu (or just press Ctrl+F5). When you add a watch, you'll need to choose the proper output format, and for the more complex expressions, enter some text. For simple values, you can just give the command when the identifier is selected in the editor.

**FIGURE 20.4:**

The Evaluate/Modify dialog box can be used to inspect the value of a variable and also to change it.

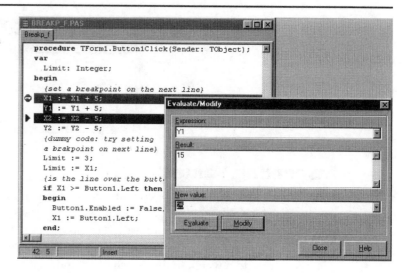

**FIGURE 20.5:**

An example of the use of the Watch List window.

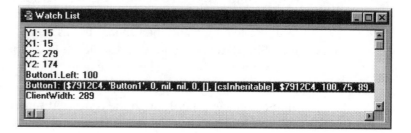

You can see the value of a variable only when the program is stopped in the debugger, not when it is running. Additionally, you can inspect only the variables that are visible in the current scope, because they must exist in order for you to see them! You can also add watches for (or inspect) entire components, but the result is not easy to understand, as you can see in Figure 20.5 above. It is far more common to inspect or watch individual properties of a component.

## More on Breakpoints

When a program reaches a breakpoint, it stops the execution and shows the current line in the editor. When the editor is activated, however, its window might cover some portions of the form of your program. When the code you are going to execute step by step involves output, the form appears from behind the editor but disappears again quickly, without letting you view its new contents.

If possible, position the editor window and the form of your program manually so that they do not overlap (or overlap only partially). With that arrangement, you'll be able to execute a program step by step and actually see its output on the screen.

This becomes particularly important for OnPaint handlers. You can try this with the BREAKP example. Open that program again, set a breakpoint in the FormPaint method, and run it. If the editor window and the form overlap, you'll enter an endless series of breakpoints. Each time the form is repainted, the breakpoint stops the program, moving the editor window in front of the form and causing the form to be repainted again, which stops the program on the same breakpoint—over and over again.

The solution is simply to arrange the forms on the screen side by side. In this arrangement, you can see the execution of the FormPaint code step by step and let the program run without any problems. As an alternative, if you only need to know when the OnPaint code is executed, you can disable the breakpoint as it is reached, and later enable it again. In fact, you can add and remove breakpoints easily while the program is stopped in the debugger.

To stop a program on a breakpoint only at certain times, you can use *conditional breakpoints*. For example, we might want to stop the Button1Click method's execution (in the BREAKP example) only when the lines have moved near the button. You can set a breakpoint as usual, then open the Breakpoint list, double-click on the breakpoint to open the Edit Breakpoint dialog box, and enter this condition:

```
Button1.Top - Y1 < 10
```

The condition is also added to the Breakpoint List window, as you can see in Figure 20.6. Now you can run the program and click on the button a number of times. Until the condition is met (when Button1.Top - Y1 is less than 10), the breakpoint is ignored. Only after you click several times will the program actually stop in the debugger.

**NOTE**   There are some special cases in Windows when a message-driven debugger, such as Delphi's integrated debugger, cannot stop at a breakpoint. In these cases, Windows is said to be in *hard mode*. This happens during menu drawing and some kernel operations. When Delphi finds a breakpoint in such a special code areas, it will warn you with a special message.

**FIGURE 20.6:**

The breakpoint list window, with a conditional breakpoint.

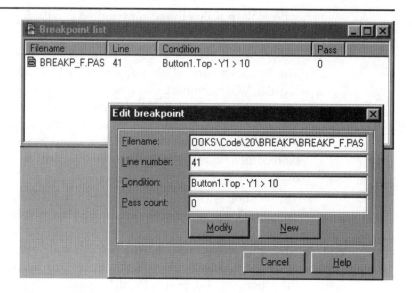

# Tracing through the VCL Source Code

If you own the VCL source code, one of its key uses is in debugging your applications. If you want to understand the effects of accessing VCL component properties or calling VCL methods (besides what the documentation tells you), you can include the library source code in your program and use the debugger to trace its execution. Of course, you need to be bold enough and have enough free time to delve into the intricacies of the VCL source code. But when nothing else seems to work, this just might be the only solution.

To include the library source code, simply add the name of the directory with the VCL source code (by default, C:\Program Files\Borland\Delphi) in the Search Path combo box of the Directories/Conditional page of the Project Options dialog box. Then rebuild the whole program and start debugging. When you reach statements containing method or property calls, you can trace the program and see the VCL code executed line after line. Naturally, you can do any common debugging operation with the VCL code that you can do with your own code.

**WARNING**    It seems that the inclusion of the VCL source code doesn't always work, although I'm not sure why. At first I thought it had problems when the project I was compiling was on a different hard disk, but then I realized this is not the only reason. Closing Delphi and running it again solved the problem most of the time.

As an example, Figure 20.7 shows the Call Stack window after tracing the Invalidate call of the button's OnClick event handler. Notice that you can see a lot of activity before the Button1Click method is called (the topmost element in the Call Stack window is the most recent call, and the highlighted method is almost at the top).

The Call Stack window when debugging a program that includes the VCL source code.

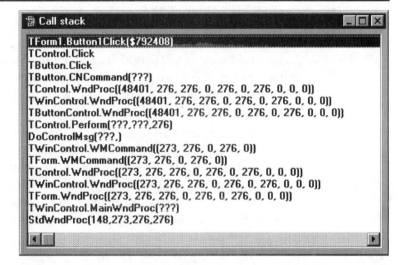

```
Call stack
TForm1.Button1Click($792408)
TControl.Click
TButton.Click
TButton.CNCommand(???)
TControl.WndProc((48401, 276, 276, 0, 276, 0, 276, 0, 0, 0))
TWinControl.WndProc((48401, 276, 276, 0, 276, 0, 276, 0, 0, 0))
TButtonControl.WndProc((48401, 276, 276, 0, 276, 0, 276, 0, 0, 0))
TControl.Perform(???,???,276)
DoControlMsg(???,)
TWinControl.WMCommand((273, 276, 0, 276, 0))
TForm.WMCommand((273, 276, 0, 276, 0))
TControl.WndProc((273, 276, 276, 0, 276, 0, 276, 0, 0, 0))
TWinControl.WndProc((273, 276, 276, 0, 276, 0, 276, 0, 0, 0))
TForm.WndProc((273, 276, 276, 0, 276, 0, 276, 0, 0, 0))
TWinControl.MainWndProc(???)
StdWndProc(148,273,276,276)
```

If you compare Figure 20.7 with the contents of the Call Stack window without the VCL source code loaded (shown earlier in Figure 20.3), you'll see the different level of detail available. This amount of detail is both an advantage and a disadvantage. It's good because you have all the details you need to get an idea of the status of your program. But how do you pick out the valuable information from all these items, unless you become an expert on the VCL message dispatching mechanism?

# Alternative Debugging Techniques

One common use of breakpoints is to know that a program has reached a certain stage, but there are other ways to get this information besides setting breakpoints. A common technique is to show simple messages (using the ShowMessage procedure) on specific lines for debugging purposes. There are many other manual techniques, such as sending the output to a terminal window, changing the text of a label in a special form, writing to a log file, or adding a line in a list box or a memo field.

All of these alternatives serve a basic purpose: to let you know that a certain statement of the code has been executed, or let you watch some values, without actually stopping the program. These approaches avoid the side effects related to stopping and restarting a program (such as the painting problems described earlier), but adding a statement to produce some output is not as easy or fast as setting a breakpoint and removing it.

# Debugging with a Terminal Window

Delphi's debugging tools are also much more powerful than the homemade techniques. Being able to step though a program, watching the value of a variable change or tracing through a series of calls, perhaps even those made by the VCL source code, is an invaluable programming aid.

However, homemade debugging techniques have their role, too. As an example, consider debugging the BACKPROC example presented in Chapter 19. This program involves a timer, idle-time computing, and other techniques that would be affected by stopping the program in a debugger. To avoid stopping the program, we could display some debug information in a secondary window. This is what I've done in the new version of the program, which is named BACK2.

The BACK2 version includes a second form I've called DebugForm, with a list box covering its entire client area. The form's unit also includes a procedure you can use to add a line of text to the debugging form's list box:

```
procedure WriteLine (Text: String);
begin
  if not DebugForm.Visible then
    DebugForm.Show;
  with DebugForm.Listbox1 do
    ItemIndex := Items.Add (Text);
end;
```

As you can see, this is not a method, but rather a global procedure, which makes it simpler to write the code calling it. Now you can simply add a call to WriteLine to each method of the form class, as in the following code:

```
procedure TForm1.IdleButtonClick(Sender: TObject);
begin
  WriteLine ('IdleButtonClick');
  IdleNPrimes := 0;
  {same code as before...}
```

The only place where this code wasn't added is in the IsPrime function, because that function is called too often.

Now you can just run the program, and you'll see a lot of output in the debug window. Some of the functions, in fact, are called for each number to test. In these cases, I've improved the output slightly by adding the current number to the output:

```
procedure TForm1.IdleProc (Sender: TObject; var Done: Boolean);
begin
  WriteLine ('IdleProc' + IntToStr (IdleNumber));
  if IdleNumber < IdleMax then
      ...
end;
```

You can see an example of a debugging session made with the terminal window in Figure 20.8.

**FIGURE 20.8:**
The output of the BACK2 example, with its debug window.

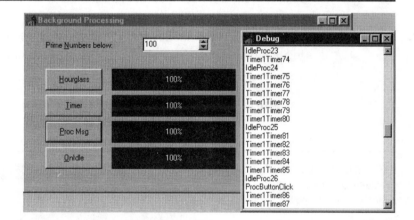

## Debug and Release Versions

Adding debugging code to an application is certainly interesting, as the example above demonstrates, but this approach has a serious flaw. In the final version of the program, the one you give to your customers, you need to disable the debugging output, and possibly remove all of the debugging code, to reduce the size of the program. At first, you might think that this is too big of a problem and that a terminal window is not a professional solution. If you are a C/C++ programmer, however, you might have some ideas on how to do this. The solution to this problem, in fact, lies in a typical C technique known as *conditional compilation*. The idea is simple: you write some lines of code that you want to compile only in certain circumstances and skip on other occasions.

In Delphi, you can use some conditional compiler directives for this:

```
$IFDEF
$IFNDEF
$IFOPT
$ELSE
$ENDIF
```

For example, in our code, we can replace any occurrence of the WriteLine procedure with the following:

```
{$IFDEF DEBUG}
  WriteLine ('IdleProc' + IntToStr (IdleNumber));
{$ENDIF}
```

This code is included in the compilation only if there is a DEBUG defined before the line, or if the DEBUG symbol has been defined in the Project Options dialog box, as shown in Figure 20.9.

You can even conditionally include the unit defining the debug form, simply writing the following code into the `implementation` part of the unit:

```
{$IFDEF DEBUG}
uses DebugF;
{$ENDIF}
```

**FIGURE 20.9:**

The definition of a symbol in the Project Options dialog box.

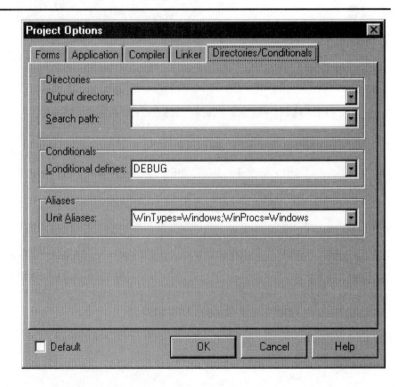

Now you can compile the program adding the DEBUG symbol (or any other symbol you choose) in the Project Options dialog box and see the debug output in the terminal window. Then you can remove the symbol definition, choose the Build All command from Delphi's Compile menu, and run it again without the terminal window. The size of the executable file will probably change slightly between the two versions because some source code is removed. Note that each time you change the symbol definitions in the Project Options dialog box, you need to rebuild the whole program. If you simply run it, the older version will be executed since the executable file is up-to-date compared to the source files.

**WARNING**  You should use conditional compilation for debugging purposes with extreme care. In fact, if you debug a program with this technique and later change its code (when removing the DEBUG define), you might introduce new bugs or expose bugs that were hidden by the debug process. For this reason, it is generally better to debug the final version of your application carefully, without making any more changes to the source code.

# Viewing a Compiled Program with the Object Browser

Another way you can explore a compiled program is with Delphi's Object Browser. The Browser doesn't show the values of the objects and variables of a program; it shows its data types and classes. Once a program is successfully compiled, you can open the Browser and see the whole hierarchy of classes included in your application, as shown in the example in Figure 20.10. The Browse Objects window displays both VCL classes and those defined by your program.

Delphi's Object Browser is similar to the corresponding tool included in many C++ compilers and in previous versions of Borland Pascal. Basically, you can use the Browser to see all of the methods, properties, and data fields—both local and inherited—of any class.

If you prefer a partial view, you can choose only a subset of the elements of a class by using the Show buttons at the top of the Browse Objects window. These buttons activate filters for the kind of definition; filter the definitions present in the parent class; and filter methods, fields, and properties by their visibility, as shown in Figure 20.11.

Besides exploring the hierarchy of classes, you can see the elements of each class, and even the details of the definition of each of these elements. You can see when there are references to particular elements in the source code of your application.

**FIGURE 20.10:**

An example of the output of the Object Browser.

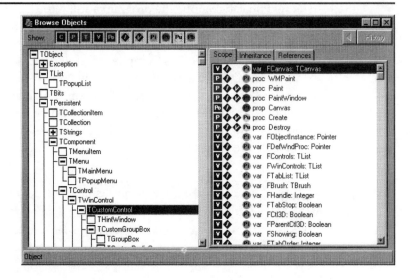

**FIGURE 20.11:**

The Object Browser's speed buttons.

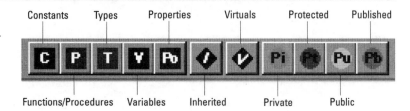

As with the debugger, if you compile the program including the VCL source files, you can see the references to the VCL source, too, and easily reach the definition of each method, property, or class in the source code. In fact when you select a reference, the Browser opens the corresponding source file in the editor, moving to the proper line.

There are other ways to use this tool. The Browser SpeedMenu offers four choices:

- The Objects command shows the inheritance tree, as shown before in Figure 20.10, with all of the classes of the application.

- The Units command shows the list of units included in the current project.

- The Globals command shows a list of global symbols.

- The Symbol command lets you enter the name of a symbol and move directly to it.

For example, you can choose the WinProcs unit and see a complete list of the functions of the Windows API, or choose WinTypes to see the definition of all Windows constants.

The Browser is a powerful tool that allows you to explore a complex program, or a not-so-complex program written by another programmer (or by you, but a long time ago), because you can easily jump back and forth from it to the editor. Each time you find a symbol in the editor that you don't recognize, you can select it and use the Browse Symbol at Cursor command on the editor's SpeedMenu to jump to the symbol definition in the Browser. There you can see where the symbol is defined or used, and then jump back to that file in the editor. If you include the VCL source code in the compilation, you'll be able to jump to these source code files, too.

The Object Browser lets you explore a program only after you have compiled it, because it uses debugging information generated by the compiler. This means that if you change the source code and the program stops compiling because you have introduced an error in your editing, you cannot use the Browser to understand what is happening. To avoid this problem, Delphi lets you save the Browser symbols. To do this, select the Desktop and Symbols radio button in the Preferences page of the Environment Options dialog box.

Now each time you compile a program, the information required by the Browser is saved to a file with the *DSM* extension. With this file, you can use the Object Browser for the program, even if it cannot be built anymore due to an error. The Browser can read the DSM file instead of rebuilding the same information in memory. The drawback is that DSM files are very big. Therefore, you might turn on this option only when you really need it; that is, when you are developing a complex program.

Do not save Browser symbols just to look at examples, or your hard disk will soon be filled with almost useless files. If you prefer leaving this option on, you should remember to occasionally search your hard disk for DSM files and delete the old ones.

# Exploring the Message Flow

The two tools we have discussed so far in this chapter, the integrated debugger and the Object Browser, provide common ways to explore the source code of a program. In Windows, however, this is often not enough. When you want to understand the details of the interaction between your program and the environment, other Windows-related tools are handy.

One of them is WinSight, a multiple-purpose tool included in Delphi. Others are memory-spying programs. Delphi doesn't include this type of program, but they are available from many sources, including a number of shareware programs, and many samples are included in books and magazine articles.

## Using WinSight

We have already seen in previous chapters how the WinSight application can be used to explore an application. Here, I'll provide a short overview, with some new details and tips. WinSight can be used for three different actions:

- to build a hierarchical graph of the windows that are currently open
- to display detailed information about the message flow
- to list all of the window classes registered in the system (a feature that is not enabled in the version of WinSight shipping with Delphi 2)

These three actions can be activated by the first three commands on WinSight's View menu: Class List (this feature is actually grayed), Window Tree, and Message Trace. You can also choose all three views at the same time, placing them in different vertical or horizontal panes, as shown in Figure 20.12.

**FIGURE 20.12:**

Two of WinSight's panes: the window tree and the message flow.

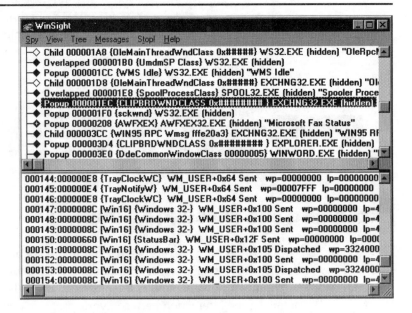

To become a proficient user of WinSight and understand all of the information it delivers, you need to have an in-depth knowledge of the structure of Windows and of the Windows applications. Although it might seem beyond the scope of this book, I've decided to give you a brief summary of the information displayed by WinSight, focusing on the information related to Delphi programming.

## The Class List and the WNDCLASS Structure

As I mentioned, the version of WinSight that ships with Delphi 2 does not display the class list. However, since I'm quite confident Borland will solve this problem, and because the technical information related to it is very important, I've decided to discuss this topic anyway.

The idea of the class list is that of a list of all the *window classes registered in the system*. Some of you might not know what this means. In short, to create a window of any kind (ranging from the main window of an application to a small control), the Windows environment requires you to specify the class of the window and formally register that class. For this reason, the code of a Windows application written in C often registers a class before creating a window  (to ensure that the class will be available). Every window in the system relates to a class, also known as WNDCLASS from the type name of the data structure used in the registration code (which is TWndClass in Delphi).

But note that *class* as a Windows term has only a limited relationship with the same term in object-oriented programming languages. Windows' WNDCLASS data structures have a fixed number of fields, one of which is the address of a procedure (called the *window procedure* or WndProc). This single procedure is used to respond to all of the messages sent by the system to the windows of that class. For this reason, the typical window procedure is made of a big case statement, with a branch for each message you want to handle. (It is obvious that the object-oriented approach to Windows programming offered by Delphi and some C++ class libraries is far superior to the original approach.)

The class list in WinSight shows all of the classes defined in the system, including Windows system classes (some of which are completely undocumented, by the way). However, most of the classes are registered by other running Windows applications. If you run a program you have written with Delphi, it registers some window classes, too.

> **NOTE**
>
> Borland engineers were smart enough to use an internal class name that is the same as the name of the Object Pascal class, such as TForm1 or TButton. I've mentioned this good choice because other programming environments use unbelievably complex naming schemes.

Using WinSight, we will be able to access some information about the window class when looking at the details of a window (as you will see in a figure in the next section). Class information includes the name of the class, the name of the executable file (or dynamic link library) that has registered it, the address of the Windows procedure of that class, and some style flags for that class.

## The Windows Tree: Parents and Children

The Window Tree view in WinSight contains a hierarchical tree of windows. The hierarchical view clarifies the relationship between parent and child windows, which is very important both in Windows and in Delphi (see the Parent and Controls properties). An important feature of WinSight is that it also lists hidden windows and other windows that aren't visible (for example, windows reduced to a single pixel). You can also see windows completely covered by other windows, such as a panel covered by a notebook, and obtain some details about a program's internal structure.

Of course, you can get the details of the structure of any Windows application, even the Delphi development environment or WinSight itself. If you try to explore an application you have written in Delphi, you'll see the forms and the controls within them. However, notice that some Delphi components don't appear in this list. This is because they are graphical components which don't create their own window. The "one visual element-one window" rule, which is a native Windows programming rule, doesn't apply to Delphi or to applications you create with Delphi, which is to our advantage. In fact, non-windowed graphical components tend to be faster and save some system resources, something that was much more important in Windows 3.1 than it is now in Windows 95 or NT.

For each node of the window tree, WinSight first displays the window's type: overlapped, pop-up, or child. Basically, child windows live within a parent window; overlapped and pop-up windows, even if they have a parent, take their pixels from the whole desktop. The different groups of window types also denote a different default behavior determined by the system.

After the window type comes the value of the window handle, a number in hexadecimal format, such as *28C8*. This value is a unique code that the system uses to identify the window. Since this is the parameter of a number of Window API functions, the handle of a form or of a windowed component is available in Delphi as the Handle property, a run-time and read-only property. The handle's value is determined by the system when the window is created.

**NOTE**    Not all Handle properties of Delphi components refer to the handle of a window. There are also icon handles, bitmap handles, menu handles, and so on. Also, not all the other Handle properties are read-only.

Next is the name of the class, the name of the executable file, the position and the size of the window, and its title or caption. You can open a detail view of the window system data (see Figure 20.13), which also includes the handle of the application that created the window (the one stored in the HInstance global variable discussed in Chapter 19), the handle of the menu, the window procedure associated with the window, the client rectangle, and the names of the flags that make up the window style. At the end are the details related to the class of the window, which we have already seen in the previous section.

**FIGURE 20.13:**

The WinSight window with detailed information about a window and its class. In this case, it is a window of a Delphi application.

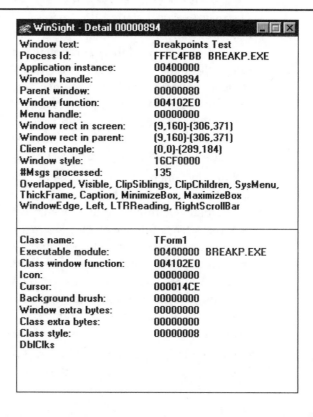

> **NOTE**
>
> If you are an experienced Windows programmer, you might notice that the window procedure of the class and that of the window do not match. By default, each window uses the window procedure registered for its class unless someone changes this value for that particular window, a technique known as *subclassing* (although it has nothing to do with the definition of a subclass in Object Pascal terms). Subclassing is used extensively in the VCL to let you specify the behavior of a windowed object through event handlers. Windows procedures in Delphi elements are so hidden away in the VCL that you'll seldom notice them. Technically, for all TWinControl and descendent classes, every object instance gets a unique window procedure address to bind to its window handle. Windows calls the window procedure of the window, and that window procedure takes you directly into the associated object instance. In contrast, traditional Windows programs use a common window procedure for all the instances of a given window class. The Delphi approach has much greater flexibility.

## Message Flow and Delphi Events

The main reason I started this analysis of WinSight was to help you understand how to spy on (or to examine; *spy* is used in programming jargon, since the original program that allowed this operation was named Spy) the message flow of the Delphi applications. Now, after some digressions, we have reached that point. To become an expert Delphi programmer, you must learn to study the message flow following an input action by a user. As you know, Delphi programs (like Windows applications in general) are event-driven. Code is executed in response to an event. Windows messages are the key element behind Delphi events, although there isn't a one-to-one correspondence between the two.

In Windows, there are many more messages than there are events in Delphi, but some Delphi events are higher level than Windows messages. For example, in Windows, there is a limited amount of support for mouse dragging, while Delphi components offer a full set of mouse-dragging events. Of course, WinSight knows nothing about Delphi events, so you'll have to figure out the correspondence between many events and messages by yourself (or study the VCL source code, if you have it). WinSight can show you all of the Windows messages that reach a window, indicating the destination window, its title or class, and the parameters in a readable format. You can use the Options command from WinSight's Messages menu to filter out some of the messages, and see only the groups you are interested in.

Usually, for Delphi programmers, spying the message flow can be useful when you are faced with some bugs related to the order of windows activation and deactivation, or to receiving and losing the input focus (OnEnter and OnExit events), particularly when message boxes or other modal windows are involved. This is a quite common area of problems, and you can often see why things went wrong by looking at the message flow. You also might want to see the message flow when you want to handle a Windows message directly (instead of using event handlers). Using WinSight, you can get more information about when that message arrives and the parameters it carries (other than those parameters listed in the Help file).

## A Look at Posted Messages

Another way to see the message flow is to trap some Windows messages directly in a Delphi application. If you limit this analysis to posted messages, excluding sent messages, it becomes almost trivial, since there is a specific event of the TApplication class we can use: the OnMessage event. This event is intended to give the application a chance to filter all of the messages it receives and to handle messages for specific windows. For example, you can use it to handle the messages for the window connected with the Application object itself, which has no specific event handlers.

In this example, however, we'll take a look at all of the messages extracted from the message queue of the application (that is, the posted messages). A description of each message is added to a list box covering the form of the example, beside a simple toolbar. For this list box, I've chosen Courier font because it is a non-proportional, or *monospaced*, font and this will produce output formatted with the same fields on each line of the list box.

The speed buttons in the toolbar can be used to turn message viewing on and off, empty the list box, and skip consecutive, repeated messages. For example, if you move the mouse you get many consecutive wm_MouseMove messages, which can be skipped without losing much information.

To let you make some real tests, the program has a second form (launched by the fourth speed button), filled with various kinds of components (chosen at random), used to see the message flow of a standard form. Figure 20.14 shows an example of the output of the MSGFLOW program when the second form is visible.

The basic idea of this example is quite simple. Just define a handler for the OnMessage event of the application, such as the following:

```
type
  TForm1 = class(TForm)
    ...
  private
    Skipping, Spying: Boolean;
    LastMessage: TMsg;
  public
    procedure HandleMessage (var Msg: TMsg;
      var Handled: Boolean);
  end;
```

**FIGURE 20.14:**

The MSGFLOW program at run-time, with a copy of the second form.

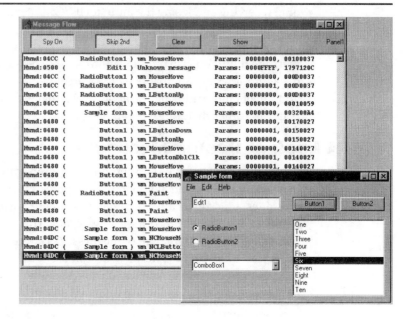

and install it in the FormCreate event:

```
procedure TForm1.FormCreate(Sender: TObject);
begin
  Application.OnMessage := HandleMessage;
  Skipping := False;
  Spying := False;
end;
```

Note the definition and initial values of some Boolean flags toggled by the toolbar buttons in the above code fragments. These flags and the value of the last message (I'll describe the TMsg structure below) determine if a message reaching the application has to be displayed. The core of the HandleMessage method is executed only if three conditions are satisfied:

- The Spying Boolean flag is set to True. A user can easily toggle this Boolean value by clicking on the Spy On button, which behaves like a check box.

- The message is not a message for the list box, to avoid a recursive call (since adding a message to the list generates a new message).

- If the Skipping flag is enabled (by clicking on the Skip 2nd button in the toolbar), the message and its destination window should be different from those of the previous message. Mouse-move messages are often sent in series; with this flag, only the first message of the series is shown.

These conditions are expressed by the following complex if statement:

```
if Spying and (Msg.Hwnd <> Listbox1.Handle) and not
  (Skipping and (LastMessage.Message = Msg.Message) and
  (LastMessage.Hwnd = Msg.Hwnd)) then
```

In the code of the HandleMessage method, you can add a line to the list box for each message. The goal is to fetch some meaningful information. The parameter of the handler of the OnMessage event, in fact, is of the TMsg type. This is a collection of low-level information about the message, including the handle of the destination window, the code of the message, and some numeric parameters. This is actually the information Windows passes to the application. Instead of using the data directly, I've made it more readable in two ways.

First, the MSGFLOW program displays the caption of the window along with its handle. This caption is retrieved using a Windows API function, GetWindowText, which works for any kind of window or component. This text is formatted in a 15-character space, using Delphi's Format function, and then it is added to the Line string that I'll add to the list box at the end. Before adding the formatted text to the Line string, however, if the string is empty (the window has no caption), the *Unknown* string is used. Here is the final code of the first part of this method:

```
procedure TForm1.HandleMessage (var Msg: TMsg;
  var Handled: Boolean);
var
  Line, Caption: string;
begin
  // initialize long strings
  SetLength (Line, 200);
  SetLength (Caption, 50);
  if Spying and (Msg.Hwnd <> Listbox1.Handle) and not
    (Skipping and (LastMessage.Message = Msg.Message) and
    (LastMessage.Hwnd = Msg.Hwnd)) then
  begin
    // output the hex value of the handle
    Line := 'Hwnd:' + IntToHex (Msg.Hwnd, 4);
    {get the caption from the handle,
    using an API function}
    GetWindowText (Msg.Hwnd, PChar (Caption),
      Length (Caption));
    Caption := PChar (Caption); // recast
    if Caption = '' then
      Caption := 'Unknown';
    // format the caption in 15 characters
    AppendStr (Line, Format (' ( %15s ) ', [Caption]));
```

Notice I have to cast the PChar back to a string with this *recast*: I cast it again to a PChar, and Delphi converts it back again to a string. This recast to itself forces the compiler to recalculate the string's length byte by scanning for the null terminator in the initializing string, as I've already discussed in Chapter 5.

The second key improvement is the output of the name of the message, instead of its code. This is not so simple, because message names are not real strings, but are rather names of constants defined in the MESSAGES.PAS system file. Here is an excerpt of this file, with the definition of the first few messages:

```
const
  wm_Null       = $0000;
  wm_Create     = $0001;
  wm_Destroy    = $0002;
  wm_Move       = $0003;
  wm_Size       = $0005;
  wm_Activate   = $0006;
  wm_SetFocus   = $0007;
  wm_KillFocus  = $0008;
```

This information is important but not usable in our example. However, we can use this text, with some semiautomatic transformations (using search and replace techniques) in an associative list of strings.

The problem is that we cannot simply define an array, because not all of the possible message numbers actually correspond to a message. As an alternative, you might recall that the TStringList class has both strings and objects. Storing an object in a StringList means storing four bytes, so we might use a trick and add the message number instead of a real object. The code above becomes the following:

```
var
  MsgList: TStringList;
...
  MsgList := TStringList.Create;
  MsgList.AddObject ('wm_Null        ', TObject($0000));
  MsgList.AddObject ('wm_Create      ', TObject($0001));
  MsgList.AddObject ('wm_Destroy     ', TObject($0002));
  MsgList.AddObject ('wm_Move        ', TObject($0003));
  MsgList.AddObject ('wm_Size        ', TObject($0005));
  MsgList.AddObject ('wm_Activate    ', TObject($0006));
  MsgList.AddObject ('wm_SetFocus    ', TObject($0007));
  MsgList.AddObject ('wm_KillFocus   ', TObject($0008));
```

This code (it's actually a couple of pages long) has been obtained by replacing the text *wm* with the text *MsgList.AddObject ('wm*, replacing the equal sign with the typecast code, and adding two parentheses at the end. The typecast used from a number to a TObject is really a dirty low-level trick, the kind of thing I usually hate; in this case, I could find no other simple solution to extract the strings from this list using the message number as the key.

I've placed this code in a separate unit, called MLIST.PAS. The interface portion of this unit has also a function, returning a string corresponding to the message:

```
function GetMessageName (Msg: Integer): string;
var
  N: Integer;
```

```
begin
  N := MsgList.IndexOfObject (TObject(Msg));
  if N >= 0 then
    Result := MsgList.Strings [N]
  else if Msg >= wm_User then
    Result := 'wm_User message       '
  else
    Result := 'Unknown message       ';
end;
```

This text is added to the string with the description of the message, followed by the hexadecimal value of the two message parameters. Here is the second part of the code of the if statement of the HandleMessage method (the first part was shown before):

```
AppendStr (Line, GetMessageName (Msg.Message));
{add the hexadecimal output of the two message parameters}
AppendStr (Line, 'Params: ' + IntToHex (Msg.wParam, 8) +
  ', ' + IntToHex (Msg.lParam, 8));
{add the line, selecting it}
ListBox1.ItemIndex := ListBox1.Items.Add (Line);
{store the message, to compare it with the next one}
LastMessage := Msg;
end; // end if
```

At the end, the string is added to the list. The return value of the Add method is used to select the new item of the list box, to keep it in sight. Then the current message structure is saved, so we can compare it with the one of the next messages we receive and eventually decide to skip it if they refer to the same message.

If you run the program, you'll see only a portion of the messages reaching the windows, since we are scanning only posted messages. Most of these messages will probably relate to mouse actions, and some of them to mouse actions on the form's border (the *nc*, or non-client, messages). Notice that you can see the caption of the panel window. I haven't removed it to improve the readability of the output of the messages related to this window (since the caption of the window is displayed) and to its speed buttons, which are not Windowed components and do not receive messages by the system. For Windows, clicking on a speed button is like clicking on the panel holding it.

# The Memory Image of an Application

In Windows 95 and in Windows NT, each application has a 4 GByte address space in a single huge chunk of memory. Actually, Windows 95 and NT allow a program to use only part of that memory, since other portions are used by system DLLs accessible from the application.

Notice that each application has a similar theoretical amount of memory for code, data, and everything else, but has no way to access the memory of other applications running at the same time. All applications, of course, can access the code (but not the data) of system libraries, which use the upper memory area. In Windows 95, the executable files (including the code of DLLs) are loaded in memory using memory-mapped files, so they are visible to all applications. This means the two programs sharing the same executable file (or two instances of the same program) do not need to load it twice in memory. Notice that in Windows NT, instead, executable files and libraries are generally mapped separately for each application, making the system far more stable (if an application crashes a system library, other applications are not affected), but raising the overall memory requirements.

To get information about the size of the different portions of the memory image of your own application, you can use the Information command on Delphi's Compiler menu. The Information dialog box (see Figure 20.15) lists the size of the compiled code and of the global data, plus the size of the stack, which depends on project settings. Going back to the memory of an application, in Windows 95 and NT, there are almost no limits: you can create very long strings or huge arrays without any trouble (although you need to have some RAM and some free disk space for the swap file). Much of the application's code is not loaded from the executable file when the program starts, but only when it is needed, and can even be discarded at run-time when memory is low. This is possible because once the code can be loaded again from the original executable file.

Besides the actual compiled code, the executable file also contains the definition of some resources, such as icons, bitmaps, cursors, tables of strings, and so on. In addition, resources are usually loaded in memory when they are needed, and can be automatically discarded. The use of resources in a Delphi application is the topic of the next chapter.

FIGURE 20.15:

The compilation information for the MSGFLOW example.

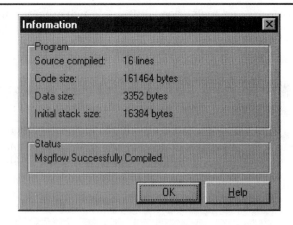

Besides the code and resources, which are loaded from the executable file, the memory of an application contains an area for global data, the space for the stack, and a lot of space for dynamically allocated memory. The size of your program's global data area depends on the global variables you've defined program and those defined by the VCL. For a small project, you will end up with few kilobytes in this area. In Delphi, the common way to determine the size of your program's global data is through the Compiler Information dialog box.

The initial size of the stack is indicated by the Linker project options, together with its maximum size (usually a very large number). The stack is used for procedure, function, and method calls. The local variables, parameters, and return value (if it is a function) are stored on the stack temporarily. Even when you call a DLL, including system libraries, the functions in the DLL use the stack of the caller application to store its local data. It was quite difficult to overcome the limitations of the stack size in Windows 3.1: in Windows 95 or NT, the stack is so huge that you can generally consider it endless.

The rest of the memory, the heap, stores all the dynamically allocated data, including all Delphi objects (instances of a class). Windows 3.1 allowed you to use two different heaps: the small but efficient local heap and the large but slightly less efficient global heap. In Windows 95 and Windows NT, each application has its own local heap, which can be as large as you need (provided it doesn't overcome the enormous 1GB or 2GB memory size "limits"). As I mentioned earlier, a common, global heap doesn't exist anymore in Windows 95 and Windows NT.

**TIP**    You can explore the internal structure of an executable file in several ways. In Windows 95, you can use QuickView from the local menu of the explorer to have this low-level system information. Delphi includes a command line tool, TDUMP, which provides similar details about a program, the functions it exports and imports from DLLs, the resources it contains, and so on. There are also specific programs that extract resources from an executable file, as we will see in the next chapter.

# Windows System Memory

Besides requiring memory in its own data segments, a Windows application consumes some system memory, too. For example, the Windows libraries, like any other DLL, have their own memory segments. These were limited to 64 KB each in Windows 3.1, but now they are almost unlimited. There are three key libraries in Windows: Kernel, User, and GDI (Graphics Device Interface).

The Kernel DLL creates and maintains a number of small global memory blocks to contain information about processes and modules. The list of modules includes each executable file loaded in the system, including programs, dynamic libraries, system drivers, and many other files in executable format.

The User DLL creates and maintains heaps that store information about windows and menus. In particular, it maintains a heap that has an entry for each window class and each window in the system. This was the cause of many headaches in Windows 3.1 programming. By creating a number of windows (particularly of different types), in fact, you could rapidly exhaust this system space, bringing the whole system to a halt.

Fortunately, Delphi 1.0 offered a number of ways to reduce the number of windows used within an application. As we have already seen, not all Delphi components are actual windows. Using windowless components, you could and can still save some memory space in the User heap. Examples of windowless components are the SpeedButton, Image, and Label components, but there are many others. Since all the windowless components are subclasses of TGraphicsControl, you can easily find them by looking at the VCL components hierarchy (see Chapter 6).

The User DLL's heap has one big advantage. When you exit from an application, all the heap entries for the windows it has created are destroyed automatically, freeing this memory space. Unfortunately, this doesn't happen in GDI heaps.

The GDI DLL stores information about graphic objects, such as pens, brushes, fonts, bitmaps, and so on. Each time you create such an object, you're responsible for deleting it. If you don't delete the graphic object, this system memory won't be released, not even after the application terminates.

**NOTE**  Even though GDI objects are usually much smaller than the window structures in the User heap, and Windows 95 provides a lot of space, a poorly written program that creates and forgets to destroy a number of these small GDI objects can create problems.

## Free System Memory

The GDI and User heaps are known as system *resources*. This is an unfortunate name, because the term *resources* is also used in Windows to denote graphical portions (and other elements) of a program included in its executable file, as discussed in the previous sections. The two uses of the term *resource* have nothing in common at all.

Windows users are familiar with the use of the term to describe the heaps, instead of a free system resources monitoring program, because the standard About box of many Windows 3.1 and Windows 95 applications shows the percentage of free system resources. (By the way, we used this same About box in the SHABOUT example in Chapter 12.) You can check the system About box occasionally to make sure you're not running out of system resources. However, this is not usually a problem in Windows 95.

I've decided to write a simple program displaying global memory status, instead of a free system resources monitoring program, because the Win16 functions to access system resources are no longer available in Windows 95. It is still possible to call the 16-bit version of the functions, but this is not very simple. For these reasons I've decided to go for a different example.

As I'll show you in a while, you can instead access system memory status information by using the GlobalMemoryStatus API function. The form I've built for this example, MEM, has two gauges (with pie charts), two labels to describe them, and a timer. It is much better to update the value of the system resources from time to time (hence the need for a timer) instead of asking the user to click on a button or select a menu command to see the new value.

The only method of this form is the handler of the OnTimer event of the Timer component. In this procedure, we access some of the values of the structure filled by the call to GlobalMemoryStatus. This function returns (among other information) the amount of free RAM and the amount of available RAM, and also the amount of free virtual memory (the swap file) and the available virtual memory. By dividing these values you can get the percentage of free space in these two areas:

```
procedure TMemForm.Timer1Timer(Sender: TObject);
var
  MemInfo : TMemoryStatus;
begin
  MemInfo.dwLength := Sizeof (MemInfo);
  GlobalMemoryStatus (MemInfo);
  RamGauge.Progress := MemInfo.dwAvailPhys div
    (MemInfo.dwTotalPhys div 100);
  VirtualGauge.Progress := MemInfo.dwAvailPageFile div
    (MemInfo.dwTotalPageFile div 100);
  Caption := Format ('Mem: = %d - %d',
    [RamGauge.Progress, VirtualGauge.Progress]);
  Application.Title := Caption;
  {if value is low, turn color to red}
  if (RamGauge.Progress < 5) then
    RamGauge.ForeColor := clRed
  else
    RamGauge.ForeColor := clLime;
  if (VirtualGauge.Progress < 20) then
    VirtualGauge.ForeColor := clRed
  else
    VirtualGauge.ForeColor := clLime;
end;
```

As you can see, the final values are also copied to the caption of the form and to the title of the application. This allows you to see the value while it changes directly on the TaskBar, even if the program has been minimized. Of course, looking at the colored gauges of the form (which are always on top) is much better than simply reading the two numbers. In fact, the color of the gauges even changes when the free value is low. You can see an example of the output of this program in Figure 20.16.

**FIGURE 20.16:**

An example of the output of the MEM example.

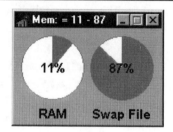

# Summary

In this chapter, we have seen that there are a number of approaches you can use to explore a compiled program or a running application, both by itself and as a whole in the Windows system.

Windows applications do not live in a world by themselves. They have a strong relationship with the system and, usually less directly, with the other applications that are running. The presence of other running Windows applications can affect the performance of your programs, as well as their stability (particularly under Windows 3.1).

In Windows 95 and NT, applications experience significantly fewer memory problems than in Windows 3.1. Every application resides in its own large memory space that cannot be accessed by other programs, which eliminates a number of potential problems for programmers.

There is only one concept that we have not discussed yet—the role of resources within an application. I didn't mention this topic in Chapter 19, which covered the Application object, or in this chapter's discussion of the memory structure of an application, for a simple reason: resources are the topic of the next chapter.

# CHAPTER

## TWENTY-ONE

# Using Resources

- Delphi's Image Editor

- Loading Windows resources

- Icons for minimized forms

- Alternative icons for status changes

- Predefined and custom cursors

- String tables and language translations

21

**A**s we saw in the previous chapter, the executable files of a Windows application can include special data, known as *resources*. The resources of a Windows program generally include icons, bitmaps, and cursors, which are graphical resources. Other resource types include lists of strings, templates used to build menus and dialog boxes, and other elements.

Most Delphi applications use resources, since at the very least they display an icon. And, as we have seen in earlier examples, you can add a bitmap to the resource section of an EXE, so that you don't need to ship the bitmap in a separate file. This chapter provides an overview of the use of resources in Windows and in Delphi and includes some interesting examples.

# Resources in Windows

In Chapter 20 we discussed the role of resources in Windows from a memory perspective. We have seen that resources are stored in separate blocks in the executable file of an application, that these blocks are loaded in memory on demand and are discardable, and that resources can be considered as read-only data. However, we still have not described the different types of resources and their individual uses. Table 21.1 provides a comprehensive summary of Windows resources.

**TABLE 21.1:** Types of Windows Resources

| Resource | Description |
|---|---|
| Icons | Small bitmaps, generally 32 × 32 pixels or 16 × 16 pixels, with a limited set of colors. Used to identify windows graphically. |
| Cursors | Small bitmaps, generally 32 × 32, which use only four colors (black, white, transparent, and reverse). Used to indicate the position of the mouse cursor on the screen. Delphi supports a set of predefined cursors, but you can add your own cursors, too. |
| Menu Templates | Define the structure of a menu. They aren't used in Delphi applications. |
| Dialog Box Templates | Define the structure of a dialog box. They aren't used in Delphi applications. |
| Bitmaps | Define general-purpose bitmaps. Delphi has no direct support for bitmap resources, but you can load a bitmap from the resources instead of from a file. |
| Fonts | Define new fonts within a single program. Custom font resources are seldom used in Windows. More often, new fonts are installed in the system. |

**TABLE 21.1:** Types of Windows Resources (continued)

| Resource | Description |
|---|---|
| String Tables | Collections of strings, which are placed in resources for flexibility and efficiency, and are used to solve translation problems. Delphi does not directly support string tables, but they can be useful in some situations. |
| Accelerator Tables | List the shortcut keys of menu commands. They are not used in Delphi applications. |
| Version Information | A special resource used to indicate the version and author of a program. This is particularly important for DLLs, in which version handling can be a problem. Delphi does not directly support version information. |
| Custom Resources | Resources in user-defined formats. Although you'll seldom define your own custom resources, Delphi uses a custom resource format for the binary description of forms. |

Before looking at special uses of resources in Delphi, let's take a look at the tools you can use to prepare resources. Delphi includes an Image Editor for bitmap, icon, and cursor manipulation, but in some cases, you might still prefer to use a full resource editor, such as Borland's Resource Workshop (which is not included when you purchase Delphi).

# Using Resource Editors

You can activate Delphi's Image Editor by choosing the corresponding command from the Tools menu. Image Editor lets you manipulate four kinds of files. Three are file types that contain specific resource types (ICO, CUR, and BMP), and the last is a file format for compiled resource files (RES), which can contain all three kinds of graphical resources. Individual RES files can contain one or more resources of any type (including the graphical resource types). You can add the resources from a RES file to a Delphi application using the $R compiler directives (discussed later in this chapter).

In Image Editor, you can prepare any kind of icons, cursors, and bitmaps. For icons, you can provide a specific bitmap for the standard $32 \times 32$ icon and the Windows 95 $16 \times 16$ icon (as shown in Figure 21.1), as well as use a different number of colors. Notice that a single icon resource can contain all these images, not just one. For cursors, you can set the *hot-spot* position, which designates which pixel is indicated by the cursor.

Delphi's Image Editor, with the different kinds of images you can define for an icon resource.

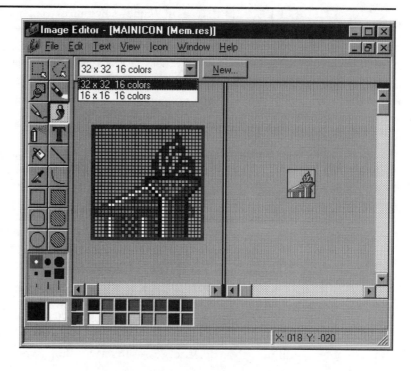

There are basically two ways to use Image Editor:

- Prepare specific files (particularly bitmaps and icons) to be loaded in the Delphi environment at design-time (using properties), or at run-time (using some of the LoadFromFile methods in your code).

- Prepare a number of big resource files, and load the resources at run-time in the code, using Windows API calls, as described in next section. When you work with graphical resource files in Image Editor, a tabbed notebook lets you see a list of elements of each group, as in the example shown in Figure 21.2.

The Image Editor is a functional tool, but its capabilities are somewhat limited, although the version you find in Delphi 2 is much more powerful than the older Delphi 1 version. When you need a full-fledged resource editor, you can use Borland's Resource Workshop (or another commercial resource editor). The Resource Workshop lets you open and edit any resource file. You can also use this tool to extract the resources from a compiled program, a DLL, a VBX, or any other executable-format file. (However, this doesn't mean that it is always legal to do so.)

If you open a Delphi application with the Resource Workshop, you will discover that it actually contains a series of resources, in addition to the icon present in its

**FIGURE 21.2:**

A list of bitmaps included in a resource file, as displayed by Image Editor (from the MINES example in Chapter 10).

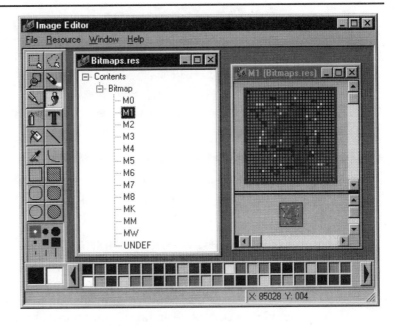

RES file. By default, a Delphi application's executable file contains a string table with system messages, captions, and other generic strings (such as the names of the months), binary data in a custom resource (describing the form in the custom RCDATA format), some cursors, and one icon. Figure 21.3 shows the list of resources for the SCREEN example from Chapter 19, which is a relatively simple program. More complex programs may have many more resources, depending on the number of forms, the system units you include, the icons and bitmaps you add to the project, and so on.

**FIGURE 21.3:**

The list of resources of a compiled Delphi application in the Resource Workshop (from the SCREEN example in Chapter 19).

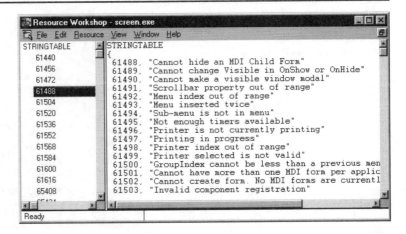

> **TIP**
>
> Among its sample programs Delphi includes an interesting one named Resource Explorer. This program allows you to open an executable file (EXE or DLL) and see most of its resources, just like Resource Workshop does. Resource Explorer has no integrated resource editors, but allows you to easily copy a resource, which you can then paste into a resource file for your Delphi application using another resource Editor.

## Loading Resources in Delphi

As I've mentioned above, there are basically two ways to define resources and load them in Delphi: by loading them as a form or component property or by defining your own resource file and importing the resources using code.

### Loading an Icon or Bitmap as a Property

The simplest approach is to load a resource as a property. Currently however, the only resources that you can load using properties are icons and bitmaps. For example, you can place an Image component as the background of a dialog box and load a bitmap into it. Figure 21.4 shows an example of a program, named BACKBMP, that uses a bitmap as a background. In this case, the bitmap is an embedded resource of the application, which means that you do not need to ship the original BMP file. (In the example, the original BMP file is in the Delphi Image library, stored by default in the IMAGE subdirectory.)

However, in BACKBMP and similar examples, the image is not added to the executable file as a stand-alone bitmap resource. It is included in the binary description of the form. The advantage of this approach is that no one can easily use a

**FIGURE 21.4:**

An example of a program (BACKBMP) using a bitmap as a background.

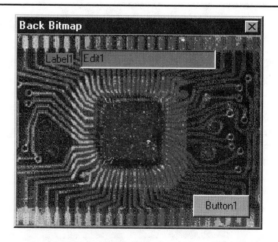

resource editor to steal your bitmap. However, keep in mind that it is possible to extract a custom Delphi form resource using a tool such as Resource Workshop, save that resource to a RES-format file (but with a DFM extension), and load it back as a DFM file in the Delphi editor. To do this, someone simply needs to know that your application was created using Delphi.

In contrast, form and application icons are placed in the compiled file in a standard resource format, to let applications such as the Explorer or the Windows 95 shell extract them and use them as a hint for the user.

## The Manual Approach to Loading Resources

The second technique you can use to access resources in Delphi is the manual approach. For this method, you must first define a separate resource file with the resources you need. The second step is to include the resource file in the project, using the $R compiler directive. In fact, contrary to the typical C/C++ approach, Delphi projects can have a number of resource files.

> **WARNING**
>
> Don't customize the default resource file—the one that has the same name as the project—because sometimes Delphi changes that file, and you might lose your customizations. Simply add other RES files to the current directory, and add a compiler directive to load them.

For example, in the MINES example of Chapter 10 (see Figure 21.2 shown earlier), I've added the mine bitmaps to a separate resource file, loaded in the program within the implementation section of the form:

```
{$R *.DFM}
{$R BITMAPS.RES}
```

These two lines look suspiciously similar. The first loads a special resource file that has the same name as the Pascal file, but with a DFM extension. This is the form file that corresponds to this unit. In this compiler directive, in fact, the star doesn't mean *any file*, but rather *the file with the same name as this one*. This also shows that Delphi compiled form files are used by the environment as custom resources.

Once you have defined some resources and included them in your application, you can use the following Windows API functions LoadAccelerators, LoadBitmap, LoadCursor, LoadIcon, LoadMenu, LoadResource, and LoadString to load resources. Each of these functions loads a specific resource type except for the Load-Resource function, which is used for custom resources. The first parameter of these functions is the handle of the instance of the application, which in Delphi is stored in the HInstance global variable. The second parameter is the name of the resource you want to load. Of course, each application can have a number of icons, bitmaps, and other resources, and you access each of them by name. The LoadString function has some other parameters to specify the buffer in which to copy the string and the size of this buffer.

In contrast, the other loading functions simply return a handle to the loaded resource as the result. You can assign this handle directly to the corresponding VCL object, as in the following code:

```
Bmp.Handle := LoadBitmap (HInstance, Name);
```

In this code, Name is a null-terminated string (a PChar) that contains the name of the bitmap, and Bmp is an object of the class TBitmap. This code is actually extracted from the source of the MINES example I've mentioned before. Study that example and its description in Chapter 10 to see how you can store several bitmaps as resources of an application and the advantages of using this approach.

Since we have placed bitmaps in the resources of this and other applications in previous examples (including the WORLD2 example in Chapter 10, which loaded a series of bitmaps from the resources into a list), I won't build other bitmap examples now. Instead, we'll focus on the use of icons, cursors, and string tables.

# The Icons for Applications and Forms

In Delphi, each form has its own Icon property. You can use this property to specify the icon of the form when it is minimized. When this property is not set, the program uses the value of the Icon property of the Application object as the default icon for minimized forms other than the main form. You can see and change this default application icon via the Application page of the Project Options dialog box.

The most common use of an icon is to provide a bitmap that identifies a minimized window. When you minimize an application in Windows 95, it actually displays a small icon (or a compressed version of the large icon if you don't provide a small icon) in the Windows task bar. However, you already know that the windows that appear in the task bar for Delphi applications are the windows for the corresponding application objects. In addition, the task bar always uses the application's icon, which can be different from the icon of the main window (the main form of a Delphi application).

All these scenarios are demonstrated by a sample program I've written called ICONS. The form of this example is divided in two parts: on the left there is a label, an image component, and two buttons referring to the icon of the form; on the right there are similar components referring to the icon of the application. In addition, we've added a bevel to separate the two areas and an OpenDialog component that we'll use to browse for icon resource files.

Notice that I've defined the Icon property of the form (using the BB.ICO file), as well as that of the application (using the AA.ICO file). I prepared the two icon files using Image Editor.

Each time you click on one of the Change buttons, a new icon is loaded from an external file:

```
procedure TForm1.Button1Click(Sender: TObject);
begin
  with OpenDialog1 do
    if Execute then
    begin
      Application.Icon.LoadFromFile (Filename);
      Image1.Picture.LoadFromFile (Filename);
    end;
end;
```

When one of the two Remove buttons is pressed, the corresponding icon is simply removed:

```
procedure TForm1.Button3Click(Sender: TObject);
begin
  Application.Icon := nil;
  Image1.Picture := nil;
end;
```

You can use this program to see how the two icon properties affect the icon of the minimized application. Some examples are shown in Figure 21.5.

**FIGURE 21.5:**

Some of the effects of the ICONS application.

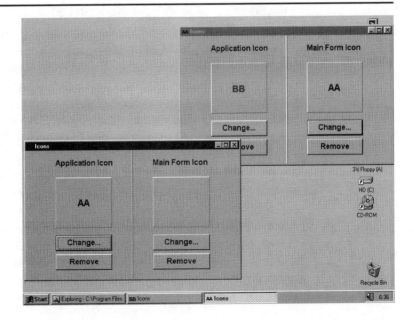

717

When you launch the ICONS application in the Explorer, Explorer will automatically use the application icon when you minimize the form, and not the icon of the main form. This is because the icon of the form is hidden inside the custom resources describing the form (the DFM file), while the icon of the application is stored in an icon resource that's bound to the executable file in the traditional manner.

# Adding Alternative Icons for Different Conditions

In the ICONS example, you can change the icon of an application by loading it from an external file. This approach has two disadvantages:

- You need to ship the icon files with your program.

- Loading an external file tends to be slightly slower (although, for resources, it won't make much difference).

However, there is also an advantage to this approach: users can replace your icon with any icon file they have on their computers.

A technique you may find useful is to add icons to the resources of an application and use them as alternative icons for the program. There are many Windows applications that use different icons to alert the user that the status of the program has changed. For example, mail applications often have an empty mailbox icon and a full mailbox icon. Another common use is in memory monitoring programs, such as the MEM example we built in Chapter 20.

In the MEM example, the title of the application changes continuously to show the current level of memory usage, and a gauge turns red when the usage reaches a low level. An improvement would be to switch the task bar icon when the gauges on the main form change color. The next example, named MEM2, uses three simple icons representing a green gauge, a yellow gauge, and a red gauge. These three icons are part of a new resource file, named RYG.RES, created with Image Editor. The green color is used to indicate that there is available free RAM, the yellow color is used to indicate the common situation of full RAM but available virtual memory (the swap file) and red indicates an almost-full swap file (a very dangerous state).

Additionally, I've changed the color of the gauges themselves to improve the user interface. Instead of changing the color of the gauges from green to red, I've chosen their foreground color to be green and their background color to be either yellow (for the RAM gauge) or red (for the virtual memory gauge). The reason is that in the MEM example, when you have no available RAM, the RAM gauge is almost completely white, with only the borders in red. In the new version, the gauge becomes completely yellow in this same situation. Similarly, when you exhaust virtual memory, the MEM2 virtual memory gauge will become completely red, and you should start to worry!

The default green icon for the task bar is loaded at run-time at the beginning of the FormCreate method:

```
procedure TMemForm.FormCreate(Sender: TObject);
begin
  Application.Icon.Handle :=
    LoadIcon (HInstance, 'GREEN');
  {update the output ASAP}
  Timer1Timer (self);
end;
```

Notice that you need to set the default icon before computing the initial value with the call to the timer event handler. Otherwise, the program might prevent the On-Timer handler from displaying the correct icon, simply replacing it always with the green icon at program startup. In the Timer1Timer method I've removed the code to change the color of the gauges, because of the new approach to colors mentioned before, and added the code to load the proper color icon for the application window, depending on the level of free memory. This code is at the end of the new version of the Timer1Timer method:

```
procedure TMemForm.Timer1Timer(Sender: TObject);
var
  MemInfo : TMemoryStatus;
begin
  MemInfo.dwLength := Sizeof (MemInfo);
  GlobalMemoryStatus (MemInfo);
  RamGauge.Progress := MemInfo.dwAvailPhys div
    (MemInfo.dwTotalPhys div 100);
  VirtualGauge.Progress := MemInfo.dwAvailPageFile div
    (MemInfo.dwTotalPageFile div 100);

  Caption := Format ('Mem: = %d - %d',
    [RamGauge.Progress, VirtualGauge.Progress]);

  {copy the form caption to the
  application title on the taskbar}
  Application.Title := Caption;

  {set icon color}
  if RamGauge.Progress > 5 then
    Application.Icon.Handle :=
      LoadIcon (HInstance, 'GREEN')
  else if VirtualGauge.Progress > 20 then
    Application.Icon.Handle :=
      LoadIcon (HInstance, 'YELLOW')
  else
    Application.Icon.Handle :=
      LoadIcon (HInstance, 'RED');
end;
```

Now that we have explored the use of icons, we can move to a different type of resource: cursors.

# Using the Cursor in Delphi

Delphi's support for cursors is extensive, so it takes much less work to customize cursors than it does to customize icons. For example, Delphi includes a number of predefined cursors. Some of these are Windows default cursors, but others are added by Delphi. The use of cursors in Delphi is straightforward: simply use the Object Inspector to select the corresponding value for the Cursor or DragCursor property of a component. If you need to set a global cursor for the whole application for a certain amount of time, you can set the Cursor property of the global Screen component. (However, you can't make this change using the Object Inspector; you have to do it in code.) This is a common way to display the wait cursor (the hourglass) for the application while a long task is executing:

```
Screen.Cursor := crHourglass;
{time-consuming code}
Screen.Cursor := crDefault;
```

Here is a safer way to write this code:

```
Screen.Cursor := crHourglass;
try
  {time-consuming code}
finally
  Screen.Cursor := crDefault;
end;
```

This version uses exception handling to ensure that if something goes wrong in the execution of the time-consuming code, the default cursor is restored. The Cursor property of the form and other components and the Cursor property of the Screen object are both of type TCursor. If you look up the definition of this data type in Delphi's help, you are in for a surprise. TCursor is not a class, but rather an integer type.

Technically speaking, a TCursor is an integer value that references an array of cursor handles, stored in the Cursors property (notice the final s in *Cursors*) of the Screen object. This array can also be used to load a new cursor from an application's resources.

## Designing a Custom Cursor

Our next example, named MYCUR, demonstrates how to add a custom cursor to a program, as well as how to use the Cursors property of the Screen object in general. This example uses a new resource file, which contains a new hand cursor, as shown in Figure 21.6. This figure also shows the Hot Spot dialog box for the cursor.

When you create a new cursor, always remember to set its *hotspot*. This is a single pixel, inside boundaries of the cursor bitmap, which indicates the exact mouse position. If you are not an artist, remember that you can browse through the collection of cursors available in the Delphi Image Library (located by default in the IMAGES\CURSORS directory).

**FIGURE 21.6:**

When preparing a resource file with a custom cursor remember to set its *hotspot*.

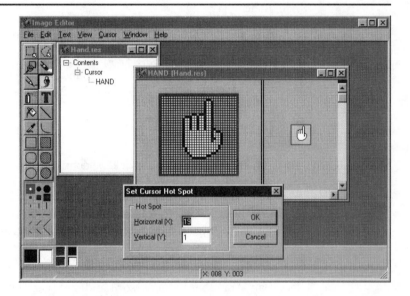

This resource file, named HAND.RES, is included in the source code using the {$R HAND.RES} directive. The example, which is based on a form with two panels and a combo box displays a list of available cursors, as you can see in Figure 21.7. When the program starts, the FormCreate method loads the custom cursor from the application's resources, using the LoadCursor API function. This cursor is then stored in the Cursors array, using a user-defined constant, crHand.

**FIGURE 21.7:**

The form of the HAND.RES example, with two panels and a combo box, displays a list of available cursors.

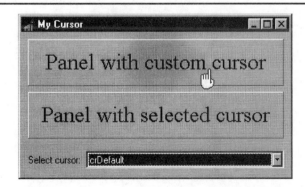

The value of this constant is set to 1. You need to do so because by using positive values, you can avoid overwriting existing cursors, which start from 0 and go backward (we will get to cursor numbering soon). Once the new cursor has been loaded, it can be used like any other cursor. Here is the implementation code:

```
$R HAND.RES}

const
  crHand = 1;

procedure TForm1.FormCreate(Sender: TObject);
begin
  {load a custom cursor from the resources}
  Screen.Cursors [crHand] := LoadCursor (HInstance, 'HAND');
  {use the new cursor for the first panel}
  Panel1.Cursor := crHand;
  {select the crDefault line}
  ComboBox1.ItemIndex := 1;
end;
```

Just two lines of code do the trick. Selecting a cursor for the second panel using the combo box is even simpler—a single line of code:

```
procedure TForm1.ComboBox1Change(Sender: TObject);
begin
  Panel2.Cursor := 1 - ComboBox1.ItemIndex;
end;
```

Strange code, isn't it? As I mentioned before, the Cursors property of the Screen object is an array that has a cursor handle for each entry. The TCursor type used for the Cursor property is actually an integer. This integer is used by Delphi as the index of the Cursors property to fetch the cursor handle. So when you write this code:

```
Form1.Cursor := crArrow;
```

the code is actually translated as

```
Form1.Cursor := -3;
```

This is exactly what I have done for the custom cursor; I've defined a constant and used it to specify a cursor within the Screen.Cursors array. With this idea in mind, we can go back to the strange statement above. The trick is that I've added the text identifier of each cursor constant to the StringList property of the combo box in the same order as the corresponding constants. Or rather, in the reverse order, since the default Delphi cursors have negative values, ranging from 0 down to –17. Since I've added the custom cursor at the beginning of the list, the first item in the list box (with ItemIndex 0) corresponds to cursor 1, the second (with ItemIndex 1) to cursor 0, the third (with ItemIndex 2) to cursor -1, and so on.

**WARNING**    The Delphi Help file lists the values for all of the cursor constants, but some of them are wrong or missing. Their order (the reverse order, I mean) is correct, but some numerical values are mistakenly repeated.

## A Flexible Cursor

In the MYCUR example discussed in the previous section, you can choose a `crNone` cursor, which isn't listed in the Object Inspector as a proper value for the Cursor property. This is reasonable, because when you select this value, or any index value outside the boundaries of the `Screen.Cursors` array, the cursor disappears. If you specify this value for the Cursor property of a specific component, the cursor will disappear when you position it over the corresponding component, and then reappear when you move the cursor over a different component.

This behavior is possible because Windows allows you to define different cursors for some areas of a window. In fact, if a form or a component does not have a specific cursor assigned to it, you can specify the cursor manually in a `wm_SetCursor` message handler, just like you would in a traditional Windows program.

The next example, FLEXCUR, shows how this can be done. The form of this application is covered by an blank Image component. This offers us a Canvas connected to a memory bitmap, so that the image we build is saved in memory, and the surface of the window can be automatically repainted. The Image component covers most of the client area, but is not aligned with it, leaving a thin empty border. In a moment, we will see why this border is necessary.

What is the goal of this example, besides demonstrating the use of a flexible cursor? Think of it as a circle painter with erasing capability. You can click on the form at run-time to paint a small circle (you can easily choose color). You can also click on any pixel inside an existing circle to erase that circle. The result of clicking on the form is indicated by the use of two different cursors; that is, the cursor changes state depending on whether the mouse is moving over one of the circles you've painted, indicating that you can delete it.

To accomplish this, the program sets the cursor of the form to `crNone` and supplies a message handler for the Windows `wm_SetCursor` message:

```
type
  TForm1 = class(TForm)
    Image1: TImage;
    procedure Image1MouseDown(Sender: TObject;
      Button: TMouseButton;
      Shift: TShiftState; X, Y: Integer);
    procedure FormCreate(Sender: TObject);
```

```
public
  procedure WmSetCursor (var Msg: TWMSetCursor);
    message wm_SetCursor;
end;
```

Inside this message handler, we perform two different tests. First, we need to check whether the mouse is over the client area of the form or over its borders. This can be done using the HitTest parameter of the message and looking for the htClient value, which means that the cursor is over the client area. (For a list of the HitTest codes, see the Windows API Help file, under the wm_NCHitTest message.)

> **NOTE**
>
> Windows sends the wm_SetCursor message to a window each time the mouse changes its position over the window. This is the message that the FLEXCUR program monitors. By default, Delphi uses the Cursor property of forms and components to determine which cursor it should display at the current mouse position, but you can easily change this. A simpler technique is to use the OnMouseMove handler to change the cursor. However, in this approach, the cursor will flicker, because the system will display the default cursor (crNone) just before you change it.

When the mouse pointer is over non-client areas, the message handler of the parent class is invoked using the inherited keyword, to implement the default behavior for Delphi forms. If the cursor is over the client area, we need to check the color of the pixel that's currently beneath the pointer. Since the wm_SetCursor message has no coordinate parameters, I've added a call to the GetCursorPos API procedure, which returns the cursor position in screen coordinates. The program then translates that point into coordinates of the Image component, and uses these coordinates to check the color of the corresponding pixel, using the Pixels array of the Image component's Canvas property. Here is the code of this message handling method:

```
procedure TForm1.WmSetCursor (var Msg: TWMSetCursor);
var
  CurPos: TPoint;
begin
  {get the position of the cursor, and converts
  it to client coordinates}
  GetCursorPos (CurPos);
  CurPos := Image1.ScreenToClient (CurPos);
  if Msg.HitTest = htClient then
    if Image1.Canvas.Pixels [CurPos.X, CurPos.Y] = clWhite then
      {if the pixel is white}
      SetCursor (Screen.Cursors [crCross])
    else
```

```
      {if the pixel is black}
      SetCursor (Screen.Cursors [crUpArrow])
  else
    {if the mouse is outside the client area}
    inherited;
  Msg.Result := 1;
end;
```

As you can see above, depending on the result of the color test, the program calls the SetCursor function of the Windows API, passing as a parameter the handle of the cursor, not its identifier (crCross or crUpArrow). To transform the identifier into a handle, the code uses the Cursors property of the Screen, accessing the proper item of the array.

Notice the last line in the code above sets the return value for the message handler (Msg.Result := 1). Return values are seldom used in Windows messages, but if you omit them when they are needed, the system might try to respond to a message you've already handled. With this message, for example, we need to tell Windows that the system should not bother setting a default cursor because we have already set one.

The program uses a cross cursor (crCross) for the white surface and the up arrow cursor (crUpArrow) for the black pixels. Here, the up arrow cursor is used as a visual hint for the flood-fill operation that erases the colored area. This erases not just a single circle, but also contiguous ones, as you can see in the two consecutive images shown in Figure 21.8.

If the pixel beneath the location of the mouse click is already black, the FloodFill method is called inside the Image1MouseDown handler in place of the default Ellipse method:

```
procedure TForm1.Image1MouseDown(Sender: TObject;
  Button: TMouseButton;
  Shift: TShiftState; X, Y: Integer);
begin
  if Image1.Canvas.Pixels [X, Y] = clWhite then
  begin
    {paint a black circle}
    Image1.Canvas.Pen.Color := clBlack;
    Image1.Canvas.Brush.Color := clBlack;
    Image1.Canvas.Ellipse (X-15, Y-15, X+15, Y+15);
  end
  else
  begin
    {erases the contiguous black pixels}
    Image1.Canvas.Brush.Color := clWhite;
    Image1.Canvas.FloodFill (X, Y, clWhite, fsBorder);
  end;
end;
```

**FIGURE 21.8:**

The FloodFill method used in the FLEXCUR example erases a group of circles at a time, as you can see by comparing the two images. The bottom image was taken after a single click. Note the two cursors.

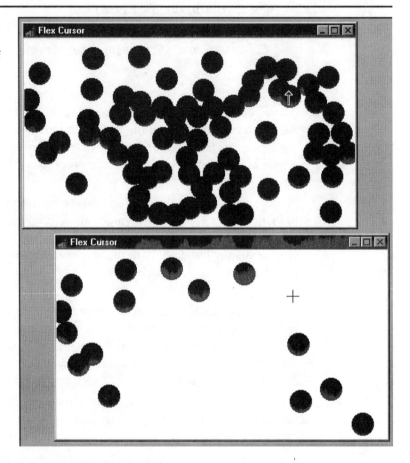

By calling FloodFill, we face the risk of also filling the form's border (if it is black) if a circle is too close to it. This is the reason for the one-pixel gap between the form and the Image component.

# Using String Table Resources

The third kind of resources we will explore in this chapter are string table resources. Although there is a limited amount of support for these resources in Delphi, I thought it was a good idea to show you a simple example of their use, because string tables play an important role in traditional Windows programming.

There are two main reasons programmers have used string tables instead of hard-coding strings in a Windows program. The first is memory usage. Strings use your application's memory directly, while string tables are loaded in separate, discardable memory blocks that the application loads when they're needed. Since string tables save memory, they were more important in Windows 3.1 than they are in Windows 95 or NT, but they might still be useful for big 32-bit applications.

The second reason is localization, or translation of a program into another language (such as from English to German). To localize a traditional program, you would have to search through each source file, locate the embedded text, translate the text, and then recompile the entire program. In contrast, when you localize a Windows application that uses string tables, you simply translate the text embedded included in the resources, recompile only the resources (a very brief process), and then bind the new resources to the previously compiled EXE code.

In Delphi, the process of localizing an application is similar. Localizing most of your user interface will involve translating the caption for components by modifying the textual description of form files (opening DFM files using the Delphi code editing window). However, programs usually need to display messages to the user, and you won't want to create a separate form to display each message. Instead of doing this, or possibly hard-coding these messages into your application using Object Pascal strings, you can put those messages into string tables. This makes your Delphi program as easy to localize as a traditional one that loads the strings using calls to Windows API functions alone. This is exactly what happens in the next example, named STRINGT. Its form has two areas marked by two bevels. One area has a button, and the other has a button and a spin edit control (with its label).

The key to the example is in a new resource compiler source file (traditionally indicated by the RC extension). This is a text file with some resource statements, documented in the Windows API Help file. Here is the text of the S_TABLE.RC file:

```
STRINGTABLE
BEGIN
    1, "Hello"
    2, "String Table Test"
    11, "First message"
    12, "Second message"
    13, "Third message"
    14, "Fourth message"
    ...
    20, "Tenth message"
END
```

For the definition of a string table resource, you need to include the resource statement (STRINGTABLE) and a list of identifiers followed by the corresponding strings (the comma separator is optional). Note that the strings must be in C-language format—they must use double quotation marks instead of the Pascal single quotation marks. However, the indicators at the beginning and end of the resource block can be either the Pascal ones (BEGIN and END, uppercase), as shown in the listing, or the C brackets, { and }.

> **WARNING**  You can number the strings as you like, but you must consider that Delphi uses several strings itself, so you should be careful to avoid duplicate entries. Delphi reserves string identifiers of 61000 and up; any lower value shouldn't create any problems.

Once you have written this file, you need to compile it into a RES file, the only kind of resource file you can include directly in a Delphi project. This is easier than you might expect, because Delphi includes a full-scale resource compiler, BRCC32, although it is a command-line tool and not a Windows application. Simply start a DOS session, move to the subdirectory with the project files, and issue the following command:

```
BRCC32 S_TABLE.RC
```

Of course, you should also provide the proper path for BRCC32, which is that of the Delphi BIN subdirectory. As an alternative, you can call the BRC32 resource compiler, passing to it the -R parameter. (The BRC32 resource compiler automatically tries to bind the resulting RES file to the EXE file. The -R parameter tells it to compile the RC file but not perform the binding step.)

Once the resource file has been generated, we can include it in the code, as usual:

```
{$R S_TABLE.RES}
```

Now we can actually start writing the code of our program. We'll want to load the first string and display it when the form's Hello button is pressed. The API function is LoadString, which has a buffer for a null-terminated string as its third parameter. The return value of the function indicates the number of characters that have been loaded from the resource, or 0 in case of an error (for example, if the string has not been found). For this reason, we can test the return value:

```
procedure TForm1.HelloButtonClick(Sender: TObject);
var
  Text: array [0..255] of Char;
  N: Integer;
begin
  N := LoadString (HInstance, 1, Text, SizeOf (Text));
  if N > 0 then
    ShowMessage (StrPas (Text));
end;
```

This code works, but it is quite complex. As a much better alternative, we can use Delphi's LoadStr function, which encapsulates the Windows API call and loads a string from the resources directly into a Pascal string. This is the second version of the same method:

```
procedure TForm1.HelloButtonClick(Sender: TObject);
var
```

```
  StrMsg: string;
begin
  StrMsg := LoadStr (1);
  if StrMsg <> '' then
    ShowMessage (StrMsg);
end;
```

There is also a second Delphi function used to load strings in Delphi, FmtLoadStr, which uses the string table string as the format template for the given data parameters. It is a mix of the LoadStr and the Format functions.

We can call LoadStr again to change the title of the window (and of the minimized window), using the second string:

```
procedure TForm1.FormCreate(Sender: TObject);
var
  StrTitle: string;
begin
  StrTitle := LoadStr (2);
  if StrTitle <> '' then
  begin
    Caption := StrTitle;
    Application.Title := StrTitle;
  end;
end;
```

The code of the Show button is only slightly more complex. Instead of displaying a fixed string, it uses the current value of the spin edit box to determine which string to use in the range of 10 to 20:

```
procedure TForm1.ShowButtonClick(Sender: TObject);
var
  StrMsg: string;
begin
  StrMsg := LoadStr (10 + SpinEdit1.Value);
  if StrMsg <> '' then
    ShowMessage (StrMsg);
end;
```

You can see the effect of this method in the output of Figure 21.9.

This last method highlights another traditional use of strings. We refer to a group of ten string-based messages, but it is quite simple to add new entries to the string table, increase the value of the SpinEdit component's MaxValue property, and let the program display the new strings without any change to the source code. However, if you change component properties, you'll have to rebuild the project to rebind the custom form resource to the EXE, unless you add the value of the property (MaxValue in this case) in another string and load it dynamically.

FIGURE 21.9:

An example of the STRINGT program's output when the Show button is pressed.

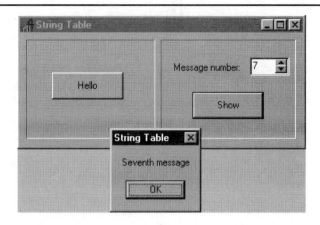

## Translating the Strings into Another Language

The program we have written works fine, but its real advantage over a program that uses hard-coded strings is that now we can easily localize the application. Simply submit the RC file to a language translator (not necessarily a programmer) and recompile the translated version with the resource compiler. If the file has a different name, you can replace the file name in the compiler directive used to include the resources and rebuild the program. That's all you need to do. (You might even skip this minor name change by using the project file's name or by merging the resources with the external resource compiler.)

For this localization, I first translated the string into another language (my actual first choice, Italian). Here is the result (stored in the file S_TAB_IT.RC):

```
STRINGTABLE
BEGIN
  1, "Ciao"
  2, "Prova Tabella Stringhe"
  11, "Primo messaggio"
  12, "Secondo messaggio"
  13, "Terzo messaggio"
  ...
  20, "Decimo messaggio"
END
```

Then I recompiled the resource file and changed a line of the source code to the following:

```
{$R S_TAB_IT.RES}
```

By recompiling and running this program, the title of the form and the messages are now in Italian, as you can see in Figure 21.10.

**FIGURE 21.10:**

**FIGURE 21.10:**

The output of the Italian version of the STRINGT example.

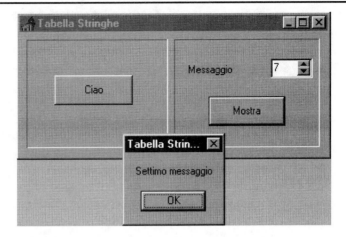

The program, however, is not completely localized. The Delphi portion (the textual description of the form) should be translated, too, to correct the names of the two buttons. To accomplish this, you can load the textual description of the form into the Delphi editor and translate all of the strings, such as captions and list items. Do not change the internal identifiers, such as the value of the Name property.

I've performed this operation and saved the new version of the form description in the file STRI_F_I.DFM. This file is loaded by replacing this statement:

```
{$R *.DFM}
```

with this one:

```
{$R STRI_F_I.DFM}
```

Now both the captions and the messages are in Italian, but we use the same source file for the code of the program. To make it simpler to compile either one of the versions from the same source code base, you can use the conditional compilation directives for resource inclusion:

```
{$IFNDEF ITALIAN}
  {$R *.DFM}
  {$R S_TABLE.RES}
{$ELSE}
  {$R STRI_F_I.DFM}
  {$R S_TAB_IT.RES}
{$ENDIF}
```

In a complex program, after this step, you also need to translate the Delphi system strings, such as those you can find in VCL source files (for example, CONST.RC or DBCONSTS.RC). This will complete the program localization.

There is also another approach to creating multilingual programs. You can prepare several different groups of strings, one for each language, using a standard numbering schema. For example, English strings might start from 1, French strings from 10001, German strings from 20001, and so on.

Now each time you need to load a string (say, string 235), you can write:

```
MyText := LoadStr (nLanguage * 10000 + 235);
```

In this case, nLanguage is a code corresponding to the current language setting (0 for English, 1 for French, 2 for German, and so on). Then you can add a dialog box to let the user change the language at run-time, setting a new code. The last thing you should consider is that referring to the string by number in the source code is a good way to make it almost unreadable. For this reason, you should define a number of constants corresponding to each string's identifier, and use the constant instead of the numeric code.

# Summary

In this chapter, we have examined some details about the role, definition, and use of Windows resources in traditional applications and demonstrated how to use them in Delphi programming. Like many other visual programming environments, Delphi lets you build most of the elements of an application graphically, making use of custom techniques instead of relying on Windows resources and traditional techniques.

At times, however, resources have a role. We have seen in previous chapters some examples of loading a bitmap from the resources of an application, and in this chapter, how you can load an icon and a cursor.

We have also explored a non-graphical resource type that is useful in Delphi as well as traditional environments: string tables. However, building string tables using plain text files is so simple that we can use them quite easily even without specific support from the Delphi environment.

This chapter ends this section of the book, which is devoted to the Application object, applications in general, memory, debugging, and resources. With the next chapter, we start exploring other advanced topics that have plenty of specific support in Delphi.

# CHAPTER

**TWENTY-TWO**

# Adding Printing Capabilities to Delphi Applications

- Standard and custom print dialog boxes

- Printing graphics

- Print preview

- Printing text

- Printing database forms

- QuickReport reporting components

- Using ReportSmith

**A**lthough we have explored many different Delphi programming topics up to now, including some advanced techniques, there are some important topics that we still haven't covered. One of these topics is printing, which is the subject of this chapter.

Some printing capabilities are present even in the most simple real-life programs, such as the ones we've built in previous chapters. Many of the examples in this chapter are improved versions of earlier examples, with support for these important capabilities.

This chapter covers two different printing-related topics. The first part discusses printing forms, including text and graphics. The second part is about printing reports. Delphi provides plenty of support for both of these printing areas, so adding these features to existing programs is easy to do.

# Printing a Whole Form

Printing a form in Delphi at run-time is fairly simple. The TForm class has a Print method, which prints the entire client area of the form and any visual components it contains. Calling this method is all you need to do to print. For example, we might add a Print button to a form and write this code:

```
procedure TForm1.PrintButtonClick (Sender: TObject);
begin
  Print;
end;
```

The effect of this code is to print a bitmap corresponding to the form's client area (the form without its caption and border) using the current printer.

To determine the actual size of the printed output, you can adjust the form's PrintScale property before you call the Print method. By default, this property has the value poProportional. This means that the printout will be proportional to the image on the screen, using the PixelPerInch property of the form relative to the screen size and the DPI (dots per inch) setting of the current printer relative to the page size. For example, if the form width is half of the screen, the printout will cover half of the printed page.

There are two other possible values for this property: poNone and poPrintToFit. With poNone, no scaling is used. Because of the higher pixel-per-inch capability of printers, the resulting image will generally be quite small. If you use the poPrintToFit parameter, the printout will be stretched to fill the whole page, but will maintain its horizontal to vertical proportion.

With `poPrintToFit` as the form's PrintScale property setting, you typically get much bigger images. However, since the bitmap corresponding to the form is stretched for the printed image, the print quality decreases as the image size increases.

## A Custom Print Dialog Box

Although Delphi has a specific component encapsulating the standard Windows Print dialog box, to keep this first example simple, I've decided not to use it. Instead, I've built a simple custom dialog box with three radio buttons (actually a radio group with three items), which lets you choose one of the three values of the PrintScale property. I've added this Print dialog box to an example application from Chapter 11, COMBOBAR. The name of the new version is COMBO2. You can see the main form and print dialog box of this example in Figure 22.1. I've added a Print command to the File menu and changed the background color of the label that covers the form's client area to white.

I chose this example because it has a simple form and because you can change the caption's font in a number of ways and see the effect both on the screen and on paper. The only problem is that the printed output contains not only the label's text, but also the image of the toolbar. If you don't want to print the toolbar, you can hide it by using the Visible command on the Toolbar menu or on the toolbar's Speed-Menu (just click the right mouse button over the toolbar to see its local menu). So the program can actually be used to print the text of the caption by itself on a page. Now add a dialog box with an edit or memo field to change the text of the caption, and you can print any text. Why buy an expensive word processor?

**FIGURE 22.1:**
The COMBO2 example at run-time.

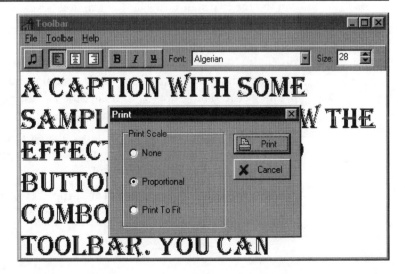

The example's code is simple. When the user issues the Print command, our custom dialog box is displayed. If the user clicks on the Print button (which has an `mrOk` value for its ModalResult property), the current scaling selection is set via the PrintScale property, and the form is printed:

```
procedure TToolbarForm.Print1Click(Sender: TObject);
begin
  if PrintDlg.ShowModal = mrOk then
  begin
    case PrintDlg.RadioGroup1.ItemIndex of
      0: PrintScale := poNone;
      1: PrintScale := poProportional;
      2: PrintScale := poPrintToFit;
    end;
    Print;
  end;
end;
```

The dialog box itself requires no code other than the class definition generated by Delphi. If we wanted to go further, we could add a panel that displays a preview of the printed image. In fact, the TForm class defines a GetFormImage method, which returns a bitmap of the form. This is the same bitmap that is sent to the printer when you call the Print method's code.

What is not simple is simulating the print scaling that shows the form's bitmap inside an area corresponding to the printed page. I'll show you an example (PRINTBMP) that includes a print preview dialog box later in this chapter. You could use that code to improve the COMBO2 example, too.

## The Standard Print Dialog Boxes

As an alternative to the custom Print dialog box used in the COMBO2 example, you can use the two standard Windows dialog boxes related to printing that are encapsulated in Delphi's PrintDialog and PrinterSetupDialog components.

This is the approach we'll take in the next version of our example, named (not surprisingly) COMBO3. This example has the same dialog box as in the previous version, this time used as a Print Options dialog box, plus the standard print and printer setup dialog boxes. To reflect the additions, the example's File menu has been rearranged, as you can see in Figure 22.2.

The two new components for the two dialog boxes have no special properties and are used in a simple way. To set up the printer, you just call the Execute method of the PrinterSetupDialog1 component:

```
procedure TToolbarForm.PrinterSetup1Click(Sender: TObject);
begin
  PrinterSetupDialog1.Execute;
end;
```

**FIGURE 22.2:**

The File menu of the COMBO3 example inside Delphi's Menu Designer.

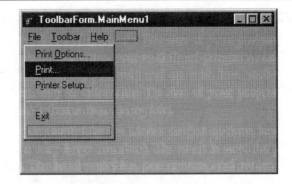

In contrast, when you call the PrintDialog component's Execute method, you need to check the return value to see if the user really wants to print. I've also added code to implement the only Print dialog box option that is always present: the selection of the number of copies. The COMBO3 example does not print all the copies automatically. It prints the first one, checks to see if the user requested more than one copy, and then asks if the user really wants to print the remaining copies:

```
procedure TToolbarForm.Print1Click(Sender: TObject);
var
  I: Integer;
begin
  if PrintDialog1.Execute then
  begin
    Print;
    if (PrintDialog1.Copies > 1) and
      (MessageDlg ('Do you actually want to print ' +
        IntToStr (PrintDialog1.Copies - 1) + ' more copies?',
        mtConfirmation, [mbYes, mbNo], 0) = mrYes) then
      for I := 1 to PrintDialog1.Copies - 1 do
        Print;
  end;
end;
```

Notice that this dialog box can activate the Printer Setup dialog box, as you can see in Figure 22.3. We could have omitted the Printer Setup command and the corresponding dialog box component without any real problems. This is the approach used in many real-world applications.

**FIGURE 22.3:**

The standard Windows 95 Print dialog box used by the COMBO3 example.

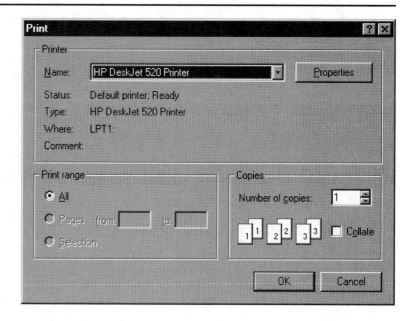

When the user selects the Print Options command, the custom dialog box from the previous example appears and the PrintScale property is set, but nothing is printed:

```
procedure TToolbarForm.PrintOptions1Click(Sender: TObject);
begin
  if PrintDlg.ShowModal = mrOk then
    case PrintDlg.RadioGroup1.ItemIndex of
      0: PrintScale := poNone;
      1: PrintScale := poProportional;
      2: PrintScale := poPrintToFit;
    end;
end;
```

This code has one less statement than the previous version, but its result changes radically: it doesn't directly print anything! Instead, I've added an OK button to save the change to the PrintScale setting and close this dialog box, and I've changed the meaning of the Print button, which now invokes the standard Print dialog box directly. As Figure 22.4 shows, you can open the Print Options dialog box, invoke the Print dialog box, and then open the Print Setup dialog box from there. You end up with three levels of dialog boxes, which can be quite useful as long as there is a way to reach each of them directly from the menu. If you don't provide the separate menu items, the users might not like being forced to navigate through the dialog boxes to set an option. (By the way, in the COMBO3 example, you can probably navigate through one or two more levels, depending on the setup options of your printer driver.)

**FIGURE 22.4:**

You can use the Print Options dialog box to open the Print dialog box, which you can use to access to the Print Setup dialog box.

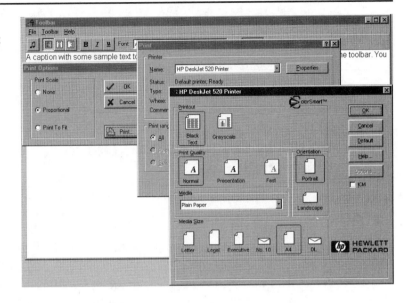

# Accessing the Printer Object

Other than for basic operations (such as printing the whole form), you'll use the global Printer variable to manipulate a printer from a Delphi program. This function returns an object of class TPrinter, defined in the Printers unit.

**NEW**

In Delphi 1, Printer was the name of a global object of the TPrinter class. In Delphi 2, there is still a global object of class TPrinter, but it is now local to the printer unit. To access this global object, you can use the Printer function. This makes the new code highly compatible with the older ones. For example, you can still write `Printer.Canvas.Font` to change the current printing font for text. The reason for this change is that in Delphi 2 there is also a SetPrinter function, which can be used to change the global object. This allows you to create more than one printer object (with different settings) and assign one of them to the "current printer object" as needed.

You can use the object returned by the Printer to access some global properties related to the printer, such as a list of installed drivers or printer fonts. However, its key property is its canvas. You can use the canvas of a printer the same way that you use the canvas of a form; that is, you can print text, graphics, and everything else.

To use this canvas, you need to call the printer's BeginDoc method to start the printing job, use the canvas methods to produce the output, and then call the EndDoc method to actually send the output to the printer. As an alternative, you can call the Abort method to discard the print job, or call the NewPage method to send the output to the printer and start working on a new page.

## Printing Graphics and Using Print Preview

Our first example of the use of the global printer object (using the Printer function) is a simple application you can use to print bitmaps. Basically, this is an extension to the TABONLY example presented in Chapter 13. That example used a TabControl to let the user browse though a series of bitmaps.

As shown in Figure 22.5, the preview form of the PRINTBMP example has a toolbar with four buttons at the top and a ScrollBox component that contains an Image component. If the image is bigger than the form, you can use the ScrollBox component to scroll the image without affecting the toolbar. This preview dialog box is opened from the new File ➤ Print menu command.

The Print Preview form lets you compare the size of the resulting bitmap with the printed page (indicated by the size of the image component) and scale the bitmap as necessary, to increase its size.

**FIGURE 22.5:**

The Print Preview form of the PRINTBMP example at design-time.

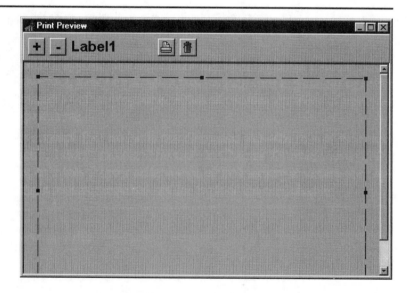

**NOTE**  Changing the image size affects the screen output in both the preview form and the printed output. The reason for scaling a bitmap prior to printing is that bitmaps printed at their standard pixel-per-inch ratio tend to appear quite small on the printed page (but at a higher resolution).

The code is based on the StretchDraw method of the TCanvas class, which I've used to generate the preview bitmap and the actual output bitmap. The StretchDraw method has two parameters, a rectangle, indicating the output region, and a graphic object (the source image). The result is an image stretched to fit the output rectangle. Now let's review some of the code. The main form responds to the Print command by initializing and running the Preview form:

```
procedure TForm1.Print1Click(Sender: TObject);
begin
  {double-checks if an image is selected}
  if Image1.Picture.Graphic <> nil then
  begin
    {set a default scale, and start the preview}
    PreviewForm.Scale := 2;
    PreviewForm.SetPage;
    PreviewForm.DrawPreview;
    PreviewForm.ShowModal;
  end;
end;
```

The check at the beginning could have been omitted, since the Print menu item is disabled until an image file is selected, but it ensures that a file is selected in any case. This code sets a public field of the PreviewForm object (Scale), calls two methods of this form (SetPage and DrawPreview), and finally displays it as a modal form. Figure 22.6 shows an example of the Print Preview form.

The SetPage method sets the size of the Print Preview form's Image component, using the size of the printed page:

```
procedure TPreviewForm.SetPage;
begin
  Image1.Width := Printer.PageWidth div 5;
  Image1.Height := Printer.PageHeight div 5;
  {output the scale to the toolbar}
  Label1.Caption := IntToStr (Scale);
end;
```

The size of the page is divided by five to make it fit into a reasonable area of the screen. You might use a parameter instead of this fixed value to add a zooming feature on the preview page. However, I thought that having a button to increase the size of the printed image and another button to increase it only in the preview was quite confusing, so I decided to skip the zooming capability.

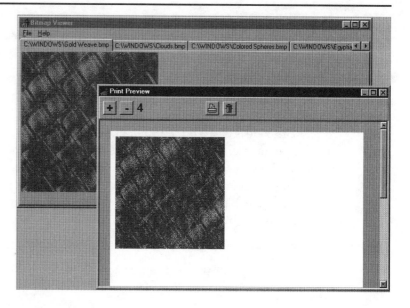

The heart of the Preview form's code is in the DrawPreview method, which has
three different sections. At the beginning, it computes the destination rectangle,
leaving a 10-pixel margin, scaling the image, and using the fixed zoom factor of five
(as you can see in the following listing). The second step erases the old image that
is still on the screen by drawing a white rectangle over it. The third step calls the
StretchDraw method of the canvas, using the rectangle calculated before and
the current image from the image component of the main form (Form1.Image1.
Picture.Graphic). To access this information, we need to add a uses clause in the
implementation portion of the code. Here is the code for this method:

```
procedure TPreviewForm.DrawPreview;
var
  Rect: TRect;
begin
  {compute the rectangle for the bitmap preview}
  Rect.Top := 10;
  Rect.Left := 10;
  Rect.Right := 10 +
    (Form1.Image1.Picture.Graphic.Width * Scale) div 5;
  Rect.Bottom := 10 +
    (Form1.Image1.Picture.Graphic.Height * Scale) div 5;
  {remove the current image}
  Image1.Canvas.Pen.Mode := pmWhite;
  Image1.Canvas.Rectangle (0, 0, Image1.Width, Image1.Height);
  {stretch the bitmap into the rectangle}
  Image1.Canvas.StretchDraw (Rect,
    Form1.Image1.Picture.Graphic);
end;
```

All of this code is executed just to initialize the form. The startup code is split into two methods, but only because DrawPreview will be called again later. When initialization is done and the modal form is visible, the user can click on the four toolbar buttons to resize the image, print it, or skip it (throw it in the garbage can, as the bitmap of the button suggests).

The two resize methods are simple, because they just set the new scale value and call the DrawPreview procedure to update the image:

```
procedure TPreviewForm.ScalePlusButtonClick(Sender: TObject);
begin
  Scale := Scale * 2;
  Label1.Caption := IntToStr (Scale);
  DrawPreview;
end;
```

The PrintButtonClick method of the Print Preview form is almost a clone of Draw-Preview. The only differences are that the destination rectangle is not zoomed by the five factor and the bitmap is sent to the printer in a new document (a new page):

```
procedure TPreviewForm.PrintButtonClick(Sender: TObject);
var
  Rect: TRect;
begin
  {compute the rectangle for the printer}
  Rect.Top := 10;
  Rect.Left := 10;
  Rect.Right := 10 +
    (Form1.Image1.Picture.Graphic.Width * Scale);
  Rect.Bottom := 10 +
    (Form1.Image1.Picture.Graphic.Height * Scale);
  {print the bitmap}
  Printer.BeginDoc;
  Printer.Canvas.StretchDraw (Rect,
    Form1.Image1.Picture.Graphic);
  Printer.EndDoc;
end;
```

# Painting to the Printer

Instead of printing a whole form or copying an existing bitmap to the printer canvas, you can actually write standard output code using the printer canvas as a form or component canvas. Since you can execute the same methods on a printer canvas as on any other canvas, you can write programs with two output methods—one for the screen and one for the printer—using similar code. Even better, you can write a single output method to use for both kinds of output.

As an example of this approach, I've built a new version of the SHAPE4 example from Chapter 9, which stored the description of a list of shapes in memory and later used this description in the OnPaint method. (You might want to review the text describing this example and its code before you go on reading.) The new version is named SHAPE6 (because a SHAPE5 example already exists). As with the other examples in this chapter, the only change in the description of its form is a new Print command in the File menu.

The interesting point is that I've moved the code of the FormPaint example into another method I've defined, called CommonPaint. This new method has two parameters, the canvas and a scale factor, and it outputs the list of shapes to the canvas passed as parameter, using the proper scale factor:

```
procedure TShapesForm.CommonPaint (
  Canvas1: TCanvas; Scale: Integer);
var
  I: Integer;
  CurShape: ShapeData;
begin
  for I := 0 to ShapesList.Count - 1 do
  begin
    CurShape := ShapesList.Items [I];
    with CurShape do
    begin
      Canvas1.Pen.Color := PenColor;
      Canvas1.Pen.Width := PenSize;
      Canvas1.Brush.Color := BrushColor;
      if Circle then
        Canvas1.Ellipse ((X-Size) * Scale, (Y-Size) * Scale,
          (X+Size) * Scale, (Y+Size) * Scale)
      else
        Canvas1.Rectangle ((X-Size) * Scale, (Y-Size) * Scale,
          (X+Size) * Scale, (Y+Size) * Scale);
    end;
  end;
end;
```

Once you've written this code, the FormPaint and Print1Click methods are simple to implement. To print the image on the screen, you can call CommonPaint without a scaling factor:

```
procedure TShapesForm.FormPaint(Sender: TObject);
begin
  CommonPaint (Canvas, 1);
end;
```

To paint the contents of the form to the printer instead of the form, you can reproduce the output on the printer canvas, using a proper scaling factor. Instead of letting the user choose a scale (in a simple Print dialog box with a SpinEdit or a ScrollBar component), I decided to compute it automatically. The idea is to print the shapes on the form as large as possible, by sizing the form's client area so that it takes up the whole page. The code is probably simpler than the description:

```
procedure TShapesForm.Print1Click(Sender: TObject);
var
  Scale, Scale1: Integer;
```

```
begin
  Scale := Printer.PageWidth div ClientWidth;
  Scale1 := Printer.PageHeight div ClientHeight;
  if Scale1 < Scale then
    Scale := Scale1;
  Printer.BeginDoc;
  CommonPaint (Printer.Canvas, Scale);
  Printer.EndDoc;
end;
```

Of course, you need to remember to call the specific commands to start printing (BeginDoc) and commit the output (EndDoc) before and after you call the CommonPaint method.

# Printing Text

In the two previous examples, we used the global printer object's canvas to print graphics. At the beginning of the chapter, we saw another example that could be used to print text, but its code was far from adequate. Printing text is really an important topic, so it deserves some specific attention.

One approach to printing text from a Delphi program is similar to the one we used in the COMBO2 example. If you prepare the text in a form (or, in general, in a bitmap), you can later print the corresponding image to the screen. This is useful in a few cases, such as when you have text in a data-entry form, but it is not generally useful because you can only print a limited amount of text and the print quality is usually quite poor.

Another approach to printing text is to draw the text, using the TextOut method of the canvas or other text-related drawing functions. This allows you precise control over the text's position, and you can obtain high-resolution output. The drawback is that there is a lot of work involved, since you must determine the length and position of each line on the page, the height of the font, and many other details. Power never comes free.

The free ride, however, comes from a third approach. In Delphi, you can associate a file with the printer, then print to the file—send text to the printer—using the standard Writeln procedure. This is much simpler than the other methods because the system automatically determines the height of the lines, relieving you of much of the work. The print resolution is good, but the control you have over the output is less precise. Long lines are automatically wrapped to the next line, which is helpful but can produce wildly unformatted output.

We could try to build a full-scale word processor that could produce output both to the screen and to the printer using TextOut calls (using an approach similar to the SHAPE6 example). But I've decided to just update the NOTES2 example from

Chapter 8, which already had a menu with the proper printing-related commands in the File menu.

In such a simple example, which uses a single font for the whole text and has no special page-handling capabilities (page numbers, header and footers, and so on), using the Writeln procedure on a file connected with the printer is a reasonable approach. We might even extend the example a bit, adding some page-handling capabilities, and still be able to use this technique without any problems.

Technically, the key to this approach is the use of the AssignPrn procedure, which connects a file with the printer. After starting the write process, you can start using Write and Writeln to print the text by calling the Rewrite procedure. In the new version, named NOTES3, the program simply prints each of the Memo component's lines, using a `for` loop from the first to the last line:

```
procedure TNotesForm.Print1Click(Sender: TObject);
var
  PrintFile: TextFile;
  I: Integer;
begin
  if PrintDialog1.Execute then
  begin
    {assign the printer to a file}
    AssignPrn (PrintFile);
    Rewrite (PrintFile);
    {set the font}
    Printer.Canvas.Font := Memo1.Font;
    {copy all the text of the memo to the printer file}
    for I := 0 to Memo1.Lines.Count - 1 do
      Writeln (PrintFile, Memo1.Lines [I]);
    System.CloseFile (PrintFile);
  end;
end;
```

**WARNING**  When you copy the current font of a component or the current font to a form or to the printer, consider that not all the screen fonts are available as printer fonts. A notable example is the MS Sans Serif font often used by default: this font won't print properly. I suggest that you use only TrueType fonts when the printer is involved, because you are sure these fonts are available both on the screen and the printer, and they have a better correspondence.

I could have easily customized this printer function, adding a dialog box to select the range of lines to print, but I decided to use the standard Print dialog box, as you can see in Figure 22.7.

**FIGURE 22.7:**
The standard Print dialog box used by the NOTES3 example.

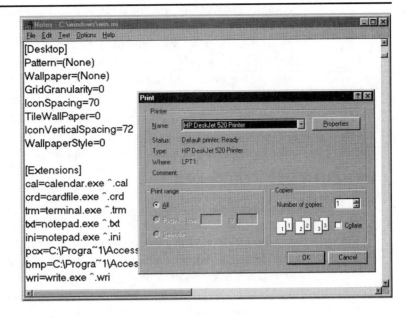

Adding the support for page selection is more complex. First, we must compute the number of lines per page, using the printer's PageHeight property and the height of the font of the printer canvas. Once this calculation is made, we need to check whether each line of text will fit in a printed line or be wrapped to the next line (or even the next two lines), and modify the number of lines in the memo field on a given page.

When you want to start a new page, however, you cannot call the printer object's EndPage method. If you do, the printer will eject the page, but the remaining output will begin in the middle of the page, as if nothing happened. To start a new page when using an output file connected to the printer, you can simply close the output file, then reopen it again. Closing the file terminates the current page. The new page will start from the first line (after a custom header and the page number).

# Printing Database Records and Tables

Using Delphi's printing capabilities, we can easily output our program's database-related forms. Basically, if a form shows a record from a database table, you can use the form's Print method to output the data. Of course, if you intend to print your data, you might as well build the form and arrange the components so that the printed output will look good.

As an alternative to printing a bitmap corresponding to the full client area of the form, you might develop a print function that temporarily removes the form's toolbar and the status bar, prints the whole surface of the form, and then restores the toolbar and status bar. Even better, you can open up a preview form, copy the bitmap of the form, and print only a portion of that bitmap, excluding the toolbar, status bar, and other extraneous elements.

This is not the only approach you can use to print records (or full tables, if they fit on the screen) using database-related forms. You can also apply any of the techniques described in the previous section to print text. In particular, using the file-printing approach, you can print the name of the field and its value on each line of a page, printing one or all of the table's records.

Our first example of database-related output is the PRINTNAV application, which is an extension of the NAVIG1 example in Chapter 17. The new form of the example has the older version's elements, plus three print buttons below the DBNavigator component, as shown in Figure 22.8. As you might remember from Chapter 17 (or as you might guess by looking at the figure), the Table component is connected to the COUNTRY.DB sample table, and the data-aware components are connected to it via the data source.

**FIGURE 22.8:**

The form of the PRINTNAV example at design-time.

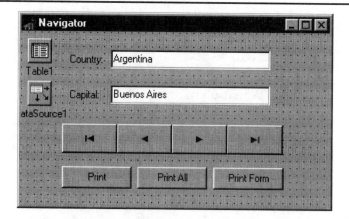

The three buttons perform three different actions involving some type of printer output. The first button simply prints the data of the current record's two visible fields, using the text of the two labels and two edit boxes:

```
procedure TNavigator.PrintButtonClick(Sender: TObject);
var
  PrintFile: TextFile;
begin
  {assign the printer to a file}
  AssignPrn (PrintFile);
```

```
    Rewrite (PrintFile);
    try
      {set the font of the form, and output each element}
      Printer.Canvas.Font := Font;
      Writeln (PrintFile, Label1.Caption,
        ' ', DBEdit1.Text);
      Writeln (PrintFile, Label2.Caption,
        ' ', DBEdit2.Text);
    finally
      {close the printing process}
      System.CloseFile (PrintFile);
    end;
end;
```

This code follows the usual assignment of the printer output to the PrintFile file. What is new in this method is that the database access and output operations are executed within a try-finally block (to avoid skipping the code that closes the print job in case of an error). The code of the second button, Print All, is more complex. It prints the two visible fields for each database record, not just the current one. The program scans the whole table with a code similar to that used in the TO-TAL example of Chapter 17. As you can see in the code below, at the beginning it sets a bookmark and disables the controls, then it scans all of the records in a while loop. For each record, the program outputs a caption followed by the field's text. The program extracts the field with the table's FieldByName method and reads its text using the AsString property of the TField class:

```
procedure TNavigator.PrintAllButtonClick(Sender: TObject);
var
  Bookmark: TBookmark;
  PrintFile: TextFile;
begin
  {assign the printer to a file}
  AssignPrn (PrintFile);
  Rewrite (PrintFile);
  {set the font of the form, and output each element}
  Printer.Canvas.Font := Font;
  {store the current position, creating a new bookmark}
  Bookmark := Table1.GetBookmark;
  Table1.DisableControls;
  try
    Table1.First;
    while not Table1.EOF do
    begin
      {output the two fields, and a blank line}
      Writeln (PrintFile, 'Country: ',
        Table1.FieldByName ('Name').AsString);
      Writeln (PrintFile, 'Capital: ',
        Table1.FieldByName ('Capital').AsString);
      Writeln (PrintFile);
      Table1.Next;
    end;
```

```
    finally
      {go back to the bookmark and destroy it}
      Table1.GotoBookmark (Bookmark);
      Table1.FreeBookmark (Bookmark);
      Table1.EnableControls;
      System.CloseFile (PrintFile);
    end;
end;
```

The Print Form button has the simplest code. To print the output of the form, the PrintFormButtonClick method simply calls the form's Print method. I've added this last button to the program simply to let you test the three different ways to output the data from a database form. You can improve each of these methods by adding headers and comments, printing other fields, and so on. This example is intended to give you an idea of the basic code involved.

By expanding on this idea, you can build complex and sophisticated kinds of output, and also create custom reports and different versions of printed output. As an alternative, you can use specific tools included in Delphi to generate reports: the Delphi QuickReport components or ReportSmith.

# The QuickReport Components

The professional editions of Delphi 2 include QuickReport, a collection of reporting components tightly integrated with Delphi and licensed to Borland by QSD AS (a Norwegian company). There are other similar Delphi components available from other third party companies, but I'll focus on this simply because it will be readily available to most Delphi developers.

QuickReport uses a form to build a report visually and in a way very similar to the way you use forms to build windows visually. However, you'll use this report form only to develop the report; it is never actually shown on screen at run-time. To print or display the report, you can call the Print or Preview methods of the QuickReport component which you place on each report form. (Placing a QuickReport component on a form turns that form into a report form.)

Using QuickReport, a report is constructed from *bands*, or horizontal regions of information. You can use a band to output data, to provide a header and footer in each printed page, or to include totals and other special information. To build a report, you simply place the QuickReport component in a secondary form (not the application's main form), add one or more bands, and then place on those bands some of the QuickReport data-aware reporting components which connect to a Delphi data source in the usual way. The data can actually come from one or more tables or queries, as in the standard data access components.

# A Quick Example

To demonstrate the QuickReport component, I've extended the main form of the last example (PRINTNAV) by adding a full report to it. I've named the new example NAVRPT. Besides adding another button to the three already available, I've added a new form named ReportForm to the project. The new form has a QuickReport component and three QRBand components, as shown in Figure 22.9.

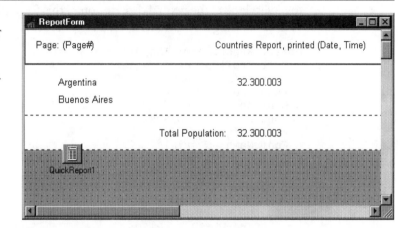

One of the key properties of the QRBand component is BandType, used to indicate the role of the band in the report. In this example, the first band is of type rbPage-Header, the second of type rbDetail, and the third of type rbPageFooter. Other types of bands you can use include rbTitle, included before or after the first page's header; rbSummary, printed only at the end of the report; rdGroupHeader and rbGroupFooter for groups defined with the specific QRGroup component; rbCo-lumnHeader for multicolumn reports; and a few others.

In the example, I've placed two QRSysData components in the first band (the page header). The QRSysData components display the page number, date, and time, and have a description in their Text property. You can print many other types of system information using this component, as indicated by this component's Data property. I've also set a border for the enclosing band, using its Frame property (which is actually a TPen object).

The second band contains the real data from the database. As a detail band, it is replicated on the report for each record that appears in the data source, so you have to specify the data source for each report component. In this case, I've used the Data-Source1 from the program's main form (after choosing File ➤ Use Unit). This same data source is also connected with the three QRDBText components placed in the second band. As is the case with the standard Delphi data-aware components, the report components have also a DataField property, but no inherent formatting capability. To display the population value with comma separators for the thousands, I created field components with the fields editor of the Table1 component and modified the DisplayFormat property of the Table1Population field.

In the last band, I've added a QRDBCalc component to display the total population of the countries in the report (actually in all the records up to the current page). This component can do some basic operations (such as counting or computing a total) without writing code. The report is based on a form, so I think it might be worth it to have a look at the textual description of this form (this is actually another advantage of building a report based on a Delphi form):

```
object ReportForm: TReportForm
  HorzScrollBar.Range = 1200
  VertScrollBar.Range = 2000
  AutoScroll = False
  Caption = 'ReportForm'
  Font.Color = clBlack
  Font.Height = -13
  Font.Name = 'Arial'
  TextHeight = 16
  object QRBand1: TQRBand
    Align = alTop
    BandType = rbPageHeader
    Color = clWhite
    ForceNewPage = False
    Frame.Color = clTeal
    Frame.Width = 2
    Ruler = qrrNone
    object QRSysData1: TQRSysData
      AlignToBand = False
      Data = qrsPageNumber
      Text = 'Page: '
    end
    object QRSysData2: TQRSysData
      AlignToBand = False
      Data = qrsDateTime
      Text = 'Countries Report, printed '
    end
  end
  object QRBand2: TQRBand
    Align = alTop
    BandType = rbDetail
    Color = clWhite
    ForceNewPage = False
    Frame.Width = 0
    Ruler = qrrNone
    object QRDBText1: TQRDBText
      DataSource = Navigator.DataSource1
      DataField = 'Name'
    end
```

```
      object QRDBText2: TQRDBText
        DataSource = Navigator.DataSource1
        DataField = 'Capital'
      end
      object QRDBText3: TQRDBText
        Alignment = taRightJustify
        DataSource = Navigator.DataSource1
        DataField = 'Population'
      end
    end
  object QRBand3: TQRBand
    Align = alTop
    BandType = rbPageFooter
    Color = clWhite
    ForceNewPage = False
    Frame.Width = 0
    Ruler = qrrNone
      object QRDBCalc1: TQRDBCalc
        Alignment = taRightJustify
        DataSource = Navigator.DataSource1
        DataField = 'Population'
        Operation = qrcSUM
        PrintMask = '###,###,###,###'
      end
      object QRLabel3: TQRLabel
        Caption = 'Total Population:'
        AlignToBand = False
      end
    end
  object QuickReport1: TQuickReport
    DataSource = Navigator.DataSource1
    Columns = 1
    DisplayPrintDialog = True
    Orientation = poPortrait
    ReportTitle = 'Countries'
    RestartData = True
    TitleBeforeHeader = False
  end
end
```

Having designed the report, you can simply test it by double-clicking on the report component. This displays the print preview form, which you can use directly to print the report without even compiling the program. You can obtain the same print preview (see Figure 22.10) by writing the following in the main form's code:

```
procedure TNavigator.ReportButtonClick(Sender: TObject);
begin
  ReportForm.QuickReport1.Preview;
end;
```

The QuickReport component is the one I'll certainly turn to in most of my Delphi applications. I haven't written many examples of its use only because I think it is

**FIGURE 22.10:**

The NAVPRT example's print preview form, based on the QuickReport components.

quite simple to manage. Using QuickReport is generally faster and simpler than accessing the printer directly, as discussed in the first part of this chapter, or using ReportSmith, as described in the following section. I'll show another example of how to use QuickReport to build a report with groups at the end of this chapter, comparing it with the corresponding ReportSmith approach.

# Creating ReportSmith Reports

When you want to build a professional report in Delphi, you can take advantage of the Report component, a very simple interface to the ReportSmith engine. This component is not particularly rich by itself. Its properties include the name of the report file you want to print, its directory, plus some other information. You can call the Report component's Run method to view a report (using the ReportSmith runtime engine) and to print it. The stand-alone version of ReportSmith, on the other hand, is a very powerful reporting tool that you can use by itself (with no connection with Delphi). ReportSmith has many more capabilities than the QuickReport component, but it requires a big set of run-time DLLs (which you must install along with your program), and it requires a fair amount of RAM to achieve usable speed. In contrast, the QuickReport reporting components require no run-time DLLs and are very fast, but they also have more limited reporting capabilities. QuickReport is also more integrated with Delphi, accessing databases using the Table and Query Delphi components, while ReportSmith uses it own approach.

Just to test ReportSmith's behavior, I've written a bare program, named PRINTRPT, which loads and runs a report (a file with the RPT extension). When you call the Report1 object's Run method, the ReportSmith engine is loaded, and you can see and print the report. This is because the Report component's Preview property is set to True. When the Preview property is set to False, the report is printed as soon as you call the Run method.

As an alternative, once the report is loaded in memory using the Run method, you can use the Print method to send a Dynamic Data Exchange (DDE) message to the ReportSmith engine, asking it to actually print the report. Do not call Print before running the report, because it will have no effect. The PRINTRPT example's form has four components: a file open dialog box to let the user select a report, a Report component, a check box to select the preview mode, and a button to start the operation. When the user clicks on the Report button, the program opens the dialog box so that the user can select a file, and then runs the engine:

```
procedure TForm1.ReportButtonClick(Sender: TObject);
begin
  Report1.Preview := PreviewCheckBox.Checked;
  if OpenDialog1.Execute then
  begin
    Report1.Reportname := OpenDialog1.FileName;
    Report1.Run;
  end;
end;
```

Since I've set the AutoUnload property, the ReportSmith run-time engine is automatically unloaded from memory when the report terminates. Otherwise, you must add a specific statement in the form's OnClose event, calling the Report component's CloseApplication method.

As I mentioned above, the effect of this code changes depending on the status of the Preview check box. If the Preview property is set to False, the ReportSmith run-time engine immediately starts printing. Otherwise, the ReportSmith RunTime window is displayed as shown in Figure 22.11. The ReportSmith window will appear in the same screen position as it was the last time you used it, and you can see the output, which is the preview. From the preview, you can make changes, choose the pages you want to print, and select from many other options.

Notice that the connection between Delphi and the ReportSmith run-time engine is somewhat loose. ReportSmith is a stand-alone reporting application, which can be driven by Delphi, but can also be used independently. What you cannot do is see the report preview inside a Delphi window. Fortunately, ReportSmith has DDE support and an API to let Delphi applications drive it; this integration has actually been improved in Delphi 2. The starting point of this integration is Delphi Report component.

**FIGURE 22.11:**

The report preview takes place inside the ReportSmith RunTime window. Notice the form of the PRINTRPT example above it.

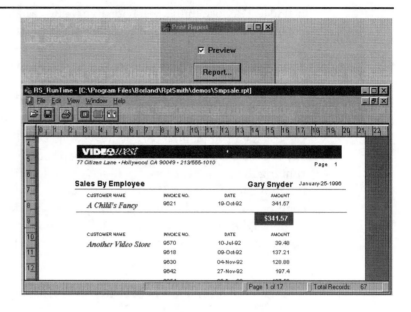

## Building a Custom Report

Using the PRINTRPT program, you can print (or preview) any existing report, but you cannot create new ones. In other words, if you use this approach in your own applications, the users will not be able to create their own reports, unless they own a copy of ReportSmith. In that case, of course, they will be able to print any existing report file.

> **NOTE**
>
> Actually, you can use Delphi to create new reports using DDE or the new API to drive the ReportSmith_Runtime without having the stand-alone package, but this is not the easiest way to build a report.

In general, you will need to build one or more reports when you are developing your program, attach them to the Delphi application, and let the user print them using menu commands.

Building a new report is not really related to Delphi programming. You start ReportSmith (the full version, not the engine) and prepare a report by choosing one of the standard layouts, accessing one or more database tables, and designing a proper layout. For more information about ReportSmith's features, refer to the manuals or on-line Help files. Here we will take a look at two examples of reports and their connection with a simple Delphi program.

TIP **You can perform many operations in ReportSmith simply by selecting an output element and clicking the right mouse button to display a local menu. The toolbar also has some powerful commands.**

Our example is a new version of another program presented in Chapter 17, called HANDGRID. This new version, HANDGRID3, has the same grid as the previous version, plus a menu that lets you print a couple of reports in different ways. The structure of the program is simple. There is a DBGrid connected to a table (again COUNTRY.DB). The program has a plain Print command, which uses the standard dialog box just to let the user confirm the action:

```
procedure TForm1.Print1Click(Sender: TObject);
begin
  if PrintDialog1.Execute then
    Print;
end;
```

The other three menu items (two in the File menu and one in the Table menu) are related to two reports. You can either print the first report directly or open it in preview mode, using the File menu's two commands. The second report always has the Preview property set to True, and is activated using the Table menu's only command. All three menu command handlers have the following structure:

```
procedure TForm1.PrintReport1Click(Sender: TObject);
var
  CurrentPath: String;
begin
  // set the report path to the application path
  CurrentPath := ExtractFilePath (CmdLine);
  Delete (CurrentPath, 1, 1);
  Report1.ReportDir := CurrentPath;
  Report1.Preview := False;
  Report1.Run;
end;
```

Before printing the report, you have to indicate its directory properly. Since I don't want to use a fixed directory, it is better to extract its name from the full path name of the application, passed in the CmdLine parameter (see Chapter 19). Since the path name in the CmdLine parameter starts with double quotes, I've removed the first character of the string.

What changes in the other two cases is the value of the Preview property and the Report component used. The form and the code of this program are simple. All of the work to build the two reports is actually done with ReportSmith. I'll discuss the first report here and the second one in the next section, because the second report uses some advanced features of ReportSmith.

The first report I've built for the HANDGRID3 example, COUNTRY.RPT, does nothing more than output the contents of the database, using a label format. To re-build it, start ReportSmith, create a new report, choose the label style, and select the proper database table (notice that the BDE aliases are not available here). Next, drag some of the fields to the report page, then add a standard label with the proper check box. You can see a step of the report's creation in Figure 22.12.

**FIGURE 22.12:**

Creating a report in ReportSmith is as simple as dragging a few labels.

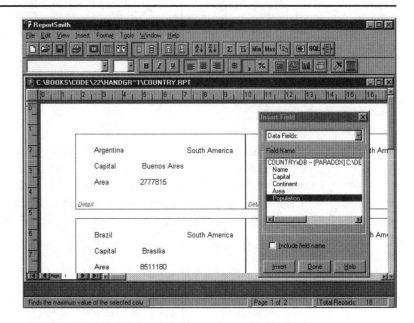

When you are done with the report's layout, save the file and enter its name in the Report1 component's ReportName property in the HANDGRID3 example. Now you can run the program and print or preview the report. It really is that simple.

**WARNING**

In the report file and in the HANDGRID3 program, there are some hard-coded directory names, particularly the name of the directory that contains the database table used by the report. If your installation does not use the default Delphi directories, you might have problems running the program without modification.

# Writing a ReportSmith Macro

The HANDGRID3 example's second report, TABLE.RPT, is more complex. It uses a columnar report format rather than the label style. Select the table (again COUNTRY.DB), and all of its fields are arranged in columns. You can resize the columns to make them fit on the page and set a proper format for the numeric output, such as including thousand separators, as you can see in Figure 22.13.

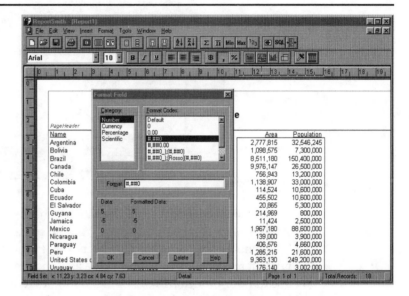

**FIGURE 22.13:**

The initial development steps of the new report include resizing the columns and choosing proper formats.

Continue building the report, entering a proper title, sorting it by continent and by name, and grouping the report by continent. Then add a footer to each of the report's groups. In the footer, place a count of the countries for each continent, the total population of each continent, and the total surface of each continent.

Finally, you can move to the tough part: adding a calculated field to show the population density, as we did in examples in Chapters 17 and 18. The problem here is that you cannot use a SQL statement with the definition of the calculated field, because this feature is not supported by ReportSmith for Paradox tables. The only technique available is to define a ReportSmith macro. You can use the Derived fields command on the Tools menu to add a new field name, defined by a ReportBasic macro. I've used the name Density. Then you can give the macro a name, such as GetDensity, and write its code.

When you click on the New or Edit buttons in the Choose a Macro dialog box, the Edit Macro dialog box appears, as shown in Figure 22.14. You can write the text of the macro directly in this macro editor, or you can use the three list boxes at the top

FIGURE 22.14:

The ReportSmith macro editor, where you can write code in BASIC for a Delphi application.

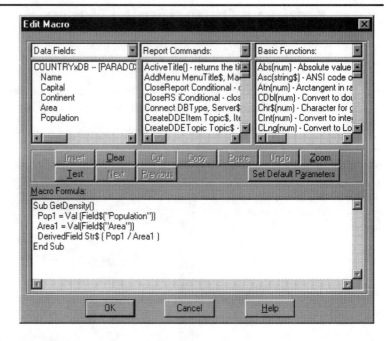

to select table fields, commands, functions, and so on. Notice that each of the three list boxes has a combo box above it. You can use each combo box to select a group of elements for the corresponding list box. For example, the last list box can display four different groups of elements: Basic Functions, Basic Statements, Dialog Box Functions, or Branching & Looping. Using these lists of available commands and functions can be helpful in writing macros, but you still need to know at least the basics of the language of the ReportSmith macro editor, ReportSmith Basic.

**NOTE**     When I first realized that I needed to write BASIC language code for this Delphi project, I considered skipping it. After some struggling with the manuals, I came up with the solution for the Density field definition macro, and decided to keep the example in the book. As you have probably guessed, I'm not too fond of BASIC in any of its incarnations, although it was one of my first programming languages in my early days of computing. But if you want to take advantage of the power of ReportSmith, some background in BASIC will help.

Here is the code of the macro for the new field:

```
Sub GetDensity()
  Pop1 = Val (Field$("Population"))
  Area1 = Val (Field$("Area"))
  DerivedField Str$ ( Pop1 / Area1 )
End Sub
```

This code defines two temporary variables (no declaration is necessary in BASIC), and stores the value of two fields in those variables. The `Field$` function returns the text of the field's contents for the current record, and the `Val` function extracts the numeric value from the string. The last statement computes the population density and transforms it back into a string, using the `Str$` function. This value is assigned to the `DerivedField` identifier, which automatically refers to the field we are computing with the macro.

You can see the result of this effort in Figure 22.15, which shows the final report displayed by the HANDGRID3 example in the ReportSmith RunTime window.

**FIGURE 22.15:**

The preview of the TABLE.RPT report shown by the HANDGRID3 example.

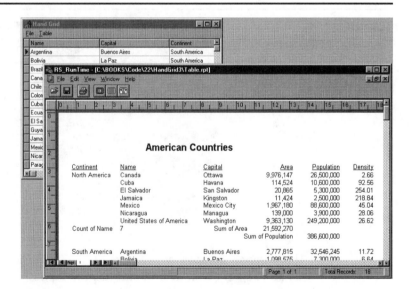

## Quicker than ReportSmith

We have seen how much trouble it takes to write this custom report, using calculated fields in ReportSmith. As I mentioned, the problem is the loose integration ReportSmith has with Delphi. Are there better solutions than the one I outlined in the HANDGRID3 example? Actually, there are two. The first is to use Delphi to build a new database table containing the actual data you want to output. In this case we need to create a temporary database table with the population density field, and then we can copy the data to it before starting a report that uses the temporary table as data source.

Another solution is to forget about ReportSmith and use the QuickReport components. As we already saw in the NAVRPT example, it is very simple to add totals to this type of report. However, we can also use the QuickReport component to group records and print the totals of each group, obtaining an output very similar to that of the last ReportSmith report, but with less work.

To test this, I've taken the CALC example from Chapter 17 and turned it into the new QRCALC example. The new report is based on the reporting form shown in Figure 22.16. The report is made of four bands: a title band (rbTitle), a group header band (rbGroupheader), a normal band (rbDetail), and a group footer band (rbGroupFooter). The two group-related bands are also specified in the QRGroup1 component's HeaderBand and FooterBand properties. This component also has DataSource and DataField properties to specify which table field you want to use to arrange the data into groups. I've chosen the Continent field.

**FIGURE 22.16:**

The QuickReport form of the QRCALC example at design-time.

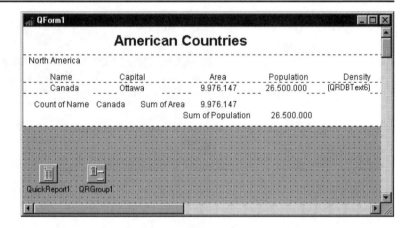

The different bands have various QRLabel, QRDBText, and QRDBCalc components. The very thin detail band has the values of the fields, with the continent name in the header band along with a few labels. The footer band displays the number of records, plus the area and population totals.

It is quite simple to build a similar QuickReport form, but connecting it to the COUNTRY.DB table won't work. The records in the table are sorted by name, so you'll end up with many groups made of just a few records, and with repeated groups for each continent. In fact, the QRGroup component simply starts a new group each time the value of the monitored field changes.

To solve this problem, I could have added a secondary index to the Paradox table. Instead, I've decided to use a Query component to access the data instead of using the Table component, and I've decided to sort the countries by continent inside the SQL query:

```
select * from country
  order by continent, name
```

After this major change, I had to define the fields of the query, add the new calculated field (Density), and modify the OnCalcFields event handler to refer to Query fields instead of Table fields.

---

**NOTE**
> You can find this code on the companion CD: I haven't reported it here because it is very similar to the code of the CALC3 example.

---

What is the result of this effort? We can now use the QuickReport components to access the calculated field, just like any other field of the Query. Compared with the ReportSmith approach, this is much simpler (and *quicker*). In addition, the result is almost the same, as you can see in Figure 22.17.

---

**FIGURE 22.17:**

The report with groups built using the QuickReport component in the QRCALC example.

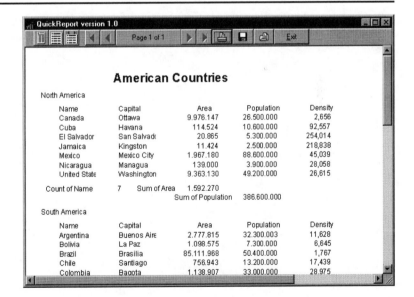

# Summary

In this chapter, we have explored Delphi's printing support. We have seen that it is easy to output the image of a form or to connect a text file with the printer and output data. The Canvas property of the Printer object can also be used to build all types of output, even complex ones. In Delphi, you work with a canvas to produce both advanced screen output and printer output. This means that you can share the code of these two operations, to produce a WYSIWYG (What You See is What You Get) application, as we saw in the SHAPE6 example.

When you work with database-related forms, you can produce printer output using three completely different approaches. You can drive the printer directly, use QuickReport reporting components, or use the ReportSmith application included in Delphi to build more complex reports. These three techniques offer increasing capabilities, but the simplest one to implement is probably the approach that uses QuickReport components.

You can use ReportSmith with less Delphi code, because it uses a version of the BASIC language for customizing reports. This might be easy for Delphi programmers with a Visual Basic background, but less simple for the rest of us. Using ReportSmith is the least integrated approach of the three, and the one I suggest you keep as a last resort.

Having discussed how to print from a program, we need to focus on another important output of an application: saving data to files.

# CHAPTER

**TWENTY-THREE**

# Adding File Support to Applications

- Handling text files with Object Pascal

- A text case conversion program

- Delphi's file system components

- Delphi's file stream support

- Component persistency

**S**aving and loading data to files is vital for most of the programs you write. We have already seen several techniques for saving and loading data in Delphi, and also a number of examples that use the standard file open and save dialog boxes. We even created a File Manager clone in Chapter 14.

Although we've covered several aspects of file support, Delphi provides many for you to use to interact with files.

We can broadly categorize Delphi file support in three areas:

- Object Pascal language file support—identified by the file keyword and by other data types and functions defined in the System unit.

- VCL file support—offered by the TStream and TComponent classes, by the TIniFile class, and by the file loading and storing methods present in several components.

- Database support—provided primarily for file-based formats, such as dBASE and Paradox tables.

In this chapter, we'll explore the first two approaches in detail. We won't cover database support here, since that was the topic of Chapters 17 and 18.

# Files and the Pascal Language

One of the peculiarities of Pascal compared with other programming languages is its built-in support for files. As you might recall from Chapter 4 (or from your knowledge of Pascal), the language has a file keyword, which is a type specifier, like array or record. You use the file keyword to define a new type, and then you can use the new data type to declare new variables:

```
type
  IntFile: file of Integers;
var
  IntFile1: IntFile;
```

It is also possible to use the file keyword without indicating a data type, which specifies an untyped file. Alternatively, you can use the TextFile type defined in the System units to declare files of ASCII characters. Each kind of file has its own pre-defined routines, as we will see later in this chapter.

> **NOTE**  The TextFile type is used in Delphi instead of the Text type from earlier versions of Borland Pascal, because Text is a property name of some components, notably TEdit and TMemo.

Once you have declared a file variable, you can assign it to a real file in the file system using the AssignFile method. The next step is usually to call Reset to open the file for reading at the beginning, Rewrite to open (or create) it for writing, and Append to add new items to the end of the file without removing the older items. Once the input or output operations are done, you should call CloseFile. This operation should typically be done inside a `finally` block, to avoid leaving the file open in case the file handling code generates an exception.

Delphi includes many other file management routines, as you can see in the list below.

| | |
|---|---|
| Append | FileSearch |
| AssignFile | FileSeek |
| BlockRead | FileSetAttr |
| BlockWrite | FileSetDate |
| ChangeFileExt | FileSize |
| CloseFile | FileWrite |
| DateTimeToFileDate | FindClose |
| DeleteFile | FindFirst |
| DiskFree | FindNext |
| DiskSize | Flush |
| Eof | GetDir |
| Eoln | IOResult |
| Erase | MkDir |
| ExpandFileName | Read |
| ExtractFileExt | Readln |
| ExtractFileName | Rename |
| ExtractFilePath | RenameFile |
| FileAge | Reset |
| FileClose | Rewrite |
| FileCreate | RmDir |

| | |
|---|---|
| FileDateToDateTime | Seek |
| FileExists | SeekEof |
| FileGetAttr | SeekEoln |
| FileGetDate | SetTextBuf |
| FileOpen | Truncate |
| FilePos | Write |
| FileRead | Writeln |

These routines are not defined in standard Pascal, but have been part of Borland Pascal for a long time. You can find detailed information about these routines in Delphi's Help files. Here, I'll show you three simple examples to help clarify how these features can be used.

## Handling Text Files

One of the most commonly used file formats is that of text files. As I mentioned before, Delphi has some specific support for text files, most notably the TextFile data type defined by the System unit. We have already used text files in the previous chapter to output text to the printer, by simply assigning the printer to the file variable using the AssignPrn procedure. In a similar way, we can output text to a real file, simply assigning the real file to a file variable.

For this reason, our first example is an extension of the PRINTNAV application presented in Chapter 22. The new version, named PRINTN2, has the same form with the addition of a PrintDialog component. The Print to File check box of this dialog box determines whether to output the text to a file or to print it.

Clicking on the form's Print button now opens the print dialog box instead of printing immediately, as you can see in Figure 23.1. You can test whether Print to File is checked by looking at the value of the Print dialog box's PrintToFile property. In this case, instead of sending the text file to the printer, the program asks the user to choose a file (using the File Save dialog box) and then writes the text to that file.

The key operation is assigning the text file to the file variable:

```
AssignFile (PrintFile, SaveDialog1.FileName);
```

Now you can write to the file, after a call to the Rewrite procedure:

```
Rewrite (PrintFile);
Writeln (PrintFile, Label1.Caption, ' ', DbEdit1.Text);
Writeln (PrintFile, Label2.Caption, ' ', DbEdit2.Text);
CloseFile (PrintFile);
```

**FIGURE 23.1:**
The Print dialog box opened by the
PRINTN2 example. Notice the Print
to File check box.

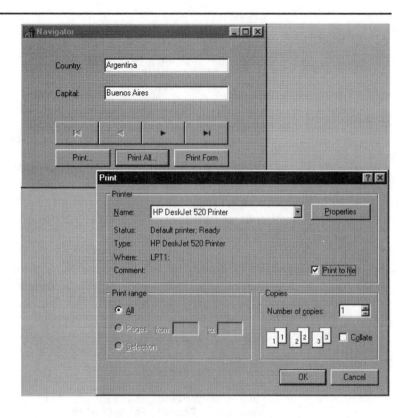

As I mentioned before, to make things safer, you can use a `try` block for the output
operations and place the CloseFile call in a `finally` block, so that it is executed
even if there is an input/output error. In addition, since the actual output code is
duplicated for printing and file output, I've rearranged the code to write the output
operations only once, as you can see in the full source code of the PrintButtonClick
method:

```
procedure TNavigator.PrintButtonClick(Sender: TObject);
var
  OutputFile: TextFile;
begin
  {show the Print dialog box}
  if PrintDialog1.Execute then
  begin
    {if the Print to File check box is selected}
    if PrintDialog1.PrintToFile then
    begin
      {choose a file name}
      if SaveDialog1.Execute then
        {output the text to a file}
        AssignFile (OutputFile, SaveDialog1.FileName);
    end
```

```
      else
      begin
        {output the text to the printer}
        AssignPrn (OutputFile);
        {set the printer font to the form font}
        Printer.Canvas.Font := Font;
      end;
      try
        Rewrite (OutputFile);
        Writeln (OutputFile, Label1.Caption,
          ' ', DBEdit1.Text);
        Writeln (OutputFile, Label2.Caption,
          ' ', DBEdit2.Text);
      finally
        CloseFile (OutputFile);
      end;
    end;
end;
```

The other button, Print All, has more complex output operations, so I've decided to follow a slightly different approach, writing a procedure that outputs the database table to a text file, which can either be connected to the printer or associated with a real file. Here is the output procedure:

```
procedure TNavigator.TableToFile (var TFile: TextFile);
var
  Bookmark: TBookmark;
begin
  {store the current position, creating a new bookmark}
  Bookmark := Table1.GetBookmark;
  Table1.DisableControls;
  try
    Rewrite (TFile);
    Table1.First;
    while not Table1.EOF do
    begin
      {output the two fields, and a blank line}
      Writeln (TFile, 'Country: ',
        Table1.FieldByName ('Name').AsString);
      Writeln (TFile, 'Capital: ',
        Table1.FieldByName ('Capital').AsString);
      Writeln (TFile);
      Table1.Next;
    end;
  finally
    {go back to the bookmark and destroy it}
    Table1.GotoBookmark (Bookmark);
    Table1.FreeBookmark (Bookmark);
    Table1.EnableControls;
    CloseFile (TFile);
  end;
end;
```

In the code of the PrintAllButtonClick method, if you've selected the Print to File check box, the program calls the TableToFile method, passing to it an actual file or one associated with the printer:

```
procedure TNavigator.PrintAllButtonClick(Sender: TObject);
var
  File1: TextFile;
begin
  if PrintDialog1.Execute then
    if PrintDialog1.PrintToFile then
    begin
      if SaveDialog1.Execute then
      begin
        {assign the output to a real file}
        AssignFile (File1, SaveDialog1.FileName);
        TableToFile (File1);
      end;
    end
    else
    begin
      {assign the printer to a file}
      AssignPrn (File1);
      {set the font of the form, and output the file}
      Printer.Canvas.Font := Font;
      TableToFile (File1);
    end;
end;
```

You can run this example, save a table to a text file, then open the resulting file (even in the Delphi editor) to see the result.

## A Text File Converter

In the first example of handling files, we produced a text file using the contents of a database table. In our next example, we'll process an existing file, creating a new one with a modified version of the contents. The program, named FILTER, can convert all the characters in a text file to uppercase, capitalize only the initial word of each sentence, or ignore the characters from the upper portion of the ASCII character set.

The form of the program has two read-only edit boxes for the names of the input and output files, and two buttons to select input and output files using the standard dialog boxes. The form's lower portion contains a RadioGroup component and a bitmap button (named ConvertBitBtn) to apply the current conversion to the selected files. The radio group has three items, as you can see from the following portion of the form's textual description:

```
object RadioGroup1: TRadioGroup
  Caption = 'Conversion'
  Items.Strings = (
    '&Uppercase'
```

```
                    'Capitalize &sentences'
                    'Remove s&ymbols')
```

The user can click on the two buttons to choose the names of the input and output files, displayed in the two edit boxes:

```
procedure TForm1.Button1Click(Sender: TObject);
begin
  if OpenDialog1.Execute then
    Edit1.Text := OpenDialog1.Filename;
end;
```

The second button activates the SaveDialog1 dialog box. The real code of the example is in the three conversion routines that are called by the bitmap button's On-Click event-handler. These calls take place inside the case statement in the middle of the ConvertBitBtn button's OnClick handler:

```
procedure TForm1.ConvertBitBtnClick(Sender: TObject);
var
  F: file of Byte;
begin
  if (Edit1.Text <> '') and (Edit2.text <> '') then
  begin
    {compute the length of the first file}
    AssignFile (F, Edit1.Text);
    try
      Reset (F);
      FileLength := FileSize (F);
    finally
      CloseFile (F);
    end;
    {open the text files}
    AssignFile (FileIn, Edit1.Text);
    try
      AssignFile (FileOut, Edit2.Text);
      {prepare the user interface}
      ConvertForm.Show;
      ConvertForm.BitBtn1.Enabled := False;
      ConvertBitBtn.Enabled := False;
      try
        {move to the beginning of the two files}
        Reset (FileIn);
        Rewrite (FileOut);
        {conversion...}
        case RadioGroup1.ItemIndex of
          0: ConvUpper;
          1: ConvCapitalize;
          2: ConvSymbols;
        end;
      finally
        {close the files and reset the UI}
        CloseFile (FileOut);
        ConvertBitBtn.Enabled := True;
        ConvertForm.BitBtn1.Enabled := True;
```

```
      end;
    finally
      CloseFile (FileIn);
    end;
  end
  else
    ShowMessage ('Enter file names');
end;
```

Before calling one of the conversion procedures, this event-handler displays a dialog box (ConvertForm) with a ProgressBar component, to show the user that the conversion is taking place (as you can see in Figure 23.2). This method does most of the work related to handling the files—it opens the input file as a `file of bytes` (a file storing data as plain bytes) the first time, so that it can use the FileSize procedure, which is not available for text files. Then this file is closed and reopened as a text file.

**FIGURE 23.2:**

The conversion procedures update the secondary form's progress bar to let the user see the percentage of the file already processed.

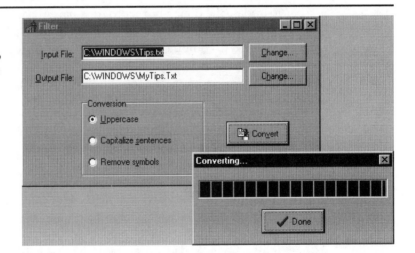

Since the program opens two files, and each of these operations can fail, it uses two nested `try` blocks to ensure a high level of protection, although using the standard dialog boxes to select file names already provides a good confirmation of file selection. Now, let's take a look at one of the conversion routines in detail. The simplest of the three conversion routines is ConvUpper, which converts every character in the text file to uppercase. Here is its code:

```
procedure TForm1.ConvUpper;
var
  Ch: Char;
  Position: LongInt;
begin
  Position := 0;
```

```
  while not Eof (FileIn) do
  begin
    Read (FileIn, Ch);
    Ch := UpCase (Ch);
    Write (FileOut, Ch);
    Inc (Position);
    ConvertForm.ProgressBar1.Position :=
      Position * 100 div FileLength;
    Application.ProcessMessages;
  end;
end;
```

It reads each character from the source file until the program reaches the end of the file (Eof). Each single character is converted and copied to the output file. As an alternative, it is possible to read and convert one line at a time (that is, a string at a time) using string handling routines. This will make the program significantly faster. The approach I've used here is reasonable only for an introductory example.

The conversion procedure's actual code, however, is complicated by the fact that it has to update the dialog box's progress bar. At each step of the conversion, a long integer variable with the current position in the file is incremented. This variable's value is used to compute the new percentage of work completed, as you can see in the code above.

The conversion procedure for removing symbols is very simple:

```
while not Eof (FileIn) do
  begin
    Read (FileIn, Ch);
    if Ch < Chr (127) then
      Write (FileOut, Choose);
    ...
```

The procedure used to capitalize the text, in contrast, is really a complex piece of code. It is based on a case statement with four branches:

- If the letter is uppercase, and it is the first letter after an ending punctuation mark (as indicated by the Period Boolean variable), it is left as is; otherwise, it is converted to lowercase. This conversion is not done by a standard procedure, simply because there isn't one for single characters. It's done with a low-level function I've written (called LowCase, as you can see below).

- If the letter is lowercase, it is converted to uppercase only if it was at the beginning of a new sentence.

- If the character is an ending punctuation mark (period, question mark, or exclamation mark), Period is set to True.

- If the character is anything else, it is simply copied to the destination file.

Here is the actual code:

```pascal
function LowCase (C: Char): Char;
begin
  if C in ['A'..'Z'] then
    LowCase := Chr (Ord (C) - Ord ('A') + Ord ('a'))
  else
    LowCase := C;
end;
procedure TForm1.ConvCapitalize;
var
  Ch: Char;
  Period: Boolean;
  Position: LongInt;
begin
  Period := True;
  Position := 0;
  while not Eof (FileIn) do
  begin
    Read (FileIn, Ch);
    case Ch of
      'A'..'Z':
        if Period then
        begin
          Write (FileOut, Ch);
          Period := False;
        end
        else
        begin
          Ch := LowCase (Ch);
          Write (FileOut, Ch);
          Period := False;
        end;
      'a'..'z':
        if Period then
        begin
          Ch := UpCase (ch);
          Write (FileOut, Ch);
          Period := False;
        end
        else
        begin
          Write (FileOut, Ch);
          Period := False;
        end;
      '.', '?', '!':
      begin
        Period := True;
        Write (FileOut, Ch);
      end;
      else
        Write (FileOut, Ch);
    end; {end of case}
    Inc (Position);
```

```
    ConvertForm.ProgressBar1.Position :=
        Position * 100 div FileLength;
  end; {end of while}
end;
```

Figure 23.3 is an example of this code's effect; it shows a text file before and after the conversion. This program is far from adequate for professional use, but it is a first step toward building a full-scale letter case conversion program. Its biggest drawbacks are that it frequently converts proper nouns to lowercase, and capitalizes any letter after a period (even if it's the first letter of the extension of a file name!).

**FIGURE 23.3:**

The result of running the FILTER example's Capitalize conversion.

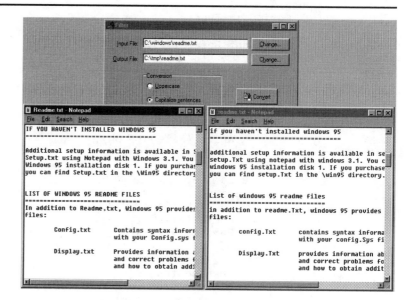

## Saving Generic Data

In addition to using text files, you can save data to a file using any data type, such as integers, real numbers, records, and other data types besides classes. (We will discuss Delphi's support for saving objects and components later in this chapter.) Using a custom file type instead of a text file may be an advantage because it might take less space (the textual version of a number usually takes much more space than its binary value), but this approach won't let the user browse through the files using a text editor (which might be an advantage, too).

Examining the examples in previous chapters, I found one that might benefit from file support—one that is based on a file of integer values rather than on a text file. Our next example, CHART2, builds on the CHART application from Chapter 16.

This program used the First Impression OLE control (OCX) to display the collected data in a grid. Since the data is basically a series of numbers, it makes sense not to save it as text, although the grid actually stores the values of the items as a table of strings.

The form of the example now has a menu with a File pull-down menu and a Help menu with the About command. The key elements are the three file-related commands: Open, Save, and Save As. The rest of the code has just a few changes from the older version.

How do you save a series of integers to a file? Simply by reading them from or writing them to a file. First of all you have to define a file as shown:

```
SaveFile: file of Integer;
```

Then you need to assign the real file to the file variable, operate on it inside a `try` block, and close it in a `finally` block. The program uses a string to hold the name of the current file (CurrentFile) and a Boolean value to track whether the data has changed (Modified):

```
TForm1 = class(TForm)
  ...
  private
    Modified: Boolean;
    CurrentFile: string;
```

First of all, I've set the Modified flag to True in the methods that affect the data (pressing the update button or changing the selected graph type in the combo box). This flag is used by the Save1Click method:

```
procedure TForm1.Save1Click(Sender: TObject);
var
  SaveFile: file of Integer;
  I, J, Value: Integer;
begin
  if Modified then
    if CurrentFile = '' then
      {call save as}
      SaveAs1Click (self)
    else
    begin
      {save to the current file}
      AssignFile (SaveFile, CurrentFile);
      try
        Rewrite (SaveFile);
        {write the value of each grid element}
        for I := 1 to 5 do
          for J := 1 to 4 do
          begin
            Value := StrToIntDef (Trim (
              StringGrid1.Cells [I, J]), 0);
            Write (SaveFile, Value);
```

```
        end;
      Value := ComboBox1.ItemIndex;
      Write (SaveFile, Value);
      Modified := False;
    finally
      CloseFile (SaveFile);
    end;
  end;
end;
```

To save the data to a file, the program saves each value of the string grid (after converting it into a number), and then saves the code of the current graph. To accomplish this, the program uses two nested for loops to scan the grid and then appends the code of the combo box selection at the end of the file. Notice the use of the temporary Value variable: the Write and Read procedures require a parameter passed by reference (var), so you cannot pass a property, since it doesn't correspond directly to a memory location.

Of course, the data should be read in the same order it is written, as you can see in the Open1Click method:

```
procedure TForm1.Open1Click(Sender: TObject);
var
  LoadFile: file of Integer;
  I, J, Value: Integer;
begin
  if OpenDialog1.Execute then
  begin
    CurrentFile := OpenDialog1.Filename;
    Caption := 'Chart [' + CurrentFile + ']';
    {load from the current file}
    AssignFile (LoadFile, CurrentFile);
    try
      Reset (LoadFile);
      {read the value of each grid element}
      for I := 1 to 5 do
        for J := 1 to 4 do
        begin
          Read (LoadFile, Value);
          StringGrid1.Cells [I, J] := IntToStr(Value);
        end;
      Read (LoadFile, Value);
      ComboBox1.ItemIndex := Value;
    finally
      CloseFile (LoadFile);
    end;
    ComboBox1Change (self);
    UpdateButtonClick (self);
    Modified := False;
  end;
end;
```

At the end of the above code, the program updates the combo box (to make the current selection effective) and copies the data to the grid (simulating a click on the Update button). The third method of the group is used to handle the File ➤ Save As menu command:

```
procedure TForm1.SaveAs1Click(Sender: TObject);
begin
  if SaveDialog1.Execute then
  begin
    CurrentFile := SaveDialog1.Filename;
    Caption := 'Chart [' + CurrentFile + ']';
    {call save}
    Modified := True;
    Save1Click (self);
  end;
end;
```

As you can see, the Save1Click and SaveAs1Click methods call each other. Save1Click calls the other method to ask for a file name when the file has changed and no file name has been assigned to the CurrentFile variable. This string is also copied to the caption of the form each time it changes (both when you load a file and when you save the current one with a new name). SaveAs1Click, in turn, calls Save1Click to actually save the file once a new file name is provided.

To complete file handling, you must set the properties of the SaveDialog and OpenDialog components. They both have a special filter, *Chart files (\*.chr)*, and some standard options. Notice that the CHR file extension is something I've invented myself, and is used only by this program. It is not something related to the First Impression OLE component. You can see an example of one of the two standard dialog boxes used by the CHART2 program in Figure 23.4.

The last portion of the code I want to show you is the check done when the user tries to close the program:

```
procedure TForm1.FormCloseQuery(Sender: TObject; var CanClose:
Boolean);
var
  Code: Word;
begin
  if Modified then
  begin
    Code := MessageDlg (
      'Data has changed, do you want to save it?',
      mtConfirmation, mbYesNoCancel, 0);
    if Code = idYes then
      Save1Click (self);
    if Code = idCancel then
      CanClose := False
    else
```

```
      CanClose := True;
   end
   else
      CanClose := True;
end;
```

The form closes or stays open, depending on the user input, and the user eventually saves the file before exiting.

**FIGURE 23.4:**

Saving a file with a new name in the CHART2 example.

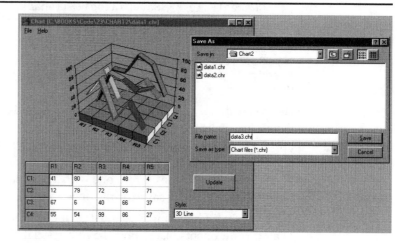

# File Support in Delphi Components

Besides the standard Pascal language file support, Delphi includes a number of other options for manipulating files. Several components have methods to save or load their contents from a file such as a text or a bitmap file, and there are other specific classes to handle files. Many component classes have the SaveToFile and Load-FromFile methods. In this book, we have used these methods for TBitmap, TPicture, and TStrings classes (used in TMemo, TListBox, and many other component classes). They are also available for some data-aware components (TBlobField, TMemoField, and TGraphicField), for other graphic formats (TGraphic, TIcon, and TMetaFile), for OLE (Object Linking and Embedding) containers, and for outlines.

Similar methods are available in TMediaPlayer class. These methods are named Open and Save, and they have a slightly different syntax and meaning than their LoadFromFile and SaveToFile counterparts. Another file-related class we've already used (in Chapter 19) is TIniFile. This class is a file wrapper specifically intended for Windows initialization files, or for any custom file using the same format. The new topics we will cover here are file system components, streaming components, and the components that implement object persistency.

# File System Components

The Delphi file system components are located in the System page of the Components palette: TDirectoryListBox, TDriveComboBox, TFileListBox, and TFilterCombo-Box. We have used these components in the TABONLY2 example in Chapter 13 and the File Manager clone example in Chapter 14. Not surprisingly, these components are well-known to many Delphi programmers (including those of you who have read the book up to this point). However, what isn't well known is that the same FileCtrl unit that defines these components also contains three interesting routines:

- DirectoryExists, which is used to check whether a directory exists.
- ForceDirectories, which can create several directories at once.
- SelectDirectory, which shows a predefined Delphi dialog box.

Our next example demonstrates the use of these little-known routines. The example, named DIRS, has a simple form with an edit box and three buttons, as you can see in Figure 23.5. The first two buttons are disabled at design-time, and they are automatically enabled only when there is some text in the edit box:

```
procedure TForm1.Edit1Change(Sender: TObject);
begin
  if Edit1.TExt <> '' then
  begin
    TestButton.Enabled := True;
    CreateButton.Enabled := True;
  end
  else
  begin
    TestButton.Enabled := False;
    CreateButton.Enabled := False;
  end;
end;
```

The method associated with the first button tests the existence of the current directory and produces a corresponding message (see Figure 23.5):

```
procedure TForm1.TestButtonClick(Sender: TObject);
begin
  if DirectoryExists (Edit1.Text) then
    MessageDlg ('OK, the directory ' +
      Edit1.Text + ' exists', mtInformation, [mbOk], 0)
  else
    MessageDlg ('Sorry, the directory ' + Edit1.Text +
      ' doesn''t exist', mtError, [mbOk], 0);
end;
```

**FIGURE 23.5:**

The output of the DIRS example when the current directory exists.

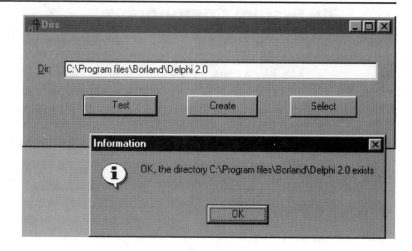

The method associated with the second button asks the user to confirm the operation, then creates the directory (or, at least it tries to, because the specified path might be invalid):

```
procedure TForm1.CreateButtonClick(Sender: TObject);
begin
  if MessageDlg ('Are you sure you want to create the ' +
      Edit1.Text + ' directory', mtConfirmation,
      [mbYes, mbNo], 0) = mrYes then
    ForceDirectories (Edit1.Text);
end;
```

The last button's OnClick event handler, which is always enabled, simply displays Delphi's Select Directory dialog box, as you can see in Figure 23.6. The three flags passed to the SelectDirectory function let the dialog box create a new directory, prompting the user for confirmation:

```
procedure TForm1.SelectButtonClick(Sender: TObject);
var
  Text: String;
begin
  if SelectDirectory (Text, [sdAllowCreate,
      sdPerformCreate, sdPrompt], 0) then
    Edit1.Text := Text;
end;
```

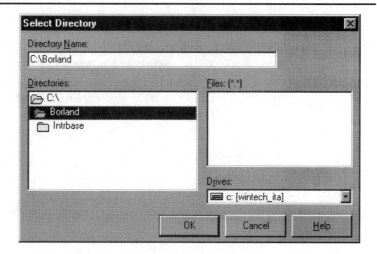

**FIGURE 23.6:**

The Select Directory dialog box is a little-known Delphi system dialog box.

# Streaming Data

Another interesting topic is Delphi's support for file streams. The VCL defines the abstract TStream class and three subclasses: TFileStream, THandleStream, and TMemoryStream. The parent class, TStream, has just a few properties, but it also has an interesting list of methods you can use to save or load data.

The various methods are described in Delphi's Help file, but it's not easy to find them. To help you locate the information, you can search the method names in Delphi Help file one by one. The following list of class methods will help you locate the information:

```
function Read(var Buffer; Count: LongInt): LongInt;
function Write(const Buffer; Count: LongInt): LongInt;
function Seek(Offset: LongInt; Origin: Word): LongInt;
procedure ReadBuffer(var Buffer; Count: LongInt);
procedure WriteBuffer(const Buffer; Count: LongInt);
function CopyFrom(Source: TStream; Count: LongInt): LongInt;
function ReadComponent(Instance: TComponent): TComponent;
function ReadComponentRes(Instance: TComponent): TComponent;
procedure WriteComponent(Instance: TComponent);
procedure WriteComponentRes(const ResName: string;
  Instance: TComponent);
procedure ReadResHeader;
```

Most of these functions relate to components and are used only by component writers, but some of them, such as ReadBuffer and WriteBuffer, can easily be used by anyone.

Creating a TStream instance makes no sense, because this class provides no support to actually save data. Instead, you can use the two file-based streams to load data from or store it to an actual file. THandleStream is used when you already have the Windows handle for a file. Use TFileStream when you have just a file name. Both classes have special Create methods used to pass file information. The third stream class is TMemoryStream, which manipulates memory locations and not an actual file. However, this class has special methods to copy its contents to or from another stream, which can be a file stream. Creating and using a file stream is as simple as creating a file variable:

```
var
  S: TFileStream;
begin
  if OpenDialog1.Execute then
  begin
    S := TFileStream.Create (OpenDialog1.FileName,
      fmOpenRead);
    try
      {use the stream S ...}
    finally
      S.Free;
    end;
  end;
end;
```

As you can see in this code, the Create method for file streams has two parameters: the name of the file and a flag indicating the requested operation. In this case, the operation is reading the file (fmOpenRead). Streams can actually be used instead of traditional files, although they might be less intuitive to use at first. A big advantage of streams, for example, is that you can work with memory streams and then save them to a file, or you can perform the reverse operation. This might be a way to improve the speed of a file-intensive program. Here is a snippet of code, a file-copying function, to give you an idea of how you can use streams (notice that this code should be protected with a try-finally block):

```
procedure CopyFile (SourceName, TargetName: String);
var
  Stream1, Stream2: TFileStream;
begin
  Stream1 := TFileStream.Create (SourceName, fmOpenRead);
  Stream2 := TFileStream.Create (TargetName,
    fmOpenWrite or fmCreate);
  Stream2.CopyFrom (Stream1, Stream1.Size);
  T.Free;
  S.Free;
end;
```

Another important use of streams (both file streams and memory steams) is to handle database BLOB fields or other large fields directly. In fact, you can export table fields data to a stream or read it from one by simply calling the corresponding method.

# The Idea of Persistency

A particularly interesting characteristic of streams is their ability to stream components. All the VCL component classes are subclasses of TPersistent, a special class used to save objects to streams, and they have methods for saving and loading all of the properties and public fields. For this reason, all TComponent descendant classes can actually save themselves to a stream, or they can be created automatically when loaded from a stream. A program can use the WriteComponent and ReadComponent methods of a stream to accomplish this, as we'll see in the next example.

Before the example, however, I would like to give you an idea of how the process works, so you can extend your exploration of this topic. Basically, the stream classes know nothing specific about reading or writing components. The methods of the TStream class simply use two other classes: TReader and TWriter, both subclasses of TFiler, to provide the necessary information. TReader and TWriter objects read and write to the stream that owns them, and are capable of adding special signatures to it to perform a check on the data format. A TWriter object can save the signature of a component, and then save the component, all of its properties, and all of the components it contains. Accordingly, it has a method called WriteRootComponent, which writes the component passed as parameter and also writes each of the components it contains. Similarly, the TReader class has a ReadRootComponent method, which is capable of creating new objects using the class information stored in the stream. This is possible with one condition: the component name must be registered by the application.

After this general introduction, let's look at the example, named CREF2. As the 2 in the name suggests, this is the second version of an older example, CLASSREF, from Chapter 5. With the original example, a user could create several components of three different types inside a form. With the new version, a user can also save these components to a file or load them from an existing file. The program is not a general-purpose application; it works only with files created by Delphi.

The form of the CREF2 example is quite simple. It has only a panel with three radio buttons. As in the older version, the example uses class references to determine the kind of component to create each time a user clicks in the form's client area. This portion of the code is similar to the original version. What's new is the code of the method related to the menu commands: New, Open, SaveAs, Exit, and About.

The New1Click method deletes all of the existing components, except for the panel used as the toolbar. To accomplish this, it scans the form's Controls array in reverse order (downto). In fact, each time a new component is removed, the Controls property changes. Using the reverse order, the changes are limited to the controls that have an order above the loop counter value (I), so they have no influence on the following operations. Notice that this method resets the component's Counter value, too:

```
procedure TForm1.New1Click(Sender: TObject);
var
  I: Integer;
begin
  {delete all existing components, except the panel}
  for I := ControlCount - 1 downto 0 do
    if Controls[I].ClassName <> 'TPanel' then
      Controls[I].Free;
  Counter := 0;
end;
```

The SaveAs1Click method uses a standard loop to save each of the components to a stream, as described earlier. Again, the code skips the TPanel component. The program uses a try-finally block to close the stream even if an error occurs:

```
procedure TForm1.SaveAs1Click(Sender: TObject);
var
  S: TFileStream;
  I: Integer;
begin
  if SaveDialog1.Execute then
  begin
    {open or create the stream file}
    S := TFileStream.Create (SaveDialog1.FileName,
      fmOpenWrite or fmCreate);
    try
      {save each component except the panel}
      for I := 0 to ControlCount - 1 do
        if Controls[I].ClassName <> 'TPanel' then
          S.WriteComponent (Controls[I]);
    finally
      S.Free;
    end;
  end;
end;
```

In Figure 23.7, you can see the Save As dialog box displayed by this program's SaveAs1Click method.

The Open1Click method is not much different. This time, the program loops until it reaches the end of the stream. In the loop, it calls the ReadComponent method, passing a nil parameter to indicate that it needs to create a new component. Instead of creating a new component, you can assign the value read from the stream to an existing component (which must be of the same type):

```
procedure TForm1.Open1Click(Sender: TObject);
var
  S: TFileStream;
  New: TComponent;
begin
```

```
if OpenDialog1.Execute then
begin
  {remove existing controls}
  New1Click (self);
  {open the stream}
  S := TFileStream.Create (OpenDialog1.FileName,
    fmOpenRead);
  try
    while S.Position < S.Size do
    begin
      {read a component and add it to the form}
      New := S.ReadComponent (nil);
      InsertControl (New as TControl);
      Inc (Counter);
    end;
  finally
    S.Free;
  end;
end;
end;
```

**FIGURE 23.7:**

You can use the CREF2 example to save component files, but you'll only be able to open those files with this program.

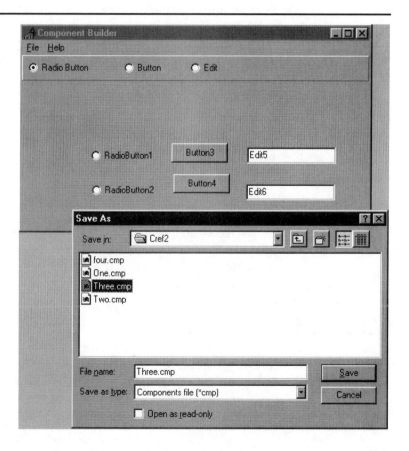

Each time a new component is loaded, it is added to the form list of controls, using the InsertControl method (which requires a parameter of TControl type, of course). Then, the counter is increased to avoid creating duplicate names later on when you add new components to the form.

To make the stream reading operations possible, I've added a call to the Register-Classes system procedure to the `initialization` section of the unit, which creates a list of class names and class references used by the stream reader. This means that the program can read only files with the components types registered in this function. If you want to extend the program with new components, you can add the corresponding classes to this list:

```
initialization
  RegisterClasses ([TRadioButton, TEdit, TButton]);
end.
```

Once you have saved a single component's data, there is little you can do with it. A better alternative might be to save the entire form using the standard Delphi DFM format. In other words, we want to save the whole form with its components in a Windows resource file, the standard format used by Delphi. In fact, DFM files are just RES files that contain custom resources.

The code we use to accomplish this is actually much simpler than what we have seen. You can simply call the WriteComponentResFile procedure, which requires a filename parameter (not a stream) and the name of the form you want to save. This is the sample code from the File ➤ Save Form File command of the CREF2 example (which uses a second SaveDialog component):

```
procedure TForm1.SaveAs2Click(Sender: TObject);
begin
  if SaveDialog2.Execute then
    WriteComponentResFile
      (SaveDialog2.Filename, self);
end;
```

Once you have saved a form using this method, you can open it in a Delphi editor as a DFM file. Of course you'll find all of the components, including the panel and the menu, but you'll be unable to use this file unless you create the header of a corresponding Pascal source code file.

# Summary

Manipulating files is a key function of most applications, and you'll find plenty of file support available in Delphi. Several components have specific methods to save their contents (usually text or bitmaps) to a file, and there are several specific classes related to files, such as the stream classes and the TIniFile class.

In addition, you can always use traditional Pascal file support, which is a key feature of the language. However, an important concept in Delphi is that each component class is persistent—it can save itself to a stream or a file. This leads to a number of interesting options for writing Delphi add-on tools (something that is beyond the scope of this book).

Typically, files are used to save data for a later use, but they are also a means of data exchange between different applications, provided that they can read and write the same file format. However, there are several other features you can use to exchange data between programs in Windows, including the Clipboard, DDE, and OLE. These three features are the subject of the next two chapters.

# Exchanging Data

- Working with the Windows Clipboard

- Adding Clipboard support to your programs

- An overview of DDE

- Adding DDE support to your programs

- Simple client/server applications

- An automatic server and graphical DDE client

24

**W**indows users frequently run several applications at a time. Each application typically has its own window, and each window seems to be isolated from the other application windows. However, from a technical point of view, this is far from true. As a result, users can benefit from various forms of data exchange between applications available in Windows.

The three main Windows features that implement data exchange are the Clipboard, DDE, and OLE. These three features have many differences, both from the user's standpoint and from the programmer's standpoint. The focus of this chapter is on the use of the Clipboard and DDE. As you'll see, these data-exchange techniques frequently work cooperatively, and it is not always easy to draw a clear line to separate them.

# What Is the Clipboard?

Basically, the Windows Clipboard is a storage area for a unit of information. This information can be a portion of text, a bitmap, some data in a proprietary format, an OLE object, and so on. Since there is a specific format for any given data type, each time an application copies data to the Clipboard, it also must specify a Clipboard format. This can be one of the standard formats or a new Clipboard format defined by the application using the `RegisterClipboardFormat` API function.

Actually, the situation is even more complex. The unit of information in the Clipboard can be available in several different formats at the same time, since an application can copy data in a custom format *and* in a standard format. The application accessing this data can use the custom format if it knows how to handle it. If not, it can take the copy in the standard format, usually losing some of the information.

As an example, consider the case of passing data from your favorite word processor to the Windows Notepad. The word processor copies the data with font and text format information, but Notepad cannot access that information; it can only retrieve the basic text, which the word processor copied to the Clipboard as a second version of the data in plain text format.

To see the contents of the Clipboard, you can use the Clipboard Viewer application, which shows the data in one of the standard formats and also lists all of the currently available formats, as you can see in Figure 24.1. If you are new to Clipboard programming, the Clipboard Viewer can help you understand how the Clipboard works.

The Clipboard offers *user-driven data exchange*. The user must copy (or cut) data to the Clipboard from the source application, switch to the destination program, and

**FIGURE 24.1:**

The Windows 95 Clipboard Viewer, with a list of available formats. Notice that inside the Clipboard there is a bitmap with an image of the screen containing the Clipboard Viewer itself, with a Delphi component inside.

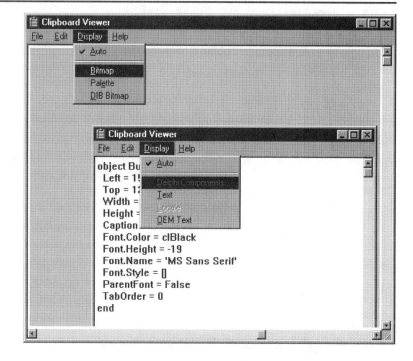

paste the data there. The user has control over the entire operation. A drawback to this approach is that if the original data changes, the user needs to repeat the whole process again. As a result, DDE and OLE were developed to overcome this limitation. In two completely different ways, these techniques can connect data directly to the source application.

Another key element is that the Clipboard supports a single-copy/multiple-paste operation. This means that when you copy new data to the Clipboard, the previous contents are lost, but the paste operation is nondestructive—after you have pasted some data to an application, it is still available in the Clipboard for another paste operation.

As you know, the Clipboard-related commands are located in the Edit menu of an application. These commands are named Cut, Copy, and Paste, and have new shortcut keys (Ctrl+X, Ctrl+C, and Ctrl+V, respectively), replacing the older Ctrl+Ins, Ctrl+Del, and Shift+Ins. The same Edit menu often contains other Clipboard-related commands, such as Paste Link and Paste Special, which are actually DDE and OLE commands, as we will see later in the chapter.

# The Clipboard in Delphi

In Delphi, Clipboard support comes in two different forms:

- Some components have specific Clipboard-related methods. For example, TMemo, TEdit, and TDBImage, among other components, have the CopyTo-Clipboard, CutToClipboard, and PasteFromClipboard methods.

- There is a specific global Clipboard object of the TClipboard class, which has a number of specific Clipboard features. For full Clipboard support, the use of the Clipboard object, defined in the Clipboard unit, is required.

A program can use the Clipboard object to see if a certain format is available (using the HasFormat method), to list all the available formats, and to place data in the Clipboard (when this function isn't handled directly by other components). The Clipboard object can also be used to open the Clipboard and copy data in different formats. This is the only case in which you need to open and close the Clipboard in Delphi—something that is also required when using the Windows API directly.

## Copying and Pasting Text

Our first example using the Clipboard is a new version of the NOTES program. After adding printing support, which we did in Chapter 22, we can now build the final version, NOTES 4. There isn't much to do to add Clipboard support to this program. Simply enable the Cut, Copy, and Paste commands, set their shortcut keys properly, and write the following three simple methods:

```
procedure TNotesForm.Copy1Click(Sender: TObject);
begin
  Memo1.CopyToClipboard;
end;

procedure TNotesForm.Cut1Click(Sender: TObject);
begin
  Memo1.CutToClipboard;
end;

procedure TNotesForm.Paste1Click(Sender: TObject);
begin
  Memo1.PasteFromClipboard;
end;
```

Now you can run the program and work with the Clipboard. Notice that the first two commands, Cut and Copy, operate on the text selected inside the Memo component. Paste can either replace the current selection (if any) or add the text at the current insertion point. The program works, but these three commands don't always perform their intended tasks. For example, when there is no selection, there is nothing to copy or cut; and when the Clipboard doesn't hold data in text format, there is nothing you can paste. The solution is to enable only the menu items that are appropriate, by testing the current selection and the current contents of the Clipboard.

But where do we write this code? We can't insert the test in the event-handlers of the menu items, because it is too late. It can't be when responding to a user action in the Memo component, because we won't know if another application has changed the contents of the Clipboard. The correct location for the test is in the OnClick event of the Edit pull-down menu itself. By adding the Edit1Click method to the form, the program behaves as it should:

```
procedure TNotesForm.Edit1Click(Sender: TObject);
begin
  {if some text is selected in the memo,
  enable the cut and copy commands}
  if Memo1.SelLength > 0 then
  begin
    Copy1.Enabled := True;
    Cut1.Enabled := True;
  end
  else
  begin
    Copy1.Enabled := False;
    Cut1.Enabled := False;
  end;
  {if the Clipboard contains some text,
  enable the Paste command}
  if Clipboard.HasFormat (CF_TEXT) then
    Paste1.Enabled := True
  else
    Paste1.Enabled := False;
end;
```

To compile this program, remember to add a uses statement referring to the Clipboard unit. You can test the effect of this code by running the program. Figure 24.2 shows an example of the program when no text is selected but the Clipboard has data in text format.

In the listing above you can see a first example of the use of the global Clipboard object. The Delphi Help file documents five different formats for the HasFormat method:

| | |
|---|---|
| CF_TEXT | CF_BITMAP |
| CF_METAFILE | CF_PICTURE |
| CF_OBJECT | |

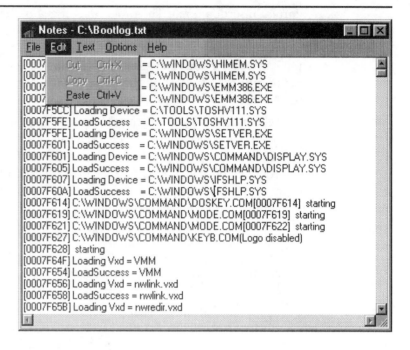

These are the formats typically used by Delphi and by VCL components. The Windows API, however, defines many more formats, including the following:

| | |
|---|---|
| CF_BITMAP | CF_OWNERDISPLAY |
| CF_DIB | CF_PALETTE |
| CF_DIF | CF_PENDATA |
| CF_DSPBITMAP | CF_RIFF |
| CF_DSPMETAFILEPICT | CF_SYLK |
| CF_DSPTEXT | CF_TEXT |
| CF_METAFILEPICT | CF_TIFF |
| CF_OEMTEXT | CF_WAVE |

You can use these Windows formats without any particular problems, although there isn't specific support in Delphi to retrieve these types of data. In this example, we have used two methods of the TMemo class to perform the Clipboard operations, but we could have accomplished the same effect with some of the text-related features of the TClipboard class. For instance, we could have used the AsText property (used to copy or paste Pascal strings), and the SetTextBuf and GetTextBuf methods (used to handle PChar strings). The TClipboard class has specific support only for text. When you want to work with other elements, you need to use the Assign method or work with handles.

# Copying and Pasting Bitmaps

The most common technique for copying or pasting a bitmap in Delphi is to use the Assign method of the TClipboard and TBitmap classes. As a slightly more advanced example of the use of the Clipboard, I've made a new version of the PRINTBMP example in Chapter 22, which was an improved version of the TABONLY example in Chapter 13.

The new example can show bitmaps from a selected file or from the Clipboard, if available, and print them (with the Preview dialog box). The structure of the form is always the same, with a TabControl component covering the whole form and an Image component inside it. The menu, however, is slightly more complex, because it now has the commands from the Edit pull-down menu.

When you select the Edit ➤ Paste command of the COPYBMP example, a new tab named Clipboard is added to the tab set (unless it is already present), as you can see in Figure 24.3. Then the number of the new tab is used to change the active tab:

```
procedure TForm1.Paste1Click(Sender: TObject);
var
  TabNum: Integer;
begin
  if TabControl1.Tabs.IndexOf ('Clipboard') < 0 then
    {create a new page for the Clipboard}
    TabNum := TabControl1.Tabs.Add ('Clipboard')
  else
    {locate the page}
    TabNum := TabControl1.Tabs.IndexOf ('Clipboard');
  {go to the Clipboard page and force repaint}
  TabControl1.TabIndex := TabNum;
  TabControl1Change (self);
end;
```

At the end of the Paste1Click method, the program calls TabControl1Change, the event-handler associated with the selection of a new tab, which can load the bitmap from the current file or paste it from the Clipboard:

```
procedure TForm1.TabControl1Change(Sender: TObject);
var
  TabText: string;
begin
  Image1.Visible := True;
  TabText := TabControl1.Tabs [TabControl1.TabIndex];
  if TabText <> 'Clipboard' then
    {load the file indicated in the tab}
    Image1.Picture.LoadFromFile (TabText)
  else
    if Clipboard.HasFormat (cf_Bitmap) then
```

```
begin
  {if the tab is 'Clipboard' and a bitmap
  is available in the Clipboard}
  if Image1.Picture.Graphic = nil then
    Image1.Picture.Graphic := TBitmap.Create;
  Image1.Picture.Graphic.Assign (Clipboard);
end
else
begin
  {else remove the Clipboard tab}
  TabControl1.Tabs.Delete (TabControl1.TabIndex);
  if TabControl1.Tabs.Count = 0 then
    Image1.Visible := False;
end;
end;
```

Notice that if the Picture property of the Image component is still not initialized, you must create the bitmap before calling the Assign method. If you forget to create the new bitmap and no graphic is associated with the picture, the Assign operation will fail (raising an exception). This is because the Assign method isn't a constructor; it is a method of an object, and if the object has not been created, you'll get a GPF error when you try to call one of its methods.

**FIGURE 24.3:**

The Clipboard page of the COPYBMP example tab set shows the current contents of the Clipboard if it is a bitmap. Notice that there is an image within the image, as in Figure 24.1.

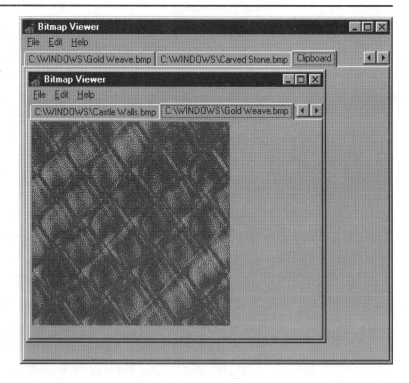

The Assign method doesn't make a copy of the actual bitmap. Its effect is to let two TBitmap objects refer to the same bitmap memory image and refer to the same bitmap handle.

Notice that the code of the example pastes the bitmap from the Clipboard each time you change the tab. The program, in fact, stores only one image at a time, and has no way to store the Clipboard bitmap. However, as soon as the Clipboard content changes, if the bitmap format is no longer available, the Clipboard tab is automatically deleted (as you can see in the listing above). If no more tabs are left, the Image component is hidden. An image can also be removed by using two menu commands: Delete and Cut. Delete simply removes the current tab. Cut removes the tab after making a copy of the bitmap to the Clipboard. In practice, the Cut1Click method does nothing besides calling the Copy1Click and the Delete1Click methods:

```
procedure TForm1.Cut1Click(Sender: TObject);
begin
  Copy1Click (self);
  Delete1Click (self);
end;
procedure TForm1.Delete1Click(Sender: TObject);
begin
  with TabControl1 do
  begin
    if TabIndex >= 0 then
      Tabs.Delete (TabIndex);
    if Tabs.Count = 0 then
      Image1.Visible := False;
  end;
end;
```

The Copy1Click method is responsible for copying the current image to the Clipboard:

```
procedure TForm1.Copy1Click(Sender: TObject);
begin
  Clipboard.Assign (Image1.Picture.Graphic);
end;
```

The rest of the code has to do with opening new files and adding them to the tabs as in the previous versions of the program, and enabling and disabling menu items in the File1Click and Edit1Click methods:

```
procedure TForm1.File1Click(Sender: TObject);
begin
  if TabControl1.Tabs.Count > 0 then
    Print1.Enabled := True
  else
    Print1.Enabled := False;
end;
```

```
procedure TForm1.Edit1Click(Sender: TObject);
begin
  if Clipboard.HasFormat (cf_Bitmap) then
    Paste1.Enabled := True
  else
    Paste1.Enabled := False;
  if TabControl1.Tabs.Count > 0 then
  begin
    Cut1.Enabled := True;
    Copy1.Enabled := True;
    Delete1.Enabled := True;
  end
  else
  begin
    Cut1.Enabled := False;
    Copy1.Enabled := False;
    Delete1.Enabled := False;
  end;
end;
```

# Copying Delphi Components to the Clipboard

Along with using text and bitmaps, you can copy any other kind of data to the Clipboard, including custom data. In fact, Delphi does this when it copies components. Actually, when Delphi copies a component to the Clipboard, it copies both the custom definition (binary code) and the textual description, which is readable with any text editor, as we saw in Chapter 2. The specific commands to copy or paste components to the Clipboard are the GetComponent and SetComponent methods of the TClipboard class. At first I thought these methods could be useful for programmers writing Delphi add-on tools, but they are really not very helpful, as we will see later.

We can use these methods to extend the CREF2 example presented in the previous chapter (the new example is CREF3). The form of the example remains the same, with the addition of a new pull-down menu with the Copy and Paste commands. When a user copies a component to the Clipboard, the program shows a list of components in a dialog box, as shown in Figure 24.4, so that the user can choose the component to paste.

The dialog box includes a default list box, a label, and two standard bitmap buttons inside a new form, named ListForm. All of the code to manipulate this form is in the Copy1Click of the main form:

```
procedure TForm1.Copy1Click(Sender: TObject);
var
  I, Index: Integer;
begin
  {fill the list of the dialog box}
  ListForm.Listbox1.Clear;
```

**FIGURE 24.4:**

The Paste command of the CREF3 example opens a dialog box with a list of available components.

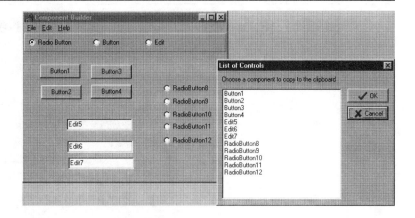

```
for I := 0 to ControlCount - 1 do
  if Controls[I].ClassName <> 'TPanel' then
    ListForm.Listbox1.Items.Add (Controls[I].Name);
if ListForm.ShowModal = mrOk then
begin
  Index := ListForm.Listbox1.ItemIndex + 1;
  {copy the component and change its name}
  Clipboard.SetComponent (Controls[Index]);
  Controls[Index].Name :=
    Controls[Index].Name + 'C';
  Controls[Index].Width :=
    Controls[Index].Width + 10;
end;
end;
```

The ItemIndex property of the list box—which identifies the position of the selected element—is used as a counter of the Controls array. The trick here is to add 1 to the ItemIndex to allow for the presence of the panel, which is always the first control of the array.

Notice that once the component is copied, its name is changed (by appending a C) to avoid any problem in case the copy is pasted back to the same form, as shown in Figure 24.5. This happens each time; therefore, if you copy the same component several times, many Cs are added to the name. An alternative would be to set the Name property to an empty string and give a meaningful value to the Caption property, but I preferred to adjust the names in both methods to try to give each component a unique identifier.

**FIGURE 24.5:**

When you copy a component with the CREF3 example, the name of the original object is changed. Pasted objects are indicated with a *P*.

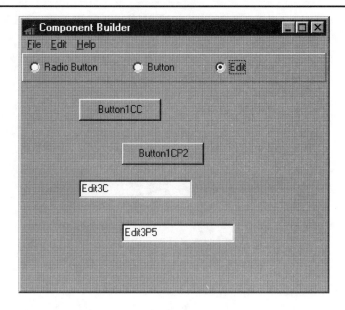

The Paste1Click method simply pastes the current component on the Clipboard, changing its position, name, and width (to accommodate the longer name):

```
procedure TForm1.Paste1Click(Sender: TObject);
var
  New: TComponent;
begin
  {retrieve the component, moving it slightly}
  New := Clipboard.GetComponent (self, self);
  (New as TControl).Left :=
    (New as TControl).Left + 50;
  (New as TControl).Top :=
    (New as TControl).Top + 50;
  Inc (Counter);
  New.Name := New.Name + 'P' + IntToStr (Counter);
  (New as TControl).Width :=
    (New as TControl).Width + 10;
end;
```

The most complex piece of code is in the Edit1Click method, which enables or disables the Copy and Paste commands. To determine whether to enable the Copy menu item, we check to see if the form contains any components other than the panel. To do so, we test whether ControlCount is greater than 1. To determine whether to enable the Paste menu item, we need to verify that there is a component in the Clipboard. By using the Clipboard Viewer, you can see the name of the Clipboard format defined by Delphi, then write the code accordingly. To check whether component format is on the Clipboard, we can call the `RegisterClipboardFormat` function of the Windows API, passing the name of the format as a parameter. The return value is a system-wide format code. This means that if two applications use the same format name, they end up with the same format code:

```
procedure TForm1.Edit1Click(Sender: TObject);
var
  Format: Cardinal;
begin
  Format := RegisterClipboardFormat ('Delphi Component');
  if Clipboard.HasFormat (Format) then
    Paste1.Enabled := True
  else
    Paste1.Enabled := False;
  if ControlCount > 1 then
    Copy1.Enabled := True
  else
    Copy1.Enabled := False;
end;
```

The CREF3 programs works, although it can be improved in a number of ways. For example, if you paste the same component twice, the older object is covered. However, the major problem I discovered is that the format used by this Clipboard method is not the same format used internally by Delphi's form editor. Besides the fact that it also copies the textual description of the component, the Delphi form editor uses a different format, *Delphi Components*. Unfortunately, this format is not compatible with the *Delphi Component* (without the *s*) format used by the SetComponent method of the TClipboard class. Therefore, this program is probably not a good example of how to develop add-on tools for Delphi.

## Copying Custom Data to the Clipboard

Our next example adds Clipboard support to a program with a generic, custom data type. To accomplish this, we can use the SetAsHandle and GetAsHandle method of the TClipboard class, which in turn call the `SetClipboardData` and `GetClipboardData` functions of the Windows API. These methods manipulate a handle for a Windows global memory block, allocated via the `GlobalAlloc` function. (For advanced uses of the Clipboard, we need to learn how to handle Windows memory blocks, something that will be useful for DDE, too.)

**NOTE**  In Delphi 1.0, the SetAsHandle method documentation did not include a parameter for the handle, which is obviously an error. The correct syntax for the SetAsHandle method is procedure `SetAsHandle (Format: Word; Value: THandle)`.

The goal of this example is to prepare a memory block with the information in a custom format. To accomplish this, we need to call some Windows API functions to allocate some memory (this is the easy part) and then fill the memory block with the data. The most common approach for this is to use a pointer to set or retrieve values from the memory area. So this is another first—the first example in the book that uses pointers (this *is* the advanced section, isn't it?).

This example is a new version of the CHART2 example from Chapter 23. This version, named CHART3, has a new Edit menu, with Copy and Paste commands and the usual three functions connected to Copy, Paste, and the selection of the Edit pull-down menu itself. Other than the changes in the menu, the form of the application is exactly the same as in the previous version. The most interesting part of the program is probably the Copy1Click method.

As I mentioned, you can allocate a memory block in Windows using the `GlobalAl-loc` function, which requires as a parameter a flag indicating the type of memory, and the size of the block. The return value is a handle to the memory block, which can be passed to the `GlobalLock` API function to return a pointer to the first location of the memory block:

```
HMem := GlobalAlloc (ghnd, 25 * Sizeof (Integer));
PInt := GlobalLock (HMem);
```

Note that in Delphi you skip these two steps and simply create an object. However, in this case, we actually need to bypass Delphi memory management, because we need a standard memory block for the Clipboard. When we pass this block to the Clipboard, it becomes the owner of the block, and we have no more rights to it.

Once we have a valid PInt pointer, we can iterate the memory block and fill it with values. This is generally done using pointers to integers; that is treating the block of memory as if it is an array of integers. In our case, we end up calling these two statements over and over (inside a loop):

```
PInt^ := Value;
Inc (PInt);
```

The first statement stores a value in the memory location referred to by the pointer, and the second moves the pointer to the next memory slot. When the memory block is ready, we can simply call the SetAsHandle method of the Clipboard object, as shown by the full code of the method:

```
procedure TForm1.Copy1Click(Sender: TObject);
var
  ClipForm, HMem: Cardinal;
  Text: String;
  PInt: ^Integer;
  I, J, Value: Integer;
begin
```

```
      {register a custom Clipboard format}
      ClipForm := RegisterClipboardFormat ('Chart_Data');

      {allocate a memory block and retrieve a pointer to it}
      HMem := GlobalAlloc (ghnd, 25 * Sizeof (Integer));
      PInt := GlobalLock (HMem);
      Text := '';

      {build the data, in both versions}
      for I := 1 to 5 do
        for J := 1 to 4 do
        begin
          {add the number for each cell of the grid}
          Value := StrToIntDef (
            Trim(StringGrid1.Cells [I, J]), 0);
          PInt^ := Value;
          Inc (PInt);
          AppendStr (Text,
            StringGrid1.Cells [I, J] + ';');
        end;

      {add the code of the combo box}
      Value := ComboBox1.ItemIndex;
      PInt^ := Value;
      AppendStr (Text, 'Style:' +
        IntToStr (ComboBox1.ItemIndex));

      {open the Clipboard, to copy multiple
      versions of the data}
      Clipboard.Open;
      Clipboard.SetAsHandle (ClipForm, HMem);
      Clipboard.AsText := Text;
      Clipboard.Close;
    end;
```

The code above has another feature. The program copies the current information to the Clipboard in two different formats: a custom format and a textual format (a string). To copy two formats of the data to the Clipboard, you need to hold its control for the time required for all operations, using the Open and Close methods of the TClipboard class. Without them, the second data format you copy to the Clipboard will hide the first one. Instead, using these methods, you can copy several versions of the data, as you can see in Figure 24.6 in the Clipboard Viewer window and in the Notepad where I've copied the data.

Notice also that I've declared a custom Clipboard format, Chart_Data, which is in the Edit1Click method, to see whether some proper information is available:

```
procedure TForm1.Edit1Click(Sender: TObject);
var
  ClipForm: Cardinal;
begin
  ClipForm := RegisterClipboardFormat ('Chart_Data');
```

```
    if Clipboard.HasFormat (ClipForm) then
      Paste1.Enabled := True
    else
      Paste1.Enabled := False;
end;
```

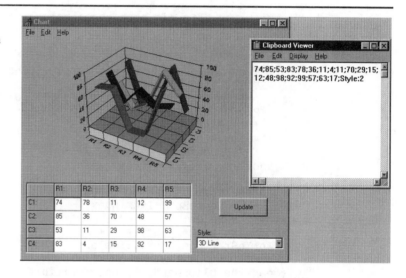

**FIGURE 24.6:**

The CHART3 data can be pasted to a text editor, because the program copies data to the Clipboard using two different formats.

The program could be improved to accept text data input (from the Clipboard), too. However, scanning the string to see if the data is in a valid format and extracting the proper information is somewhat too complex for this example. For this reason, only a Chart_Data memory block can be pasted back, as you can see in the code of the Paste1Click method:

```
procedure TForm1.Paste1Click(Sender: TObject);
var
  HMem, ClipForm: Cardinal;
  PInt: ^Integer;
  I, J, Value: Integer;
begin
  {get the memory block from the Clipboard}
  ClipForm := RegisterClipboardFormat ('Chart_Data');
  HMem := Clipboard.GetAsHandle (ClipForm);
  PInt := GlobalLock (HMem);

  {read each number}
  for I := 1 to 5 do
    for J := 1 to 4 do
    begin
      Value := PInt^;
      StringGrid1.Cells [I, J] := IntToStr(Value);
      Inc (PInt);
```

```
      end;

   {read the graph type}
   Value := PInt^;
   ComboBox1.ItemIndex := Value;

   {update everything}
   ComboBox1Change (self);
   UpdateButtonClick (self);
end;
```

The Paste command handler performs basically the reverse operation of the Copy handler. It iterates through the memory block, again using an integer pointer, and retrieves the data. More specifically, the program retrieves the handle to the memory block from the Clipboard, then uses the GlobalLock function to access it. Note that you should not attempt to store the memory handler the Clipboard passes to you. You need to read it immediately (as I've done in this example), or make a copy in a new memory block. In fact, the next time some information is copied to the Clipboard, the Clipboard will release the memory block.

# Dynamic Data Exchange (DDE): A Technical Overview

As stated at the beginning of this chapter, the Clipboard is basically user-driven. If you want to allow an application to move data to another application automatically, without a specific action by the user, the standard approach is to use Windows DDE. DDE allows two applications to establish a connection and use this connection to pass data. There are different actions DDE can perform, such as sending data on request or performing a continuous update of a changing data item.

The first version of DDE was primarily used as an add-on to MS Excel spreadsheets. It was a message-based protocol, which means that applications sent special Windows messages to each other to exchange information. The protocol was basically a set of message rules you could use to communicate with applications written by other programmers.

Things have changed over time. DDE has become an integral part of Windows. A new version, named DDEML (DDE Management Library), was added to Windows 3.1. DDEML has a sort of repository where information about the current DDE activities is stored. Instead of communicating directly with another application, DDEML works as an intermediary between the two connected programs, solving problems that arise. This makes DDE far more reliable.

## DDE Conversations

DDE is used to let two applications conduct in a *conversation*. One of the two applications involved in the conversation acts as the server, and the second as the client. The server is basically the information provider; the client is the application that controls the process. A DDE compatible application can act as a server to multiple clients, as a client for multiple servers, or as a client and a server at the same time. You can see a graphical example of some DDE conversations in Figure 24.7.

**FIGURE 24.7:**
Examples of DDE conversations.

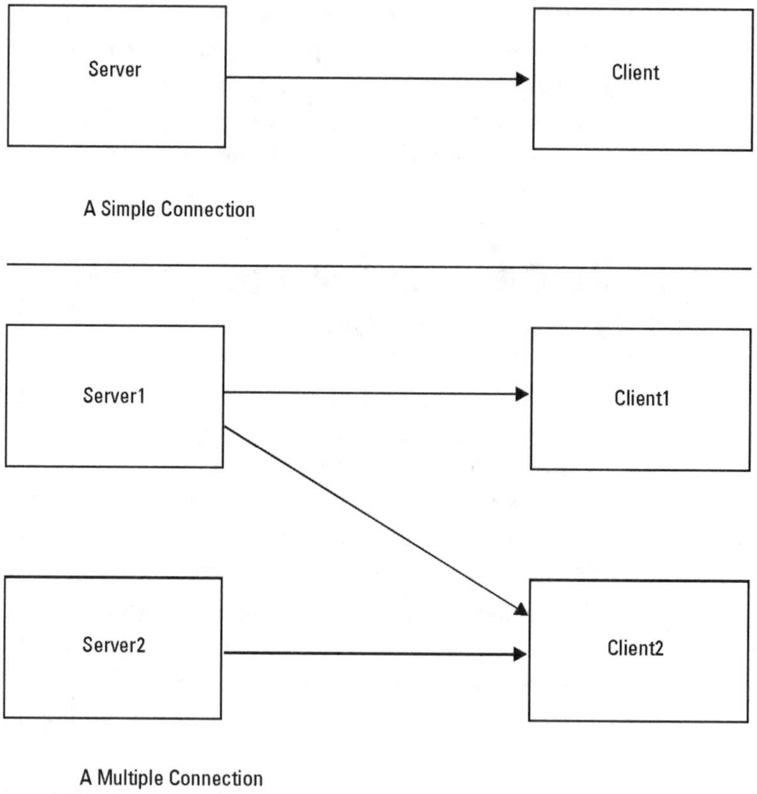

A Simple Connection

A Multiple Connection

## Roles of the Server and Client

What actual roles do the server and client play? What can happen when a DDE conversation is active between two applications? The role of the server is essentially to send data to the client upon request. The role of the client is to start the conversation, request the data from the server, send unsolicited data to the server (*poke*), or ask the server to execute commands (*execute*).

The central task is certainly sending data. Once a conversation is active, the client can ask for data from the server (*request*) or start an *advise loop*. Starting an advise loop means that the client can ask the server for notification of any change to a certain piece of data. The server will forward either a notification or a new copy of the data each time it changes. To determine which server you can connect to and the subject of the data exchange, DDE uses three elements:

- *Service* is basically the name of the DDE server application. It can be the name of the executable (without the extension), but it can also a different name determined by the server itself.

- *Topic* is the global theme of a conversation. It can be a data file, a window of the server, or anything else. A DDE conversation is established between a client and a server about a certain topic.

- *Item* is an identifier of a specific data element. It can be a field of a database, a cell of a spreadsheet, or a stock in an exchange market. Within a single conversation, a client and a server can exchange data about multiple items.

# DDE in Delphi

After this general introduction, it is time to return to Delphi and explore its DDE support. The System page of the Components palette contains four DDE-related components:

- DdeServerConv handles a description of the conversation (including the name of the topic) from the server side, supporting execute operations.

- DdeClientConv handles a conversation from the client side, specifies the current server and topic, and is required to start a conversation.

- DdeServerItem refers to a data item within a conversation for the server. This is the data that is usually sent to the client, or received from it in the case of a poke operation. The name of this component specifies the DDE item.

- DdeClientItem refers to data received from the server (or sent to it with the poke operation). It refers to the DDE item of the server, and relates to a conversation.

## A Simple Example of DDE

To build a DDE server and client, you can simply place some of these components in two different forms of two different applications, and write a few lines of code. Of course, the aim of DDE is to communicate with applications written by other programmers. However, since I don't know which DDE-enabled programs you have on your computer, several of our examples here will include both the server and client applications. I'll also show you examples of the use of different clients and servers.

Our first program for this example is probably the simplest possible server, which will soon be connected to the simplest possible client. Then the application will evolve into a more complex one.

## Building a Simple Server

The form of the first server (FIRSTSER) example has an edit box and a DdeServerItem component. This form doesn't include a DdeServerConv component, since this is required only to provide a custom name and to handle 'execute' commands. The service name will be the name of the application, without the .EXE extension, and the topic name will be the title of the form containing the DdeServerItem.

The code of this program is extremely simple. It copies the contents of the edit to the DdeServerItem's Text property each time the Edit component changes:

```
procedure TForm1.Edit1Change(Sender: TObject);
begin
  DdeServerItem1.Text := Edit1.Text;
end;
```

You can run this server application, but it will be far more interesting after we build the client application.

## Building a Simple Client

The first client application, FIRSTCLI, is just slightly more complex than the first server program. The form of this example has both a DdeClientConv and a DdeClientItem component, plus an edit box. The DdeClientItem1 component is connected to the conversation component (DdeClientConv1), using the DdeConv property, but there is no design-time connection from DdeClientConv1 to the server. The connection is initialized when the form is created:

```
procedure TForm1.FormCreate(Sender: TObject);
begin
  if DdeClientConv1.SetLink ('firstser', 'First Server') then
  begin
    ShowMessage ('Connected');
    DdeClientItem1.DdeItem := 'DdeServerItem1';
  end
  else
    ShowMessage ('Error');
end;
```

**WARNING**  In Delphi 1, this same code could also be executed in response to the OnClick event of a button. With Delphi 2, this code works only in the creation method, although it is not clear why. Borland added some undocumented functions, and I hope they'll clarify how to use them as soon as possible.

The program calls the SetLink method, passing as parameters the service (the name of the server) and the topic (the title of the form). If the connection is successful, besides showing a message, the application connects the DdeItem property of the client item to the server item. When the connection is set and the link is active, the server application starts sending data to the client each time the data on the server changes. The client application can simply copy the data it receives to its own edit box:

```
procedure TForm1.DdeClientItem1Change(Sender: TObject);
begin
  Edit1.Text := DdeClientItem1.Text;
end;
```

When the connection and the link are established (when both the client and server programs are running), everything the user types in the server edit box is automatically copied to the client edit box. Figure 24.8 shows an example of a server edit box change and the corresponding change in the client edit box. (Of course, you should run both of these programs yourself to fully appreciate their capabilities.)

**FIGURE 24.8:**
When the connection and the link are established, everything you type in the server edit box is copied to the client edit box.

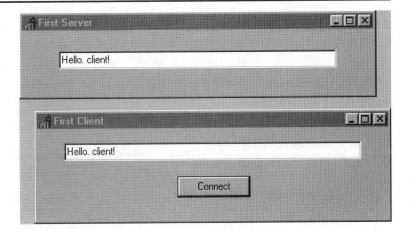

Notice that the DDE link is between the DdeServerItem component of the server application and the DdeClientItem component of the client application. Each time the Text property of the server item changes, this change is automatically reflected in the Text property of the client item. However, since we have established a link between the text of the two Text properties of the DDE items and the corresponding properties of the two Edit components, in effect, we have connected the two edit boxes via DDE.

> **NOTE**
>
> What we have built in these DDE applications in Delphi is a *DDE advise loop* (also known as a *hot link*) using the DDEML library. Writing the same code in C takes a while, because DDEML is not exactly the simplest Windows API. Delphi's support for advise loops makes this program even simpler than a DDE conversation based on a request by the client, which is based on the RequestData method of the DdeClientConv component.

## Design-Time DDE Connections

In this DDE example, we made the connection at run-time. However, in Delphi it is also possible to make DDE connections at design-time. To test this, run the server application, open the client project, select the DdeClientConv1 component, and open the property editor of the DdeService or DdeTopic property. In the dialog box that follows, enter the required information, as shown in the example in Figure 24.9.

Now you can select the client item, select the proper conversation, and enter the name of the DdeItem property, and the connection is established. Make a change in the server, and the new text appears in the Object Inspector, as you can see in Figure 24.10.

**FIGURE 24.9:**

The property editor of the DdeService and DdeTopic properties of the DdeClientConv component.

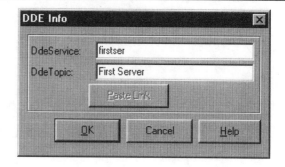

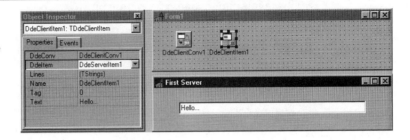

**FIGURE 24.10:**
If the server is running (see the lower-right corner) when you set the connection and the link, the Text property of the client item is automatically updated with the server text.

If you set the connection and the link at design-time, you can actually remove the Connect button and its code. Simply running the client program sets up the DDE connection, and the application will work immediately (as long as the server is running). In general, I prefer the run-time connection approach, which doesn't require the user to start the two applications in a fixed order.

This example could be extended to support poke operations and macro execution, direct requests for data from the client, and provide some information about the current links. However, the result of such efforts would be similar to the DDE examples available in Delphi itself, so I decided to work in a different direction.

# Copying and Pasting DDE Links

Our next step will be to add the DDE version of Copy and Paste support to the DDE program, by changing it a bit and enabling its interaction with other third-party applications.

## Copying Link Data to the Clipboard

As when we started, the first step in building a new version of the DDE example is to build a server. The form of the new paste server program (PASTESER) has three edit boxes, three DdeServerItem components, and three buttons. This version also uses a DdeServerConv component. The code of this program is still quite simple, although a bit more repetitive. When the form is first created at run-time, the text of the edit boxes is copied to the corresponding server items:

```
procedure TForm1.FormCreate(Sender: TObject);
begin
  DdeServerItem1.Text := Edit1.Text;
  DdeServerItem2.Text := Edit2.Text;
  DdeServerItem3.Text := Edit3.Text;
end;
```

This text is copied again each time one of the edit boxes changes. Here is one of the three methods:

```
procedure TForm1.Edit2Change(Sender: TObject);
begin
  DdeServerItem2.Text := Edit2.Text;
end;
```

The new code is in the OnClick handlers of the three buttons. When the user clicks on a button, the text in the edit box and the link are both copied to the Clipboard:

```
procedure TForm1.CopyButton1Click(Sender: TObject);
begin
  Clipboard.Open;
  Clipboard.AsText := DdeServerItem1.Text;
  DdeServerItem1.CopyToClipboard;
  Clipboard.Close;
end;
```

The copy operation of the server item copies information about the link. This information is not the actual data, the text. If you make only the link, many third-party applications won't recognize this data, because you don't specify anything about the format. For this reason, both copies are needed.

With this code, you can copy the text of one of the edit boxes from this program and paste it into almost any DDE client. For example, in Microsoft Word for Windows you can either Paste or Paste Link this data. Simply run the PASTESER program, copy one of the messages, open a Word document, and choose Edit ➤ Paste Special. In the Paste Special dialog box, select the Paste Link radio button and click on OK to establish a connection.

Now the text is inserted into your Word document, but when you move to the server and change the text, it will change in the Word document as well. This should not surprise you, since this is equivalent to our previous example. You should be able to obtain this same effect with many other Windows applications, using menu commands named similarly to Paste Special or Paste Link.

You can see an example of the effect I can obtain in Word in Figure 24.11. I've pasted the contents of each of the server's three edit boxes, making a connection with the second line, but I've also pasted them without a connection (using the Paste command in the first and third cases). Only the copy that has an active link changes while I type in the server edit boxes. Note that if you close the server, the link is temporarily broken, but you can later restore it. Usually, DDE client applications have a specific Links command in the Edit menu to support restoring a broken link.

FIGURE 24.11:
Word links the text changes as I type in the server edit boxes—not a bad result for four lines of Delphi code.

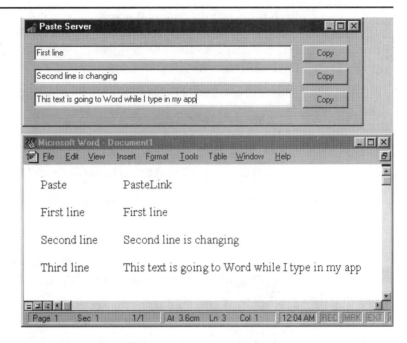

# DDE with Timers and Graphics

Most of the DDE examples in Delphi use text as a data-exchange element. This is because Delphi has specific support for text items. It is possible to use Delphi DDE support and call some functions of the DDEML API, to overcome this limit. However, it is generally easier to convert data to and from text and use DDE support than to try to use Delphi undocumented features and direct API calls.

To test Delphi's DDE capabilities beyond handling text items, I've built an example that involves graphics, although the data exchange passes a string. This example is different from the previous ones for two reasons. First, the server data is automatically updated, using a timer. Second, the client shows a graphical version of the data.

## The Automatic Server

The server, named DATASERV, has a simple form with a read-only Memo component, a timer, a Copy button, and a DdeServerItem component. When the form is created, it starts the random number generation and calls the Randomize function:

```
procedure TForm1.FormCreate(Sender: TObject);
begin
  Randomize;
end;
```

Each time the timer interval elapses, the values of the five lines of the memo are changed by adding a random value between –10 and 10 (adding or subtracting a number from 1 to 10). At the end of the handler, the text of the memo is copied to the DdeServerItem:

```
procedure TForm1.Timer1Timer(Sender: TObject);
var
  I, Value: Integer;
begin
  for I := 0 to 4 do
  begin
    Value := StrToIntDef (Memo1.Lines [I], 50);
    Value := Value + Random (21) - 10;
    Memo1.Lines [I] := IntToStr (Value);
  end;
  DdeServerItem1.Lines := Memo1.Lines;
end;
```

The other method we'll write is a copy-to-Clipboard operation you should already be familiar with. Besides copying the data, we also copy the DDE link:

```
procedure TForm1.CopyButtonClick(Sender: TObject);
begin
  Clipboard.Open;
  Clipboard.AsText := Memo1.Text;
  DdeServerItem1.CopyToClipboard;
  Clipboard.Close;
end;
```

When we copy from this server and paste link the result in any application, the data will change automatically, without any user assistance. You can see an example using Microsoft Word in Figure 24.12.

**FIGURE 24.12:**

You can copy the DATASERV data to WinWord, and it will automatically change at each timer interval.

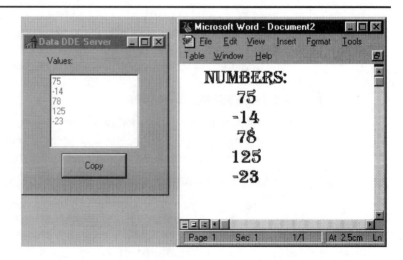

# A Graphical DDE Client

Showing the numbers that change automatically in a third-party application is certainly interesting, but this is just text. The client application that works with this server will show the data graphically. The form of the VIEWDATA client contains just the two typical DDE client conversations and DDE client item components, without any special property set. Since the form is so bare, you might expect the code to be complex, and it really is.

When the form is created, the DDE connection is established:

```
procedure TForm1.FormCreate(Sender: TObject);
begin
  if DdeClientConv1.SetLink ('dataserv', 'Data DDE Server') then
    DdeClientItem1.DdeItem := 'DdeServerItem1'
  else
    ShowMessage ('Start the server before the client');
end;
```

Instead of simply showing a message, you might try to actually run the server, using the WinExec API. However, this can get complicated if it doesn't reside in the same directory or in one of the directories of the system path.

Each time the DDE item data changes, the new values are extracted from the string and copied to an array of integers, defined as a private data member of the TForm1 class:

```
Values: array [0..4] of Integer;
```

At first, I thought that the lines of the server item were copied to the lines of the client item, so that this code simply needed to extract and convert each string. But the program ended up with a single string containing all of the numbers. After some trials, I found my error. The FormatChars property of the DdeClientConv component should be set to True, to prevent it from skipping the new-line characters. When you have set this property, simply write the following code:

```
procedure TForm1.DdeClientItem1Change(Sender: TObject);
var
  I: Integer;
begin
  {extract the numbers}
  for I := 0 to 4 do
    if I < DdeClientItem1.Lines.Count then
      Values [I] := StrToIntDef (DdeClientItem1.Lines[I], 50);
  Invalidate;
end;
```

The if statement might seem redundant, but it is not. This method is called at startup, when the values are still not there.

Now for the core code. The last line of the OnChange event handler of the DdeClientItem component, above, calls Invalidate to repaint the form. The FormPaint method is quite complex. It draws five vertical bars, in the range −100 to 200, equally spaced in the form. At startup, the program computes some internal values. The width of each bar, DX, is computed by dividing the width of the client area of the form by 11, because there are five bars and six empty spaces around them. The DY value serves as a reference value of one hundred (of the data), and to draw the reference line. You can see the effect, with some hints, in the graph shown in Figure 24.13.

**FIGURE 24.13:**

The Y axis of the VIEWDATA output.

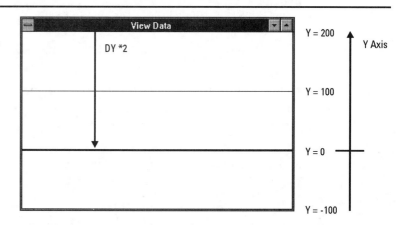

For each value of the array, the program draws a rectangle, at a fixed horizontal position, which depends on its array index. The vertical position range starts at the origin (DY*2) and reaches the value of the element, sized to the proper scale. If the number becomes negative, there is no problem, since the parameters of the Rectangle method are considered as the sides of the rectangle. Here is the code:

```
procedure TForm1.FormPaint(Sender: TObject);
var
  I, DX, DY: Integer;
  Scale: Real;
begin
  {DX is the width of each band}
  DX := ClientWidth div 11;
  {DY is the height corresponding to a value of 100}
  DY := ClientHeight div 3;
  Scale := DY / 100;

  {draw axis, at Y=0}
  Canvas.Pen.Width := 3;
  Canvas.MoveTo (0, DY * 2);
  Canvas.LineTo (ClientWidth, DY * 2);
```

```
{draw 100 mark}
Canvas.Pen.Width := 1;
Canvas.MoveTo (O, DY);
Canvas.LineTo (ClientWidth, DY);

for I := 0 to 4 do
begin
  {green for positive values,
  red for negative values}
  if Values [I] > O then
    Canvas.Brush.Color := clGreen
  else
    Canvas.Brush.Color := clRed;
  {draw the bar}
  Canvas.Rectangle (DX * (2 * I + 1),
    DY * 2 - Round (Values [I] * Scale),
    DX * (2 * I + 2),
    DY * 2);
  end;
end;
```

You can see the result of this painting code in Figure 24.14, where two copies of the program are running to show that the image is automatically scaled to the form size.

**FIGURE 24.14:**

Two examples of the output of the VIEWDATA program.

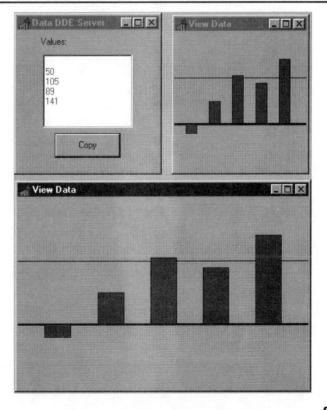

The bars of the VIEWDATA example change automatically over the time, without any user assistance, both on the client program and on the server application.

# Summary

In this chapter, we have seen how you can add Clipboard and DDE support to existing or new Delphi programs, and we have seen the similarities and differences between the two features. The use of the Clipboard is very common in Windows applications, and those you write should be no exception. Fortunately, adding Clipboard support is generally quite simple (even when you write Windows programs using the API). In contrast, DDE support can be a significant enhancement to your program. Letting a user copy and paste links, and not only data, between two programs you have written is certainly interesting. Even better, with DDE links, users of your programs can exchange data with other popular Windows applications.

DDE support in Delphi is simple, particularly if you compare it with the code behind the scenes. The only drawback is that it is not very well documented, and that not all of the DDE features are easily accessible. Delphi's support, however, is good enough for most programmers. Now it is time to look to the third Windows data-exchange technique, OLE, which is the subject of the next chapter.

# CHAPTER

**TWENTY-FIVE**

# The Power of OLE

- A simple OLE container

- Embedding and linking objects

- In-place editing and the user-interface

- Loading and saving objects to files

- OLE Automation: Clients and Servers

- Making OLE applications interact

**25**

**F**or several technical reasons, OLE can be considered an extension of the other data-exchange techniques we discussed in the previous chapter, such as the Clipboard and DDE. OLE was developed later, it used DDE connections behind the scenes in the first version, and it is often activated using Copy and Paste menu commands. As with DDE, OLE connections can originate from the Clipboard.

OLE merits an entire chapter because it comes in several flavors, involves client and server applications, exists in two main versions, offers features similar to DDE execute (indicated as OLE automation), and is one of the key elements of Microsoft's software and operating system strategy.

Although this chapter begins with a short introduction to OLE and its terminology, you won't find details about the many aspects of OLE—there are whole books devoted to that topic. I assume that you have some experience as a user of OLE-enabled applications. Our focus here is on Delphi OLE support, which is available in the form of OLE *container* applications, OLE Automation Servers, OLE Automation clients, and OLE Control containers (already discussed in Chapter 16). With Delphi, you can call any API function, so you can therefore create any Windows application, including OLE servers and OLE Controls. However, to build a server or control, you need to work with low-level OLE API calls, without any help from the Delphi environment.

In the first part of this chapter, I'll discuss the OLE technology in its original incarnation (OLE objects and documents), and in the second part I'll focus on OLE Automation in its two versions.

# What Is an OLE Object?

OLE objects have two different capabilities: *embedding* and *linking*. One way to think of object embedding is as a smart version of the copy and paste operations you can make with the Clipboard. The key difference is that when you copy an OLE object from a server application and paste it into a container application, you can automatically activate the server application from within the container to edit the data. Of course, there is much more to it than this. For example, you can create new OLE objects in an application, you can create a server that doesn't run directly (some OLE servers are built-in DLLs, so they cannot be executed at all), and you can benefit from the compound document model (saving to disk an OLE object inside another OLE object).

A good way to think of object linking is as an advanced version of DDE advise loops. You generally activate object linking by using the Clipboard and making a paste-link operation. However, the server application doesn't need to be running when you begin to change its data. (In fact, it doesn't need to be running explicitly at all.) From the OLE container application, you can call functions in the server application and work on the original data.

As with embedding, there is much more to it than this. Object linking has a number of advanced features you won't find in DDE, and it is generally quite easy for users to work with linked objects.

When you have a linked object, if you open the server to edit the object, it always appears in a separate window. However, when you have an embedded object from an OLE 2.0 server, the container can support visual (or *in-place*) editing, which means that you can modify the object in context, inside the container's main window. The server and container application windows, their menus, and their toolbars are merged automatically, allowing the user to work within a single window on a number of different object types—and therefore with a number of different OLE servers—without leaving the window of the container application.

Another key difference between embedding and linking is that the data of an embedded object is stored and managed by the container application. The container saves the embedded object in its own files. In contrast, a linked object physically resides in a separate file, which is handled by the server exclusively, even if the link refers only to a small portion of the file.

In both cases, the container application doesn't have to know how to handle the object and its data—not even how to display it—without the help of the server. Accordingly, the server application has a lot of work to do, even when you are not editing the data. Container applications often make a copy of the image of an OLE object and use the bitmap to represent the data, which speeds up some operations with the object itself. The drawback of this approach is that many commercial OLE applications end up with bloated files (because two copies of the same data are saved). If you consider this problem along with the relative slowness of OLE and the amount of work necessary to develop OLE servers, you can understand why the use of this powerful approach is still somewhat limited.

## The Flavors of OLE

OLE comes in several flavors, and there are currently Windows applications using compatible but different versions of OLE. The first version, included in Windows 3.1, has been replaced by version 2.0, which uses 32-bit code but is also compatible with 16-bit Windows. OLE 2 has several important features:

- *in-place* or visual editing
- better support for object storage

- support for automation
- support for the development of OLE controls

There are also two kinds of OLE servers:

- Full servers are stand-alone applications, which have file support and are available for any possible use of OLE.
- Mini servers are servers that reside in DLLs, which cannot be executed by themselves and don't provide their own storage (they use the storage of the host application). Mini servers support only embedding, not linking.

On the other side, containers can support OLE in varying degrees. Without considering the different versions, there are several ways you can place an object in a container:

- You can insert a new object, using a specific menu command to create an embedded object.
- You can paste an object from the Clipboard, creating a new embedded object.
- You can paste-link an object from the Clipboard, creating a new linked object.
- You can create a new object from a file generated by a server. This can result in either an embedded object or a linked object.
- You can drag an object from a server to a container, if the two applications support OLE drag-and-drop.
- You can create an object inside another object, if the server application can also act as a container.

Once the object is placed inside the container, you can then perform operations on it, using the server's available *verbs*, or actions. Usually the *edit verb* is the default action—the action performed when you double-click on the object. For other objects, *play* is defined as the default action. You can typically see the list of actions supported by the current container object when it is not active (when you are not editing it) by selecting the Object menu item, which is generally in the Edit pull-down menu. The Object menu item should have a submenu that lists the available verbs for the current object. Recent applications tend to use the local menu of the OLE object itself to select its verbs and other commands, instead of the Edit ➤ Object menu item.

## OLE behind the Scenes

We object-oriented programmers (Delphi programmers are legitimately included in this group) think in terms of variables corresponding to specific data types. Each data type provides methods we can apply to the objects of that type. Objects have unique values for properties and data, but we manipulate the object by using its public interface, and often know nothing about the details of the implementation.

In OLE, objects are similar to the objects in object-oriented languages. We know very little about their implementation (that is, the code of the server application), and can use only their public interface. Since it is based on the C language, this public interface is basically an array of function pointers—*procedural types* in Object Pascal terms. Most of these functions are internal to OLE, and you won't call or use them directly. They are used to ask the server to draw an object, print it, activate its menus, determine the toolbar arrangement, and so on. Some of the functions correspond to the verbs.

When implemented in Object Pascal, an OLE object contains data and not code. As we mentioned earlier, in an OOP language, the methods of the object that are available are determined using the object's type information. In OLE, every object has a connection (through a unique ID) to a description of the server, which is stored in a central repository, the registration database or registry. As we have already seen in Chapter 19, this database can be browsed using the Windows REGEDIT application or accessed by your applications using Delphi TRegistry class.

The Registration Editor has, among many other things, a display that tells you where the server resides on the computer, and it can activate this application or library by running it or by activating it within the context of the current application. In any case, to work on the object in the container, the server application must be loaded in memory. Once this has happened, the container and the server start to communicate and exchange data. For this purpose, the two applications access some OLE DLLs, but these DLLs keep in contact using the DDEML (the DDE Management Library, mentioned in the previous chapter).

That's enough for a minimal overview of technical OLE details. Now we will move on to the real topic of this chapter: writing OLE-enabled applications in Delphi.

# OLE Support in Delphi

OLE container support in Delphi comes through the TOleContainer component. This component is defined in the OleCtnrs unit. Here, we will look at an OLE example built step-by-step, which creates a final effect similar to the OLE examples that come with Delphi.

**NEW**

Notice that OLE container support in Delphi 2 is quite different from its Delphi 1 counterpart. The name of the component remained the same, but the unit defining it has changed (it was ToCtrl), the OLE helper functions have disappeared (replaced by new methods of the TOleContainer class), and the creation of new OLE objects is completely different. Overall, the new Delphi 2 approach is simpler, and tends to work better.

## Building the Minimum OLE Container

To create a simple OLE container application in Delphi, place an OLE container component in a form. Then select the component and click the right mouse button to activate its local menu, which will have an Insert Object command. When you select this command, Delphi displays the standard OLE Insert Object dialog box. This dialog box allows you to choose from one of the registered server applications, as shown in Figure 25.1. The list of servers that appears in this dialog box depends on the OLE applications and OLE Controls installed on your system and stored in the registration database. In fact, you can choose to insert an OLE server object or an OCX.

The OLE object inserted in the container will have several more menu items added to the local menu of the form (when the Delphi OLE control container component is selected). The new menu items include commands to change the properties of the OLE object, insert another one, copy the existing object, or remove it. The list also includes the verbs of the object (such as Edit, Open, or Play).

**FIGURE 25.1:**
The standard OLE Insert Object dialog box allows you to insert an OLE object from one of the servers installed on your system.

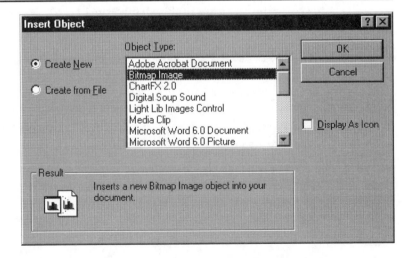

Once you have inserted an OLE object in the container, the corresponding server will launch to let you edit the new object. As soon as you close the server application, Delphi updates the object in the container and shows it at design-time in the form of the Delphi application you are developing, as shown in Figure 25.2.

**FIGURE 25.2:**

The Paint OLE object inside the form of the OLECONT1 example at design-time.

I haven't made any other relevant changes to this program, named OLECONT1, besides aligning the OLE container to the client area and setting its SizeMode to smCenter (to show the OLE object in the center of the container component). If you look at the textual description of this form (using the View as Text command of the local menu of the form), you'll notice a Data property, which contains the actual data of the OLE object.

This means that the OLE object is *embedded* (its data is saved in the server) and that OLE data can be stored together with the other form properties and data. As we've just seen, the data of an embedded OLE object is actually stored inside the form, which is then stored in the executable file of the program. This can increase the size of the program a lot, depending on the type of server you're using and the amount of data. Another problem is that you can run this program only on a computer that has the required server installed. Otherwise, you'll get a run-time error when the OLE container tries to launch the server application to edit the object.

**NOTE**
This is true for the sample program: you can run OLECONT1 only if the Microsoft Paint server is installed on your computer. (This server is included in the default Windows 95 installation.)

When you run the OLECONT1 example, you can simply double-click on the OLE container component, and the server editing controls will show up inside the window of your application, as shown in Figure 25.3. Object editing becomes active when you double-click on the object because of the value of the AutoActivate property, which is aaDoubleClick by default. Other alternatives are aaGetFocus and aaManual. When the value is aaManual, you can use the Active property to start the server via code; when the value is aaGetFocus, the server is activated as soon as you move the input focus on the object (for example, by clicking on it).

> **NOTE**  Notice that you cannot always use the Active property to end editing; if the server has its own window, the user generally closes it.

**FIGURE 25.3:**
The OLECONT1 example at run-time, with visual editing in action.

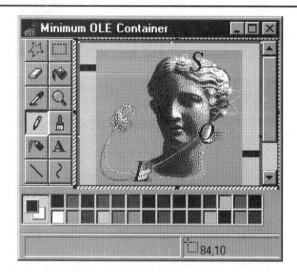

To improve visual editing by importing the menus from the server application, you can add a menu bar to the form, as we'll do in the next section.

## The Minimal Menu of an OLE Container

To build a better version of the sample OLE container application, OLECONT2, I've created a new form, which includes an OLE container component, a menu, and a panel with a combo box. In this version, the container does not contain an OLE object specified at design-time. A new OLE object will be created when you select File ➤ New, one of the few menu items that are enabled.

An important feature of an OLE container application that provides menus and supports in-place editing is *menu merging*. When the OLE object is activated in-place, some of the pull-down menus of the server application's menu bar are added to the menu bar of the container application. At the same time, some of the corresponding pull-down menus of the container application will disappear.

OLE menu merging is handled almost automatically by Delphi. You need only to set the proper indexes for the menu items of the container, using the GroupIndex property. Basically, the menu items with an odd index are replaced by the corresponding elements of the active OLE object.

More specifically, the File (0) and Window (4) pull-down menus belong to the container application. The Edit (1), View (3), and Help (5) pull-down menus (or the groups of pull-down menus with those indexes) are those of the OLE server. A sixth group, named Object and indicated with the index 2, can be used by the container to display another pull-down menu between the Edit and View groups, even when the OLE object is active.

In our example, the GroupIndex properties are 0 for File, 1 for Edit, and 5 for Help. Figure 25.4 shows an example of menu merging, using a Paint OLE object.

The only menu item we need to code is the New command, which we'll use to insert a new OLE object in the container. In Delphi 1, the code of this method was based on the InsertOleObjectDlg global function. In Delphi 2, you can instead call the InsertObjectDialog method of the TOleContainer class to display the standard Insert OLE Object dialog box (which is exactly the same dialog box we already saw in Figure 25.1).

**FIGURE 25.4:**

The menu merging of an active OLE object (only the File menu is that of the container application).

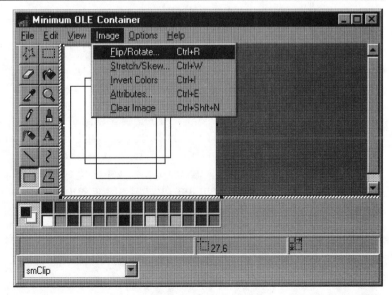

The InsertObjectDialog method shows the dialog box, takes care of deleting the resulting OLE object, and provides the new object initialization. However, it doesn't automatically activate the OLE object. For this reason, it is common to write the following code to activate the object:

```
procedure TForm1.New1Click(Sender: TObject);
begin
  if OleContainer1.InsertObjectDialog then
    OleContainer1.DoVerb (
      OleContainer1.PrimaryVerb);
end;
```

Once a new object has been created, you can execute its primary verb using the DoVerb method. Besides this code, the program also has a combo box inside a panel. You can use this combo box to set the SizeMode property of the OLE object component to one of the possible values of the TSizeMode enumeration (which include viewing the component as is, centering it in the container, resizing it, or stretching it). The selection is quite simple because I've added five elements in the combo box in the same order they appear in the enumeration. Here is the textual definition of the component:

```
object ComboBox1: TComboBox
  Style = csDropDownList
  Items.Strings = (
    'smClip'
    'smCenter'
    'smScale'
    'smStretch'
    'smAutoSize')
  OnChange = ComboBox1Change
end
```

And here is the code of the OnClick event handler:

```
procedure TForm1.ComboBox1Change(Sender: TObject);
begin
  OleContainer1.SizeMode := TSizeMode (
    ComboBox1.ItemIndex);
end;
```

This combo box also provides a way to deactivate the OLE container component, by selecting something else. Just click on the combo box and on the container to toggle the focus between the two components. To keep this panel visible while in-place editing is occurring, you should set its Locked property to True. This allows the panel to remain present in the application and not be replaced by a toolbar of the server, as we will see in the next version of the example.

# Visual Editing and Toolbars

If you use the OLECONT2 example to activate an OLE object in-place (which may or may not be possible, depending on the kind of server you are using), and the server has toolbars, the result can be awkward, although the new Delphi 2 OLE container component has way fewer problems than the older Delphi 1 component. To improve the user interface, we can add a toolbar to the example. If you add a panel to the form, align it to the top, and place some buttons on it, this new toolbar will be replaced with that of the active OLE server.

> To make all the automatic resizing operations work more smoothly, you should place the OLE container component in a panel component and align both of them to the client area of the form.

In the OLECONT3 example, I've added some speed buttons to the toolbar of the form, as you can see near the top of Figure 25.5. When in-place editing launches a server application that displays a toolbar, that server's toolbar replaces the container's toolbar, as you can see in the lower part of Figure 25.5.

**FIGURE 25.5:**

The toolbar of the OLECONT3 example (top), and the toolbar of the server, which replaces it (bottom).

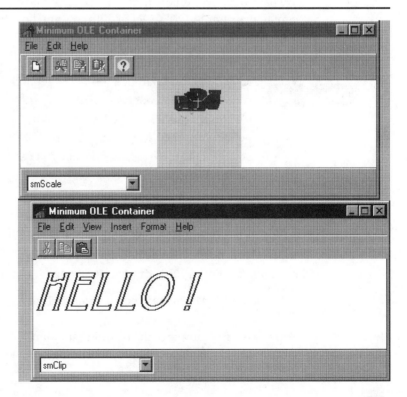

# The OLE Standard Dialog Boxes

In our previous examples, we have been able to create new OLE objects at run-time using the InsertObjectDialog method. However, there are other ways to create OLE objects. One way is to use a similar function, PasteSpecialDialog. Another way to create an OLE object is by dragging, but we won't explore this technique in the book. Creating new OLE objects is not as simple as the Delphi interface might lead you to believe, but for Delphi programmers, there are no special problems.

In the fourth version of our example, named OLECONT4, I've added Paste Special support and some other Clipboard support to the OLE container. Another addition to the example is its handling of OLE links. This is another operation available via a standard dialog box, wrapped in a Delphi function.

There are several standard dialog boxes in OLE. Some of them are directly available in Delphi using the special methods:

- InsertObjectDialog
- ObjectPropertiesDialog
- PasteSpecialDialog

We have already seen the first of these dialog boxes. In the new version of the OLE container example, OLECONT4, I'll show you how to use the other two, while adding full Clipboard support to the application.

**TIP**  Notice, by the way, that information about the methods of the OLE container component is not easily accessible from the Help file: you have to choose TOleContainer, then TOleContainer Methods in the detail information. This part of the Help file is in fact a last minute addition, and it is not fully indexed. You can reach it from the *VCL Additions* help topic.

The OLECONT4 example uses essentially the same form as the previous version, with a new Object Properties item in the Edit pull-down menu. Here is the code triggered by this menu item:

```
procedure TForm1.Object1Click(Sender: TObject);
begin
  OleContainer1.ObjectPropertiesDialog;
end;
```

You can see an example of the resulting standard OLE dialog box in Figure 25.6. Obviously, this dialog box changes depending on the nature of the active OLE object in the container.

**FIGURE 25.6:**

The standard OLE properties dialog box, available in the OLECONT4 example.

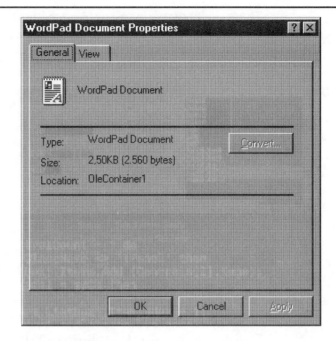

In addition, the program now handles the Clipboard, using cut, copy, paste, and paste special operations. Here is the code for these methods (which are used to handle both menu commands and toolbar buttons):

```
procedure TForm1.Paste1Click(Sender: TObject);
begin
  OleContainer1.Paste;
  UpdateUI;
end;

procedure TForm1.PasteSpecial1Click(Sender: TObject);
begin
  OleContainer1.PasteSpecialDialog;
  UpdateUI;
end;

procedure TForm1.Copy1Click(Sender: TObject);
begin
  OleContainer1.Copy;
  UpdateUI;
end;

procedure TForm1.Cut1Click(Sender: TObject);
begin
  OleContainer1.Copy;
  OleContainer1.Destroy;
  UpdateUI;
end;
```

These methods perform simple operations, complementing PasteSpecial1Click, which shows another standard OLE dialog box, as you can see in Figure 25.7.

**FIGURE 25.7:**

The standard OLE Paste Special dialog box.

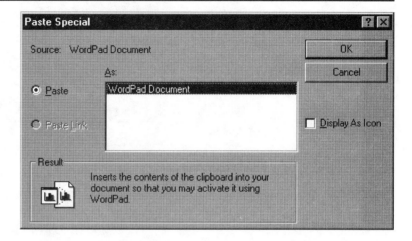

Each of these handlers (and also the Edit1Click method that responds to the selection of the Edit pull-down menu) calls an UpdateUI procedure I've added to the form:

```
procedure TForm1.UpdateUI;
begin
  Cut1.Enabled := OleContainer1.State <> osEmpty;
  Copy1.Enabled := OleContainer1.State <> osEmpty;
  Object1.Enabled := OleContainer1.State <> osEmpty;
  Paste1.Enabled := OleContainer1.CanPaste;
  PasteSpecial1.Enabled := OleContainer1.CanPaste;
  PasteSpeedButton.Enabled := Paste1.Enabled;
  CutSpeedButton.Enabled := Cut1.Enabled;
  CopySpeedButton.Enabled := Copy1.Enabled;
end;
```

This private method simply enables or disables the menu items and the toolbar buttons depending on the State property and the CanPaste method of the OLE container object.

## Loading and Saving Objects in Files

The last enhancement we'll make in the series of OLE container examples involves adding support for files. This is actually one of the simplest additions we can make, because the OLE container component already provides file support.

The form of the new example, OLECONT5, has two standard dialog components (OpenDialog1 and SaveDialog1), and its source code adds just a few more lines:

```
procedure TForm1.Open1Click(Sender: TObject);
begin
  if OpenDialog1.Execute then
    OleContainer1.LoadFromFile (
      OpenDialog1.FileName);
  UpdateUI;
end;

procedure TForm1.SaveAs1Click(Sender: TObject);
begin
  if SaveDialog1.Execute then
    OleContainer1.SaveToFile (
      SaveDialog1.FileName);
end;
```

Again, the code calls two methods of the TOleContainer class. Notice that there is another method, CreateObjectFromFile, which has a completely different meaning from the LoadFromFile method. (LoadFromFile is simply used to re-load files saved with the SaveToFile method.) In this example, I've given these files the extension .DOL (for Demo OLe files).

In contrast, CreateObjectFromFile is used to insert new OLE objects into the container, loading their data from a file. In this case, the file is a file generated by the server, and its extension is used to determine the server type.

That's a lot of OLE capabilities, although it still isn't a complete sample of all the available capabilities. For example, the program doesn't support creating objects from files (which I've just mentioned) or OLE object drag-and-drop.

# Multiple OLE Containers

All of the previous examples we've created could display only one OLE object at a time, because we created one permanent OLE container component in each example. Our next example, named MULTIOLE, shows how to manipulate multiple OLE container components in the same form.

**NOTE**   At first, I thought of using the MDI approach to build this example, but then I realized that there is already an example of this kind in the Delphi package. That is why I decided to write a different one, capable of displaying multiple OLE objects in a single form. You can compare the approach in this example with the MDI approach in Delphi's example.

The MULTIOLE example can actually display both Shapes (only squares) and OLE containers. Components of these two types are created when the user double-clicks on the surface of the form, and they are placed in the position of the click event. The choice between the two components depends on the status of the two speed buttons of the toolbar, which behave like radio buttons (they have the same value of the GroupIndex property) and have the following code:

```
procedure TForm1.SpeedButton1Click(Sender: TObject);
begin
  OleObj := True;
end;

procedure TForm1.SpeedButton2Click(Sender: TObject);
begin
  OleObj := False;
end;
```

The example also has other capabilities. You can move each shape or OLE container and still click on an OLE container to activate it. You can also select an OLE container and then use its pop-up menu to call its verbs.

## Creating OLE Containers at Run-Time

One of the key elements of the source code is the FormDblClick method, which is used to create new components when the user double-clicks on the surface of the form. You can see the effect of executing this code several times in Figure 25.8.

**FIGURE 25.8:**

With the MULTIOLE example, you can create several OLE containers and shapes.

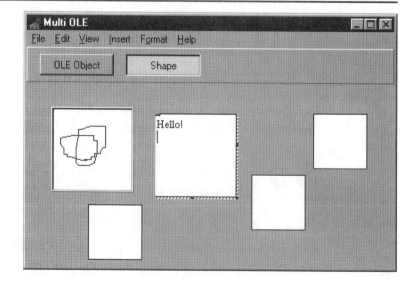

Actually, there is another related event-handling method, FormMouseDown, used to store the position of the mouse:

```
procedure TForm1.FormMouseDown (
  Sender: TObject; Button: TMouseButton;
  Shift: TShiftState; X, Y: Integer);
begin
  X1 := X;
  Y1 := Y;
end;
```

In fact, the OnDblClick event handler provides no information regarding the mouse position. The FormDblClick has two distinct parts: the creation of a shape and the creation of an OLE container. The choice between the two depends on the currently selected speed button. I suggest that you look first at the second part of the code, used to create shapes, because it is simpler:

```
procedure TForm1.FormDblClick(Sender: TObject);
var
  OleCont: TOleContainer;
  Pan: TPanel;
  Shape: TShape;
begin
  if OleObj then
  begin
    // create a panel to host the OLE container
    Pan := TPanel.Create (self);
    Pan.Parent := Self;
    Pan.Top := Y1;
    Pan.Left := X1;
    Pan.Width := 100;
    Pan.Height := 100;
    // create OLE container
    OleCont := TOleContainer.Create (self);
    OleCont.Parent := Pan;
    OleCont.Align := alClient;
    // generate a unique name
    Inc (OleCount);
    OleCont.Name := 'OleContainer' + IntToStr (OleCount);
    // set the position object
    OleCont.InsertObjectDialog;
    // enable dragging
    OleCont.DragMode := dmAutomatic;
    OleCont.OnDragDrop := OleContainerDragDrop;
    OleCont.OnDragOver := OleContainerDragOver;
  end
  else
  begin
    // create a new shape
    Shape := TShape.Create (self);
    Shape.Parent := self;
    // define a unique name and set the position
    Inc (ShapeCount);
```

```
      Shape.Name := 'Shape' + IntToStr (ShapeCount);
      Shape.Left := X1;
      Shape.Top := Y1;
      // activate dragging
      Shape.DragMode := dmAutomatic;
    end;
end;
```

To show a new shape, the above code creates a new Shape component, sets its Parent property, and gives it a unique name. Then it sets the position of the shape, using the two values stored when the user clicked the mouse button, and activates dragging by setting the DragMode property. For dragging to work properly, we need to handle a couple of events of the form, as we will see later.

To create a new OLE container, the code performs similar operations, but creates the component inside of a panel, then calls the InsertObjectDialog function. Again, the code sets the DragMode property to dmAutomatic to enable dragging, but a problem occurs: if you double-click on an OLE container, this operation is ignored, because the mouse clicks are trapped by the dragging code. Instead of customizing the dragging code, I've decided to initiate object editing when the user clicks on the OLE container; that is, when the dragging operation terminates on the same component that started it. To accomplish this, the program dynamically defines a handler for the OnDragDrop and OnDragOver events of the OLE container components.

## Dragging Components and Activating OLE Containers

The program has four dragging-related methods: two that are connected to the form and used for real dragging operations, and two that are used to activate the OLE containers:

```
procedure TForm1.FormDragOver(
  Sender, Source: TObject; X, Y: Integer;
  State: TDragState; var Accept: Boolean);
begin
  {dragging of OLE containers and shapes is allowed}
  if (Source is TOleContainer)
      or (Source is TShape) then
    Accept := True;
end;

procedure TForm1.FormDragDrop(
  Sender, Source: TObject; X, Y: Integer);
begin
  if Source is TShape then
  begin
    (Source as TControl).Left := X;
    (Source as TControl).Top := Y;
  end
```

```
      else
      begin
        // move the panel
        (Source as TControl).Parent.Left := X;
        (Source as TControl).Parent.Top := Y;
      end;
  end;

procedure TForm1.OleContainerDragOver(
    Sender, Source: TObject; X, Y: Integer;
    State: TDragState; var Accept: Boolean);
begin
  {if dragging onto itself, that is, clicking,
  activate the OLE object, starting the server}
  if Sender = Source then
    Accept := True;
end;

procedure TForm1.OleContainerDragDrop(Sender, Source: TObject;
    X, Y: Integer);
begin
  {allow dragging over the same component,
  an operation which is considered a click}
  if Sender = Source then
    with (Sender as TOleContainer) do
      DoVerb (PrimaryVerb);
end;
```

As you can see in the listing above, the form accepts dragging from TOleContainer and TShape components, and simply changes the position of the component to the location where the drop event took place. Using the coordinates passed by the Form-DragDrop method to set the Left and Top properties of the component (or the panel holding it) is not a perfect solution. You should also consider the relative position of the mouse click to the upper-left corner of the component when the dragging operation starts.

The other two dragging-related methods are much simpler. The key code is in two lines of the OleContainerDragOver procedure:

```
if Sender = Source then
  Accept := True;
```

You should remember that these two methods are connected to the OLE container components at run-time, when the components are created.

# OLE Automation

After this detailed description of the use of the OLE Container component, this second part of the chapter focuses on OLE Automation. OLE Automation relates to OLE in much the same way that DDE Execute relates to DDE: these are not data exchange techniques *per se*, but techniques to control a second application or DLL. Since the use of DDE Execute has never become widespread, the OLE Automation interfaces are increasingly common. It is quite simple to drive other applications using OLE Automation from many programming languages and macro languages.

OLE Automation is a promising programming feature, and the extended support for it in Delphi 2 is welcome. As I've said for other standard techniques (including DDE), OLE Automation's fundamental purpose is to let applications cooperate, even if they have been written by different programmers in software houses, often in different programming languages.

Of course you can also use OLE Automation to write Delphi applications that interact. I'll show an example of this mainly because I don't know which other OLE-enabled programs you may have on your system. OLE Automation in Delphi is so simple to implement that you can actually use it as a tool to make your programs interact, even though when you are building both the client and the server program there are other techniques you can use.

## Sending Data to Word

Before showing you how to write an OLE automation server, let me start with a simple example. (There is a similar program among Delphi demos, but the idea is so important I really want to stress it here again.) What I want to do is to extract some data from a database table, using Delphi, and use it to build a Microsoft Word document, driving Word though its OLE Automation interface.

The basic idea is that you can easily manipulate an OLE server by declaring a variable of the `variant` data type (its general implications were discussed briefly in Chapter 4), and assigning the OLE object to it:

```
var
  Word: Variant;
begin
  Word := CreateOleObject ('Word.Basic');
```

The CreateOleObject function is defined in the OleAuto unit. Now you can call any method or access any properties of the *Word.Basic* OLE server, as documented in the help files of that application.

> **WARNING**
>
> With versions of Word prior to Word 7 for Windows 95, the application used a different OLE automation interface for each foreign language it was translated into, making it difficult to write a generic program. The new version has a common English interface, although it still retains the localized interfaces. This is not just a Word problem: many OLE servers (including Microsoft ones) provide different OLE interfaces for each localized version. In the following example, I'll use the English version of Word, which means the example might not work if you have a localized version prior to 7.0.

To show you an example of an OLE automation *controller* (this is the term for a program that controls an OLE automation server), I've extended the PRINTN2 example from Chapter 24. This program can save the contents of a database table to a text file or print it. In PRINTN3, I've replaced the caption of one of its buttons with *Print to Word* and changed its code as follows:

```
procedure TNavigator.PrintWordButtonClick(Sender: TObject);
var
  Word: Variant;
  Bookmark: TBookmark;
  Lines: Integer;
begin
  // store the current position
  Bookmark := Table1.GetBookmark;
  Table1.DisableControls;
  try
    // create the automation object
    Word := CreateOleObject ('Word.Basic');
    Word.AppShow;
    Word.FileNew;
    // insert header (in bold font)
    Word.Bold;
    Word.Insert ('Country'#9'Capital'#13);
    // scan the database table
    Table1.First;
    Lines := 1;
    while not Table1.EOF do
    begin
      // send the two fields
      Word.Insert (
        Table1.FieldByName ('Name').AsString + #9 +
        Table1.FieldByName ('Capital').AsString + #13);
      Table1.Next;
      Inc (Lines);
    end;
  finally
    // go back to the bookmark and destroy it
    Table1.GotoBookmark (Bookmark);
```

```
      Table1.FreeBookmark (Bookmark);
      Table1.EnableControls;
      // convert Word text to table
      Word.LineUp (Lines, 1);
      Word.TextToTable;
  end;
end;
```

This method creates an OLE object (inside a try block, because the server application might not be available on the computer), launches the server application, and creates a new document. Then it inserts a caption with the names of the database table columns, using a bold font (notice the tab (#9) and newline (#13) characters included in the text using their ASCII codes). The program continues adding a line of text for each record of the database table and counts each line. At the end, the program selects all the lines with the LineUp method (the second parameter is a Boolean used to indicate if the text has to be selected) and transforms the text to a Word table. The tab separators and newline characters are used to automatically determine the columns and lines of the table. You can see the result of this code in Figure 25.9.

**NOTE**  The Delphi OLE container demo program passes some parameters to the TextToTable method and uses the comma as separator, but this approach has problems in localized versions of Windows (not Word), which use the semicolon as separator.

**FIGURE 25.9:**

The Word document produced by the PRINTN3 OLE controller example.

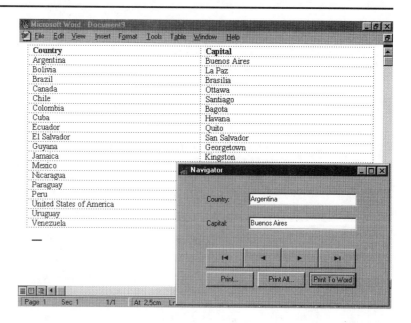

# Writing an OLE Automation Server

If it is very simple to write an OLE Automation controller, with Delphi 2 it is even easier to write an OLE automation server. To create an OLE Automation object, you can use Delphi's Automation Object Expert. Open the Object Repository by selecting File ➤ New, and choose OLE Object in the *New* page. In the expert (see Figure 25.10), first enter the internal name of the OLE automation class. The registered name of the OLE automation class (the external name—similar to *Word.Basic* above) is automatically generated, adding the program name and removing the *T* in front of the internal class name. Then you can write a description of the object and indicate if the object allows multiple instances (the general behavior for DLLs) or a single instance (the general behavior of programs).

**FIGURE 25.10:**

The Automation Object Expert.

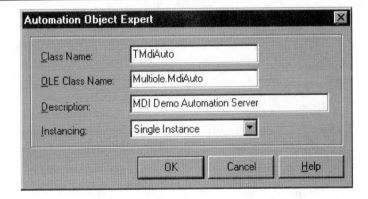

This is the code automatically generated by the Delphi Automation Object Expert, with the input values you can see in Figure 25.10:

```
interface

uses
  OleAuto;

type
  TMdiAuto = class(TAutoObject)
  private
    { Private declarations }
  automated
    { Automated declarations }
  end;

implementation

procedure RegisterMdiAuto;
```

```
const
  AutoClassInfo: TAutoClassInfo = (
    AutoClass: TMdiAuto;
    ProgID: 'Mdidemo.MdiAuto';
    ClassID: '{F51AEEE0-703E-11CF-AEC2-444553540000}';
    Description: 'MDI Demo Automation Server';
    Instancing: acSingleInstance);
begin
  Automation.RegisterClass(AutoClassInfo);
end;

initialization
  RegisterMdiAuto;
end.
```

The RegisterMdiAuto procedure uses Delphi's OLE Automation manager, the global Automation object. The procedure calls the RegisterClass method of the global Automation object, using the values indicated in the Automation Object Expert, plus a GUID (*Globally-Unique IDentifier*) generated for the server by the Automation Object Expert.

There are two key technical elements to writing OLE Automation Servers: you have to derive a new class from the TAutoObject class, and you must add to this class a public OLE interface, indicated by the `automated` keyword.

After this keyword, you can indicate either methods (procedures and functions) or properties with a read and a write method (it is not possible to create an automated property that accesses a field directly, as with standard Delphi properties). Since this OLE automation interface should be accessible by programs written in any language, there are also some restrictions related to the data types you can use for the properties and parameters or return values of methods. These data types include most basic data types such as Integer, SmallInt, Byte, Single, Double, String, Variant, and WordBool (but not Boolean).

## Automating an MDI Application

To build an example of an automated server, I've started with the MDIDEMO4 example from Chapter 15. Then I've activated the Automation Object Expert, providing the values indicated in the last section. The next step is to write the automation interface of the OLE object. Here is the code:

```
type
  TMdiAuto = class (TAutoObject)
  private
    function GetColor: Integer;
    procedure SetColor (Col: Integer);
    function GetChildCount: Integer;
  automated
    procedure NewCircle;
    procedure NewSquare;
```

```
    procedure Tile;
    procedure Next;
    property Color: Integer read GetColor write SetColor;
    property ChildCount: Integer read GetChildCount;
  end;
```

The four procedures can be used to create new MDI child windows of two different types, tile the child windows, or activate the next one. The two properties can be used to retrieve or change the color of the element of the window (either a moving shape or a circle) and to get the number of current child windows. To implement these properties, I've written three private methods, too.

The code of most of the methods of this class is quite simple. Three methods call three event handlers of the main form:

```
procedure TMdiAuto.NewCircle;
begin
  MainForm.New1Click (self);
end;

procedure TMdiAuto.NewSquare;
begin
  MainForm.New2Click (self);
end;

procedure TMdiAuto.Tile;
begin
  MainForm.Tile1Click (self);
end;
```

The other two methods require a simple access to the main form:

```
function TMdiAuto.GetChildCount: Integer;
begin
  Result := MainForm.MDIChildCount;
end;

procedure TMdiAuto.Next;
begin
  MainForm.Next;
end;
```

Only the two methods related to manipulating the color are more complex. In fact, the code used to access the color is different depending on the type of the current child window. By the way, we need to cast the data type from Integer to TColor and vice-versa, since the OLE automation interface provides no support for Delphi data types:

```
function TMdiAuto.GetColor: Integer;
begin
  if MainForm.ActiveMdiChild is TCircleChildForm then
    Result := Integer (TCircleChildForm (
      MainForm.ActiveMdiChild).FillColor)
```

```
  else
    Result := Integer ((
      MainForm.ActiveMdiChild as TBounceChildForm).
      Shape1.Brush.Color)
end;

procedure TMdiAuto.SetColor (Col: Integer);
begin
  if MainForm.ActiveMdiChild is TCircleChildForm then
    with TCircleChildForm (MainForm.ActiveMdiChild) do
    begin
      FillColor := TColor (Col);
      Invalidate;
    end
  else
    (MainForm.ActiveMdiChild as TBounceChildForm).
      Shape1.Brush.Color := TColor (Col);
end;
```

# Registering the Automation Object

Once you have written the application, you have to register its OLE object. This is quite simple to accomplish: you need only to run the application on the target machine (the computer where you want to install the OLE automation server), passing to it the */regserver* parameter on the command line. You can do this by selecting Start ➤ Run, by using the Explorer or File Manager, or by running the program within Delphi after you've entered a command line parameter (using the Run ➤ Parameters command).

This command line parameter is intercepted by the `Application.Initialize` call Delphi places in the source code of the project, which registers the OLE server and immediately terminates the program. Another command line parameter, */unregserver* is used to remove this server from the registration database.

> **TIP**
>
> The Delphi 2 Help files fail to discuss this topic, and describe a different approach. You can refer to the documentation in the OLE Automation examples to find more information.

# Writing a Test Program

Once the server is successfully registered, you can use nearly any language and programming environment that supports OLE automation to control it. Needless to say, I've decided to write a Delphi program for the test, named OLETEST. The form of this program is very simple: it has a number of buttons to call the various methods and properties of the server, and has a ColorGrid component to choose the current color. You can see the program at run-time, with the server running behind it, in Figure 25.11.

**FIGURE 25.11:**

The OLETEST example, which drives the OLE automation server you can see behind it.

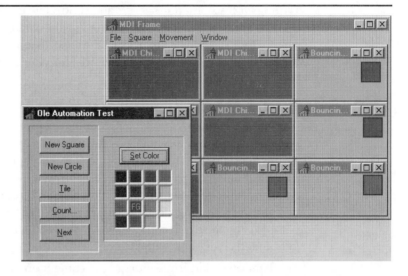

The program creates the OLE server object, opening the server window, at startup:

```
procedure TForm1.FormCreate(Sender: TObject);
begin
  Server := CreateOleObject ('Mdidemo.MdiAuto');
end;
```

In this example, I've provided no code to check if the server object can be created, to suggest that users install the server application if necessary, and to terminate the program if the server cannot be found. This is something you could easily add by testing the Boolean return value of the CreateOleObject function.

The other methods are terribly simple, since they correspond to automation functions available in the server. Here are some examples (including the most complex ones):

```
procedure TForm1.Button2Click(Sender: TObject);
begin
  Server.NewCircle;
end;
```

```
procedure TForm1.Button3Click(Sender: TObject);
begin
  Server.Color := Integer (ColorGrid1.ForegroundColor);
end;
```

```
procedure TForm1.Button5Click(Sender: TObject);
```

```
begin
  ShowMessage (Format ('Child windows: %d',
    [Integer(Server.ChildCount)]));
end;
```

Writing OLE automation servers and controllers is really quite simple. Once you've become accustomed to the use of the variant data type and to the automated definitions, there is little else to do but study the documentation of the servers you want to drive and plan appropriate interfaces for your own automation servers.

# The Future of OLE

As you have seen in this and the previous chapter, OLE is the most important technology for data exchange and application interoperability. This is one of the Windows technologies with the brightest future, at least according to Microsoft. The company has clear intentions of promoting OLE support in Windows 95, Windows NT, and forthcoming object-oriented (or OLE-based) operating systems. This is paralleled by the explosion of new APIs based on the same COM (Component Object Model) layer, such as the Games API or the DAO (Database Access Object).

The Windows platform is going to become more and more OLE-centric in the future, including Network OLE (that is, connecting an OLE automation client computer on a machine with an OLE Automation server located elsewhere on the computer network) and Microsoft projects to push OLE technology toward the Internet. Certainly, the extensive OLE support in Delphi 2 will ease this transition for many programmers. In this respect, my bet is that OLE Automation might turn out to be a key element of the future OLE technology, and the Object Pascal language extensions supporting it (the variant data type and the automated keyword) are really a big plus.

# Summary

In this chapter we have focused on Microsoft OLE technology, and Delphi capabilities to support it. We have discussed the use of the new Ole Container class and have seen how to build OLE Automation controllers and server applications. This still doesn't cover the full spectrum of OLE capabilities, but they are the key elements, and those directly supported by the Delphi visual environment.

Now we'll take a break with a more relaxing topic (multimedia applications) in the next chapter, and then we will be ready for the last part of the book, which covers building components and DLL libraries.

# CHAPTER

**TWENTY-SIX**

# Multimedia Fun

- Windows default sounds, from beeps to music

- The Media Player component

- Playing sounds and running videos

- Applications for Audio CD drives

26

**S**ince we've already discussed the printer and the file system (Chapters 22 and 23), I want to focus on other devices that might be attached to your PC, such as a sound card or a CD-ROM drive. Besides being physically connected to your computer, these devices must be properly installed in Windows for you to access them.

Windows provides a specific API to handle external devices, including video, MIDI, and CD drives. This API is known as the *Multimedia API*. Delphi includes a corresponding help file along with an easy-to-use component, the Media Player, to manipulate most multimedia devices. Before discussing this component, which is the main topic of the chapter, we'll look at some simpler ways to produce sound in Windows, beyond the simple beeps we have used previously.

# Windows Default Sounds

In the book's earlier examples, every time I wanted to notify the user of an error or a specific event, I called a Windows API function, `MessageBeep`, passing to it parameter either `0` or `Cardinal (-1)`. Since the data type of a parameter is declared as an unsigned value, you should use the hexadecimal value 0xFFFFFFFF, which corresponds to –1 converted into an unsigned value, as `Cardinal (-1)`. The Windows 3.1 help file actually suggested to use –1 for this value, which produces a compiler error in Delphi, while the Win32 help file properly suggests 0xFFFFFFFF. However, you cannot use such a large hexadecimal constant in Object Pascal.

Besides this value used to produce a standard beep, the `MessageBeep` function can also accept other values. Here are the names of the acceptable constants listed with the corresponding Windows sounds they produce (these are the sound names available in Control Panel):

| | |
|---|---|
| `mb_IconAsterisk` | SystemAsterisk sound |
| `mb_IconExclamation` | SystemExclamation sound |
| `mb_IconHand` | SystemHand sound |
| `mb_IconQuestion` | SystemQuestion sound |
| `mb_Ok` | SystemDefault sound |

You can change the association between system events and sound files using the Control Panel (see Figure 26.1), which lists the sounds under the names shown in the right column above. These associations are stored in the Windows System Registry.

Notice that these constants are also the possible values of the `MessageBox` API function, encapsulated in the MessageBox method of the TApplication class. It is common to produce the corresponding sound when the message box is displayed. This

**FIGURE 26.1:**

Setting Windows default sounds
with the Control Panel.

feature is not directly available in the Delphi MessageDlg function (which displays a message box with a corresponding icon), but we can extend it easily by building a SoundMessageDlg function, as demonstrated by the following example.

## Every Box Has a Beep

To show you the capabilities of the MessageBeep API function, I've prepared a simple example, BEEPS. The form of this example has a RadioGroup with some radio buttons from which the user can choose one of the five valid constants of the MessageBeep function. Here is the definition of the RadioGroup, from the textual description of the form:

```
object RadioGroup1: TRadioGroup
  Caption = 'Parameters'
  ItemIndex = 0
  Items.Strings = (
    'mb_IconAsterisk'
    'mb_IconExclamation'
    'mb_IconHand'
    'mb_IconQuestion'
    'mb_Ok')
end
```

The program plays the sound corresponding to the current selection when the user clicks on the Beep Sound button (one of the push buttons of the form). This button's OnClick event-handler first determines which constant's radio button was selected, using a case statement, and then plays the sound using that same constant:

```
procedure TForm1.BeepButtonClick(Sender: TObject);
var
  BeepConstant: Cardinal;
begin
  case RadioGroup1.ItemIndex of
    0: BeepConstant := mb_IconAsterisk;
    1: BeepConstant := mb_IconExclamation;
    2: BeepConstant := mb_IconHand;
    3: BeepConstant := mb_IconQuestion;
    4: BeepConstant := mb_Ok;
  else
    BeepConstant := 0;
  end;
  MessageBeep (BeepConstant);
end;
```

The else clause of the case is provided mainly to prevent an annoying (but not dangerous) compiler warning. To compare the selected sound with the default beep sound, click on the second button of the column (labeled *Beep –1*), which has the following code:

```
procedure TForm1.BeepOneButtonClick(Sender: TObject);
begin
  MessageBeep (Cardinal (-1));
end;
```

Remember you can also pass the corresponding $FFFFFFFF value, to the Message-Beep function. There is actually no difference between the two approaches. To test whether a sound driver is installed in your system (with or without a sound card, since it is possible to have a sound driver for the PC speaker), click on the first button (labeled *Test*), which uses a multimedia function, WaveOutGetNumDevs, to perform the test:

```
procedure TForm1.TestButtonClick(Sender: TObject);
begin
  if WaveOutGetNumDevs > 0 then
    SoundMessageDlg ('Sound is supported',
      mtInformation, [mbOk], 0)
  else
    SoundMessageDlg ('Sound is NOT supported',
      mtError, [mbOk], 0);
end;
```

Notice that to compile this function, you need to add the MmSystem unit to the uses clause. If your computer has no proper sound driver installed, you will hear only standard beeps, regardless of which sound is selected. The last two buttons have a similar aim: they both display a message box and play the corresponding sound (see Figure 26.2). The handler of the OnClick event of the Message Box button uses the traditional Windows approach. It calls the `MessageBeep` function and then the `MessageBox` method of the Application object soon afterward. The effect is that the sound is played when the message box is displayed. In fact, playing a sound doesn't stop other Windows operations. (Well, this actually depends on the sound driver, so this is only the suggested behavior.)

**FIGURE 26.2:**

The output of the MessageBox call, accompanied by sound (above), and the output of the SoundMessageDlg function, which plays a system sound and shows a Delphi message box (below).

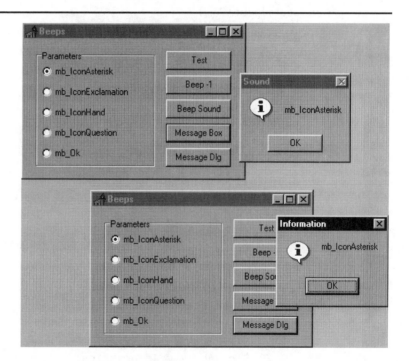

Here is the code related to this fourth button:

```
procedure TForm1.BoxButtonClick(Sender: TObject);
var
  BeepConstant: Cardinal;
begin
  case RadioGroup1.ItemIndex of
    0: BeepConstant := mb_IconAsterisk;
    1: BeepConstant := mb_IconExclamation;
    2: BeepConstant := mb_IconHand;
    3: BeepConstant := mb_IconQuestion;
  else {including 4:}
    BeepConstant := mb_Ok;
  end;
  MessageBeep (BeepConstant);
```

```
Application.MessageBox (
  PChar (RadioGroup1.Items [RadioGroup1.ItemIndex]),
  'Sound', BeepConstant);
end;
```

If you click on the last button, the program calls the SoundMessageDlg function, which is not an internal Delphi function. It's one I've added to the program, but you can use it in your applications. The only suggestion I have is to choose a shorter name if you want to use it frequently. SoundMessageDlg plays a sound, depending on the type parameter, and then displays the Delphi standard message box (see again Figure 26.2):

```
function SoundMessageDlg (const Msg: string;
  AType: TMsgDlgType; AButtons: TMsgDlgButtons;
  HelpCtx: Longint): Integer;
var
  BeepConstant: Cardinal;
begin
  case AType of
    mtWarning: BeepConstant := mb_IconExclamation;
    mtError: BeepConstant := mb_IconHand;
    mtInformation: BeepConstant := mb_IconAsterisk;
    mtConfirmation: BeepConstant := mb_IconQuestion;
  else
    BeepConstant := mb_Ok;
  end;
  MessageBeep(BeepConstant);
  Result := MessageDlg (Msg, AType,
    AButtons, HelpCtx);
end;

procedure TForm1.MessDlgButtonClick(Sender: TObject);
var
  DlgType: TMsgDlgType;
begin
  case RadioGroup1.ItemIndex of
    0: DlgType := mtInformation;
    1: DlgType := mtWarning;
    2: DlgType := mtError;
    3: DlgType := mtConfirmation;
  else {including 4:}
    DlgType := mtCustom;
  end;
  SoundMessageDlg (
    RadioGroup1.Items [RadioGroup1.ItemIndex],
    DlgType, [mbOK], 0);
end;
```

SoundMessageDlg is a simple function, but your programs can really benefit from its use.

# From Beeps to Music

When you use the `MessageBeep` function, your choice of sounds is limited to the default system sounds. Another Windows API function, `PlaySound`, can be used to play a system sound, as well as any other waveform file (WAV). (The `PlaySound` Win32 function replaces the outdated `SndPlaySound` Win16 function, still available in Win32 only for compatibility reasons.) Again, I've built a simple example to show you this approach. The example is indicated as EXTBEEP, Extended Beep, and has the simple form shown in Figure 26.3.

**FIGURE 26.3:**

The form of the EXTBEEP example.

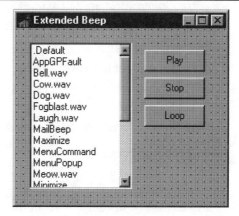

The list box of this example lists the names of some system sounds and some WAV files, available in the current directory (that is, the directory of the example itself). When the user clicks on the Play button, the `PlaySound` function (defined in the MmSystem unit) is called:

```
procedure TForm1.PlayButtonClick(Sender: TObject);
begin
  PlaySound (PChar (Listbox1.Items [
    ListBox1.ItemIndex]),
    0, snd_Async);
end;
```

The first parameter is the name of the sound—either a system sound, a WAV file, or a specific sound resource (see the Win32 API Help file for details). The second parameter specifies where to look for the resource sound, and the third indicates that the function should return immediately and let the sound play asynchronously. The alternative to the third parameter's value is `snd_Sync` parameter. If you use this value, the function won't return until the sound has finished playing. In the first case, asynchronous play, you can interrupt a long sound by calling the

PlaySound function again, using nil for the first parameter:

```
procedure TForm1.StopButtonClick(Sender: TObject);
begin
  PlaySound (nil, 0, 0);
end;
```

This is the code executed by the EXTBEEP example when the user clicks on the Stop button. This button is particularly useful for stopping the repeated execution of the sound started by the Loop button with this code:

```
procedure TForm1.LoopButtonClick(Sender: TObject);
begin
  PlaySound (PChar (Listbox1.Items [
    ListBox1.ItemIndex]),
    0, snd_Async or snd_Loop);
end;
```

The only other method of the example, FormCreate, selects an item from the list box at startup, to avoid run-time errors if the user clicks on the button before selecting an item from the list box:

```
procedure TForm1.FormCreate(Sender: TObject);
begin
  ListBox1.ItemIndex := 0;
end;
```

You can test this example by running it, and by adding the names of the other WAV files or system sounds (listed in the registration database). I suggest you also test other values for the third parameter of the function.

# The Media Player Component

By browsing through the other API functions related to multimedia in the Windows API Help file, you can learn many other techniques for playing sounds and controlling external media devices. Instead of delving into this topic directly, I prefer to move back to Delphi and use the Media Player component. The Delphi TMedia-Player class encapsulates most of the capabilities of the Windows Media Control Interface (MCI), a high-level interface for controlling internal and external media devices.

As you probably remember, we already used the Media Player component to play WAV files in the FILEMAN2 example in Chapter 14. This is exactly what we're going to do in the next example. Before we move to the examples, however, let me give you some general information about this component.

First, consider the DeviceType property of the TMediaPlayer component. Its value can be dtAutoSelect, indicating that the type of the device depends on the file extension of the current file (the FileName property). As an alternative, you can select a specific device type, such as dtAVIVideo, dtCDAudio, dtWaveAudio, or many others.

Once the device type (and eventually the file) has been selected, you can open the corresponding device (or set AutoOpen to True), and the buttons of the Media Player component will be enabled. Notice that the component has a number of buttons, not all of which are appropriate for each media type. There are actually three properties referring to the buttons: VisibleButtons, EnabledButtons, and Colored-Buttons. The first determines which of the buttons are present in the control, the second determines which buttons are enabled, and the third determines which buttons have colored marks. By using the first two of these properties, you can permanently hide or temporarily disable some of the buttons.

My last comment concerns the component's events. The OnClick event is different than usual because it contains one parameter indicating which button was pressed and a second parameter you can use to disable the button's default action. The On-Notify event later informs the component of the success of the action generated by the button. Another event, OnPostClick, is sent either when the action starts or when it ends, depending on the value of the Wait property. This property determines whether or not the operation on the device should be synchronous.

## Playing Sound Files

The first example using the Media Player is very simple. The form of the MMSOUND example has some labels describing the current status, a button to select a new file, an OpenDialog component, and a Media Player component with the following settings:

```
object MediaPlayer1: TMediaPlayer
  VisibleButtons = [btPlay, btPause, btStop, btNext, btPrev]
  OnClick = MediaPlayer1Click
  OnNotify = MediaPlayer1Notify
end
```

**NOTE**
At first I wanted to name the example SOUND, not MMSOUND, but this name is in conflict with that of a system library, preventing the program from loading. Delphi even refuses to generate a program with this name, claiming that it is already running.

When a user opens a new file, a wave table, or a MIDI file, the program enables the Media Player, and you can play the sound and use the other buttons, too:

```
procedure TForm1.NewButtonClick(Sender: TObject);
begin
  if OpenDialog1.Execute then
```

```
  begin
    FileLabel.Caption := OpenDialog1.Filename;
    MediaPlayer1.Filename := OpenDialog1.Filename;
    MediaPlayer1.Open;
    MediaPlayer1.Notify := True;
  end;
end;
```

Since I set the Notify property to True, the Media Player invokes the corresponding event handler, which outputs the information to a label:

```
procedure TForm1.MediaPlayer1Notify(Sender: TObject);
begin
  case MediaPlayer1.NotifyValue of
    nvSuccessful : NotifLabel.Caption := 'Success';
    nvSuperseded : NotifLabel.Caption := 'Superseded';
    nvAborted    : NotifLabel.Caption := 'Aborted';
    nvFailure    : NotifLabel.Caption := 'Failure';
  end;
  MediaPlayer1.Notify := True;
end;
```

Notice that you need to set the Notify property to True every time the OnNotify event handler is called in order to receive further notifications. Another label is updated to display the requested command, as you can see in Figure 26.4.

```
procedure TForm1.MediaPlayer1Click(Sender: TObject; Button:
TMPBtnType;
  var DoDefault: Boolean);
begin
  case Button of
    btPlay: ActionLabel.Caption := 'Playing';
    btPause: ActionLabel.Caption := 'Paused';
    btStop: ActionLabel.Caption := 'Stopped';
    btNext: ActionLabel.Caption := 'Next';
    btPrev: ActionLabel.Caption := 'Previous';
  end;
end;
```

**FIGURE 26.4:**

A notification message displayed by the MMSOUND example.

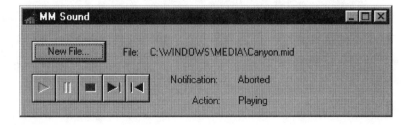

# Running Videos

Up to now, we have worked with sound only. Now it is time to move to another kind of media device: video. You indeed have a video device on your system, but to play video files (such as AVI files), you need a specific driver (directly available in Windows 95). If your computer can display videos, writing a Delphi application to do so is almost trivial: place a Media Player component in a form, select an AVI file in the FileName property, set the AutoOpen property to True, and run the program. As soon as you click on the Play button, the system opens a second window and shows the video in it, as you can see in Figure 26.5.

**FIGURE 26.5:**

By default, an AVI file is displayed in its own window.

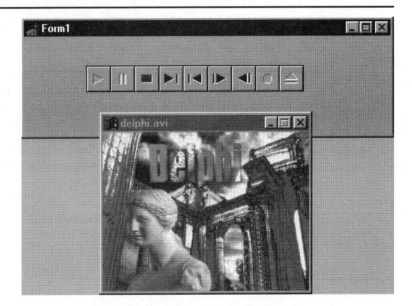

In this case, I've chosen the DELPHI.AVI file distributed by Borland. Instead of playing the file in its own window, we can add a panel (or any other windowed component) to the form and use the name of this panel as the value of the Media Player's Display property. As an alternative, we can set the Display and the DisplayRect properties to indicate which portions of the output window the video should cover.

For example, the MMVIDEO example has the output shown in Figure 26.6.

**FIGURE 26.6:**

The output of an AVI file into a panel. Compare this figure with the previous one, which shows the video in a default window.

Although it is possible to create a similar program with no code at all, to do so I would have to know which AVI files reside on your computer, and specify the full path of one of them in the FileName property of the Media Player component. As an alternative, I've written a simple routine to open and start playing a file automatically. You only have to click on the panel (as the caption suggests).

```
procedure TForm1.Panel1Click(Sender: TObject);
begin
  if OpenDialog1.Execute then
  begin
    MediaPlayer1.FileName := OpenDialog1.Filename;
    MediaPlayer1.Open;
    MediaPlayer1.Perform (wm_LButtonDown, 0, $00090009);
    MediaPlayer1.Perform (wm_LButtonUp, 0, $00090009);
  end;
end;
```

After opening the Media Player, I could have called its Play method immediately to start it. However, in doing so, the buttons are not properly enabled and disabled. So I decided to simulate a click in position 9 on the x axis and 9 on the y axis of the Media Player window (instead of building the 32-bit value including both coordinates with a function, you can use the Hexadecimal value directly, as in the code above). To avoid errors, I disabled all the buttons at design-time, until the simulated click takes place. I automatically close the player when the application is closed:

```
procedure TForm1.FormClose(Sender: TObject;
  var Action: TCloseAction);
begin
  MediaPlayer1.Close;
end;
```

# A Video in a Form

The Media Player component has some limits regarding the window it can use to produce the output. You can use many components, but not all of them. A strange thing you can try is to use the Media Player component itself as the video's output window. This works, but there are two problems. First, the Media Player component cannot be aligned, and it cannot be sized at will. If you try to use big buttons, their size will be reduced automatically at run-time. The second problem is that if you click on the Pause button, you'll see the button in front of the video, while the other buttons are still covered. I suggest you try this approach, anyway, for fun.

One thing you cannot do easily is display the video in a form. In fact, although you cannot set the form as the value of the Media Player's Display property at design-time, you can set it at run-time.

To try this, simply place a hidden Media Player component (set the Visible property to False) and an OpenDialog component in a form. Set a proper title and hint for the form itself, and enable the ShowHints property. Then write the following code to load, start, and stop the video when the user clicks on the form:

```
procedure TForm1.FormClick(Sender: TObject);
begin
  if MediaPlayer1.FileName = '' then
    if OpenDialog1.Execute then
    begin
      MediaPlayer1.FileName :=
        OpenDialog1.FileName;
      MediaPlayer1.Open;
      Playing := False;
    end
    else
      exit; // stop if no file is selected
  if Playing then
  begin
    MediaPlayer1.Stop;
    Playing := False;
    Caption := 'MM Video (Stopped)';
    Hint := 'Click to play video';
  end
  else
  begin
    MediaPlayer1.Display := self;
    MediaPlayer1.DisplayRect := ClientRect;
    MediaPlayer1.Play;
    Playing := True;
    Caption := 'MMV (Playing)';
    Hint := 'Click to stop video';
  end;
end;
```

In this code, Playing is a private Boolean field of the form. Notice that the program shows the video using the full client area of the form. In case the form is resized, simply stretch the output accordingly:

```
procedure TForm1.FormResize(Sender: TObject);
begin
  MediaPlayer1.DisplayRect := ClientRect;
end;
```

The best way to look at the video is to use the original size, but with this program you can actually stretch it, and even change its proportions, as you can see in Figure 26.7 (which also shows the hint).

**FIGURE 26.7:**

A stretched video (with very poor resolution) and the hint indicating the current effect of a click.

Of course, the Media Player can also stop when it reaches the end of a file or when an error occurs. In both cases, we receive a notification event:

```
procedure TForm1.MediaPlayer1Notify(Sender: TObject);
begin
  Playing := False;
  Caption := 'MMV (Stopped)';
  Hint := 'Click to play video';
end;
```

# Working with a CD Drive

In addition to audio and video files, the MCI interface is generally used to operate external devices. There are many examples, but the most common MCI device connected to a PC is probably a CD-ROM drive. Most CD-ROM drives can also read normal audio CDs, sending the output to an external speaker.

You can use the MCI interface and the Media Player component to write applications that handle such a device. Basically, you need to set the DeviceType property to dtCDAudio, make sure no file is selected in the FileName property, and be ready with a CD player.

In fact, just by placing a Media Player component in a form, setting the above properties, and compiling and running the program, you end up with a fully functional audio CD player. When you start customizing the player, though, not everything is as simple as it seems at first glance. I've built an example using some more capabilities of this component and of Windows multimedia support related to audio CDs. The form of this program has a couple of buttons, some labels to show the current status, a timer, and a SpinEdit component you can use to choose a track from the disk.

The idea is to use the labels to inform the user of the number of tracks on a disk, the current track, the current position within a track, and the length of the track, monitoring the current situation using the timer.

In general, if you can, use the tfTMSF value (Track, Minute, Second, Frame) for the Time Format property of the Media Player component to access positional properties (such as Position and Length. Extracting the values is not too complex if you use the proper functions of the MmSystem unit, such as the following:

```
CurrentTrack := Mci_TMSF_Track (MediaPlayer1.Position);
```

Here are the two functions computing the values of the whole disk and the current track:

```
procedure TForm1.CheckDisk;
var
  NTracks, NLen: Integer;
begin
  NTracks := MediaPlayer1.Tracks;
  NLen := MediaPlayer1.Length;
  DiskLabel.Caption := Format (
    'Tracks: %.2d, Length:%.2d:%.2d',
    [NTracks, Mci_TMSF_Minute (NLen),
    Mci_TMSF_Second (NLen)]);
  SpinEdit1.MaxValue := NTracks;
end;

procedure TForm1.CheckPosition;
```

```
var
  CurrentTrack, CurrentPos, TrackLen: Integer;
begin
  CurrentPos := MediaPlayer1.Position;
  CurPosLabel.Caption := Format (
    'Position: %.2d:%.2d',
    [Mci_TMSF_Minute (CurrentPos),
    Mci_TMSF_Second (CurrentPos)]);
  CurrentTrack := Mci_TMSF_Track (CurrentPos);
  TrackLen := MediaPlayer1.TrackLength [CurrentTrack];
  TrackNumberLabel.Caption := Format (
    'Current track: %.2d, Length:%.2d:%.2d',
    [CurrentTrack, Mci_MSF_Minute (TrackLen),
    Mci_MSF_Second (TrackLen)]);
end;
```

The code is complex only because of the many conversions. Notice in particular that the length of the current track (stored in the TrackLength property) is not measured using the default format, as the online help suggests, but with the MSF (Minute Second Frame) format.

The result of displaying this information is visible in Figure 26.8. The global values for the disk are computed only at start up and when the New CD button is clicked:

```
type
  TForm1 = class (TForm)
  ...
  public
    procedure CheckDisk;
    procedure CheckPosition;
  end;
procedure TForm1.FormCreate(Sender: TObject);
begin
  MediaPlayer1.TimeFormat := tfTMSF;
  MediaPlayer1.Open;
  CheckDisk;
  CheckPosition;
end;

procedure TForm1.NewButtonClick(Sender: TObject);
begin
  CheckDisk;
  CheckPosition;
end;
```

The value for the current track and position are computed this way each time the timer interval elapses:

```
procedure TForm1.Timer1Timer(Sender: TObject);
begin
  CheckPosition;
end;
```

FIGURE 26.8:
The CDPLAYER example running.

This is far from perfect, because if you want to play an audio CD while using other programs, a timer accessing the Media Player information often slows down the system too much. Of course, this mainly depends on your hardware.

Besides advising the user of what is going on, the form has the Media Player component to allow the user to start and stop playing, change track, and so on. The operations on this component activate and halt the timer:

```
procedure TForm1.MediaPlayer1PostClick(Sender: TObject;
  Button: TMPBtnType);
begin
  if MediaPlayer1.Mode = mpPlaying then
    Timer1.Enabled := True
  else
    Timer1.Enabled := False;
  CheckPosition;
end;
```

An alternative is to use the Go button to jump to the track selected in the SpinEdit component, where the MaxValue property is set by the CheckDisk method. Here is the code I've written:

```
procedure TForm1.GoButtonClick(Sender: TObject);
var
  Playing: Boolean;
begin
  Playing := (MediaPlayer1.Mode = mpPlaying);
  if Playing then
    MediaPlayer1.Stop;
  MediaPlayer1.Position :=
    MediaPlayer1.TrackPosition[SpinEdit1.Value];
```

```
  CheckPosition;
  if Playing then
    MediaPlayer1.Play;
end;
```

A good extension of this program would be to connect it to a CD database with the title of each CD you own and the title of each track. (I would have done it if it hadn't been for the time it would have taken to enter the title and track of each of my disks.) Remember, anyway, that a similar program is already available in Windows 95.

# Summary

In this chapter, we have seen some audio capabilities we can add to Delphi applications in general and have looked at the Media Player component. We have seen how to add sound effects to respond to user actions, although this should generally be a program option that a user can turn off (besides disabling sounds in Windows). We have also seen three examples how to use the Media Player, using sound files, video files, and an external device (an audio CD). As the hardware becomes more powerful and CD-ROM players become faster, video will become an important feature of many applications. Don't underestimate this area of programming simply because you are writing *serious* business programs.

This chapter ends the part of the book devoted to advanced Windows programming topics. One of the most interesting areas of Delphi development awaits you in the next chapter: building Delphi components.

# PART IV

## Creating Components and Libraries

# Creating Components

- Extending the VCL library

- Customizing existing components

- Building graphical components

- Defining custom events

- Using array properties

- Writing a custom property editor

- Placing a dialog box in a component

**D**elphi offers two main approaches to programming: using components and writing components. While most Delphi programmers are probably component users, many of them need to write simple components or customize existing ones. One of the most interesting aspects of Delphi is that creating components is simple. For this reason, even though this book is for Delphi programmers and not Delphi tool writers, this chapter will cover the topic of creating components.

In this chapter, I'll give you an overview of writing Delphi components and a number of simple examples. There is no space for the source code and description of very complex components, but I hope the ideas in this chapter can help you write any kind of component.

# Extending the VCL

When you write a new component, you basically extend one of the classes of the VCL. To do this, you use many features of the Object Pascal language that component users seldom need. I've presented an overall description of the language in Chapters 4 and 5, so I'm not going to outline language concepts here. Instead, I'll focus on some Object Pascal constructs specific to components, such as the definition of properties, that I didn't cover before in detail.

**NOTE**  Chapter 6 presented an overview of the VCL, together with some hierarchy graphs and a discussion of the role of properties, methods, and events. If you skipped that chapter or do not feel confident with the basic ideas about VCL, read it before continuing with this chapter.

## Delphi Components Are Classes

Delphi components are classes, and the VCL library is the collection of all the classes defining Delphi components. Each time you add a new component to Delphi, you actually extend the VCL with a new class.

**NOTE**  Technically, the code of the components installed in Delphi is stored in the COMPLIB.DCL file, a component library file, which also happens to be a DLL. When you install a new component, you extend the VCL by actually adding new components to the current component library.

This new class will be derived from one of the existing component-related classes. You can inherit a new component from an existing component to add new capabilities, or inherit from an abstract component class—one that does not correspond to a usable component. The VCL hierarchy includes many of these intermediate classes to let you choose a default behavior for your new component and to change its properties. In fact, when you subclass a component with a specific property, you cannot remove that property from the inherited component; you can only add new properties. If a component class contains a property you do not want, you should choose a higher-level class in the VCL hierarchy.

## Static Linking Components

Another very important element in understanding Delphi components is their linking. (I discussed this topic in Chapter 16, where I compared Delphi components to OLE controls.) Although we won't focus on dynamic linking in Windows until the next chapter, the basic idea is that the code of a Delphi component ends up embedded in the executable code of a compiled Delphi application.

Once you write a component (or purchase it), you have to install it in Delphi. Installing a component means adding its code to the current component library (by default, the file COMPLIB.DCL in the Delphi BIN subdirectory). Once your component's code is part of the library and its icon has been added to the Components palette, you can use it in any Delphi project. When you compile the project, the required code is copied from the library to the application's executable file. This means that to run the program, a user doesn't need to have a separate file for the component, unlike what happens with other kinds of external controls.

## Rules for Writing Components

Some general rules govern the writing of components. You can find a detailed description of most of them in the *Delphi Component Writer's Guide*. This manual is certainly required reading for Delphi component writers, but the information in it is somewhat limited. For this reason, it is important to delve into the details of component creation using *Delphi's Component Writer's Help*, an online reference with many details about components that are not available in the basic Delphi help because they are interesting for component writers, not for component users. The VCL source code and the VCL reference manual (which are part of the Delphi Developer and Delphi Client/Server Suite packages) are other important references for component writers.

Here is my own summary of the rules for component writers:

- Study the Object Pascal language with care, particularly inheritance, method overriding, the difference between public and published sections, and the definition of properties and events.

- Study the structure of the VCL hierarchy and have a graph with the classes at hand (see Chapter 6 or some third-party VCL posters).

- Be ready to write *real* code and forget the Delphi visual programming environment. Writing components generally means writing code without visual support.

- Follow the Borland naming conventions. There are many of them for components, as we will see, and following these rules makes it easier for other programmers to interact and further extend your components.

- Keep components simple, mimic other components, and avoid dependencies. These three rules basically mean that a user of the components you write should be able to use them as easily as Delphi pre-installed components. If you try to use similar property, method, and event names whenever possible, it helps. If users can avoid learning complex rules about the use of the component (that is, if the dependencies between methods or properties are limited) and can simply access properties with meaningful names, they'll be happy.

- Use exceptions. When something goes wrong, the component should raise an exception. When you are allocating resources of any kind, you must protect them with `try-finally` blocks, and destructor calls.

- Test a component in a sample form before installing it in the system. Installing a component with bad errors can blow up Delphi, and reinstalling a component over and over takes more time than compiling new test programs. For this reason you should make a back-up copy of the VCL library before installing any component, including those discussed in this chapter of the book.

- To complete a component, add a bitmap to it for the Components palette, and if you want to sell it, also add a proper Help file.

# Introducing Some Simple Components

Before going on with the theory and looking at complete examples of components, I would like to show you a couple of simple, almost trivial, components. The aim of this section, which skips most of the details, is to give you an idea of how easy it is to write new components.

## The Fonts Combo Box

Many applications have a toolbar with a combo box you can use to select a font. There was a similar example, COMBOBAR, in Chapter 11. Now, if you happen to use a similar customized combo box, why not make it a component? It would probably take less than a minute.

Close any active projects in the Delphi environment and start the Component Expert by choosing Component ➤ New. As an alternative, you can select File ➤ New to open the Object Repository, then choose Component in the New page. Using either approach, you start the Component Expert. In the window of this expert, enter a name for the class of the new component and choose a parent class (see Figure 27.1). Then select the page of the Component palette where you want to display the new component. When you click on OK, the Component Expert generates a simple Pascal source file, with the structure of your component.

Here is the generated code:

```pascal
unit Unit1;
interface
uses
  Windows, Messages, SysUtils, Classes, Graphics,
  Controls, Forms, Dialogs, StdCtrls;

type
  TFontCombo = class(TComboBox)
  private
    { Private declarations }
  protected
    { Protected declarations }
  public
    { Public declarations }
  published
    { Published declarations }
  end;

procedure Register;

implementation

procedure Register;
begin
  RegisterComponents('Samples', [TFontCombo]);
end;

end.
```

**FIGURE 27.1:**

The definition of the new TFontCombo component with the Components Expert.

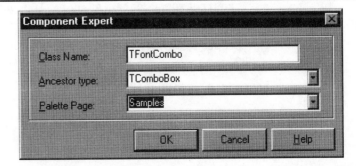

One of the key elements of this listing is the class definition, which begins by indicating the parent class. The other critical portion is the Register procedure.

You can see that the Component Expert does its work, but it is not a lot of work. Now you can start writing code. That's all it takes to build a component. Of course, in this example the code is very simple. We need only copy all the system fonts to the Items property of the combo box at startup. To accomplish this, we might try to override the Create method in the class declaration, adding the statement Items := Screen.Fonts. However, if we tried to add this component to the component library, the component would not be usable. The problem is that we cannot access the combo box's Items property, which refers to the strings that will appear in the combo box, before the component is completely constructed. This is because some key properties (such as the Parent property, which refers to the form containing the component) won't be set up correctly until the component construction is finished.

Instead of assigning the new strings in the Create constructor, we must perform this operation in the CreateWnd procedure, which is called to create the window control after the component is constructed. Again, we execute the default behavior, and then we can write our custom code. I could have skipped the Create constructor and written all the code here, but I prefer using both startup methods to let you see the difference between them. Here you can see the complete source code of the TFontCombo component (available in the FONTBOX project on the companion CD):

```
unit Fontcomb;
interface

uses
  SysUtils, WinTypes, WinProcs, Messages, Classes, Graphics,
    Controls, Forms, Dialogs, StdCtrls;

type
  TFontCombo = class(TComboBox)
  private
    { Private declarations }
  protected
    { Protected declarations }
  public
    constructor Create (AOwner: TComponent); override;
    procedure CreateWnd; override;
  published
    property Style default csDropDownList;
  end;

procedure Register;

implementation

constructor TFontCombo.Create (AOwner: TComponent);
```

```
begin
  inherited Create (AOwner);
  Style := csDropDownList;
end;

procedure TFontCombo.CreateWnd;
begin
  inherited CreateWnd;
  Items := Screen.Fonts;
end;

procedure Register;
begin
  RegisterComponents('Samples', [TFontCombo]);
end;

end.
```

Notice that besides giving a new value to the component's Style property, in the Create method, I've redefined this property by setting a value with the `default` keyword. We have to do both operations because adding the default keyword to a property declaration has no direct effect on the property's initial value. The reason to specify a property's default value is that properties that have a value equal to the default value are not streamed with the form definition (and you can see they don't appear in the textual description of the form). The default keyword tells the streaming code that the component initialization code will handle setting the value of that property.

Now we have to install the component in the system library. Select the Install command from the Components menu and select the file that defines the new component. (Of course, you have to save the file with a proper name first.) When you have added a new file, it is added to the Installed Units list box and its path is added to the Search Path edit box, as shown in Figure 27.2.

Once you click on OK in the Install Components dialog box, Delphi updates the component library, compiling the new component. If you open this dialog box again later on and select the name of the unit you've added, you'll see the list of the components it defines (in this case, only one).

**NOTE**    In this and the following examples in this chapter, I'll always make changes to the COMPLIB.DCL component library, but you should make a copy of this library and work on that copy. Delphi, in fact, allows you to easily switch between multiple component libraries and choose the one you want to use each time (for each project).

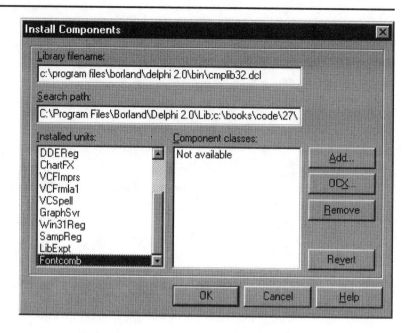

The other effect of compiling the new component is that a bitmap for it is added to the Samples page of the Components palette, as indicated by the Register function. By default, the bitmap used will be the same as the parent class, because we haven't provided a custom bitmap (we will do this in future examples). Notice also that the new component will display the name of the class without the initial *T* as its pop-up hint.

## Using the Fonts Combo Box

Now you can create a new Delphi program to test the fonts combo box. Move to the palette, select the component, and add it to a new form. A traditional-looking combo box will appear. However, if you open the Items Property Editor, you'll see the font names as the default element. To build a simple text example, I've added a Memo component to the form and selected some text inside it (actually, it is the text of the Pascal file defining the new component). The program has little code. When a user selects a new font in the combo box, the new value is used as the Memo component's font:

```
procedure TForm1.FontCombo1Change(Sender: TObject);
begin
  Memo1.Font.Name :=
    FontCombo1.Items [FontCombo1.ItemIndex];
end;
```

At the beginning, the reverse action is performed; the name of the Memo component's font is displayed in the combo box:

```
procedure TForm1.FormCreate(Sender: TObject);
begin
  with FontCombo1 do
    ItemIndex := Items.IndexOf (Memo1.Font.Name);
end;
```

The aim of this simple program (see Figure 27.3 for its output) is only to test the behavior of the new component we have built. The component is not very useful—we could have written a couple of lines of code in any example to obtain the same effect—but looking at a couple of simple components is useful to give you an idea of what is involved in component building.

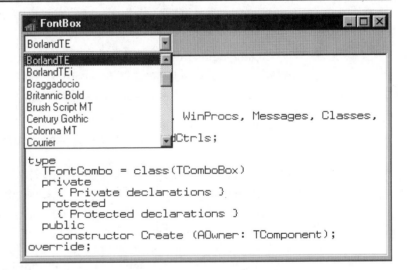

## Creating a Tabbed List Box

The Delphi TListBox component lacks a feature that is generally useful in Windows list boxes: the use of tab characters to display list data in columns. We can build a new, simple component extending the standard Delphi list boxes with this capability. Since tabbed columns are difficult to maintain, as we will see later in this chapter, Borland's choice is not coincidental. Instead of extending the behavior of list boxes, Borland programmers have chosen a radical solution: the Grid family of components.

From a technical point of view, a list box can accept tab characters if it was created using the lbs_UseTabStops window style. Luckily, we can use a hook to change the control creation. We saw in the earlier example that the window connected to a windowed component is created in a second step, via the CreateWnd method. When this method is executed, we have a choice of examining the parameters of the Windows API CreateWindow function and changing the values before the actual window creation takes place. This method is CreateParams, and its parameter is a reference of type TCreateParams.

> **NOTE**
>
> Experienced Windows programmers might already know that the TCreateParams type is a record with fields corresponding to each parameter of the CreateWindow API function. A pointer to this parameter is passed to the window being created in the wm_Create message.

The CreateParams method is used in Delphi components to change some of the standard values used in component creation. For example, we can write this code:

```
procedure TTabList.CreateParams (var Params: TCreateParams);
begin
  inherited CreateParams (Params);
  Params.Style := Params.Style or lbs_UseTabStops;
end;
```

This code sets the default parameters, calling the method of the parent class, and then adds the lbs_UseTabStops flag to the specified window style.

Now we can use this list box and display tab characters inside it to display the text in multiple columns. However, we can do something more. We could add a property to set the horizontal position of the tab stops. However, since this is quite complex, I'll skip it for the moment. In fact, this addition requires the use of an array property, which I'll show you later on in this chapter, when I finish this example.

For the moment, I've stayed with the simpler example. I've opened the Component Expert and chosen a name for the class of the new component, TTabList; a parent component, TListBox; and a page in the palette, Samples. In the automatically generated Pascal file, I've deleted some useless declarations and written the method above, including the declaration inside the class:

```
type
  TTabList = class(TListBox)
  public
    procedure CreateParams (
      var Params: TCreateParams); override;
  end;
```

The code of this example is another demonstration that writing a component can be an easy task. Again, I've written a program to test the new component, the TAB-TEST example.

## Testing the Tab List Component

To test the TTabList component, I've created a new project and added to its main form the new component and a normal list box, side by side. The form also has three edit boxes and a button, used to add new strings to the list. After adding these components to the form, I entered the new strings for both list boxes, using the same lines of text, including tabs. In Figure 27.4, you can see the text I used for both list boxes with the embedded tabs. In the background of the figure, you can already see how this text is displayed by the two list boxes.

**FIGURE 27.4:**

The form of the TABTEST example at design-time.

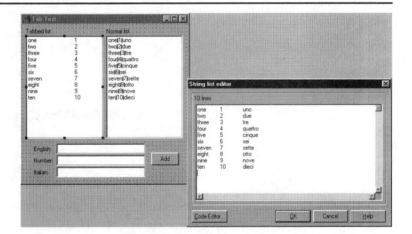

**TIP**

To enter tabs while you're in the String List Property Editor, simply press Ctrl+Tab instead of the Tab key alone.

When you run this program, besides looking at the differences between the two list boxes, you can actually add new entries. The text of the three edit boxes is used to form a string, with two tabs between the three parts. This string is added to both list boxes, with this code:

```
procedure TForm1.AddButtonClick(Sender: TObject);
var
  NewItem: String;
begin
  if Edit1.Text <> '' then
```

```
begin
  NewItem := Edit1.Text + #9 + Edit2.Text +
    #9 + Edit3.Text;
  TabList1.Items.Add (NewItem);
  ListBox1.Items.Add (NewItem);
end;
end;
```

You can see an example of the effect of this code in Figure 27.5, where I've added the number 20 to the list of English and Italian numbers. There is no other code in the test program.

**FIGURE 27.5:**

The TABTEST example shows the difference between a standard Delphi list box and the tab list component.

# Building Brand-New Components

The simple components we have built were just extensions of existing ones, with limited changes. This is what you'll probably do most of the time. At other times, however, you'll define brand-new components or components derived from generic classes, such as the TCustomXXX classes. When you write a brand-new component, you can subclass one of these higher-level classes:

- TWinControl is the parent class of components based on a window. In this case, the control can receive the input focus and get Windows messages from the system. You can also use its window handle when calling API functions.

- TGraphicControl is the parent class of visible components that have no Windows handle, thus saving some Windows resources. These components cannot receive the input focus or respond to windows messages directly.

- TComponent is the parent class of all components and can be used as a direct parent class for nonvisual components.

In the rest of the chapter, we will build some components using various parent classes, looking at the differences among them.

# A Graphical Component Built Step by Step

The graphical component I want to build is an arrow component. Arrows are often useful in graphical programs and other applications—you can use such a component to indicate a flow of information, an action, and many other elements. Instead of showing you the final version of the component, which is quite complex, I've built it in consecutive steps. To avoid rebuilding the component library each time, I've tested this component in a program that creates it at run-time. I'll install the component into the Delphi VCL only at the end of the process.

## Defining an Enumerated Property

After generating the new component with the Component Expert and choosing TGraphicControl as the parent class, we can start to customize its source code. The arrow can point in four different directions: up, down, left, and right. To express these choices, I've defined an enumerated type:

```
TArrowDirection = (adUp, adDown, adLeft, adRight);
```

This enumerated type defines a private data member of the component and a parameter of the procedure used to change it:

```
TArrow = class(TGraphicControl)
  private
    FDirection: TArrowDirection;
    procedure SetDirection (Value: TArrowDirection);
  ...
```

Now that we have private data and a method to set it, we can define a corresponding property as follows:

```
published
  property Direction: TArrowDirection
    read FDirection write SetDirection default adRight;
```

The property, which is of the same TArrowDirection data type, is read directly from the FDirection field and is written using the SetDirection procedure. The default value is adRight.

You should notice several things here. First, look at the naming conventions:

- The private data field is named with an *F* (field) at the beginning, followed by the name of the property.

- The property has a meaningful name.

- The function used to change the value of the property has the word *Set* at the beginning.

- A corresponding function used to read the property would be named *Get*Direction.

These are just naming conventions. The compiler doesn't enforce them; they are only guidelines to make programs more readable. In all likelihood, such a standard approach could be used to write tools to generate the basic code of new properties.

Another important element is the definition of the property, since this is the first property we've defined. The simplest way to define a property is to specify direct access to a field of the component (which should be a private field):

```
property NewProperty
  read FNewProperty write FNewProperty;
```

This direct approach is seldom used because in general, when you change the value of a property, you need to repaint the component or cause other side effects. Each of these cases requires a procedure. For the arrow component, this is code of the SetDirection method:

```
procedure TArrow.SetDirection (Value: TArrowDirection);
begin
  if FDirection <> Value then
  begin
    FDirection := Value;
    Invalidate;
  end;
end;
```

Notice that the side effect takes place only if the property is really changing its value. Otherwise, the code is skipped and the method ends immediately. This code structure is very common, and we will use it for most of the Set procedures of properties. The last thing we have to remember is to write a constructor to set the default value of the property in the code:

```
constructor TArrow.Create (AOwner: TComponent);
begin
  inherited Create (AOwner);
  FDirection := adRight;
end;
```

In fact, the default value specified in the property declaration is used only to determine whether or not to save the value to disk. This constructor is defined in the public section of the type definition of the new component:

```
type
  TArrowDirection = (adUp, adDown, adLeft, adRight);
  TArrow = class(TGraphicControl)
  private
    FDirection: TArrowDirection;
    procedure SetDirection (Value: TArrowDirection);
  protected
    procedure Paint; override;
  public
    constructor Create (AOwner: TComponent); override;
  published
    property Direction: TArrowDirection
      read FDirection write SetDirection default adRight;
  end;
```

# Drawing the Arrow Component

What is quite complex in this example is drawing the arrow. I've overridden the Paint method in the protected section of the type definition (as shown in the listing above), and used the Canvas property (automatically available for each TGraphicControl component). With a series of MoveTo and LineTo calls, you can draw the arrow in the different directions, as shown in Figure 27.6 for the adUp direction.

**FIGURE 27.6:**

The code used to draw the adUp arrow and the resulting effect.

```
1) MoveTo (XCenter, Height-1);
2) LineTo (XCenter, YCenter);
3) LineTo (Width 1, YCenter);
4) LineTo (XCenter, 0);
5) LineTo (0, YCenter);
6) LineTo (XCenter, YCenter);
```

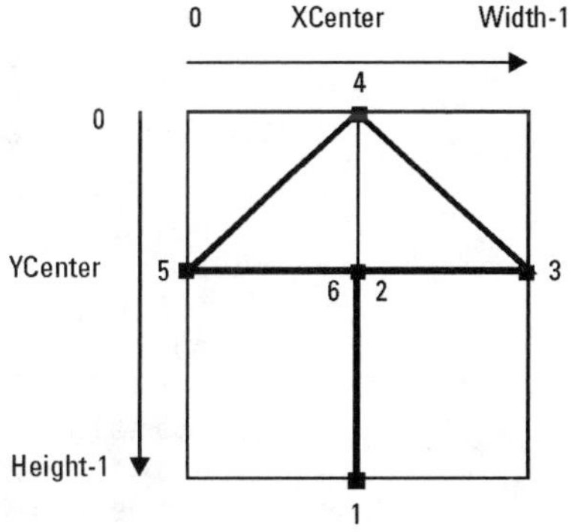

The code computes the center of the component area and uses it to determine the position of the arrow and the division between its two parts (the line and the triangle). Notice that the drawing fills the whole surface of the component, something quite common, since you can then resize the drawing to set the size of the component. Here is the code of the Paint method:

```pascal
procedure TArrow.Paint;
var
  XCenter, YCenter: Integer;
begin
  {compute the center}
  YCenter := (Height - 1) div 2;
  XCenter := (Width - 1) div 2;

  {draw the line and the arrow}
  case FDirection of
    adUp:
      with Canvas do
      begin
        MoveTo (XCenter, Height-1);
        LineTo (XCenter, YCenter);
        LineTo (Width-1, YCenter);
        LineTo (XCenter, 0);
        LineTo (0, YCenter);
        LineTo (XCenter, YCenter);
      end;
    adDown:
      with Canvas do
      begin
        MoveTo (XCenter, 0);
        LineTo (XCenter, YCenter);
        LineTo (Width - 1, YCenter);
        LineTo (XCenter, Height - 1);
        LineTo (0, YCenter);
        LineTo (XCenter, YCenter);
    end;
    adLeft:
      with Canvas do
      begin
        MoveTo (Width - 1, YCenter);
        LineTo (XCenter, YCenter);
        LineTo (XCenter, Height - 1);
        LineTo (0, YCenter);
        LineTo (XCenter, 0);
        LineTo (XCenter, YCenter);
      end;
    adRight:
      with Canvas do
      begin
        MoveTo (0, YCenter);
        LineTo (XCenter, YCenter);
        LineTo (XCenter, Height - 1);
        LineTo (Width - 1, YCenter);
```

```
        LineTo (XCenter, 0);
        LineTo (XCenter, YCenter);
      end;
  end;
end;
```

# Testing the Arrow

Now, instead of installing this component in the palette, we can write a test program to see whether it works properly. We cannot place the new component in the form of this example, ARROW1, because it is still not installed in the Delphi component library. Instead, we can create it at run-time.

> **NOTE** By the way, notice that ARROW1 is the name of the directory where you can find the code of the component, while the actual name of the project file is ATEST.

The form of this example has other components, which are used to set some of the arrow's properties. There are two spin edit components to set the width and height of the arrow, a button to accept these changes (*Size*), and a second button to turn the arrow (*Turn*), changing its Direction property. When the form is built, it creates a new arrow component:

```
procedure TForm1.FormCreate(Sender: TObject);
begin
  A := TArrow.Create (self);
  A.Parent := self;
  A.Left := 150;
  A.Top := 150;
  A.Width := 20;
  A.Height := 30;
end;
```

In this code, A is a private field of the form, declared with the TArrow component type:

```
private:
  A: TArrow;
```

The arrow component changes when one of the two buttons is pressed. The Size button uses the values of the two Spin Edit components to change the Arrow component's height and size:

```
procedure TForm1.SizeButtonClick(Sender: TObject);
begin
  A.Width := SpinEdit1.Value;
  A.Height := SpinEdit2.Value;
end;
```

The other button, Turn, changes the direction of the arrow. It reads the current value of the Direction property we have defined and increases its value by calling the system Succ procedure. In case the highest value of the set has been reached, the lowest value is selected (extreme values of the enumeration are computed using the High and Low functions). This is the code of the Turn button's OnClick event-handler:

```
procedure TForm1.TurnButtonClick(Sender: TObject);
begin
  if A.Direction = High (TArrowDirection) then
    A.Direction := Low (TArrowDirection)
  else
    A.Direction := Succ (A.Direction);
end;
```

As you can see in Figure 27.7 and test yourself by running the program, the new component works. The problem is that its capabilities are very limited. We have no way to change the size of the arrow point or to act on the colors used and the size of the lines. We will address these problems in the next versions.

**FIGURE 27.7:**

The ARROW1 example after some changes on the arrow component.

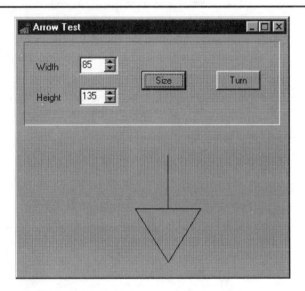

## The Point of the Arrow, Plus a Pen and a Brush

To determine the aspect of the point of the arrow, I've added two properties to the component, ArrowHeight and Filled:

```
type
  TArrow = class(TGraphicControl)
  private
```

```
    FArrowHeight: Integer;
    FFilled: Boolean;
    ...
    procedure SetArrowHeight (Value: Integer);
    procedure SetFilled (Value: Boolean);
  published
    property ArrowHeight: Integer
      read FArrowHeight write SetArrowHeight default 10;
    property Filled: Boolean
      read FFilled write SetFilled default False;
    ...
  end;
```

The ArrowHeight property determines the size of the arrow's point, and the Filled property determines whether or not it should be colored. The color used for the point is determined by the current brush of the canvas, so we should add one more property to change the brush. While we are at it, why not add another property for the pen? We have a lot of work to do for the new version of the component.

First of all, we have to implement the two properties above, ArrowHeight and Filled. Both have a corresponding private field in the class, as well as a private access function, as indicated in the declaration of the property. Their code is simple:

```
procedure TArrow.SetArrowHeight (Value: Integer);
begin
  if FArrowHeight <> Value then
  begin
    FArrowHeight := Value;
    Invalidate;
  end;
end;

procedure TArrow.SetFilled (Value: Boolean);
begin
  if FFilled <> Value then
  begin
    FFilled := Value;
    Invalidate;
  end;
end;
```

The biggest effect of these new properties, in fact, is on the Paint method, which should now correctly display the size of the arrow's point and its color. Here is an excerpt from the Paint method:

```
adUp:
  with Canvas do
  begin
    MoveTo (XCenter, Height-1);
    LineTo (XCenter, FArrowHeight);
    LineTo (Width-1, FArrowHeight);
    LineTo (XCenter, 0);
    LineTo (0, FArrowHeight);
```

```
    LineTo (XCenter, FArrowHeight);
    if FFilled then
      FloodFill (XCenter, FArrowHeight div 2,
        Pen.Color, fsBorder);
  end;
```

You can see a graph with the effect of this code in Figure 27.8 and compare it with the older version in Figure 27.6. To fill a surface with FloodFill, you have to use the first two parameters to indicate a point inside it. I've chosen a point approximately in the center of the arrowhead, but any other point within the boundaries of the arrow's triangle would do.

---

**FIGURE 27.8:**

A schema of the new version of the Paint code for the up arrow.

1) MoveTo (XCenter, Height-1);
2) LineTo (XCenter, FArrowHeight);
3) LineTo (Width -1, FArrowHeight);
4) LineTo (XCenter, 0);
5) LineTo (0, FArrowHeight);
6) LineTo (XCenter, FArrowHeight);
   if FFilled then
7) FloodFill (XCenter, FArrowHeight
   div 2, Pen.Color, fsBorder);

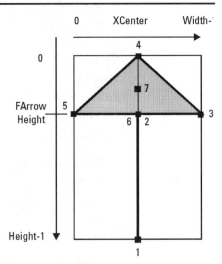

---

You can use the FloodFill method with two different techniques. In this case, I've applied the fsBorder style to fill all of the area included within a line of the pen color. As an alternative, I could have filled all of the area of a given color. (See Delphi Help about this method for the details.)

The other two new properties are defined as follows:

```
type
  TArrow = class(TGraphicControl)
  private
    FPen: TPen;
    FBrush: TBrush;
    ...
    procedure SetPen (Value: TPen);
    procedure SetBrush (Value: TBrush);
    procedure RepaintRequest (Sender: TObject);
```

```
published
  property Pen: TPen read FPen write SetPen;
  property Brush: TBrush read FBrush write SetBrush;
end;
```

These properties refer to VCL classes (or *VCL objects*, to use a standard term), so handling them is slightly different. Each of them again is implemented as a private field of the form, and uses a set method, with similar code:

```
procedure TArrow.SetPen (Value: TPen);
begin
  FPen.Assign(Value);
  Invalidate;
end;

procedure TArrow.SetBrush (Value: TBrush);
begin
  FBrush.Assign(Value);
  Invalidate;
end;
```

The problem, however, is that at design-time or run-time, the value of one of the Pen object's fields might change without changing the whole pen. Pens, Brushes, and other GDI classes have a specific event for this: OnChange. If you assign a method to the OnChange event of these components, the method will be called each time one of the parameters or properties of the class changes.

In the Arrow component, I've added this code to the Create method:

```
FPen.OnChange := RepaintRequest;
FBrush.OnChange := RepaintRequest;
```

The RepaintRequest handler is declared in the private section of the component as you already saw above. Its effect, as the name suggests, is to repaint the component by calling the Invalidate method:

```
procedure TArrow.RepaintRequest (Sender: TObject);
begin
  Invalidate;
end;
```

Now, to actually use the pen and brush for the drawing, you have to modify the Paint method accordingly:

```
procedure TArrow.Paint;
var
  XCenter, YCenter: Integer;
begin
  YCenter := (Height - 1) div 2;
  XCenter := (Width - 1) div 2;
  Canvas.Pen := FPen;
  Canvas.Brush := FBrush;
```

```
case FDirection of
  adUp:
    with Canvas do
    ...
```

The last thing to notice is that FPen and FBrush are two objects, and as with any other objects that are not built-in data types, they must be initialized. For this reason, I've added two more lines to the Create method:

```
constructor TArrow.Create (AOwner: TComponent);
begin
  {call the parent constructor}
  inherited Create (AOwner);
  {set the default values}
  FDirection := adRight;
  FArrowHeight := 10;
  FFilled := False;
  {create the pen and the brush}
  FPen := TPen.Create;
  FBrush := TBrush.Create;
  {set a handler for the OnChange event}
  FPen.OnChange := RepaintRequest;
  FBrush.OnChange := RepaintRequest;
end;
```

Then I added a destructor to the component and wrote its code as follows:

```
destructor TArrow.Destroy;
begin
  FPen.Free;
  FBrush.Free;
  inherited Destroy;
end;
```

This is probably the first time we have used a destructor effectively in an example. As I mentioned at the beginning of this chapter, writing components requires the use of many features of Object Pascal that are seldom used in other cases. To sum things up, here is the complete declaration of the new version of the TArrow class:

```
type
  TArrow = class(TGraphicControl)
  private
    FDirection: TArrowDirection;
    FArrowHeight: Integer;
    FFilled: Boolean;
    FPen: TPen;
    FBrush: TBrush;
    procedure SetDirection (Value: TArrowDirection);
    procedure SetArrowHeight (Value: Integer);
    procedure SetFilled (Value: Boolean);
    procedure SetPen (Value: TPen);
    procedure SetBrush (Value: TBrush);
    procedure RepaintRequest (Sender: TObject);
```

```
protected
  procedure Paint; override;
public
  constructor Create (AOwner: TComponent); override;
  destructor Destroy; override;
published
  property Direction: TArrowDirection
    read FDirection write SetDirection default adRight;
  property ArrowHeight: Integer
    read FArrowHeight write SetArrowHeight default 10;
  property Filled: Boolean
    read FFilled write SetFilled default False;
  property Pen: TPen read FPen write SetPen;
  property Brush: TBrush read FBrush write SetBrush;
end;
```

## Testing the Second Version of the Arrow

To test the new version of the arrow component, still without installing it in Delphi, I've extended the last test example. The new version has a form with some additional components: some more buttons, a check box, a ColorDialog component, and a track bar, as you can see in Figure 27.9 at run-time.

**FIGURE 27.9:**

An example of the output of the ARROW2 test program.

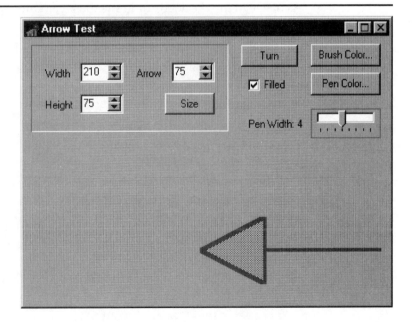

The code of the example is simply an extension of the previous version. The value of the new Spin Edit control is used when the user clicks on the Size button:

```
procedure TForm1.SizeButtonClick(Sender: TObject);
begin
  A.Width := SpinEdit1.Value;
  A.Height := SpinEdit2.Value;
  A.ArrowHeight := SpinEdit3.Value;
end;
```

The buttons related to the color of the pen and the brush use the ColorDialog component:

```
procedure TForm1.BrushButtonClick(Sender: TObject);
begin
  ColorDialog1.Color := A.Brush.Color;
  if ColorDialog1.Execute then
    A.Brush.Color := ColorDialog1.Color;
end;

procedure TForm1.PenButtonClick(Sender: TObject);
begin
  ColorDialog1.Color := A.Pen.Color;
  if ColorDialog1.Execute then
    A.Pen.Color := ColorDialog1.Color;
end;
```

A change in the check box or in the track bar automatically causes a change in the properties of the component, as well as of its user interface:

```
procedure TForm1.FilledCheckBoxClick(Sender: TObject);
begin
  A.Filled := not A.Filled;
end;
procedure TForm1.TrackBar1Change(Sender: TObject);
begin
  PenLabel.Caption := 'Pen Width: ' +
    IntToStr (TrackBar1.Position);
  A.Pen.Width := TrackBar1.Position;
end;
```

# Defining a New Custom Event

To complete our development of the Arrow component, I want to add a custom event. Most of the time, new components use the event of the parent classes. For example, in the third version of Arrow, I've made some standard events available simply by re-declaring them in the published section:

```
type
  TArrow = class(TGraphicControl)
    ...
  published
    property OnClick;
```

```
property OnDragDrop;
property OnDragOver;
property OnEndDrag;
property OnMouseDown;
property OnMouseMove;
property OnMouseUp;
```

Simply by means of this declaration, the above events (originally declared in a parent class) will now be available in the Object Inspector when we install the component. What is more interesting, of course, is to see how you can add a custom event, although this operation is not often necessary. Most of the components will work well enough if you simply redefine existing events, thereby changing their behavior.

To define a brand-new event, you first need to add a field to the class, defining the type of the event-handler. This field is actually a method pointer. Here is the definition I've added in the private section of the TArrow class:

```
FArrowDblClick: TNotifyEvent;
```

Around this field I've defined a very simple published property, with direct access to the data:

```
property OnArrowDblClick: TNotifyEvent
  read FArrowDblClick write FArrowDblClick;
```

Notice again the standard naming convention, with properties starting with *On*. The FArrowDblClick method pointer is activated (executing the corresponding function) inside the specific ArrowDblClick dynamic method. This happens only if an event-handler has been specified:

```
procedure TArrow.ArrowDblClick;
begin
  if Assigned (FArrowDblClick) then
    FArrowDblClick (self);
end;
```

This method is defined in the protected section of the type definition to allow future subclasses both to call and change it. Basically, the ArrowDblClick method is called by the handler of the wm_LButtonDblClk Windows message, but only if the double-click took place inside the arrow's point. To test this condition, we can use some of the Windows API's region functions. A *region* is an area of the screen enclosed by any shape. For example, we can build a polygonal region using the three vertices of the arrow-point triangle. The only problem is that to fill the surface properly, we must define an array of TPoints in a clockwise direction (see the description of the CreatePolygonalRgn in the Windows API Help for the details of this strange approach).

Once we have defined a region, we can test whether the point where the double-click occurred is inside the region by using the PtInRegion API call. You can see the complete source code of this procedure in the following listing, with the new elements of the type definition of the TArrow class:

```
type
  TArrow = class(TGraphicControl)
  private
    FArrowDblClick: TNotifyEvent;
    procedure WMLButtonDlbClk (var Msg: TWMLButtonDblClk);
      message wm_LButtonDblClk;
    ...
  protected
    procedure ArrowDblClick; dynamic;
    ...
  published
    property OnArrowDblClick: TNotifyEvent
      read FArrowDblClick write FArrowDblClick;
    ...
  end;

procedure TArrow.WMLButtonDblClk (
  var Msg: TWMLButtonDblClk);
var
  ArrowPoints: array [0..2] of TPoint;
  XCenter, YCenter: Integer;
  HRegion: HRgn;
begin
  {perform default handling}
  inherited;

  {compute the points}
  YCenter := (Height - 1) div 2;
  XCenter := (Width - 1) div 2;
  case FDirection of
    adUp:
    begin
      ArrowPoints [0] :=
        Point (0, FArrowHeight);
      ArrowPoints [1] :=
        Point (XCenter, 0);
      ArrowPoints [2] :=
        Point (Width-1, FArrowHeight);
    end;
    adDown:
    begin
      ArrowPoints [0] := Point (
        XCenter, Height - 1);
      ArrowPoints [1] := Point (
        0, Height - 1 - FArrowHeight);
      ArrowPoints [2] := Point (
        Width - 1, Height - 1 - FArrowHeight);
    end;
    adLeft:
    begin
```

```
      ArrowPoints [0] :=
        Point (FArrowHeight, Height - 1);
      ArrowPoints [1] :=
        Point (0, YCenter);
      ArrowPoints [2] :=
        Point (FArrowHeight, 0);
    end;
    adRight:
    begin
      ArrowPoints [0] := Point (
        Width - 1 - FArrowHeight, Height - 1);
      ArrowPoints [1] := Point (
        Width - 1 - FArrowHeight, 0);
      ArrowPoints [2] := Point (
        Width - 1, YCenter);
    end;
  end;

  {check whether the click took place
  in the arrow-point region}
  HRegion := CreatePolygonRgn (
    ArrowPoints, 3, WINDING);
  if PtInRegion (HRegion, Msg.XPos, Msg.YPos) then
    ArrowDblClick;
  DeleteObject (HRegion);
end;
```

## Testing the OnArrowDblClick Event

Now that we have defined the complete version of the component, we can make one last test on the new event before installing it in Delphi. The third version of the test program, saved in the ARROW3 directory, uses the same form as the previous version. Its code, though, contains the new method, ArrowDoubleClick. This procedure is declared in the public portion of the form and is defined as follows:

```
procedure TForm1.ArrowDoubleClick (Sender: TObject);
begin
  ShowMessage ('You have double-clicked ' +
    'on the point of the arrow');
end;
```

It is a handler of the same type as that required by the Arrow component's OnArrowDblClick event, so we can set it with the new line at the end of the form's Create method:

```
procedure TForm1.FormCreate(Sender: TObject);
begin
  A := TArrow.Create (self);
  A.Parent := self;
  A.Left := 200;
  A.Top := 200;
```

```
  A.Width := 20;
  A.Height := 30;
  A.ArrowHeight := 15;
  A.OnArrowDblClick := ArrowDoubleClick;
end;
```

The result of this code? If you run the program and double-click inside the triangular point of the arrow, a message is displayed, as shown in Figure 27.10. If, instead, you double-click on the component but outside the arrow point, nothing happens.

**FIGURE 27.10:**

The output message displayed by the ARROW3 example when a user clicks on the arrow's point.

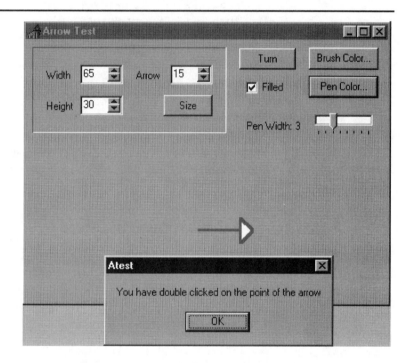

## Adding a Bitmap for the Components Palette

Now that we have written the component's code, before installing it we have to take a further step: we must define a bitmap for the Component palette. The first two components we defined in this chapter had no specific bitmap, so they used those of their parent class. In this case, since there is no parent class with a bitmap, we'll get a default Delphi bitmap. Luckily, defining a new bitmap is easy, once you know the rules. First of all, open the Image editor, start a new project, and select the DCR (Dynamic Component Resource) project type.

**TIP**

DCR files are simply standard RES files with a different extension. If you prefer, you can create them with any resource editor, including the Borland Resource Workshop, which is certainly a more powerful tool than the Delphi Image editor. When you finish creating the resource file, simply rename the RES file with a DCR extension.

Add a new bitmap to the resource, choosing a size of 24 × 24 pixels. Now you are ready to draw the bitmap. The only precaution you have to take is to choose dark yellow (`clOlive` in Delphi terms) for the background color, because this is the color the Component palette replaces with the default grays for the selected or unselected component. The other important rule refers to naming. In this case, the rules do not just define a naming convention; they are enforced by the system:

- The name of the bitmap resource must match the name of the component, including the initial *T*. In this case, the name of the bitmap resource is TARROW.

- The name of the bitmap resource must be in uppercase. Delphi will ignore a bitmap resource named with mixed case (such as *TArrow*).

- The name of the DCR file must match the name of the compiled unit that defines the component, which is the same as the name of the Pascal source code file. In this case, the file name must be ARROW3.DCR. The file must be saved in the same directory as the component.

Notice that the source code does *not* include the resource. The component's bitmap is used by the Delphi environment, and in particular the Component palette, not the final program. For this reason, the component's bitmaps are not linked in the VCL, and, of course, are not part of your compiled applications.

When the bitmap for the component is ready, you can install the component in Delphi using the standard approach. Choose the Install command from the Components menu, select the new file, ARROW3.PAS, and click on OK. The component is added to the VCL, and its bitmap appears on the palette.

# The Final Test of the Arrow Component

Now that the component is installed, we can write a small example to test it. This time, we will be able to use the component like any standard component, setting properties and events with the Object Inspector.

This type of test, after we have written the program, is very important. Often, when you create a component at run-time, some elements may be different from what you would expect. Also, by testing various values for the properties, you can find errors the initial tests did not show. In fact, when testing the component for this example, I found two errors in the code I had written.

The first error is that the component has no default size, so when you place it in a form, its size will be a single pixel. The second error occurs when you select most of the alternative pen styles. In many cases, the filling algorithm doesn't work anymore, as you can see in Figure 27.11.

Since these problems are fairly common, I've left the ARROW3 code as it was (that is, with bugs) and made the changes in a new version, ARROW4. You can install one of the two versions at a time in Delphi to test them: when you install a version, you have to remove the other one because you cannot have two components—two classes in the components library—with the same name.

**FIGURE 27.11:**

If you try to use a dotted pen in the ARROW3 component, a problem in the filling code emerges at design-time.

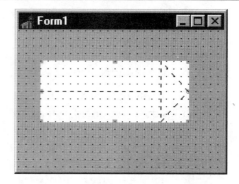

## Correcting Bugs in the Arrow Component

The first change in the Arrow component is adding the default values for the Width and Height properties, both in the description of these properties and in the Create method:

```
property Width default 50;
property Height default 20;
```

The above is simply a re-declaration of the properties, already defined by a parent class, with a new default value. Actually, providing a default value for the height and width is not common in Delphi, but I thought it was a good idea anyway. In fact, if the programmer doesn't change these standard values, they won't show up in the textual description of the form.

The other changes are related to the FloodFill method. If you use FloodFill, the region should have a continuous (unbroken) border. Dashed lines don't qualify as continuous borders, so FloodFill *leaks* outside the proper area. As a result, it is time for a complete rewrite of the component's Paint method, using the PolyLine and Polygon methods of the TCanvas class instead of FloodFill. The difference between PolyLine and Polygon is that the first draws a line and the second fills the resulting polygon with the current brush. Polygon fills its interior using pure vectors. It doesn't matter what is on the screen; the polygon will be filled properly. So in this case Polygon is a better choice than FloodFill.

We have already seen how to build a polygon with an array of points to test whether the click was on the arrow point. A similar code can be used now. The only problem is that the PolyLine procedure doesn't automatically close the polygon. To draw a triangle, it requires a fourth point in the same position as the first one. You can see the new Paint function in Listing 27.1, together with the complete source code of the final version of the arrow component.

### Listing 27.1: The final version of the Arrow component, in file ARROW4.PAS.

```
unit Arrow4;

interface

uses
  SysUtils, WinTypes, WinProcs, Messages, Classes,
  Graphics, Controls, Forms, Dialogs;

type
  TArrowDirection = (adUp, adDown, adLeft, adRight);
  TArrow = class(TGraphicControl)
  private
    FDirection: TArrowDirection;
    FArrowHeight: Integer;
    FFilled: Boolean;
    FPen: TPen;
    FBrush: TBrush;
    FArrowDblClick: TNotifyEvent;
    procedure SetDirection (Value: TArrowDirection);
    procedure SetArrowHeight (Value: Integer);
    procedure SetFilled (Value: Boolean);
    procedure SetPen (Value: TPen);
    procedure SetBrush (Value: TBrush);
    procedure RepaintRequest (Sender: TObject);
    procedure WMLButtonDlbClk (var Msg: TWMLButtonDblClk);
      message wm_LButtonDblClk;
  protected
    procedure Paint; override;
    procedure ArrowDblClick; dynamic;
  public
    constructor Create (AOwner: TComponent); override;
    destructor Destroy; override;
  published
```

## Listing 27.1: The final version of the Arrow component, in file ARROW4.PAS (continued).

```pascal
      property Width default 50;
      property Height default 20;
      property Direction: TArrowDirection
         read FDirection write SetDirection default adRight;
      property ArrowHeight: Integer
         read FArrowHeight write SetArrowHeight default 10;
      property Filled: Boolean
         read FFilled write SetFilled default False;
      property Pen: TPen read FPen write SetPen;
      property Brush: TBrush read FBrush write SetBrush;
      property OnClick;
      property OnDragDrop;
      property OnDragOver;
      property OnEndDrag;
      property OnMouseDown;
      property OnMouseMove;
      property OnMouseUp;
      property OnArrowDblClick: TNotifyEvent
         read FArrowDblClick write FArrowDblClick;
   end;

procedure Register;

implementation

constructor TArrow.Create (AOwner: TComponent);
begin
   {call the parent constructor}
   inherited Create (AOwner);
   {set the default values}
   FDirection := adRight;
   Width := 50;
   Height := 20;
   FArrowHeight := 10;
   FFilled := False;
   {create the pen and the brush}
   FPen := TPen.Create;
   FBrush := TBrush.Create;
   {set a handler for the OnChange event}
   FPen.OnChange := RepaintRequest;
   FBrush.OnChange := RepaintRequest;
end;

destructor TArrow.Destroy;
begin
   {delete the two objects}
   FPen.Free;
   FBrush.Free;
   {call the parent destructor}
```

**Listing 27.1: The final version of the Arrow component, in file ARROW4.PAS (continued).**

```pascal
  inherited Destroy;
end;

procedure TArrow.SetDirection (Value: TArrowDirection);
begin
  if FDirection <> Value then
  begin
    FDirection := Value;
    Invalidate;
  end;
end;

procedure TArrow.SetArrowHeight (Value: Integer);
begin
  if FArrowHeight <> Value then
  begin
    FArrowHeight := Value;
    Invalidate;
  end;
end;

procedure TArrow.SetFilled (Value: Boolean);
begin
  if FFilled <> Value then
  begin
    FFilled := Value;
    Invalidate;
  end;
end;

procedure TArrow.SetPen (Value: TPen);
begin
  FPen.Assign(Value);
  Invalidate;
end;

procedure TArrow.SetBrush (Value: TBrush);
begin
  FBrush.Assign(Value);
  Invalidate;
end;

procedure TArrow.RepaintRequest (Sender: TObject);
begin
  Invalidate;
end;

procedure TArrow.Paint;
var
  XCenter, YCenter: Integer;
```

**Listing 27.1: The final version of the Arrow component, in file ARROW4.PAS  (continued).**

```
  ArrowPoints: array [0..3] of TPoint;
begin
  YCenter := (Height - 1) div 2;
  XCenter := (Width - 1) div 2;

  {use the current pen and brush}
  Canvas.Pen := FPen;
  Canvas.Brush := FBrush;

  {draw a line and compute the triangle
  for the arrow point}
  case FDirection of
    adUp:
    begin
      Canvas.MoveTo (XCenter, Height-1);
      Canvas.LineTo (XCenter, FArrowHeight);
      ArrowPoints [0] :=
        Point (0, FArrowHeight);
      ArrowPoints [1] :=
        Point (XCenter, 0);
      ArrowPoints [2] :=
        Point (Width-1, FArrowHeight);
      ArrowPoints [3] :=
        Point (0, FArrowHeight);
    end;
    adDown:
    begin
      Canvas.MoveTo (XCenter, 0);
      Canvas.LineTo (XCenter, Height - 1 - FArrowHeight);
      ArrowPoints [0] := Point (
        XCenter, Height - 1);
      ArrowPoints [1] := Point (
        0, Height - 1 - FArrowHeight);
      ArrowPoints [2] := Point (
        Width - 1, Height - 1 - FArrowHeight);
      ArrowPoints [3] := Point (
        XCenter, Height - 1);
    end;
    adLeft:
    begin
      Canvas.MoveTo (Width - 1, YCenter);
      Canvas.LineTo (FArrowHeight, YCenter);
      ArrowPoints [0] :=
        Point (FArrowHeight, Height - 1);
      ArrowPoints [1] :=
        Point (0, YCenter);
      ArrowPoints [2] :=
        Point (FArrowHeight, 0);
      ArrowPoints [3] :=
        Point (FArrowHeight, Height - 1);
```

**Listing 27.1: The final version of the Arrow component, in file ARROW4.PAS (continued).**

```pascal
    end;
    adRight:
    begin
      Canvas.MoveTo (0, YCenter);
      Canvas.LineTo (Width - 1 - FArrowHeight, YCenter);
      ArrowPoints [0] := Point (
        Width - 1 - FArrowHeight, Height - 1);
      ArrowPoints [1] := Point (
        Width - 1 - FArrowHeight, 0);
      ArrowPoints [2] := Point (
        Width - 1, YCenter);
      ArrowPoints [3] := Point (
        Width - 1 - FArrowHeight, Height - 1);
    end;
  end;

  {draw the arrow point, eventually filling it}
  if FFilled then
    Canvas.Polygon (ArrowPoints)
  else
    Canvas.PolyLine (ArrowPoints);
end;

procedure TArrow.WMLButtonDblClk (
  var Msg: TWMLButtonDblClk);
var
  ArrowPoints: array [0..2] of TPoint;
  XCenter, YCenter: Integer;
  HRegion: HRgn;
begin
  {perform default handling}
  inherited;

  {compute the points}
  YCenter := (Height - 1) div 2;
  XCenter := (Width - 1) div 2;
  case FDirection of
    adUp:
    begin
      ArrowPoints [0] :=
        Point (0, FArrowHeight);
      ArrowPoints [1] :=
        Point (XCenter, 0);
      ArrowPoints [2] :=
        Point (Width-1, FArrowHeight);
    end;
    adDown:
    begin
      ArrowPoints [0] := Point (
        XCenter, Height - 1);
```

**Listing 27.1: The final version of the Arrow component, in file ARROW4.PAS (continued).**

```pascal
      ArrowPoints [1] := Point (
        0, Height - 1 - FArrowHeight);
      ArrowPoints [2] := Point (
        Width - 1, Height - 1 - FArrowHeight);
    end;
    adLeft:
    begin
      ArrowPoints [0] :=
        Point (FArrowHeight, Height - 1);
      ArrowPoints [1] :=
        Point (0, YCenter);
      ArrowPoints [2] :=
        Point (FArrowHeight, 0);
    end;
    adRight:
    begin
      ArrowPoints [0] := Point (
        Width - 1 - FArrowHeight, Height - 1);
      ArrowPoints [1] := Point (
        Width - 1 - FArrowHeight, 0);
      ArrowPoints [2] := Point (
        Width - 1, YCenter);
    end;
  end;

  {check whether the click took place
  in the arrow-point region}
  HRegion := CreatePolygonRgn (
    ArrowPoints, 3, WINDING);
  if PtInRegion (HRegion, Msg.XPos, Msg.YPos) then
    ArrowDblClick;
  DeleteObject (HRegion);
end;

procedure TArrow.ArrowDblClick;
begin
  {call the handler, if available}
  if Assigned (FArrowDblClick) then
    FArrowDblClick (self);
end;

procedure Register;
begin
  RegisterComponents('Samples', [TArrow]);
end;

end.
```

## Arrows and Shapes

Now that everything should work fine, we can test this component in an example project, TARROW (which stands for *Test Arrow*). The form of this program has four arrows, four shapes, and a timer. The aim of the example is to see a colored element move around the surface of the form. The color, indicating a hypothetical active element of a process, moves from a square to the following arrow, then to the next square, and so on.

This is the reason for having a timer. When the form is created, the program stores the four shapes and the four arrows in an array of graphical components, defined as follows:

```
private
  Graph: array [1..8] of TGraphicControl;
```

Here is the code of the FormCreate method:

```
procedure TForm1.FormCreate(Sender: TObject);
var
  I: Integer;
begin
  Active := 1;
  Shape1.Brush.Color := clYellow;
  for I := 1 to 4 do
  begin
    Graph [I * 2 - 1] :=
      (FindComponent ('Shape' + IntToStr (I))
      as TGraphicControl);
    Graph [I * 2] :=
      (FindComponent ('Arrow' + IntToStr (I))
      as TGraphicControl);
  end;
end;
```

Well, I've managed to show you something new about the use of components in Delphi even in this example. The FindComponent method simply returns a component with the given name of the form, scanning the form's Components array. When this array has been built, you can change the color of the active element quite easily (as you can see in Figure 27.12). Remember that you also need to restore the color of the element that was active before:

```
procedure TForm1.Timer1Timer(Sender: TObject);
begin
  // disables the active elements
  if Graph [Active] is TArrow then
    TArrow (Graph [Active]).Brush.Color := clWhite
  else
    TShape (Graph [Active]).Brush.Color := clWhite;
  // compute the new active element
  Active := Active mod 8 + 1;
  // enables the active element
```

```
    if Graph [Active] is TArrow then
      TArrow (Graph [Active]).Brush.Color := clRed
    else
      TShape (Graph [Active]).Brush.Color := clYellow;
  end;
```

FIGURE 27.12:

The output of the TARROW example.

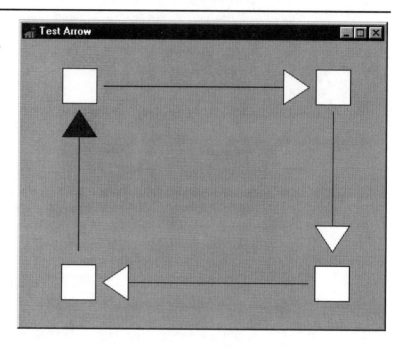

That's all—well, almost all. In fact, why not show a message when the user double-clicks exactly on the arrow point of an active arrow? The following method is connected to all four arrow components, using the Object Inspector:

```
procedure TForm1.ArrowDoubleClick(Sender: TObject);
begin
  if (Sender as TArrow).Brush.Color = clRed then
    ShowMessage ('Click on active arrow');
end;
```

This example, which might be the output of a simulation program, ends the part of the chapter devoted to the step-by-step development of the arrow component. Now it is time to move to another component: a digital clock.

# The Clock Components

The next component I want to focus on is a clock. I'll actually build two components: a digital clock and an analog clock, and I'll put both components in a single source file. This example has some interesting features. First, it embeds components (a Timer) in another component; second, it shows the live-data approach; and third, it shows how to place two components in a single source file.

# The Digital Clock

We will focus first on the digital clock. Since it will provide some text output, I considered subclassing the TLabel component. However, if you do this, a user can change the label's caption—that is, the text of the clock. To avoid this problem, I simply used the TCustomLabel component as the parent class. A TCustomLabel object has the same capabilities as a TLabel object, but few published properties. In other words, a TCustomLabel subclass can decide which properties should be available and which should remain hidden.

Besides re-declaring some of the properties of the parent class, TDigClock has one of its own, Active. This property indicates whether or not the clock is working. As you might have guessed, the clock contains a Timer component. However, the Timer is not made public through a property since I don't want programmers to access it directly. Instead, I made the Enabled property of the Timer available, wrapping it inside the Active property of the digital clock. Here is the full type declaration for the component:

```
type
  TDigClock = class (TCustomLabel)
  private
    FTimer: TTimer;
    function GetActive: Boolean;
    procedure SetActive (Value: Boolean);
  protected
    procedure UpdateClock (Sender: TObject);
  public
    constructor Create (AOwner: TComponent); override;
    destructor Destroy; override;
  published
    property Align;
    property Alignment;
    property Color;
    property Font;
    property ParentColor;
    property ParentFont;
    property ParentShowHint;
    property PopupMenu;
    property ShowHint;
    property Transparent;
    property Visible;
    property Active: Boolean
      read GetActive write SetActive;
  end;
```

Notice that we need a method both to write and to read the value of the Active property, because it is not local data, but rather refers to a member of the embedded component, the Timer:

```
function TDigClock.GetActive: Boolean;
begin
  Result := FTimer.Enabled;
end;

procedure TDigClock.SetActive (Value: Boolean);
begin
  FTimer.Enabled := Value;
end;
```

The other problems of the example relate to the use of the Timer. We have to override both the constructor and the destructor of the class and provide a function to connect to the OnTimer event.

The Create method calls the corresponding method of the base class and initializes the Timer:

```
constructor TDigClock.Create (AOwner: TComponent);
begin
  inherited Create (AOwner);
  FTimer := TTimer.Create (self);
  FTimer.OnTimer := UpdateClock;
  FTimer.Enabled := True;
end;
```

The destructor simply frees the Timer object:

```
destructor TDigClock.Destroy;
begin
  FTimer.Free;
  inherited Destroy;
end;
```

The key piece of the component's code is the UpdateClock procedure, which is just one statement:

```
procedure TDigClock.UpdateClock (Sender: TObject);
begin
  Caption := TimeToStr (Time);
end;
```

It uses Caption, which is an unpublished property, so that a user of the component cannot modify it. The result of this code statement is to display the current time. This happens continuously, since we have a Timer connected to it.

## The Analog Clock

We can build the code of the analog clock using some of the code of the digital clock, but we cannot derive the code from it. After all, it makes no sense to say the analog clock is a Label. Instead, I've derived the TAnalogClock component from the TGraphicComponent class. As a result, some of the code of the digital clock has been duplicated. As before, this clock has a Timer, an Active property, and so on. However, it has much more code because it must draw the hands of the clock, including the second hand and the marks for the hours. Certain properties determine the presence of these optional elements, while other properties determine the color of the various elements. Actually, I've limited the color choices to two—one for the second hand and the other for the other elements—but you can easily extend the example to include additional properties. Here is the declaration of the class of the new component:

```
TAnalogClock = class (TGraphicControl)
private
  FTimer: TTimer;
  FSeconds: Boolean;
  FHourMarks: Boolean;
  FColorHands: TColor;
  FColorSeconds: TColor;
  Hour, Minute, Second: Word; {current time}
  OldMinute: Word;
  function GetActive: Boolean;
  procedure SetActive (Value: Boolean);
  procedure SetSeconds (Value: Boolean);
  procedure SetHourMarks (Value: Boolean);
  procedure SetColorHands (Value: TColor);
  procedure DrawHand (XCenter, YCenter, Radius,
    BackRadius: Integer; Angle: Real);
protected
  procedure UpdateClock (Sender: TObject);
  procedure Paint; override;
public
  constructor Create (AOwner: TComponent); override;
  destructor Destroy; override;
published
  property Align;
  property Color;
  property ParentColor;
  property ParentShowHint;
  property PopupMenu;
  property ShowHint;
  property Visible;
  property Active: Boolean
    read GetActive write SetActive;
  property Seconds: Boolean
    read FSeconds write SetSeconds default True;
  property HourMarks: Boolean
    read FHourMarks write SetHourMarks default True;
  property ColorHands: TColor
    read FColorHands write SetColorHands default clBlue;
```

```
property ColorSeconds: TColor
  read FColorSeconds write FColorSeconds default clRed;
end;
```

Most of the code of this component has actually been borrowed from the CLOCK2 and CLOCK3 examples from Chapter 19. However, I could not use the last optimized version, CLOCK3, as it was written. At design-time, the TGraphicControl component can only produce output via a Paint method, probably because it does not own its own window. Trying to draw the second hand with the xor pen mode, as I did in CLOCK3, failed in design mode. Of course, everything worked fine at run-time, but I liked the idea of showing a working analog clock at design-time.

Accordingly, I decided to build a non-optimized version of the component, which has some flickering when the second hand is present. To reduce this problem, I tried to speed up the Paint method, limiting the changes on pens, drawing pixels instead of circles for the hour marks, and so on:

```
procedure TAnalogClock.Paint;
var
  Angle: Real;
  I, X, Y, Radius, XCenter, YCenter: Integer;
begin
  {compute the middle of the component}
  XCenter := Width div 2;
  YCenter := Height div 2;
  if XCenter > YCenter then
    Radius := YCenter - 1
  else
    Radius := XCenter - 1;
  {draw hour marks}
  if FHourMarks then
  begin
    for I := 0 to 11 do
    begin
      Angle := 2 * Pi * (I + 9) / 12;
      X := XCenter - Round (Radius * Cos (Angle));
      Y := YCenter - Round (Radius * Sin (Angle));
      Canvas.Pixels [X, Y] := FColorHands;
      Canvas.Pixels [X+1, Y] := FColorHands;
      Canvas.Pixels [X, Y+1] := FColorHands;
      Canvas.Pixels [X+1, Y+1] := FColorHands;
    end;
  end;

  {draw the minutes hand}
  Canvas.Pen.Color := FColorHands;
  Angle := 2 * Pi * (Minute + 45) / 60;
  DrawHand (XCenter, YCenter,
    Radius * 90 div 100, 0, Angle);

  {draw the hours hand}
  Angle := 2 * Pi * (Hour + 9 + Minute / 60) / 12;
```

```
DrawHand (XCenter, YCenter,
  Radius * 70 div 100, 0, Angle);

if FSeconds then
begin
  {draw the seconds hand}
  Canvas.Pen.Color := FColorSeconds;
  Angle := 2 * Pi * (Second + 45) / 60;
  DrawHand (XCenter, YCenter, Radius,
    Radius * 30 div 100, Angle);
end;
end;
```

This code uses the DrawHand method, already presented in Chapter 19. The code handling the Timer is very similar to that of the Digital Clock component (presented in the last section). The other properties have very simple Set methods:

```
procedure TAnalogClock.SetSeconds (Value: Boolean);
begin
  if not (FSeconds = Value) then
  begin
    FSeconds := Value;
    Invalidate;
  end;
end;

procedure TAnalogClock.SetHourMarks (Value: Boolean);
begin
  if not (FHourMarks = Value) then
  begin
    FHourMarks := Value;
    Invalidate;
  end;
end;

procedure TAnalogClock.SetColorHands (Value: TColor);
begin
  if not (FColorHands = Value) then
  begin
    FColorHands := Value;
    Invalidate;
  end;
end;
```

Here is the code of the constructor, which in addition to creating the Timer, also provides some default property values:

```
constructor TAnalogClock.Create (AOwner: TComponent);
begin
  inherited Create (AOwner);
  FTimer := TTimer.Create (self);
  FTimer.OnTimer := UpdateClock;
  FTimer.Enabled := True;
  {set default values}
```

```
  Width := 100;
  Height := 100;
  FSeconds := True;
  FHourMarks := True;
  FColorSeconds := clRed;
  FColorHands := clBlue;
  {get the current time before
  the clock is first painted}
  UpdateClock (self);
end;
```

Finally, here is the core method, UpdateClock, which is now more complex:

```
procedure TAnalogClock.UpdateClock (Sender: TObject);
var
  HSec: Word;   {temporary value, not used}
begin
  OldMinute := Minute;
  DecodeTime (Time, Hour, Minute, Second, HSec);
  if FSeconds or not (Minute = OldMinute) then
    Invalidate;
end;
```

If you want to optimize the repaint operations of this component, you should change the if statement of the method above to something like this:

```
if Minute = OldMinute then
  begin
  if FSeconds then
    InvalidateSeconds;
  end
  else
    Invalidate;
```

What is not easy is writing the InvalidateSeconds method. You have to invalidate both the area of the hand's previous position and the area of the new position. If you invalidate a rectangular area, you have to consider that its upper-left and lower-right corners change depending on the hand's position. You can get the position of the two extreme points of the hand, see which has the lower and higher $X$ and $Y$ values, and use the result to build the rectangle. Then, of course, you are still invalidating too much. Instead of a rectangle, it might be better to build a region just around the hand. Even though computing it requires some time, you'll actually save a good deal of paint time and reduce flickering to a minimum.

If you try to do this—an interesting exercise—remember also that you should invalidate a portion of the area of the parent component. To do this, you should use the parent's handle as the first parameter of the InvalidateRect or InvalidateRgn call. Then, remember to define the rectangle or region in the coordinates of the parent form, adding the value of the component's Top and Left properties to each vertical and horizontal coordinate, respectively. Another alternative to this is to use an off-screen bitmap, so that you'll copy only the final bitmap to the screen, avoiding the flickering.

What might be really interesting instead is to improve the component, making it more flexible. Basically, we should look at the Paint method and move all the constants to properties. Here are some suggestions: add a property for the color of each element, one for the length of each hand (in both directions), and other properties for the hour marks (none; only 4; 12, as it is now; 60) and their style.

# A First Test

Now that we have our two new components, we need to test them. I actually built a test program while I was developing these components, not after, in a process similar to that of the arrow example. However, for these new components, I decided to show you only their final code and the final version of the test program, which is very simple. The form of the DIGTEST example (present in the DIG-CLOCK subdirectory along with the component code) is empty, and all its code is in the FormCreate and FormDestroy methods. The three clock components used in this program are defined in the form as follows:

```
private
  Clock1: TDigClock;
  Clock2, Clock3: TAnalogClock;
```

The FormCreate functions is where most of the work takes place:

```
procedure TForm1.FormCreate(Sender: TObject);
begin
  Clock1 := TDigClock.Create (self);
  Clock1.Parent := self;
  Clock1.Left := 10;
  Clock1.Top := 10;

  Clock2 := TAnalogClock.Create (self);
  Clock2.Parent := self;
  Clock2.Left := 10;
  Clock2.Top := 50;
  Clock2.HourMarks := False;

  Clock3 := TAnalogClock.Create (self);
  Clock3.Parent := self;
  Clock3.Left := 150;
  Clock3.Top := 50;
  Clock3.Seconds := False;
  Clock3.ColorHands := clRed;
end;
```

Similarly, the FormDestroy method calls Free for each of the three clock objects. When you run this program, you can only see the clocks on the screen; you have no way to change their properties. The output of the example is shown in Figure 27.13.

FIGURE 27.13:

The output of the DIGTEST example, with the two clock components.

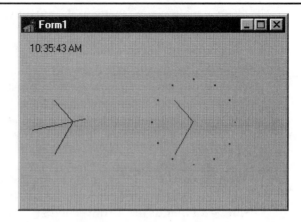

## Installing the Clock Components

Since the components seem to work in the test program, it is time to install them in the Delphi VCL. You should know the process by now, so I won't describe it again. However, notice that for the bitmaps you need to create a single DCR file, named after the source code file. This time, the single DCR file should contain two bitmaps, one for each component, with the names of the classes.

Now that the components are installed in the components library and on the palette, you can see an example of the live-data Delphi approach. As soon as you place a digital or an analog clock on a form, it starts working, showing the current time, and is automatically updated by the hidden timer. At this point, you can create any example that uses clocks. You can place a graphical clock on a toolbar or a digital clock on a status bar or simply use one of them in a form.

# Defining an Array Property

Now that we have built some interesting components, the arrow and the two clocks, we can move back to the example introduced at the beginning of the chapter, the tabbed list box. We can now complete this example using (for the first time) an array property. There is actually nothing strange about the definition of an array property, but this is not documented in detail, so I decided to provide a specific example. When implementing this example, we will face another confusing issue: dialog box units.

# The New Tabbed List

The new version of the tabbed list box has a new property, which sets the position of the tabs. This is the definition of the array property:

```
property TabStops [Index: Integer]: Integer
  read GetTabStops write SetTabStops;
```

This property cannot be added to the published portion of the unit because its type is not an `object` data type or a simple (built-in) type. However, we can declare it in the public portion of the class declaration, effectively making it a run-time property. Although it is not necessary, I've added an array field to the component to store the current tab stop values, based on a custom array data type, as you can see in the complete declaration of the component class:

```
type
  TTabsArray = array [0..9] of Integer;

  TTabList = class(TListBox)
  private
    FTabStops: TTabsArray;
    function GetTabStops (Index: Integer): Integer;
    procedure SetTabStops (Index, Value: Integer);
  protected
    procedure UpdateTabStops;
  public
    procedure CreateParams (
      var Params: TCreateParams); override;
    procedure CreateWnd; override;
    property TabStops [Index: Integer]: Integer
      read GetTabStops write SetTabStops;
  end;
```

The overridden CreateWnd method initializes the array with fixed values, then updates the actual values of the list box by calling the UpdateTabStops method (a custom method I've added to copy the values from the private integer array to the actual Windows list box):

```
procedure TTabList.CreateWnd;
var
  I: Integer;
begin
  inherited CreateWnd;
  for I := Low (FTabStops) to High (FTabStops) do
    FTabStops [I] := I * 100;
  UpdateTabStops;
end;
```

This method sets the initial values, but what is really important is the definition of the two access methods for the property, which have an unusual structure. In fact, this time both the Get function and the Set procedure have one more parameter: the index used to access the property. The code of these two methods is quite simple:

```
procedure TTabList.SetTabStops (Index, Value: Integer);
begin
  if FTabStops [Index] <> Value then
  begin
    FTabStops [Index] := Value;
    UpdateTabStops;
    Invalidate;
  end;
end;

function TTabList.GetTabStops (Index: Integer): Integer;
begin
  Result := FTabStops [Index];
end;
```

SetTabStops simply updates the array, calls the UpdateTabStops method, and then calls Invalidate to repaint it. The UpdateTabStops method is actually the key element of this component. It sets the tab stops in the list box control that is owned by the component. To accomplish this, a program has to send an lb_SetTabStops message to the list box, passing as parameters the number of tabs you want to set and a pointer to an array of integers, with these tab values:

```
SendMessage (Handle, lb_SetTabStops,
  1 + High (ConvertedTabs) - Low (ConvertedTabs),
  LongInt (@ConvertedTabs));
```

## Using Dialog Box Units

In the code above, ConvertedTabs is another TTabsArray variable. You cannot pass the FTabStops array directly because the list box uses different units of measurement. In fact, the list box tab stops are expressed in dialog box units, even if you place the list box in a generic window (or any kind of form or container component). However, I don't want to force programmers to use these units; I want to let them work in pixels. For this reason, I've added some conversion code to the UpdateTabStops method.

First of all, what are dialog box units? *Dialog box units* are a unit of measure based on the dialog's font size because the controls of a dialog box (such as list boxes, labels, and edit boxes) base their size on the current font. (Consider that Windows' native font handling for controls is less flexible than the one offered by Delphi.) Dialog box units are computed by taking the average character width and height and dividing them by 4 and 8, respectively. Now, how do you make this a conversion to dialog box units? The Windows API function GetDialogBaseUnits returns the base value of the dialog box units (the *x* in the low word and the *y* in the high word), so you might think you could write this code:

```
XDialog := XPixels * 4 div LoWord (GetDialogBaseUnits);
```

However, this function is not reliable. It works only for dialog boxes (or list boxes) using the system font. Instead, you can compute the average width of the font in your code. You should use only the same code Windows itself uses, which is based on the GetTextExtent API function. In Delphi, we can use the TextWidth method of the TCanvas class instead. The standard Windows approach is to take the 26 uppercase and 26 lowercase characters, measure the total width, and compute the average by dividing by 52:

```
HUnits := Canvas.TextWidth (
  'ABCDEFGHIJKLMNOPQRSTUVWXYZabcdefghijklmnopqrstuvwxyz')
  div 52;
```

Of course, you should set the font first, as you can see in the following listing. When you have the base dialog box unit, you can easily compute the new value for each of the tabs and set them in the Windows list box control. So, after this detailed discussion, here is the code of the UpdateTabStops method:

```
procedure TTabList.UpdateTabStops;
var
  I: Integer;
  HUnits: Integer;
  ConvertedTabs: TTabsArray;
begin
  {determine the horizontal dialog box units
  used by the list box, which depend on
  its current font}
  Canvas.Font := Font;
  HUnits := Canvas.TextWidth (
    'ABCDEFGHIJKLMNOPQRSTUVWXYZabcdefghijklmnopqrstuvwxyz')
    div 52;

  {convert the array of tab values}
  for I := Low (ConvertedTabs) to High (ConvertedTabs) do
    ConvertedTabs [I] := FTabStops [I] * 4 div HUnits;

  {activate the tabs stops in the list box,
  sending a Windows list box message}
  SendMessage (Handle, lb_SetTabStops,
    1 + High (ConvertedTabs) - Low (ConvertedTabs),
    LongInt (@ConvertedTabs));
end;
```

## Installing the Component

You can now install the component as usual and provide a new bitmap instead of using the one for the list box. In addition to solving the problem mentioned earlier (fixing the length of the path), you should remove the older tabbed list box component before you try installing the new one. Up to now, we have always installed components from source code files to the Component palette, which makes them available to other applications. However, as soon as you add a component you have defined to a form, its source file is included in the list of units of the uses statement. You add only the compiled unit to the VCL, but since Delphi static links component code directly into your EXEs, you need to supply a source file with the interface section of the unit declaring the component.

Remember that if you want to build the compiled unit of a component, among other approaches, you can open its source file as if it were a project file (using the Delphi Open Project command). When you have done this, you can check the syntax of the component and compile it into the DCU format.

## A Header and a Tabbed List Box

Before adding a finishing touch to this component, I want to test the tabbed list box with the most typical example: adding a Header component above it to let the user adjust the tabs at run-time. The form of this example, TABTEST2, is similar to the one of the previous version, TABTEST1, beside a THeader component aligned at the top of the form. The positions of the tab stops in the list box are set at the beginning, in the FormCreate method, and then each time one of the header separators is moved, in the Header1Sized method. Both procedures are based on a similar array, which computes the tab positions by adding the size of each header to those of the preceding headers. In fact, tabs have an absolute value, while the position of the header component's separators is indicated as the width of each section relative to the previous one. Here is the code common to both methods:

```
for I := 0 to Header1.Sections.Count - 1 do
begin
  TabList1.TabStops [I] :=
    Header1.SectionWidth [I] + Last;
  Last := Header1.SectionWidth [I];
end;
```

The FormCreate method has another for loop to set the other tab stops to a high value (the actual number used is not important) so that they won't interfere:

```
for I := Header1.Sections.Count to 9 do
  TabList1.TabStops [I] := 1000;
```

When you use this code, the list box tabs are automatically resized with the header sections, giving you a nice effect. As you can see in Figure 27.14, this works with any font, not just the system font. The critical code is not in this example, but in the tabbed list box component it uses. That's the power of Delphi components. Notice that we might further extend this example by creating a single component that features a tabbed list box with a header. This would indeed be a useful component, if

The output of the TABTEST2 example.

Microsoft had not added to Windows 95 a specific ListView control with this capability built in.

On the down side, notice that the tab characters of the list box are indeed tabs. This means that if you move the second column too close to the first, some of the tabs will disappear, depending on the length of the words in the first column. You can see an example of this behavior, which is not a bug but is *as designed,* in Figure 27.15. For example, you might compute the size of a tab by checking the length of each of the strings in the first column with the current font.

# Writing a Property Editor

We have written a nice component with a very complex property, but how can the users of our component work with it? Their only choice is to set it at run-time, as we have seen in this last example. Instead, I would like to find a way to let fellow programmers set the initial value of this property (the array of integers with the tab stop values) at design-time.

Fortunately, Delphi allows programmers to define their own property editors for special component properties. For simple properties, there is generally no need to do so, because the default editors available in the Delphi Object Inspector are good enough. However, for a more complex property such as our TabListBox's TabStops,

**FIGURE 27.15:**

The behavior of the tabbed list box when tabs are too short.

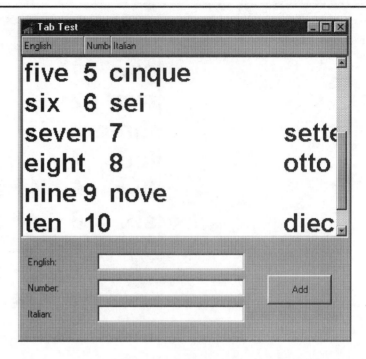

the Object Inspector does not know how to handle a list of integers, which is not even a published property. Even if it were, we are out of luck, because Delphi doesn't allow us to edit array properties directly. The solution to this problem is to define a TCollection property and a TCollectionItem subtype to store the integer values. Although this is the official Delphi 2 solution to the problem, I've chosen a simpler (although less clean) path.

I've added a new property to the tabbed list box, a string with the values of the tabs, so I can let programmers see and modify it at design-time. Here are the new elements of the code of the class:

```
TTabList = class(TListBox)
private
  function GetTabsString: string;
  procedure SetTabsString (Value: string);
  ...
published
  property TabsString: string
    read GetTabsString write SetTabsString;
end;
```

The two access methods are not simple to write—particularly the SetTabsString procedure, which has to scan the string looking for the number separators and convert each substring back into a number:

```
function TTabList.GetTabsString: string;
var
  Text: string;
  I: Integer;
begin
  SetLength (Text, 100);
  Text := '';
  for I := Low (FTabStops) to High (FTabStops) do
    Text := Text + IntToStr (FTabStops [I]) + ';';
  Result := Text;
end;
procedure TTabList.SetTabsString (Value: string);
var
  Text: string;
  I, Len : Integer;
begin
  Text := Value;
  for I := Low (FTabStops) to High (FTabStops) do
  begin
    Len := Pos (Text, ';');
    FTabStops [I] := StrToIntDef (
      Copy (Text, 1, Len), 0);
    Delete (Text, 1, Len);
  end;
  UpdateTabStops;
  Invalidate;
end;
```

Once we've added the new property, we can manipulate it directly like any other string at design-time. However, it isn't very convenient to input the substrings in a line of the Object Inspector, using semicolons as separators. Instead, we should provide a custom property editor. I don't want to describe all the ideas behind writing a property editor here; I simply want to show you a practical example and give you some general guidelines.

Every property editor must be a subclass of the abstract TPropertyEditor class, defined in the DsgnIntf (Design Interface) system unit. However, Delphi already defines some specific property editors for strings (TStringProperty), integers (TInteger-Property), characters (TCharProperty), and enumerations and sets (TEnumProperty and TSetProperty). Then, there are many custom property editors for color, font, pen, string lists, and many other Delphi objects and components.

Since we want to edit strings, it's better to inherit from the string property editor, as you can see in the following listing that shows the definition of my new property editor class:

```
TIntListProperty = class (TStringProperty)
public
  function GetAttributes: TPropertyAttributes; override;
  procedure Edit; override;
end;
```

In every custom property editor, you have to redefine the GetAttributes function, which simply returns one or more values (in a set) indicating the capabilities of the editor:

paValueList  The property editor provides a list of values to display in a combo box of the Object Inspector. The property editor must override the GetValues method to provide the list of values to Delphi.

paSubProperties  The property editor provides some subproperties of the property, displayed when the user clicks on the plus sign beside the property name. The property editor must override the GetProperties method to define a list of subproperties.

paDialog  The property editor provides a custom editor in a stand-alone dialog box, deployed when the user clicks on the ellipsis button on the right of the editing area of the Object Inspector. The property editor must override the Edit method and display the dialog box in it.

paMultiSelect  The property should be listed in the Object Inspector even if the user selects more than one component of the same kind, or components of different kinds sharing that property. This option is quite common.

paAutoUpdate  The property is updated continuously as the user changes a value in the editor (for example, while you type the value of the Caption of a component, you see it change on the screen). If this is not set, the value is updated only at the end of the editing process.

paSortList  The values of the list displayed by the Object Inspector (if also paValueList is set) are alphabetically sorted.

paReadOnly  The Object Inspector doesn't allow you to modify the property (although the property cannot be a read-only property and be available in the Object Inspector). This is actually what we need in order to show the string with the tabs at design-time, but prevent the user from changing it directly in the Object Inspector.

In the case of the TabsString property, I want to provide a custom editor in a dialog box, so this is the code of the method:

```
function TIntListProperty.GetAttributes: TPropertyAttributes;
begin
  Result := [paDialog, paReadOnly];
end;
```

I don't want to allow the user to select multiple components, because this will affect the code of the Edit method. In this code, in fact, I want to access the array of component tabs directly, without having to use the TabsString property (the property the editor will be manipulating). Here is the code of the Edit method:

```
procedure TIntListProperty.Edit;
var
  PEForm: TIntListPEForm;
  Tabs: TTabList;
  I: Integer;
begin
  PEForm := TIntListPEForm.Create (Application);
  try
    Tabs := GetComponent (0) as TTabList;
    for I := Low (TTabsArray) to High (TTabsArray) do
      PEForm.Memo1.Lines.Add (IntToStr (Tabs.TabStops [I]));
    if PEForm.ShowModal = mrOK then
    begin
      for I := Low (TTabsArray) to High (TTabsArray) do
        Tabs.TabStops [I] := StrToIntDef (
          PEForm.Memo1.Lines [I], 0);
    end;
  finally
    PEForm.Free;
  end;
end;
```

This code uses a form I've built in a separate unit (included in this one), which has only a memo component to edit the numbers and three bitmap buttons to accept or reject the changes, or to restore the standard values of the property. The important code is in the Edit method above. There, the property editor accesses the component it is editing, calling the GetComponent (0) method (the parameter there to handle the case of an editor used to update several components at once, something I've disabled). Once you begin editing the component, the Edit method can access its TabsStops array property directly, reading its values at the beginning and setting the modified ones at the end.

This code performs very limited input checking, simply setting values to 0 when the input is invalid. A real tabs property editor should check to make sure that the input is made up only of numbers (and no text) and see whether the relative values are reasonable for the tabs. For example, it should make sure that the values of the tabs are always increasing.

After you've written this code (or you can find it in the TABLIST3 directory), you can install the component and its property editor in Delphi. To accomplish this, you have to add the following statement to the Register procedure of the unit:

```
RegisterPropertyEditor (TypeInfo (string),
  TTabList, 'TabsString', TIntListProperty);
```

This call registers the editor specified in the last parameter for use with properties of type string (first parameter), but only for a specific component and for a property with a specific name. These last two values can be omitted to provide more general editors. This code allows the Object Inspector to inspect the component's properties and use the dialog box called by the Edit method to enter new tab stop values, as you can see in Figure 27.16.

**FIGURE 27.16:**

The TabStrings property in the Object Inspector and the property's editor at design-time.

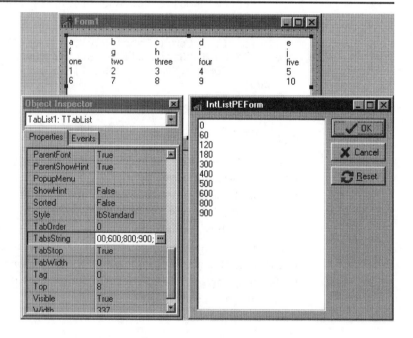

# Forms Are Components, Too

The last component we examine in this chapter will be completely different from the ones we have seen up to now. Now that I have built controls (such as the tabbed list box) and many graphic components (that is, windowless components), I'm going to build a nonvisual component.

The basic idea is that forms are components. When you have built a form that might be particularly useful in a number of projects, you can add it to the Object Repository or make a component out of it. The second approach is more complex than the first one, but it makes using the new form easier and allows you to distribute the form without its source code, which is not possible with templates. As an example, I'll build a component based on a custom dialog box, trying to mimic as much as possible the standard Delphi dialog box components.

## A Dialog Box in a Component

The first step in building a dialog box in a component is to write the code of the dialog box itself, using the standard Delphi approach. Just define a new form and work on it as usual. When a component is based on a form, you can almost visually design the component. Of course, once the dialog box has been built, you have to define a component around it by writing code.

The standard dialog box I want to build is based on a list box since it is common to let a user choose a value from a list of strings. I've customized this common behavior in a dialog box first and then used it to build a component. The simple ListBox-Form form I've built has a list box and the typical OK and Cancel buttons. The only method of this dialog box form relates to the double-click event of the list box, which closes the dialog box as though the user clicked on the OK button:

```
procedure TListBoxForm.ListBox1DblClick(Sender: TObject);
begin
  ModalResult := mrOk;
end;
```

Once this form works, we can start arranging its source code, adding the definition of a component, removing the declaration of the form variable, and moving the form's type definition to the implementation portion. The most important of these operations is the definition of the TListBoxDialog component, a nonvisual component.

What determines that this component is nonvisual is that its immediate ancestor class is TComponent. The component has three published properties and a public one. These are the three published properties:

- Lines is a TStrings object, which is accessed via two methods, GetLines and SetLines. This second method uses the Assign procedure to copy the new values to the private field corresponding to this property. This object is initialized in the Create method and destroyed in the Destroy procedure.

- Selected is an integer that directly accesses the corresponding private field. It stores the selected element of the list of strings.

- Title is a string used to change the title of the dialog box (it might have been a write-only property).

The public property is SelItem, a read-only property that automatically retrieves the selected element of the list of strings. Notice that this property has no storage and no data: it simply accesses other properties, providing a virtual representation of data:

```
type
  TListBoxDialog = class (TComponent)
  private
    FLines: TStrings;
    FSelected: Integer;
    FTitle: string;
    function GetSelItem: string;
    procedure SetLines (Value: TStrings);
    function GetLines: TStrings;
  public
    constructor Create(AOwner: TComponent); override;
    destructor Destroy; override;
    function Execute: Boolean;
    property SelItem: string
      read GetSelItem;
  published
    property Lines: TStrings
      read GetLines write SetLines;
    property Selected: Integer
      read FSelected write FSelected;
    property Title: string
      read FTitle write FTitle;
  end;
```

Most of the code of this example is in the Execute method, a function that returns True or False depending on the modal result of the dialog box. This is consistent with the Execute method of most standard Delphi dialog box components. The Execute function creates the form dynamically, sets some of its values using the component's properties, shows the dialog box, and if the result is correct, updates the current selection:

```
function TListBoxDialog.Execute: Boolean;
var
  ListBoxForm: TListBoxForm;
begin
  if FLines.Count = 0 then
    raise EStringListError.Create ('No items in the list');
  ListBoxForm := TListBoxForm.Create (self);
  try
    ListBoxForm.ListBox1.Items := FLines;
    ListBoxForm.ListBox1.ItemIndex := FSelected;
    ListBoxForm.Caption := FTitle;
    if ListBoxForm.ShowModal = mrOk then
    begin
      Result := True;
      Selected := ListBoxForm.ListBox1.ItemIndex;
    end
    else
      Result := False;
  finally
    ListBoxForm.Destroy;
  end;
end;.
```

Notice that the code is contained within a `try-finally` block, so if a run-time error occurs when the dialog box is displayed, the form will be destroyed. I've also used exceptions to raise an error if the list is empty when a user runs it. This error is by design, and using an exception is a good technique to enforce it. The other methods of the component are quite straightforward:

```
constructor TListBoxDialog.Create(AOwner: TComponent);
begin
  inherited Create (AOwner);
  FLines := TStringList.Create;
  FTitle := 'Choose a string';
end;

destructor TListBoxDialog.Destroy;
begin
  FLines.Free;
  inherited Destroy;
end;

function TListBoxDialog.GetSelItem: string;
begin
  if Selected >= 0 then
    Result := FLines [Selected]
  else
    Result := '';
end;
```

```
function TListBoxDialog.GetLines: TStrings;
begin
  Result := FLines;
end;

procedure TListBoxDialog.SetLines (Value: TStrings);
begin
  FLines.Assign (Value);
end;
```

Of course, since we are manually writing the code of the component (without the help of the Component Expert), we have to remember to write the Register procedure. This is one of the many changes I've made to the typical structure of a form's code, as you can see from the full listing on the companion CD (in the LISTDIAL subdirectory).

## Using the Nonvisual Component

Now that the component is ready, you must provide a bitmap. For nonvisual components, bitmaps are very important because they are used not only for the Component palette, but also when you place the component on a form. Now let's prepare the bitmap, install the component, and write a simple project to test it. The form of this test program has simply a button, an edit box, and our new nonvisual component, as you can see in Figure 27.17.

**FIGURE 27.17:**
The form of the LDTEST example, with the new nonvisual component.

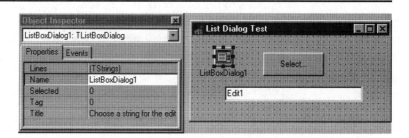

Now you can write a few lines of code, corresponding to the OnClick event of the button:

```
procedure TForm1.Button1Click(Sender: TObject);
begin
  if ListBoxDialog1.Execute then
    Edit1.Text := ListBoxDialog1.SelItem;
end;
```

That's all you need to run the dialog box we have placed in the component, as you can see in Figure 27.18. I think this is an interesting approach to the development of some common dialog boxes.

**FIGURE 27.18:**
The LDTEST example can show the dialog box we encapsulated in the ListDial component.

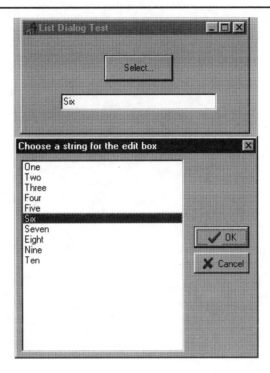

# Summary

This chapter was devoted to the design and creation of Delphi components. We have seen how to define various types of properties, how to add events, and how to define and override component methods. We have seen different examples of components, including simple changes to existing ones, new graphical components, and, in the final section, a dialog box inside a component. While building these components, we have faced some new Windows programming challenges. In general, it is not uncommon to have to use the Windows API directly when writing new components.

However, building components in Delphi is not simply an activity for a few experts, as it is in the Visual Basic approach, but is something any experienced Delphi programmer should learn to do.

Notice again that Delphi components are based on a traditional compile-and-link approach, which has nothing to do with Windows' dynamic linking. Writing and using DDLs, however, is another interesting approach to component software development in general, particularly when you need to build projects using several Windows programming environments at a time. Writing DLLs is the topic of the next chapter.

# CHAPTER

## TWENTY-EIGHT

# Dynamic Link Libraries

- DLLs in Windows 95 and NT

- Using a C++ DLL in Delphi

- Using a Delphi form in Paradox

- A DLL of icons

- Calling DLL functions at run-time

**W**indows executable files come in two flavors: *programs* and *dynamic link libraries* (DLLs). When you write a Delphi application, you typically generate a program file, an EXE. However, Delphi applications often use calls to functions stored in DLLs. While Delphi itself relies more on static linking than on dynamic linking for its own components and code, each time you call a Windows API function directly, you actually access a DLL.

Besides generating programs, Delphi can generate new dynamic link libraries. The New page of the Object Repository includes a DLL skeleton generator, which offers very limited support, but in fact it is very simple to generate a DLL in the Delphi environment. However, some problems arise from the nature of DLLs. Writing a DLL in Windows is not always as simple as it seems, and debugging programs with multiple executable files (the main program and one or more DLLs) is often a headache.

This chapter, the last in the book, covers the basics of DLL programming from the Delphi point of view. As usual, I'll show you some examples of what you can place in a Delphi DLL, or in a DLL in general. However, I'll also show you a couple of examples using other programming languages and environments, simply because one of the key reasons for writing a DLL in Delphi is to be able to call the DLL from a program written with another development environment and a different programming language.

# The Role of DLLs in Windows

Before delving into the development of DLLs, both in Delphi and in other programming languages, I'll give you a short technical overview of DLLs in Windows, highlighting the key elements.

We will start by looking at dynamic linking, at the way Windows uses DLLs, and at the differences between DLLs and executable files, ending with some general rules to follow when writing DLLs.

## What Is Dynamic Linking?

First of all, you need to understand the difference between static and dynamic linking of functions or procedures. When a subroutine is not directly available in a source file, the compiler adds it to an internal table, which includes all external symbols. Of course, the compiler must have seen the declaration of the subroutine and know about its parameters and type, or it will issue an error.

After compilation of a normal—*static*—subroutine, the linker fetches the subroutine's compiled code from a Delphi compiled unit (or static library) and adds it to the executable. The resulting EXE file includes all the code of the program and of the units involved. Actually, the Delphi linker is smart enough to include only the minimum amount of code of the units included in the program, not all of it.

In the case of dynamic linking, which occurs when your code calls a DLL-based function, the linker simply uses the information of the `external` declaration of the subroutine to set up some tables in the executable file. When the executable file is loaded in memory, it loads all the DLLs it requires first; then the program starts. During this loading process, the program's internal tables are filled with the addresses of the functions in memory, since each DLL has been loaded and is now available. If for some reason the DLL is not found, the program won't start.

Each time the program calls an external function, the call is forwarded to the DLL code (which is now located in the program's address space). Notice that this scheme does not involve two different applications. The DLL becomes part of the current program, and (as we will see later in this chapter) all the parameter passing takes place on the stack as with any static function call.

You can see a sketch of how the program calls statically or dynamically linked functions in Figure 28.1. Notice that I haven't yet discussed compilation of the DLL—because I wanted to focus on the two different linking mechanisms.

> **NOTE**
>
> The term *dynamic linking*, as used when referring to DLLs, has nothing to do with the late-binding feature of the object-oriented programming language. Virtual and dynamic methods in Object Pascal have nothing to do with DLLs. Unfortunately, the same term is used for both kinds of procedures and functions, which causes a lot of confusion. When I speak of dynamic binding in this chapter, I am referring not to polymorphism but to DLLs.

**FIGURE 28.1:**

Static and dynamic binding in Windows.

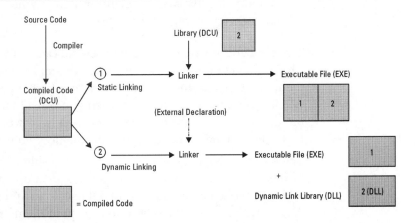

There is also another, less common approach to using DLLs, which is even more dynamic than the one we have just discussed. In fact, at run-time, you can load a DLL in memory, search for a function (provided you know its name), and call the function by name. This approach requires much more complex coding and is generally slower, but you don't need to have the DLL available to start the program. We will use this approach in an example at the end of the chapter.

## What Are DLLs For?

Now that you have a general idea of how DLLs work, we can focus on the reasons for their use. Here are some of the reasons to use dynamic link libraries in Windows:

- If the same code is used by different programs, it is loaded in memory only once in Windows 95, thus sparing some system memory. In Windows 95, DLLs are mapped into the private address space of each process (each running application), but their code is loaded in memory only once, using a memory mapped file. This file is placed at the same address in each process address space into which the library is loaded. In Windows NT, instead, memory mapped files are not shared. For this reason, each process loads the DLLs into its memory space at a separate address: DLLs are loaded more than once, saving no memory (the only exceptions are the system libraries).

- You can provide a different version of a DLL, replacing the current one. If the subroutines in the DLL have the same parameters, you can run the program with the new version of the DLL without having to recompile it. If the DLL has new subroutines, it doesn't matter at all. Problems might arise only if a procedure of the older version of the DLL is missing in the new one.

- You can use a DLL as a central repository of information that each of the programs using it can access. For example, a DLL can provide an interface to a device and take care of disciplining its use by different applications. Sharing memory directly is not available in Win32, where applications should use memory mapped files instead.

These generic advantages apply in several cases. If you have some complex algorithm or some complex windows that several applications require, you can store them in a DLL and then include them in different programs. In Windows 95, this will let you save some memory when you run all the programs at the same time, but unless the size of this program portion is very big, the work of moving to the DLL approach might not be worth the memory you save.

The second advantage is particularly applicable to complex applications. If you have a very big program that requires frequent updates and bug fixes, dividing it into many executables and several DLLs allows you to distribute a DLL that contains only the code that has been fixed to your clients, not one single big executable.

This makes sense for Windows system libraries in particular. If Borland makes a new version of the Database Engine libraries and writes new SQL Links to access other SQL server databases, you probably won't need to recompile your application to take advantage of the changes.

Another common technique is to use DLLs to store nothing except resources. You can build a version of the DLL with strings for each language and then change the language at run-time, or you can prepare a library of icons and bitmaps and then use them in different applications. Another key advantage, as I already mentioned, is that DLLs are language-independent. Actually, DLL functions and procedures use a calling convention that's a hybrid of the C and Pascal language models, since the date types of the parameters are based on C with some Windows additions, but the parameter passing technique is that of Pascal.

In any case, most Windows programming environments, including most macro languages of end-user applications, allow a programmer to call a subroutine stored in a DLL. This means you can build a DLL in Delphi and call it from C++, Visual Basic, Paradox, dBASE, Excel, WordPerfect, and many other Windows applications.

## The System DLLs

The three key advantages of DLLs I've highlighted are all used by the Windows system DLLs. For this reason, it is worth examining them. First of all, Windows has many system DLLs. There are the three central portions of Windows—Kernel, User, and GDI—which are implemented using DLLs. (You can find these files in the WINDOWS\SYSTEM directory.)

Actually, in Windows 95 the three key system libraries are duplicated in 16-bit versions (KRNL386.EXE, USER.EXE, and GDI.EXE) and 32-bit versions (KERNEL32.DLL, USER32.DLL, and GDI32.DLL). These two versions often call each other, in a process called *thunking*. In fact, it is generally not possible for a 16-bit program or DLL to call 32-bit DLL, and vice versa. In Windows NT, the system libraries have only 32-bit code.

Other system DLLs are operating system extensions (such as the DLL for common dialog boxes and controls, the DLL for DDEML, the OLE DLLs, and so on), device drivers, fonts, VBX controls, and others.

In the case of Windows itself, using DLLs is extremely important. In fact, DLLs are one of the key technical foundations of the Windows operating systems. Since each application uses the system DLLs for anything from creating windows to producing output, every program is linked to those DLLs. Let's take a minute to look at why you might have different versions of the same library. First, consider device drivers: when you change your printer, you do not need to rebuild your application, or even buy a new version of the Windows GDI library, which manages the printer output. You need only to provide a specific driver, which is a DLL called by the GDI, to access your printer. Each printer type has its own driver, or DLL, making the system extremely flexible. From a different point of view, version handling is important for the system itself. If you have an application compiled for Windows 3.1, you should be able to run it on Windows 95. Each version of Windows has different system code (and Windows 95 16-bit support actually corrects some Windows 3.1 quirks), but since each new version contains the older API functions, the old code still works, even though it cannot take advantage of the new API functions.

However, old code can indeed take advantage of new features when an existing function's code changes. An obvious example is the user interface: if you build an application for Windows 3.1, you can run it on Windows 95, and it will automatically have different user interface elements. You have not recompiled your program; it used the features of the new system libraries, which were linked dynamically to it.

The system DLLs are also used as system information archives. For example, the User module maintains a list of all the active windows in the system, and any application can directly access this list. The same holds for the GDI system library.

# Differences between DLLs and EXEs

Now that you know the basic elements of dynamic linking and some reasons to use it, we can focus on the difference between a normal executable file (an EXE file) and a dynamic link library (a DLL file). For the most part, the internal structure of an EXE file and a DLL file is the same; the key difference is the file extension.

It is when a DLL is loaded in memory that things change. As I mentioned earlier, a DLL can be loaded in memory only once in Windows 95, while they are loaded once for each process in Windows NT. In both cases, each process has its own copy of the of the DLL data. An executable file, on the other hand, can have multiple instances, even if its code is still loaded in memory only once in Windows 95 (again using a memory mapped file). For the DLLs, a proper usage-count mechanism ensures that the code and data segments of a library are not unloaded too early.

Another important difference is that a library, even when loaded in memory, is not a running program. It is only a collection of procedures and functions that other programs can call. These procedures and functions use the stack of the calling program (the *calling thread*, to be precise). So another key difference between a program and a library is that a library doesn't create its own stack—it uses the stack of the program calling it. In Win32, since the DLL is loaded into the application's address space, any local allocations of the DLL or any global data it creates are in that same address space.

# Rules for DLL Writers

What I've described so far can be summarized in some rules for DLL programmers. A DLL function or procedure to be called by external programs must follow these guidelines:

- It has to be declared as `export` and has to be listed in the DLL's `exports` clause. This makes the routine visible to the outside world. In Delphi 2, exported functions should also be declared as `stdcall`, to disable an optimization that uses registers for parameter passing (the *fastcall* mechanism, discussed in Chapter 4).

- It should use the Pascal calling convention (this is easy in Delphi), which is the default Windows calling convention.

- In Win32, a DLL can use global data that won't be shared by calling applications. Each time the application is loaded by a different process, the DLL global data is duplicated in the address space of the calling application (as we will see in the DLLMEM example later on).

- In Delphi, exceptions should never cross the DLL boundary. Every function or procedure that might raise an exception should have a comprehensive `try` block to catch all possible exceptions.

# Win16 and Win32 DLLs

Another important aspect of DLLs is that in Windows, they come in two different flavors. There are Windows 3.1 (Win16) DLLs, and Windows NT or Windows 95 (Win32) DLLs. Libraries written with the first version of Delphi are of the first kind. Libraries compiled with Delphi 2 are of the latter kind.

Unfortunately, as I already mentioned, 16-bit and 32-bit DLLs are *not* compatible. For example, you cannot call a 16-bit DLL from a Delphi 2 program. This is not a Delphi limitation, but is rather a general Windows problem. There is actually a solution: you can use Microsoft's thunk compiler to create the proper entry points for the different DLL type. This is what Windows 95 does to call 16-bit system libraries from a 32-bit application, or to accomplish the opposite (call new 32-bit system libraries from old 16-bit applications). However, using the thunk mechanism is quite complex, provides low performance, and requires you to own this specific Microsoft tool. For these reasons, I'm not going to show you an example of how to accomplish this in the book.

Remember that the libraries we are going to build with Delphi 2 won't be compatible with 16-bit applications, and that you cannot use old third-party 16-bit libraries in Delphi 2. Of course if you have the source code, you can try to recompile the library (something that's not always easy). If you recompile 16-bit DLLs in Delphi, for example, you must remember to add the `stdcall` directive to disable the fast-call mechanism.

# Using Existing DLLs

Before writing DLLs in Delphi, what about using them? Well, we have done that in a number of examples in the book, when calling Windows API functions. As you might remember, all the API functions are declared in the system Windows unit. In the interface portion of the unit, functions are declared, as shown here:

```
function PatBlt(DC: HDC; X, Y, Width, Height: Integer;
  Rop: DWORD): BOOL; stdcall;
function Pie(DC: HDC; X1, Y1, X2, Y2,
  X3, Y3, X4, Y4: Integer): BOOL; stdcall;
function PlayMetaFile(DC: HDC;
  MF: HMETAFILE): BOOL; stdcall;
function PaintRgn(DC: HDC;
  RGN: HRGN): BOOL; stdcall;
function PolyPolygon(DC: HDC; var Points;
  var nPoints; p4: Integer): BOOL; stdcall;
function PtInRegion(RGN: HRGN;
  p2, p3: Integer): BOOL; stdcall;
```

Then, in the implementation portion, instead of providing their code, the unit refers to the external definition in a DLL:

```
function PatBlt; external gdi32 name 'PatBlt';
function Pie; external gdi32 name 'Pie';
function PlayMetaFile; external gdi32 name 'PlayMetaFile';
function PaintRgn; external gdi32 name 'PaintRgn';
function PolyPolygon; external gdi32 name 'PolyPolygon';
function PtInRegion; external gdi32 name 'PtInRegion';
```

The external definition of these functions refers to the name of the DLL they use. This is the internal name of the module, which often, but not always, matches the name of the file without the extension. The other element is the name of the DLL function itself. This is not necessary if the Pascal function (or procedure) name matches the DLL function name.

**NOTE**  Notice that in Delphi 2, you can no longer use the `index` directive to match DLL functions by ordinal value as you can in Delphi 1.

To call a function from a DLL, you can provide these declarations and external definitions, as shown above, or you can merge them in a single declaration. Once the function is properly defined, you can call it in the code of your Delphi application as though it were a non-DLL function. There is nothing special about the calling syntax; it is just a normal function or procedure call.

# Calling a C++ DLL

As an example of how to call a DLL, I've decided to write a new, very simple DLL in C++, with some useless functions, and show you how to call it from a Delphi application. I won't comment the C++ code in detail (it is basically C code, anyway) but will focus instead on the calls between the Delphi application and the C++ DLL. This is important because it is common in Delphi to use a DLL written in C or C++.

## The C++ DLL

In the following listing, you can see the source code of the C++ file used to build the CPPDLL library. Needless to say, this is actually Borland C++ code, compiled with version 4.5 of the compiler, but most of the things I discuss here will also work with any other C++ compiler:

```
#include <windows.h>
#include <bwcc.h>

BOOL WINAPI DllMain (HINSTANCE hinst,
  DWORD reason, LPVOID reserved)
{
  return TRUE;
}

void WINAPI _export Beep ()
{
  MessageBeep (-1);
}

extern "C"
int WINAPI _export Double (int n)
{
  return n * 2;
}

extern "C"
void WINAPI _export ShowMessage (
  HWND hwnd, LPSTR text)
{
  BWCCMessageBox (hwnd, text, "Message",
MB_OK | MB_ICONINFORMATION);
}
```

This code is very simple, but it contains at least one useful element: a function wrapping the call to the message box of the Borland Windows Custom Controls library (BWCC). We could have called this library directly from Delphi, but I have just used it to illustrate parameter passing. Notice that all the functions are defined as WINAPI _export to indicate that they use the standard PASCAL calling convention (implied in the WINAPI define), and that they should be exported to be made available to other programs. Two of these C++ functions also use the C naming convention (indicated by the extern ""C"" statement), but one doesn't. We will see what changes when we call these functions from a Delphi application. The first function, DllMain, is a special function called on DLL startup and cleanup. This is a new feature of the Win32 API, corresponding to the LibMain and WEP functions in Windows 3.1. The file above is the only source file of the CPPDLL project (the corresponding Borland C++ project file is available on the companion CD).

## Declaring the DLL Functions in Delphi

Now that I've written this DLL in C++, we can write a Delphi program to call it. The example, named CALLCPP and stored in the same directory as the C++ DLL (CPPDLL) on the companion CD, is simple. Its form has three buttons to call each function of the DLL, plus a Spin Edit component and an edit box to provide some input values for the parameters.

The first thing you have to do to write this program is provide a proper definition of the functions. To accomplish this we might first look into the DLL to see the names of the exported functions. If you are running Windows 95 and have installed the viewer for the executable files, which comes with the system, you can simply move to the DLL file in the Explorer, click on it with the right mouse button, and choose the Quick View command. (If you are using Windows NT, you can test this on a Windows 95 machine, or use many other command prompt tools, such as the TDUMP program that comes with Delphi, to have similar details.) The viewer that appears lists a lot of low-level technical information (available for each executable file). What we are interested in right now is the *Export Table* section you can see in Figure 28.2.

**NOTE**
Notice that each of the three functions has a name and also an index number (indicated as Ordinal). This index number was generally used for binding DLL functions in Windows 3.1. In Win32, Microsoft suggests that you bind DLL functions by name, which is what Delphi does.

The internal names of the three functions correspond to their names in the C++ source code file, except for the Beep function. In fact, we didn't use the extern "C" clause for it, so Borland C++ used the standard C++ name mangling (the way function names are transformed to include information about the number and type of parameters), leading to the funny name you can see in Figure 28.2. This is actually the name we have to use in our Delphi example to call the Beep DLL function.

**FIGURE 28.2:**

Windows 95 Quick View lets you
explore DLLs and EXEs. Here is the
Export Table of CPPDLL.DLL.

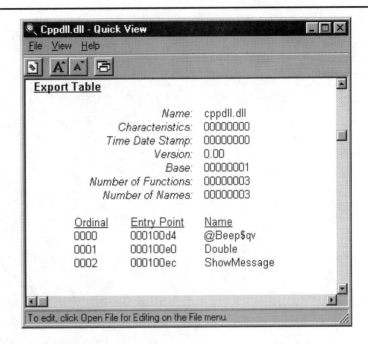

This is the declaration of the three functions in the Delphi CALLCPP example:

```
procedure Beep; stdcall;
  external 'CPPDLL' name '@Beep$qv';
function Double (N: Integer): Integer;
  stdcall; external 'CPPDLL';
procedure ShowBWCCMessage (Handle: Hwnd; Text: PChar);
  stdcall; external 'CPPDLL' name 'ShowMessage';
```

As you can see above, you can provide an alias name for an external function. I've done it for the first function (there was no alternative, because the exported DLL function name @Beep$qv is not a valid Pascal identifier) and for the third (simply to make the name shorter and simpler to call). If the two names match, you can omit the name directive, as we did for the second function above.

Remember to add the stdcall directive to each definition, so that the caller and the callee pass and return parameters on the stack in the same way. The problem is that if you fail to do so, you do not always get a run-time error, but instead get a random function call result, which is the worst outcome, since you might have trouble tracing this bug.

The output of the CALLCPP program is very simple. When you click on the Beep button, the system beeps; when you click on the Message button, a BWCC-style message box appears (see Figure 28.3); and when you click on the Double button, the value of the Spin Edit component changes.

FIGURE 28.3:
The output of the CALLCPP
example when the ShowMessage
DLL function is called.

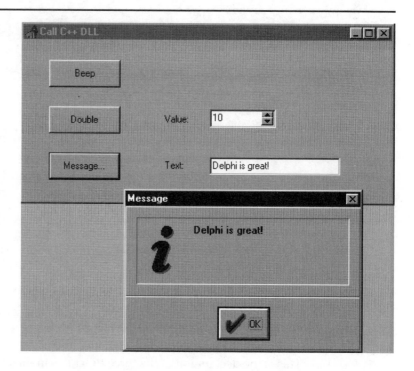

Here is the code of the three OnClick event handlers:

```
procedure TForm1.BeepButtonClick(Sender: TObject);
begin
  Beep;
end;
procedure TForm1.DoubleButtonClick(Sender: TObject);
begin
  SpinEdit1.Value := Double (SpinEdit1.Value);
end;
procedure TForm1.MessageButtonClick(Sender: TObject);
begin
  ShowBWCCMessage (Handle, PChar (Edit1.Text));
end;
```

**WARNING**   To run this program you must have installed the BWCC DLL that
Borland C++ and other Borland products install on your system.

# Creating a DLL in Delphi

Besides using DLLs written with other environments, you can use Delphi to build DLLs that can be used in Delphi itself or with any other tool. Note that Delphi is probably the only visual programming tool that can build DLLs. This is because Delphi is based on a real compiler, something other visual programming environments are not. Despite this, I would discourage you from building DLLs in Delphi to be used in other Delphi projects unless the application you are building is huge and you want to use this technique to split the work among several programmers. Instead of building DLLs, consider whether working with static libraries (that is, compiled units), form templates, and components instead would be a better solution.

By building DLLs, you might think you are sparing some memory, but you'll probably end up requiring more. In fact, each Delphi executable includes the same runtime library code and probably a lot of standard VCL code also. If you build an EXE and a DLL, this code will be duplicated, so even if two applications share the DLL, you might end up needing more memory than if you had used static linking.

Static linking is also more selective, and it allows Delphi to link only the code you really use to the program. When you load a DLL, you load it all, at least in theory, since some code modules might actually remain on the disk and be loaded on request. As you might guess, it is not easy to give a definitive statement, because there are many parameters. My suggestion to not write Delphi DLLs for a Delphi program (unless it is a really big project) is just a general guideline. Later in the chapter, I'll show you some cases in which it makes sense to do so.

## Routines, Methods, Objects, and DLLs

Another reason not to use DLLs when they are not required is that DLLs typically export routines, functions, and procedures, not methods, objects, or components. When you work with Delphi visual tools, turning your code into a DLL is generally more complex than turning it into a component. You do not need to write more code. You need a paradigm shift, thinking in terms of functions and procedures instead of classes and methods. One solution to this problem is to write DLLs that export a COM interface (an OLE interface). This way, the program can export objects for use by other programs. If you need this, however, you can probably use OLE automation, which is directly supported by Delphi. OLE automation also provides a standard approach to inter-process communication and to the development of big programs divided in modules.

In general, when you build complex Delphi applications, you can also use object-oriented programming techniques to define your application's structure. If you later divide the application's code among its DLLs, you lose this advantage. A better way to use Delphi DLLs is to implement algorithms and access resources or other elements using Pascal code instead of Object Pascal. When you write this kind of code, you can consider placing it in a DLL. In this case, if you use no VCL code, the memory overhead is minimal, too.

Aside from these special cases, the only reason to write DLLs in Delphi is to provide functionality for programmers working in other environments.

## A First Simple Delphi DLL

Before studying a real example, a form in a DLL, I'll show you a very simple DLL built in Delphi. This is more or less a new version of the DLL we already built in C++. The primary focus of this example will be to see the syntax you use to define a DLL in Delphi. To start, select the File ➤ New command and choose the DLL option in the New page of the Object Repository. This creates a very simple source file starting with the following definition:

```
library Project1;
```

The `library` statement (which replaces the standard `program` statement) indicates we want to build a DLL instead of an executable file.

Now you can add the functions, marked with the `export` keyword, and list these functions in a new `exports` statement:

```
procedure Beep; export; stdcall;
begin
  MessageBeep (Cardinal (-1));
end;

function Double (N: Integer): Integer; export; stdcall;
begin
  Double := N * 2;
end;

exports
  Beep, Double;
```

Since I call an API function in the Beep procedure, I also added Windows to the list of units in the uses statement. By using Delphi, you can build the DLL with the Build All or Compile command on the Run menu. You can also issue the Run command, but Delphi will complain that it cannot run a DLL, of course. Since we have not included any VCL code, the resulting DLL is quite small—about 45 Kbytes. By removing the Classes and SysUtils units from the uses statement, you can reduce it to a mere 10 Kbytes (in theory, the smart linker should be capable of removing all unused code, but at times you can help it a little…). Instead, if you now add the

Dialogs unit to the uses statement and add a line to the Beep procedure, as follows:

```
procedure Beep; export;
begin
  MessageBeep (Cardinal (-1));
  ShowMessage ('Beep');
end;
```

the total size of the DLL will become more than 150 Kbytes. The difference is that now a lot of code from the VCL is included in the DLL executable file. All this is to demonstrate that you can trim the size of a DLL to a minimum when you're not using the Delphi VCL and classes, but are writing a plain Pascal DLL, such as the FIRSTDLL example.

How can you use this library? Well, you can call it from within another Delphi project or from other environments. As a sample, I've built a new version of the CALLCPP example, named CALLFRST, that defines the two external functions as shown here:

```
procedure Beep; far;
  stdcall; external 'FIRSTDLL';
function Double (N: Integer): Integer;
  stdcall; external 'FIRSTDLL';
```

This is similar to the preceding code. This time, however, we have no problems with function names. Besides this change and the removal of the third button, the code of the example remains the same as in the CALLCPP example, so I haven't listed it in the text (of course, you can find it on the companion CD).

It is useful to build libraries of small functions if the same functions have to be called from different environments. In particular you can write fast-compiled DLLs and call them from interpreted environments such as Visual Basic. Of course, if it is possible, just build the whole program in Delphi. Another interesting case for DLLs is when they are subject to change, because you can provide different versions of these libraries for different users (as happens with device drivers).

## Placing a Form in a DLL

What is even more interesting, particularly if you work in other development environments, is placing a complete form built with Delphi into a DLL. This can be a dialog box or any other kind of form.

To build the FORMDLL example, I've started with a *very* old form, the main form of the SCROLLC example from Chapter 7. You can see the new version of the form, with two bitmap buttons, in Figure 28.4. The only other change I made was to set the BorderStyle property of the form to bsDialog.

FIGURE 28.4:

The new version of the SCROLLC
form, with two bitmap buttons.

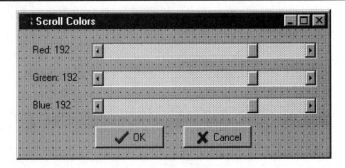

The source code of the form, its type definition, and its code have no other changes.
I've only added a new function to the unit, defined in the interface portion as
shown:

```
function GetColor (Col: LongInt): LongInt; stdcall; export;
```

The color passed as a parameter is used as the initial color, and the return value is
the final color (which is the same as the initial color if the user clicked on the Cancel
button). Here is the code of the function:

```
function GetColor (Col: LongInt): LongInt;
begin
  FormScroll := TFormScroll.Create (Application);
  {initialize the data}
  FormScroll.Color := Col;
  FormScroll.ScrollBarRed.Position :=
    GetRValue (ColorToRGB (Col));
  FormScroll.ScrollBarGreen.Position :=
    GetGValue (ColorToRGB (Col));
  FormScroll.ScrollBarBlue.Position :=
    GetBValue (ColorToRGB (Col));
  try
    {show the form}
    if FormScroll.ShowModal = mrOK then
      Result := ColorToRGB (FormScroll.Color)
    else
      Result := Col;
  finally
    FormScroll.Free;
  end;
end;
```

When you want to place a Delphi component (such as a form) in a DLL, you cannot
make the component available to DLL users (for example, to place a Button component in a window); you can only provide some functions that create, initialize,
or run the component or access its properties and data. The simplest approach is to
have a single function that sets the data, runs the component, and returns the result,

as in the current example. However, for complex cases, you might have to provide complex data structures as parameters. For actual examples, you can look at the Windows API functions for the common dialog boxes (such as `GetOpenFileName` or `ChooseColor`) in the Help file.

Another important element is the structure of the code of the GetColor function. The code creates the form at the beginning, sets some initial values, and then runs the form in a protected block (`try-finally`). By checking the return value of the ShowModal method, it determines the result of the function. Notice also that I've passed as a parameter a long integer, which corresponds to the Windows COLOR-REF data type. Using TColor, a Delphi type, might have caused problems with non-Delphi applications, even though a TColor is very similar to a COLORREF. When you write a DLL, my suggestion is to use Windows' native data types.

Now that we have written the unit's code, we can move to the project code, which becomes the following:

```
library Scrollc;

uses
  Scroll_f in 'SCROLL_F.PAS' {FormScroll};

exports
  GetColor;

begin

end.
```

## Calling the DLL Form from Delphi

We can now test the form we have placed in the DLL in a Delphi program. I consider this just a test because, as I've already mentioned, doing this for real projects makes no sense. On the companion CD, the test example, USECOL, is in the same directory (FORMDLL). The reason for this approach is that the DLL must reside in the same directory as the program that uses it, in a directory of the PATH, in the Windows directory, or in the Windows system directory. Using the current directory is the ideal solution for a simple test as well as for many complex applications.

The USECOL example is simple. Its form contains only a button. When the user presses the button, the DLL function is called. Here is the definition of this function and the code of the Button1Click method:

```
function GetColor (Col: LongInt): LongInt;
  stdcall; external 'SCROLLC';
procedure TForm1.Button1Click(Sender: TObject);
var
  Col: LongInt;
```

```
begin
  Col := ColorToRGB (Color);
  Color := GetColor (Col)
end;
```

When you run this program (see Figure 28.5), the dialog box is displayed, using the current background color of the main form. If you change the color and click on OK, the new color is used as the background color for the main form.

**FIGURE 28.5:**

The execution of the USECOL test program when it calls the dialog box we have placed in a DLL.

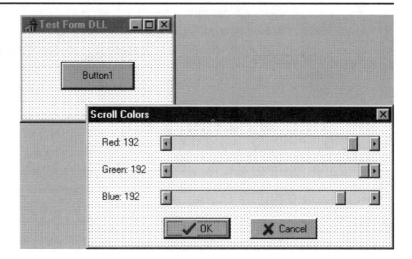

## Calling a Delphi DLL from Other Languages

What is interesting in this example is that we can display this dialog box from other programming languages. Calling this DLL from C or C++ is easy. You need to declare the function as follows:

```
extern COLORREF GetColor (COLORREF);
```

Then you can call it as usual:

```
MyColor = GetColor (OldColor);
```

To link this application, you need to generate an import library (using the IMPLIB utility) and add the resulting LIB file to the project. Since I've already used Borland C++ in this chapter, instead of completing this example, I want to write a similar one with Paradox. To start, create a new Paradox form and place a button and an ellipse in it. The button is named *MyButton* and the ellipse *MyEllipse*. Then choose a color for the ellipse and for the form. Now, define the button's pushButton method and write the following code:

```
uses ScrollC
  GetColor (AColor CLONG) CLONG
enduses

method pushButton(var eventInfo Event)
var
  MyColor LongInt
endvar
  MyColor = MyEllipse.Color
  MyColor = GetColor (MyColor)
  MyEllipse.Color = MyColor
endmethod
```

The first three lines declare the GetColor function of the DLL. To avoid problems, you can copy the DLL file in the WINDOWS\SYSTEM directory so any application can access it. The CLONG type is the ObjectPal definition of the Windows long integer type. The rest of the code simply calls the function, passing to it the color of the ellipse and using the return value as the new color for the shape. The PDOXCALL directory on the companion CD contains the CALLCOL.FSL file for this example. Of course, you need to have Paradox to run it.

# A DLL of Icons

Dynamic link libraries in Windows have many other uses. As an example, we'll build a DLL of icons and then load icons dynamically in a program. This will be the first time we access a DLL from an application at run-time, without the usual compile-time link. As a result, the program will run even if the DLL is not available.

To build a DLL out of icons or other Windows resources, you need only prepare a resource file and link it as a library. For example, I've prepared a file with three resources, named *Icon_A*, *Icon_B*, and *Icon_C*, representing the corresponding letters. Once the resource file is ready (in this case, it is named ICONS.RES), you can write the simple source code for the DLL:

```
library Iconsdll;

{$R ICONS.RES}

begin
end.
```

Build this program, and the ICONSDLL.DLL library will be ready to use. Consider this DLL as a collection of icons and other resources, such as standard strings for error messages or bitmaps with company logos, used by several applications at the same time. In fact, in Windows 95 (but not in Windows NT) if two applications will use this DLL, only one copy of the resources will be in memory. Instead, if the same resource file is included in several programs, it will be duplicated.

## Loading the Icons from the DLL

Now that we have built the DLL, we have to load it in a program. For this purpose, I've built a simple example, USEICONS (saved in the ICONSDLL directory), which allows users to enter the name of the icon they want to see. The form of this application contains an edit box with a corresponding label, a button, and an image component with a bevel around it. When the form is created, it tries to open the DLL, calling the LoadLibrary API function:

```
procedure TForm1.FormCreate(Sender: TObject);
begin
  HInst := LoadLibrary ('Iconsdll.dll');
  begin
    LoadButton.Enabled := False;
    ShowMessage ('Icons DLL not found');
  end;
end;
```

LoadLibrary returns the instance handle of the library. If this value is NULL, it means that an error occurred. (To determine what happened, you'll have to call the GetLastError function.) The library's handle is saved in a private field of the form, HInst:

```
type
  TForm1 = class(TForm)
    ...
  private
    HInst: THandle;
  end;
```

This value is later used in the LoadButtonClick method to load an icon from the DLL (notice that the button is enabled only if the library was successfully loaded). The icon is indicated by name, using the text of the Edit component. Once the icon's handle has been loaded, it is used to set the new image (see Figure 28.6):

```
procedure TForm1.LoadButtonClick(Sender: TObject);
var
  HIcon: THandle;
begin
  HIcon := LoadIcon (HInst, PChar(Edit1.Text));
  if HIcon = 0 then
    ShowMessage ('Icon not found')
  else
    Image1.Picture.Icon.Handle := HIcon;
end;
```

Of course, there's a chance the icon won't be found. In this case, the user sees an error message, and the image does not change. The last part of the program is very

**FIGURE 28.6:**
The output of the USEICONS
program.

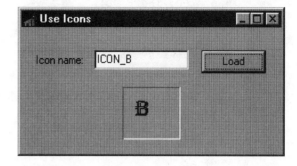

important, too. When you load a library manually by using LoadLibrary, you
must remember to free it by using the FreeLibrary call:

```
procedure TForm1.FormDestroy(Sender: TObject);
begin
  FreeLibrary (HInst);
end;
```

If you forget to do this, the library will remain in memory until you exit the application (or run one of the special utilities capable of removing a DLL from the memory), and you won't be able to recompile it.

# Calling a DLL Function at Run-Time

Now that we know how to access resources in a DLL at run-time, we might want
to use this approach to access a DLL-based function. Since this is quite uncommon,
I've built a very simple example that doesn't make much sense. Let me show you
the example first, and then I'll describe when this approach might be interesting.
The example is named DYNACALL and uses the FIRSTDLL library we built earlier
in this chapter. Instead of declaring the Beep function and using it as a plain Delphi
function, this example obtains the same effect with much more code.

The form of this example simply contains a button. When this button is pressed, the
only method of the program is executed. First, it calls the LoadLibrary function.
Then, if the handle of the library instance is valid, it calls the GetProcAddress API
function. This function searches the DLL, looking for the name of the function
passed as a parameter. If it finds a match, it returns a pointer to the requested
procedure:

```
type
  Proc = procedure;

procedure TForm1.Button1Click(Sender: TObject);
var
  HInst: THandle;
```

```
    FPointer: TFarProc;
    MyProc: Proc;
begin
  HInst := LoadLibrary ('Firstdll.dll');
  if HInst > 32 then
  begin
    FPointer := GetProcAddress (HInst, 'Beep');
    if FPointer <> nil then
    begin
      MyProc := Proc (FPointer);
      MyProc;
    end
    else
      ShowMessage ('DLL function not found');
    FreeLibrary (HInst);
  end
  else
    ShowMessage ('Library not found');
end;
```

How do you call a procedure in Delphi, once you have a pointer to it? One solution is to convert the pointer to a procedural type and then call the procedure using the procedural type variable. This is the solution the DYNACALL example uses. Notice that the procedural type you define must be compatible with the definition of the procedure of the DLL function you access. This is the Achilles' heel of this method: there is no check of the parameter types.

What is the advantage of this approach? In theory, you can use it to access any function of any DLL at any time. In practice, it is useful when you have different DLLs with compatible functions (or a single DLL with several compatible functions) and you want to be able to access these functions at run-time.

With this code, the compiler and the linker ignore the existence of the DLL. When the program is loaded, the DLL is ignored, too. We might mimic the last example and let the user enter the name of the DLL to use—or even the name of the function to use, provided it is compatible with a given procedural type. In some cases, this is a great advantage. A user might make a DLL switch while running the program that uses the DLL, something the direct approach does not allow.

Note that this approach to loading DLL functions is common in macro languages and is used by many visual programming environments. Also, the Paradox code we saw earlier in this chapter probably uses this approach to call the external DLL function. Only a system based on a compiler and a linker, such as Delphi, can use the direct approach, which is generally more reliable and also a little bit faster. I think the indirect loading approach the DYNALINK example uses is generally not useful. However, when you really need it, it can be extremely powerful. A special case for its use relates to showing a splash screen when your application starts. An application requiring several DLLs, in fact, cannot show anything on screen until all the DLLs have been loaded. If you load the DLL libraries dynamically, instead, you can easily show a splash screen first. The drawback is that the code becomes much more complex to write and less reliable, because of the limited compile checks on functions parameters.

## A DLL in Memory

We can use this technique based on the GetProcAddress API function to test to which memory address of the current process a function has been loaded. We will use the same example to prove that two Win32 programs can access the same global data of a DLL with no problem, since they replicate this data in the private address space.

This example (indicated as DLL_MEM) is based on two projects, a Delphi DLL and a Delphi application. Here is the full source code of the DLLMEM.DLL:

```
library dllmem;

uses
  SysUtils, Classes, Windows;

// global DLL data
var
  Data: Integer;

procedure SetData (I: Integer); stdcall; export;
begin
  if I <> Data then
    Data := I
  else
    MessageBeep ($FFFFFFFF);
end;

function GetData: Integer; stdcall; export;
begin
  Result := Data;
end;

exports
  SetData, GetData;

begin
  // initialization
  Data := 1;
end.
```

The program has two simple routines that read or write a global memory location, initialized with a value of 1. When you store the same value again, the library emits a warning sound.

The code of the program using this DLL is very simple. The form of this application has two edit boxes (one with an UpDown control connected), three buttons, and a label. The first button saves the value of the first edit box, getting the value from the connected UpDown control:

```
procedure TForm1.Button1Click(Sender: TObject);
begin
  SetData (UpDown1.Position);
end;
```

If you press the second button, the program copies the DLL data to the second edit box:

```
procedure TForm1.Button2Click(Sender: TObject);
begin
  Edit2.Text := IntToStr(GetData);
end;
```

Finally, the third button is used to display in a label the memory address of the Set-Data function of the DLL:

```
procedure TForm1.Button3Click(Sender: TObject);
var
  HDLLInst: THandle;
begin
  HDLLInst := LoadLibrary ('dllmem');
  Label1.Caption := Format ('Address: %p', [
    GetProcAddress (HDLLInst, 'SetData')]);
  FreeLibrary (HDLLInst);
end;
```

If you run two copies of this program (see Figure 28.7), you can see that each of them has its own value for the global data of the DLL. On the other hand, in Windows 95, each copy of the program should refer to the same memory address for the function, while in Windows NT values might be different.

Actually, this is not proof that the DLL is loaded in memory once and then mapped to the same address in the process space of each application, rather than being loaded multiple times at the same address. In fact, the global memory data is probably at the same address in each process space, but is mapped to different physical memory locations.

# Summary

This chapter about DLL programming ends the book. We have seen how you can use application DLLs created in C++ or other languages and how to create DLLs using Delphi itself. Although I haven't emphasized this, Delphi DLLs are as fast, reliable, and usable in other programming environments as C or C++ DLLs—there is no real difference.

**FIGURE 28.7:**

By running two copies of the USEMEM program, you can see that the global data in the USEMEM.DLL is not shared.

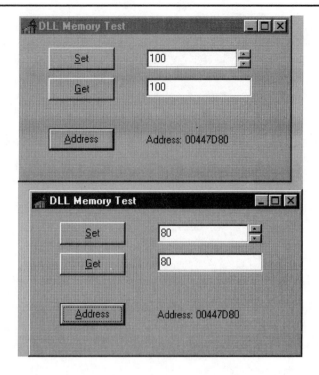

To understand DLL programming, we have examined a number of general concepts about DLLs in Windows. Although many of these concepts weren't demonstrated by the simple examples we built, the examples did provide some hints for the development of Delphi DLLs. In closing, I do discourage you from building DLLs for Delphi projects. The alternatives, such as compiled units, template forms, and components, are generally more powerful and easier to use. They are more closely related to the Delphi environment and approach, too.

Delphi and Windows share many elements, but also have different "views" of programming. When possible, follow the Delphi object-oriented approach over the Windows one, and you'll probably benefit a lot.

Delphi is a great programming environment: now that you can master Delphi, enjoy it.

# APPENDICES

# APPENDIX

## A

# A Short Overview of OOP Concepts

- The OOP concept of class

- Inheritance and class definitions

- Object polymorphism

- Types of OOP languages

**T**he Delphi language, Object Pascal, is an object-oriented programming (OOP) language. Chapter 5 describes the object-oriented features of the language, but it doesn't include much information about OOP in general. This appendix provides an overview of the key elements of OOP.

# Abstraction in Programming Languages

The foundation of OOP lies in the idea of abstraction. Programming languages were invented and are used to describe a process at a higher level than the CPU machine code. Traditionally, the abstraction offered by programming languages could be divided into two categories, related to the representation of data and control structures.

The fundamental idea of abstraction in the representation of data is the concept of the *data type*. Historically, the first generation of programming languages introduced the concept of type, and the second generation (including the original Pascal language) added the idea of user-defined data types, such as records and arrays.

Later on, the idea of the data type evolved into the concept of the *abstract data type*, a type associating the representation of data with the operations used to manipulate it. In an abstract data type, the representation of the data is usually hidden to its users. In these languages, a new data type is perceived as an extension of the type system provided by the language. Classes, as defined by OOP languages, can be considered an extension of the concept of abstract data types.

On the side of control structures, the first programming languages introduced statements for jumps, broaches, and loops. Then came the idea of subroutines (in the form of procedures and functions). With the advent of subroutines, many programming theories were developed, including *functional top-down decomposition*. The abstraction of subroutines is illustrated by the fact that you can call them and know *what* they do, but you don't need to know *how* they do it. Similarly to abstract data types, new subroutines can be considered extensions of the programming language.

# Classes

The first key element of OOP is the concept of *class*. A class can be defined as the abstract description of a group of objects, each with a specific state but all capable of performing the same operations.

For instance, a bottle is an object that has a state (it can be empty or full and can have different contents, often indicated by a label) and that allows some operations, such as filling it, pouring it, opening it, closing it, changing its contents, and so on. Of course, some operations depend on the state—pouring from an empty bottle doesn't make much sense.

In different words, a class is a type definition that has some fields (the data representing the status of an object of that class) and some methods (the operations), which generally depend on the object's status.

> **NOTE**
>
> Note that in OOP, the term *class* refers to the data type and the term *object* to an instance of the data type, a variable. Unfortunately, some OOP languages (including older versions of Object Pascal) use different terminology.

Within a program, classes have two main purposes:

- Classes define the abstraction they relate to. You can use them to define real-world entities, no matter how complex they are. If the entity is very complex, you can use classes to describe some of its subelements (or subsystems). As I mentioned, you can view classes as extensions of the data types of the program. In the same way, you can consider the new Delphi components you write as extensions of the original VCL shipped with Delphi.

- Classes are the basis of the modularity of a program. In Object Pascal, you can place each new class (defining a form or another element) in its own unit, dividing even a big application into small, manageable pieces. The way Delphi handles the source code of forms naturally leads to this kind of approach. According to the idea of modularity, each class should hide, or encapsulate, some of its elements.

Being based on classes is not the only requirement for a language to be defined as object-oriented. Two other key features are inheritance and polymorphism.

# Inheritance

By using inheritance, you can build a new class by defining it in terms of another existing class, instead of by building the class from scratch. A subclass inherits both fields and methods from its parent class.

In the example of the bottle given in the previous section, you can inherit, from the generic bottle, plastic bottles, glass bottles, or specific ones (such as beer or wine bottles). Each bottle has its own form, is handled in a different way, and might have a liquid inside. However, all the bottles share some common characteristics, properties, and methods.

Inheritance is a very powerful language construct, but it is not always easy to understand and use. Here are some guidelines and tips:

- In theory, inheritance represents *specialization*. You can consider a subclass as a special case of the parent class. This is often expressed using an *is a* relationship (as in "a plastic bottle *is a* bottle").

- At times, inheritance is used to express *generalization*. If you have a class for managers, one for secretaries, and one for accountants, you can come up with a generic employee class you can use as the parent class for each other class. You can use this parent class to share the common elements, as well as some common code.

- In practice, inheritance is a way to avoid code duplication. Instead of using copy-and-paste techniques to build two similar classes, it is much easier to use one as the parent class of the second. Besides saving some code, you can save some debugging time and handle future changes more easily because there is only one version of the code.

- Another reason to use inheritance is that the compiler *does* understand it. A parent class and a subclass have some form of type compatibility, as described in the next section.

# Polymorphism

The other key feature of OOP languages (besides classes and inheritance) is *polymorphism*, which literally indicates the ability of an object to take many forms. In other words, polymorphism allows you to refer to objects of different classes by means of the same program variable. It also allows you to perform operations on that variable in different ways, according to the data type, the class, and the object currently associated with that variable at the moment.

For example, I can declare a generic variable of the bottle class (say, MyBottle) and then assign to it objects of the TWineBottle or TBeerBottle class. (The T in front of the name is a common Borland notation.) Now suppose every class has an Open procedure, each with a different implementation. This method must use dynamic binding. In Object Pascal, this means declaring it in the parent class as `virtual` or `dynamic` (as discussed in Chapter 5) and redefining it with the `override` keyword.

When you apply the Open method to MyBottle, what happens? The Open procedure of the current type of the object is called. If MyBottle is currently a TWineBottle object, the cork is extracted using a proper opener. Opening a beer bottle involves a different action and a different tool.

You can use inheritance and polymorphism together to build programs based on class hierarchies. Writing hierarchy-based code is probably the ultimate OOP approach.

# A Definition of OOP

Now that we know what classes, inheritance, and polymorphism are, we can say an OOP language is a language that has at least these three key capabilities. To be more precise, there are three degrees of object-orientedness:

- Object-based languages support objects—that is, elements with a set and a state.

- Class-based languages have both objects and classes. Every object is an instance of a class, which defines the operations and the representation of the data.

- Object-oriented languages also have inheritance and polymorphism, two elements that are often related.

There are other more complex and complete definitions of OOP, but each author tends to gear them toward the language he or she prefers, giving a biased opinion.

# OOP Languages

There are many OOP languages. Some consider Simula67 the first one, but Smalltalk was the first language to provide a complete implementation of the OOP concepts. Then came hybrid languages (that is, OOP languages built on existing languages), such as C++, Objective-C, CLOS (a LISP derivative), and Object Pascal. Other important, and more theoretically sound, OOP languages include Eiffel and Sather. But new OOP languages appear frequently, with Java being the most recent case.

You can use two key categories to group OOP languages:

- *Pure versus hybrid:* Pure OOP languages are languages that do not allow other programming models. You cannot write a function by itself if it is not part of a class. You cannot declare a global variable. Examples of pure OOP languages are Smalltalk and Eiffel. With hybrid languages, you can do whatever you want, including forgetting to apply OOP principles completely. Examples of hybrid OOP languages are all those compatible with an existing one, such as C++ or Object Pascal.

- *Static versus dynamic:* Static languages are based on the notion of the data type and perform much compile-time type-checking. Dynamic languages have a weaker type notion and perform most of the checks at run-time. Dynamic languages, such as Smalltalk, are generally interpreted. Static languages, such as Object Pascal, are always compiled.

# Object-Oriented Analysis and Design

You can use an OOP language in many ways, particularly when it is an extension of an existing language. However, to exploit the full power of OOP languages, particularly in complex projects, you should probably analyze and design the program following object-oriented principles.

There are several methodologies of object-oriented analysis (OOA) and many object-oriented design (OOD) approaches. Refer to the literature on these specific subjects for information.

# Summary

Do not underestimate the role of OOP in Delphi. If you are not familiar with OOP, spend some time learning it, besides delving into Delphi elements and features. A clear comprehension of OOP concepts will allow you to better understand Delphi's inner structure and to write better programs.

Templates, classes, and components are great tools for re-usability, but without proper design, applications bigger than the sample programs in this book can get messy. To gain the benefits of OOP (re-usability, easy maintenance, and so on), you must know what you are doing, not only how to use an OOP tool.

# APPENDIX

## B

# An Introduction to SQL

- A definition of SQL

- The Select statement and its clauses

- The distinct keyword for eliminating duplicates

- Multiple table joins

- Other SQL statements

**W**hen you use the TQuery component in a Delphi database application, you need to write a SQL statement for its SQL property, as we saw in Chapter 17. If you own the Client-Server version of Delphi, you can use the Visual Query Builder tool instead of writing a SQL statement from scratch.

In both cases, you need to understand the SQL language. In Chapters 17 and 18, we used some simple SQL statements without describing them in detail. This appendix serves as an introduction to the basics of SQL programming for programmers who have never used SQL.

You can test these SQL statements using the Database Desktop tool. All the SQL statements in this appendix work with the Database Desktop, provided you have selected the proper alias (DBDEMO) with the Alias command of the SQL menu.

# What Is SQL?

Before looking at SQL statements and how SQL works, we should have a definition of what SQL is. The SQL acronym stands for *Structured Query Language*, but this term is often pronounced according to its former name, *SEQUEL* (for Structured English QUEry Language). SQL is the standard language used to construct and access relational database management systems (RDBMS) of different kinds and on many hardware platforms. Although it is a standard language, there are differences among the SQL dialects implemented in SQL databases.

Here, I'll refer just to a few elements of the language, which, as far as I know, should be common to each SQL dialect. Note that although the name refers to queries, you can use SQL for many other operations besides queries, such as for deleting or updating a database.

# The Select Statement

The most important SQL statement is probably the Select statement, which is built around three clauses:

- The `select` clause indicates a list of fields you want in the result of the query; by using the asterisk symbol (*) instead of a list of fields, you can select all of them.

- The `from` clause indicates the tables you want to consider to build the query.

- The `where` clause indicates some selection criteria. If the `where` clause is missing, all the fields are selected.

For example, if you want to select all the rows (or records) of the COUNTRY.DB table (as in the NAVIG2 example in Chapter 17), you can write the following code:

```
select * from Country
```

To specify the rows (or records) you want to consider in the result, you can write this code:

```
select Name, Capital
  from Country
```

## The Where Clause

If you want only some of the rows instead of all of them, you can add a where clause:

```
select Name, Capital
  from Country
  where Population > 20000000
```

This returns only the countries that have more than 20 million inhabitants. In the where clause, you can write several different expressions, including an expression to look for a single element, as in:

```
select *
  from Country
  where Name = "Argentina"
```

Of course, you can also write multiple conditions at the same time. You can merge two conditions with and to indicate that they must be met at the same time, or use or to indicate the record should meet one of the conditions:

```
select *
  from Country
  where Continent = "South America"
  and Population < 10000000

select Name, Capital
  from Country
  where Name <= "Brazil"
  or Capital >= "Ottawa"
```

The first statement selects the South American countries with fewer than 10 million inhabitants. The second statement selects the countries that have a name alphabetically preceding *Brazil* and those that have a capital with a name following *Ottawa*.

## Avoiding Duplicates

Now suppose you want to have a list of continents for the countries. You can write this code:

```
select Continent from Country
```

However, like any Select statement in general, this returns the same continent several times. To avoid duplicate elements in the result, you can add one more SQL keyword, `distinct`, which forces duplicate removal:

```
select distinct Continent
  from Country
```

# Making a Join

In most cases, SQL statements refer to two or more tables. When you work with two tables, you can join them or use the result of a table to express the condition used in the second one.

When you work on two or more source tables, you'll generally join them. In SQL, there is no specific statement or clause to express a join (although this is possible in the SQL dialect of some RDBMSs, including InterBase).

You can simply work on two tables and join them properly using the `where` clause to match the value of two fields. For example, we can join the Orders and Customer tables to find the date of each order and the company involved by writing the following code:

```
select Orders.OrderNo, Orders.SaleDate,
    Customer.Company, Customer.Contact
  from Orders, Customer
  where Orders.CustNo = Customer.CustNo
```

In exactly the same way, you can join three tables using two conditions. In this case, we also want to know the name of the employee who processed the order:

```
select Orders.OrderNo, Orders.SaleDate,
    Customer.Company, Customer.Contact,
    Employee.LastName
  from Orders, Customer, Employee
  where Orders.CustNo = Customer.CustNo
    and Orders.EmpNo = Employee.EmpNo
```

With the following SQL statement, we retrieve the amount paid by each customer who ordered something by *Johnson:*

```
select Orders.AmountPaid, Customer.Company
  from Orders, Customer, Employee
  where Orders.CustNo = Customer.CustNo
    and Orders.EmpNo = Employee.EmpNo
    and Employee.LastName = "Johnson"
```

# More Select Clauses

Besides `select`, `from`, and `where`, you can use other clauses in a Select statement. You can use an ordering clause or a grouping clause, and you can make some computations on tables or groups in a SQL statement.

## Choosing an Order

Another SQL clause is `order by` (two separate words), which determines the order of the values in the resulting query:

```
select *
  from Country
  where Population > 10000000
  order by Continent, Name
```

This statement returns a table with countries ordered by continent first and then by name.

## Computing Values

In the `select` clause, instead of a field of a table, you can have the result of a computation. For example, you can compute the number of employees with this statement:

```
select count (*)
  from Employee
```

For a more complex example, you can compute the number of orders taken by an employee, the total amount, and the average:

```
select Sum (Orders.AmountPaid),
    Count (Orders.AmountPaid), Avg (Orders.AmountPaid)
  from Orders, Employee
  where Orders.EmpNo = Employee.EmpNo
    and Employee.LastName = "Johnson"
```

## Defining Groups

Besides making a computation on the result of a query, you can compute a value for each group of elements, as indicated by the `group by` clause:

```
select Employee.LastName, Sum(Orders.AmountPaid)
  from Orders, Employee
  where Orders.EmpNo = Employee.EmpNo
  group by Employee.LastName
```

The result is a list of employees, each with the total amount of the orders that employee has taken.

# Beyond Select

Select statements are just a part of SQL, although a very important one and also the main topic of this appendix. However, there are other SQL statements you should be aware of. Here are the most important ones:

- `Insert` adds data to a table. Generally, it is also possible to insert the result of a sub-table into a table, although the Database Desktop doesn't allow this.
- `Update` changes the values of a table.
- `Delete` removes some of the rows of a table.
- `Create Table` defines a new table.
- `Alter Table` restructures an existing table, adding or removing columns.
- `Drop Table` removes a table.
- `Create Index` builds a new index for a table.
- `Drop Index` removes an existing index.

# Summary

This appendix has presented a very concise exploration of SQL, aimed at beginners. If you want to become a fluent SQL programmer, I suggest that you refer to books on database theories in general, because a good understanding of the basic database concepts is required to write complex SQL statements. Do not overlook how writing the same SQL statement in different ways can affect performance, because this is another important topic, mostly related to the SQL servers you work with.

# INDEX

**Note to the Reader:** Page numbers in *italics* refer to figures or tables; page numbers in **bold** refer to primary discussions of the topic.

## Symbols & Numbers

{$} (braces with dollar sign), for compiler directive, 100–101

% Speedbutton, OnClick event, 556

^ (caret), to define pointer type, 93

& (ampersand)
  for menu command shortcuts, 262
  for shortcut keys, 145, 216, 342

* (intersection) set operator, 106

* operator, *105*

(* (parentheses with star), for comments, 100

* (star symbol), in SQL statement, 527, 966

… (ellipsis)
  in button caption, 234
  in menus, 260

+ operator, *105*, 106

+ (set union) operator, 106

:= (assignment) operator, 17, 107

; (semicolon)
  for Pascal program statement, 14, 101, 107
  and syntax error from if statement, 108

<> (not equal) relational operator, *106*

< (less than) relational operator, *106*

= (equal) operator, 17, *106*, 107

{ and } (braces), for comments, 100

> (greater than) relational operator, *106*

[ and ] (square brackets)
  to indicate values in set, 90
  for strings, 95

- (difference) set operator, 106

- (subtraction) operator, *105*

! (exclamation mark), in menu bar, 258

? (question mark), in form title bar, 304

/ (division) operator, *105*, 106

@ operator, 93, 105

| character, to separate substrings, 287, 398–399

3D effect
  Bevel component to define, 341
  color and, *202*, 450

8-bit (ANSI) characters, data type for, 78

8-bit representation, for enumerations, 88

#13 character, 320

16-bit applications, recompiling source code for Delphi 2, 937–938

16-bit integers, vs. 32-bit, 79

16-bit representation, for enumerations, 88

16-bit (Unicode) characters, data type for, 78

16-bit version, of Windows system libraries, 935

16-color adapters (VGA), 203

32-bit integers, vs. 16-bit, 79

32-bit representation, for enumerations, 88

32-bit version, of Windows system libraries, 935

64-bit representation, for Currency data type, 81

## A

aaDoubleClick AutoActivate property value, 828

aaGetFocus AutoActivate property value, 828

aaManual AutoActivate property value, 828

Abort method, 740

About boxes, **425–427**
  custom hidden screen for, **426–427**
  for Delphi, 39
  predefined, 60

absolute paths, 71

abstract data type, 960

abstract keyword, 163, 166

abstract methods, **163–166**
  redefining in inherited forms, 433

abstraction, **960**

accelerator tables, as Windows resource, *711*

Accept parameter, for OnDragOver method, 223

# C

# F

# G

# J

# K

# M

# O

# Q

# R

## S

## T

# x

# y

# z

# Mastering Delphi 2 Companion CD-ROM

The CD includes:

- Source code for the examples in the book (including Pascal files, form description files, project files, and resource files)
- Compiled executable files to let you test the behavior of each program without even loading it in Delphi
- Several Delphi components and tools
- Freeware and shareware components
- Demo versions of commercial components
- Delphi magazines along with issues of a special Delphi newsletter

## Installation

Since you can use the material from the CD directly, there is no installation program. Some of the components and third-party tools have their own setup programs, but I have included an installed version for many of them to allow you to view a demo before deciding whether or not to install them.

## Navigation

To help you navigate through the CD, I suggest using the "CD-View" program included in the root directory. As you select a directory, CD-View automatically loads and shows the text of the README.TXT file included in the directory. From CD-View's list of files, you can:

- Run programs
- Load TXT, PAS, DPR, and other text files
- See a preview of BMP and WAV files

## On-Line Author

If you have any complaints or suggestions about the CD or the book, you can address them to me over CompuServe at 100273,2610. I also suggest you check the book errata at my home page:

Http://ourworld.compuserve.com/homepages/marcocantu